Conference of the North American Chapter of the Association for Computational Linguistics: Human Language Technologies (NAACL HLT 2022)

Student Research Workshop

Online
10 - 15 July 2022

ISBN: 978-1-7138-5621-4

Printed from e-media with permission by:

Curran Associates, Inc.
57 Morehouse Lane
Red Hook, NY 12571

CURRAN ASSOCIATES INC. proceedings.com

Some format issues inherent in the e-media version may also appear in this print version.

Printed with permission by Curran Associates, Inc. (2022)

Association for Computational Linguistics
209 N. Eighth Street
Stroudsburg, Pennsylvania 18360

Phone: 1-570-476-8006
Fax: 1-570-476-0860

acl@aclweb.org

Additional copies of this publication are available from:

Curran Associates, Inc.
57 Morehouse Lane
Red Hook, NY 12571 USA
Phone: 845-758-0400
Fax: 845-758-2633
Email: curran@proceedings.com
Web: www.proceedings.com

NAACL 2022

The 2022 Conference of the North American Chapter of the Association for Computational Linguistics: Human Language Technologies

Proceedings of the Student Research Workshop

July 10-15, 2022

The NAACL organizers gratefully acknowledge the support from the following sponsors.

SRW Sponsors

NSF

Google Research

Microsoft

Order copies of this and other ACL proceedings from:

Association for Computational Linguistics (ACL)
209 N. Eighth Street
Stroudsburg, PA 18360
USA
Tel: +1-570-476-8006
Fax: +1-570-476-0860
acl@aclweb.org

Introduction

Welcome to the NAACL 2022 Student Research Workshop.

The NAACL 2022 Student Research Workshop (SRW) is a forum for student researchers in computational linguistics and natural language processing. The workshop provides a unique opportunity for student participants to present their work and receive valuable feedback from the international research community as well as from faculty mentors.

Following the tradition of the previous student research workshops, we have archival and non-archival tracks for research papers and thesis proposals. The research paper track is a venue for Ph.D. students, Masters students, and advanced undergraduates to describe completed work or work-in-progress along with preliminary results. The thesis proposal track is offered for advanced Masters and Ph.D. students who have decided on a thesis topic and are interested in feedback on their proposal and ideas about future directions for their work.

This year, we received 96 submissions in total: 8 thesis proposals and 88 research papers. We accepted 5 thesis proposal and 41 research papers, resulting in an acceptance rate of 63% for thesis proposals and 47% for research papers. Out of the 41 research papers, 9 were non-archival and 33 are presented in these proceedings. Out of the 5 thesis proposals, 1 was non-archival and 4 are presented in these proceedings.

Mentoring is at the heart of the SRW. In line with previous years, we had a pre-submission mentoring program before the submission deadline. A total of 28 papers participated in the pre-submission mentoring program. This program offered students the opportunity to receive comments from an experienced researcher to improve the writing style and presentation of their submissions.

We are deeply grateful to our sponsors, the National Science Foundation, Microsoft and Google. We thank the program committee members for their careful reviews of each paper and all of the mentors for donating their time to provide feedback to the student authors. We thank our faculty advisors, Danqi Chen and Nianwen Xue, for their essential advice and guidance, and the NAACL 2022 organizing committee for their support. Finally, we thank all the student authors for submitting their work and participating in the NAACL 2022 edition of the SRW.

Program Committee

Student Research Workshop Student Chairs

Daphne Ippolito, University of Pennsylvania
Liunian Harold Li, University of California, Los Angeles
Maria Leonor Pacheco, Purdue University

Faculty Advisors

Danqi Chen, Princeton University
Nianwen Xue, Brandeis University

Pre-submission Mentors

Archita Pathak, Amazon
Arkaitz Zubiaga, Queen Mary University of London
Atul Kumar Ojha, National University of Ireland, Galway
Dan Goldwasser, Purdue University
Eduardo Blanco, Arizona State University
Greg Durrett, University of Texas at Austin
Hao Tan, Adobe
Kasturi Bhattacharjee, AWS AI
Kristen Johnson, Michigan State University
Mascha Kurpicz-Briki, Bern University of Applied Sciences
Melissa Roemmele, RWS Language Weaver
Mihir Kale, Google
Muhao Chen, University of Southern California
Nedjma Ousidhoum, The University of Cambridge
Rajaswa Patil, TCS Research
Sunipa Dev, University of California, Los Angelesv
Shomir Wilson, Pennsylvania State University
Valerio Basile, University of Turin
Vincent Ng, University of Texas at Dallas
Vivek Srivastava, TCS Research
Yonatan Bisk, Carnegie Mellon University

Program Committee

Abeer Aldayel, King Saud University
Abhinav Joshi, Indian Institute of Technology, Kanpur
Adithya Pratapa, Carnegie Mellon University
Adithya Shah, Virginia Polytechnic Institute and State University
Agnieszka Falenska, University of Stuttgart
Alessandra Teresa Cignarella, University of Turin
Alexander Panchenko, Skoltech
Alina Karakanta, Fondazione Bruno Kessler
Andrea Varga, Theta Lake Ltd
Arjun Subramonian, University of California, Los Angeles

Arkaitz Zubiaga, Queen Mary University London
Arya McCarthy, Johns Hopkins University
Ashima Suvarna, University of California, Los Angeles
Ayushi Pandey, University of Dublin, Trinity College
Beatrice Savoldi, Fondazione Bruno Kessler
Bonnie Webber, University of Edinburgh
Brian Davis, Dublin City University
Bruno Martins, InstituInstituto Superior Técnico
Bryan Li, University of Pennsylvania
Chenglei Si, University of Maryland, College Park
Dage Särg, University of Tartu
Dan Goldwasser, Purdue University
Eduardo Blanco, Arizona State University
Esma Balkir, National Research Council Canada
Evgeniia Tokarchuk, University of Amsterdam
Fajri Koto, The University of Melbourne
Fatemehsadat Mireshghallah, University of California, San Diego
Fernando Alva-Manchego, Cardiff University
Francielle Vargas, Universidade de São Paulo
Gabriel Bernier-Colborne, National Research Council Canada
Gemma Boleda, ICREA
Hai Pham, Carnegie Mellon University
Haoyu Wang, University of Pennsylvania
Hossein Rouhizadeh, Shahid Beheshti University
Hritik Bansal, University of California, Los Angeles
J. Alberto Conejero, Universidad Politécnica de Valencia
Jakob Prange, Georgetown University
Jakob Prange, Georgetown University
Jasy Suet Yan Liew, Universiti Sains Malaysia
Joseph Marvin Imperial, University of Bath
Julia Kiseleva, Microsoft Research
Koichi Takeda, Nagoya University
Kristen Johnson, Michigan State University
Labiba Jahan, Augustana College
Laurie Burchell, University of Edinburgh
Lei Li, Peking University
Lina Maria Rojas-Barahona, Orange Labs
Luca Soldaini, Allen Institute for Artificial Intelligence
Maaz Amjad, Instituto Politecnico Nacional
Maria Antoniak, Cornell University
Maria Kunilovskaya, University of Wolverhampton
Marija Stanojevic, Temple University
Masaaki Nagata, NTT Corporation
Mascha Kurpicz-Briki, Bern University of Applied Sciences
Max Müller-Eberstein, IT University of Copenhagen
Meishan Zhang, Harbin Institute of Technology, Shenzhen
Michael Miller Yoder, Carnegie Mellon University
Michael Sejr Schlichtkrull, University of Cambridge
Mike Zhang, IT University of Copenhagen
Mingda Chen, Toyota Technological Institute at Chicago
Mona Jalal, Boston University

Neville Ryant, Linguistic Data Consortium
Nikhil Mehta, Purdue University
Parsa Bagherzadeh, Concordia University
Peiyuan Liao, Praxis Pioneering
Prashant Kodali, International Institute of Information Technology Hyderabad
Qing Lyu, University of Pennsylvania
Qing Lyu, University of Pennsylvania
Rajkumar Pujari, Purdue University
Ritam Dutt, Carnegie Mellon University
Ryohei Sasano, Nagoya University
Ryohei Sasano, Nagoya University
Sandeep Mathias, Presidency University, Bangalore
Sashank Santhanam, Apple
Satwik Dutta, University of Texas at Dallas
Shabnam Behzad, Georgetown University
Shamik Roy, Purdue University
Shubham Mittal, Indian Institute of Technology Delhi
Shubhanshu Mishra, Twitter
Sowmya Vajjala, National Research Council Canada
Stan Szpakowicz, University of Ottawa
Sunny Rai, Mahindra University
Surangika Ranathunga, University of Moratuwa
Tanmay Parekh, University of California, Los Angeles
Tatiana Litvinova, Voronezh State Pedagogical University
Tom Sherborne, University of Edinburgh
Tsvetomila Mihaylova, Instituto de Telecomunicações, Portugal
Tunazzina Islam, Purdue University
Vincent Nguyen, Australian National University
Vivek Srivastava, Tata Consultancy Services Limited, India
Xabier Soto, University of the Basque Country UPV/EHU
Xiang Dai, CSIRO
Yoshinari Fujinuma, AWS AI Labs
Younghun Lee, Purdue University
Yuan Zhang, Google
Zhong Zhou, Carnegie Mellon University

Table of Contents

Program

Tuesday, July 12, 2022

08:00 - 09:00 *Virtual Poster Q&A Session 1*

Explicit Use of Topicality in Dialogue Response Generation
Takumi Yoshikoshi, Hayato Atarashi, Takashi Kodama and Sadao Kurohashi

Automating Human Evaluation of Dialogue Systems
Sujan Reddy A

Probe-Less Probing of BERT's Layer-Wise Linguistic Knowledge with Masked Word Prediction
Tatsuya Aoyama and Nathan Schneider

Regularized Training of Nearest Neighbor Language Models
Jean-Francois Ton, Walter Talbott, Shuangfei Zhai and Joshua M. Susskind

Analysing the Correlation between Lexical Ambiguity and Translation Quality in a Multimodal Setting using WordNet
Ali Hatami, Paul Buitelaar and Mihael Arcan

12:15 - 10:45 *Panel Discussion for Starting Researchers*

14:15 - 15:45 *In-Person Poster Session*

Systematicity Emerges in Transformers when Abstract Grammatical Roles Guide Attention
Ayush K Chakravarthy, Jacob Labe Russin and Randall O'Reilly

Grounding in social media: An approach to building a chit-chat dialogue model
Ritvik Choudhary and Daisuke Kawahara

ExtraPhrase: Efficient Data Augmentation for Abstractive Summarization
Mengsay Loem, Sho Takase, Masahiro Kaneko and Naoaki Okazaki

Neural Retriever and Go Beyond: A Thesis Proposal
Man Luo

Tuesday, July 12, 2022 (continued)

Unifying Parsing and Tree-Structured Models for Generating Sentence Semantic Representations
Antoine Simoulin and Benoit Crabbé

Defending Compositionality in Emergent Languages
Michal Auersperger and Pavel Pecina

Exploring the Effect of Dialect Mismatched Language Models in Telugu Automatic Speech Recognition
Aditya Yadavalli, Ganesh Sai Mirishkar and Anil Vuppala

Multimodal large language models for inclusive collaboration learning tasks
Armanda Lewis

16:15 - 17:45 *Thesis Proposals*

Methods for Estimating and Improving Robustness of Language Models
Michal Stefanik

Retrieval-augmented Generation across Heterogeneous Knowledge
Wenhao Yu

Neural Retriever and Go Beyond: A Thesis Proposal
Man Luo

Multimodal large language models for inclusive collaboration learning tasks
Armanda Lewis

Wednesday, July 13, 2022

08:00 - 09:00 *Virtual Poster Q&A Session 3*

Again, Dozens of Refugees Drowned: A Computational Study of Political Framing Evoked by Presuppositions
Qi Yu

Impact of Training Instance Selection on Domain-Specific Entity Extraction using BERT
Eileen Salhofer, Xing Lan Liu and Roman Kern

Text Style Transfer for Bias Mitigation using Masked Language Modeling
Ewoenam Kwaku Tokpo and Toon Calders

Differentially Private Instance Encoding against Privacy Attacks
Shangyu Xie and Yuan Hong

Methods for Estimating and Improving Robustness of Language Models
Michal Stefanik

Static and Dynamic Speaker Modeling based on Graph Neural Network for Emotion Recognition in Conversation
Prakhar Saxena, Yin Jou Huang and Sadao Kurohashi

Simulating Feature Structures with Simple Types
Valentin D. Richard

09:15 - 10:15 *Virtual Poster Q&A Session 4*

Dr. Livingstone, I presume? Polishing of foreign character identification in literary texts
Aleksandra Konovalova, Antonio Toral and Kristiina Taivalkoski-Shilov

Zuo Zhuan Ancient Chinese Dataset for Word Sense Disambiguation
Xiaomeng Pan, Hongfei Wang, Teruaki Oka and Mamoru Komachi

Few-shot fine-tuning SOTA summarization models for medical dialogues
David Fraile Navarro, Mark Dras and Shlomo Berkovsky

Systematicity Emerges in Transformers when Abstract Grammatical Roles Guide Attention

Ayush Chakravarthy[*]
Department of Computer Science
University of California Davis
akchakravarthy@ucdavis.edu

Jacob Russin[*]
Center for Neuroscience
University of California Davis
jlrussin@ucdavis.edu

Randall O'Reilly
Department of Computer Science
Center for Neuroscience
University of California Davis
One Shields Ave. Davis, CA 95616
oreilly@ucdavis.edu

Abstract

Systematicity is thought to be a key inductive bias possessed by humans that is lacking in standard natural language processing systems such as those utilizing transformers. In this work, we investigate the extent to which the failure of transformers on systematic generalization tests can be attributed to a lack of linguistic abstraction in its attention mechanism. We develop a novel modification to the transformer by implementing two separate input streams: a role stream controls the attention distributions (i.e., queries and keys) at each layer, and a filler stream determines the values. Our results show that when abstract role labels are assigned to input sequences and provided to the role stream, systematic generalization is improved.

1 Introduction

Transformers have achieved state-of-the-art performance on many natural language processing (NLP) tasks (Brown et al., 2020; Devlin et al., 2019; Vaswani et al., 2017), but it has been suggested that they remain inferior to human language learners when it comes to sample efficiency (Linzen, 2020) and more difficult generalization problems (Baroni, 2020; Lake and Baroni, 2018; Lake et al., 2019; Keysers et al., 2020). These architectures have proven to scale remarkably well (Brown et al., 2020), but may lack the strong inductive biases that contribute to these human abilities (Battaglia et al., 2018; Lake et al., 2017).

Systematicity, or the capacity to leverage structural or grammatical knowledge to compose familiar concepts in novel ways (Fodor and Pylyshyn, 1988; Smolensky, 1990), has been highlighted as one potential inductive bias present in humans (Lake et al., 2019; O'Reilly et al., 2021) that deep learning architectures may lack (Lake and Baroni, 2018; Lake et al., 2017). It has been argued that in humans, the ability to understand sentences such as "John loves Mary" necessarily implies the ability to understand certain other sentences, e.g., those that are constructed from the same elements and grammatical relations such as "Mary loves John" (Fodor and Pylyshyn, 1988).

The SCAN dataset (Lake and Baroni, 2018) was introduced to evaluate the systematic generalization capabilities of deep neural networks. In SCAN, instructions generated from an artificial grammar must be translated into action sequences, and train-test splits require models to generalize to novel compositions of familiar words. Although deep learning models achieve good generalization performance when train and test data are split randomly, their performance suffers on these systematic generalization tests (Lake and Baroni, 2018), even though humans perform well on analogous generalization problems (Lake et al., 2019).

The mechanisms underlying human systematicity remain unclear, but a number of candidates have been proposed, including tensor-product representations (Schlag et al., 2019; Smolensky, 1990) and specialized attention mechanisms (Goyal et al., 2019; Bengio, 2017; Russin et al., 2020; Webb et al., 2021). Attention is central to the transformer architecture (Vaswani et al., 2017) and has been leveraged in mechanisms resembling systematic symbolic processing (Graves et al., 2014; Webb et al., 2021), thus making it a key potential target for encouraging systematicity (Russin et al., 2020).

In this work, we explore the connection between attention and systematicity using a novel transformer architecture designed to leverage structural or abstract information in its attention mechanism.

[*]equal contribution

Proceedings of the 2022 Conference of the North American Chapter of the Association for Computational Linguistics: Human Language Technologies: Student Research Workshop, pages 1 - 8
July 10-15, 2022 ©2022 Association for Computational Linguistics

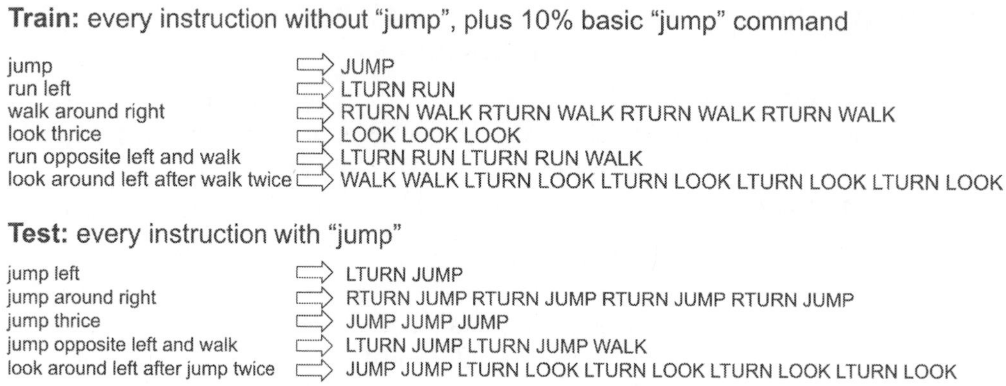

Figure 1: Examples from the add-jump split of SCAN. All except the simplest instructions with the word "jump" are held out of the training set, requiring models to generalize its usage to more complicated constructions.

We hypothesized that systematicity would improve if attention distributions in the transformer were strictly determined from abstract inputs containing minimal token-specific information, as this may prevent memorization of spurious relationships in the training data. Previous work has experimented with incorporating additional linguistic inputs into NLP systems (e.g., Sachan et al., 2021), but here we propose a novel way of utilizing additional linguistic knowledge: a separate "role" input stream is introduced to the transformer, which determines the attention distributions at each layer but is kept separate from the typical ("filler") input stream used to directly generate outputs. Many kinds of information can be passed to the role input stream (including the original tokens themselves), thereby allowing us to explore the kinds of inputs that, when used to determine attention, result in improved systematicity. In our preliminary work, we explore the use of abstract grammatical roles to determine attention in the transformer on the SCAN dataset.

2 Related Work

2.1 SCAN

The SCAN dataset (see Figure 1) uses a simple finite phrase-structure grammar to generate instruction sequences that must be translated into sequences of actions (Lake and Baroni, 2018). In the *simple split*, train and test examples are sampled randomly from the set of all possible instructions. In the systematic generalization test called the *add-jump split*, all instruction sequences containing one of the primitive verbs ("jump") are systematically held out of the training set, except in its simplest form ("jump" $\rightarrow$ JUMP). The original work showed that recurrent neural networks such as long short-term memory (LSTM) succeed at the simple split but fail on the add-jump split (Lake and Baroni, 2018).

Subsequent work introduced a new framework for generating systematic generalization tests called distribution-based compositionality assessment, and showed that transformers perform poorly on these tests in addition to the original add-jump split (Keysers et al., 2020). Although standard deep learning architectures consistently fail at this task, a number of non-standard approaches have demonstrated some success, including a meta-learning (Lake, 2019), recurrent networks that factorize alignment and translation (Russin et al., 2020) or are designed for primitive substitution (Li et al., 2019), masked language model pretraining (Furrer et al., 2021); iterative back-translation (Guo et al., 2020), use of analytic expressions (Liu et al., 2020), and auxiliary sequence prediction (Jiang and Bansal, 2021). Our preliminary work presents a new approach that has many commonalities with these previous ideas.

2.2 Utilizing Linguistic Knowledge

Prior work has shown that a remarkable amount of linguistic structure emerges in the representations learned by large transformers self-supervised on natural language (Linzen and Baroni, 2021; Manning et al., 2020; Tenney et al., 2019), and that transformers can learn to approximate a compositional process for solving math problems (Russin et al., 2021). These findings may cast doubt on the idea that injecting explicit linguistic structure will aid these models in producing the kinds of systematic behavior observed in human language learners. However, given their poor systematic generalization performance observed on tasks like SCAN (Lake and Baroni, 2018), and their reliance on certain syntactic heuristics that lead to predictable failures on challenging sentences (McCoy et al., 2019; Linzen and Baroni, 2021), it stands to reason that these models may benefit from access to explicit linguistic knowledge (Sachan et al., 2021).

Some work has attempted to incorporate linguistically-informed labels such as part-of-speech tags or syntactic parses into the inputs or training regiments of deep learning models (Sachan et al., 2021; Sennrich and Haddow, 2016; Strubell et al., 2018), showing some improvements on machine translation (Sennrich and Haddow, 2016) and semantic role labeling (Strubell et al., 2018). A number of methods have been used to inject linguistic knowledge into these models, including the use of graph neural networks (Marcheggiani and Titov, 2017; Sachan et al., 2021) and multi-task learning (Strubell et al., 2018). In this work, we develop a novel approach that attempts to establish an explicit link between linguistic structure and the attention mechanism of transformers to improve their systematic generalization capabilities.

3 Methods

3.1 Architecture

The transformer architecture (Vaswani et al., 2017) utilizes multi-head attention layers that take as input query (Q), key (K), and value (V) vectors:

$$\text{Attn}(Q, K, V) = \text{softmax}(\frac{QK^T}{\sqrt{d_k}})V \quad (1)$$

where d_k is the dimension of the keys (K). Note that the probability distribution over the sequence length produced by the softmax is determined by the queries (Q) and keys (K) alone. We modified the existing transformer architecture by separating two streams of processing (see Figure 2): 1) the "filler" stream determines the values at each layer, which will be averaged according to the weights given by the attention distributions and contribute directly to the output of the model, and 2) the "role" stream determines at each layer the queries (Q) and keys (K) — and therefore the attention distributions — but otherwise does not directly contribute to the output of the model. This was achieved by introducing a separate set of embeddings for each input stream (M for the fillers and X for the roles). The existing attention mechanism was modified so that the roles in layer $l+1$ are determined from a weighted combination of the keys in layer l:

$$\begin{aligned} M &= \text{Attn}(Q, K, V) \\ X &= \text{Attn}(Q, K, K) \end{aligned} \quad (2)$$

This ensures that no information from the filler stream can enter into the determination of the attention distributions at each layer, and that the roles can only affect the output of the model through their control over the attention, similar to Russin et al. (2020). The attention at each layer can have multiple heads in the usual way (Vaswani et al., 2017), and the separation between the two streams is maintained throughout both the encoder and the decoder (see Figure 2). Because the role stream determines the way information from the input tokens will be combined throughout the architecture (through its influence on the attention distributions), positional encodings are added to the role embeddings rather than the filler embeddings.

Note that this setup allows us flexibility in terms of the kind of information that is passed to the role input stream. The original tokens themselves can be embedded separately and passed to the role stream, in which case the architecture becomes very similar to the original transformer, with the exception of the modification to the attention depicted in Figure 2. Here, we embed abstract roles for the tokens in the SCAN dataset to investigate the relationship between abstraction in the attention mechanism and systematic generalization behavior.

3.2 Role Auxiliary Loss

Each transformer layer returns two sets of vectors (X and M). The output of the filler stream (M) is a sequence of target predictions that are used to compute the usual cross entropy loss before back-propagation ("Filler loss"). The output of the role stream (X) can optionally be used in an auxiliary cross-entropy loss on the roles assigned to the target sequence ("Role loss"). We performed experiments with and without this auxiliary loss, and results are reported for both.

3.3 Thresholded Attention

Drawing inspiration from Rahaman et al. (2021), we also experimented with thresholding the encoder-decoder attention:

$$\text{threshold}(A_{ij}) = \begin{cases} A_{ij} & \text{if } A_{ij} > \tau \\ 0 & \text{otherwise} \end{cases} \quad (3)$$

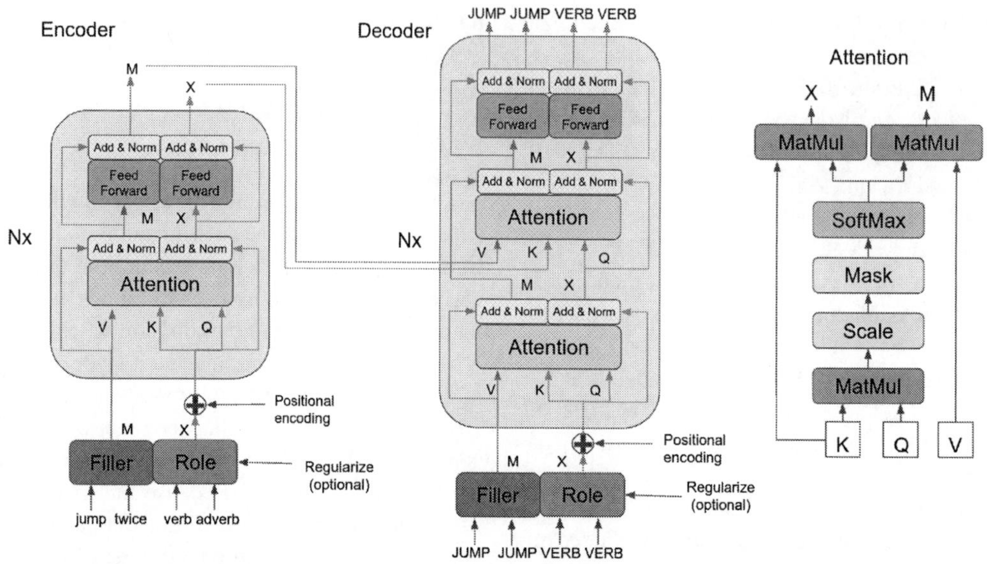

Figure 2: Modified transformer architecture. The architecture imposes two separate role and filler streams throughout the encoder (left) and decoder (middle). The filler stream determines the values (V) at each layer while the role stream determines the keys (K) and queries (Q), and therefore the attention distributions. This was accomplished by modifying the original attention mechanism (right).

Where τ is the attention threshold and $A = \text{softmax}(\frac{QK^T}{\sqrt{d_k}})$. The thresholded attention matrix is then re-normalized and multiplied by the value matrix as in equation 1.

3.4 Implementation Details

The encoder and decoder had 2 layers with 8 attention heads and used a thresholding parameter (τ) of 0.08. The embedding dimension was 256, the hidden dimension was 512, and the dimension of the query, key and value vectors was 256. The model was optimized for 400 epochs using Adam (Kingma and Ba, 2015) with a learning rate of 2.5×10^{-4}. Experiments were performed using both absolute positional encodings (Vaswani et al., 2017) and relative positional embeddings (Dai et al., 2019); absolute positional encodings were found to lead to slightly better performance with reduced variance, so for simplicity we only report those results.

4 Experiments

To test our hypothesized link between attention, linguistic abstraction, and systematic generalization, we developed abstract roles to label each token in the SCAN vocabulary, and performed experiments testing our architecture with and without these abstract roles. We report results on the difficult add-jump split of the SCAN dataset, and compare against previous work. Our main purpose is to show that systematic generalization is improved in the transformer when linguistic abstractions are used as inputs to the role stream for determining attention, and that there is an asymmetry in the transformer such that these abstractions should be used to determine attention (i.e., keys and queries) and not to directly produce outputs (i.e., values).

4.1 SCAN Roles

The phrase-structure grammar used in SCAN is very simple, so the grammatical roles used as additional inputs were relatively straightforward to implement. In the case of the add-jump split, we hypothesized that the best abstract role scheme would be one that assigned all primitive verbs to a single role ("prim") in both the instructions (source) and the actions (target). Except where indicated (section 4.2.2), all results used this scheme.

4.2 Results

Our main results are shown in Table 1. We reproduce previous work and show that the baseline transformer (Vaswani et al., 2017) achieves perfect accuracy on the simple split of the SCAN dataset,

Model	Simple	Add jump
LSTM+Attn (Keysers et al., 2020)	99.9 ± 2.7	0.0 ± 0.0
Syntactic Attention (Russin et al., 2020)	100.0 ± 0.0	78.4 ± 27.4
CGPS-RNN (Li et al., 2019)	99.9 ± 0.0	98.8 ± 1.4
T5-11B (Furrer et al., 2021)	X	98.3 ± 3.3
Semi-Sup (Guo et al., 2020)	X	100.0 ± 0.0
LANE (Liu et al., 2020)	100.0 ± 0.0	100.0 ± 0.0
Aux. seq. (Jiang and Bansal, 2021)	X	98.32 ± 0.3
Transformer	100.0 ± 0.0	0.19 ± 0.18
Filler loss, no thresh (ours)	99.9 ± 0.01	16.2 ± 25.1
Filler loss, thresh (ours)	99.9 ± 0.01	85.6 ± 1.15
Filler + Role loss, no thresh (ours)	99.9 ± 0.02	87.4 ± 5.6
Filler + Role loss, thresh (ours)	100.0 ± 0.0	92.7 ± 3.3

Table 1: Performance (average accuracy $\pm$ standard deviation) on the simple and add-jump splits of SCAN.

but fails dramatically on the add-jump split testing its systematic generalization capabilities. Our architecture improves performance on the add-jump split when the role labels are used as inputs to the role stream. Marginal improvement relative to baseline was observed without the use of attention thresholding and without backpropagating the auxiliary role loss ("Filler loss, no thresh"). Each of these two tweaks improved performance ("Filler loss, thresh", "Filler + Role loss, no thresh") and when both were used ("Filler + Role loss, thresh"), the architecture achieved 92.7% accuracy on the test set of the add-jump split.

4.2.1 Abstraction in Roles vs. Fillers

To further investigate the connection between attention and systematicity, we varied the inputs used in each of the filler and role streams of the architecture (see Table 2). When the filler tokens (i.e., the words from the original SCAN vocabulary) were used as inputs to both the role and filler streams, our architecture resembled the original transformer architecture, as these inputs were used to simultaneously determine the outputs (i.e., the values) and the attention (i.e., the keys and queries) at each layer. This was confirmed in the performance on the SCAN task, where using the fillers in both streams ("Fillers-Fillers") resulted in similar performance to the baseline transformer.

As a sanity check, we also reversed the role and filler inputs, so that the role labels were inputs to the filler stream and the words from the original SCAN vocabulary were used as inputs to the role stream ("Roles-Fillers"). In this case, performance again matched the baseline transformer on the add-jump split, confirming our intuition that linguistic abstractions are best used to determine attention distributions, not values.

Model	Simple	Add jump
Transformer	100.0 ± 0.0	0.19 ± 0.18
Fillers-Fillers	100.0 ± 0.0	2.8 ± 1.6
Roles-Fillers	100.0 ± 0.0	0.22 ± 0.16
Fillers-Roles	100.0 ± 0.0	92.7 ± 3.3

Table 2: Performance on the add-jump split only improved when abstract annotations were used in the role stream ("Fillers-Roles").

4.2.2 Varying the Level of Abstraction

We believe that the previous result highlights a strength of our setup, as it allows us the flexibility to diverge from the original transformer in a continuous way by varying the amount of abstraction used in the inputs to the role stream. For example, in a natural language task it would be possible to vary the kinds of abstract labels or annotations supplied as input to the role stream from highly abstract part-of-speech tags to more complex annotations from more sophisticated automated parses.

To test this idea in the SCAN setting, we experimented with different schemes for assigning roles that varied in their level of abstraction, as measured by the empirical entropy of the resultant source role vocabulary (see Figure 3). After our initial role-assignment scheme, we made roles progressively more abstract by assigning additional instruction words to the same role (e.g., "left" and "right" to "dir", "twice" and "thrice" to "num", etc.). Results validated the assumption that the best scheme was one that used a single role for each of the primitive verbs, and assigned a different role to each of the

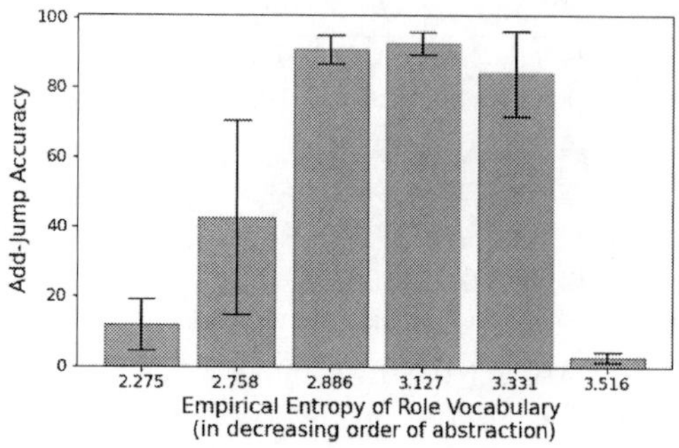

Figure 3: Add-jump performance varies with the level of abstraction in the inputs to the role stream (highest performance outlined in red).

other words (entropy = 3.127). This experiment shows that there is an ideal level of abstraction to use in the role stream: too much abstraction results in an inability to distinguish relevant distinctions, and too little results in the unsystematic memorization typical of the vanilla transformer.

5 Conclusion

Our preliminary work establishes a connection between linguistic abstraction, the attention mechanism used in transformers, and systematic generalization behavior as measured by performance on the SCAN dataset: when abstract roles are assigned to inputs and used to determine the attention at each layer, systematic generalization improves. We developed an architecture that may facilitate greater understanding of the original transformer (Vaswani et al., 2017) by allowing more precise investigation into the relative contributions of attention distributions and representation learning. Future work will test our setup on other compositional or systematic generalization tasks (Keysers et al., 2020; Kim and Linzen, 2020) and determine the kinds of linguistic abstraction that allows success on these tasks. In addition, future work will experiment with using our novel architecture on natural language datasets using varying levels of linguistic abstraction.

The extent to which human-level language understanding requires stronger inductive biases than those currently implemented in deep learning systems remains an open question. Our work shows that utilizing linguistic abstraction in the attention mechanism of transformers may be a promising approach for improving the systematic generalization capabilities of deep neural networks.

Acknowledgements

We would like to thank the members of the Computational Cognitive Neuroscience lab at UC Davis, Paul Smolensky, Roland Fernandez, and other members of the Deep Learning Group at Microsoft Research, as well as reviewers for helpful comments and discussions. The work was supported by: ONR grants ONR N00014-20-1-2578, N00014-19-1-2684 / N00014-18-1-2116, N00014-18-C-2067.

References

Marco Baroni. 2020. Linguistic generalization and compositionality in modern artificial neural networks. *Philosophical Transactions of the Royal Society B: Biological Sciences*, 375(1791):20190307.

Peter W. Battaglia, Jessica B. Hamrick, Victor Bapst, Alvaro Sanchez-Gonzalez, Vinicius Zambaldi, Mateusz Malinowski, Andrea Tacchetti, David Raposo, Adam Santoro, Ryan Faulkner, Caglar Gulcehre, Francis Song, Andrew Ballard, Justin Gilmer, George Dahl, Ashish Vaswani, Kelsey Allen, Charles Nash, Victoria Langston, Chris Dyer, Nicolas Heess, Daan Wierstra, Pushmeet Kohli, Matt Botvinick, Oriol Vinyals, Yujia Li, and Razvan Pascanu. 2018. Relational inductive biases, deep learning, and graph networks. *arXiv:1806.01261 [cs, stat]*.

Yoshua Bengio. 2017. The Consciousness Prior. *arXiv:1709.08568 [cs, stat]*.

Tom B. Brown, Benjamin Mann, Nick Ryder, Melanie Subbiah, Jared Kaplan, Prafulla Dhariwal, Arvind Neelakantan, Pranav Shyam, Girish Sastry, Amanda Askell, Sandhini Agarwal, Ariel Herbert-Voss, Gretchen Krueger, Tom Henighan, Rewon Child, Aditya Ramesh, Daniel M. Ziegler, Jeffrey Wu, Clemens Winter, Christopher Hesse, Mark Chen, Eric Sigler, Mateusz Litwin, Scott Gray, Benjamin Chess, Jack Clark, Christopher Berner, Sam McCandlish, Alec Radford, Ilya Sutskever, and Dario Amodei. 2020. Language Models are Few-Shot Learners.

Zihang Dai, Zhilin Yang, Yiming Yang, Jaime Carbonell, Quoc Le, and Ruslan Salakhutdinov. 2019. Transformer-XL: Attentive language models beyond a fixed-length context. In *Proceedings of the 57th Annual Meeting of the Association for Computational Linguistics*, pages 2978–2988, Florence, Italy. Association for Computational Linguistics.

Jacob Devlin, Ming-Wei Chang, Kenton Lee, and Kristina Toutanova. 2019. BERT: Pre-training of deep bidirectional transformers for language understanding. In *Proc. of the 2019 Conf. of the NA Chapt. of the Assoc. for Comp. Ling.*, pages 4171–4186, Minneapolis, MN, USA. Association for Computational Linguistics.

Jerry A. Fodor and Zenon W. Pylyshyn. 1988. Connectionism and cognitive architecture: A critical analysis. *Cognition*, 28(1-2):3–71.

Daniel Furrer, Marc van Zee, Nathan Scales, and Nathanael Schärli. 2021. Compositional Generalization in Semantic Parsing: Pre-training vs. Specialized Architectures. *arXiv:2007.08970 [cs]*.

Anirudh Goyal, Alex Lamb, Jordan Hoffmann, Shagun Sodhani, Sergey Levine, Yoshua Bengio, and Bernhard Schölkopf. 2019. Recurrent Independent Mechanisms. *arXiv:1909.10893 [cs, stat]*.

Alex Graves, Greg Wayne, and Ivo Danihelka. 2014. Neural Turing Machines. *arXiv:1410.5401 [cs]*.

Yinuo Guo, Hualei Zhu, Zeqi Lin, Bei Chen, Jian-Guang Lou, and Dongmei Zhang. 2020. Revisiting Iterative Back-Translation from the Perspective of Compositional Generalization. *arXiv:2012.04276 [cs]*.

Yichen Jiang and Mohit Bansal. 2021. Inducing Transformer's Compositional Generalization Ability via Auxiliary Sequence Prediction Tasks. In *Proceedings of the 2021 Conference on Empirical Methods in Natural Language Processing*, pages 6253–6265, Online and Punta Cana, Dominican Republic. Association for Computational Linguistics.

Daniel Keysers, Nathanael Schärli, Nathan Scales, Hylke Buisman, Daniel Furrer, Sergii Kashubin, Nikola Momchev, Danila Sinopalnikov, Lukasz Stafiniak, Tibor Tihon, Dmitry Tsarkov, Xiao Wang, Marc van Zee, and Olivier Bousquet. 2020. Measuring compositional generalization: A comprehensive method on realistic data. page 38.

Najoung Kim and Tal Linzen. 2020. COGS: A Compositional Generalization Challenge Based on Semantic Interpretation. In *Proceedings of the 2020 Conference on Empirical Methods in Natural Language Processing (EMNLP)*, pages 9087–9105, Online. Association for Computational Linguistics.

Diederik P. Kingma and Jimmy Ba. 2015. Adam: A Method for Stochastic Optimization. In *3rd International Conference on Learning Representations, ICLR 2015, San Diego, CA, USA, May 7-9, 2015, Conference Track Proceedings*.

Brenden M Lake. 2019. Compositional generalization through meta sequence-to-sequence learning. In H. Wallach, H. Larochelle, A. Beygelzimer, F. Alché-Buc, E. Fox, and R. Garnett, editors, *Advances in Neural Information Processing Systems 32*, pages 9788–9798. Curran Associates, Inc.

Brenden M. Lake and Marco Baroni. 2018. Generalization without systematicity: On the compositional skills of sequence-to-sequence recurrent networks. In *Proc. of the 35th Intern. Conf. on Mach. Lear.*, volume 80 of *Proceedings of Machine Learning Research*, pages 2879–2888, Stockholmsmässan, Stockholm, Sweden. PMLR.

Brenden M. Lake, Tal Linzen, and Marco Baroni. 2019. Human few-shot learning of compositional instructions. In *Proceedings of the 41th Annual Meeting of the Cognitive Science Society, CogSci 2019: Creativity + Cognition + Computation, Montreal, Canada, July 24-27, 2019*, pages 611–617. cognitivesciencesociety.org.

Brenden M. Lake, Tomer D. Ullman, Joshua B. Tenenbaum, and Samuel J. Gershman. 2017. Building machines that learn and think like people. *The Behavioral and Brain Sciences*, 40:e253.

Yuanpeng Li, Liang Zhao, Jianyu Wang, and Joel Hestness. 2019. Compositional Generalization for Primitive Substitutions. In *Proceedings of the 2019 Conference on Empirical Methods in Natural Language Processing and the 9th International Joint Conference on Natural Language Processing (EMNLP-IJCNLP)*, pages 4293–4302, Hong Kong, China. Association for Computational Linguistics.

Tal Linzen. 2020. How Can We Accelerate Progress Towards Human-like Linguistic Generalization? In *Proceedings of the 58th Annual Meeting of the Association for Computational Linguistics*, pages 5210–5217, Online. Association for Computational Linguistics.

Tal Linzen and Marco Baroni. 2021. Syntactic Structure from Deep Learning. *Annual Review of Linguistics*, 7(1):null.

Qian Liu, Shengnan An, Jian-Guang Lou, Bei Chen, Zeqi Lin, Yan Gao, Bin Zhou, Nanning Zheng, and Dongmei Zhang. 2020. Compositional Generalization by Learning Analytical Expressions. *arXiv:2006.10627 [cs]*.

Christopher D. Manning, Kevin Clark, John Hewitt, Urvashi Khandelwal, and Omer Levy. 2020. Emergent linguistic structure in artificial neural networks trained by self-supervision. *Proceedings of the National Academy of Sciences*.

Diego Marcheggiani and Ivan Titov. 2017. Encoding Sentences with Graph Convolutional Networks for Semantic Role Labeling. In *Proceedings of the 2017 Conference on Empirical Methods in Natural Language Processing*, pages 1506–1515, Copenhagen, Denmark. Association for Computational Linguistics.

R. Thomas McCoy, Ellie Pavlick, and Tal Linzen. 2019. Right for the Wrong Reasons: Diagnosing Syntactic Heuristics in Natural Language Inference. *arXiv:1902.01007 [cs]*.

R. C. O'Reilly, Charan Ranganath, and Jacob L. Russin. 2021. The Structure of Systematicity in the Brain. *arXiv:2108.03387 [q-bio]*.

Nasim Rahaman, Muhammad Waleed Gondal, Shruti Joshi, Peter V. Gehler, Yoshua Bengio, Francesco Locatello, and Bernhard Schölkopf. 2021. Dynamic inference with neural interpreters. *CoRR*, abs/2110.06399.

Jacob Russin, Roland Fernandez, Hamid Palangi, Eric Rosen, Nebojsa Jojic, Paul Smolensky, and Jianfeng Gao. 2021. Compositional Processing Emerges in Neural Networks Solving Math Problems. In *Proceedings for the 43rd Annual Meeting of the Cognitive Science Society*.

Jacob Russin, Jason Jo, Randall C O'Reilly, and Yoshua Bengio. 2020. Systematicity in a Recurrent Neural Network by Factorizing Syntax and Semantics. In *Proceedings for the 42nd Annual Meeting of the Cognitive Science Society*, page 7.

Devendra Singh Sachan, Yuhao Zhang, Peng Qi, and William Hamilton. 2021. Do Syntax Trees Help Pre-trained Transformers Extract Information? *arXiv:2008.09084 [cs]*.

Imanol Schlag, Paul Smolensky, Roland Fernandez, Nebojsa Jojic, Jürgen Schmidhuber, and Jianfeng Gao. 2019. Enhancing the Transformer with Explicit Relational Encoding for Math Problem Solving. *arXiv:1910.06611 [cs, stat]*.

Rico Sennrich and Barry Haddow. 2016. Linguistic Input Features Improve Neural Machine Translation. In *Proceedings of the First Conference on Machine Translation: Volume 1, Research Papers*, pages 83–91, Berlin, Germany. Association for Computational Linguistics.

Paul Smolensky. 1990. Tensor product variable binding and the representation of symbolic structures in connectionist systems. *Artificial Intelligence*, 46(1-2):159–216.

Emma Strubell, Patrick Verga, Daniel Andor, David Weiss, and Andrew McCallum. 2018. Linguistically-Informed Self-Attention for Semantic Role Labeling. In *Proceedings of the 2018 Conference on Empirical Methods in Natural Language Processing*, pages 5027–5038, Brussels, Belgium. Association for Computational Linguistics.

Ian Tenney, Dipanjan Das, and Ellie Pavlick. 2019. BERT Rediscovers the Classical NLP Pipeline. *arXiv:1905.05950 [cs]*.

Ashish Vaswani, Noam Shazeer, Niki Parmar, Jakob Uszkoreit, Llion Jones, Aidan N. Gomez, Lukasz Kaiser, and Illia Polosukhin. 2017. Attention is All you Need. In *Advances in Neural Information Processing Systems 30: Annual Conference on Neural Information Processing Systems 2017, 4-9 December 2017, Long Beach, CA, USA*, pages 5998–6008.

Taylor W. Webb, Ishan Sinha, and Jonathan D. Cohen. 2021. Emergent Symbols through Binding in External Memory. *arXiv:2012.14601 [cs]*.

Grounding in social media: An approach to building a chit-chat dialogue model

Ritvik Choudhary
Waseda University
ritvik@fuji.waseda.jp

Daisuke Kawahara
Waseda University
dkw@waseda.jp

Abstract

Building open-domain dialogue systems capable of rich human-like conversational ability is one of the fundamental challenges in language generation. However, even with recent advancements in the field, existing open-domain generative models fail to capture and utilize external knowledge, leading to repetitive or generic responses to unseen utterances. Current work on knowledge-grounded dialogue generation primarily focuses on persona incorporation or searching a fact-based structured knowledge source such as Wikipedia. Our method takes a broader and simpler approach, which aims to improve the raw conversation ability of the system by mimicking the human response behavior through casual interactions found on social media. Utilizing a joint retriever-generator setup, the model queries a large set of filtered comment data from Reddit to act as additional context for the seq2seq generator. Automatic and human evaluations on open-domain dialogue datasets demonstrate the effectiveness of our approach.

1 Introduction

Humans have long wanted to talk with the machine and have them comprehend and generate natural language. The task of chit-chat dialogue response generation can be described as one of the major goals in natural language processing. As such, there has been considerable interest in the sub-field of open-domain dialogue models.

Nevertheless, the existing dialogue response generation models still suffer from some very fundamental problems: lack of interesting ("Ok", "I see", etc.) or uninformative responses ("I don't know") (Li et al., 2016a, Shao et al., 2017, Ghazvininejad et al., 2017). The primary cause for this is that, unlike humans, the models do not have access to knowledge, experience about out-of-domain topics or human conversational habits and hence can only produce limited unengaging generic responses.

Recent work has proposed considering additional context information such as multi-turn conversational history (Zhang et al., 2018), persona (Li et al., 2016b) or a fact-based knowledge base (Dinan et al., 2019). Among these, our work approaches this problem from a more general standpoint of improving the raw conversational ability of generative models. We attempt this by taking inspiration from how humans learn to converse, i.e., through mimicking social interactions. Applying this in the context of dialogue models, we use a human-readable external knowledge base consisting solely of unstructured **s**ocial **m**edia **i**nteractions (hereinafter referred to as SMIkb), which tends to include a more diverse language structure and hence improve generated responses.

For our approach, we jointly train a generator-retriever model where the retriever searches through pre-indexed SMIkb and feeds the related information together with the input utterance to the generative seq2seq model, allowing for additional context at the time of generation.

In particular, we utilize the Dense Passage Retriever proposed by Karpukhin et al. (2020) on top of BART (Lewis et al., 2020a) as our generational model trained on a mix of open-domain dialogue datasets, together with a collection of Reddit submissions and comments as our main source of social interactions. Experiments showed that our approach outperformed the existing vanilla seq2seq baseline (BART) across all of the automatic and human evaluation metrics. By making use of interactions grounded in social media, the generated responses were not only more engaging but were also shown to be much more relevant and natural, thus establishing the effectiveness of our approach.

2 Related Work

Dialogue Systems In recent years, major breakthroughs beginning with the Transformer (Vaswani et al., 2017) and BERT (Devlin et al., 2019) have

Proceedings of the 2022 Conference of the North American Chapter of the Association for Computational Linguistics: Human Language Technologies: Student Research Workshop, pages 9 - 15
July 10-15, 2022

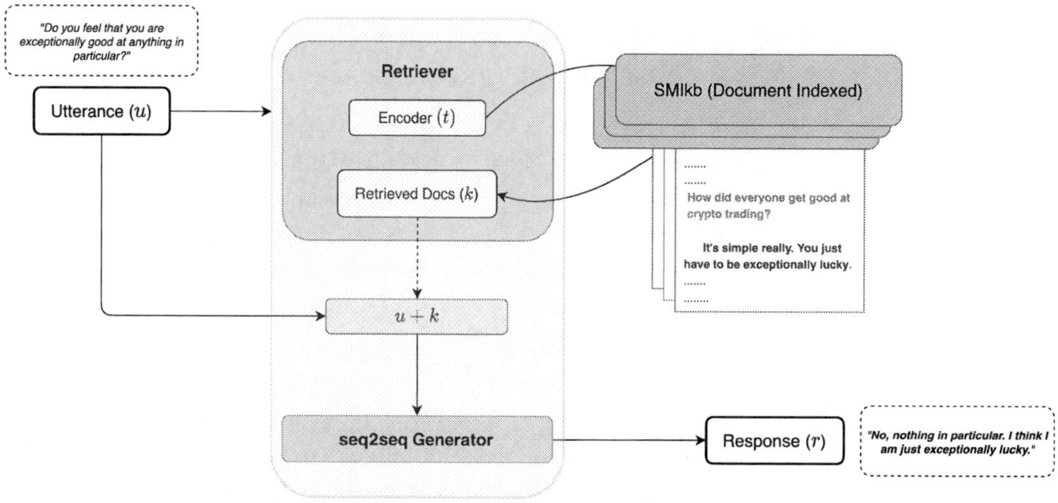

Figure 1: Our proposed dialogue response generation approach grounded in SMIkb through a jointly trained retriever-seq2seq generator setup. Utterance u is encoded and matched against titles (in red) where the respective comments (k, in blue) are retrieved from the SMIkb. These act as an additional context for the generator to generate the final dialogue response r.

quickly shifted the landscape of modern NLP research. These were shortly followed by auto-regressive seq2seq models (T5 (Raffel et al., 2020), BART) that significantly improved performance on generation-based tasks such as dialogue systems. We adopt the widely accessible BART as our strong baseline.

Knowledge-based Conversational Models Incorporating additional context or external information into existing models has been a field of much interest lately. Persona-chat (Zhang et al., 2018) or Empathetic Dialogues (Rashkin et al., 2019) take into account persona or empathetic information. Furthermore, advancements making use of knowledge bases in the area of open-domain dialogue systems have become increasingly common (Ghazvininejad et al., 2017; Dinan et al., 2019). The closest work to ours, in terms of including a retrieval step for dialogue generation, is Weston et al. (2018), which proposed an approach involving pre-training the retriever and generating only over the candidates retrieved in advance from the training set. More recently Roller et al. (2021) also tested retrieval-based dialogue generation. However, similar to Weston et al. (2018), they utilized a retrieval model that was kept fixed during training. Our work meanwhile follows a different direction that does not require pre-training of the retriever but fine-tunes it along with the generator to retrieve over a much larger knowledge base of interactions at generation time.

We would also like to mention Shuster et al. (2021), which investigates factual hallucination in dialogue retrieval-generation models with a fact-based knowledge base such as Wikipedia. Our work takes a more generalized approach, focusing solely on improving the raw conversational ability of dialogue models. Instead of factual accuracy, we propose a simple approach for generating an engaging conversation grounded in unstructured social media interactions.

3 Proposed Approach

In this section, we discuss our approach to introducing social media interactions as an external knowledge base (SMIkb) to ground in for more natural and human-like response generation. We begin with formulating the task of dialogue generation and then proceed to explain our joint retriever-generator model as the proposed setup for utilizing the aforementioned unstructured data source. Note that in this work, we primarily focus on response generation for single-turn dialogues or dialogues. We decided that other settings such as a multi-turn case were best addressed in future work.

3.1 Task Formulation

Our task of response generation grounded in external knowledge can be formulated as training a model to predict a response $\mathbf{r} = (r_1, r_2, ..., r_m)$ of

m words when given an input utterance $\mathbf{u}$ and a set of documents $\mathcal{D}$ that might contain relevant knowledge. We define our goal as to allow the model to learn the parameters such that when given an input utterance $\mathbf{u}$ and a knowledge base $\mathcal{D}$, the model can generate a response $\mathbf{r}$ following the probability $p(r_i|\mathbf{u}, \mathbf{r}_{<i}, \mathcal{D}; \theta)$, where θ refers to the parameters of the model.

3.2 Model

Inspired by recent advances in retrieval assisted QA (Guu et al., 2020; Lewis et al., 2020b), we adopt a simple joint retriever-generator setup to the task of dialogue generation. Concretely, we utilize BART, a seq2seq model pre-trained on a denoising objective, as our generative model along with the pre-trained neural Dense Passage Retriever (DPR) (Karpukhin et al., 2020) as the retriever of choice. DPR is a highly efficient neural retriever pre-trained for retrieving the top-$\boldsymbol{k}$ similar documents to an input query $\boldsymbol{u}$. It executes this by encoding both the query and the entire knowledge base through independent BERT-based encoders (as $\boldsymbol{t}$). Furthermore, we follow Karpukhin et al. (2020) to build an offline searchable dense vector index of these embeddings for our SMIkb using the FAISS (Johnson et al., 2017) library for faster lookup. An overview of our architecture is shown in Figure 1. Application of our model to dialogue response generation can be formulated as a two-step process: (1) the retriever searching top-k documents from the pre-indexed interaction knowledge base, relevant to the input utterance, and (2) the generator predicting the response to the previous utterance along with the retrieved context.

Following the notion set in Section 3.1, the probability of generating the response $\mathbf{r}$ given the utterance $\mathbf{u}$ and each of the top-k documents d_j from the knowledge base $\mathcal{D}$ can be defined as

$$p(\mathbf{r}|\mathbf{u}; \theta, \lambda) = \textstyle\sum_j^k p_\lambda(d_j|\mathbf{u}; \lambda) \prod_i p_\theta(r_i|\mathbf{u}, \mathbf{r}_{<i}, d_j; \theta), \quad (1)$$

where θ and λ are parameters for the generator and retriever, respectively. They are both fine-tuned jointly in an end-to-end fashion, with the retriever providing additional context that is concatenated together with the input at the time of generation. As there is no "correct" document source in the knowledge base, we consider it to be a latent variable. Therefore, during decoding we marginalize these probabilities over all the retrieved documents to return the most probable (best) response using beam search.

Dataset	Total (turns)	Train	Valid	Test
DailyDialog	76,743	53,721	11,511	11,511
DailyDialog++	39,913	27,939	5,987	5,987
Cornell Movie-Dialogs	221,088	154,762	33,163	33,163
Reddit (pseudo extracted)	200,000	140,000	30,000	30,000

Table 1: Overview of datasets in use.

4 Experiments

We evaluate our model together with various external knowledge datasets on a mixture of open-domain dialogue datasets. The results are then compared with two BART-based baselines.

4.1 SMIkb

Aiming to improve the raw communication ability of dialogue systems by mimicking human response behavior, we built our external knowledge base of unstructured social media interactions (SMIkb). It comprises of entries from top thread titles and their top 100 comments from Reddit, an American social news aggregation and discussion site, throughout 2020 (January-November). A total of 1.6 million entries were first scraped through the open-sourced Pushshift API (Baumgartner et al., 2020) of which a random selection of 600,000 (due to memory limitations) makes up our SMIkb. A snapshot of the same is shared in Table 5.

Furthermore, to verify the effectiveness of using a conversational knowledge base like Reddit, we compared ours to a pure Wikipedia knowledge base (ref. "Wiki") of the same size (random sample of 600k entries) containing the wiki page title and the leading 100 words. Additionally, we also tested a 1:1 combination of the above two bases (ref. "Mix").

4.2 Datasets

We fine-tune our models on a variety of open-domain and scraped dialogue datasets.

Open-domain datasets We use a combination of DailyDialog (Li et al., 2017) and DailyDialog++ (Sai et al., 2020) as high-quality daily life-based dialogue sets. We also consider the Cornell Movie-Dialogs Corpus (Danescu-Niculescu-Mizil and Lee, 2011), which is a corpus of scripts of movie dialogues.

Reddit Furthermore we extract another 200,000 comment pairs from Reddit, distinct from the

Model Setup	Training Data	Knowledge Base (Retrieval)				BLEU-4	Dist-1	Dist-2			
Baseline 1	ODD	None				1.31	0.20	0.96			
Baseline 2	ODD + SMIkb	None				1.05	0.12	0.47			
			$k = 3$			$k = 5$			$k = 7$		
			BLEU-4	Dist-1	Dist-2	BLEU-4	Dist-1	Dist-2	BLEU-4	Dist-1	Dist-2
Ours (SMIkb)	ODD	SMIkb	**9.78**	**2.80**	**16.90**	**10.51**	**5.50**	**26.63**	**10.48**	**5.51**	**26.62**
Ours (Wiki)	ODD	Wiki	6.93	2.57	14.91	7.14	4.94	23.38	7.11	5.02	23.79
Ours (Mix)	ODD	SMIkb + Wiki	6.03	2.45	14.08	6.20	4.71	22.25	6.21	4.71	22.23

Table 2: Automatic evaluation of generated responses across various values of k for top-k document retrieval. The baselines do not have a retrieval step and therefore do not have an effect due to changing k. **bold** refers to the best scores across all k among the generated responses. ODD is the collection of **O**pen-**D**omain **D**atasets from Section 4.2.

Model Setup	Human Eval.		
	Relevance	Engagement	Knowledge
Gold (Test-Data)	3.50	3.33	3.47
Baseline 1	2.82	2.35	3.00
Baseline 2	3.03	3.02	2.89
Ours (SMIkb)	**3.84**	3.75	3.60
Ours (Wiki)	3.40	3.75	**3.76**
Ours (Mix)	3.62	**3.80**	3.71

Table 3: Human evaluation of responses for the best $k = 5$.

SMIkb, to act as a pseudo dialogue dataset to supplement our knowledge base.

An overview of the datasets is listed in Table 1.

4.3 Experimental Setup

Implementation Details Our joint retriever-generator model consists of a pre-trained Dense Passage Retriever and BART-large (24 layers, 406M), which are later fine-tuned together on SMIkb and dialogue datasets. The model is trained mostly with the default parameters, batch size of 1, and an initial learning rate of 3×10^{-5}. We further experiment with various values of k for our top-k document retrieval, while beam search with size of 5 is used as our response decoding strategy.

Baseline We consider two strong baselines based on a vanilla BART-large with no retriever to investigate the effectiveness of our approach. The first is fine-tuned solely on the datasets mentioned in Section 4.2 (ref. "Baseline 1") with no SMIkb. Next to confirm the effectiveness of our providing external data through our retriever-generator setup, we merge the entire SMIkb interactions into our training data, and simply fine-tune the vanilla model on this new extended set. (ref. "Baseline 2"). Note that although we choose BART as our generator and baseline for its size and relative ease in training, our proposed SMIkb based modeling setup could possibly also be extended to larger models.

4.4 Evaluation

To measure the impact of social media interactions, the generated responses were evaluated through both automatic and human evaluations. The results are compiled in Tables 2 and 3.

Automatic We perform a series of automatic evaluations on the generated responses. Starting with the BLEU (Papineni et al., 2002) score for relevancy, we also calculate Distinct-N (Li et al., 2016a) for the amount of diversity introduced.

Human It has been widely reported that automatic metrics do not sufficiently evaluate the actual quality of the generated outputs (Liu et al., 2016). Thus, we additionally performed human evaluation of the responses with the highest BLEU ($k = 5$) through Amazon Mechanical Turk, on the following three metrics: *Relevance*, whether the response is relevant to the utterance; *Engagement*, whether the response makes the conversation engaging; and *Knowledge*, whether the response seems knowledgeable or sensible. The evaluators were asked to score 100 responses selected at random from the test set, on a scale of 1-5. Each response was scored by 7 different evaluators, and their average was calculated. We selected our evaluators to be English speakers from the United States with an approval rate of over 90%.

4.5 Discussion

First, with automatic evaluation, we observe that our method of introducing social interactions through a retriever at generation time maintains task performance and allows for a more diverse set of responses, as shown with an increase in all of the

Input Utterance	SMIkb	Wiki	Mix	Baseline
Here comes the birthday cake.	Wow, what a lovely cake. I'll have a piece.	Wow, what a beautiful cake. It must have tasted as good as I expected.	Really? Wow. Happy birthday to you! You look so healthy.	Thank you.
I'd better go. I gotta get up early. Go over to my parents'.	What are you going to do for breakfast?	You mean you don't wanna go with me?	Why don't you stay at my place? I'll cook dinner.	I don't think so.
Something's burning?	Oh my goodness, it's on fire!	Oh my goodness, it ' s burning!	Oh, my bread! It's burning!	No, it's not.
Would you mind if we just called it an early night?	Even I couldn't. I have work tomorrow.	I'd love to. But I've got to work tomorrow.	What are you talking about? We just ate?	I don't think so.
Isn't it wonderful walking here?	What do you mean? Was it bad?	Not at all. The air is fresh, the walk is easy and the sunshine is kind.	Yes, you can see the whole city from here.	Yes, it's very beautiful.

Table 4: A comparison of responses generated from various sources.

SMIkb	
title	text
LPT: If you borrow something like a tool or a generator from someone, return it in BETTER shape than you got it.	My dad always said that returning something in the same condition you received it is the absolute bare minimum.
SoftBank Nears $40 Billion Deal to Sell Arm Holdings to Nvidia	Nvidia is priced decentlyfor what they offer.
Apple to Give Employees Paid Time Off to Vote in U.S. Election	This exactly. A large majority of disenfranchised communities work jobs that don't observe federal holidays.
Apple may be working on a foldable iPhone	I can confirm that Apple would be stupid to not be working on one. Whether they ever release one is up for debate, but they're definitely working on one.

Table 5: Snapshot of SMIkb.

measured metrics over both the baselines. Moreover, our Reddit-based SMIkb model outperformed other combinations, confirming an increase in response quality. Furthermore, experiments comparing the effect of top-k on generation quality showed $k = 5$ as the sweet spot with the highest BLEU, which was then evaluated further.

Similar to the automatic evaluation, all of the proposed combinations showed improvements over the baseline in human evaluation. In line with our initial hypothesis, the SMIkb model recorded the highest score in terms of conversational relevance. Meanwhile, the mix of SMIkb and Wikipedia seems to find the appropriate balance between conversational ability and "knowledgeability" with the metrics even exceeding the gold score. We hypothesize that this is not just due to high generation quality but also the nature of our task, which might make our model responses more relevant to a worker when assessed in a single-turn context. Overall, the results verified our proposed approach of learning directly from social media interactions leading to large improvements over the baseline in all metrics of interest. Furthermore, significance tests of bootstrap re-sampling showed that the above evaluation score differences between baselines and our models were statistically significant ($p < 0.01$). Examples of the various generated responses across all the models are shared in Table 4.

In addition, we looked at cases where our model struggles or fails at generating a natural response, a select few of which are compiled in Table 6. In some of these particular cases, the baseline generations, although generic, turn out to be more relevant. We believe some of these long responses with unrelated information to be an artifact of our generation model being overly dependent on the

Input Utterance	SMIkb	Wiki	Mix	Baseline
Who was the conductor?	Oh speaking of the conductor, he was indeed a genius. A descendent of Chinese.	I don't remember the name.	Oh, speaking of the conductor, he did an excellent job.	I know.
Oh god you scared me!	Ahahah! We need a fitness instructor.	I'm sorry.	Sorry. I was trying to scare you.	Is something wrong?

Table 6: Selected examples where the proposed model struggles or fails at generating a relevant response.

knowledge base. While social media may simulate human-like conversations in a large variety of situations, it is still far from being a perfect stand-in for real-life dialogue. Therefore, our future work in this direction should look at not only the quality and scope of the knowledge base, but also consider selecting *when* to ground and make use of the said knowledge during response generation.

5 Conclusion

We aimed to improve the raw conversational ability of dialogue systems by grounding the responses in much more human-like social media interactions. Our approach involved a neural retriever-seq2seq generator model fine-tuned jointly, where relevant knowledge was retrieved at the time of generation to assist a more engaging and natural dialogue response. Our experiments showed significant improvements with both automatic and human evaluation metrics ranking the SMIkb-grounded replies to be much more diverse, engaging, and relevant.

Acknowledgements

This work was supported by a joint research grant from LINE Corporation.

References

Jason Baumgartner, Savvas Zannettou, Brian Keegan, Megan Squire, and Jeremy Blackburn. 2020. The pushshift reddit dataset. In *Proceedings of the Fourteenth International AAAI Conference on Web and Social Media, ICWSM 2020, Held Virtually, Original Venue: Atlanta, Georgia, USA, June 8-11, 2020*, pages 830–839. AAAI Press.

Cristian Danescu-Niculescu-Mizil and Lillian Lee. 2011. Chameleons in imagined conversations: A new approach to understanding coordination of linguistic style in dialogs. In *Proceedings of the 2nd Workshop on Cognitive Modeling and Computational Linguistics*, pages 76–87, Portland, Oregon, USA. Association for Computational Linguistics.

Jacob Devlin, Ming-Wei Chang, Kenton Lee, and Kristina Toutanova. 2019. BERT: Pre-training of deep bidirectional transformers for language understanding. In *Proceedings of the 2019 Conference of the North American Chapter of the Association for Computational Linguistics: Human Language Technologies, Volume 1 (Long and Short Papers)*, pages 4171–4186, Minneapolis, Minnesota. Association for Computational Linguistics.

Emily Dinan, Stephen Roller, Kurt Shuster, Angela Fan, Michael Auli, and Jason Weston. 2019. Wizard of wikipedia: Knowledge-powered conversational agents. In *International Conference on Learning Representations*.

Marjan Ghazvininejad, Chris Brockett, Ming-Wei Chang, Bill Dolan, Jianfeng Gao, Wen-tau Yih, and Michel Galley. 2017. A knowledge-grounded neural conversation model. *arXiv preprint arXiv:1702.01932*.

Kelvin Guu, Kenton Lee, Zora Tung, Panupong Pasupat, and Ming-Wei Chang. 2020. Realm: Retrieval-augmented language model pre-training.

Jeff Johnson, Matthijs Douze, and Hervé Jégou. 2017. Billion-scale similarity search with gpus. *arXiv preprint arXiv:1702.08734*.

Vladimir Karpukhin, Barlas Oguz, Sewon Min, Patrick Lewis, Ledell Wu, Sergey Edunov, Danqi Chen, and Wen-tau Yih. 2020. Dense passage retrieval for open-domain question answering. In *Proceedings of the 2020 Conference on Empirical Methods in Natural Language Processing (EMNLP)*, pages 6769–6781, Online. Association for Computational Linguistics.

Mike Lewis, Yinhan Liu, Naman Goyal, Marjan Ghazvininejad, Abdelrahman Mohamed, Omer Levy, Veselin Stoyanov, and Luke Zettlemoyer. 2020a. BART: Denoising sequence-to-sequence pre-training for natural language generation, translation, and comprehension. In *Proceedings of the 58th Annual Meeting of the Association for Computational Linguistics*, pages 7871–7880, Online. Association for Computational Linguistics.

Patrick Lewis, Ethan Perez, Aleksandra Piktus, Fabio Petroni, Vladimir Karpukhin, Naman Goyal, Heinrich Küttler, Mike Lewis, Wen-tau Yih, Tim Rocktäschel, Sebastian Riedel, and Douwe Kiela. 2020b.

Retrieval-augmented generation for knowledge-intensive nlp tasks. In *Advances in Neural Information Processing Systems*, volume 33, pages 9459–9474. Curran Associates, Inc.

Jiwei Li, Michel Galley, Chris Brockett, Jianfeng Gao, and Bill Dolan. 2016a. A diversity-promoting objective function for neural conversation models. In *Proceedings of the 2016 Conference of the North American Chapter of the Association for Computational Linguistics: Human Language Technologies*, pages 110–119, San Diego, California. Association for Computational Linguistics.

Jiwei Li, Michel Galley, Chris Brockett, Georgios Spithourakis, Jianfeng Gao, and Bill Dolan. 2016b. A persona-based neural conversation model. In *Proceedings of the 54th Annual Meeting of the Association for Computational Linguistics (Volume 1: Long Papers)*, pages 994–1003, Berlin, Germany. Association for Computational Linguistics.

Yanran Li, Hui Su, Xiaoyu Shen, Wenjie Li, Ziqiang Cao, and Shuzi Niu. 2017. DailyDialog: A manually labelled multi-turn dialogue dataset. In *Proceedings of the Eighth International Joint Conference on Natural Language Processing (Volume 1: Long Papers)*, pages 986–995, Taipei, Taiwan. Asian Federation of Natural Language Processing.

Chia-Wei Liu, Ryan Lowe, Iulian Serban, Mike Noseworthy, Laurent Charlin, and Joelle Pineau. 2016. How NOT to evaluate your dialogue system: An empirical study of unsupervised evaluation metrics for dialogue response generation. In *Proceedings of the 2016 Conference on Empirical Methods in Natural Language Processing*, pages 2122–2132, Austin, Texas. Association for Computational Linguistics.

Kishore Papineni, Salim Roukos, Todd Ward, and Wei-Jing Zhu. 2002. Bleu: a method for automatic evaluation of machine translation. In *Proceedings of the 40th Annual Meeting of the Association for Computational Linguistics*, pages 311–318, Philadelphia, Pennsylvania, USA. Association for Computational Linguistics.

Colin Raffel, Noam Shazeer, Adam Roberts, Katherine Lee, Sharan Narang, Michael Matena, Yanqi Zhou, Wei Li, and Peter J. Liu. 2020. Exploring the limits of transfer learning with a unified text-to-text transformer.

Hannah Rashkin, Eric Michael Smith, Margaret Li, and Y-Lan Boureau. 2019. Towards empathetic open-domain conversation models: A new benchmark and dataset. In *Proceedings of the 57th Annual Meeting of the Association for Computational Linguistics*, pages 5370–5381, Florence, Italy. Association for Computational Linguistics.

Stephen Roller, Emily Dinan, Naman Goyal, Da Ju, Mary Williamson, Yinhan Liu, Jing Xu, Myle Ott, Eric Michael Smith, Y-Lan Boureau, and Jason Weston. 2021. Recipes for building an open-domain chatbot. In *Proceedings of the 16th Conference of the European Chapter of the Association for Computational Linguistics: Main Volume*, pages 300–325, Online. Association for Computational Linguistics.

Ananya B. Sai, Akash Kumar Mohankumar, Siddhartha Arora, and Mitesh M. Khapra. 2020. Improving dialog evaluation with a multi-reference adversarial dataset and large scale pretraining. *Transactions of the Association for Computational Linguistics*, 8:810–827.

Yuanlong Shao, Stephan Gouws, Denny Britz, Anna Goldie, Brian Strope, and Ray Kurzweil. 2017. Generating high-quality and informative conversation responses with sequence-to-sequence models. In *Proceedings of the 2017 Conference on Empirical Methods in Natural Language Processing*, pages 2210–2219, Copenhagen, Denmark. Association for Computational Linguistics.

Kurt Shuster, Spencer Poff, Moya Chen, Douwe Kiela, and Jason Weston. 2021. Retrieval augmentation reduces hallucination in conversation.

Ashish Vaswani, Noam Shazeer, Niki Parmar, Jakob Uszkoreit, Llion Jones, Aidan N. Gomez, Lukasz Kaiser, and Illia Polosukhin. 2017. Attention is all you need.

Jason Weston, Emily Dinan, and Alexander Miller. 2018. Retrieve and refine: Improved sequence generation models for dialogue. In *Proceedings of the 2018 EMNLP Workshop SCAI: The 2nd International Workshop on Search-Oriented Conversational AI*, pages 87–92, Brussels, Belgium. Association for Computational Linguistics.

Saizheng Zhang, Emily Dinan, Jack Urbanek, Arthur Szlam, Douwe Kiela, and Jason Weston. 2018. Personalizing dialogue agents: I have a dog, do you have pets too? In *Proceedings of the 56th Annual Meeting of the Association for Computational Linguistics (Volume 1: Long Papers)*, pages 2204–2213, Melbourne, Australia. Association for Computational Linguistics.

ExtraPhrase: Efficient Data Augmentation for Abstractive Summarization

Mengsay Loem, Sho Takase, Masahiro Kaneko, and **Naoaki Okazaki**
Tokyo Institute of Technology
{mengsay.loem, sho.takase, masahiro.kaneko}@nlp.c.titech.ac.jp
naoaki.okazaki@c.titech.ac.jp

Abstract

Neural models trained with large amount of parallel data have achieved impressive performance in abstractive summarization tasks. However, large-scale parallel corpora are expensive and challenging to construct. In this work, we introduce a low-cost and effective strategy, **ExtraPhrase**, to augment training data for abstractive summarization tasks. ExtraPhrase constructs pseudo training data in two steps: extractive summarization and paraphrasing. We extract major parts of an input text in the extractive summarization step and obtain its diverse expressions with the paraphrasing step. Through experiments, we show that ExtraPhrase improves the performance of abstractive summarization tasks by more than 0.50 points in ROUGE scores compared to the setting without data augmentation. ExtraPhrase also outperforms existing methods such as back-translation and self-training. We also show that ExtraPhrase is significantly effective when the amount of genuine training data is remarkably small, i.e., a low-resource setting. Moreover, ExtraPhrase is more cost-efficient than the existing approaches[1].

1 Introduction

Neural encoder-decoders have achieved remarkable performance in various sequence-to-sequence tasks including machine translation, summarization, and grammatical error correction (Bahdanau et al., 2015; Rush et al., 2015; Yuan and Briscoe, 2016). Recent studies indicated that neural methods are governed by the scaling law for the amount of training data (Koehn and Knowles, 2017; Brown et al., 2020). In short, the more training data we prepare, the better performance a neural model achieves. In this paper, we address increasing the training data for summarization to improve the performance of neural encoder-decoders on abstractive summarization tasks.

In sequence-to-sequence tasks, we need a parallel corpus to train neural encoder-decoders. Since it is too costly to construct genuine (i.e., human-generated) parallel corpora, most studies explored the way to construct pseudo training data automatically. Back-translation is a widely used approach to construct pseudo training data for sequence-to-sequence tasks (Sennrich et al., 2016a; Edunov et al., 2018; Caswell et al., 2019). In the back-translation approach, we construct a model generating a source side sentence from a target side sentence, and apply the model to a target side corpus to generate a pseudo source side corpus. In addition to machine translation, back-translation is also used in grammatical error correction (Kiyono et al., 2019) and summarization (Parida and Motlicek, 2019) tasks. However, back-translation on summarization is an unrealistic problem because a model is required to restore deleted information in the given summary without any guide.

He et al. (2020) indicated that the self-training approach, which makes a model generate target sentences from source sentences and use the pairs to train a model, can improve the performance on machine translation and summarization. However, pseudo data generation for summarization by self-training is hard to generate diverse summaries (Gu et al., 2018). Moreover, self-training and back-translation approaches require expensive computational cost because we need to train additional neural encoder-decoders on a large amount of training data to obtain high-quality pseudo data (Imankulova et al., 2019).

To solve these issues, we propose a novel strategy: **ExtraPhrase** consisting of **extra**ctive summarization and para**phrase** to construct pseudo training data for abstractive summarization. Firstly, ExtraPhrase extracts an important part from a source text as a summary without requiring additional model training. Then, we apply a paraphrasing technique to the extracted text to obtain diverse

[1]The datasets used in our experiments are available at https://github.com/loem-ms/ExtraPhrase.

Proceedings of the 2022 Conference of the North American Chapter of the Association for Computational Linguistics: Human Language Technologies: Student Research Workshop, pages 16 - 24
July 10-15, 2022

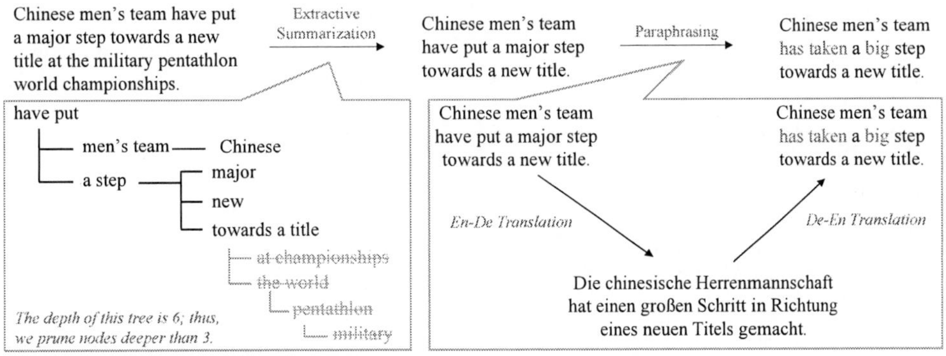

Figure 1: Example of pseudo summary generated by **ExtraPhrase**. The upper part shows output sentences in each step of ExtraPhrase. Paraphrased words after paraphrasing (round-trip translation) in step-2 are highlighted in blue.

pseudo summaries.

We conduct experiments on two summarization tasks: headline generation and document summarization tasks. Experimental results show that pseudo training data constructed by our proposed strategy improves the performance on both tasks. In detail, the pseudo data raises more than 0.50 in ROUGE F1 scores on both tasks. Moreover, we show that ExtraPhrase is robust in low-resource settings and is much more cost-efficient than previous self-training and back-translation approaches.

2 Proposed Method: ExtraPhrase

As described in Section 1, our ExtraPhrase consists of two steps: extractive summarization and paraphrasing. Figure 1 illustrates the overview of ExtraPhrase briefly. ExtraPhrase receives a (genuine) sentence as an input, and generates a pseudo summary corresponding to the input sentence. When we construct a pseudo summary from a document, we independently apply ExtraPhrase to multiple sentences included in the given document.

2.1 Step-1: Extractive Summarization

In this extractive summarization step, we extract important parts of a given source sentence with sentence compression. Previous studies proposed various sentence compression methods such as rule-based methods (Dorr et al., 2003), the approach detecting important parts in a syntax tree (Turner and Charniak, 2005; Filippova and Altun, 2013; Cohn and Lapata, 2009), sequential labeling approach (Hirao et al., 2009), and neural-based methods (Filippova et al., 2015; Kamigaito et al., 2018).

In this study, we adopt the most straightforward approach: a rule-based method based on the syntax tree of the given sentence. Because the rule-based approach does not require any training corpus, we can use it in the situation where we do not have genuine parallel corpus. We emphasize that we can use more sophisticated way if we need because we do not have any restrictions for the summarization method in this step.

We define a rooted subtree of the syntax tree for the given sentence as important parts of the sentence. First, we parse the given sentence to obtain its dependency tree. Follow Filippova and Altun (2013), we combine functional words with their heads on the dependency tree. Then, we prune the dependency tree to obtain a smaller rooted subtree. We can roughly control the output summary length (the number of words) by the depth of the subtree. The left lower part of Figure 1 illustrates these processes. Finally, we linearize the extracted rooted subtree to obtain its sequential representation by following the word order of the original sentence.

2.2 Step-2: Paraphrasing

The constructed summaries by the previous step consist of words included in the source sentences only. To increase the diversity of the summaries, we apply the paraphrasing method to the summaries. For paraphrasing, we adopt the approach using machine translation models (Sun and Zhou, 2012; Mallinson et al., 2017) because some studies published high-quality neural machine translation models (Ott et al., 2018; Ng et al., 2019). In this approach, we obtain paraphrases by conducting round-trip translation that translates a sentence into a different language and the translated sentence into the original language. The right lower part of Figure 1 illustrates this process.

3 Experiments

To investigate the effect of ExtraPhrase, we conduct experiments on two summarization tasks: headline generation and document summarization tasks.

3.1 Datasets

For the headline generation task, we use the de-facto headline generation dataset constructed by Rush et al. (2015). The dataset contains pairs of the first sentence and headline extracted from the annotated English Gigaword (Napoles et al., 2012). We use the same splits for train, valid, and test as Rush et al. (2015). We use the byte pair encoding (Sennrich et al., 2016b) to construct a vocabulary set with the size of 32K by sharing vocabulary between source and target sides.

For the document summarization task, we use CNN/DailyMail dataset (See et al., 2017). The training set contains 280K pairs of news articles and abstractive summary extracted from CNN and DailyMail websites. We construct a vocabulary set with the byte pair encoding (Sennrich et al., 2016b) and set the vocabulary size to 32K with sharing vocabulary between source and target sides.

3.2 Comparison Methods

We compare ExtraPhrase with several existing methods to increase the training data size as follows. We use the training set of each dataset described in Section 3.1 to construct pseudo data.

Oversampling This strategy is the simplest approach to increase the dataset size. We sample source-summary pairs from the genuine training set and add the sampled instances to training data. Thus, the training data constructed by this approach contains genuine data only.

Back-translation In back-translation, we train a neural encoder-decoder that generates a source text from a summary by using each training set. Then, we input summaries in the training set to the neural encoder-decoder to generate corresponding source texts[2]. We use the pairs of pseudo source texts and genuine summaries as pseudo training data.

Self-training In self-training, we train a neural encoder-decoder that generates a summary from a source text by using each training set. Then, we input source texts in the training set to the neural encoder-decoder to generate the corresponding summaries. We use the pairs of pseudo summaries and genuine source texts as pseudo training data.

ExtraPhrase We apply ExtraPhrase to each training set. In the headline generation task, we construct pseudo summaries from the source sentence in the training data. Because ExtraPhrase generates pseudo summary in sentence unit, the number of sentences in generated summary is not reduced in the case of multi-sentence source text. Thus, we use the first three sentences in the source document to reduce the number of input sentences beforehand in the document summarization task. As described in Section 2, we apply ExtraPhrase to each sentence one-by-one, and then concatenate them in the original order. In this study, we use spaCy[3] (Honnibal et al., 2020) for dependency parsing and prune nodes whose depths are deeper than half of the dependency tree in the extractive summarization step. For the paraphrasing step, we use English-to-German and German-to-English translation models[4] constructed by Ng et al. (2019). We translate sentences with beam width 5.

For all pseudo training data, we attach a special token, <Pseudo>, to the front of the source text because Caswell et al. (2019) indicated that this strategy improves the performance in training on pseudo data.

3.3 Encoder-Decoder Architecture

We use the de-facto standard neural encoder-decoder model, Transformer (Vaswani et al., 2017) in our experiments. We also use the Transformer for back-translation and self-training in addition to each abstractive summarization model. We use the Transformer-base setting described in Vaswani et al. (2017) as our architecture. The setting is widely used in studies on machine translation (Vaswani et al., 2017; Ott et al., 2018). In detail, we use the implementation in the fairseq[5] (Ott et al., 2019) for our experiments.

[2]For the back-translation approach in machine translation, we generate sentences in the source language from monolingual corpus in the target language. In the abstractive summarization, we need summaries as sentences in the target language but it is hard to obtain corpus containing summaries only. Thus, we use genuine summaries in training data as an input of back-translation.

[3]https://spacy.io/

[4]https://github.com/pytorch/fairseq/tree/main/examples/translation

[5]https://github.com/pytorch/fairseq

Method	Headline Generation				Document Summarization			
	Training Data	R-1	R-2	R-L	Training Data	R-1	R-2	R-L
Genuine only	3.8M	37.95	18.80	35.05	280K	39.76	17.55	36.75
Oversampling	7.6M	38.26	19.14	35.41	560K	40.14	17.86	37.05
Back-translation	7.6M (3.8M)	38.49	19.24	35.63	560K (280K)	39.93	17.74	36.85
Self-training	7.6M (3.8M)	38.32	19.06	35.37	560K (280K)	40.19	17.87	37.21
ExtraPhrase	7.6M (3.8M)	38.51	**19.52**	35.72	560K (280K)	**40.57**	**18.22**	**37.51**
w/o paraphrasing	7.6M (3.8M)	**38.85**	19.43	**35.86**	560K (280K)	40.32	17.94	37.28
w/o extractive	7.6M (3.8M)	38.52	19.32	35.71	560K (280K)	40.33	18.10	37.38

Table 1: ROUGE F1 scores (R-1, 2, and L) for the headline generation and document summarization tasks. The number of genuine training data is shown in parentheses.

3.4 Results

Table 1 shows F1 based ROUGE-1, 2, and L scores for each setting on the headline generation and document summarization tasks. We use the same size of training data for each method except for Genuine only.

Table 1 indicates that Oversampling outperforms Genuine only. This result indicates that the more training data we prepare, the better performance an encoder-decoder achieves even if the training data contains many duplications. For Back-translation and Self-training, they achieve better performance than Genuine only, but their scores are comparable to ones of Oversampling in both tasks. These results imply that the improvements in their approaches are not based on the quality of their generated pseudo data, but based on the increase of training data. Since Back-translation and Self-training require training an additional model to construct pseudo data, these approaches are more costly than Oversampling.

In contrast, our ExtraPhrase achieves better performance than other approaches. In particular, our pseudo training data significantly improves the ROUGE-2 score compared to Genuine only setting in the headline generation. For the document summarization, our pseudo training data significantly improves all ROUGE scores[6]. These results indicate that ExtraPhrase is more effective than existing approaches including oversampling, back-translation, and self-training to construct pseudo data for the abstractive summarization tasks.

In addition to configurations described in Section 3.2, we also report results when using each step of the proposed method to generate pseudo training data to investigate the effect of each step.

[6]These results are statistically significant according to Student's t-test ($p < 0.05$) in comparison with Genuine only.

ExtraPhrase w/o paraphrasing in Table 1 refers to applying only the extractive summarization described in 2.1 on source articles of genuine training data to obtain pseudo summaries. Similarly, ExtraPhrase w/o extractive refers to applying only the paraphrasing described in 2.2 on summaries of genuine training data.

For the headline generation task, ExtraPhrase w/o paraphrasing achieves better performance than Genuine only setting. Surprisingly, although with a small margin, this result also outperforms ExtraPhrase, where the paraphrasing step is applied after the extractive summarization, in ROUGE-1 and ROUGE-L. ExtraPhrase w/o extractive achieves comparable ROUGE-1 and ROUGE-L scores compared to ExtraPhrase, but with a decrease in ROUGE-2 score. However, this result is better than Oversampling, where duplicated data is used, which infers that the paraphrasing step effectively boosts the diversity in augmented training data.

For the document summarization task, summarization performance decreases in both ExtraPhrase w/o paraphrasing and ExtraPhrase w/o extractive. These results imply that ExtraPhrase is better than using each composing step alone.

4 Analysis

4.1 Low-resource Setting

In this section, we investigate the effectiveness of ExtraPhrase when the amount of genuine training data is small.

We randomly sample 1K source text and summary pairs from each training set in the headline generation and document summarization tasks. Then, we conduct the same experiments in Section 3 by using the sampled 1K instances as genuine training data. We construct pseudo training data from the rest of each training data and combine

Method	Headline Generation				Document Summarization			
	Training Data	R-1	R-2	R-L	Training Data	R-1	R-2	R-L
Genuine only	1K	4.84	0.58	4.66	1K	2.48	0.29	2.45
Oversampling	3.8M	9.89	1.39	9.30	280K	13.63	0.89	12.63
Back-translation	3.8M (1K)	12.19	2.43	11.31	280K (1K)	9.73	0.50	8.92
Self-training	3.8M (1K)	7.27	1.07	6.98	280K (1K)	14.37	1.52	13.36
ExtraPhrase	3.8M (1K)	**23.58**	**6.56**	**21.12**	280K (1K)	**34.47**	**12.91**	**31.36**
w/o paraphrasing	3.8M (1K)	22.56	5.25	19.87	280K (1K)	32.95	12.07	29.44
Extractive	–	18.72	4.26	17.09	–	28.52	8.02	23.83

Table 2: ROUGE F1 scores (R-1, 2, and L) for the headline generation and document summarization tasks in low-resource setting. The number of genuine training data is shown in parentheses.

Task	Method	BLEU	BERTScore
Headline generation	Self-training	28.64	92.44
	ExtraPhrase	1.51	86.19
Document summarization	Self-training	19.91	90.02
	ExtraPhrase	5.89	87.33

Table 3: BLEU scores and F1 based BERTScores between genuine and pseudo training data.

the pseudo data with the sampled genuine data for training. For Self-training and Back-translation, we train neural encoder-decoders with the sampled 1K instances, and then apply them to the rest of training data for the pseudo data construction.

Table 2 shows the F1 based ROUGE scores of each method on the headline generation and document summarization tasks when we have a small amount of genuine training data. This table indicates that Back-translation and Self-training outperform Genuine only. These results are consistent with the result in Section 3.4. However, the performance improvement by Back-translation and Self-training are smaller compared to ExtraPhrase. These results show that Back-translation and Self-training tend to be ineffective when the amount of genuine training data is small (see appendix A).

For ExtraPhrase, it achieves significantly better performance than others in both tasks. Thus, ExtraPhrase is more effective when the amount of the genuine training data is small. The lowest parts of Table 2 shows the results of ExtraPhrase without paraphrasing for the ablation study. In ExtraPhrase w/o paraphrasing setting, we train the model with genuine and pseudo training data generated by ExtraPhrase without the paraphrasing step. Moreover, Extractive in these parts shows the ROUGE scores of summaries generated by the extractive summarization step. These parts indicate that ExtraPhrase outperforms the one without paraphrasing. Thus, we need the paraphrasing step to improve the quality of the pseudo training data, although the setting excluding paraphrasing significantly outperforms others. Moreover, ROUGE scores of Extractive are much lower than ones of ExtraPhrase. This result implies that we need to train a neural encoder-decoder by using the pseudo data as the training data to generate better abstractive summaries.

4.2 Diversity of Pseudo Summaries

We assume that our ExtraPhrase can generate more diverse summaries in comparison with the self-training approach. To verify this assumption, we compare pseudo summaries generated by Self-training and ExtraPhrase.

Table 3 shows BLEU scores (Papineni et al., 2002) between genuine summaries in each training data and generated pseudo summaries. In addition, this table also shows F1 based BERTScores (Zhang et al., 2020) of them as the indicator of semantic similarities. This table indicates that both BERTScores of Self-training and ExtraPhrase are remarkably high. This result implies that the generated summaries are semantically similar to genuine summaries. Thus, generated summaries are suitable as pseudo data semantically.

In contrast, the BLEU score of ExtraPhrase is much lower than one of Self-training. This result indicates that ExtraPhrase generates pseudo summaries that contain many different phrases from the genuine summaries in comparison with Self-training. Therefore, ExtraPhrase can generate

Task	Method	Training	Generation	Cost
	Back-translation	256 H	7 H	333 USD
Headline generation	Self-training	256 H	4 H	328 USD
	ExtraPhrase	–	7 H	12 USD
	Back-translation	384 H	16 H	511 USD
Document summarization	Self-training	320 H	8 H	417 USD
	ExtraPhrase	–	15 H	26 USD

Table 4: Cost on pseudo data generation using Amazon Elastic Compute Cloud (Amazon EC2). Consuming times are calculated in case of one GPU.

much more diverse summaries than Self-training.

5 Efficiency of Pseudo-data Generation

Our proposed ExtraPhrase does not require additional neural encoder-decoders such as the back-translation and self-training approaches. We discuss the advantage of this property.

Table 4 shows time required by each pseudo data construction method. This table also shows costs when we use Amazon EC2, which is a cloud computing service, to construct pseudo data. This table indicates that Back-translation and Self-training require much time to train their neural encoder-decoders. In contrast, for ExtraPhrase, we do not spend any time on such training. Therefore, ExtraPhrase is much more cost-efficient than others.

6 Related Work

Data Augmentation Back-translation and self-training are widely used techniques in data augmentation for sequence-to-sequence tasks (Sennrich et al., 2016a; Kiyono et al., 2019; Parida and Motlicek, 2019; He et al., 2020).

Sennrich et al. (2016a) proposed back-translation to augment training data for machine translation by translating monolingual data on the target side to generate source side pseudo data. Edunov et al. (2018) reported the effectiveness of the back-translation approach in large-scale monolingual settings for machine translation. In addition, Hoang et al. (2018) introduced an iterative version by repeatedly applying back-translation several times. Back-translation is an effective approach for machine translation but it is unrealistic to apply the approach to abstractive summarization.

In self-training, we train a model on genuine data and apply it to generate pseudo data. Zhang and Zong (2016) applied self-training to enlarge parallel corpus for neural machine translation. He et al. (2020) introduced noisy self-training that uses dropout as the noise while decoding in self-training. These studies reported the effectiveness of self-training but self-training is hard to generate diverse pseudo data (Gu et al., 2018).

Perturbation Using perturbation that is a small difference from genuine data can be regarded as data augmentation (Kobayashi, 2018). Takase and Kiyono (2021) investigated the performance of various perturbations including adversarial perturbations (Goodfellow et al., 2015), word dropout (Gal and Ghahramani, 2016), and word replacement on various sequence-to-sequence tasks. Since these perturbations are orthogonal to our ExtraPhrase, we can combine them with ours. In fact, Takase and Kiyono (2021) reported that simple perturbations such as word dropout are useful on pseudo data generated by back-translation.

7 Conclusion

This paper proposes a novel strategy, ExtraPhrase, to generate pseudo data for abstractive summarization tasks. ExtraPhrase consists of two steps: extractive summarization and paraphrasing. We obtain the important parts of an input by the extractive summarization, and then obtain diverse expressions by the paraphrasing. Experimental results indicate that ExtraPhrase is more effective than other pseudo data generation methods such as back-translation and self-training. Moreover, we show that ExtraPhrase is much more cost-efficient than others in pseudo data construction.

Acknowledgements

This work was partially supported by JSPS KAKENHI Grant Number 19H01118 and JP21K17800. These research results were obtained partially from the commissioned research (No. 225) by National Institute of Information and Communications Technology (NICT), Japan.

References

Dzmitry Bahdanau, Kyunghyun Cho, and Yoshua Bengio. 2015. Neural machine translation by jointly learning to align and translate. In *3rd International Conference on Learning Representations (ICLR)*.

Tom Brown, Benjamin Mann, Nick Ryder, Melanie Subbiah, Jared D Kaplan, Prafulla Dhariwal, Arvind Neelakantan, Pranav Shyam, Girish Sastry, Amanda Askell, Sandhini Agarwal, Ariel Herbert-Voss, Gretchen Krueger, Tom Henighan, Rewon Child, Aditya Ramesh, Daniel Ziegler, Jeffrey Wu, Clemens Winter, Chris Hesse, Mark Chen, Eric Sigler, Mateusz Litwin, Scott Gray, Benjamin Chess, Jack Clark, Christopher Berner, Sam McCandlish, Alec Radford, Ilya Sutskever, and Dario Amodei. 2020. Language models are few-shot learners. In *Advances in Neural Information Processing Systems 33 (NeurIPS)*, pages 1877–1901.

Isaac Caswell, Ciprian Chelba, and David Grangier. 2019. Tagged back-translation. In *Proceedings of the Fourth Conference on Machine Translation*, pages 53–63.

Trevor Anthony Cohn and Mirella Lapata. 2009. Sentence compression as tree transduction. *Journal Of Artificial Intelligence Research*, pages 637–674.

Bonnie Dorr, David Zajic, and Richard Schwartz. 2003. Hedge trimmer: A parse-and-trim approach to headline generation. In *Proceedings of the 2003 Conference of the North American Chapter of the Association for Computational Linguistics: Human Language Technologies (NAACL-HLT) Text Summarization Workshop*, pages 1–8.

Sergey Edunov, Myle Ott, Michael Auli, and David Grangier. 2018. Understanding back-translation at scale. In *Proceedings of the 2018 Conference on Empirical Methods in Natural Language Processing (EMNLP)*, pages 489–500.

Katja Filippova, Enrique Alfonseca, Carlos A. Colmenares, Lukasz Kaiser, and Oriol Vinyals. 2015. Sentence compression by deletion with LSTMs. In *Proceedings of the 2015 Conference on Empirical Methods in Natural Language Processing (EMNLP)*, pages 360–368.

Katja Filippova and Yasemin Altun. 2013. Overcoming the lack of parallel data in sentence compression. In *Proceedings of the 2013 Conference on Empirical Methods in Natural Language Processing (EMNLP)*, pages 1481–1491.

Yarin Gal and Zoubin Ghahramani. 2016. A theoretically grounded application of dropout in recurrent neural networks. In *Advances in Neural Information Processing Systems 29 (NIPS)*, pages 1019–1027.

Ian Goodfellow, Jonathon Shlens, and Christian Szegedy. 2015. Explaining and harnessing adversarial examples. In *Proceedings of the 3rd International Conference on Learning Representations (ICLR)*.

Jiatao Gu, James Bradbury, Caiming Xiong, Victor OK Li, and Richard Socher. 2018. Non-autoregressive neural machine translation. In *International Conference on Learning Representations (ICLR)*.

Junxian He, Jiatao Gu, Jiajun Shen, and Marc'Aurelio Ranzato. 2020. Revisiting self-training for neural sequence generation. In *International Conference on Learning Representations (ICLR)*.

Tsutomu Hirao, Jun Suzuki, and Hideki Isozaki. 2009. A syntax-free approach to Japanese sentence compression. In *Proceedings of the Joint Conference of the 47th Annual Meeting of the ACL and the 4th International Joint Conference on Natural Language Processing of the AFNLP*, pages 826–833.

Vu Cong Duy Hoang, Philipp Koehn, Gholamreza Haffari, and Trevor Cohn. 2018. Iterative back-translation for neural machine translation. In *Proceedings of the 2nd Workshop on Neural Machine Translation and Generation*, pages 18–24.

Matthew Honnibal, Ines Montani, Sofie Van Landeghem, and Adriane Boyd. 2020. spaCy: Industrial-strength Natural Language Processing in Python.

Aizhan Imankulova, Takayuki Sato, and Mamoru Komachi. 2019. Filtered pseudo-parallel corpus improves low-resource neural machine translation. *ACM Transactions on Asian and Low-Resource Language Information Processing (TALLIP)*, pages 1–16.

Hidetaka Kamigaito, Katsuhiko Hayashi, Tsutomu Hirao, and Masaaki Nagata. 2018. Higher-order syntactic attention network for longer sentence compression. In *Proceedings of the 2018 Conference of the North American Chapter of the Association for Computational Linguistics: Human Language Technologies (NAACL-HLT)*, pages 1716–1726.

Shun Kiyono, Jun Suzuki, Masato Mita, Tomoya Mizumoto, and Kentaro Inui. 2019. An empirical study of incorporating pseudo data into grammatical error correction. In *Proceedings of the 2019 Conference on Empirical Methods in Natural Language Processing and the 9th International Joint Conference on Natural Language Processing (EMNLP-IJCNLP)*, pages 1236–1242.

Sosuke Kobayashi. 2018. Contextual augmentation: Data augmentation by words with paradigmatic relations. In *Proceedings of the 2018 Conference of the North American Chapter of the Association for Computational Linguistics: Human Language Technologies (NAACL-HLT)*, pages 452–457.

Philipp Koehn and Rebecca Knowles. 2017. Six challenges for neural machine translation. In *Proceedings of the First Workshop on Neural Machine Translation*, pages 28–39.

Jonathan Mallinson, Rico Sennrich, and Mirella Lapata. 2017. Paraphrasing revisited with neural machine translation. In *Proceedings of the 15th Conference of the European Chapter of the Association for Computational Linguistics (EACL)*, pages 881–893.

Courtney Napoles, Matthew Gormley, and Benjamin Van Durme. 2012. Annotated Gigaword. In *Proceedings of the Joint Workshop on Automatic Knowledge Base Construction and Web-scale Knowledge Extraction (AKBC-WEKEX)*, pages 95–100.

Nathan Ng, Kyra Yee, Alexei Baevski, Myle Ott, Michael Auli, and Sergey Edunov. 2019. Facebook FAIR's WMT19 news translation task submission. In *Proceedings of the Fourth Conference on Machine Translation*, pages 314–319.

Myle Ott, Sergey Edunov, Alexei Baevski, Angela Fan, Sam Gross, Nathan Ng, David Grangier, and Michael Auli. 2019. fairseq: A fast, extensible toolkit for sequence modeling. In *Proceedings of the 2019 Conference of the North American Chapter of the Association for Computational Linguistics: Human Language Technologies (NAACL-HLT) Demonstrations*, pages 48–53.

Myle Ott, Sergey Edunov, David Grangier, and Michael Auli. 2018. Scaling neural machine translation. In *Proceedings of the Third Conference on Machine Translation: Research Papers*, pages 1–9.

Kishore Papineni, Salim Roukos, Todd Ward, and Wei jing Zhu. 2002. Bleu: a method for automatic evaluation of machine translation. In *Proceedings of the 40th Annual Meeting of the Association for Computational Linguistics (ACL)*, pages 311–318.

Shantipriya Parida and Petr Motlicek. 2019. Abstract text summarization: A low resource challenge. In *Proceedings of the 2019 Conference on Empirical Methods in Natural Language Processing and the 9th International Joint Conference on Natural Language Processing (EMNLP-IJCNLP)*, pages 5994–5998.

Alexander M. Rush, Sumit Chopra, and Jason Weston. 2015. A neural attention model for abstractive sentence summarization. In *Proceedings of the 2015 Conference on Empirical Methods in Natural Language Processing (EMNLP)*, pages 379–389.

Abigail See, Peter J. Liu, and Christopher D. Manning. 2017. Get to the point: Summarization with pointer-generator networks. In *Proceedings of the 55th Annual Meeting of the Association for Computational Linguistics (ACL)*, pages 1073–1083.

Rico Sennrich, Barry Haddow, and Alexandra Birch. 2016a. Improving neural machine translation models with monolingual data. In *Proceedings of the 54th Annual Meeting of the Association for Computational Linguistics (ACL)*, pages 86–96.

Rico Sennrich, Barry Haddow, and Alexandra Birch. 2016b. Neural machine translation of rare words with subword units. In *Proceedings of the 54th Annual Meeting of the Association for Computational Linguistics (ACL)*, pages 1715–1725.

Hong Sun and Ming Zhou. 2012. Joint learning of a dual SMT system for paraphrase generation. In *Proceedings of the 50th Annual Meeting of the Association for Computational Linguistics (ACL)*, pages 38–42.

Sho Takase and Shun Kiyono. 2021. Rethinking perturbations in encoder-decoders for fast training. In *Proceedings of the 2021 Conference of the North American Chapter of the Association for Computational Linguistics: Human Language Technologies (NAACL-HLT)*, pages 5767–5780.

Jenine Turner and Eugene Charniak. 2005. Supervised and unsupervised learning for sentence compression. In *Proceedings of the 43rd Annual Meeting of the Association for Computational Linguistics (ACL)*, pages 290–297.

Ashish Vaswani, Noam Shazeer, Niki Parmar, Jakob Uszkoreit, Llion Jones, Aidan N Gomez, Ł ukasz Kaiser, and Illia Polosukhin. 2017. Attention is all you need. In *Advances in Neural Information Processing Systems 30 (NIPS)*, pages 5998–6008.

Zheng Yuan and Ted Briscoe. 2016. Grammatical error correction using neural machine translation. In *Proceedings of the 2016 Conference of the North American Chapter of the Association for Computational Linguistics: Human Language Technologies (NAACL-HLT)*, pages 380–386.

Jiajun Zhang and Chengqing Zong. 2016. Exploiting source-side monolingual data in neural machine translation. In *Proceedings of the 2016 Conference on Empirical Methods in Natural Language Processing (EMNLP)*, pages 1535–1545.

Tianyi Zhang, Varsha Kishore, Felix Wu, Kilian Q. Weinberger, and Yoav Artzi. 2020. Bertscore: Evaluating text generation with bert. In *International Conference on Learning Representations (ICLR)*.

Ratio	Difference	R-1	R-2	R-L
Headline generation				
0.86	-5	35.14	15.13	28.59
Document summarization				
0.81	-297	13.76	1.09	13.07

Table 5: F1 based ROUGE scores (R-1, 2, and L) between source texts generated by back-translation and genuine source texts. Ratio and Difference are comparisons between the number of tokens in generated source texts and genuine ones.

A Quality of Back-translation

As described in Section 1, the back-translation approach for the abstractive summarization task is essentially impossible because it requires restoring source texts from summaries without any additional information. Thus, we investigate the quality of source texts generated by Back-translation.

Table 5 shows the length difference and ratio between genuine and source text generated by Back-translation. This table indicates that the generated source texts are shorter than the original genuine data. This result implies that Back-translation fails to restore the full information in the genuine data. In other words, this result implies that it is difficult to generate source texts from summaries.

Table 5 also shows ROUGE scores of source texts generated by Back-translation when we regard the genuine source texts as the correct instances to investigate whether the generated texts correspond to the genuine data. For the document summarization, ROUGE scores are extremely low. This result also indicates that Back-translation fails to generate source texts.

On the other hand, ROUGE scores on the headline generation are much higher than ones on the document summarization. This result implies that Back-translation might restore the core parts of source texts from summaries. Because the headline generation is the task of generating a headline from a given sentence, the summary (headline) often contains the dominant part of the source sentence. We consider this property causes such high scores.

Regularized Training of Nearest Neighbor Language Models

Jean-Francois Ton* University of Oxford
Walter Talbott Apple
Shuangfei Zhai Apple
Joshua Susskind Apple

Abstract

Including memory banks in a natural language processing, architecture increases model capacity by equipping it with additional data at inference time. In this paper, we build upon kNN-LM (Khandelwal et al., 2020), which uses a pre-trained language model together with an exhaustive kNN search through the training data (memory bank) to achieve state-of-the-art results. We investigate whether we can improve the kNN-LM performance by instead training a LM with the knowledge that we will be using a kNN post-hoc. We achieved significant improvement using our method on language modeling tasks on `WIKI-2` and `WIKI-103`. The main phenomenon that we encounter is that adding a simple L2 regularization on the activations (not weights) of the model, a transformer (Vaswani et al., 2017), improves the post-hoc kNN classification performance. We explore some possible reasons for this improvement. In particular, we find that the added L2 regularization seems to improve the performance for high-frequency words without deteriorating the performance for low-frequency ones.

1 Introduction

The problem of language modeling (LM) usually consists of two main challenges. Firstly, mapping the context, i.e. the sentence prefixes, to a vector representation, and secondly using this representation to predict the subsequent word. In Khandelwal et al. (2020), the authors claim that the first problem is much easier to solve. Hence, given a pre-trained LM, they post-hoc modify the representation using a k-nearest neighbor scheme (kNN) and achieve significant improvements on challenging datasets, such as `WIKI-103`.

Given that kNN improves the overall language modeling of a pre-trained network, we examine training strategies that can make the underlying network's representations more amenable to the kNN step. Our results show improvements over applying kNN to a generic LM network.

We first explore a simple learning scheme for the language model, where during training we intentionally push representations that predict the same word closer together in the L2 sense, using a Momentum Contrastive (MOCO) (He et al., 2020) style implementation. We go on to note that this MOCO style learning can be replaced by simply adding L2 regularization to the activation of the layer used for kNN, eliminating implementation complexity. Lastly, we present some initial experiments toward understanding why this L2 regularization brings improved performance.

2 Background

Our work builds upon kNN-LM (Khandelwal et al., 2020). In essence, kNN-LM tackles the problem of how to improve a trained LM's representations, and how to adapt LMs to capture non-frequent sentences that are usually forgotten by the model during training. kNN-LMs achieve significantly higher performance through a simple interpolation between the original LM predictions and the kNN predictions.

At inference time, given a new context sentence, kNN-LM works as follows:

1. The context sentence c_i is passed through the pre-trained network to produce a representation $r_i^{context} \in \mathbf{R}^d$ as well as the corresponding logits y_i^{LM} to predict the next word.

2. $r_i^{context}$ is used to find the k-nearest neighbors in the training data. The logits y^{kNN} are computed by a weighted average of the neighbors' labels, using the inverse exponential distance as the weight for each neighbor.

3. The logits are interpolated to give the final prediction:

$$y_{final} = \lambda y^{kNN} + (1 - \lambda) y^{LM},$$

*Work done as an intern at Apple

Proceedings of the 2022 Conference of the North American Chapter of the Association for Computational Linguistics: Human Language Technologies: Student Research Workshop, pages 25 - 30
July 10-15, 2022

where λ is the interpolation parameter that can be tuned on validation data.

This simple post-hoc implementation allows Khandelwal et al. (2020) to improve upon the SOTA in LM by a significant margin. One thing to note about kNN-LM is that they do not need to retrain the LM and hence the whole algorithm can be run on CPU only. Furthermore, kNN-LM uses *FAISS*, which is an efficient library that allows them to quickly find kNNs.

One detail to note in (Khandelwal et al., 2020) which was crucial for this work was that the authors tried both the inner product and the L2 for their distance metric in kNN. They concluded that L2 worked significantly better. This observation implies the fact that the default training recipe of LMs *implicitly* prefers one distance over the other. Given that we know that a post-hoc kNN adaptation significantly improves the performance, it is natural to ask whether we could train a LM with this in mind. In the next section, we describe how to adapt the training of the LM for this purpose.

3 Proposed Method

In our initial attempt, we experimented with the idea of explicitly minimizing the L2 distance between context vectors that predict the same target word. This strategy directly mirrors the use of context vectors at the kNN step, and we hoped that training the representations in a way similar to testing will further improve the effectiveness of kNN LM. However, a naïve implementation of it is infeasible due to having to store all the representation in memory. We then resorted to a MOCO-(He et al., 2020) style training scheme. Specifically, for each target word w, we construct a queue Q of fixed length L, which stores the recent L context representations for w. During training, we optimize a regularized objective as follows:

$$\mathcal{L}_{new} = L_{CE} + \omega \sum_{j=1}^{\mathrm{N}} \sum_{i=1}^{\mathrm{L}} ||sg(Q_i^{w_j}) - r_j||^2, \quad (1)$$

where N is the batch size, r_j is the context representation of the jth word, $Q_I^{w_j}$ is the ith item in the queue corresponding to the jth target word w_j; ω is the regularization parameter; $sg(\cdot)$ is the stop gradient operator. Specifically, Q is updated with a momentum target encoding network which is initialized with the same parameters of the LM, similar to MOCO (He et al., 2020).

Empirically, we found that Equation 1 provides a practical solution and yields improved representations for the kNN LM, as shown in Fig 1. In particular, we see from the figure that there is an optimal value for ω for which the added regularization seems to improve the kNN LM model perplexity significantly i.e. from 76 to 70 at $\omega = 2$ (orange line). The interesting part to note in this case, is the fact that the standard LM (without post-hoc kNN) does not vary much up to $\omega = 5$, leading us to conclude that the added regularization has changed the representation in a way that kNN can more effectively exploit the neighbors.

However, the use of the queue and momentum target network still adds overhead to a large-scale model training as we are required to access the queue for each batch. Hence we tried to decrease Q and L, which interestingly did not decrease the performance at all and therefore, to promote efficiency, we tested an even simpler formulation, where we replace Q with all **zero** vectors. This eliminates the need to explicitly construct and update the queue, while instead encouraging the model to learn conservative representations w.r.t. the L2 norms of its context representations. The corresponding loss is as follows:

$$\mathcal{L}_{new} = L_{CE} + \omega \sum_{j=1}^{\mathrm{N}} ||r_j||^2. \quad (2)$$

To our surprise, Equation 2 yields similar performance to Equation 1 in practice see Table 1, while being much easier to implement and tune. This is a new interesting finding that we will try to explain in the ablation study below. We thus use Equation 2 as the default loss function in our experiments unless otherwise mentioned.

4 Experiments

We tested our method on the `WIKI-2` and `WIKI-103` datasets, which are widely used benchmarks for language modeling. We are interested in demonstrating two empirical results: improved performance using our approach over that of kNN-LM, and exploring a possible mechanism for this improved performance.

4.1 Experimental setup

Dataset `WIKI-2` is a benchmark with 30k word vocabulary and consists of 2M tokens. `WIKI-103`

	kNN-LM ($\omega = 0$)	$\omega = 0.1$	$\omega = 1.0$	$\omega = 10.0$
Train Ppl. LM	19.99	20.05	20.11	21.37
Valid Ppl. LM	75.96	75.68	76.37	81.29
Valid Ppl. kNN-LM	74.11	73.13	**70.63**	80.52

Table 1: Experiments on `WIKI-2` with corresponding validation perplexity using L2 regularization. We see that a weighting of $\omega = 1$ yields the best performance for our method

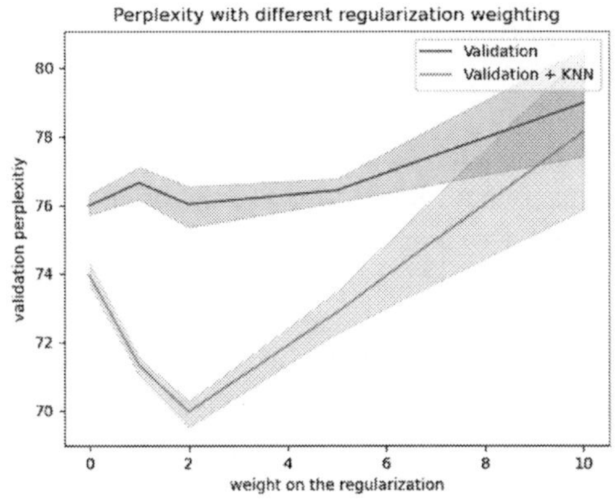

Figure 1: Validation perplexity on `WIKI-2` of the LM before (blue) and after (orange) adding kNN. NOTE: `weight=0` corresponds to the standard version that does not include our added MOCO-style regularization term i.e. kNN-LM from Khandelwal et al. (2020)

is a benchmark with 250k word vocabulary and consisting of 103M tokens (Merity et al., 2016).

Language Model Architecture For the language model architecture, we will be using the exact setup as described in (Khandelwal et al., 2020). This setup consists of the language model (Baevski and Auli, 2018), which consists of 16 layers, each with 16 self-attention heads, 1024 dimensional hidden states, and 4096 dimensional feedforward layers. Thus, following (Baevski and Auli, 2018), this LM has adaptive inputs and an adaptive softmax (Joulin et al., 2017) with tied weights (Press and Wolf, 2016) for all our experiments. We trained the each language model on a `Tesla V100` with `40GB` of RAM.

In addition, we follow the exact same training procedure as in (Khandelwal et al., 2020) and refer to their paper for further details on the training parameters. The only difference in terms of implementation is the MOCO style learner as well as the L2 regularization added to the final layer. Lastly, we would like to note that while crossvalidating though the interpolation parameter λ we note that for all models, $\lambda = 0.3$ works the best which is similar to the finding in (Khandelwal et al., 2020).

4.2 Experiments on `WIKI-2`

We first apply our proposed method on the standard `WIKI-2` dataset, where we run each configuration 5 times and plot the standard deviation, as seen in Figure 1. Note that $\omega = 0$ in Figure 1 corresponds to the standard kNN-LM version, i.e. without the added term in the loss. Comparing Figure 1 and Table 1, we see that the MOCO and L2 approaches produce similar results. From these results, we note the following phenomena:

1. A clear "U"-shape demonstrating the added benefit of our loss term on the validation perplexity of the LM for moderate values of ω.

2. Training performance does not decrease for moderate values of ω, showing that the extra term does not destroy training and generalization of the standard LM.

3. There is no difference in terms of validation perplexity between the standard LM and our version **before** applying kNN, but there is a significant difference **after** applying kNN. Our approach likely finds a different local minimum for the language model that is better suited for kNN.

The above finding supports our belief that using our added regularization, we are able to find better representations, that can subsequently be used more efficiently when for kNN LM. Next, we apply our methods on the much bigger data `WIKI-103`.

4.3 Experiments on `WIKI-103`

We illustrate our findings on the more challenging `WIKI-103` dataset and demonstrate that our L2 fix significantly improves the performance of the LM. In the Table 2, we illustrate that when changing the regularization strength we again see a significant gain in performance when adding our regularization during training of the LM. Due to the computational costs when training these models, we resort to the same hyperparameters as in

	kNN-LM ($\omega = 0$)	kNN-LM ($\omega = 1$)	kNN-LM ($\omega = 10$)
Train Ppl. LM	11.31	11.24	**11.07**
Valid Ppl. LM	18.00	17.95	**17.71**
Valid Ppl. kNN-LM	16.09	**15.89**	17.46

Table 2: Experiments on WIKI-103. We report the training and validation perplexities for standard kNN-LM i.e. ($\omega = 0$) as well as our weighted versions. Here we show that our method is much better once we apply kNN

the WIKI-2 dataset and hence present fair comparisons of the different variants of the model.

Note that again, we see significant improvements in terms of validation perplexity when using the kNN-LM scheme by simply adding an L2 regularization when training the language model.

On another note, when taking a closer look at the validation perplexity before applying kNN, we note that $\omega = 10$ seems to have the lowest validation perplexity. This better generalization phenomenon is interesting and has recently been noted in the machine vision community in the context of investigating the regularization effects of batch normalization in classification settings (Dauphin and Cubuk, 2021). This also relates to the findings of (Merity et al., 2017), those who used L2 regularization in LSTMs. In this paper, we found initial indications that the L2 regularization on the activations might be useful for Transformer models.

Finally, we believe that these two standard benchmark datasets in language modeling are sufficient evidence to demonstrate the merit our of findings. Further studies with more hyperparameters could be done on WIKI-103, however, due to computational costs, we leave this for future work.

4.4 Further investigations into the representations and possible explanations

To get a better understanding of why the L2 regularization on the activations seems to improve the performance of kNN-LM, we looked closer at the learned representations for WIKI-02.

Effect of the target word frequency on the loss: Figure 2 shows a histogram of word frequency, where the color represents the respective losses each word incurred. More concretely, each bar represents the number of words with a given frequency. For a given histogram bar, we compute the loss for each of these corresponding words. The colors represent the loss i.e. if we have a darker violet color, we incurred a higher loss for these words, and the lighter color the bar the smaller the error. Note that firstly, there is little difference in the loss for the less frequent words (right tail end of the histogram). If we shift our attention to the more frequent words (left side of the histogram) however, we see a different picture. Looking at our L2 regularized model, we note that for the most frequent words, our model seems to incur lower loss (see the brighter colors bars at the peak of the histograms) compared to the standard LM with kNN. This observation suggests that the main differences in terms of representations come from the frequent words rather than rare ones. This is an indication that L2 regularization helps representations cluster and hence when performing the interpolation between the predictions of the LM and kNN, the resulting kNN LM is more confident in these predictions hence leading us to obtain lower perplexities for common words.

Secondly, knowing that the main differences are within the words that are most frequent, we investigated these representations in more detail. In particular, we analyzed the most frequent words and divided the data into "*high loss/score* i.e. loss > -10" meaning they contributed a lot to the loss (bad predictions) and "*low loss/score* i.e. loss < -10" meaning they are good predictions i.e. they contributed a little to the loss.

We employed a simple mixture of Gaussians model (GMM) ($m = 10$) and used the log-likelihood as an indicator for how well the data are clustered. GMMs allow us to put probability mass on each of the representations and given that we are using a mixture of Gaussians, we inherently capture clusters. Intuitively, this means that if the likelihood of the GMM is high, the representations can be easily captured using a mixture of Gaussians, which is indicative of being more clustered i.e. close to one of the gaussian mixture means.

In Figure 3 we compare the distributions of the loglikelihoods for the representations that have been trained using the standard LM and our modified L2 regularization. In particular, for each representation, we obtain the corresponding likelihood from the GMM (x-axis on Figure 3). As mentioned before, we split the words into "*high loss/scores*" and "*low loss/scores*" and plot their histograms in

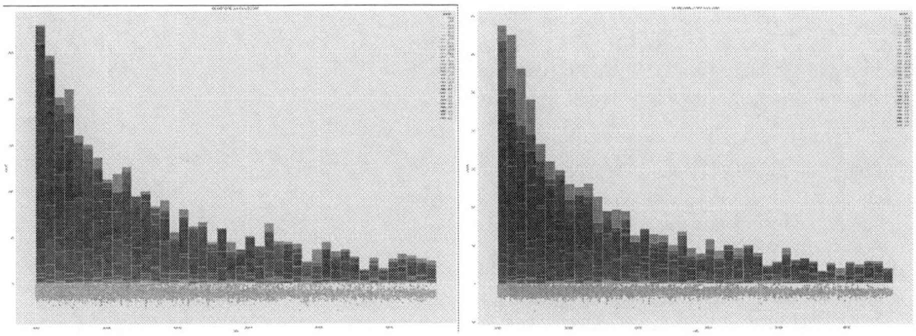

Figure 2: Frequency/Loss histograms. The x-axis denotes the frequency of the word with high-frequency words to the left. The y-axis denotes the number of words with x frequency and the colors of each bar represent the loss accumulated. (LEFT) Standard LM after kNN, (RIGHT) Our L2 regularized LM after kNN.

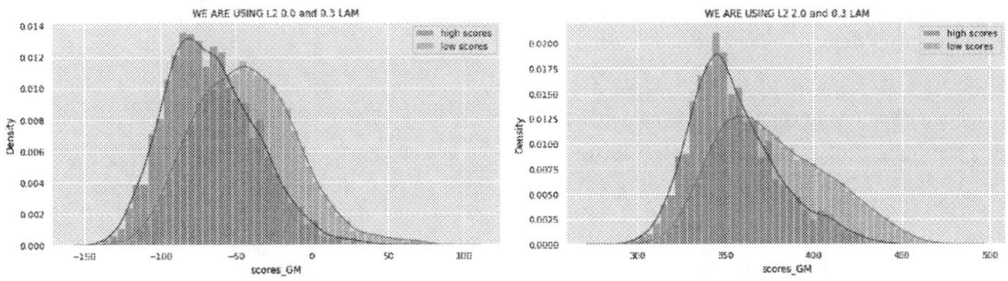

Figure 3: x-axis denotes the Loglikelihood under the Gaussian Mixture. y-axis denotes the normalized histogram. (LEFT) Standard training of the Language Model (RIGHT) using an L2 regularization for the Language Model.

blue and orange respectively. Fig. 3 demonstrates one key finding, which is that the difference between the likelihoods of the "*high loss/scores*" and "*low loss/scores*" varies much more dramatically in the L2 regularized case. Recall that the higher the likelihood, the higher the "clusterness" is. By noting that the likelihood differs much more in the L2 regularized case, we can conclude that the representations in the latter are more clustered (for the low scores) due to the regularization, which could be one potential explanation why kNN LM is improved. Hence, one of our hypotheses is that kNN-LM improves the classification accuracy mostly for the non-frequent words (Khandelwal et al., 2020), whereas our proposed method with L2 regularization, **in addition**, also improves the classification accuracy of the frequent words by clustering them closer together and hence improving kNN-LM.

5 Conclusion

In conclusion, we propose a useful training mechanism that is inspired by the fact that the post-hoc application of kNN seems to significantly improve the performance of standard LMs. We have found that training a LM with L2 regularization at the final layer, i.e. layer which is used for the post-hoc kNN search, improves validation performance. We have also found initial indications that the L2 regularization mostly improves performance for the most frequent, lower-loss words. In addition, we have found further evidence for the hypothesis proposed (Dauphin and Cubuk, 2021) which states that L2 regularization helps generalization in vision tasks. This paper found similar results when working with Transformer models in NLP tasks.

There are, however, some shortcomings in our work. Firstly, we have only given a preliminary explanation for why the added L2 regularization significantly improves upon standard kNN LM, but we believe that we have given sufficient evidence that our proposed method promotes clustering of the representations which subsequently improves the kNN. Secondly, even though we have found great and promising improvement using our findings on `WIKI-2`, further work with more compute should be done on `WIKI-103`. We however leave this for future work due to computational constraints. Lastly, we believe that training models with post-hoc kNN in mind is a promising area and hence future work will consider more diverse datasets from the NLP literature. These findings motivate exploring various regularizations in different Transformer architectures and LM tasks.

References

Alexei Baevski and Michael Auli. 2018. Adaptive input representations for neural language modeling. *arXiv preprint arXiv:1809.10853.*

Yann N Dauphin and Ekin D Cubuk. 2021. Deconstructing the regularization of batch-norm. In *International Conference on Learning Representations (ICLR).*

Kaiming He, Haoqi Fan, Yuxin Wu, Saining Xie, and Ross Girshick. 2020. Momentum contrast for unsupervised visual representation learning. In *Proceedings of the IEEE/CVF Conference on Computer Vision and Pattern Recognition*, pages 9729–9738.

Armand Joulin, Moustapha Cissé, David Grangier, Hervé Jégou, et al. 2017. Efficient softmax approximation for gpus. In *International Conference on Machine Learning*, pages 1302–1310. PMLR.

Urvashi Khandelwal, Omer Levy, Dan Jurafsky, Luke Zettlemoyer, and Mike Lewis. 2020. Generalization through Memorization: Nearest Neighbor Language Models. In *International Conference on Learning Representations (ICLR).*

Stephen Merity, Nitish Shirish Keskar, and Richard Socher. 2017. Regularizing and optimizing lstm language models. *arXiv preprint arXiv:1708.02182.*

Stephen Merity, Caiming Xiong, James Bradbury, and Richard Socher. 2016. Pointer sentinel mixture models. *arXiv preprint arXiv:1609.07843.*

Ofir Press and Lior Wolf. 2016. Using the output embedding to improve language models. *arXiv preprint arXiv:1608.05859.*

Ashish Vaswani, Noam Shazeer, Niki Parmar, Jakob Uszkoreit, Llion Jones, Aidan N Gomez, Łukasz Kaiser, and Illia Polosukhin. 2017. Attention is all you need. *Advances in neural information processing systems*, 30.

"Again, Dozens of Refugees Drowned": A Computational Study of Political Framing Evoked by Presuppositions

Qi Yu
Cluster of Excellence "The Politics of Inequality" & Department of Linguistics
University of Konstanz
qi.yu@uni-konstanz.de

Abstract

Earlier NLP studies on framing have focused heavily on shallow classification of issue framing, while framing effect arising from pragmatic cues remains neglected. We put forward this latter type of framing as *pragmatic framing*. To bridge this gap, we take presupposition-triggering adverbs such as 'again' as a study case, and investigate how different German newspapers use them to covertly evoke different attitudinal subtexts. Our study demonstrates the crucial role of presuppositions in framing, and emphasizes the necessity of more attention on *pragmatic framing* in future research.

1 Introduction

Framing, i.e., intentionally selecting certain aspects of an issue and making them more salient in a communicating text (Entman, 1993), is ubiquitous in political discourse. The release of corpora with manual annotation – mostly based on the codebook of *issue framing* by Boydstun et al. (2014) – has popularized the task of issue framing classification (see Section 2), e.g., classifying whether influx of migrants is presented from the perspective of economy or domestic security. However, the heavy focus on classification accuracy in earlier studies has resulted in very few in-depth investigations of the effects of individual linguistic cues in framing. Yet, in a study on framing strategies employed by different German newspapers in the discourse of the "European Refugee Crisis"[1] (2014–2018), we observed from an exploratory reading that iterative adverbs, including *erneut* 'again', *immer wieder* 'again and again', and *schon wieder* 'yet again', can act as subtle but effective cues of framing. Consider sentence (1):

(1) *Erneut dutzende Flüchtlinge ertrunken*
'Again dozens of refugees drowned'
(BILD, Feb. 8, 2016)

[1] For details on the event: https://en.wikipedia.org/wiki/2015_European_migrant_crisis

Iterative adverbs like 'again' in (1) are known as *presupposition-triggers* in theoretical pragmatics, as they carry *presuppositions* (see, e.g., Levinson, 1983; Beaver et al., 2021). A presupposition of an utterance is background information that is "taken for granted" by the speaker, i.e., information that is not explicitly uttered but assumed by the speaker to be shared belief of all discourse participants (Stalnaker, 1972; Beaver, 1997; Zeevat, 2002). The word 'again' in sentence (1) triggers the presupposition $\mathcal{P}$ below, as its usage assumes that all discourse participants already know $\mathcal{P}$.

(2) $\mathcal{P}$ = 'It has already happened before (at least once) that refugees got drowned.'

We argue from two aspects that presuppositions and their triggers are crucial devices for framing. First, presuppositions can smuggle additional information into hearers' belief systems: It is well studied in theoretical pragmatics that presuppositions can be *accommodated*, i.e., in many cases where the presupposition of an utterance conveys information that is new instead of known to its hearers, the hearers will just tacitly admit to this information in order to make sense of the utterance (Lewis, 1979; Stalnaker, 2002; von Fintel, 2008). A reader that did not know $\mathcal{P}$ above at the time of reading sentence (1) will normally admit to $\mathcal{P}$ silently in order to understand the author's usage of 'again'. Second, given a certain political context, presuppositions may bring up attitudinal subtextual messages as a concomitant: Once $\mathcal{P}$ above is in the belief system of the readers of sentence (1) (either because they already knew $\mathcal{P}$ before the reading, or because they *accommodated* $\mathcal{P}$), the attitudinal subtext $\mathcal{A}$ below is likely to be evoked in their mind. We use $\rightsquigarrow$ to denote the pragmatic relation that $\mathcal{P}$ does not logically entail $\mathcal{A}$, but can plausibly give rise to $\mathcal{A}$. Concomitant attitudinal subtexts of this kind can covertly bias the hearers' opinion towards the issue and thus give rise to framing effect.

Proceedings of the 2022 Conference of the North American Chapter of the Association for Computational Linguistics: Human Language Technologies: Student Research Workshop, pages 31 - 43
July 10-15, 2022 ©2022 Association for Computational Linguistics

(3) $\mathcal{P} \rightsquigarrow (\mathcal{A} =$ 'Refugees are in urgent need of help as their safety is severely threatened.')

Such framing effects that arise indirectly from cues with significant pragmatic effects, e.g., presupposition-triggers discussed above, remain neglected in existing studies on framing. We put forward this type of framing as **pragmatic framing** (see Section 3 for detailed discussion). The automated detection of *pragmatic framing* is yet a challenging task: It can be only found via a close examination of the relevant linguistic cues, and (weakly-)supervised models as proposed by numerous earlier studies (see Section 2) are not necessarily able to capture the effect of such cues, as these cues can be extremely sparse. Following our observation on the iterative adverbs, this work quantitatively investigates whether iterative adverbs in different newspapers give rise to different attitudinal subtexts via presupposition, and thus result in different pragmatic framing styles. With this study, we aim at a) validating the argued importance of presupposition in framing, and b) exploring the possibility of automatically detecting *pragmatic framing*. Our contribution is two-fold:

1) Theoretically, we put forward the notion of *pragmatic framing*, and demonstrate its significance for research on framing detection via our case study on presupposition-triggering adverbs. To the best of our knowledge, this is also the first study on the role of presuppositions in framing.

2) Methodologically, we show that consciously combining theoretically motivated linguistic cues with NLP methods can yield crucial information for more in-depth framing detection.

2 Earlier NLP Studies on Framing

Along with the release of large-scale corpora annotated with issue frames (e.g., Card et al., 2015; Liu et al., 2019), numerous studies have been done on (weakly-)supervised classification of issue framing. The methods used vary from linear classifiers such as in Baumer et al. (2015) (naïve Bayes) and Field et al. (2018) (logistic regression), probabilistic soft logic as in Johnson et al. (2017), neural networks such as in Naderi and Hirst (2017) (LSTM) and Ji and Smith (2017) (RNN), to transformer-based language models such as BERT and RoBERTa (e.g., Khanehzar et al., 2019; Huguet Cabot et al., 2020; Akyürek et al., 2020; Mendelsohn et al., 2021).

Despite the classification accuracy of these proposed models, there still lacks an in-depth drilling down into the effects of individual linguistic components. A few earlier studies have attempted to incorporate features that are motivated by theoretical linguistics: Baumer et al. (2015) validated the positive impact of various semantic and pragmatic features (including *factive verb*, *assertive word*, *entailment* and *hedging*) on the performance of a naïve Bayes classifier for frame classification. Demszky et al. (2019) investigated the usage of expressions for necessity modality (including *should*, *must*, *have to* and *need to*) among tweets about mass shooting events, as necessity modality bears the illocutionary force of calling for action or change in the discourse under discussion. Ziems and Yang (2021) examined the usage of agent-less passive constructions (e.g., using 'He was killed' instead of 'He was killed *by police*') in the discourse of police violence in view of the fact that such constructions obscure the actor entirely and thus remove blame from the actor.

Nevertheless, in the last decades theoretical linguistic researchers have uncovered many more pragmatic cues which have fundamental effects on conveying attitudes and steering the discourse development. Such cues are highly relevant for framing but remain unstudied, especially because many of them are stop words and prone to be dismissed in NLP practice. These include, but are not limited to, the aforementioned presupposition-triggers like *again* or *too* (Levinson, 1983; Beaver et al., 2021), focus particles like *even* or *only* (Rooth, 1985), modal particles like *indeed* (Zeevat, 2004; Zimmermann, 2011), and conventional implicature-bearing words like *luckily* or *confidentially* (Bach, 1999; Potts, 2005). With our case study on iterative adverbs, we aim at bridging this gap between NLP and theoretical linguistics.

3 *Pragmatic Framing* as a New Dimension of Framing

As described in Section 2, earlier NLP studies on framing detection are centered around *issue framing*, i.e., what aspects of an issue are covered in the discourse. However, our observation on the effect of presupposition-triggers in political discourse suggests that certain subtle pragmatic cues can evoke implicit, second-level subtextual communication, and this phenomenon remain neglected in the research on framing. We argue that such subtextual communication also constitutes a type of framing, as they covertly smuggle extra information into the discourse besides the information conveyed by the surface form of the text (see Section 1). Grounded in this observation, we propose the notion of *pragmatic framing* as a new dimension of framing besides the *issue framing*. Pragmatic framing differs from issue framing in two aspects:

1) **Locus:** Issue framing is a content-level phenomenon. It is typically defined as describing what specific perspectives, values or facts of an issue are presented (see, e.g., Entman, 1993; Nelson et al., 1997; Druckman, 2011; Boydstun et al., 2014). However, pragmatic framing is a linguistics-level phenomenon and describes *what specific linguistic devices are employed strategically in order to reinforce a certain perspective, value or fact.* Pragmatic framing is rooted in the usage of fine-grained pragmatic cues, and it contributes to the conveyance of issue frames in a rhetorical sense.

2) **Accessibility:** Whereas issue framing are mostly directly accessible from the surface form of the text, pragmatic framing goes beyond the surface form and can only be reached indirectly through pragmatic procedures triggered by specific cues (e.g., hearer's accommodation of presuppositions as mentioned in Section 1, or hearer's pragmatic enrichment of a certain utterance as described in Grice, 1975). From the perspective of NLP, automatically identifying pragmatic framing requires close examination of particular pragmatic cues.

The notion of pragmatic framing also applies to a wide range of other theoretical linguistic features that trigger very specific types of discursive inferencing, such as those mentioned in Section 2. We believe that more attention on in-depth pragmatic devices will be a valuable enrichment of the research on framing, as the particular ways of presenting information are the core of framing, and the usage of subtle linguistic devices is in turn an essential part of information presentation.

4 Experiment

Our study focuses on the usage of iterative adverbs in political discourse as a case of pragmatic framing, and aims at examining whether iterative adverbs give rise to different attitudinal subtexts via presuppositions in different newspapers. The data and experimental setup are described below.

4.1 Data

We used a dataset comprising of articles about the "European Refugee Crisis" published between 2014 to 2018 by the three most circulated newspapers in Germany (Statista, 2021): *BILD*, *Frankfurter Allgemeine Zeitung* (FAZ), and *Süddeutsche Zeitung* (SZ). All three are nation-wide daily newspapers, and they build a balanced sample of differing styles and political orientations.

From each newspaper, we first collected articles with at least one match of the following quasi-synonyms of 'refugee': {*Flüchtling*, *Geflüchtete*, *Migrant*, *Asylant*, *Asylwerber*, *Asylbewerber*}. We then removed articles that were: 1) duplicated, 2) from non-political sections such as *Sport*, and 3) with a ratio of the 'refugee'-synonyms lower than 0.01. Criterion 3) was experimentally defined, and it allowed us to remove most articles that mention the European Refugee Crisis only as a side-topic.

Following the observation from our exploratory reading mentioned in Section 1, we then extracted from the dataset all sentences that contain the iterative adverbs *erneut*, *immer wieder*, and *schon wieder*. We refer to these extracted sentences as *iterAdv-S*. Duplicated sentences in each newspaper were removed. Table 1 summarizes the dataset.[2]

name	type	#articles	#tokens	#sentences	#*iterAdv-S*
BILD	C, T	12,109	3,059,123	180,555	1,138
FAZ	C, B	6,700	3,342,609	168,725	558
SZ	L, B	4,561	1,766,921	93,224	557

Table 1: Overview of the dataset. (C = conservative; L = liberal; T = tabloid; B = broadsheet)

4.2 Experimental Setup

As the pragmatic framing evoked by iterative adverbs is a sentence-level phenomenon and we thus focus on *iterAdv-S* for our quantitative analysis described below, topic modelling approaches such as LDA would be inadequate due to their deficiency in handling short documents (Tang et al., 2014). Thus, we used a combination of clustering and keyword-mining methods. The experimental setup is described below stepwise. Additional details of hyperparameters are provided in Appendix A.

Vectorizing *iterAdv-S* Vectorizing the *iterAdv-S* is the basis of all following computational steps.

[2]The newspaper articles were purchased from their respective publishers. Unfortunately, due to their copyright regulations, we cannot make the dataset publicly available. But the code and model of our study are available in the following repository. All results reported in this paper can also be found in the Jupyter Notebook files there: `https://github.com/qi-yu/framing-by-presuppositions`

Given the success of transformer-based language models in issue framing classification (see the studies cited in Section 2), we decided to fine-tune the `bert-base-german-cased` model[3] (12 layers, 768 hidden units, 12 attention heads) to achieve the vectorization. Considering that all articles in our dataset are labeled with sources (i.e., BILD, FAZ, & SZ), we decided to fine-tune the BERT on a source classification task using all articles, so that the model weights better represent the overall linguistic characteristics of our very topic-specific dataset. As BERT limits the input to be no longer than 512 tokens (*tokens* here refer to WordPieces generated by BERT-tokenizer, and the special tokens [CLS] and [SEP]), whereas numerous articles exceed this limit, we divided each article into segments of maximally 200 words long as inspired by Pappagari et al. (2019) to circumvent the limit. This resulted in 45,402 segments in all (BILD: 18,131; FAZ: 17,641; SZ: 9,630). We used these segments as input to BERT and classified each with their sources. The segments were split into training set and validation set in an 80/20 fashion. The accuracy on the validation set reached 0.87, indicating that the fine-tuned model was able to capture the major linguistic characteristics of the dataset.

Next, we vectorized the *iterAdv-S* by inputting each sentence to the fine-tuned BERT and extracting the embedding of the [CLS]-token of the 11th layer. The decision of using the [CLS] of the 11th layer was based on earlier studies which have shown that: 1) the embedding of [CLS] performs better as sentence representation than the average embedding of all tokens (Kalouli et al., 2021), and 2) semantic features are mostly captured by higher layers of BERT, whereas the last (12th) layer is very close to the actual classification task and thus less suitable as *semantic* representation (Kalouli et al., 2021; Jawahar et al., 2019; Lin et al., 2019).

K-Means Clustering For each newspaper, we then conducted a k-means clustering on the vectorized *iterAdv-S* using *scikit-learn* (Pedregosa et al., 2011). The clustering allows us to divide these sentences into latent subgroups and to investigate them at a finer granularity.

As a validation of the clustering results, for each newspaper we used the optimal cluster amount found by applying *silhouette coefficient* (Rousseeuw, 1987). Silhouette coefficient is a method for validating the consistency of clusters generated by clustering algorithms. For each sample i which is assigned to cluster A by a certain clustering algorithm, its silhouette coefficient $s(i)$ is defined as the equation below, where $a(i)$ stands for the average distance between i and all other items in A (also known as *intra-cluster distance*), and $b(i)$ stands for the average distance between i and all items in the second-nearest cluster besides A (also known as *inter-cluster distance*):

$$s(i) = \frac{b(i) - a(i)}{max\{a(i), b(i)\}}$$

The value of $s(i)$ ranges between [-1, 1]. The closer it is to 1, the better i matches the cluster A. A negative value occurs when the intra-cluster distance $a(i)$ is greater than the inter-cluster distance $b(i)$, indicating that assigning i to A is suboptimal.

We monitored the silhouette coefficient of each item (i.e., each vectorized *iterAdv-S*) with respect to cluster amounts $k \in [2, 50]$. For all newspapers, the optimal amount found was 3. Additional details are provided in Appendix B.

Mining Keywords of Each Cluster Though the clustering divided the *iterAdv-S* into smaller subgroups, manually examining the sentences in each cluster would still be challenging, as each cluster still contains hundreds of sentences (see Section 5). To ease the evaluation, we further used the keyword mining approach *PMI-freq* (Jin et al., 2020) to find the most representative keywords of each cluster in each newspaper. *PMI-freq* builds upon the measure of *pointwise mutual information* (*PMI*; Church and Hanks, 1990) by incorporating the document frequency of each word into the calculation, and thus overcomes *PMI*'s shortage of preferring rare words. Given a word w and a cluster C, the *PMI-freq* of w with respect to C is defined as follows, where $df(w)$ stands for the document frequency of w:

$$\textit{PMI-freq}(w; C) \equiv \log(df(w)) \cdot \log \frac{P(w|C)}{P(w)}$$

Prior to applying *PMI-freq*, all *iterAdv-S* were tokenized and lemmatized using NLTK (Bird et al., 2009), and stop words, numbers and punctuations were removed.[4]

[3] `https://huggingface.co/bert-base-german-cased`

[4] These preprocessing steps were not applied at the sentence vectorization stage, as they would cause a loss of contextual information for BERT. However, here they are relevant, as the keyword mining step aims at examining the lexical usage of each cluster to find out their semantic characteristics.

5 Results and Discussion

Table 1 shows that the *iterAdv-S* are fairly scarce in all newspapers. However, our approach is still able to reveal stark contrasts between the pragmatic framing styles arising from them. Table 2 shows the top 15 words by *PMI-freq* in each cluster of each newspaper (translated into English; See Appendix C for the original German version together with the *PMI-freq* score of each word).

BILD The largest cluster (#2) of BILD indicates the salience of violence issues among the *iterAdv-S* in BILD, as shown by keywords like 'ISIS', 'aggressive' (German: *aggressiv*), 'violence' (*Gewalt*) and 'riot' (*randalieren*). We also found out that *iterAdv-S* which contain the keywords 'initial reception center' (*Erstaufnahmeeinrichtung*) and 'refugee camp' (*Flüchtlingsunterkunft*) are often about violent incidents in refugee camps. This salience of violence issues is furthermore reflected by several keywords in Cluster #3 including 'incident' (*Zwischenfall*), 'attack' (*Übergriff*) and 'perpetrate' (*verüben*). Example (4) depicts the typical effect of iterative adverbs in violence-related sentences: They evoke a negative subtext that refugees are a *persistent* threat of the domestic security.

(4) *Im Bahnhof* [...] *randalierten immer wieder Flüchtlinge.*
'Refugees rioted at the train station again and again.' (BILD, Sep. 1, 2018)

$\mathcal{P}$ = 'Refugees have been rioting before.'
$\rightsquigarrow \mathcal{A}$ = 'Refugees continuously threaten the public order.'

Moreover, the keywords 'ship' (*Schiff*), 'deadly' (*tödlich*) and 'port' (*Hafen*) in Cluster #3 show a slight focus of the *iterAdv-S* in BILD on security issues at the Mediterranean route. As shown before in Example (1), iterative adverbs in this context evoke the subtext that the refugees need help.

FAZ Keywords in the largest cluster (#3) of FAZ show a mixed focus on both the security situation at the Mediterranean route, e.g., 'Greece' (*Griechenland*), 'human trafficker' (*Schlepper*) and 'smuggler' (*Schmuggler*), as well as on violence issues, e.g., 'foreigner' (*Ausländer*, often used in reports on attacks against foreigners), 'police' (*Polizei*), and 'violence' (*Gewalt*). However, while two of three clusters in BILD address violence and security issues (#2 and #3), two of three clusters in FAZ (#1 and #2) show a clear focus on asylum policies. This is reflected by policy-specific words like 'right of asylum' (*Asylrecht*, #1), names of political actors like 'Prime Minister' (*Ministerpräsident*, #2), as well as words related to political negotiations like 'reproach' (*vorwerfen*, #1) and 'conversation' (*Gespräch* #2). Example (5) depicts the typical effect of iterative adverbs in sentences containing these keywords: A closer check indicates that iterative adverbs there often evoke the subtext that the execution of refugee policies is hard (and sometimes rendered as inefficient) because of *repeating* conflicts of interest between parties or countries.

(5) *Italien wird immer wieder vorgeworfen, es setze die EU-Vorschrift nicht durch.*
'Italy is again and again accused of not executing EU-regulation.' (FAZ, Sep. 7, 2015)

$\mathcal{P}$ = 'Italy has been criticized at least once.'
$\rightsquigarrow \mathcal{A}$ = 'Italy is a stumbling block in executing the EU immigration policy'.

SZ The largest cluster (#2) in SZ shows the salience of security issues at the Mediterranean route among the *iterAdv-S*, as indicated by keywords like 'Mediterranean Sea' (*Mittelmeer*), 'refugee boat' (*Flüchtlingsboot*), 'coast' (*Küste*), 'Libyan' (*libysch*) and 'Greece' (*Griechenland*). In the sentences containing these keywords, iterative adverbs evoke the same humanitarian leaning subtext as illustrated in Example (1). Moreover, the top 2 keywords 'man' (*Mann*) and 'young' (*jung*) of Cluster #3 indicate an interesting emphasis on the demographic characteristics of the refugees. In a closer check, we found out that these keywords, besides being used in narrative texts about individual experiences of the refugees, often occur in context concerning the social integration of young male refugees. Sentence (6) shows an example: In such context, the iterative adverbs evoke a subtext that appeals to immediate action to facilitate the integration. Overall, the focus on security and integration issues indicates SZ's tendency of framing the Refugee Crisis from a humanitarian aspect.

(6) *Wenn diese jungen* [...] *zu lange ohne Beschäftigung herumsitzen, kommt es immer wieder zu Streit und Massenprügeleien.*
'When these young people are idle for too long, quarrels and brawls happen

BILD		
Cluster #2: 428 Samples	Cluster #3: 381 Samples	Cluster #1: 329 Samples
today, yesterday, o'clock, direction, explain, speaker, ISIS, Syrian, aggressive, Asylum, around, planned, person, Athens, start (v.), initial reception center, thousand, violence, riot (v.), flame, grand coalition, Hannover, standing, flare up, press conference, evening, commit (a crime)/beat, refugee camp, advertise	attempt (v.), give, incident, name (n.), bring, big, get, situation, hear, ship, deadly, know, story/history, government, port, think, calm (down), help (v.), arise, manage (to do), find, attack (n.), speak, perpetrate, politics, past (n.), past (adj.)	Angela, Friday, Merkel, reject (v.), refugee policy, controversial, CSU, Monday, upper limit, attack (v.), Greece, rescue, end (n.), Seehofer, chancellor
FAZ		
Cluster #3: 223 Samples	Cluster #1: 204 Samples	Cluster # 2: 131 Samples
give, attract attention, money, aid agency, see, foreigner, help (n.), police, Greece, situation, lead, say, stand, policeman, confirm, lacking (adj.), refugee accommodation, human trafficker, smuggler, week, violence, The Greens, Austria, last (adj.), together, Greek, prognosis, civil servant, camp, security force, report (n.), accommodation, because, new	far, stay, name (v.), right of asylum, belong, go, chancellor, speak, reproach (v.), Turkey, let, number, manage (to do), country, get, The Left, Bavarian, openness, boat, yield, Munich, always, port, game, appeal to, planned, municipality, bring, show, do	city, day, Prime Minister, institution, Frankfurt, old, state government, Mayor, conversation, end (n.), population, year, letter, located, Heidelberg, non-party, inquiry, district, reason, accommodate, tell, difficulty, wild, euro, refugee policy, open (adj.), live (v.), Italian, possible, development, search (v.), political, without, demonstrate, homeland
SZ		
Cluster #2: 217 Samples	Cluster #3: 187 Samples	Cluster #1: 153 Samples
person, Mediterranean Sea, refugee boat, Calais, coast, weekend, Sunday, asylum seeker, European Commission, Libyan, thousand, Greek, Angela, pressure, Greece, Merkel, get into, Federal Office, deportation, Italy, migration, boat, before, attack (n.), number	man, young, month, past (adj.), report (v.), stand (v.), new, year, just, prevent, group, money, sentence, hear, lead, seldom, call (v.), experience (n.), along, attitude, message, find, attempt (v.)	know, Federal Office for Migration and Refugees, Bavaria, Horst, Seehofer, political, Thursday, Hungary, place (n.), correct (adj.), Wednesday, name (v.), Friday, solidarity, speak, time/once, decide, let, human rights group, international, if possible, mouth, EU state, complain, own, CSU, demand

Table 2: The top 15 keywords by *PMI-freq* in each cluster of each newspaper. The clusters in each newspaper are ordered by their size from left to right. The words are separated by a comma, and additional explanation is given in parenthesis. Note that multiple words can have equal *PMI-freq* score.

again and again.' (SZ, Feb. 19, 2016)

$\mathcal{P}$ = 'Quarrels and brawls have happened at least once.'
$\rightsquigarrow \mathcal{A}$ = 'To avoid such violence, the integration of refugees into the labor market should be taken priority.'

6 Conclusion

Grounded in established pragmatics theory, we argued for the importance of presuppositions in framing, and put forward the notion of *pragmatic framing*. This was validated by our computational study on the case of iterative adverbs. Given the sparsity of the iterative adverbs, such pragmatic framing would be difficult to detect with many of the (weakly-)supervised classification approaches pursued in earlier studies, but we showed that it can be uncovered via consciously combining deep linguistic knowledge with NLP approaches. We see our work as a step towards successfully incorporating theoretical linguistic insights into NLP applications.

Acknowledgements

This work was funded by the Deutsche Forschungsgemeinschaft (DFG - German Research Foundation) under Germany's Excellence Strategy - EXC-2035/1 - 390681379. The author greatly appreciates Kristen Johnson, her mentor of the NAACL SRW 2022, for the valuable suggestions. Furthermore, the author thanks the helpful feedback from Miriam Butt and all anonymous reviewers.

References

Afra Feyza Akyürek, Lei Guo, Randa Elanwar, Prakash Ishwar, Margrit Betke, and Derry Tanti Wijaya. 2020. Multi-label and multilingual news framing analysis. In *Proceedings of the 58th Annual Meeting of the Association for Computational Linguistics*, pages 8614–8624, Online. Association for Computational Linguistics.

Kent Bach. 1999. The myth of conventional implicature. *Linguistics and philosophy*, pages 327–366.

Eric Baumer, Elisha Elovic, Ying Qin, Francesca Polletta, and Geri Gay. 2015. Testing and comparing computational approaches for identifying the language of framing in political news. In *Proceedings of the 2015 Conference of the North American Chapter of the Association for Computational Linguistics: Human Language Technologies*, pages 1472–1482, Denver, Colorado. Association for Computational Linguistics.

David Ian Beaver. 1997. Presupposition. In *Handbook of logic and language*, pages 939–1008. Elsevier.

David Ian Beaver, Bart Geurts, and Kristie Denlinger. 2021. Presupposition. In Edward N. Zalta, editor, *The Stanford Encyclopedia of Philosophy*. Metaphysics Research Lab, Stanford University.

Benjamin Bengfort, Rebecca Bilbro, Nathan Danielsen, Larry Gray, Kristen McIntyre, Prema Roman, Zijie Poh, et al. 2018. Yellowbrick.

Steven Bird, Ewan Klein, and Edward Loper. 2009. *Natural language processing with Python: Analyzing text with the natural language toolkit*. O'Reilly Media.

Amber E. Boydstun, Dallas Card, Justin H. Gross, Philip Resnik, and Noah A. Smith. 2014. Tracking the development of media frames within and across policy issues. `https://homes.cs.washington.edu/~nasmith/papers/boydstun+card+gross+resnik+smith.apsa14.pdf`, last accessed on March 24, 2022.

Dallas Card, Amber E. Boydstun, Justin H. Gross, Philip Resnik, and Noah A. Smith. 2015. The media frames corpus: Annotations of frames across issues. In *Proceedings of the 53rd Annual Meeting of the Association for Computational Linguistics and the 7th International Joint Conference on Natural Language Processing (Volume 2: Short Papers)*, pages 438–444, Beijing, China. Association for Computational Linguistics.

Kenneth Ward Church and Patrick Hanks. 1990. Word association norms, mutual information, and lexicography. *Computational Linguistics*, 16(1):22–29.

Dorottya Demszky, Nikhil Garg, Rob Voigt, James Zou, Jesse Shapiro, Matthew Gentzkow, and Dan Jurafsky. 2019. Analyzing polarization in social media: Method and application to tweets on 21 mass shootings. In *Proceedings of the 2019 Conference of the North American Chapter of the Association for Computational Linguistics: Human Language Technologies, Volume 1 (Long and Short Papers)*, pages 2970–3005, Minneapolis, Minnesota. Association for Computational Linguistics.

James N. Druckman. 2011. What's it all about? framing in political science. *Perspectives on framing*, 279.

Robert M. Entman. 1993. Framing: Toward clarification of a fractured paradigm. *Journal of communication*, 43(4):51–58.

Anjalie Field, Doron Kliger, Shuly Wintner, Jennifer Pan, Dan Jurafsky, and Yulia Tsvetkov. 2018. Framing and agenda-setting in Russian news: a computational analysis of intricate political strategies. In *Proceedings of the 2018 Conference on Empirical Methods in Natural Language Processing*, pages 3570–3580, Brussels, Belgium. Association for Computational Linguistics.

Kai von Fintel. 2008. What is presupposition accommodation, again? *Philosophical perspectives*, 22:137–170.

Herbert P. Grice. 1975. Logic and conversation. In *Speech acts*, pages 41–58. Brill.

Pere-Lluís Huguet Cabot, Verna Dankers, David Abadi, Agneta Fischer, and Ekaterina Shutova. 2020. The Pragmatics behind Politics: Modelling Metaphor, Framing and Emotion in Political Discourse. In *Findings of the Association for Computational Linguistics: EMNLP 2020*, pages 4479–4488, Online. Association for Computational Linguistics.

Ganesh Jawahar, Benoît Sagot, and Djamé Seddah. 2019. What does BERT learn about the structure of language? In *Proceedings of the 57th Annual Meeting of the Association for Computational Linguistics*, pages 3651–3657, Florence, Italy. Association for Computational Linguistics.

Yangfeng Ji and Noah A. Smith. 2017. Neural discourse structure for text categorization. In *Proceedings of the 55th Annual Meeting of the Association for Computational Linguistics (Volume 1: Long Papers)*, pages 996–1005, Vancouver, Canada. Association for Computational Linguistics.

Yiping Jin, Dittaya Wanvarie, and Phu T.V. Le. 2020. Learning from noisy out-of-domain corpus using dataless classification. *Natural Language Engineering*, pages 1–31.

Kristen Johnson, Di Jin, and Dan Goldwasser. 2017. Leveraging behavioral and social information for weakly supervised collective classification of political discourse on Twitter. In *Proceedings of the 55th Annual Meeting of the Association for Computational Linguistics (Volume 1: Long Papers)*, pages 741–752, Vancouver, Canada. Association for Computational Linguistics.

Aikaterini-Lida Kalouli, Rebecca Kehlbeck, Rita Sevastjanova, Oliver Deussen, Daniel Keim, and Miriam Butt. 2021. Is that really a question? going beyond factoid questions in NLP. In *Proceedings of the 14th International Conference on Computational Semantics (IWCS)*, pages 132–143, Groningen, The Netherlands (online). Association for Computational Linguistics.

Shima Khanehzar, Andrew Turpin, and Gosia Mikolajczak. 2019. Modeling political framing across policy issues and contexts. In *Proceedings of the The 17th Annual Workshop of the Australasian Language Technology Association*, pages 61–66, Sydney, Australia. Australasian Language Technology Association.

Stephen C. Levinson. 1983. *Pragmatics*. Cambridge university press.

David Lewis. 1979. Scorekeeping in a language game. In *Semantics from different points of view*, pages 172–187. Springer.

Yongjie Lin, Yi Chern Tan, and Robert Frank. 2019. Open sesame: Getting inside BERT's linguistic knowledge. In *Proceedings of the 2019 ACL Workshop BlackboxNLP: Analyzing and Interpreting Neural Networks for NLP*, pages 241–253, Florence, Italy. Association for Computational Linguistics.

Siyi Liu, Lei Guo, Kate Mays, Margrit Betke, and Derry Tanti Wijaya. 2019. Detecting frames in news headlines and its application to analyzing news framing trends surrounding U.S. gun violence. In *Proceedings of the 23rd Conference on Computational Natural Language Learning (CoNLL)*, pages 504–514, Hong Kong, China. Association for Computational Linguistics.

Julia Mendelsohn, Ceren Budak, and David Jurgens. 2021. Modeling framing in immigration discourse on social media. In *Proceedings of the 2021 Conference of the North American Chapter of the Association for Computational Linguistics: Human Language Technologies*, pages 2219–2263, Online. Association for Computational Linguistics.

Nona Naderi and Graeme Hirst. 2017. Classifying frames at the sentence level in news articles. In *Proceedings of the International Conference Recent Advances in Natural Language Processing, RANLP 2017*, pages 536–542, Varna, Bulgaria. INCOMA Ltd.

Thomas E. Nelson, Rosalee A. Clawson, and Zoe M. Oxley. 1997. Media framing of a civil liberties conflict and its effect on tolerance. *American Political Science Review*, 91(3):567–583.

Raghavendra Pappagari, Piotr Żelasko, Jesús Villalba, Yishay Carmiel, and Najim Dehak. 2019. Hierarchical transformers for long document classification. In *2019 IEEE Automatic Speech Recognition and Understanding Workshop (ASRU)*, pages 838–844. IEEE.

Fabian Pedregosa, Gaël Varoquaux, Alexandre Gramfort, Vincent Michel, Bertrand Thirion, Olivier Grisel, Mathieu Blondel, Peter Prettenhofer, Ron Weiss, Vincent Dubourg, Jake Vanderplas, Alexandre Passos, David Cournapeau, Matthieu Brucher, Matthieu Perrot, and Édouard Duchesnay. 2011. Scikit-learn: Machine learning in Python. *Journal of Machine Learning Research*, 12:2825–2830.

Christopher Potts. 2005. *The logic of conventional implicatures*. Oxford University Press.

Mats Edward Rooth. 1985. *Association with focus*. Ph.D. thesis, University of Massachusetts Amherst.

Peter J. Rousseeuw. 1987. Silhouettes: A graphical aid to the interpretation and validation of cluster analysis. *Journal of computational and applied mathematics*, 20:53–65.

Robert C. Stalnaker. 1972. Pragmatics. In Donald Davidson and Gilbert Harman, editors, *Semantics of natural language*, pages 380–397. D. Reidel Publishing Company.

Robert C. Stalnaker. 2002. Common ground. *Linguistics and philosophy*, 25(5/6):701–721.

Statista. 2021. *Statistiken zum Thema Zeitungen*. `https://de.statista.com/themen/176/zeitung/#dossierKeyfigures`, last accessed on March 24, 2022.

Jian Tang, Zhaoshi Meng, Xuanlong Nguyen, Qiaozhu Mei, and Ming Zhang. 2014. Understanding the limiting factors of topic modeling via posterior contraction analysis. In *International Conference on Machine Learning*, pages 190–198.

Henk Zeevat. 2002. Explaining presupposition triggers. *Information sharing*, pages 61–87.

Henk Zeevat. 2004. Particles: Presupposition triggers, context markers or speech act markers. In *Optimality theory and pragmatics*, pages 91–111. Springer.

Caleb Ziems and Diyi Yang. 2021. To protect and to serve? analyzing entity-centric framing of police violence. In *Findings of the Association for Computational Linguistics: EMNLP 2021*, pages 957–976, Punta Cana, Dominican Republic. Association for Computational Linguistics.

Malte Zimmermann. 2011. Discourse particles. In *Handbücher zur Sprach- und Kommunikationswissenschaft/Handbooks of Linguistics and Communication Science*, pages 2012–2038. De Gruyter Mouton.

A Hyperparameters

All hyperparameters used in our experiment described in Section 4.2 are listed below:

Fine-Tuning BERT The BERT model was fine-tuned for 4 epochs with a learning rate of 2e-5 and a batch size of 16.

K-Means Clustering The k-means algorithm was run 100 times with different centroid seeds. The maximum iteration number was set to 2000, and the random state was set to 42.

B Silhouette Coefficient for Optimal Cluster Amount Searching

As described in Section 4.2, we applied silhouette coefficient to find the optimal cluster amount for clustering the *iterAdv-S* and experimented with cluster amounts $k \in [2, 50]$. Figure 1 visualizes the distribution of the silhouette coefficients under $k \in [2, 5]$ using the Python package *Yellowbrick* (Bengfort et al., 2018), with each color standing for one cluster. It can be observed that the average silhouette coefficient decreases continuously when k increases (This trend continues for all $k \in [2, 50]$, but in order to avoid redundancy, we only show the visualization of $k \in [2, 5]$ here). The best trade-off between the average silhouette coefficient and the amount of suboptimally clustered items (represented by the colored areas that stretch to left) is 3 for all three newspapers.

C Keywords of Each Cluster in German

Figure 2, 3 and 4 shows the original German keywords that are ranked top 15 by *PMI-freq* in BILD, FAZ and SZ, respectively. The plots in each figure are ordered by the cluster size from left to right. The bars stand for the *PMI-freq* score. The words are separated by a comma. Multiple words assigned to one bar indicate that they have equal *PMI-freq* score.

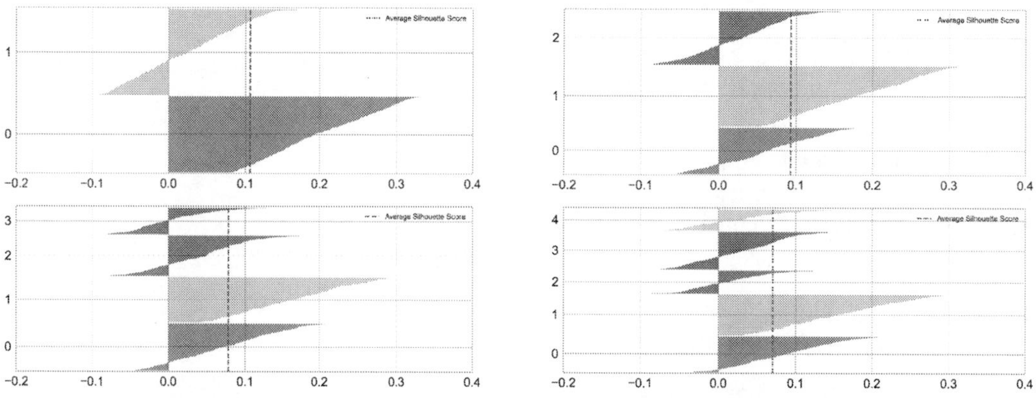

(a) BILD

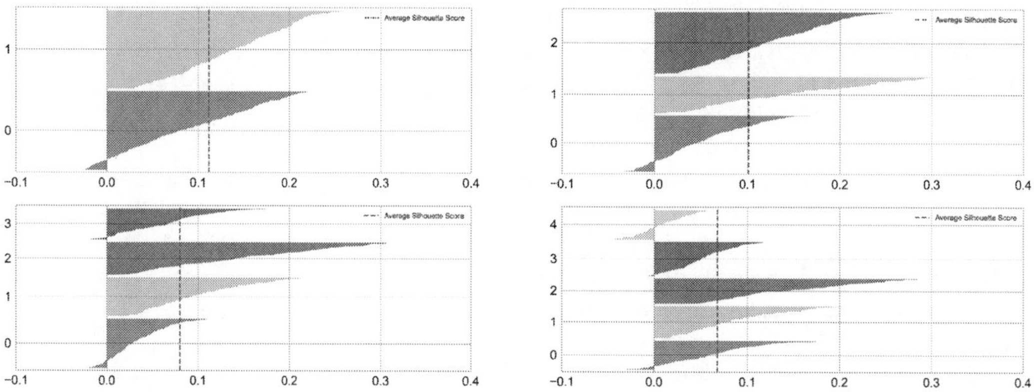

(b) FAZ

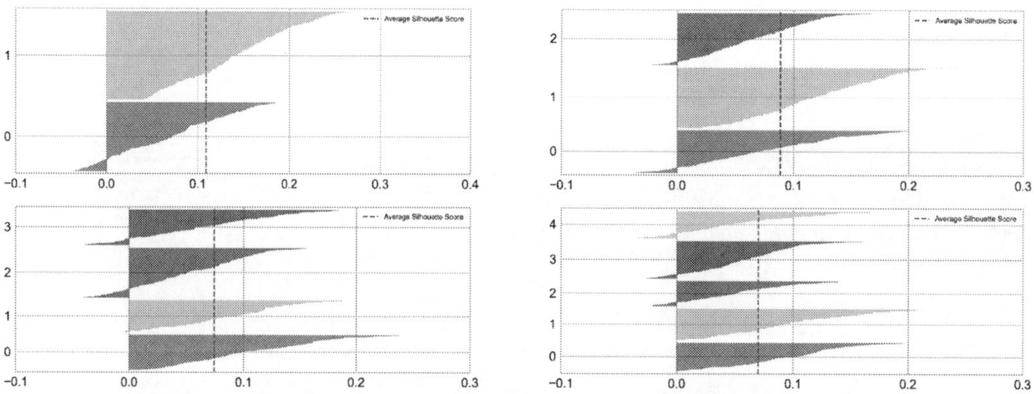

(c) SZ

Figure 1: Silhouette coefficients (represented by the horizontal axis) with respect to cluster amount $k \in [2, 5]$ (represented by the vertical axis). The red dash line represents the average silhouette coefficient.

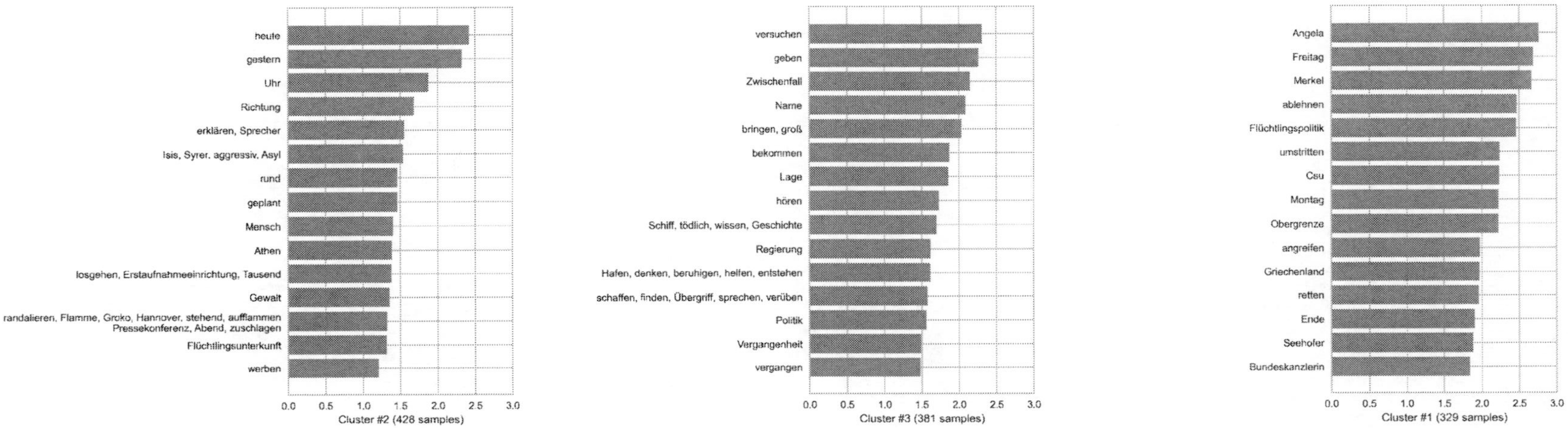

Figure 2: The top 15 keywords by *PMI-freq* in each cluster of BILD.

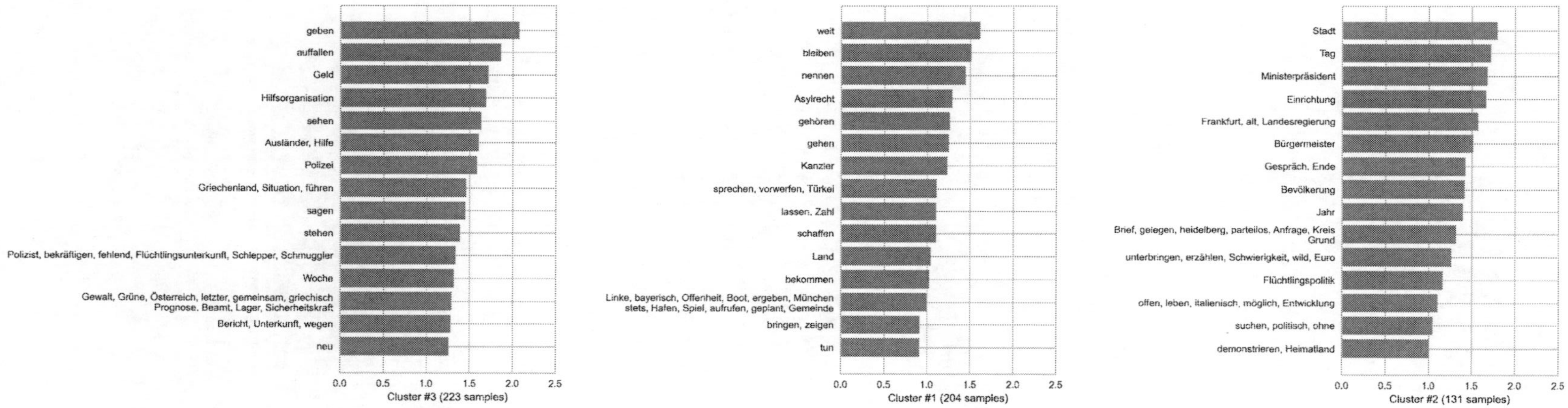

Figure 3: The top 15 keywords by *PMI-freq* in each cluster of FAZ.

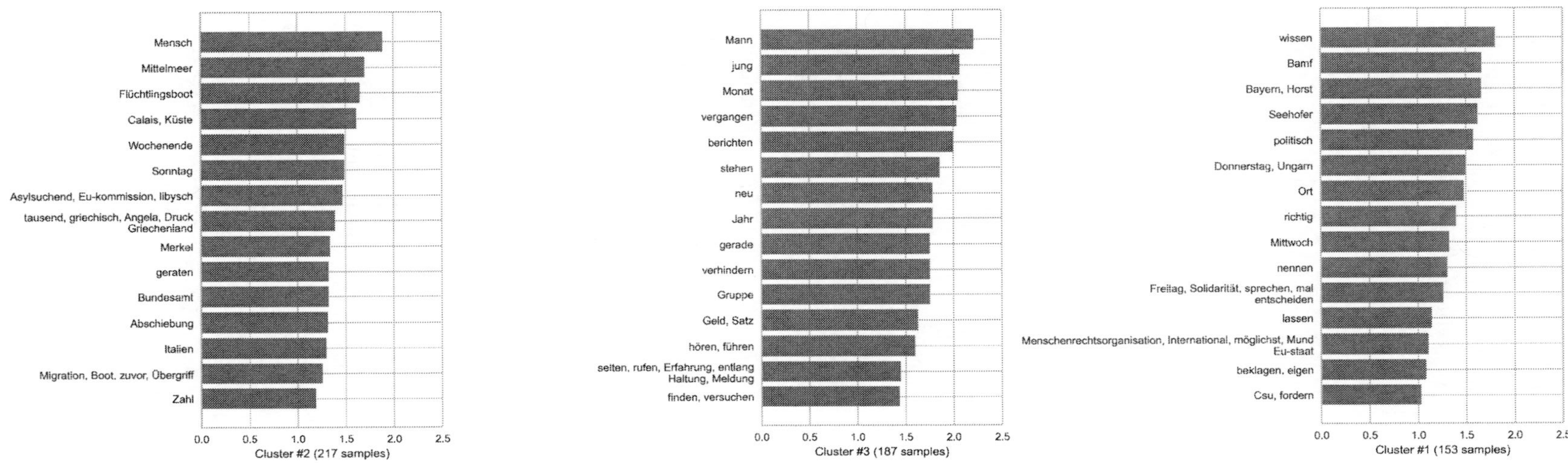

Figure 4: The top 15 keywords by *PMI-freq* in each cluster of SZ.

Methods for Estimating and Improving Robustness of Language Models

Michal Štefánik
Faculty of Informatics, Masaryk University
stefanik.m@mail.muni.cz

Abstract

Despite their outstanding performance, large language models (LLMs) suffer notorious flaws related to their preference for simple, surface-level textual relations over full semantic complexity of the problem. This proposal investigates a common denominator of this problem in their weak ability to generalise outside of the training domain. We survey diverse research directions providing estimations of model generalisation ability and find that incorporating some of these measures in the training objectives leads to enhanced distributional robustness of neural models. Based on these findings, we present future research directions towards enhancing the robustness of LLMs.

1 Introduction

The advances in language processing that we observe in recent years, mostly led by the instances of large language models (LLMs) based on the transformer architecture (Vaswani et al., 2017) raise a deserved attention of the scientific community. We find studies concluding that LLMs fine-tuned for a specific task can align with, or even outperform human accuracy on complex tasks such as question answering (Rajpurkar et al., 2016), paraphrase identification (Bowman et al., 2015), machine translation (Bahdanau et al., 2016) and others.

In contrast, critical studies demonstrate that many of the models reaching a state-of-the-art on a given task perform poorly on data sets drawn from different distribution(s). This is due to various reasons, such as training data set biases including spurious linguistic correlations (McCoy et al., 2019), different text stylistics or typos (Belinkov and Bisk, 2018), where a broad preference of LLMs towards fitting non-representative, yet easy-to-learn surface-level relations cause them to under-perform even shallow networks (Bojanowski et al., 2016). A lack of generalisation can also be caused by procedural reasons, such as training process instability, causing a convergence to local minima of distinct generalisation quality (McCoy et al., 2020). Low robustness of the consequential model towards out-of-distribution (OOD) samples limits their practical usability to the samples drawn from the training distribution, which is often impossible to ensure.

Despite that the complex language models strike an impression of a black-box, an extensive branch of research demonstrated that internal representations of LLMs correspond well to a human taxonomy in terms of morphological and syntactic decomposition (Clark et al., 2019a), or that the depth of the internal representation correlates well with the complexity of the problem as perceived by humans (Tenney et al., 2019).

The reported agility support the central presumption of this proposal; that LLMs can avoid the problems mentioned above under additional *regularisation*. We argue that such regularisation could also strenghten the implicit property of LLMs learning compositional language features and thus enhance an *interpretability* of their decision-making.

In this proposal, we survey literature from the broader area of neural networks for the reasons for better generalisation of the neural model. We find that many measures reported to correlate well with model's OOD performance can also enhance neural model generalisation when utilised within the model's training objective, as regularisers, or additional components of the training cost function. Inspired by this finding, this proposal outlines a path towards identification and utilisation of generalisation measures aimed to enhance robustness of LLMs towards distribution shift.

RQ1: "Can we *estimate* the performance of LLMs on data from OOD, without a collection of annotated data or expert feedback?"

RQ2: "Can we *adjust* the process of training LLMs to perform *better* on OOD samples?"

Proceedings of the 2022 Conference of the North American Chapter of the Association for Computational Linguistics: Human Language Technologies: Student Research Workshop, pages 44 - 51
July 10-15, 2022 ©2022 Association for Computational Linguistics

In Section 2.1 we survey the studies aiming to estimate robustness of neural models with no restrictions on a domain of application. Subsequently, in Section 2.2, we survey the training techniques reported to enhance the robustness of the trained model. Based on these findings, in Section 3 we identify promising directions and respective challenges specific for estimating (§3.1) and enhancing (§3.2) the robustness of LLMs.

1.1 Applicability

This proposal grounds the notion of model generalisation to its ability to perform well on samples drawn from distributions different than the training distribution (OOD). In this context, the term of a *distribution*, used interchangeably with *domain*, is commonly described by a specific shared property, such as topic, style, genre, or linguistic register (Ramponi and Plank, 2020).

This proposal focuses on distributional robustness in two branches of applications of current LLMs: *generative tasks*, where the problem is to generate a sequence of tokens, and *discriminative tasks*, where the task is to infer a discrete decision for each token or a sequence of tokens. Generative tasks include summarization, dialogue generation or machine translation, while discriminative tasks include classification, extractive question answering or named entity recognition.

In both cases, we propose to estimate the impact of given adjustment on model generalisation by measuring a difference in the model's performance on a set of distinct OOD domains. We note that such estimation is still only a pointwise estimation of model generalisation as some properties of the domains drawn for evaluation remain uncontrolled.

2 Background

2.1 Estimating Model Robustness (RQ1)

Having a set of true labels for some set of OOD samples X_t of target domain(s) D_t, the robustness of the model M can be estimated using standard qualitative measures, such as accuracy. This raises questions about the representativeness of the draw of X_t: do these cover *all* the domains of application of M, and are these domains accurately weighted in evaluation?

The problem is circumvented by generalisation measures based on *latent properties* of M, that do not require any labelled data of D_t. However, such an approach might come at the price of accuracy: according to Jiang et al. (2020), the Spearman's rank correlation of any unsupervised measure with out-of-distribution accuracy does not exceed 0.5 on average. The accuracy of the estimator improves using supervised approaches (Stefanik et al., 2021), but these already require some labelled data.

The situation presents a common dilemma in robustness evaluation: Ground-truth evaluation must involve a representative selection of test data. This problem can be avoided with unsupervised estimations based on the model properties, but such proxies are burdened by a certain level of inaccuracy. In the following sections, we review the measures introduced directly for evaluating model generalisation (§2.1.1) and for estimating model's expected output quality (§2.1.2), more commonly used in NLP.

2.1.1 Generalisation Measures

Traditionally, the ability of neural networks to generalise was related to the measures of their *capacity*, where the lower capacity might imply the lower *generalisation gap* (Jiang et al., 2020), i.e. a drop of performance under *distribution shift*. The capacity can be quantified in terms of *complexity* given by a number of model parameters, expressive power or others. A standard example of such a measure is a degree of a polynomial; the higher the degree, the better is the fit, but it comes at the price of generalisation loss. This group of measures is referred to as Vapnik–Chervonenkis dimension (VC-dimension), introduced by Vapnik (1999).

A large body of work aims to find such VC-dimensions that correspond well with OOD performance even with modern, over-parametrised networks. For instance, norm-based approaches (Neyshabur et al., 2015b) propose to use the p-norms used in regularisation of the training as the anchor value of generalisation and support this in theory by connecting such measure with a limitation of network capacity. Bartlett et al. (2017) conclude that a *spectral complexity* measure, that is inferred from eigenvalues of a matrix of the network weights, can be used as one of such complexity measures.

A collateral line of work, starting with Shawe-Taylor et al. (1998) show that *generalisation bounds*, denoting a range of expected performance of the given model on an arbitrary test set, can be provably associated with *VC-bounds*. Harvey et al. (2017) show that the *tightness* of such bounds for a linear subset of networks can be theoretically found.

Furthermore, Dziugaite and Roy (2017) propose a method to *optimize PAC-Bayesian bounds*, optimising the model for as tight bounds as possible.

Despite these proofs, error bounds based on VC-dimensions remain *vacuous* in practice (Dziugaite and Roy, 2017; Jiang et al., 2020): such estimates of OOD performance are too wide to be used in practice. Additionally, it is now widely observed (Novak et al., 2018; Neyshabur et al., 2015a), that in practice, an effect of over-parametrisation is in contrast with traditional VC-dimension theory and in multiple cases, over-parametrisation leads to *better* reported generalisation (Neyshabur et al., 2019).

Existing work attempts to ground *error bounds* in the underlying causal model that *describes* the target domains of interest. Meinshausen (2018) introduces a term of *Structural equation model* (SEM) defining the causal interventions consistent with a given *world* and relates domain generalisation to the model's robustness to the *interventions* defined by such SEM. Additionally, given that SEM produces a class of distributions $\mathcal{Q}$, a model M robust on $\mathcal{Q}$ is a *causal inference model* for $\mathcal{Q}$, connecting distributional robustness to a *weak form* of causal inference (Dziugaite et al., 2021). Similarly, Bühlmann (2018) ascribes the ability of causal inference on $\mathcal{Q}$ to any model whose representation is invariant to any domain $D \in \mathcal{Q}$ and proposes a method of selecting a subset of *invariant features* that picks such subset of attributes from a given set.

Practical observations of errors suggest that empirical *error bounds* are in fact significantly tighter than what can be proven in theory. Dziugaite et al. (2021) locate all bounds between the two extremes: theoretically-supported, yet vacuous bounds of methods based solely on the model property (*VC-bounds*) or behaviour (*PAC-Bayesian bounds*) and empirical, yet strictly data- and model-dependent evaluation on sample set(s) $X_t \in D_t$.

2.1.2 Quality Estimation

Quality estimation (QE) measure predicts model output quality in the absence of ground-truth reference (Fomicheva et al., 2020). Although not commonly used in this manner, QE measures also reflect on model robustness, making this branch of research applicable for OOD performance estimation (**RQ1**).

A significant line of work grounds quality estimation in model *confidence*, which can be estimated using Bayesian networks (Mackay, 1992) where standard *scalar* weights of the network are replaced with random variables, modelling the output distribution. This approach is accurate but not computationally feasible for larger networks. A branch of work *approximates* parametric distributions (Graves, 2011; Tran et al., 2019) making such uncertainty estimation practically feasible.

Model uncertainty can also be computed by ensembling variations of a given model in multiple trials, commonly referred to as *Monte Carlo* (MC) methods. Monte Carlo dropout (Gal and Ghahramani, 2016) applies dropout on inference randomly among multiple inference trials yielding an estimation of the distribution of network output, based on which the uncertainty is approximated. Lee et al. (2015) build such ensembles of estimators using *bagging*, i.e. training the ensembled models on different train sub-sets.

Model-variational methods fit well into the central *PAC-Bayesian* theory (Valiant, 1984), stating that if the error of the classifier can be bound, then also a performance of an ensemble of such classifiers can be upper-bound with arbitrarily-small bound ϵ (Guedj, 2019).

Confidence estimation can be utilised in enhanced model robustness, where prediction confidence is used as a regularizer of the main objective; in augmentation (Szegedy et al., 2014), confidence calibration (Gong et al., 2021), or in a training for consistency (Xie et al., 2019).

Jiang et al. (2020) propose to measure a regularisation decay of the weights, together with a measure of *sharpness*, reflecting on a volume of change in the model evaluation when the limited surrounding of the learnt parameter space minima is permuted (Keskar et al., 2017). Another introduced measure reflects a *variance of gradients* measured on a train set after a first training iteration. This work is the first large-scale study evaluating correlation of selected generalisation measures with true OOD performance and concludes that the mentioned sharpness and gradient-based measures correlate highest with the measured OOD performance. Consecutively, Dziugaite et al. (2021) support these findings on sharpness-based and PAC-Bayesian measures as the best-correlated in the similar methodology.

An important application of QE techniques lays in neural machine translation, where avoiding *critical errors* in translation remains an open problem. Such errors deviate the meaning of the translation in a way that may carry health, safety, legal or other implications (Specia et al., 2021). Kim et al. (2017) train a token-level estimator of machine translation output quality concurrently with the neural translation model. Fomicheva et al. (2020) additionally propose to predict output quality from *entropy of attention activations* of transformer model, but they find this approach not more accurate than the one based on simple output entropy (Kim et al., 2017), or than the MC dropout method.

2.2 Training Robust Models (RQ2)

A problem of training a model that performs well on out-of-distribution (OOD) samples can be found in the literature under the terms of *out-of-distribution generalisation* (Yi et al., 2021), *domain generalisation* (Gong et al., 2021), *distributional robustness* (Meinshausen, 2018), or simply *generalisation* (Foret et al., 2021). The variety of terminology points to the fact that the standards in this branch of research are not yet clearly set.

Despite imperfect correlations of generalisation measures with measured OOD performance, we find these measures already incorporated in novel training objectives reaching attractive enhancements of model robustness; Neyshabur et al. (2015b) investigate the impact of incorporating norm-based measures into the loss, obtaining generalisation guarantees of ℓ_2-norm. Foret et al. (2021) enrich the cross-entropy loss with a complementary component reflecting a sharpness of local optimum, based on a difference to local ϵ. Keskar et al. (2017) also demonstrate that the sharpness of the objective's optima corresponds to the model's robustness, and flatter optima can also be reached by noising the update steps by smaller training batch size.

Objective adjustments creatively utilising PAC--Bayesian measures also confirm reported correspondence of these measures to generalisation. Hinton (2002) proposes a *Product of Experts* (PoE) framework where an ensemble of identical shallow estimators eliminate model-specific biases in a dot product of ensembled outputs, resulting in superior OOD performance. Sanh et al. (2021) show an application of PoE eliminating the systematic biases on adversarial NLI data sets. Dagaev et al. (2021) adopt similar approach in debiasing image classification from *heuristical shortcuts*. Utama et al. (2020) eliminate model reliance on domain-specific attributes in a two-step process: by *identifying* the biased samples by model over-confidence, and their subsequent *down-weighting*.

Rather than encouraging specific model features, others have investigated the impact of specific *training strategies*, which becomes particularly relevant in multi-step training strategies of LLMs. Wang and Sennrich (2020) enhance robustness of the translation by fine-tuning for sentence-level Minimum Risk Training objective instead of the common token-level cross-entropy. Tu et al. (2020) show on adversarial data sets that: a) longer fine-tuning eliminates model fragility on under-represented samples, and b) *multitask learning* has a positive impact on transformer generalisation to adversarial data sets. Compliant results are reported by Xie et al. (2019) with multitask learning for both classification and output consistency to augmented samples, or by Raffel et al. (2020) on generative language multitask learning, or in cross-lingual settings by Clark et al. (2019b); Conneau et al. (2019); Lewis et al. (2020).

Similar results are reported in work addressing dataset biases. Utama et al. (2020); Nie et al. (2019); Teney et al. (2020) report that addressing only one bias in domain adaptation hurts the model generalisation on other domains. On the other hand, Wu et al. (2020) find that addressing multiple biases at once can enhance OOD generalisation, although they draw this conclusion from a single domain.

A different branch of work attempts to enhance the robustness by training strategies that work with knowledge of *domain distinction*. Gong et al. (2021) propose to approximately cover the class of *all* possible *target* domains D_t by *source* domains D_s and to learn the calibration of output probabilities from D_s that will allow to *associate* samples of a new target domain D_t to some known D_s. Yi et al. (2021) propose to use the adversarial framework, learning *indistinguishable* final-layer representation for different domains.

3 Research Proposal

Following the referenced studies on evaluation and enhancement of the generalisation of neural models, this section outlines directions in measuring and improving robustness of LLMs, respectively.

3.1 Estimating Model Robustness (RQ1)

Recently, the measures of generalisation of neural networks struck increasing attention (Jiang et al., 2020; Dziugaite et al., 2021). However, none of the referenced studies evaluates the measures on the case of LLMs. Especially within a standard *pre-training + fine-tuning* framework of modern NLP applications, quality of the measures might differ compared to the experiments on relatively small convolutional networks trained for image classification from scratch.

Hence, we first focus on evaluating the established generalisation measures, such as the ones based on spectral complexity, variance of gradients or sharpness in the case of pre-trained LLMs. A major challenge is to scale such experiments to a representative evaluation framework covering a broad set of tasks, domains, and model types. For instance, other training parameters will likely impact the metrics' quality; such covariates will have to be identified and controlled. However, even extensive evaluation will likely fail to identify some of such covariates; Due to this reason, we will delimit the scope of our results to the estimation and enhancement of robustness *with respect to* the enumerated covariates, even though it contrasts with the methodology of previous work.

We will give preference to the generalisation measures that correspond to linguistic and semantic language properties, as the practical deployment of such measures in evaluation also addresses a desire for enhancing *interpretability* of the LLMs' behaviour. Instances of linguistically-motivated measures can be a *largest common ancestor* between the parse trees of reference and hypothesis of generative model, or a coherence of output of discriminative model when a negation is introduced in the input.

In the evaluation of robustness of generative LLMs, we will prioritise *token-level* measures over conventional segment-level ones such as BLEU, as incorporating accurate token-level measures in training objectives could complement the classic token-level cross-entropy loss in sequence-to-sequence objective with its specific flaws, such as *exposure bias* (Wang and Sennrich, 2020).

The evaluation methodology will closely follow the one of Dziugaite et al. (2021), which reflects on a correlation of the measure with the measured OOD performance. If these measures reach high correlations, they might be applied directly in training regularisation or model selection. Even in cases of measures not reaching a high correlation, these can still bear the potential to improve model robustness (Foret et al., 2021).

3.2 Training Robust Models (RQ2)

Following the referenced examples adjusting training objectives with accurate generalisation measures (§2.2), e.g. norm-based measures (Neyshabur et al., 2015b), PAC-Bayesian measures (Sanh et al., 2021; Dagaev et al., 2021; Utama et al., 2020), or sharpness measure (Foret et al., 2021), we will use the accurate generalisation measures of LLMs (§3.1) as *regularizers* and *complementary objectives* of the training.

Locatello et al. (2019) theoretically prove that full distributional robustness is not possible without an *explicit* exposition of both the data and the model biases. Recently, Bengio et al. (2020) theoretically and empirically demonstrated that the model could *utilise* data biases to expose the underlying causal structure of the data in an experiment where such a structure is preliminarily known.

We will introduce training objectives that expose domain-specific data biases to the model in more explicit ways. The most direct approach is to complement the task-specific objective with another objective of distinguishing the domain(s) of origin. The domain-distinctive objective can shape a form of a binary classifier or a similarity loss of selected model representations (e.g. KL-divergence (Kullback and Leibler, 1951)).

We will investigate the impact of the *pre-training*, and *fine-tuning* objectives on the model's eventual robustness over multiple application tasks, domains and architectures, in a methodology similar to the *generalisation measures* evaluation of (Dziugaite et al., 2021).

Additionally, we will *replace* or *complement* the objectives of generative LLMs with token-level measures well-correlated with the OOD performance and compare the resulting models with computationally-expensive sentence-level objectives optimising the measures such as BLEU as their objectives.

In the case of discriminative models, we will evaluate robustness to surface-level heuristics using adversarial datasets like HANS (McCoy et al., 2019), or PAWS (Zhang et al., 2019) designed to expose the commonly-learnt biases of LLMs. For generative LLMs, we will evaluate a performance of the model on domain(s) *different* from the training domain; for instance, we will train a translation model on *subtitles* parallel corpus and evaluate on a domain of *news articles*. We will also evaluate the trained model(s) for its inclination to *critical errors* as a probability of generating a translation containing a severe error (Specia et al., 2021) in *enforced* generation.

4 Conclusion

Our work outlines potential directions in enhancing distributional robustness of LLMs to mitigate a performance drop under distribution shift. We survey and identify accurate generalisation measures (§2.1) and find multiple studies demonstrating that utilisation of these measures in the training objectives positively impacts model robustness (§2.2).

Following this observation, we propose to identify generalisation measures best-suitable for LLMs (§3.1) and outline ways how to utilise these measures in the training process. Additionally, we identify a set of other methods reported to enhance OOD performance of LLMs that we propose to compare to in the outlined methodology for evaluating generalisation measures.

Similarly, we propose methodologies for robustness estimation of both generative and discriminative LLMs (§3.2); These methodologies are based on a quality assessment on the domains covered by the enclosed set of variables, and on the robustness towards the data set(s) constructed to expose enclosed set of models' biases.

References

Dzmitry Bahdanau, Kyunghyun Cho, and Yoshua Bengio. 2016. Neural Machine Translation by Jointly Learning to Align and Translate.

Peter L. Bartlett, Dylan J. Foster, and Matus Telgarsky. 2017. Spectrally-Normalized Margin Bounds for Neural Networks. In *Proc. of the 31st International Conference on Neural Information Processing Systems*, NIPS '17, pages 6241–6250, Red Hook, NY, USA. Curran Associates Inc.

Yonatan Belinkov and Yonatan Bisk. 2018. Synthetic and Natural Noise Both Break Neural Machine Translation. In *Proc. of International Conference on Learning Representations*.

Yoshua Bengio, Tristan Deleu, Nasim Rahaman, Nan Rosemary Ke, Sebastien Lachapelle, Olexa Bilaniuk, Anirudh Goyal, and Christopher Pal. 2020. A Meta-Transfer Objective for Learning to Disentangle Causal Mechanisms. In *Proc. of International Conference on Learning Representations*.

Piotr Bojanowski, Edouard Grave, Armand Joulin, and Tomas Mikolov. 2016. Enriching Word Vectors with Subword Information. ArXiv:1607.04606.

Samuel R. Bowman, Gabor Angeli, Christopher Potts, and Christopher D. Manning. 2015. A large annotated corpus for learning natural language inference. In *Proc. of the 2015 Conference on Empirical Methods in Natural Language Processing*, pages 632–642, Lisbon, Portugal. ACL.

Peter Bühlmann. 2018. Invariance, Causality and Robustness. *CoRR*, 1812.08233v1.

Kevin Clark, Urvashi Khandelwal, Omer Levy, and Christopher D. Manning. 2019a. What Does BERT Look At? An Analysis of BERT's Attention. ArXiv:1906.04341.

Kevin Clark, Urvashi Khandelwal, Omer Levy, and Christopher D. Manning. 2019b. What does BERT look at? an analysis of BERT's attention. In *Proc. of the 2019 ACL Workshop BlackboxNLP: Analyzing and Interpreting Neural Networks for NLP*, pages 276–286, Florence, Italy. ACL.

Alexis Conneau, Kartikay Khandelwal, Naman Goyal, Vishrav Chaudhary, Guillaume Wenzek, Francisco Guzmán, Edouard Grave, Myle Ott, Luke Zettlemoyer, and Veselin Stoyanov. 2019. Unsupervised Cross-lingual Representation Learning at Scale. ArXiv:1911.02116.

Nikolay Dagaev, Brett D. Roads, Xiaoliang Luo, Daniel N. Barry, Kaustubh R. Patil, and Bradley C. Love. 2021. A Too-Good-to-be-True Prior to Reduce Shortcut Reliance. *CoRR*, abs/2102.06406v2.

Gintare K. Dziugaite and Daniel M. Roy. 2017. Computing Nonvacuous Generalization Bounds for Deep (Stochastic) Neural Networks with Many More Parameters than Training Data. *CoRR*, abs/1703.11008v1.

Gintare Karolina Dziugaite, Alexandre Drouin, Brady Neal, Nitarshan Rajkumar, Ethan Caballero, Linbo Wang, Ioannis Mitliagkas, and Daniel M. Roy. 2021. In Search of Robust Measures of Generalization. *CoRR*, abs/2010.11924v2.

Marina Fomicheva, Shuo Sun, Lisa Yankovskaya, Frédéric Blain, Francisco Guzmán, Mark Fishel, Nikolaos Aletras, Vishrav Chaudhary, and Lucia Specia. 2020. Unsupervised Quality Estimation for Neural Machine Translation. *Transactions of the ACL*, 8:539–555.

Pierre Foret, Ariel Kleiner, H. Mobahi, and Behnam Neyshabur. 2021. Sharpness-Aware Minimization for Efficiently Improving Generalization. *CoRR*, abs/2010.01412v1.

Yarin Gal and Zoubin Ghahramani. 2016. Dropout as a Bayesian Approximation: Representing Model Uncertainty in Deep Learning. In *Proc. of the 33rd International Conference on Machine Learning*, volume 48 of *Proc. of Machine Learning Research*, pages 1050–1059, New York, USA. PMLR.

Yunye Gong, Xiaoyu Lin, Yi Yao, Thomas G. Dietterich, Ajay Divakaran, and M. Gervasio. 2021. Confidence Calibration for Domain Generalization under Covariate Shift. *CoRR*, abs/2104.00742v2.

Alex Graves. 2011. Practical Variational Inference for Neural Networks. In *Advances in Neural Information Processing Systems*, volume 24. Curran Associates, Inc.

Benjamin Guedj. 2019. A Primer on PAC-Bayesian Learning. *CoRR*, abs/1901.05353v3.

Nick Harvey, Christopher Liaw, and Abbas Mehrabian. 2017. Nearly-tight VC-dimension bounds for piecewise linear neural networks. In *Proc. of the Conference on Learning Theory*, volume 65 of *PMLR*, pages 1064–1068. PMLR.

Geoffrey E. Hinton. 2002. Training Products of Experts by Minimizing Contrastive Divergence. *Neural Computation*, 14(8):1771–1800.

Yiding Jiang, Behnam Neyshabur, H. Mobahi, Dilip Krishnan, and Samy Bengio. 2020. Fantastic Generalization Measures and Where to Find Them. *CoRR*, abs/1912.02178v1.

Nitish Shirish Keskar, Dheevatsa Mudigere, Jorge Nocedal, Mikhail Smelyanskiy, and Ping Tak Peter Tang. 2017. On Large-Batch Training for Deep Learning: Generalization Gap and Sharp Minima. *CoRR*, abs/1609.04836v1.

Hyun Kim, Hun-Young Jung, Hongseok Kwon, Jong-Hyeok Lee, and Seung-Hoon Na. 2017. Predictor-Estimator: Neural Quality Estimation Based on Target Word Prediction for Machine Translation. *ACM Trans. Asian Low-Resour. Lang. Inf. Process.*, 17(1).

S. Kullback and R. A. Leibler. 1951. On Information and Sufficiency. *Annals of Mathematical Statistics*, 22:79–86.

Stefan Lee, Senthil Purushwalkam, Michael Cogswell, David J. Crandall, and Dhruv Batra. 2015. Why M Heads are Better than One: Training a Diverse Ensemble of Deep Networks. *CoRR*, abs/1511.06314v1.

Mike Lewis, Yinhan Liu, Naman Goyal, Marjan Ghazvininejad, Abdelrahman Mohamed, Omer Levy, Veselin Stoyanov, and Luke Zettlemoyer. 2020. BART: Denoising Sequence-to-Sequence Pre-training for Natural Language Generation, Translation, and Comprehension. In *Proc. of the 58th Annual Meeting of the ACL*, pages 7871–7880. ACL.

Francesco Locatello, Stefan Bauer, Mario Lucic, S. Gelly, B. Schölkopf, and Olivier Bachem. 2019. Challenging Common Assumptions in the Unsupervised Learning of Disentangled Representations. *CoRR*, 1811.12359v4.

David John Cameron Mackay. 1992. *Bayesian Methods for Adaptive Models*. Ph.D. thesis, California Institute of Technology, USA. UMI Order No. GAX92-32200.

R. Thomas McCoy, Junghyun Min, and Tal Linzen. 2020. BERTs of a feather do not generalize together: Large variability in generalization across models with similar test set performance. *CoRR*, abs/1911.02969v2.

Tom McCoy, Ellie Pavlick, and Tal Linzen. 2019. Right for the Wrong Reasons: Diagnosing Syntactic Heuristics in Natural Language Inference. In *Proc. of the 57th Annual Meeting of the ACL*, pages 3428–3448, Florence, Italy. ACL.

Nicolai Meinshausen. 2018. Causality from a Distributional Robustness Point of View. In *Proc. of IEEE Data Science Workshop (DSW 2018)*, pages 6–10.

Behnam Neyshabur, Zhiyuan Li, Srinadh Bhojanapalli, Yann LeCun, and Nathan Srebro. 2019. The role of over-parametrization in generalization of neural networks. In *Proc. of International Conference on Learning Representations*.

Behnam Neyshabur, Ryota Tomioka, and Nathan Srebro. 2015a. In Search of the Real Inductive Bias: On the Role of Implicit Regularization in Deep Learning. ArXiv:1412.6614.

Behnam Neyshabur, Ryota Tomioka, and Nathan Srebro. 2015b. Norm-based capacity control in neural networks. In *Proc. of The 28th Conference on Learning Theory*, volume 40 of *PMLR*, pages 1376–1401, Paris, France. PMLR.

Yixin Nie, Yicheng Wang, and Mohit Bansal. 2019. Analyzing Compositionality-Sensitivity of NLI Models. *CoRR*, abs/1811.07033v1.

Roman Novak, Yasaman Bahri, D. Abolafia, Jeffrey Pennington, and J. Sohl-Dickstein. 2018. Sensitivity and Generalization in Neural Networks: an Empirical Study. ArXiv:1802.08760.

Colin Raffel, Noam Shazeer, Adam Roberts, Katherine Lee, Sharan Narang, Michael Matena, Yanqi Zhou, Wei Li, and Peter J. Liu. 2020. Exploring the limits of transfer learning with a unified text-to-text transformer. *Journal of Machine Learning Research*, 21(146):1–67.

Pranav Rajpurkar, Jian Zhang, Konstantin Lopyrev, and Percy Liang. 2016. SQuAD: 100,000+ Questions for Machine Comprehension of Text. In *Proc. of the 2016 Conference on Empirical Methods in Natural Language Processing*, pages 2383–2392, Austin, USA. ACL.

Alan Ramponi and Barbara Plank. 2020. Neural unsupervised domain adaptation in NLP—A survey. In *Proc. of the 28th International Conference on Computational Linguistics*, pages 6838–6855, Barcelona, Spain (Online). International Committee on Computational Linguistics.

Victor Sanh, Thomas Wolf, Yonatan Belinkov, and Alexander M. Rush. 2021. Learning from others' mistakes: Avoiding dataset biases without modeling them. *CoRR*, abs/2012.01300v1.

J. Shawe-Taylor, P.L. Bartlett, R.C. Williamson, and M. Anthony. 1998. Structural risk minimization over data-dependent hierarchies. *IEEE Transactions on Information Theory*, 44(5):1926–1940.

Lucia Specia, Frédéric Blain, Marina Fomicheva, Chrysoula Zerva, Zhenhao Li, Vishrav Chaudhary, and André F. T. Martins. 2021. Findings of the WMT 2021 shared task on quality estimation. In *Proceedings of the Sixth Conference on Machine Translation*, pages 684–725, Online. Association for Computational Linguistics.

Michal Stefanik, Vít Novotný, and Petr Sojka. 2021. Regressive ensemble for machine translation quality evaluation. In *Proceedings of the Sixth Conference on Machine Translation*, pages 1041–1048, Online. Association for Computational Linguistics.

Christian Szegedy, Wojciech Zaremba, Ilya Sutskever, Joan Bruna, D. Erhan, I. Goodfellow, and R. Fergus. 2014. Intriguing properties of neural networks. *CoRR*, abs/1312.6199v4.

Damien Teney, Kushal Kafle, Robik Shrestha, Ehsan Abbasnejad, Christopher Kanan, and A. V. Hengel. 2020. On the Value of Out-of-Distribution Testing: An Example of Goodhart's Law. *CoRR*, abs/2005.09241v1.

Ian Tenney, Dipanjan Das, and Ellie Pavlick. 2019. BERT Rediscovers the Classical NLP Pipeline.

Dustin Tran, Michael W. Dusenberry, Mark van der Wilk, and Danijar Hafner. 2019. Bayesian Layers: A Module for Neural Network Uncertainty. In *Proc. of the 33rd International Conference on NIPS*, Red Hook, USA. Curran Associates Inc.

Lifu Tu, Garima Lalwani, Spandana Gella, and He He. 2020. An Empirical Study on Robustness to Spurious Correlations using Pre-trained Language Models. *Transactions of the ACL*, 8:621–633.

Prasetya Ajie Utama, Nafise Sadat Moosavi, and Iryna Gurevych. 2020. Towards Debiasing NLU Models from Unknown Biases. In *Proc. of the 2020 Conference on Empirical Methods in Natural Language Processing (EMNLP)*, pages 7597–7610, Online. ACL.

L. G. Valiant. 1984. A Theory of the Learnable. In *Proc. of the Sixteenth Annual ACM Symposium on Theory of Computing*, STOC '84, pages 436–445, New York, USA. ACM.

Vladimir N. Vapnik. 1999. *The Nature of Statistical Learning Theory*, second edition. Springer.

Ashish Vaswani, Noam Shazeer, Niki Parmar, Jakob Uszkoreit, Llion Jones, Aidan N. Gomez, Łukasz Kaiser, and Illia Polosukhin. 2017. Attention is All You Need. In *Proc. of the 31st International Conference on Neural Information Processing Systems*, NIPS'17, pages 6000–6010, Red Hook, NY, USA. Curran Associates Inc.

Chaojun Wang and Rico Sennrich. 2020. On exposure bias, hallucination and domain shift in neural machine translation. In *Proceedings of the 58th Annual Meeting of the Association for Computational Linguistics*, pages 3544–3552, Online. Association for Computational Linguistics.

Mingzhu Wu, N. Moosavi, Andreas Rücklé, and Iryna Gurevych. 2020. Improving QA Generalization by Concurrent Modeling of Multiple Biases. *CoRR*.

Qizhe Xie, Zihang Dai, Eduard Hovy, Minh-Thang Luong, and Quoc V. Le. 2019. Unsupervised Data Augmentation. *CoRR*, abs/1904.12848v1.

Mingyang Yi, Lu Hou, Jiacheng Sun, Lifeng Shang, Xin Jiang, Qun Liu, and Zhi-Ming Ma. 2021. Improved OOD Generalization via Adversarial Training and Pre-training. In *Proc. of the 38th ICML*, volume 139, pages 11987–11997. PMLR.

Yuan Zhang, Jason Baldridge, and Luheng He. 2019. PAWS: Paraphrase Adversaries from Word Scrambling. In *Proc. of the 2019 Conf. NAACL-HLT*, pages 1298–1308, Minneapolis, USA. ACL.

Retrieval-augmented Generation across Heterogeneous Knowledge

Wenhao Yu
University of Notre Dame, USA
wyu1@nd.edu

Abstract

Retrieval-augmented generation (RAG) methods have been receiving increasing attention from the NLP community and achieved state-of-the-art performance on many NLP downstream tasks. Compared with conventional pre-trained generation models, RAG methods have remarkable advantages such as easy knowledge acquisition, strong scalability, and low training cost. Although existing RAG models have been applied to various knowledge-intensive NLP tasks, such as open-domain QA and dialogue systems, most of the work has focused on retrieving unstructured text documents from Wikipedia. In this paper, I first elaborate on the current obstacles to retrieving knowledge from a single-source homogeneous corpus. Then, I demonstrate evidence from both existing literature and my experiments, and provide multiple solutions on retrieval-augmented generation methods across heterogeneous knowledge.

1 Introduction

In recent years, large pre-trained language models (PLMs), such as T5 (Raffel et al., 2020) and GPT-3 (Brown et al., 2020), have revolutionized the field of natural language processing (NLP), achieving remarkable performance on various downstream tasks (Qiu et al., 2020). These PLMs have learned a substantial amount of in-depth knowledge from the pre-training corpus (Petroni et al., 2019), so they can predict the outputs on downstream tasks without access to any external memory or raw text, as a parameterized implicit knowledge base (Roberts et al., 2020). The way of fine-tuning PLMs using only *input-output* pairs of target data is often referred to as *close-book* setting (Petroni et al., 2019).

While this development is exhilarating, such large-scale PLMs still suffer from the following

* This is a thesis proposal paper presented at the student research workshop (SRW) at NAACL 2022 in Seattle, USA.

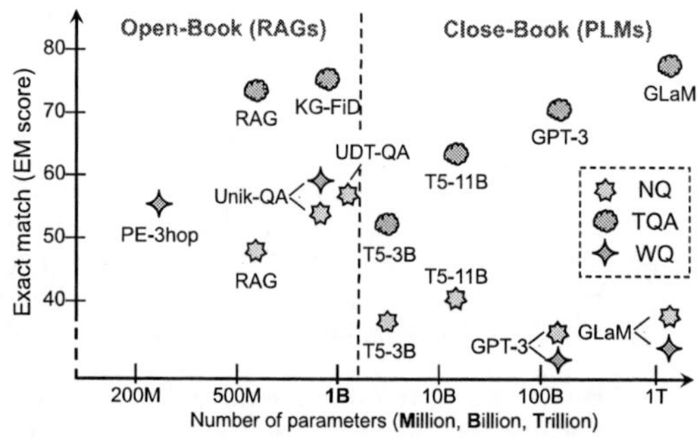

Figure 1: The RAG methods significantly outperform large-scale PLMs on three open-domain QA tasks while trained with much fewer parameters than PLMs.

drawbacks: (i) They are usually trained offline, making the model agnostic to the latest information, e.g., asking a chat-bot trained from 2011-2018 about COVID-19 (Yu et al., 2022b). (ii) They make predictions by only "looking up information" stored in its parameters, leading to inferior interpretability (Shuster et al., 2021). (iii) They are mostly trained on general domain corpora, making them less effective on domain-specific tasks (Gururangan et al., 2020). (iv) Their pre-training phase can be prohibitively expensive for academic research groups, limiting the model pre-training to only a few industry labs (Izsak et al., 2021).

The solution that seems obvious at first glance is to allow language models free access to open-world resources, such as encyclopedias and books. The way of augmenting the input of PLMs with external information is often referred to as *open-book* setting (Mihaylov et al., 2018). A prominent method in the open-book setting is retrieval-augmented generation (RAG) (Lewis et al., 2020b; Yu et al., 2022c), a new learning paradigm that fuses PLMs and traditional IR techniques, which has achieved state-of-the-art performance in many knowledge-intensive NLP tasks (Petroni et al., 2021). Compared with large-scale PLMs counterparts, e.g., GPT-3, the RAG model has some remarkable ad-

Proceedings of the 2022 Conference of the North American Chapter of the Association for Computational Linguistics: Human Language Technologies: Student Research Workshop, pages 52 - 58
July 10-15, 2022

vantages: (i) The knowledge is not implicitly stored in model parameters, but is explicitly acquired in a plug-and-play manner, leading to great scalability; (ii) Instead of generating from scratch, the model generates outputs based on some retrieved references, which eases the difficulty of text generation.

Although the RAG models have been widely used in the existing literature, most of the work has focused on retrieving unstructured text from general domain corpus, e.g., Wikipedia. However, the performance is often limited by the coverage of only one certain knowledge. For example, only a finite portion of questions could be answered from Wikipedia passages in many open-domain QA datasets, while the remaining could only rely on the input question because no supportive documents could be retrieved (Oguz et al., 2022). In this paper, I first elaborate on the current obstacles to retrieving knowledge from a single-source homogeneous corpus. Then, I demonstrate several pieces of evidence from both existing literature and my own experiments, and provide multiple potential solutions on retrieval-augmented generation methods across heterogeneous knowledge.

2 Background

I will first provide a formal definition of the RAG framework and list necessary notations. RAG aims to predict the output y based on the source input x (x, y are from a corpus $\mathcal{D}$), while a document reference set $\mathcal{Z}$ is accessible (e.g., Wikipedia). Besides, the association between a document $z \in \mathcal{Z}$ and the tuple $(x, y) \in \mathcal{D}$ is not necessarily known, though it could be provided by human annotations (Dinan et al., 2019) or weakly supervised signals (Karpukhin et al., 2020).

Overall, a general RAG framework has two major components: (i) a document retriever and (ii) a text generator, as shown in Figure 2. The objective of the RAG is to train a model to maximize the likelihood of y given x and $\mathcal{Z}$, In practice, $\mathcal{Z}$ often contains millions of documents, rendering enumeration over z impossible. Therefore, the first step of RAG is to leverage a document retriever, e.g., DPR (Karpukhin et al., 2020), to narrow down the search to a handful of relevant documents. The retriever takes x and $\mathcal{Z}$ as input and yields relevance scores $\{s_1, \cdots, s_K\}$ of the top-K documents $Z = \{z_{(1)}, \cdots, z_{(K)}\}$. Then, the second step of RAG is to use a text generator, e.g., BART (Lewis et al., 2020a) and T5 (Raffel et al.,

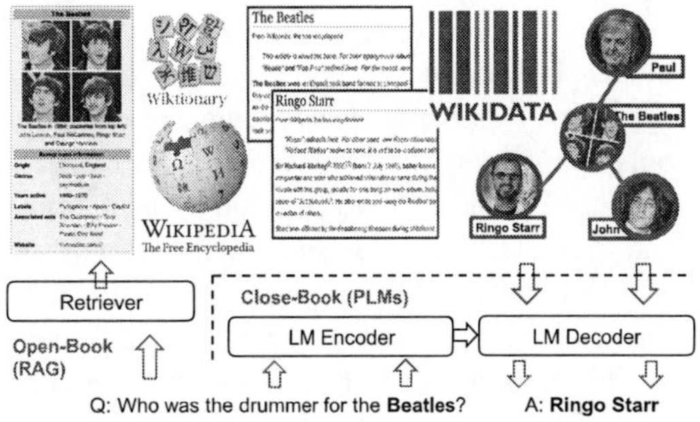

Figure 2: Compared with PLMs, RAG models directly seeks knowledge (e.g., texts, tables and KGs) from external information sources to help answer questions.

2019), to produce desired output y by taking both input x and retrieved document set Z as conditions.

Document Retriever. A neural document retriever typically employs two independent encoders like BERT (Devlin et al., 2019) to encode the query and the document separately, and estimates their relevance by computing a single similarity score between two encoded representations. For example, in DPR (Karpukhin et al., 2020), the documents Z and context queries x are mapped into the same dense embedding space. The relevance score $s(x, z)$ for each document z is computed as the vector inner product between document embedding h_z and query embedding h_x, i.e., $s(x, z) = h_x^T \times h_z$.

Text Generator. It can use any encoder-decoder framework, such as BART (Lewis et al., 2020a) and T5 (Raffel et al., 2019). The model takes input sequence, as well as the support documents to generate the desired output. A naive method for combining the input sequence with the support documents is to concatenate them sequentially (Lewis et al., 2020a). However, this method suffers from the input sequence length limitation and high computation cost. FiD (Izacard and Grave, 2021) processed passages independently in the encoder, performed attention over all the retrieved passages, which demonstrated state-of-the-art performance on many knowledge-intensive NLP tasks.

3 Proposed Work

3.1 Background and Motivation

Despite achieving remarkable performance, previous efforts of retrieval-augmented generation (RAG) works mainly exploit only a single-source homogeneous knowledge retrieval space, i.e., Wikipedia passages (Karpukhin et al., 2020; Lewis et al., 2020b; Petroni et al., 2021; Izacard and

Grave, 2021; Yu et al., 2022a). However, their model performance might be limited by the coverage of only one certain knowledge. For example, only a finite portion of questions can be answered from the Wikipedia passages in many open-domain QA datasets, while the remaining can only rely on the input query because no supportive documents can be retrieved (Oguz et al., 2022). Since much useful information cannot be fulfilled based on Wikipedia alone, a natural solution is to expand the retrieval corpus from Wikipedia to the entire World Wide Web (WWW). However, suffering from the long-tail issue and the cost of a massive workforce, it is not wise to improve the coverage by expanding the number of entries in a single-source knowledge (Piktus et al., 2021; Lazaridou et al., 2022). For example, as shown in Table 1, increasing the retrieval space from Wikipedia (22M documents) to the web-scale corpus CCNet (906M documents) even hurts model performance on NQ and HotpotQA datasets. This is most likely due to the lower quality (where quality could mean truthfulness, objectivity, lack of harmful content, source reliability, etc) of the web corpus, compared with the Wikipedia corpus (Piktus et al., 2021).

Instead of expanding the number of entries in a single-source knowledge, an alternative solution is resorting to heterogeneous knowledge sources. This is also in line with our human behavior of answering questions that often seek a variety of knowledge learned from different sources. Therefore, grounding generation across heterogeneous knowledge sources is a natural solution to improve knowledge coverage and have more room to select appropriate knowledge. It is worth mentioning that no knowledge type can always perform the best. The most suitable knowledge depends on the case, in which multiple knowledge might need to be combined for answering one question.

3.2 Evidence from Existing Literature

There are several studies in the existing literature that combine multiple knowledge to enhance language models, such as augmenting commonsense reasoning with knowledge graphs (Yu et al., 2022d), and introducing multi-modal visual features to enhance emotional dialogue (Liang et al., 2022). However, most of them use aligned knowledge from different sources (e.g., graph-text pairs, image-text pairs), without retrieving knowledge from a large-scale heterogeneous corpus.

Table 1: With a larger corpus of unstructured text retrieval – CCNet, the model performs even worse than retrieving from Wikipedia alone on the NQ and HotpotQA datasets. The model used in the table is DPR+FiD.

No.	Source	# docs	NQ	TQA	HotpotQA
1	Wikipedia	22M	**51.4**	71.0	**36.9**
2	CCNet	906M	48.6	**73.1**	31.6

Table 2: Exact match (EM-score) of retrieving heterogeneous knowledge for three open-domain QA benchmarks. The model used in the table is DPR+FiD.

No.	Knowledge type			Dataset		
	Text	Table	KG	NQ	TQA	WebQ
1	√			49.0	64.0	50.6
2		√		36.0	34.5	41.0
3			√	27.9	35.4	55.2
4	√	√		**54.1**	**65.1**	50.2
5	√	√	√	54.0	64.1	**57.8**

The most relevant works to this proposal are UniK-QA (Oguz et al., 2022) and PLUG (Li et al., 2021). In UniK-QA, Oguz et al. (2022) proposed to retrieve information from a merged corpus of structured (i.e., KG triples), semi-structured (i.e., tables) and unstructured data (i.e., text passages) for open-domain QA (Oguz et al., 2022). Their experiments were conducted on multiple open-domain QA benchmark datasets, including NaturalQuestions (NQ) (Kwiatkowski et al., 2019), TriviaQA (TQA) (Joshi et al., 2017) and WebQuestions (WebQ) (Berant et al., 2013).

The results in the first three lines in Table 2 highlight the limitation of current state-of-the-art open-domain QA models which use only one information source. Among the three types of knowledge sources, text-only methods perform best on NQ and TQA datasets, and KG-only methods perform best on WebQ datasets. This is because most of the questions in WebQ are collected from Freebase. The results in the last two lines show that adding semi-structured and structured information sources significantly improves the performance over text-only models on NQ and TQA datasets. This indicates tables and knowledge graph triples contain valuable knowledge which is either absent in the unstructured texts or harder to extract from them.

It is worth mentioning that knowledge heterogeneity can be defined not only by the format of knowledge data (i.e., structured and unstructured knowledge), but also by the scope of knowledge data (i.e., encyclopedic and common-

Table 3: Commonly used knowledge sources.

	Unstructured	(Semi-)structured
Encyclopedic knowledge	Wikipedia, AMiner	Wikidata, Freebase
Commonsense knowledge	ConceptNet, CSKG, Atomic	OMCS, ARC, Wiktionary

Table 4: Accuracy of retrieving heterogeneous knowledge for commonsense reasoning over entity tasks.

No.	Knowledge source		Dataset	
	Commonsense	Encyclopedia	CREAK	CSQA2.0
1		√	86.55	59.28
2	√		82.28	58.23
3	√	√	**87.57**	**60.49**

sense knowledge). Table 3 shows common knowledge sources under two categories. In addition of combining structured and unstructured knowledge, combining encyclopedic and commonsense knowledge also brings benefits for many NLP tasks, such as commonsense reasoning over entities. Some preliminary experiments were conducted on CREAK (Onoe et al., 2021) and CSQA2.0 (Talmor et al., 2021) datasets. CREAK is a dataset of human-authored English claims about entities that are either true or false, such as "Harry Potter can teach classes on how to fly on a broomstick *(True)*." The model is supposed to bridge fact-checking about entities with commonsense inferences. An entity fact relevant to this statement, *"Harry Potter is a wizard and is skilled at riding a broomstick"*, can be retrieved from Wikipedia. A commonsense knowledge, *"if you are good at a skill you can teach others how to do it"*, can be retrieved from the *ATOMIC* (Sap et al., 2019). By leveraging both commonsense knowledge and encyclopedic knowledge in the first-step retrieval, as shown in Table 4, the RAG model can achieve superior performance than only using either of them.

3.3 Proposed Solutions

As mentioned above, heterogeneous knowledge is often required when solving open-domain QA and many other knowledge-intensive NLP tasks. One natural assumption is to expand knowledge sources and add more data to increase the coverage of relevant contexts, thereby improving the end-to-end performance. In this section, I will present three potential solutions for grounding generation across heterogeneous knowledge.

3.3.1 Homogenize Different Knowledge to a Unified Knowledge Representation

The first solution is to homogenize different knowledge source data into a unified data format – unstructured text. This transformation will then require only one retriever, enable relevance comparison across different types of data, and offer textual knowledge to easily augment the input of generation models by concatenation. Table 3 shows some commonly used knowledge sources. For example, semi-structured tables and structured knowledge graph triples can be converted into the unstructured text by template-based methods (Bosselut et al., 2019; Oguz et al., 2022) or neural data-to-text methods (Wang et al., 2021; Nan et al., 2021).

First, the template-based method is easy to implement and requires no training process. For example, a relation triplet in a knowledge graph consists of subject, predicate, and object. It can be serialized by concatenating the surface form of the three elements to be a sequence of words. Besides, a table can also be hierarchically converted into text format: first, concatenate cell values of each row separated by commas; then combine these rows' text forms delimited by semicolons. Although the template-based method is simple but may suffer from incorrect syntax and incomplete semantics. On the contrary, the neural graph-to-text and table-to-text generation methods rely on pre-trained language models that may ensure syntax correctness and semantic completeness. Once either type of the methods converts the structured and semi-structured data to unstructured text, a dense retriever model such as DPR (Karpukhin et al., 2020) can be used to index all of them and retrieve relevant knowledge. The reader model will concatenate the retrieved text with original input and compute full attention over the entire representations through a T5 (Raffel et al., 2020) decoder. This unified knowledge index allows the models to learn knowledge of various formats and scopes of data, and the model can simultaneously retrieve information from a unified index of multiple knowledge sources to improve the knowledge coverage.

3.3.2 Multi-virtual Hops Retrieval over Heterogeneous Knowledge

Retrieved data are expected to bridge the gap between inputs and outputs of generation models. In other words, retrievers are trained to provide information that is found with the inputs as queries and related to the outputs. Ideally, they find the output-related information just once. However, that may actually take multiple hops of retrieval across knowledge sources. Thus, the second solution is to iteratively retrieve knowledge from different sources. Regarding an entity, encyclopedic knowledge usually contains its attribute information (e.g., age, duration), while commonsense knowledge includes universally recognized facts in human's daily life. For example, the entity "soup" in Wikipedia is described as "a primarily liquid food, generally served warm or hot, made by combining ingredients of meat or vegetables with stock, milk, or water"; and in the OMCS corpus (Singh et al., 2002), it contains a well-known fact "soup and salad can be a healthy lunch". Therefore, to answer the question "What are the common ingredients in a healthy lunch?", the encyclopedic corpus and commonsense corpus can provide complementary knowledge that should be both leveraged.

Besides, it also might be necessary to first read a subset of the corpus to extract the useful information, and then further retrieve information from other knowledge sources. For example, given input q, it may take k steps, each step retrieving data d_i from source $s_i \in \mathcal{S}$ with an incremental query $q_i = q \oplus d_1 \oplus \cdots \oplus d_{i-1}$ $(i \leq k)$ until the final d_k contains the information that can directly augment the generation of outputs o. Here $\mathcal{S}$ includes various sources such as text corpora, tables, and knowledge graphs. To achieve this, however, the primary challenge for training such a multi-hop retriever is that it cannot observe any intermediate document for supervision but only the final output. So, the multi-virtual hops retrieval (MVHL) needs to perform multi-hop retrieval without any intermediate signal. I will discuss two promising designs as below. First, the MVHL approach will dynamically determine when the multi-hops retrieval finishes. I denote the relevance score between query q_i and data d_i from source s_i by $r(d_i; q_i, s_i)$. The search continues at the i-th step, if $r(d_i; q_i, s_i) > r(d_i; q_{i-1}, s_{i-1} \cup s_i)$; because d_i brings new relevant information that was not able to be retrieved at the $(i-1)$-th step or any previous steps. Second, the MVHL can use sequential models instead of heuristics to control the multi-hops search. The search is expected to finish at step i, when the relevance between the retrieved data d_i and output o, which can be computed by BERTScore (Zhang et al., 2020), achieves a local maximum. In order to model the relationship between this target relevance $r_o(d_i)$ and the retrieval score $r(d_i; q_i, s_i)$, a straightforward solution is to train a multi-hop retriever with only the output o using a fixed number of hops K (5 or 10) and use the validation set to choose the best model. With that model, I can observe the K-length series of r and r_o, and train an RNN model that predicts $r_o(d_k)$ based on the first k elements in the r series. The search terminates when the predicted r_o decreases.

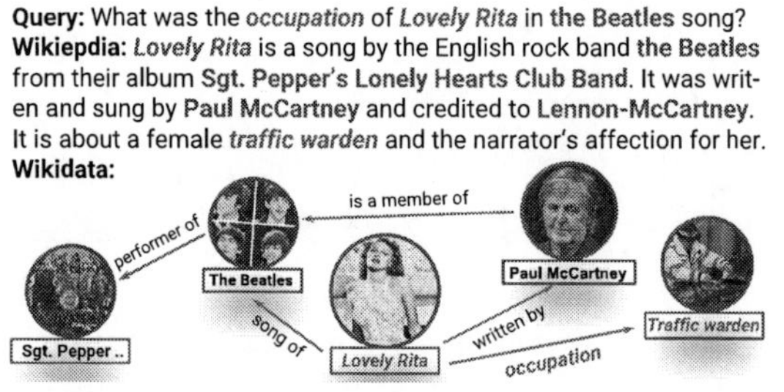

Figure 3: Reasoning over retrieved documents on structured knowledge provides explicit knowledge grounding to help answer questions. For example, in WebQ, 46.9%/56.1% of the questions can be solved by one/two-hop neighbors on the query-document subgraph.

3.3.3 Reasoning over Retrieved Documents Based on Structured Knowledge

Traditional reader modules typically concatenate the input query and retrieved documents sequentially, and then feed them into a pre-trained generation model, such as T5. Although the token-level attention can *implicitly* learning some relational patterns between the input query and retrieved documents, it does not fully utilize the structured knowledge that can provide more *explicit* grounding. As shown in Figure 3, the relational information between important entities in the input query (i.e., Lovely Rita) and the retrieved documents (i.e., traffic warden) may require reasoning over structured knowledge that is not explicitly stated in the context. So, the third solution is to perform multi-hop reasoning on structured knowledge, e.g., Wikidata, to learn relational patterns between the input query and retrieved documents. In this way, the representation of retrieved documents is further enriched by structured knowledge. To perform knowledge reasoning over retrieved documents, the idea is to first extract a query-document subgraph since direct reasoning on the entire knowledge graph is intractable. Entities on the subgraph can be mapped by given hyperlinks in Wikipedia passages. Then, a multi-relational graph encoder iteratively updates the representation of each entity node by aggregating information from its neighboring nodes and edges. Then, the embedded node and relation representations, as well as the query and document representations, are then fused into the reader model.

Acknowledgements

Many thanks to my doctoral supervisor Dr. Meng Jiang and my doctoral thesis committee members Dr. Nitesh Chawala, Dr. David Chiang, Dr. Heng Ji, Dr. Scott Yih for giving me constructive suggestions. My research is mainly funded by National Science Foundation (NSF) grants IIS-1849816, CCF-1901059, IIS-2119531, and IIS-2142827.

References

Jonathan Berant, Andrew Chou, Roy Frostig, and Percy Liang. 2013. Semantic parsing on freebase from question-answer pairs. In *Conference on Empirical Methods in Natural Language Processing (EMNLP)*.

Antoine Bosselut, Hannah Rashkin, Maarten Sap, Chaitanya Malaviya, Asli Celikyilmaz, and Yejin Choi. 2019. Comet: Commonsense transformers for automatic knowledge graph construction. In *Proceedings of the 57th Annual Meeting of the Association for Computational Linguistics (ACL)*.

Tom Brown, Benjamin Mann, Nick Ryder, Melanie Subbiah, Jared D Kaplan, Prafulla Dhariwal, Arvind Neelakantan, Pranav Shyam, Girish Sastry, Amanda Askell, et al. 2020. Language models are few-shot learners. *Advances in neural information processing systems (Neurips)*.

Jacob Devlin, Ming-Wei Chang, Kenton Lee, and Kristina Toutanova. 2019. Bert: Pre-training of deep bidirectional transformers for language understanding. In *Conference of the North American Chapter of the Association for Computational Linguistics: Human Language Technologies (NAACL)*.

Emily Dinan, Stephen Roller, Kurt Shuster, Angela Fan, Michael Auli, and Jason Weston. 2019. Wizard of wikipedia: Knowledge-powered conversational agents. In *International Conference on Learning Representations (ICLR)*.

Suchin Gururangan, Ana Marasović, Swabha Swayamdipta, Kyle Lo, Iz Beltagy, Doug Downey, and Noah A Smith. 2020. Don't stop pretraining: Adapt language models to domains and tasks. In *58th Annual Meeting of the Association for Computational Linguistics (ACL)*.

Gautier Izacard and Édouard Grave. 2021. Leveraging passage retrieval with generative models for open domain question answering. In *Proceedings of the 16th Conference of the European Chapter of the Association for Computational Linguistics (EACL)*.

Peter Izsak, Moshe Berchansky, and Omer Levy. 2021. How to train bert with an academic budget. In *Proceedings of the 2021 Conference on Empirical Methods in Natural Language Processing (EMNLP)*.

Mandar Joshi, Eunsol Choi, Daniel S Weld, and Luke Zettlemoyer. 2017. Triviaqa: A large scale distantly supervised challenge dataset for reading comprehension. In *Proceedings of the 55th Annual Meeting of the Association for Computational Linguistics (ACL)*.

Vladimir Karpukhin, Barlas Oguz, Sewon Min, Patrick Lewis, Ledell Wu, Sergey Edunov, Danqi Chen, and Wen-tau Yih. 2020. Dense passage retrieval for open-domain question answering. In *Proceedings of the 2020 Conference on Empirical Methods in Natural Language Processing (EMNLP)*, pages 6769–6781.

Tom Kwiatkowski, Jennimaria Palomaki, Olivia Redfield, Michael Collins, Ankur Parikh, Chris Alberti, Danielle Epstein, Illia Polosukhin, Jacob Devlin, Kenton Lee, et al. 2019. Natural questions: A benchmark for question answering research. *Transactions of the Association for Computational Linguistics (TACL)*.

Angeliki Lazaridou, Elena Gribovskaya, Wojciech Stokowiec, and Nikolai Grigorev. 2022. Internet-augmented language models through few-shot prompting for open-domain question answering. *arXiv preprint arXiv:2203.05115*.

Mike Lewis, Yinhan Liu, Naman Goyal, Marjan Ghazvininejad, Abdelrahman Mohamed, Omer Levy, Veselin Stoyanov, and Luke Zettlemoyer. 2020a. Bart: Denoising sequence-to-sequence pre-training for natural language generation, translation, and comprehension. In *Annual Meeting of the Association for Computational Linguistics (ACL)*.

Patrick Lewis, Ethan Perez, Aleksandra Piktus, Fabio Petroni, Vladimir Karpukhin, Naman Goyal, Heinrich Küttler, Mike Lewis, Wen-tau Yih, Tim Rocktäschel, et al. 2020b. Retrieval-augmented generation for knowledge-intensive nlp tasks. *Advances in Neural Information Processing Systems (Neruips)*.

Yu Li, Baolin Peng, Yelong Shen, Yi Mao, Lars Liden, Zhou Yu, and Jianfeng Gao. 2021. Knowledge-grounded dialogue generation with a unified knowledge representation. *arXiv preprint arXiv:2112.07924*.

Yunlong Liang, Fandong Meng, Ying Zhang, Yufeng Chen, Jinan Xu, and Jie Zhou. 2022. Emotional conversation generation with heterogeneous graph neural network. *Artificial Intelligence*.

Todor Mihaylov, Peter Clark, Tushar Khot, and Ashish Sabharwal. 2018. Can a suit of armor conduct electricity? a new dataset for open book question answering. In *Conference on Empirical Methods in Natural Language Processing (EMNLP)*.

Linyong Nan, Dragomir Radev, Rui Zhang, Amrit Rau, Abhinand Sivaprasad, Chiachun Hsieh, Xiangru Tang, Aadit Vyas, Neha Verma, Pranav Krishna, et al. 2021. Dart: Open-domain structured data record to text generation. In *Conference of the North American Chapter of the Association for Computational Linguistics: Human Language Technologies (NAACL)*.

Barlas Oguz, Xilun Chen, Vladimir Karpukhin, Stan Peshterliev, Dmytro Okhonko, Michael Schlichtkrull, Sonal Gupta, Yashar Mehdad, and Scott Yih. 2022. Unik-qa: Unified representations of structured and unstructured knowledge for open-domain question answering. *Conference of the North American Chapter of the Association for Computational Linguistics: Human Language Technologies (NAACL-HLT)*.

Yasumasa Onoe, Michael JQ Zhang, Eunsol Choi, and Greg Durrett. 2021. Creak: A dataset for commonsense reasoning over entity knowledge. In *Thirty-fifth Conference on Neural Information Processing Systems Datasets and Benchmarks Track (Neurips)*.

Fabio Petroni, Aleksandra Piktus, Angela Fan, Patrick Lewis, Majid Yazdani, Nicola De Cao, James Thorne, Yacine Jernite, Vladimir Karpukhin, Jean Maillard, et al. 2021. Kilt: a benchmark for knowledge intensive language tasks. In *Proceedings of the 2021 Conference of the North American Chapter of the Association for Computational Linguistics: Human Language Technologies (NAACL)*.

Fabio Petroni, Tim Rocktäschel, Sebastian Riedel, Patrick Lewis, Anton Bakhtin, Yuxiang Wu, and Alexander Miller. 2019. Language models as knowledge bases? In *Proceedings of the 2019 Conference on Empirical Methods in Natural Language Processing and the 9th International Joint Conference on Natural Language Processing (EMNLP-IJCNLP)*.

Aleksandra Piktus, Fabio Petroni, Vladimir Karpukhin, Dmytro Okhonko, Samuel Broscheit, Gautier Izacard, Patrick Lewis, Barlas Oğuz, Edouard Grave, Wen-tau Yih, et al. 2021. The web is your oyster–knowledge-intensive nlp against a very large web corpus. *arXiv preprint arXiv:2112.09924*.

Xipeng Qiu, Tianxiang Sun, Yige Xu, Yunfan Shao, Ning Dai, and Xuanjing Huang. 2020. Pre-trained models for natural language processing: A survey. In *Science China Technological Sciences*. Springer.

Colin Raffel, Noam Shazeer, Adam Roberts, Katherine Lee, Sharan Narang, Michael Matena, Yanqi Zhou, Wei Li, and Peter J Liu. 2019. Exploring the limits of transfer learning with a unified text-to-text transformer. *arXiv preprint arXiv:1910.10683*.

Colin Raffel, Noam Shazeer, Adam Roberts, Katherine Lee, Sharan Narang, Michael Matena, Yanqi Zhou, Wei Li, and Peter J Liu. 2020. Exploring the limits of transfer learning with a unified text-to-text transformer. In *Journal of Machine Learning Research*.

Adam Roberts, Colin Raffel, and Noam Shazeer. 2020. How much knowledge can you pack into the parameters of a language model? In *Proceedings of the 2020 Conference on Empirical Methods in Natural Language Processing (EMNLP)*, pages 5418–5426.

Maarten Sap, Ronan Le Bras, Emily Allaway, Chandra Bhagavatula, Nicholas Lourie, Hannah Rashkin, Brendan Roof, Noah A Smith, and Yejin Choi. 2019. Atomic: An atlas of machine commonsense for if-then reasoning. In *Proceedings of the AAAI Conference on Artificial Intelligence (AAAI)*.

Kurt Shuster, Spencer Poff, Moya Chen, Douwe Kiela, and Jason Weston. 2021. Retrieval augmentation reduces hallucination in conversation. In *Findings of Empirical Methods in Natural Language Processing*.

Push Singh, Thomas Lin, Erik T Mueller, Grace Lim, Travell Perkins, and Wan Li Zhu. 2002. Open mind common sense: Knowledge acquisition from the general public. In *International Conferences on the Move to Meaningful Internet Systems*. Springer.

Alon Talmor, Ori Yoran, Ronan Le Bras, Chandra Bhagavatula, Yoav Goldberg, Yejin Choi, and Jonathan Berant. 2021. Commonsenseqa 2.0: Exposing the limits of ai through gamification. In *Thirty-fifth Conference on Neural Information Processing Systems Datasets and Benchmarks Track (Neurips)*.

Luyu Wang, Yujia Li, Ozlem Aslan, and Oriol Vinyals. 2021. Wikigraphs: A wikipedia text-knowledge graph paired dataset. In *Proceedings of the Fifteenth Workshop on Graph-Based Methods for Natural Language Processing (TextGraphs-15)*.

Donghan Yu, Chenguang Zhu, Yuwei Fang, Wenhao Yu, Shuohang Wang, Yichong Xu, Xiang Ren, Yiming Yang, and Michael Zeng. 2022a. Kg-fid: Infusing knowledge graph in fusion-in-decoder for open-domain question answering. *Proceedings of the Annual Meeting of the Association for Computational Linguistics (ACL)*.

Wenhao Yu, Chenguang Zhu, Yuwei Fang, Donghan Yu, Shuohang Wang, Yichong Xu, Michael Zeng, and Meng Jiang. 2022b. Dict-bert: Enhancing language model pre-training with dictionary. *Proceedings of the Annual Meeting of the Association for Computational Linguistics (ACL)*.

Wenhao Yu, Chenguang Zhu, Zaitang Li, Zhiting Hu, Qingyun Wang, Heng Ji, and Meng Jiang. 2022c. A survey of knowledge-enhanced text generation. In *ACM Computing Survey (CSUR)*.

Wenhao Yu, Chenguang Zhu, Lianhui Qin, Zhihan Zhang, Tong Zhao, and Meng Jiang. 2022d. Diversifying content generation for commonsense reasoning with mixture of knowledge graph experts. In *Annual Meeting of the Association for Computational Linguistics (ACL)*.

Tianyi Zhang, Varsha Kishore, Felix Wu, Kilian Q Weinberger, and Yoav Artzi. 2020. Bertscore: Evaluating text generation with bert. In *International Conference on Learning Representations*.

Neural Retriever and Go Beyond: A Thesis Proposal

Man Luo
Arizona State University
mluo26@asu.edu

Abstract

Information Retriever (IR) aims to find the relevant documents (e.g. snippets, passages, and articles) to a given query at large scale. IR plays an important role in many tasks such as open domain question answering and dialogue systems, where external knowledge is needed. In the past, searching algorithms based on term matching have been widely used. Recently, neural-based algorithms (termed as neural retrievers) have gained more attention which can mitigate the limitations of traditional methods. Regardless of the success achieved by neural retrievers, they still face many challenges, e.g. suffering from a small amount of training data and failing to answer simple entity-centric questions. Furthermore, most of the existing neural retrievers are developed for pure-text query. This prevents them from handling multi-modality queries (i.e. the query is composed of textual description and images). This proposal has two goals. First, we introduce methods to address the abovementioned issues of neural retrievers from three angles, new model architectures, IR-oriented pretraining tasks, and generating large scale training data. Second, we identify the future research direction and propose potential corresponding solution[1].

1 Introduction

The convenience and advance of internet not only speed up the spread of information and knowledge, but also the generation of new information. Such phenomenon also boosts humans needs of knowledge and frequency of acquiring information, which makes Information retrieval (IR) an important task in human life. IR aims to find relevant information from a large corpus to satisfy an information need. It also plays an important role in other tasks such as open domain question answering and open domain dialogue, where external knowledge are needed. Not only that, IR can also assistant other systems to achieve a tough goal. By providing external knowledge, IR can help numerical reasoning systems to reach the correct answer (Mishra et al., 2022) , and IR can enrich or update the knowledge of large pretrained language models (PrLMs) (Petroni et al., 2019; Sung et al., 2021). By filtering and selecting examples (Liu et al., 2021; Lin et al., 2022), IR can assist in-context learning (ICL), a process allows large PrLMs do a new task instructed by prompts and few examples with few-shot tuning (Gao et al., 2021) or without any fine-tuning (Brown et al., 2020).

IR has a long history and the first automated information retrieval system can be traced back to the 1950s. In this work, we call information retrieval methods or systems as retrievers. Traditional retrievers are mainly based on term-matching, i.e. searching for information that has an overlap with terms in the query. TF-IDF and BM25 (Robertson and Zaragoza, 2009) are two strong and efficient algorithms in this category. Although these algorithms consider the importance and frequency of terms in query and document, they suffer from term-mismatch issues and lack of semantic understanding of the query and document (Chang et al., 2020). Using neural models to represent the concatenation of query and passage is a promising way to achieve semantic matching (Nogueira and Cho, 2019; Banerjee and Baral, 2020). These methods are only applicable at small scale retrieval but not at large scale. Recently, dual-encoder architecture retrievers based on large pretrained language models (PrLMs), such as BERT (Devlin et al., 2019) have shown capability to do semantic matching and can be applicable at large scale (Karpukhin et al., 2020; Guu et al., 2020; Lewis et al., 2020). Such neural retrievers (NR) involve two PrLMs which are used to compute the vector representation of queries and documents respectively. Neural retriev-

[1]Since previous work use context, documents or knowledge to represent the retrieved information given a query, we use these two terms interchangeably.

Proceedings of the 2022 Conference of the North American Chapter of the Association for Computational Linguistics: Human Language Technologies: Student Research Workshop, pages 59 - 67
July 10-15, 2022 ©2022 Association for Computational Linguistics

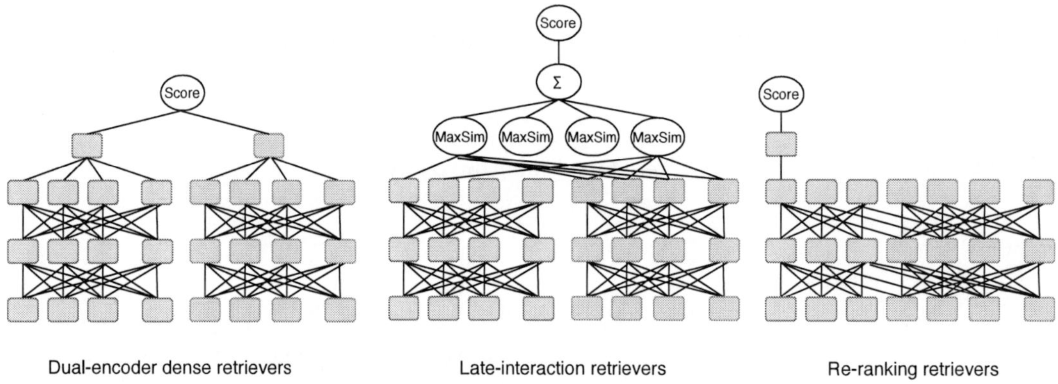

Figure 1: Architectures of three major types of retrievers. For simplicity, some lines in the figures are not drawn. Blue blocks represent the encoding for question, and the green blocks represent context or documents.

ers are trained in such a way that the documents which best answer a query maximize the dot product between the two representations. Despite the success of neural retrievers, they still face many challenges. In the next Section, we will present a brief overview of five types of retrievers and the efforts made toward building stronger retrievers. Section 3 describes four limitations of current NRs and promising solutions. Section 4 discusses three more research directions and potential solutions. We conclude the proposal in Section 5.

2 Retrievers in General

In general, the modern retrievers can be categorized in five classes (adapted from (Thakur et al., 2021)). **Lexical retrievers** such as BM25 are based on token-matching between two high-dimensional sparse vectors. The sparse vectors are represented based on the frequency of the terms in documents and thus does not require any annotated training data. Regardless of the simplicity of the algorithms, such methods perform well on new domains (Thakur et al., 2021). **Dual-encoder dense retrievers** consists of two encoders where the query encoder and context encoder generate a single dense vector representation for query and context respectively. Then the score can be computed by inner-dot product or cosine-similarity between the two representations (Karpukhin et al., 2020; Xiong et al., 2020; Hofstätter et al., 2021). Language models such as BERT (Devlin et al., 2019) are preferred choices for encoders. **Sparse retrievers** use sparse representations instead of dense representations for query and document (Dai and Callan, 2020; Zhao et al., 2021; Nogueira et al., 2019). **Late-interaction retrievers** different from dense retrievers who use sequence-level representations of query and document, they use token-level representations for the query and passage: a bag of multiple contextualized token embeddings (Khattab and Zaharia, 2020). The late-interactions are aggregated with sum of the max-pooling query term and a dot-product across all passage terms. **Re-ranking retrievers** include two stages, coarse-search by efficient methods (e.g. BM25) and fine-search by cross-attentional re-ranking models. The re-ranking model takes input as the concatenation of the query and one candidate given by the first stage and produce a score based on the cross representation (e.g. the [CLS] token), and such process is repeated for every candidate, and finally re-rank candidates based on the generated scores.

Without changing the architectures, different efforts have been made toward learning better representation of dense vectors and improving the efficiency in terms of training resources as well as short inference time. One way to improve the representation of dense vectors is to construct proper negative instances to train a neural retriever. In-batch negative training is a frequently used strategy to train dense retrievers, and the larger the batch size is, the better performance a dense retriever can achieve (Karpukhin et al., 2020; Qu et al., 2021). Using hard negative candidates is better than using random or simple in-batch negative samples, for example, Karpukhin et al. (2020) mine negative candidates by BM25 and (Xiong et al., 2020) mine negative candidates from the entire corpus using an optimized dense retriever. Hofstätter et al. (2021) selects the negative candidates from the same topic cluster, such a balanced topic aware sampling method allows the training with small batch size and still achieves high quality dense representation. ColBert (Khattab and Zaharia, 2020) is proposed to improve the efficiency of the ranking model. Since every token can be pre-indexed, it prevents inference time from getting representation of context. While Colbert is faster than single-model, it is slower compared to dual-models, thus, it is not suitable for retrieval at large scale. On the other hand, Nogueira et al. (2019) shortens the inference time by using sparse representation for queries. Zhang et al. (2021) integrates dense passage retriever and cross-attention ranker and use adversarial training to jointly both module.

Above methods are usually used to retrieve a document (e.g. a paragraph in Wikipedia) which can potentially contain the answer to a query. Some other retrievers directly retrieve the answer phrase (or entities) so that they can be directly used to answer questions without a reader (Seo et al., 2019; Lee et al., 2020; De Cao et al., 2020, 2021). While such methods can reduce the latency, it also increases the memory to store potential phrases which will be much larger than the number of raw documents. On the other hand, Lee et al. (2021a,b) use generative model to generate the entities which largely reduce the memory.

3 Research Gaps and Solutions

In this section, we will describe multiple research gaps and the proposed methods introduced in (Luo et al., 2021a,b, 2022b).

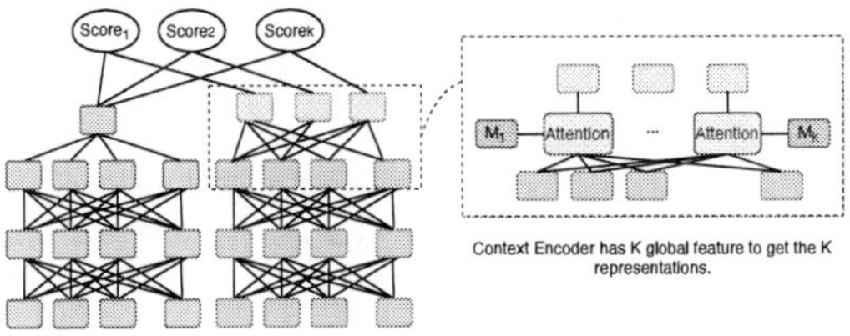

Figure 2: Poly-DPR, the context encoder uses K representations to capture the information in context.

3.1 Is One Dense Vector Enough to Capture Information?

Most of the neural retrievers use one dense representation for context (Karpukhin et al., 2020; Guu et al., 2020; Lewis et al., 2020). Previous work found that one dense vector is not enough to capture enough information in the context, especially for a long context. One dense representation is also hard to be applied to exact word matching so that it fails on entities-centric questions (Sciavolino et al., 2021). To close the gap of existing NRs, we propose a new model called Poly-DPR which builds upon two recent developments: Poly-Encoder (Humeau et al., 2020) and Dense Passage Retriever (Karpukhin et al., 2020).

Method In Poly-DPR (see Figure 2), the context encoder represents each *context* using K vectors and produces *query-specific vectors* for each context. In particular, the context encoder includes K global features $(m_1, m_2, \cdots, m_k)$, which are used to extract representation v_c^i, $\forall i \in \{1 \cdots k\}$ by attending over all context tokens vectors.

$$v_c^i = \sum_n w_n^{m_i} h_n, \text{ where} \tag{1}$$

$$(w_1^{m_i} \ldots, w_n^{m_i}) = \text{softmax}(m_i^T \cdot h_1, \ldots, m_i^T \cdot h_n). \tag{2}$$

After extracting K representations, a query-specific context representation $v_{c,q}$ is computed by using the attention mechanism:

$$v_{c,q} = \sum_k w_k v_c^k, \text{ where} \tag{3}$$

$$(w_1, \ldots, w_k) = \text{softmax}(v_q^T \cdot v_c^1, \ldots, v_q^T \cdot v_c^k). \tag{4}$$

To enable efficient search in inference (e.g. using MIPS (Shrivastava and Li, 2014) algorithms), instead of computing query-specific context representation, we simply use the inner-dot product of each K representations with the query embeddings, and apply max pooling function to get the score.

Result We evaluate Poly-DPR on BioASQ8 (Nentidis et al., 2020) dataset to see how effective the model is. Instead of using the full corpus which has 19M PubMed articles, we construct a small corpus with 133,084 articles for efficient and comprehensive experiments purpose. We also examine the impact of changing the value of K on the performance. Furthermore, we design two context length, one is two sentences no more than 128 tokens (short) and the other one is up to 256 tokens (long). In Table 1, we have three values for K, where value 0 is the same as the original DPR. We see that in both settings, Poly-DPR is better than the original DPR, and a larger value of K leads to better performance.

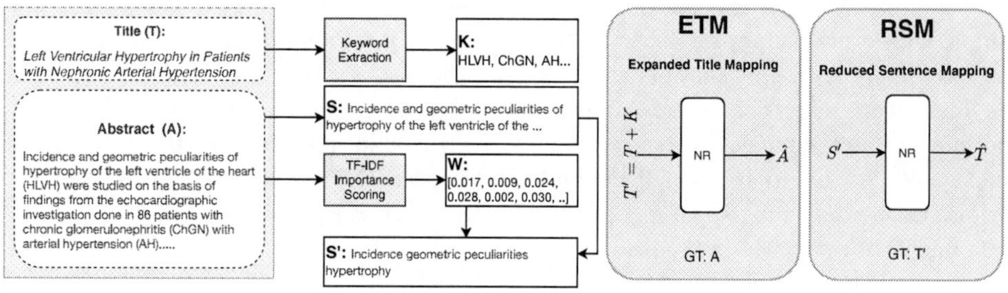

Figure 3: Two IR-oriented pretraining tasks. ETM is suitable for corpus which have titles and passages. RSM is suitable for any type of corpus.

CL	K	B1	B2	B3	B4	B5	Avg.
	0	62.06	**61.81**	61.85	66.69	61.30	62.74
Short	6	62.92	58.79	**62.94**	70.30	63.39	63.67
	12	**65.22**	60.86	62.59	**70.50**	**66.21**	**65.08**
	0	61.70	58.28	58.62	67.33	61.48	61.48
Long	6	**63.95**	**59.51**	**62.98**	66.71	62.80	63.19
	12	63.83	57.81	62.72	**70.00**	**63.64**	**63.60**

Table 1: Comparison among different values of K for Poly-DPR in both short and long context settings of BioASQ8 dataset using MRR metric. Bi stand for different testing batch.

CL	PT	B1	B2	B3	B4	B5	Avg.
Short	-	54.48	50.51	53.8	59.06	48.71	53.31
	RSM	**65.94**	**57.43**	**61.89**	**69.01**	**58.23**	**62.50**
Long	-	35.69	32.66	32.26	38.28	30.87	33.95
	ICT	54.44	**47.37**	52.61	53.69	44.38	50.50
	ETM	**56.63**	46.63	**52.79**	**56.97**	**49.61**	**52.53**

Table 2: Effect of pre-training tasks (PT) on the performance of Poly-DPR with two context lengths (CL) on the BioASQ dataset.

3.2 Is IR-oriented Pretraining Important?

PrLMs are trained on general tasks, such as masked language prediction, and next sentence prediction (Devlin et al., 2019). While these pretraining tasks help the model to learn the linguistic knowledge, the model might still lack of specific skill to perform down-stream tasks, e.g. match similar words or characterize the relation between the question and answer. Chang et al. (2020) has shown that IR-oriented pretraining tasks can help model to develop basic retrieval skill. However, their proposed methods require specific document structure, e.g. the document includes external hyperlinks.

Method We propose two new IR-oriented pretraining strategies (Figure 3). Our pre-training tasks are designed such that they can be used both for long contexts as short contexts. In **Expanded Title Mapping (ETM)**, the model is trained to retrieve an abstract, given an extended title T' as a query. T' is obtained by extracting top-m keywords from the abstract based on the TF-IDF score, denoted as $K = \{k_1, k_2, \cdots, k_m\}$, and concatenating them with the title as: $T' = \{T, k_1, k_2, \cdots, k_m\}$. The intuition behind ETM is to train the model to match the main topic of a document (keywords and title) with the entire abstract. **Reduced Sentence Mapping (RSM)** is designed to train the model to map a sentence from an abstract with the extended title T'. For a sentence S from the abstract, we first get the weight of each word $W = \{w_1, w_2, \cdots, w_n\}$ by the normalization of TF-IDF scores of each word. We then reduce S to S' by selecting the words with the top-m corresponding weights. The intuition behind a reduced sentence is to simulate a real query which usually is shorter than a sentence in an abstract.

Result We test on BioASQ dataset and use the similar experimental setting as in §3.1, where we use both short and long context length settings. From Table 2, we see that in both settings, using our pretraining tasks are much better than without any pretraining with large margins. Furthermore, in the long context setting, we also compare our method with ICT (Lee et al., 2019) pretraining task, and we see that ETM beats than ICT on average with better performance on 4 out of 5 batches.

3.3 How to Obtain Enough Training Data?

While the pretraining makes language models more easily adapted to new tasks, a decent amount of domain-specific data for fine-tuning is still crucial to achieve good performance on downstream tasks (Howard and Ruder, 2018; Clark et al., 2019). Collecting annotated data is expensive and time

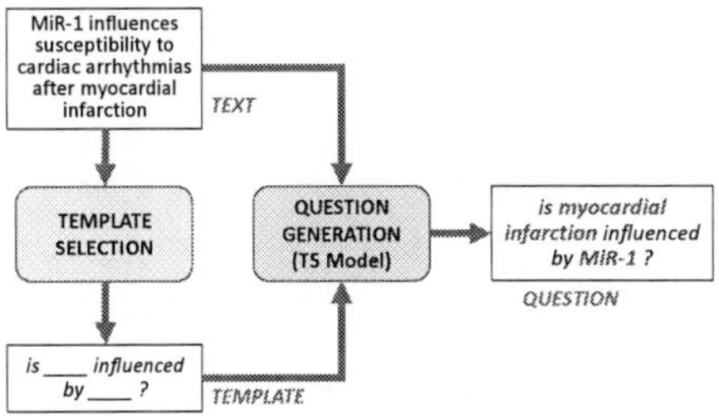

Figure 4: Template-Based Question Generation.

CL	PT	FT	B1	B2	B3	B4	B5	Avg.
Short	RSM	B	**65.94**	57.43	61.89	69.01	58.23	62.50
	RSM	A	56.84	55.79	57.52	58.68	55.15	56.80
	RSM	T	64.71	**64.92**	**64.28**	**73.11**	**66.29**	**66.66**
Long	ETM	B	56.63	46.63	52.79	56.97	49.61	52.53
	ETM	A	54.44	49.95	48.42	58.15	52.60	52.71
	ETM	T	64.57	58.51	**64.02**	68.44	62.60	**63.62**

Table 3: Comparison of fine-tuning on different downstream training data B: BioASQ A: AnsQG and T: TempQG) on the performance of Poly-DPR with two context lengths (CL) on the BioASQ small corpus test set.

consuming. Moreover, for some domains such as biomedical, annotation usually requires expert knowledge which makes the data collection harder (Tsatsaronis et al., 2012). To address this problem, Ma et al. (2021) uses a question generation model trained on existing large scale data to obtain synthetic question-answer pairs using domain articles. Still, the style of the generated questions are far away from the target-domain and limit the models' performance.

Method To address the domain adaptation issue, we propose a semi-supervised pipeline to generate questions using domain-templates (Figure 4). To do so, we assume a small amount of domain annotated question-answer data is given. We first extract templates from the questions by using a name entity recognition model to identify question-specific entities and removing such entities. A template selection model is trained to select the template for a new passage. Finally a generative model (e.g. T5) is trained to generate questions conditioned on this template and a text passage. The questions generated using domain templates are much better than the previous question generation method.

Result Again, we use BioASQ8 as testbed with similar settings as previous experiments. We compare our method with an existing question generation method which extracts answer span first and then generates questions (Chan and Fan, 2019). In Table 3, we compare three models trained on two generated questions as well as the training dataset of BioASQ8, and our proposed method is better than the other two especially with large gain (10%+) in long context setting.

3.4 How to Retrieve Information for Multi-modality Queries?

Previous discussion focuses on retrieving relevant documents to text-only queries, while in current society, lots of information is presented by multi-modalities such as text, image, speech, and video. Therefore, retrieving relevant documents to multi-modality queries can have wide application in human's life. For instance an image of a milkshake and a complementary textual description "restaurants near me" should return potential matches of nearby restaurants serving milkshakes. In literature, OK-VQA (Marino et al., 2019) is a task that requires external knowledge to answer visual questions (i.e. the query is composed of image and text.). To find the relevant knowledge for such a query, current neural retrieval can not be directly applied since the text part in the query is not completed to understand the information needs and the model is unable to look at the image information. To address this issue, we propose three types of retrievers to handle multi-modality queries.

Method *Term-based retriever*, we first extract the image information by using a captions generation model (Li et al., 2020). Then we concatenate the question and the caption as a query and obtain knowledge by BM25. The other two multi-modality retrievers are adopted from the DPR model. *Image-DPR*: we use LXMERT (Tan and Bansal, 2019) as the question encoder, which takes image and question as input and outputs a cross-modal representation. *Caption-DPR*: similar to the strategy we use in term-based retrievers, we concatenate the question with the caption of an image as a query and use standard BERT as a query encoder to get the representation. In both *Image-DPR* and *Caption-DPR*, we use standard BERT as context encoder. Figure 5 shows a comparison between these two retrievers. We find that the performance of Caption-DPR is better than Image-DPR, and the term-based retriever performs worst.

Result We evaluate three retrievers on OK-VQA dataset and use the knowledge base (with 112,724 pieces of knowledge) created in (Luo et al., 2021b)

Model	# of Retrieved Knowledge													
	1		5		10		20		50		80		100	
	P*	R*	P*	R*	P*	R*	P*	R*	P*	R*	P*	R*	P*	R*
BM25	37.63	37.63	35.21	56.72	34.03	67.02	32.62	75.90	29.99	84.56	28.46	88.21	27.69	89.91
Image-DPR	33.04	33.04	31.80	62.52	31.09	73.96	30.25	83.04	28.55	90.84	27.40	93.80	26.75	94.67
Caption-DPR	**41.62**	**41.62**	**39.42**	**71.52**	**37.94**	**81.51**	**36.10**	**88.57**	**32.94**	**94.13**	**31.05**	**96.20**	**30.01**	**96.95**

Table 4: Evaluation of three proposed visual retrievers on Precision (P) and Recall (R): Caption-DPR achieves the highest Precision and Recall on all number of retrieved knowledge.

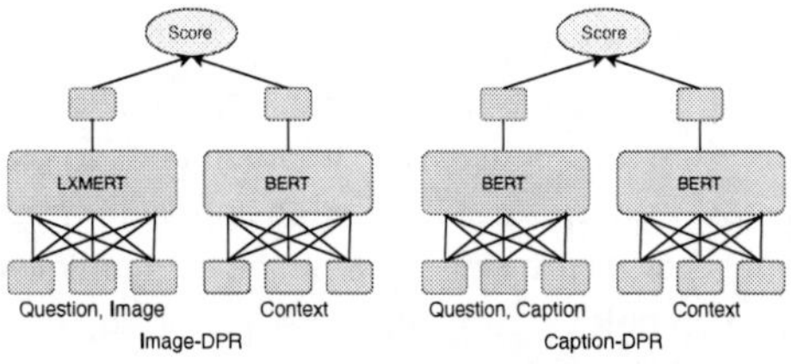

Figure 5: Comparison of two multi-modality.

as the corpus. We retrieve 1/5/10/20/50/80/100 knowledge for each question. Table 4 shows that the two neural retrievers are better than simple term-based retriever, and the Caption-DPR is the best model in all cases.

4 Future Work

Previous section describes multiple research problems for neural retrievers, while we provide some solutions, each problem can be further investigated. In the following, we identify more research directions and propose potential solutions.

Document Expansion Previous work (Nogueira et al., 2019) has shown BM25 with expended documents using generated questions is an efficient way to retrieve documents. Such a method also showed good generalization across different domains (Thakur et al., 2021). The template-based question generation proposed in this work has better domain adaptation than the previous question generation method. It is interesting to see how each module in the pipeline performs on new domain without further fine-tuning. For example, can the template selection model select good templates for passage from new domain; can the question generation model generate good questions given a new template? Evaluating how our template-based question generation pipeline works when apply it to document expansion is an interesting future work.

Distinguish Between Negative Samples Many training data only provide positive candidates but not the negative candidates. Section 2 summarizes existing methods to construct negative candidates; however, the negativeness of different candidates are different. For instance, if some candidates have the same topic as the queries while others do not, then in such cases, the former candidates should be less negative compared to the later. We propose to label the negativeness of candidates by using the similarity between the questions and the candidates and use such labels to train neural retrievers.

Generalization of Neural IR Previous work has shown that neural retrievers perform well on the same domain of the training data (IID) but poorly in out-of-domain (Thakur et al., 2021). In fact, generalization is a common issue in many other tasks such as image classification and question answering (Gokhale et al., 2022; Luo et al., 2022a). A range of methods including data augmentation, data filtering, and data debiasing methods have been proposed to improve the generalization capacity of models. Applying these methods to train neural retrievers can potentially improve their generalization capacity. Prompting or instruction learning has shown good generalization performance on many NLP tasks (Mishra et al., 2021) or in low-resource domain (Parmar et al., 2022), yet applying such method on retrieval task is less investigated, and it will be an interesting direction to explore.

5 Conclusion

In this proposal, we focus on an important task: information retrieval. From word-matching retrievers to neural retrievers, many efforts have been made toward building stronger retrievers that can achieve high recall and precision. We summarize five types of modern retrievers and methods to address some existing issues. While the development in this field is exciting, retrievers still have a long journey to go. We hope this proposal can shed some light on building a more capable retriever in future.

References

Pratyay Banerjee and Chitta Baral. 2020. Knowledge fusion and semantic knowledge ranking for open domain question answering. *ArXiv*, abs/2004.03101.

Tom Brown, Benjamin Mann, Nick Ryder, Melanie Subbiah, Jared D Kaplan, Prafulla Dhariwal, Arvind Neelakantan, Pranav Shyam, Girish Sastry, Amanda Askell, et al. 2020. Language models are few-shot learners. *Advances in neural information processing systems*, 33:1877–1901.

Ying-Hong Chan and Yao-Chung Fan. 2019. A recurrent BERT-based model for question generation. In *Proceedings of the 2nd Workshop on Machine Reading for Question Answering*, pages 154–162. Association for Computational Linguistics.

Wei-Cheng Chang, F. Yu, Yin-Wen Chang, Yiming Yang, and S. Kumar. 2020. Pre-training tasks for embedding-based large-scale retrieval. *ArXiv*, abs/2002.03932.

Kevin Clark, Minh-Thang Luong, Quoc V Le, and Christopher D Manning. 2019. Electra: Pre-training text encoders as discriminators rather than generators. In *International Conference on Learning Representations*.

Zhuyun Dai and Jamie Callan. 2020. Context-aware term weighting for first stage passage retrieval. In *Proceedings of the 43rd International ACM SIGIR conference on research and development in Information Retrieval*, pages 1533–1536.

Nicola De Cao, Gautier Izacard, Sebastian Riedel, and Fabio Petroni. 2020. Autoregressive entity retrieval. In *International Conference on Learning Representations*.

Nicola De Cao, Ledell Wu, Kashyap Popat, Mikel Artetxe, Naman Goyal, Mikhail Plekhanov, Luke Zettlemoyer, Nicola Cancedda, Sebastian Riedel, and Fabio Petroni. 2021. Multilingual autoregressive entity linking. *arXiv preprint arXiv:2103.12528*.

Jacob Devlin, Ming-Wei Chang, Kenton Lee, and Kristina Toutanova. 2019. BERT: Pre-training of deep bidirectional transformers for language understanding. In *Proceedings of the 2019 Conference of the North American Chapter of the Association for Computational Linguistics: Human Language Technologies, Volume 1 (Long and Short Papers)*, pages 4171–4186, Minneapolis, Minnesota. Association for Computational Linguistics.

Tianyu Gao, Adam Fisch, and Danqi Chen. 2021. Making pre-trained language models better few-shot learners. In *Proceedings of the 59th Annual Meeting of the Association for Computational Linguistics and the 11th International Joint Conference on Natural Language Processing (Volume 1: Long Papers)*, pages 3816–3830.

Tejas Gokhale, Swaroop Mishra, Man Luo, Bhavdeep Singh Sachdeva, and Chitta Baral. 2022. Generalized but not robust? comparing the effects of data modification methods on out-of-domain generalization and adversarial robustness. *arXiv preprint arXiv:2203.07653*.

Kelvin Guu, Kenton Lee, Z. Tung, Panupong Pasupat, and Ming-Wei Chang. 2020. Realm: Retrieval-augmented language model pre-training. *ArXiv*, abs/2002.08909.

Sebastian Hofstätter, Sheng-Chieh Lin, Jheng-Hong Yang, Jimmy Lin, and Allan Hanbury. 2021. Efficiently teaching an effective dense retriever with balanced topic aware sampling. In *Proceedings of the 44th International ACM SIGIR Conference on Research and Development in Information Retrieval*, pages 113–122.

Jeremy Howard and Sebastian Ruder. 2018. Universal language model fine-tuning for text classification. In *Proceedings of the 56th Annual Meeting of the Association for Computational Linguistics (Volume 1: Long Papers)*, pages 328–339.

Samuel Humeau, Kurt Shuster, Marie-Anne Lachaux, and J. Weston. 2020. Poly-encoders: Architectures and pre-training strategies for fast and accurate multi-sentence scoring. In *ICLR*.

V. Karpukhin, Barlas Oğuz, Sewon Min, Patrick Lewis, Ledell Yu Wu, Sergey Edunov, Danqi Chen, and Wen tau Yih. 2020. Dense passage retrieval for open-domain question answering. In *EMNLP*.

Omar Khattab and Matei Zaharia. 2020. Colbert: Efficient and effective passage search via contextualized late interaction over bert. In *Proceedings of the 43rd International ACM SIGIR conference on research and development in Information Retrieval*, pages 39–48.

Jinhyuk Lee, Minjoon Seo, Hannaneh Hajishirzi, and Jaewoo Kang. 2020. Contextualized sparse representations for real-time open-domain question answering. In *Proceedings of the 58th Annual Meeting of the Association for Computational Linguistics*, pages 912–919.

Jinhyuk Lee, Mujeen Sung, Jaewoo Kang, and Danqi Chen. 2021a. Learning dense representations of phrases at scale. In *Association for Computational Linguistics (ACL)*.

Jinhyuk Lee, Alexander Wettig, and Danqi Chen. 2021b. Phrase retrieval learns passage retrieval, too. In *Conference on Empirical Methods in Natural Language Processing (EMNLP)*.

Kenton Lee, Ming-Wei Chang, and Kristina Toutanova. 2019. Latent retrieval for weakly supervised open domain question answering. *ArXiv*, abs/1906.00300.

Patrick Lewis, Ethan Perez, Aleksandara Piktus, Fabio Petroni, Vladimir Karpukhin, Naman Goyal, Heinrich Kuttler, M. Lewis, Wen tau Yih, Tim Rocktäschel, Sebastian Riedel, and Douwe Kiela. 2020. Retrieval-augmented generation for knowledge-intensive nlp tasks. *ArXiv*, abs/2005.11401.

Xiujun Li, Xi Yin, Chunyuan Li, Pengchuan Zhang, Xiaowei Hu, Lei Zhang, Lijuan Wang, Houdong Hu, Li Dong, Furu Wei, et al. 2020. Oscar: Object-semantics aligned pre-training for vision-language tasks. In *European Conference on Computer Vision*, pages 121–137. Springer.

Bill Yuchen Lin, Kangmin Tan, Chris Miller, Beiwen Tian, and Xiang Ren. 2022. Unsupervised cross-task generalization via retrieval augmentation. *arXiv preprint arXiv:2204.07937*.

Jiachang Liu, Dinghan Shen, Yizhe Zhang, Bill Dolan, Lawrence Carin, and Weizhu Chen. 2021. What makes good in-context examples for gpt-3? *arXiv preprint arXiv:2101.06804*.

Man Luo, Kazuma Hashimoto, Semih Yavuz, Zhiwei Liu, Chitta Baral, and Yingbo Zhou. 2022a. Choose your qa model wisely: A systematic study of generative and extractive readers for question answering. In *Proceedings of the 1st Workshop on Semiparametric Methods in NLP: Decoupling Logic from Knowledge*, pages 7–22.

Man Luo, Arindam Mitra, Tejas Gokhale, and Chitta Baral. 2022b. Improving biomedical information retrieval with neural retrievers. *arXiv preprint arXiv:2201.07745*.

Man Luo, Shailaja Keyur Sampat, Riley Tallman, Yankai Zeng, Manuha Vancha, Akarshan Sajja, and Chitta Baral. 2021a. 'just because you are right, doesn't mean i am wrong': Overcoming a bottleneck in development and evaluation of open-ended vqa tasks. In *Proceedings of the 16th Conference of the European Chapter of the Association for Computational Linguistics: Main Volume*, pages 2766–2771.

Man Luo, Yankai Zeng, Pratyay Banerjee, and Chitta Baral. 2021b. Weakly-supervised visual-retriever-reader for knowledge-based question answering. In *Proceedings of the 2021 Conference on Empirical Methods in Natural Language Processing*, pages 6417–6431.

Ji Ma, Ivan Korotkov, Yinfei Yang, Keith Hall, and Ryan McDonald. 2021. Zero-shot neural passage retrieval via domain-targeted synthetic question generation. In *Proceedings of the 16th Conference of the European Chapter of the Association for Computational Linguistics: Main Volume*, pages 1075–1088.

Kenneth Marino, Mohammad Rastegari, Ali Farhadi, and Roozbeh Mottaghi. 2019. Ok-vqa: A visual question answering benchmark requiring external knowledge. In *Conference on Computer Vision and Pattern Recognition (CVPR)*.

Swaroop Mishra, Daniel Khashabi, Chitta Baral, and Hannaneh Hajishirzi. 2021. Cross-task generalization via natural language crowdsourcing instructions. *arXiv preprint arXiv:2104.08773*.

Swaroop Mishra, Arindam Mitra, Neeraj Varshney, Bhavdeep Sachdeva, Peter Clark, Chitta Baral, and Ashwin Kalyan. 2022. Numglue: A suite of fundamental yet challenging mathematical reasoning tasks. *arXiv preprint arXiv:2204.05660*.

Anastasios Nentidis, Anastasia Krithara, Konstantinos Bougiatiotis, Martin Krallinger, Carlos Rodriguez-Penagos, Marta Villegas, and Georgios Paliouras. 2020. Overview of bioasq 2020: The eighth bioasq challenge on large-scale biomedical semantic indexing and question answering. In *International Conference of the Cross-Language Evaluation Forum for European Languages*, pages 194–214. Springer.

Rodrigo Nogueira and Kyunghyun Cho. 2019. Passage re-ranking with bert. *ArXiv*, abs/1901.04085.

Rodrigo Nogueira, Jimmy Lin, and AI Epistemic. 2019. From doc2query to docttttquery. *Online preprint*, 6.

Mihir Parmar, Swaroop Mishra, Mirali Purohit, Man Luo, M Hassan Murad, and Chitta Baral. 2022. In-boxbart: Get instructions into biomedical multi-task learning. *arXiv preprint arXiv:2204.07600*.

Fabio Petroni, Tim Rocktäschel, Sebastian Riedel, Patrick Lewis, Anton Bakhtin, Yuxiang Wu, and Alexander Miller. 2019. Language models as knowledge bases? In *Proceedings of the 2019 Conference on Empirical Methods in Natural Language Processing and the 9th International Joint Conference on Natural Language Processing (EMNLP-IJCNLP)*, pages 2463–2473, Hong Kong, China. Association for Computational Linguistics.

Yingqi Qu, Yuchen Ding, Jing Liu, Kai Liu, Ruiyang Ren, Wayne Xin Zhao, Daxiang Dong, Hua Wu, and Haifeng Wang. 2021. Rocketqa: An optimized training approach to dense passage retrieval for open-domain question answering. In *Proceedings of the 2021 Conference of the North American Chapter of the Association for Computational Linguistics: Human Language Technologies*, pages 5835–5847.

S. Robertson and H. Zaragoza. 2009. The probabilistic relevance framework: Bm25 and beyond. *Found. Trends Inf. Retr.*, 3:333–389.

Christopher Sciavolino, Zexuan Zhong, Jinhyuk Lee, and Danqi Chen. 2021. Simple entity-centric questions challenge dense retrievers. In *Proceedings of the 2021 Conference on Empirical Methods in Natural Language Processing*, pages 6138–6148.

Minjoon Seo, Jinhyuk Lee, Tom Kwiatkowski, Ankur Parikh, Ali Farhadi, and Hannaneh Hajishirzi. 2019. Real-time open-domain question answering with dense-sparse phrase index. In *Proceedings of the 57th Annual Meeting of the Association for Computational Linguistics*, pages 4430–4441.

Anshumali Shrivastava and P. Li. 2014. Asymmetric lsh (alsh) for sublinear time maximum inner product search (mips). *ArXiv*, abs/1405.5869.

Mujeen Sung, Jinhyuk Lee, Sean Yi, Minji Jeon, Sungdong Kim, and Jaewoo Kang. 2021. Can language models be biomedical knowledge bases? In *Proceedings of the 2021 Conference on Empirical Methods in Natural Language Processing*, pages 4723–4734, Online and Punta Cana, Dominican Republic. Association for Computational Linguistics.

Hao Tan and Mohit Bansal. 2019. LXMERT: Learning cross-modality encoder representations from transformers. In *Proceedings of the 2019 Conference on Empirical Methods in Natural Language Processing and the 9th International Joint Conference on Natural Language Processing (EMNLP-IJCNLP)*, pages 5100–5111, Hong Kong, China. Association for Computational Linguistics.

Nandan Thakur, N. Reimers, Andreas Ruckl'e, Abhishek Srivastava, and Iryna Gurevych. 2021. Beir: A heterogenous benchmark for zero-shot evaluation of information retrieval models. *ArXiv*, abs/2104.08663.

George Tsatsaronis, Michael Schroeder, Georgios Paliouras, Yannis Almirantis, Ion Androutsopoulos, Eric Gaussier, Patrick Gallinari, Thierry Artieres, Michael R Alvers, Matthias Zschunke, et al. 2012. Bioasq: A challenge on large-scale biomedical semantic indexing and question answering. In *AAAI fall symposium: Information retrieval and knowledge discovery in biomedical text*. Citeseer.

Lee Xiong, Chenyan Xiong, Ye Li, Kwok-Fung Tang, Jialin Liu, Paul N Bennett, Junaid Ahmed, and Arnold Overwijk. 2020. Approximate nearest neighbor negative contrastive learning for dense text retrieval. In *International Conference on Learning Representations*.

Hang Zhang, Yeyun Gong, Yelong Shen, Jiancheng Lv, Nan Duan, and Weizhu Chen. 2021. Adversarial retriever-ranker for dense text retrieval. *arXiv preprint arXiv:2110.03611*.

Tiancheng Zhao, Xiaopeng Lu, and Kyusong Lee. 2021. Sparta: Efficient open-domain question answering via sparse transformer matching retrieval. In *Proceedings of the 2021 Conference of the North American Chapter of the Association for Computational Linguistics: Human Language Technologies*, pages 565–575.

Improving Classification of Infrequent Cognitive Distortions: Domain-Specific Model vs. Data Augmentation

Xiruo Ding and **Kevin Lybarger** and **Justin S. Tauscher** and **Trevor Cohen**
{xiruod, lybarger, jtausch, cohenta}@uw.edu
University of Washington, Seattle, WA, USA

Abstract

Cognitive distortions are counterproductive patterns of thinking that are one of the targets of cognitive behavioral therapy (CBT). These can be challenging for clinicians to detect, especially those without extensive CBT training or supervision. Text classification methods can approximate expert clinician judgment in the detection of frequently occurring cognitive distortions in text-based therapy messages. However, performance with infrequent distortions is relatively poor. In this study, we address this sparsity problem with two approaches: *Data Augmentation* and *Domain-Specific Model*. The first approach includes Easy Data Augmentation, back translation, and `mixup` techniques. The second approach utilizes a domain-specific pretrained language model, MentalBERT. To examine the viability of different data augmentation methods, we utilized a real-world dataset of texts between therapists and clients diagnosed with serious mental illness that was annotated for distorted thinking. We found that with optimized parameter settings, `mixup` was helpful for rare classes. Performance improvements with an augmented model, MentalBERT, exceed those obtained with data augmentation.

1 Introduction

Data augmentation first became a popular topic in computer vision, where deep neural networks have performed remarkably well. Complex architectures, such as AlexNet (Krizhevsky et al., 2012), VGG-16 (Simonyan and Zisserman, 2014), ResNet (He et al., 2016), DenseNet (Huang et al., 2017), generally require sufficient training data for model convergence, even with the help of dropout regularization and batch normalization. This situation also occurs in natural language processing (NLP) with deep learning methods and can become more problematic when limited to small datasets by data collection or data annotation constraints. In imaging, data augmentation, involving transformations such as cropping and shearing, is a common strategy to expand the amount of data available for training. Analogously, several methods have been proposed to perform data augmentation in NLP, including Easy Data Augmentation (Wei and Zou, 2019), Back Translation (Sennrich et al., 2015), GPT-2 Augmentation (Anaby-Tavor et al., 2020), and `mixup` (Zhang et al., 2017). Kumar et al. (2020) applied some of these methods to pretrained transformer models and showed an average improvement in accuracy of 1-6%. However, the low-resource scenario was simulated by simply constraining the training data from large corpuses. It remains unclear how these methods might perform when used in realistic applications, where certain classes may be of very low frequency. One exemplary case concerns NLP analysis of online therapy sessions, where large amounts of patient-generated texts must be classified, but only well-trained specialists with relevant mental health domain knowledge can perform annotation manually to ensure clinical accuracy. In this study, we used a dataset from text message conversations between clients and therapists, previously used for detecting distorted thoughts (Tauscher et al., 2022). Besides the limitation in size, we found that some types of distorted thinking are very rare, resulting in worse classification performance. To address these issues, we investigate the extent to which data augmentation methods can improve performance of the best-performing BERT model from these experiments. We compare the utility of this augmentation approach to the use of a domain-specific pretrained language model, MentalBERT. In doing so, we evaluate the utility of data augmentation techniques and a domain-specific model to improve the identification of rare classes in the context of real-world data.

Our main contributions are as follows:

- We compared different augmentation methods in a low-resource dataset. We found improve-

Proceedings of the 2022 Conference of the North American Chapter of the Association for Computational Linguistics: Human Language Technologies: Student Research Workshop, pages 68 - 75
July 10-15, 2022

ments with majority classes and that `mixup` can improve performance for rare classes.

- We adapted a domain-specific pretrained language model, MentalBERT, and showed the highest performance for majority classes, and better results for rare classes.
- We explored the hyperparameter α, controlling mixing proportions, for `mixup` and showed that a low α setting is helpful for dominant classes, and a high α for rare classes.

2 Low-resource Corpus

From our previous work (Tauscher et al., 2022), we utilized data from a randomized controlled trial of a community-based text-message intervention for individuals with serious mental illness (Ben-Zeev et al., 2020). Data were collected from 39 participants enrolled in the active intervention arm of this trial between December 2017 and October 2019. As part of the study, clients participating in standard care engaged with trained clinicians in text-message conversations up to three times a day for 12-weeks. In total, 14,312 messages were sent between clinicians and clients with 7,354 coming from clients. To build a predictive model for distorted thoughts, five common distortions were selected (Burns, 1999): Mental Filter (MF), Jumping to Conclusions (JC), Catastrophizing (C), Should Statements (SM), Overgeneralization (O). In addition, we added the label Any Distortion (AD), generated in accordance with the other assigned distortions. Two mental health specialists annotated all messages from clients by assigning these six categories, which are not mutually exclusive (Tauscher et al., 2022). This provided ground truth for labels. It is worth noting that any message could be identified as having multiple distortions, or no distortions at all, making this a multi-label multi-class problem. Table 1 shows the label frequency and inter-rater reliability.

	AD	C	MF	JC	O	SM
Frequency	24.4%	14.8%	8.6%	8.1%	3.6%	2.6%
kappa	0.51	0.44	0.33	0.53	0.46	0.39

Table 1: Label frequency and inter-rater reliability

3 Methods

Based on results by Tauscher et al. (2022), we used BERT as a starting point for our study, since it outperformed support vector machines and logistic regression (with L2 regularization), which had been used in prior work (Shickel et al., 2020; Shreevastava and Foltz, 2021). All models in this study were trained with the previously identified best hyperparameter settings for the dataset (Tauscher et al., 2022) (Section 3.1). Given the observed frequencies (Table 1), we combined results for six categories into three bins by frequency, to distinguish between effects on frequent and infrequent classes. The three bins are "high freq:AD,C", "medium freq:MF,JC", and "low freq:O,SM". For evaluation, we chose area under the precision-recall curve (AUPRC) over F_1 scores, because F_1 scores are special cases of AUPRC for a predefined cutoff and AUPRC is threshold-agnostic. For rare classes, the receiver operating characteristic curve (ROC) may lead to overly optimistic performance estimates, especially when class frequency drops to 1%, which is not the case with the precision-recall curve (Ozenne et al., 2015). Thus, we used AUPRC over others as our main metric. Macro-averaged AUPRC was calculated for each of the bins. This metric was also used to evaluate overall model performance.

We used two approaches to data augmentation, differing in the point at which augmentation occurs. The first involves directly augmenting the original text and outputting augmented examples as plain text, to be added to the original data (Section 3.2). The second approach involves augmentation in the hidden spaces of a deep neural network, and its outputs are vectors in the hidden space, rather than plain text (Section 3.3). For domain-specific model, we utilized a domain-specific pretrained language model with additional linguistic knowledge pertinent to the task at hand (Section 3.4).

3.1 BERT-based Classification

The baseline model we used is BERT (bert-base-uncased [1]) (Devlin et al., 2018). A classification layer was added on top of BERT's output and used for classifying all five cognitive distortions ("MF", "JC", "C", "SM", "O") and "AD". The maximum sequence length was set to 120 (word pieces).

The main framework for evaluation is 5-fold cross validation, and out-of-sample predictions were collected for the whole dataset. Following the original paper (Tauscher et al., 2022), we used the best hyperparameter settings for each of the iterations, as shown in Table 2. Also, losses were

[1] https://huggingface.co/bert-base-uncased

weighted inversely proportional to label frequencies.

Iteration	#1	#2	#3	#4	#5
number of epochs	14	14	10	14	8
dropout	0.2	0.3	0.1	0.2	0.2

Table 2: BERT hyperparameter settings

We repeated 5-fold cross validation five times with fixed folds but different random instantiations of the classification layer to assess the robustness of the results. This is the base setting for our experiments and was used across all other methods. This baseline model is labeled as "BERT (no aug)".

3.2 Augmentation of text data

3.2.1 EDA: Easy Data Augmentation

Wei and Zou (2019) proposed Easy Data Augmentation (EDA), which comprises of four main operations on the original text: Synonym Replacement (SR), Random Insertion (RI), Random Swap (RS), and Random Deletion (RD). EDA was evaluated on five different tasks and showed an increased performance of 0.8% on average.

We adopted authors' recommended setting for the parameter α, 0.1, that controls the percentage of words in a sentence changed by each augmentation method. This is labeled as "BERT (EDA)".

3.2.2 Back Translation

Sennrich et al. (2015) proposed Back Translation for data augmentation, where sentences are first translated into another language and then back to the original language. This technique has been explored for the task of neural machine translation (Sugiyama and Yoshinaga, 2019). To generate new texts, we applied Back Translation with two intermediate languages: German and Spanish. During the augmentation, each original message was translated into German or Spanish and then back to English to get a corresponding message. Class labels of the original text were inherited. We did not repeat these experiments because we found little to no variation in generated texts upon repetition. The two backtranslation models are labeled as "BERT (BT:German)" and "BERT (BT:Spanish)".

3.2.3 GPT-2

Anaby-Tavor et al. (2020) propose using GPT-2 for data augmentation, by fine-tuning the model to generate text corresponding to a class of interest. Following their proposed approach, and using a publicly available GPT-2 model[2], we implemented two variations of GPT-2 for data augmentation.

Context-agnostic GPT-2: we first reconstructed our text messages as follows:

$$y_i[SEP]x_i[EOS]$$

for each of the messages i, where y_i indicates the label of a message, and x_i the message content. GPT-2 was then fine-tuned on this new structure of data for 20 epochs. New messages were generated by feeding in the prompt of "$y[SEP]$". This is labeled as "BERT (GPT-2: no context)".

Contextual GPT-2: Texts in our dataset are derived from conversations. To utilizing this contextual information, we reorganized inputs as follows:

$$y_i[SEP]x_{i-1}[SEP]x_i[EOS]$$

where x_{i-1} is the previous message. The GPT-2 model was then fine-tuned on this structure. Given the prompt of "$y_i[SEP]x_{i-1}[SEP]$", new messages were generated according to the class label y_i and and the preceding message for a representative example as context. This is labeled as "BERT (GPT-2: contextual)".

For text generation, we followed same steps described in Kumar et al. (2020). Due to computational time requirements, we did this once only.

3.3 Augmentation of Hidden Spaces: `mixup`

Zhang et al. (2017) proposed `mixup` for data augmentation. The authors claim that this method extends the training distribution by incorporating the prior knowledge that linear interpolations of feature vectors should lead to linear interpolations of the associated targets, providing data are modeled on vicinity relation across examples of different classes. `mixup` operates as follows:

$$\tilde{x} = \lambda x_i + (1 - \lambda)x_j,$$
$$\tilde{y} = \lambda y_i + (1 - \lambda)y_j$$

where $\lambda \sim Beta(\alpha, \alpha)$ for $\alpha \in (0, +\infty)$. This paper did not examine the hyperparameter α across different NLP applications, with results reported only for Google speech commands, a dataset of 65,000 one-second utterances[3]. However, the authors did report improved results when using

[2] https://huggingface.co/gpt2

[3] https://ai.googleblog.com/2017/08/launching-speech-commands-dataset.html

$\alpha = 0.3$ for this task, and in general proposed a small $\alpha \in [0.1, 0.4]$, based on results on ImageNet-2012. They also acknowledge that model error is less sensitive to large α when increasing model capacity. Sun et al. (2020) applied `mixup` to the transformer architecture and showed improvements on eight GLUE benchmarks. Across all of their experiments, α was fixed at 0.5, which is a reasonable extension from the originally proposed range (Zhang et al., 2017).

From the previous two studies (Zhang et al., 2017; Sun et al., 2020), it is not clear what hyperparameter setting of α should be used with other data sets. Given the probability density function controlled by α (demonstrated in Supplementary Figure 1), other settings when α is large may make more sense for scenarios in which we want to make two examples contribute more evenly. This leads to augmented examples lying in the margin between two categories, which may be appropriate for categories that are difficult to distinguish. In our case, the cognitive distortion dataset is relatively small compared with those evaluated previously, and some classes (O, SM) are quite rare. We wished to assess whether the `mixup` method could help with data augmentation in this context. We did an extended search in the hyperparameter space of α: 0.02, 0.2, 0.5, 1, 2, 4, and 8. The models are labeled as "BERT (`mixup`: $alpha = X$)".

3.4 Domain-Specific Model: MentalBERT

To investigate the utility of domain-specific models for transfer learning, we identified a domain-specific pretrained language model. Ji et al. (2021) describe MentalBERT and MentalRoBERTa, two language models developed specifically for mental health NLP. Starting with pretrained base models, and following standard BERT and RoBERTa pretraining protocols, MentalBERT and MentalRoBERTa were further pretrained on subreddits in the mental health domain, including "r/depression", "r/SuicideWatch", "r/Anxiety", "r/offmychest", "r/bipolar", "r/mentalillness", and "r/mentalhealth". These subreddits made up a pretraining corpus of over 13 million sentences. Upon evaluation, this additional pretraining improved performance in classifying mental conditions, including depression, stress, and anorexia. However, the evaluation sets used texts from online or SMS-like platforms, which were not fully annotated by specialists. In our work, we used MentalBERT, available from HuggingFace [4]. The same hyperparameters as the BERT model were used for comparison purposes. The baseline MentalBERT model is referred as "MentalBERT (no aug)". We also applied the best-performing data augmentation methods to MentalBERT, including back translation (Spanish) and explored some α settings for `mixup`.

4 Results

Performance for all models is shown in Table 3.

BERT: For the baseline BERT model, BERT (no aug), we obtain an AUPRC of 0.5179 for the most frequent classes (AD,C). When frequency decreases (classes MF,JC), the AUPRC also drops to 0.3718, and it drops further to 0.2139 for the rarest class of O,SM. This trend applies to all models. When data augmentation is applied to the base BERT model, we see improved results with different models. For the most frequent class of AD,C, back translation using Spanish achieves the highest AUPRC of 0.5208, followed by `mixup`: $\alpha = 0.02$. However, none of these results are significant improvements over baseline BERT. For the less frequent classes (MF,JC), back translation outperforms baseline BERT by 1.5%. `mixup` does not offer a performance boost here. When it comes to the rarest classes (O,SM), improvement is clearer: EDA, back translation (Spanish), and most settings of `mixup` can offer a boost in AUPRC. Among them, `mixup` ($\alpha = 4$) shows the biggest improvement in AUPRC by around 1.6%, which is statistically significant ($t(8) = 3.24, p\text{-}value = .012$ from t test). It is also notable that both GPT-2 based data augmentation methods decrease the performance of the base BERT model substantially (0.47 vs 0.52 for AD,C and 0.14 vs 0.21 for O,SM).

MentalBERT: When comparing MentalBERT results with BERT results, we can see improved performance for all classes, with the highest change for AD,C and MF,JC of 1.3%-1.8%. Similar to BERT models, performance is highly related to class frequencies, with highest being 0.5359 for the most frequent class of AD,C, dropping to 0.3846 for MF,JC then 0.2171 for O,SM. This trend holds for different augmentation settings. For augmentation effects, the base model performs best for both AD,C and MF,JC, as compared with augmented models. For rare class of O,SM, there is a small improvement from back translation (Spanish) of

[4] `https://huggingface.co/mental/mental-bert-base-uncased`

model	AUPRC (high freq:AD,C)	AUPRC (medium freq:MF,JC)	AUPRC (low freq:O,SM)	macro-AUPRC
BERT (no aug)	0.518 ± 0.0055	0.372 ± 0.0054	0.214 ± 0.0039	0.368 ± 0.0030
BERT (EDA)	0.517 ± 0.0062	0.378 ± 0.0071	0.228 ± 0.0091*	**0.374± 0.0067**
BERT (BT: German)	0.517	0.375	0.216	0.369
BERT (BT: Spanish)	**0.521**	**0.386**	0.222	0.376
BERT (GPT-2: contextual)	0.472	0.290	0.143	0.302
BERT (GPT-2: no context)	0.460	0.306	0.155	0.307
BERT (mixup: $\alpha = 0.02$)	0.519 ± 0.0013	0.372 ± 0.0026	0.218 ± 0.0078	0.370 ± 0.0041
BERT (mixup: $\alpha = 0.2$)	0.515 ± 0.0060	0.369 ± 0.0027	0.218 ± 0.0061	0.367 ± 0.0041
BERT (mixup: $\alpha = 0.5$)	0.510 ± 0.0058	0.367 ± 0.0058	0.213 ± 0.0034	0.363 ± 0.0033
BERT (mixup: $\alpha = 1$)	0.504 ± 0.0072	0.367 ± 0.0076	0.221 ± 0.0047	0.364 ± 0.0055
BERT (mixup: $\alpha = 2$)	0.505 ± 0.0043	0.366 ± 0.0046	0.222 ± 0.0054*	0.364 ± 0.0021
BERT (mixup: $\alpha = 4$)	0.505 ± 0.0048	0.367 ± 0.0027	**0.229 ± 0.0081***	0.367 ± 0.0038
BERT (mixup: $\alpha = 8$)	0.504 ± 0.0045	0.366 ± 0.0057	0.218 ± 0.0059	0.363 ± 0.0030
MentalBERT (no aug)	**0.536 ± 0.0029***	**0.385 ± 0.0059***	0.217 ± 0.0018	**0.379 ± 0.0032***
MentalBERT (BT: Spanish)	0.520	0.380	**0.222**	0.374
MentalBERT (mixup: $\alpha = 0.02$)	0.529 ± 0.0050*	0.379 ± 0.0031*	0.211 ± 0.0052	0.373 ± 0.0022*
MentalBERT (mixup: $\alpha = 0.2$)	0.523 ± 0.0033	0.382 ± 0.0049*	0.216 ± 0.0030	0.374 ± 0.0030*
MentalBERT (mixup: $\alpha = 1$)	0.520 ± 0.0064	0.381 ± 0.0056*	0.214 ± 0.0068	0.372 ± 0.0020*
MentalBERT (mixup: $\alpha = 4$)	0.515 ± 0.0028	0.379 ± 0.0021*	0.215 ± 0.0063	0.370 ± 0.0028
MentalBERT (mixup: $\alpha = 8$)	0.515 ± 0.0049	0.377 ± 0.0037	0.213 ± 0.0060	0.368 ± 0.0044

Table 3: AUPRC (mean ± std) for combined labels by frequency. *: significantly > BERT (no aug), unpaired t-test.

0.5%. None of the mixup configurations provide a benefit over the base MentalBERT model.

mixup: We explored an extensive range of the hyperparameter α with the BERT model. In Table 3, the best results usually come with a small α (0.02) for the dominant classes of AD,C and MF,JC. This best setting shows an increase of 1-2%. With an increasing α, the performance drops. For the rare classes of O,SM, a small α is no longer favored. The performance of AUPRC is not monotonic: with an increasing α, it first increases then drops, with its peak of 0.2285 at $\alpha = 4$. A similar trend is also observed for the MentalBERT model, although mixup did not perform best in this case.

Overall model performances is consistent with some of the preceding observations: (1) data augmentation improves overall performance, but only by a small margin; (2) in-domain pretraining of the language model (MentalBERT) provides the most improvement in performance; (3) for mixup, a small α is favored (0.02 for BERT and 0.2 for MentalBERT).

5 Discussion

We examined several data augmentation methods and explored their applications in BERT and MentalBERT for detecting distorted thinking in a modestly-sized set of text-based therapy messages. Grouping distortion classes by frequency, we found that most of data augmentation methods do not improve performance for frequent classes (frequency: 8-25%). For rare classes (3%), mixup significantly improved AUPRC results by 1.6%. In comparison, the domain-specific pretrained language model, MentalBERT, offered the highest benefit for dominant classes. However, MentalBERT also performs relatively poorly with rare classes. This may be due to the limited number of training examples. Another reason might be the fact that our text messages sometimes represent general conversations related to case management (e.g. appointment reminders) rather than the specific mental health related concerns that predominate in mental-health-related subreddits.

We also explored different settings for the hyperparameter α for the mixup method. For dominant classes, mixup favors a small α, which corresponds with previous work (Zhang et al., 2017). This indicates the model performs better with limited mixing of two random samples, generating cases where only one example predominates. In comparison, a larger α is favored for rare classes. According to Supplementary Figure 1, this means the model tends toward mixes in which the influence of individual texts is diluted, a possible way to create more variation in this low-resource scenario for the model to learn from. However, progressing to more extreme values ($\alpha = 8$) harms performance, and this cutoff point may change in other settings. Taken together, our results suggest that mixup is helpful for rare classes, but may compromise performance on frequent classes. Future work with mixup should include increasing the number of training epochs, since Zhang et al. (2017) sug-

label	Generated Text
JC	Yes you understand that it's incredibly frustrating and a lot of hard work but it's not at all stressful
C	Okay, i will do that, eventually

Table 4: GPT-2 generated text

gest that errors may be further reduced with more iterations of training.

Contrary to expectations, GPT-2-based data augmentation harmed performance in this context. It appears that GPT-2 generated texts (Table 4) do not express cognitive distortions as intended. This is likely because the data are not large enough to fully train a "distorted" GPT-2 model. Another reason may be that our prompts are not associated with distorted text by GPT-2. Designing better prompts may be a fruitful direction for future work.

6 Conclusions

We compared a range of data augmentation strategies and a domain-specific pretrained language model for their utility in improving identification of infrequently observed cognitive distortions. Using a domain-specific pretrained language model (MentalBERT) provided the greatest improvements, especially for dominant classes, whereas data augmentation did not improve performance with this model. In contrast, some data augmentation methods significantly improved performance with the base BERT model, but we did not find a method to improve performances for all classes universally, nor did we find a consistent hyperparameter setting to improve performance across these class frequencies. `mixup` appears helpful for rare classes, but a relatively large hyperparameter setting for α should be used. However, this may compromise the performance on frequent classes to some degree. Taken together our results suggest that the domain-specific model may be a better strategy for frequent classes, and that the best data augmentation strategy for infrequently observed classes varies across frequency ranges. As future work, two areas of interest include: (1) modified loss functions, such as the Label-Distribution-Aware Margin (LDAM) Loss (Cao et al., 2019) and Class-Balanced (CB) Loss (Cui et al., 2019), which have been proposed in the field of computer vision to address class imbalance; (2) unsupervised learning frameworks to address the inherent uncertainty of labels for augmented data, such as Confident Learning (Northcutt et al., 2021) and Unsupervised Data Augmentation (UDA) (Xie et al., 2020).

Acknowledgements

This work was supported by the UW Medicine Garvey Institute for Brain Health Solutions; National Institute of Mental Health grant (R56MH109554); and in part by the National Institutes of Health, National Library of Medicine (NLM) Biomedical and Health Informatics Training Program at the University of Washington (Grant Nr. T15LM007442). The content is solely the responsibility of the authors and does not necessarily represent the official views of the National Institutes of Health.

References

Ateret Anaby-Tavor, Boaz Carmeli, Esther Goldbraich, Amir Kantor, George Kour, Segev Shlomov, Naama Tepper, and Naama Zwerdling. 2020. Do not have enough data? deep learning to the rescue! In *Proceedings of the AAAI Conference on Artificial Intelligence*, volume 34, pages 7383–7390.

Dror Ben-Zeev, Benjamin Buck, Suzanne Meller, William J Hudenko, and Kevin A Hallgren. 2020. Augmenting evidence-based care with a texting mobile interventionist: a pilot randomized controlled trial. *Psychiatric Services*, 71(12):1218–1224.

David D Burns. 1999. *Feeling Good: The New Mood Therapy*. Harper Collins, New York, NY.

Kaidi Cao, Colin Wei, Adrien Gaidon, Nikos Arechiga, and Tengyu Ma. 2019. Learning imbalanced datasets with label-distribution-aware margin loss. *Advances in neural information processing systems*, 32.

Yin Cui, Menglin Jia, Tsung-Yi Lin, Yang Song, and Serge Belongie. 2019. Class-balanced loss based on effective number of samples. In *Proceedings of the IEEE/CVF conference on computer vision and pattern recognition*, pages 9268–9277.

Jacob Devlin, Ming-Wei Chang, Kenton Lee, and Kristina Toutanova. 2018. Bert: Pre-training of deep bidirectional transformers for language understanding. *arXiv preprint arXiv:1810.04805*.

Kaiming He, Xiangyu Zhang, Shaoqing Ren, and Jian Sun. 2016. Deep residual learning for image recognition. In *Proceedings of the IEEE conference on computer vision and pattern recognition*, pages 770–778.

Gao Huang, Zhuang Liu, Laurens Van Der Maaten, and Kilian Q Weinberger. 2017. Densely connected convolutional networks. In *Proceedings of the IEEE conference on computer vision and pattern recognition*, pages 4700–4708.

Shaoxiong Ji, Tianlin Zhang, Luna Ansari, Jie Fu, Prayag Tiwari, and Erik Cambria. 2021. Mentalbert: Publicly available pretrained language models for mental healthcare. *arXiv preprint arXiv:2110.15621.*

Alex Krizhevsky, Ilya Sutskever, and Geoffrey E Hinton. 2012. Imagenet classification with deep convolutional neural networks. *Advances in neural information processing systems*, 25.

Varun Kumar, Ashutosh Choudhary, and Eunah Cho. 2020. Data augmentation using pre-trained transformer models. *arXiv preprint arXiv:2003.02245.*

Curtis Northcutt, Lu Jiang, and Isaac Chuang. 2021. Confident learning: Estimating uncertainty in dataset labels. *Journal of Artificial Intelligence Research*, 70:1373–1411.

Brice Ozenne, Fabien Subtil, and Delphine Maucort-Boulch. 2015. The precision–recall curve overcame the optimism of the receiver operating characteristic curve in rare diseases. *Journal of clinical epidemiology*, 68(8):855–859.

Rico Sennrich, Barry Haddow, and Alexandra Birch. 2015. Improving neural machine translation models with monolingual data. *arXiv preprint arXiv:1511.06709.*

Benjamin Shickel, Scott Siegel, Martin Heesacker, Sherry Benton, and Parisa Rashidi. 2020. Automatic detection and classification of cognitive distortions in mental health text. In *2020 IEEE 20th International Conference on Bioinformatics and Bioengineering (BIBE)*, pages 275–280. IEEE.

Sagarika Shreevastava and Peter Foltz. 2021. Detecting cognitive distortions from patient-therapist interactions. In *Proceedings of the Seventh Workshop on Computational Linguistics and Clinical Psychology: Improving Access*, pages 151–158.

Karen Simonyan and Andrew Zisserman. 2014. Very deep convolutional networks for large-scale image recognition. *arXiv preprint arXiv:1409.1556.*

Amane Sugiyama and Naoki Yoshinaga. 2019. Data augmentation using back-translation for context-aware neural machine translation. In *Proceedings of the Fourth Workshop on Discourse in Machine Translation (DiscoMT 2019)*, pages 35–44.

Lichao Sun, Congying Xia, Wenpeng Yin, Tingting Liang, Philip S Yu, and Lifang He. 2020. Mixup-transformer: dynamic data augmentation for nlp tasks. *arXiv preprint arXiv:2010.02394.*

Justin Tauscher, Kevin Lybarger, Xiruo Ding, Ayesha Chander, William Hudenko, Trevor Cohen, and Dror Ben-Zeev. 2022. Automated detection of cognitive distortions in text exchanges between clinicians and people with serious mental illness. *Psychiatric Services (in review).*

Jason Wei and Kai Zou. 2019. Eda: Easy data augmentation techniques for boosting performance on text classification tasks. *arXiv preprint arXiv:1901.11196.*

Qizhe Xie, Zihang Dai, Eduard Hovy, Thang Luong, and Quoc Le. 2020. Unsupervised data augmentation for consistency training. *Advances in Neural Information Processing Systems*, 33:6256–6268.

Hongyi Zhang, Moustapha Cisse, Yann N Dauphin, and David Lopez-Paz. 2017. *mixup*: Beyond empirical risk minimization. *arXiv preprint arXiv:1710.09412.*

A Appendix

Supplementary Figure 1

Figure 1: Probability Density Function of $Beta(\alpha, \alpha)$

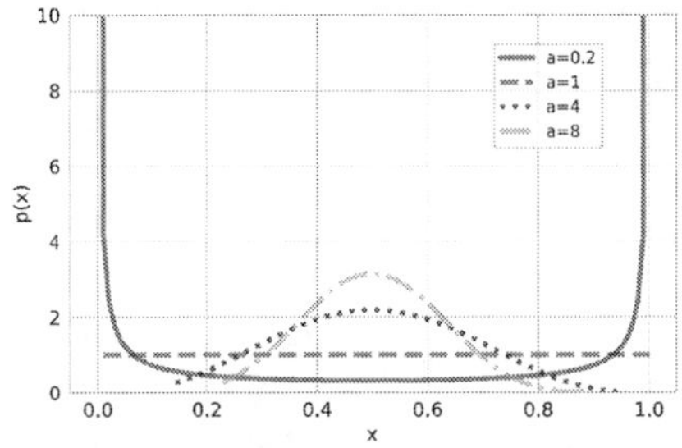

In the paper of `mixup`, a special form of $Beta(\alpha, \beta)$ distribution was used where $\alpha = \beta$. The figure shows PDF of different α settings and this could affect the distributions of how the weights of two samples are assigned.

Generate, Evaluate, and Select: A Dialogue System with a Response Evaluator for Diversity-Aware Response Generation

Ryoma Sakaeda and **Daisuke Kawahara**
Waseda University
{s.ryoma6317@akane., dkw@}waseda.jp

Abstract

We aim to overcome the lack of diversity in responses of current dialogue systems and to develop a dialogue system that is engaging as a conversational partner. We propose a generator-evaluator model that evaluates multiple responses generated by a response generator and selects the best response by an evaluator. By generating multiple responses, we obtain diverse responses. We conduct human evaluations to compare the output of the proposed system with that of a baseline system. The results of the human evaluations showed that the proposed system's responses were often judged to be better than the baseline system's, and indicated the effectiveness of the proposed method.

1 Introduction

Dialogue systems based on deep neural networks (DNNs) have been widely studied. Although these dialogue systems can generate fluent responses, they often generate dull responses such as "yes, that's right" and lack engagingness as a conversation partner (Jiang and de Rijke, 2018). To develop an engaging dialogue system, it is necessary to generate a variety of responses not to bore users.

However, dialogue systems that are capable of generating diverse responses are difficult to automatically evaluate. A commonly used evaluation metric is BLEU (Papineni et al., 2002) used in machine translation, which measures the degree of n-gram agreement with the reference response. However, due to the diversity of responses, i.e., the one-to-many nature of dialogue (Zhao et al., 2017), which means the existence of multiple appropriate responses to an utterance, methods that compare the response to reference responses are not appropriate. Therefore, there is a need for evaluation methods that do not use reference responses, and one of them is supervised evaluation. It trains DNNs using human evaluations of responses generated by humans and models (Zhao et al., 2020; Ghazarian et al., 2019). DNN-based evaluations correlate to some extent with human evaluations.

We aim to develop a dialogue system that is more engaging as a conversational partner by combining independently studied response generation and response evaluation models into a single dialogue system. Specifically, we propose a generator-evaluator model in which multiple responses are generated by the generation model, evaluated by the evaluation model, and the response with the highest evaluation score is selected. By generating multiple responses, we can obtain diverse responses. This can be enabled by the response evaluator that does not require reference responses.

Our methods of generating multiple responses include a method with multiple decoding schemes and a method that uses a model that can generate responses with a specified Dialogue Act (DA). Generating responses by specifying various DAs leads to a variety of responses.

To evaluate the proposed method, we conducted human evaluation by crowdsourcing to compare the outputs of the proposed system and a baseline system. The evaluation results show that the proposed system outputs better responses, and indicate the effectiveness of the proposed method.

We target Japanese dialogue systems and construct datasets of Japanese dialogues.

2 Related Work

Methods for evaluating responses by dialogue systems can be divided into human and automatic evaluations. Automatic evaluation can be further classified into evaluation with or without reference responses. As an automatic evaluation metric, BLEU (Papineni et al., 2002) is mainly used. It evaluates responses in terms of n-gram agreement with the reference sentence. However, it has been shown that there is no correlation at all between BLEU and human evaluations (Liu et al., 2016). One reason for this is the one-to-many nature of di-

Proceedings of the 2022 Conference of the North American Chapter of the Association for Computational Linguistics: Human Language Technologies: Student Research Workshop, pages 76 - 82

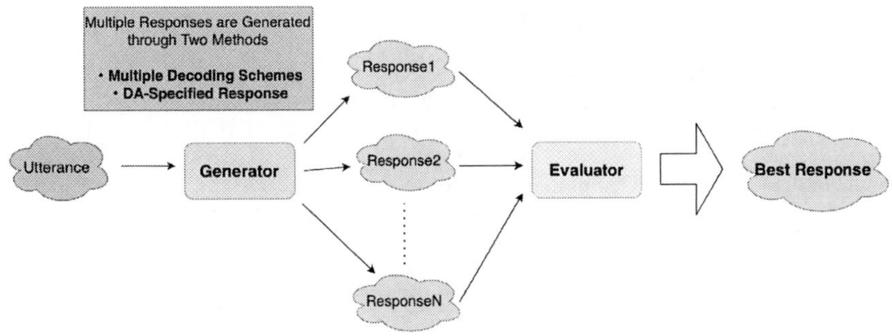

Figure 1: The architecture of our proposed system, the generator-evaluator model. It generates multiple responses from the generator, evaluates them with the evaluator, and selects the best response.

alogue (Zhao et al., 2017), which means that there are multiple appropriate responses to an utterance. Considering this nature, a method that measures the degree of n-gram agreement with the reference response is inappropriate for evaluating responses. Therefore, automatic evaluation methods without any reference responses have been studied (Zhao et al., 2020; Ghazarian et al., 2019). They trained BERT (Devlin et al., 2019) on a dataset of human evaluations to perform response evaluation that correlates with the human evaluations.

DA represents the role of an utterance in a dialogue. There are some datasets annotated with DAs such as SwDA (Stolcke et al., 2000) and MRDA (Shriberg et al., 2004). However, such datasets exist only for English, and we construct a DA dataset in Japanese. Raheja and Tetreault (2019); Ahmadvand et al. (2019) constructed a model that classifies a DA for an utterance. Kawano et al. (2019) proposed a model to generate responses with a specified DA. This was achieved through adversarial learning. In this study, we use a more straightforward method to control responses.

3 A Generator-Evaluator Model for an Engaging Dialogue System

3.1 Generator-Evaluator Model

We propose a generator-evaluator model that generates multiple responses, evaluates these responses, and selects the response with the highest evaluation score for output. The overview of the proposed model is shown in Figure 1. Two methods are used to generate multiple responses: multiple decoding schemes and a model that can generate DA specified responses. For the evaluator, BERT is fine-tuned with the Response-Evaluation dataset described in Section 4.2.

3.2 Multiple Response Generators

We use T5 (Raffel et al., 2020) as a generator by fine-tuning it with the method described below.

3.2.1 Multiple Decoding Schemes

The first method for obtaining multiple responses is to use multiple decoding schemes. Three types of decoding methods are used: greedy search, beam search, and sampling. In particular, to repeat sampling is thought to generate diverse responses. We use the top-50 sampling (Fan et al., 2018).

3.2.2 DA-Specified Response Generation

The second method to obtain multiple responses is to use a model that can generate responses with specified DAs. We achieve such a model by training a response generation model based on utterance-response pairs attached with prompts that specify the DA of a response. The dataset format is as follows: (1a) represents the input and (1b) represents the response. The italic span denotes the prompt specifying a DA.

(1) a. *Return a response of advice to tne interlocutor* I haven't done the assignment yet.

b. You should read this book before you do it.

To train this model, we need a dialogue corpus annotated with DA labels. We use the DA dataset described in Section 4.3. A dialogue corpus without DA labels is also used as responses with a *general* DA. Its prompt is *Return a response*.

4 Dataset

Since there is not a sufficiently large corpus of Japanese dialogues, we start from corpus construction.

Viewpoint	Response	Amount
Relevance	Twitter/decoding model	4,000/4,000
Interestingness	Twitter	2,000
Engagingness	Twitter/decoding model/DA model	4,000/4,000/4,000
Empathy	Twitter	2,000

Table 1: Amount of data for each viewpoint in the Response-Evaluation dataset. "Response" indicates where the response derives from. Due to the collection cost, more data were collected for the more important viewpoints.

Dialogue Act	Description
Advice	advice or instruction given to the partner
Emotion	emotion experienced by speaker
Opinion	opinion about a particular topic
Inform	give information about oneself(speaker)
Schedule	what the speaker plans to do or wants to do
Question	questioning the partner
Agree	agree about the partner's opinion or feeling

Table 2: DA types and their descriptions. Crowdworkers are shown this description and asked to choose which DA applies to each response.

Dialogue Act	Amount
Advice	853
Emotion	1,433
Opinion	1,323
Inform	1,131
Schedule	718
Question	342
Agree	1,136

Table 3: Amount of data for each DA.

4.1 Twitter Dataset

Our dialogue dataset is collected from Twitter using the Twitter API. Some of the conversations are collected from single-turn conversations only (Twitter-Single), while the others are collected from multi-turn conversations (Twitter-Multi).

4.2 Response-Evaluation Dataset

Our Response-Evaluation dataset contains evaluations of how well a response meets certain viewpoints when looking at a single-turn utterance and response. We use the following four evaluation viewpoints: relevance, interestingness, engagingness, and empathy.

We use two types of utterance-response pairs to ensure corpus diversity: the first is the Twitter-Single dataset described in Section 4.1, and the second is the utterances from the Twitter-Single dataset and the responses generated from generator models. We use two types of generator models: the model with the multiple decoding schemes and the model that can generate responses with specified DAs. In the datasets using responses from the generator models, the evaluations of multiple responses to an utterance are collected. They represent how evaluations differ when different responses are generated to the same utterance. The evaluations are collected through crowdsourcing. We ask a five-grade question to five people, and the average was taken as the evaluation value. The statistics of the dataset is shown in Table 1.

4.3 DA Dataset

We assign DAs for each utterance in the Twitter-Multi dataset described in Section 4.1. By using the dataset of multi-turn conversations, we intended to make a dataset to capture the transition of DAs in a long conversation. We adopt seven DA types shown in Table 2. The number of DA types was reduced to seven because the 42 types in the previous study (Stolcke et al., 2000) were too fine-grained to be annotated by crowdsourcing. Since there are utterances that do not settle on a single DA, we allow multiple DAs for each utterance. DAs are collected through crowdsourcing. We ask a question to five people and adopt the DA with at least three votes. The amount of utterances for each DA is shown in Table 3. Since the amount of data is not sufficient to be used for training the generator model described in Section 3.2.2, this dataset is used to train DA classifiers that are applied to the Twitter-Single dataset for data augmentation.

Augmentation with DA Classifiers

We build DA classifiers by fine-tuning BERT with the DA dataset described above. These DA classifiers are binary classifiers that determine whether a response belongs to each of the DAs. The results of DA classification by each DA classifier are shown

Dialogue Act	Precision	Recall	F1
Advice	0.52	0.57	0.54
Emotion	0.54	0.37	0.44
Opinion	0.60	0.51	0.55
Inform	0.44	0.55	0.49
Schedule	0.41	0.47	0.44
Question	0.88	0.51	0.65
Agree	0.69	0.53	0.60

Table 4: Results of DA classification by five-fold cross validation.

Dialogue Act	Amount
Advice	2,284
Emotion	4,195
Opinion	6,580
Inform	63,652
Schedule	89,990
Question	33,629
Agree	70,557

Table 5: Amount of data for each DA obtained by data augmentation with the DA classifiers.

in Table 4. Metrics are precision, recall, and F1. They are computed using five-fold cross validation. From this table, the predicted DAs do not seem sufficiently precise to be used for data augmentation. However, we manually examined a part of predicted DAs and found that their precision was around 70%, which made us decide to use them for data augmentation.

We augment the DA dataset by applying the classifiers to an unlabeled dialogue corpus. We apply each binary classifier to 1.6M responses of the Twitter-Single dataset, and assign DA labels to responses judged to be positive. The amount of data obtained for each DA is shown in Table 5.

5 Experiments

We do the evaluation by crowdsourcing. Workers are shown the outputs of the two systems and asked which of the system they would prefer to continue the conversation with. We ask a question to three workers and take a majority vote as the result. The test corpus consists of 2,000 sentences from the Twitter-Single dataset described in Section 4.1 which are not used for training.

5.1 Experimental Setup

The proposed systems use two types of generators: one by the multiple decoding schemes (**DE**) and one by DA specified responses (**DA**). Also, by combining DE and DA, the DA generator can generate responses using the multiple decoding schemes (**DADE**). We define **DE Best**, **DA Best**,

Comparison	Win	Lose	Even
DE Best vs DE Greedy	**44%**	21%	35%
DE Best vs DE Random	**50%**	24%	26%
DA Best vs DA General	**42%**	25%	33%
DA Best vs DA Random	**44%**	21%	35%
DADE Best vs DE Greedy	**44%**	43%	12%
DADE Best vs DE Random	**48%**	41%	11%
DADE Best vs DA General	**49%**	33%	17%
DADE Best vs DA random	**55%**	28%	17%
DADE Best vs DADE Random	**73%**	14%	13%
DADE Best vs DE Best	38%	**51%**	11%
DADE Best vs DA Best	**45%**	32%	22%

Table 6: Result of one-to-one comparison between a proposed system and a baseline system.

and **DADE Best**, which refer to the response judged to be the best among multiple responses by the evaluators in DE, DA, and DADE, respectively. Here, in DE, seven responses were generated by repeating sampling five times in addition to greedy search and beam search. In DA, seven responses were obtained by generating responses for the general DA and excluding the emotion DA, whose classifier did not perform accurately. Multiple DAs were allowed for dataset construction, but only one DA was specified for generation. In DADE, seven responses are obtained for each of the seven DAs, resulting in a total of 49 responses. We perform a one-to-one comparison of each proposed system's response with the baseline system's response following Roller et al. (2021). There are five types of responses to be compared, which are shown below.

DE Greedy a response generated by greedy search

DE Random a randomly selected response from seven responses

DA General a response generated by specifying the general DA

DA Random a randomly selected response from seven DAs responses

DADE Random a randomly selected response from 49 responses

5.2 Training

We use T5 (Raffel et al., 2020) pretrained with a Japanese corpus[1] as a generator in DE. We fine-tune it with 800,000 pairs from the Twitter-Single dataset described in Section 4.1. The generator model used in DA is further fine-tuned from the DE generator model with the augmented DA dataset in

System	Utterance	Scheme/DA	Response	Eval
DE	美味しいですよね。台湾茶。大好き。(It's delicious. Taiwanese tea. I love it.)	Beam	ありがとうございます。台湾茶は美味しいですよね。(Thank you. Taiwanese tea is delicious.)	3.6
		Sampling1	美味しいですよね。味も飲みやすくて、お値段の割にちょっぴり高級感があって良いですね(^-^) (It's delicious. It tastes easy to drink and has a little bit of luxury for the price (^-^) .)	3.9
		Sampling2	台湾茶は美味しいですよねー。私も大好きです〜。(Taiwanese tea is delicious! I love it too!)	3.8
DA	充電がすぐ切れるんだね。(I see that the charge runs out quickly.)	General	充電がすぐ切れるのね。(You see the charge runs out quickly, don't you.)	3.4
		Advice	充電が切れるなら、バッテリー交換した方がいいよ。(If it's going to run out of charge, you should replace the battery.)	3.3
		Opinion	充電切れたので、今日はお休みにします。(I'm out of charge, so I'm taking the rest of the day off.)	3.1

Table 7: Diverse responses from the proposed system. We think that the best responses for humans are the responses of "Sampling1" for DE and "Advice" for DA. This best response gets the highest evaluation in DE. However, this is not the case in DA. This may be one reason why the experimental results for DA are inferior to one for DE.

Section 4.3 and a part of the Twitter-Single dataset as general DA responses. It has the same size as the augmented DA dataset (270,000 pairs).

The evaluator is a fine-tuned BERT model and constructed for each of DE and DA. The dataset used for fine-tuning is the Engagingness data of the Response-Evaluation dataset described in Section 4.2. It consists of 4,000 pairs derived from Twitter and 4,000 pairs from either of the DE and DA generators. For DADE, we use the same evaluator as DA.

5.3 Result

The evaluation results of our experiments are shown in Table 6. It shows the effectiveness of generating multiple responses and selecting the best response by the evaluator. However, the results of **DADE Best vs DE Greedy** and **DADE Best vs DE Best** show the responses of the DA generator were not rated better than the responses of the DE generator. This can be attributed to the fact that the distribution of the dataset was skewed by data augmentation, and further study is needed. Example responses generated by the proposed system are shown in Table 7.

6 Analysis

6.1 Out-of-Domain Evaluator

In the experiments in Section 5, each evaluator of DE and DA was trained using the human evaluations of the corresponding generator responses for each of DE and DA. However, it is not practical to use human evaluations for each generator. Therefore, we investigate the impact of using different generation methods and datasets used for evaluators. The same comparisons are made as the comparisons in Section 5. The results are shown in Table 8. We see that the proposed systems defeat the baseline in this case as well.

[1]https://huggingface.co/sonoisa/t5-base-japanese

Comparison	Win	Lose	Even
DE Best' vs DE Greedy	47%	24%	28%
DE Best' vs DE Random	47%	27%	26%
DA Best' vs DA General	36%	25%	40%
DA Best' vs DA Random	45%	25%	30%

Table 8: One-to-one comparison between a proposed system with an OOD evaluator and a baseline system.

Decoding Scheme	Ratio
Greedy-Search	12%
Beam-Search	15%
Sampling (x5)	73%

Table 9: Analysis of which decoding scheme is selected. Sampling was repeated five times, and the percentage of any of the five responses chosen was 73%.

6.2 Which Response is Chosen?

We analyzed which decoding methods or DAs are selected by the evaluator model. The more equally the choices are divided, the more effective the proposed method is. This is because the proposed method cannot be surpassed by using any one specific decoding scheme or DA. The results of the

DA	Ratio
General	16%
Advice	8%
Schedule	16%
Question	11%
Inform	14%
Agree	9%
Opinion	25%

Table 10: Analysis of DA selection.

analysis are shown in Tables 9 and 10. The choices are scattered, and thus the proposed method can generate diverse responses.

7 Conclusion

We developed a dialogue system that can generate engaging responses by incorporating a response evaluator within the dialogue system. We proposed a generator-evaluator model, which consists of multiple response generation through multiple decoding schemes or specified DAs, responses evaluations, and the best response selection. Human evaluation showed that responses generated by the generator-evaluator model are more engaging than those by the baseline systems. However, it is still necessary to improve the quality of responses generated with specified DAs in the future.

Acknowledgements

This work was supported by a joint research grant from LINE Corporation.

References

Ali Ahmadvand, Jason Ingyu Choi, and Eugene Agichtein. 2019. Contextual dialogue act classification for open-domain conversational agents. In *Proceedings of the 42nd International ACM SIGIR Conference on Research and Development in Information Retrieval*, SIGIR'19, page 1273–1276, New York, NY, USA. Association for Computing Machinery.

Jacob Devlin, Ming-Wei Chang, Kenton Lee, and Kristina Toutanova. 2019. BERT: Pre-training of deep bidirectional transformers for language understanding. In *Proceedings of the 2019 Conference of the North American Chapter of the Association for Computational Linguistics: Human Language Technologies, Volume 1 (Long and Short Papers)*, pages 4171–4186, Minneapolis, Minnesota. Association for Computational Linguistics.

Angela Fan, Mike Lewis, and Yann Dauphin. 2018. Hierarchical neural story generation. In *Proceedings of the 56th Annual Meeting of the Association for Computational Linguistics (Volume 1: Long Papers)*, pages 889–898, Melbourne, Australia. Association for Computational Linguistics.

Sarik Ghazarian, Johnny Wei, Aram Galstyan, and Nanyun Peng. 2019. Better automatic evaluation of open-domain dialogue systems with contextualized embeddings. In *Proceedings of the Workshop on Methods for Optimizing and Evaluating Neural Language Generation*, pages 82–89, Minneapolis, Minnesota. Association for Computational Linguistics.

Shaojie Jiang and Maarten de Rijke. 2018. Why are sequence-to-sequence models so dull? understanding the low-diversity problem of chatbots. In *Proceedings of the 2018 EMNLP Workshop SCAI: The 2nd International Workshop on Search-Oriented Conversational AI*, pages 81–86, Brussels, Belgium. Association for Computational Linguistics.

Seiya Kawano, Koichiro Yoshino, and Satoshi Nakamura. 2019. Neural conversation model controllable by given dialogue act based on adversarial learning and label-aware objective. In *Proceedings of the 12th International Conference on Natural Language Generation*, pages 198–207, Tokyo, Japan. Association for Computational Linguistics.

Chia-Wei Liu, Ryan Lowe, Iulian Serban, Mike Noseworthy, Laurent Charlin, and Joelle Pineau. 2016. How NOT to evaluate your dialogue system: An empirical study of unsupervised evaluation metrics for dialogue response generation. In *Proceedings of the 2016 Conference on Empirical Methods in Natural Language Processing*, pages 2122–2132, Austin, Texas. Association for Computational Linguistics.

Kishore Papineni, Salim Roukos, Todd Ward, and Wei-Jing Zhu. 2002. Bleu: a method for automatic evaluation of machine translation. In *Proceedings of the 40th Annual Meeting of the Association for Computational Linguistics*, pages 311–318, Philadelphia, Pennsylvania, USA. Association for Computational Linguistics.

Colin Raffel, Noam Shazeer, Adam Roberts, Katherine Lee, Sharan Narang, Michael Matena, Yanqi Zhou, Wei Li, and Peter J. Liu. 2020. Exploring the limits of transfer learning with a unified text-to-text transformer. *Journal of Machine Learning Research*, 21(140):1–67.

Vipul Raheja and Joel Tetreault. 2019. Dialogue Act Classification with Context-Aware Self-Attention. In *Proceedings of the 2019 Conference of the North American Chapter of the Association for Computational Linguistics: Human Language Technologies, Volume 1 (Long and Short Papers)*, pages 3727–3733, Minneapolis, Minnesota. Association for Computational Linguistics.

Stephen Roller, Emily Dinan, Naman Goyal, Da Ju, Mary Williamson, Yinhan Liu, Jing Xu, Myle Ott, Eric Michael Smith, Y-Lan Boureau, and Jason Weston. 2021. Recipes for building an open-domain chatbot. In *Proceedings of the 16th Conference of the European Chapter of the Association for Computational Linguistics: Main Volume*, pages 300–325, Online. Association for Computational Linguistics.

Elizabeth Shriberg, Raj Dhillon, Sonali Bhagat, Jeremy Ang, and Hannah Carvey. 2004. The ICSI meeting recorder dialog act (MRDA) corpus. In *Proceedings of the 5th SIGdial Workshop on Discourse and Dialogue at HLT-NAACL 2004*, pages 97–100, Cambridge, Massachusetts, USA. Association for Computational Linguistics.

Andreas Stolcke, Klaus Ries, Noah Coccaro, Elizabeth Shriberg, Rebecca Bates, Daniel Jurafsky, Paul Taylor, Rachel Martin, Carol Van Ess-Dykema, and Marie Meteer. 2000. Dialogue act modeling for automatic tagging and recognition of conversational speech. *Computational Linguistics*, 26(3):339–374.

Tiancheng Zhao, Ran Zhao, and Maxine Eskenazi. 2017. Learning discourse-level diversity for neural dialog models using conditional variational autoencoders. In *Proceedings of the 55th Annual Meeting of the Association for Computational Linguistics (Volume 1: Long Papers)*, pages 654–664, Vancouver, Canada. Association for Computational Linguistics.

Tianyu Zhao, Divesh Lala, and Tatsuya Kawahara. 2020. Designing precise and robust dialogue response evaluators. In *Proceedings of the 58th Annual Meeting of the Association for Computational Linguistics*, pages 26–33, Online. Association for Computational Linguistics.

Impact of Training Instance Selection on Domain-Specific Entity Extraction using BERT

Eileen Salhofer
Know-Center GmbH
esalhofer@know-center.at

Xinglan Liu
Know-Center GmbH
lliu@know-center.at

Roman Kern
Graz University of Technology
Know-Center GmbH
rkern@know-center.at

Abstract

State of the art performances for entity extraction tasks are achieved by supervised learning, specifically, by fine-tuning pretrained language models such as BERT. As a result, annotating application specific data is the first step in many use cases. However, no practical guidelines are available for annotation requirements. This work supports practitioners by empirically answering the frequently asked questions (1) how many training samples to annotate? (2) which examples to annotate? We found that BERT achieves up to 80% F1 when fine-tuned on only 70 training examples, especially on biomedical domain. The key features for guiding the selection of high performing training instances are identified to be pseudo-perplexity and sentence-length. The best training dataset constructed using our proposed selection strategy shows F1 score that is equivalent to a random selection with twice the sample size. The requirement of only a small number of training data implies cheaper implementations and opens door to wider range of applications.

1 Introduction

Information extraction (IE) is the process of turning unstructured texts into structured data (Jurafsky and Martin, 2021), and is one of the most widely used natural language processing (NLP) tasks in industrial applications. Named entity recognition (NER) is an IE task of tagging entities in text with their corresponding types. Most existing NER methods require either handcrafted features, and/or a large number of annotated examples (Jurafsky and Martin, 2021), both of which are labor intensive.

Recent advances in transformers (Vaswani et al., 2017) and BERT (Devlin et al., 2019) changed the landscape for many NLP tasks. Significant performance gain can be achieved by fine-tuning language models on a small number of training examples due to transfer learning. As a result, the pipeline of annotating – fine-tuning becomes common practice. Following this pipeline, the first step for each use case is to annotate application specific data. It is therefore beneficial to estimate in advance how many training samples need to be annotated, as well as which samples to annotate.

This work answers these two frequently asked questions through empirical studies on the NER task. Specifically, we repeatedly down-sample benchmark datasets and fine-tune BERT models for the downstream task of token classification. Two benchmark datasets (1) general domain Conll2003 (F. and De Meulder, 2003) and (2) biomedical domain BC5CDR (Li et al., 2016) are used in this study.

In summary, our main contributions are:

- Empirically identified the relation between sample size and model performance on the entity extraction task for corpora of different domains.
- Proposing key measures for selecting training examples that yield high performances in our evaluation, which can serve as a promising starting point for many other application scenarios.

2 Experimental Setting

The goal of the experiments is to answer beforementioned questions on how many and which training samples to annotate for the named entity extraction task.

We repeatedly down-sample benchmark NER datasets and compared model performances fine-tuned on different number of training examples and different samples. Two datasets of different domains, and two BERT models pretrained on different datasets are used in this study.

2.1 Fine-Tuning Language Models

As recommended in Devlin et al. (2019), the NER task is formulated as a token-level classification

Proceedings of the 2022 Conference of the North American Chapter of the Association for Computational Linguistics: Human Language Technologies: Student Research Workshop, pages 83 - 88

split	n-sentence	CoNLL2003 *(news)* n-token *mean*	n-LOC *mean*	n-MISC *mean*	n-ORG *mean*	n-PER *mean*	BC5CDR *(PubMed, PMC)* n-sentence	n-token *mean*	n-Disease *mean*	n-Chemical *mean*
train	14042	14.50	0.51	0.24	0.45	0.47	4612	24.95	0.91	1.13
validation	3251	15.80	0.57	0.28	0.41	0.57	4607	24.81	0.92	1.16
test	3454	13.44	0.48	0.20	0.48	0.47	4819	25.02	0.92	1.12

Table 1: Number of sentences, the mean of the number of tokens and entities for CoNLL2003 and BC5CDR datasets. On average, sentences in BC5CDR are nearly twice as long as those in CoNLL2003.

task. Namely, a pretrained BERT model is stacked with a linear layer on top of the hidden-states output, before fine-tuned on training examples. The transformers library from Hugging Face (Wolf et al., 2020) is used for fine-tuning. Two BERT models are compared: (1) BERT[1] pretrained on BooksCorpus (Zhu et al., 2015) and Wikipedia, which represent general domain. (2) BioBERT[2] (Lee et al., 2020) where also PubMed abstracts and PMC articles are added to the pretraining data. As a result, the pretraining data for BioBERT also covers the biomedical domain. For both pretrained models, we choose the base setting with 12 transformer layers and 768 hidden embedding sizes. Following recommendations from both Devlin et al. (2019) and Lee et al. (2020), the cased vocabulary is used for the NER task.

2.2 Datasets

Two NER datasets with different domains were used and statistics for both graphs are provided in Table 1.

CoNLL2003 (English) dataset (F. and De Meulder, 2003)) is one of the most commonly used NER datasets. The corpus consists of 1.4K news articles with four types of entities (LOCations, ORGanizations, PERsons, and MISCellaneous) being annotated.

BC5CDR dataset (Li et al., 2016) consists of 1.5K PubMed articles, where two types of entities (chemical and disease) are annotated.

2.3 Down-Sample

To study the relation between model performance and training sample size, we uniformly draw N ($N \in \{50, 150, 500, 1000, 2000\}$) sentences at random from the training split, with the constraint that at least one instance from each IOB (Inside–Outside–Beginning) class is present in the sample.

[1]https://huggingface.co/bert-base-cased

[2]https://huggingface.co/dmis-lab/biobert-v1.1

3 Results

We first establish a baseline using the full dataset, which also serves as an upper bound. Next, we compare the F1 scores for each dataset for different random sample-sizes and for the training subset selected using our proposed method. Finally, we conclude the analysis with a recommended workflow for training instance selection.

3.1 Corpora Domain for Pretraining and Fine-Tuning

We first select a pretrained BERT model for each dataset. Table 2 shows the best F1 score on the test data for CoNLL2003 and BC5CDR datasets, using pretrained BioBERT and BERT.

	CoNLL2003	BC5CDR
BERT	**91.4**	84.9
BioBERT	89.1	**88.2**

Table 2: F1 score on test data for CoNLL2003 and BC5CDR datasets, using different pretrained models BioBERT and BERT. Best performance is observed when the domain for pretraining matches that of the downstream task.

Similar to previous work (Lee et al., 2020; Gururangan et al., 2020), best performance is observed when the domain for language model pretraining matches that of the downstream task. For further experiments, we choose pretrained BERT model for CoNLL2003 dataset and BioBERT for BC5CDR dataset.

3.2 Effect of Sample Size

Next, we fine-tune a BERT language model on the randomly down-sampled datasets of different size, and the F1 performance in entity extraction on the test split is summarized in Figure 1. For sample size below 200 sentences, the model performance

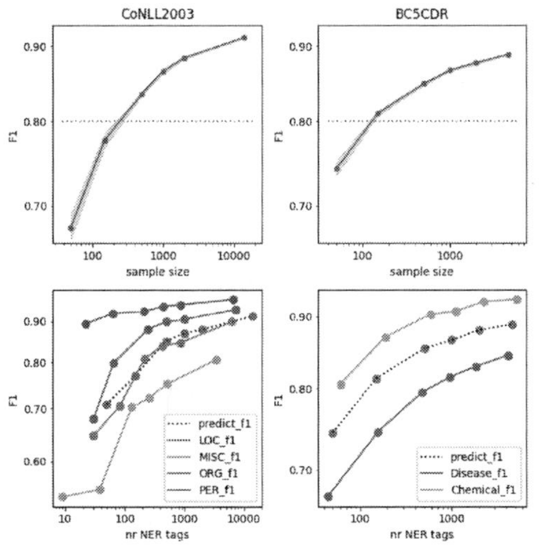

Figure 1: *Top*: performance (micro F1) in entity extraction on the test split for random selection of the training data subset of different sample sizes (number of sentences). The shading represent 95% confidence interval over 8 different runs using the same data and same training parameter. To reach F1 score of 80%, only 150 and 300 sentences are needed for BC5CDR and CoNLL2003 dataset, respectively. *Bottom*: F1 per NER class as a function of the number of tokens tagged per class. We observe a difference in performance between the NER classes, which cannot be explained by the number of respective tokens in the training set.

increases very fast . Above 200 sentences, the increase in F1 score slows down when more training examples become available.

Different fine-tuning runs show very low variance (shown as shaded band in Figure 1). The variance, however, increases as the sample size decreases, as expected.

Within each sample, the number of observations for each entity class may be different from each other. Would the same scaling hold for each entity class? In other words, can the differences in F1 score per class be explained by the differences in the number of observations? Figure 1 plots F1 score per class as a function of number of tokens tagged with that class. We observe that although NER classes with less observations show lower F1 score than those with a larger number of observations, the curves per class do not fall on the same line. This suggests that the difference in the number of observations is not the only reason for the differences in F1 per NER class.

Furthermore, for CoNLL2003, the F1 score for MISC entities shows the lowest value for all sample sizes. The MISC class has the lowest number of observations (see also Table 1), which causes the lower F1-MISC, which in turn reduces the overall F1 score.

3.3 Effect of Sample Seed

In this experiment, we empirically investigate if fine-tuning on different training samples results in similar performance.

10 different random samples of size 50 are generated, following Section 2.3, and F1 performances of the BERT models fine-tuned on the different samples are reported in Table 3. 7 to 8 points difference in F1 score observed between best and worst random samples, which is much higher than the variations between different runs of the same sample. The difference is the highest for the lowest sample size, suggesting the importance of sampling optimization, especially when annotated data is limited.

3.4 Training Instance Selection

The large difference in model performance between different random training samples raises the pos-

	BC5CDR	
sample size	50	150
variation runs std	1.3	0.5
variation runs min-max	3.4	1.4
worst random	66.6	79.3
best random	74.4	81.3
best kernel density	78.5	83.4
	CoNLL2003	
sample size	50	150
variation runs std	2.0	1.3
variation runs min-max	5.3	3.5
worst random	61.6	73.5
best random	70.8	78.2
best kernel density	71.6	75.6

Table 3: F1 score on test split for CoNLL2003 and BC5CDR datasets, finetuned on different training samples (random or selected via our proposed method) of size 50 and 150. The best random sample shows up to 8 points higher F1 than the worst random sample, which is much higher than the variations between 8 different runs of the same sample. The sample guided by kernel density (see section 3.4) improves further over the best random sample.

sibility to improve training instance selection. In order to identify the key features that differentiate a "good" random sample from a "bad" one, we first investigate several potential features to characterise the different random samples, before selecting the two most differential features. Finally, we propose a sampling strategy guided by the identified key features.

Identifying Key Features

Since the goal is to select training instances before annotation, we only include features that can be computed without labeled data. Three types of features are investigated for characterising the training examples. (1) Descriptive statistics including sentence-length and coverage over different documents. (2) "Fluency" measures include perplexity and pseudo-perplexity (Salazar et al., 2020) for masked language model like BERT, which are computed by masking tokens one by one. (3) Diversity measures as recommended in Mccarthy and Jarvis (2010).

The most differentiating features turn out to be sentence length (number of tokens) and pseudo-perplexity, while all three diversity measures are very similar across different samples. Thus we omitted diversity measures in this study and leave it to future research.

Figure 2 top row shows median sentence-length per random sample vs median pseudo-perplexity, where the coloring represents F1 score on the evaluation split when model is trained on this random sample. Fine-tuning model on samples on the periphery tend to result in higher F1 score than those in the center.

Training Instance Selection

2-dimensional kernel density estimation is used to capture the observed relation between sentence length, pseudo-perplexity and F1 score (Figure 2 *bottom*). We then proceed to generate training instances based on the kernel density profile[3]. Different sampling ratios are tested, and the best performing setting is to sample 85% of the training instances from the 15% sentences at the lowest density. The results on the improved training sample can be found in Table 3.

For the BC5CDR dataset, the best sampling achieves F1 of 78.5 and 83.4 for sample size of 50 and 150, respectively. Using the relation in

[3]We release all code for future studies at https://github.com/tugraz-isds/kd

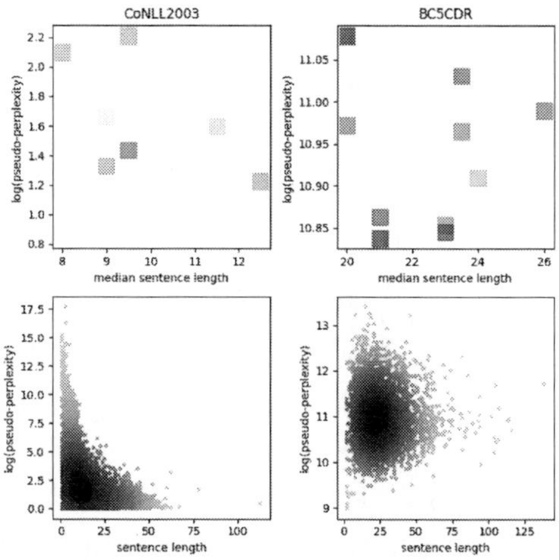

Figure 2: *Top*: Median sentence-length per random sample vs median pseudo-perplexity, where the coloring represents F1 score on the evaluation split when model is trained on this random sample. Fine-tuning model on samples on the periphery result in higher F1 score than those in the center. *Bottom*: Sentence-length vs pseudo-perplexity for all training samples, colored by kernel-density. The random samples with higher F1 scores have median pseudo-perplexity and median sentence length values that are located around the periphery, i.e. the lower density area, especially for the BC5CDR dataset.

Figure 1, this level of F1 is equivalent to the performance of a random sample with size 120 and 400, respectively. In other words, a smart sampling is worth more than twice as many training examples.

For the CoNLL2003 dataset, the F1 score of the optimized sample does not consistently outperform random sampling. Possibly because the Gaussian kernel density estimator does not fit very well to the map with pseudo-perplexity vs sentence length. In addition, the CoNLL2003 dataset shows larger variation over different finetuning runs, and contains sentences that are not as "clean" as those in the BC5CDR dataset. For instance, sentences like *"4-6 7-6 (7-4)"* or *"————————"*.

Compared to the full training set, our best sample with sample size 150 is only 5 points lower in F1, albeit with less than 4% of training data size.

The optimised sampling can also be intuitively understood: (1) longer sentences have higher chance to contain more NER tagged tokens; (2) instances with higher perplexities offer more "learnings" for the pretrained model; (3) samples that weigh more on rare instances are apparently more enabling for BERT language models.

We notice that although our best sampling leads

to 2 - 4 points improvement in F1 over the best random samples, our empirical way for sample selection is possibly only at a local maximum.

Training instance selection work flow

Based on this result, our recommended workflow for training instance selection is summarized in Figure 3.

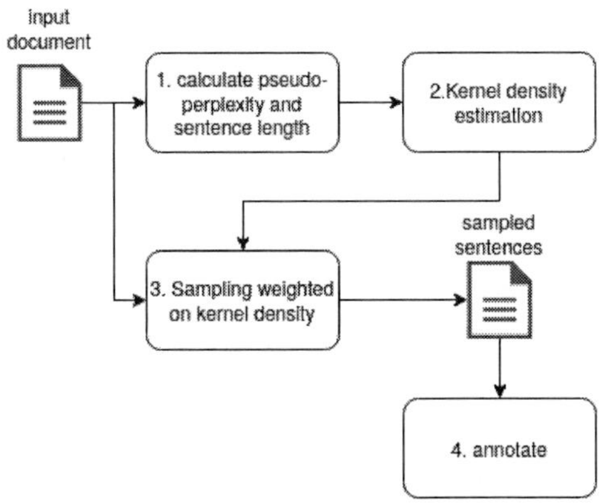

Figure 3: Recommended workflow for annotating customised dataset.

To select the best sample for annotation, first of all, pseudo-perplexity and sentence length should be calculated for all unlabelled text. A kernel density estimator can then be used to fit the relation. Finally, the optimised samples can be drawn weighing on kernel density, before being annotated.

We notice that the proposed workflow differs from typical active learning (Olsson, 2009) approaches, in the sense that no active feedback or interaction with oracle is included. It is thereby a complementary simpler approach for training instance selection.

4 Conclusions

It can be shown that domain-specific pre-trained BERT performs well even when fine-tuned only on small amounts of training samples. Initial increase in amount of data leads to large performance gain before saturating at around 200 training examples. For small data sizes, the F1 scores of different random samples vary greatly.

A sampling strategy is proposed in this work which uses kernel density estimate to balance the instance selection between pseudo-perplexity and sentence length.

The F1 scores of BERT models fine-tuned on training sets constructed using our method are equivalent to the same model fine-tuned on a random sample using twice as many training examples.

This work provides practical guidelines for annotation requirements, namely, data size and sampling strategy. Given the reduced number of training instances needed due to sampling optimisation, data annotation becomes less expensive and can be achievable in more use cases.

Acknowledgements

The research was conducted under the framework of the ECSEL AI4DI "Artificial Intelligence for Digitising Industry" project. The project has received funding from the ECSEL Joint Undertaking (JU) under grant agreement No 826060. The Know-Center is funded within the Austrian COMET Program—Competence Centers for Excellent Technologies under the auspices of the Austrian Federal Ministry of Transport, Innovation and Technology, the Austrian Federal Ministry of Economy, Family and Youth and by the State of Styria. COMET is managed by the Austrian Research Promotion Agency FFG. We acknowledge useful comments and assistance from our colleagues at Know-Center and at Infineon.

References

Jacob Devlin, Ming Wei Chang, Kenton Lee, and Kristina Toutanova. 2019. BERT: Pre-training of deep bidirectional transformers for language understanding. *NAACL HLT 2019 - 2019 Conference of the North American Chapter of the Association for Computational Linguistics: Human Language Technologies - Proceedings of the Conference*, 1(Mlm):4171–4186.

Tjong Kim Sang Erik F. and Fien De Meulder. 2003. Introduction to the CoNLL-2003 shared task: Language-independent named entity recognition. In *Proceedings of the Seventh Conference on Natural Language Learning at HLT-NAACL 2003*, pages 142–147.

Suchin Gururangan, Ana Marasović, Swabha Swayamdipta, Kyle Lo, Iz Beltagy, Doug Downey, and Noah A. Smith. 2020. Don't stop pretraining: Adapt language models to domains and tasks. In *Proceedings of ACL*.

Dan Jurafsky and James H. Martin. 2021. *Speech and Language Processing*.

Jinhyuk Lee, Wonjin Yoon, Sungdong Kim, Donghyeon Kim, Sunkyu Kim, Chan Ho So, and Jaewoo Kang. 2020. BioBERT: A pre-trained biomedical language representation model for biomedical text mining. *Bioinformatics*, 36(4):1234–1240.

Jiao Li, Yueping Sun, Robin J. Johnson, Daniela Sciaky, Chih-Hsuan Wei, Robert Leaman, Allan Peter Davis, Carolyn J. Mattingly, Thomas C. Wiegers, and Zhiyong Lu. 2016. Biocreative V CDR task corpus: a resource for chemical disease relation extraction. *Database*.

Philip Mccarthy and Scott Jarvis. 2010. Mtld, vocd-d, and hd-d: A validation study of sophisticated approaches to lexical diversity assessment. *Behavior research methods*, 42:381–92.

Fredrik Olsson. 2009. A literature survey of active machine learning in the context of natural language processing.

Julian Salazar, Davis Liang, Toan Q. Nguyen, and Katrin Kirchhoff. 2020. Masked Language Model Scoring. pages 2699–2712.

Ashish Vaswani, Noam Shazeer, Niki Parmar, Jakob Uszkoreit, Llion Jones, Aidan N Gomez, Ł ukasz Kaiser, and Illia Polosukhin. 2017. Attention is all you need. In *Advances in Neural Information Processing Systems*, volume 30. Curran Associates, Inc.

Thomas Wolf, Lysandre Debut, Victor Sanh, Julien Chaumond, Clement Delangue, Anthony Moi, Pierric Cistac, Tim Rault, Rémi Louf, Morgan Funtowicz, Joe Davison, Sam Shleifer, Patrick von Platen, Clara Ma, Yacine Jernite, Julien Plu, Canwen Xu, Teven Le Scao, Sylvain Gugger, Mariama Drame, Quentin Lhoest, and Alexander M. Rush. 2020. Transformers: State-of-the-art natural language processing. In *Proceedings of the 2020 Conference on Empirical Methods in Natural Language Processing: System Demonstrations*, pages 38–45, Online. Association for Computational Linguistics.

Yukun Zhu, Ryan Kiros, Rich Zemel, Ruslan Salakhutdinov, Raquel Urtasun, Antonio Torralba, and Sanja Fidler. 2015. Aligning books and movies: Towards story-like visual explanations by watching movies and reading books. In *2015 IEEE International Conference on Computer Vision (ICCV)*, pages 19–27.

Analysing the Correlation between Lexical Ambiguity and Translation Quality in a Multimodal Setting using WordNet

Ali Hatami, Paul Buitelaar and Mihael Arcan
Insight SFI Research Centre for Data Analytics,
Data Science Institute, National University of Ireland Galway
firstname.lastname@insight-centre.org

Abstract

Multimodal Neural Machine Translation is focusing on using visual information to translate sentences in the source language into the target language. The main idea is to utilise information from visual modalities to promote the output quality of the text-based translation model. Although the recent multimodal strategies extract the most relevant visual information in images, the effectiveness of using visual information on translation quality changes based on the text dataset. Due to this, this work studies the impact of leveraging visual information in multimodal translation models of ambiguous sentences. Our experiments analyse the Multi30k evaluation dataset and calculate ambiguity scores of sentences based on the WordNet hierarchical structure. To calculate the ambiguity of a sentence, we extract the ambiguity scores for all nouns based on the number of senses in WordNet. The main goal is to find in which sentences, visual content can improve the text-based translation model. We report the correlation between the ambiguity scores and translation quality extracted for all sentences in the English-German dataset.

1 Introduction

In recent years, Neural Machine Translation (NMT) model is widely used in translation tasks and represents remarkable performance in terms of fluency and precision compared with the previous generations of machine translation. Recurrent Neural Network (RNN)-based NMT with Attention mechanism has found broad application in different fields of NLP tasks such as machine translation. The transformer model as a Self-attention based model has been introduced by Google in 2017 as a new architecture for NMT (Vaswani et al., 2017). The self-attention mechanism uses cross-lingual attention that allows the input words to interact with each other (self) and find out which one should pay more attention to (attention). In addition to the mechanism of cross-lingual attention, the transformer model uses a stacked self-attention layer that follows with a point-wise feed-forward component. Recently many studies in machine translation have been increasingly focusing on using visual content well as textual to improve the translation quality. Therefore, Multimodal Neural Machine Translation (MNMT) as a subarea of NMT has been introduced to use visual information extracted from other modalities such as speech, image or video to translate a sentence in a source language into the target language.

MNMT is an area of research that plays an important role in machine translation tasks since multimodal resources have been increasingly used in deep learning techniques. MNMT tries to extend the ability of the NMT models by taking visual context such as images as an additional input to better translate the source text. The main idea behind this is that the textual context does not provide sufficient information for the text-based NMT model in some situations to translate ambiguous sentences (ambiguous terms or grammatical gender). Due to this, visual information can enrich text-best NMT systems by adding extra information to disambiguate the input words and provide correct translations on the target side.

One of the main ideas of using multimodality in Machine Translation is that visual information can help the textual context to find the correct sense of ambiguous words in the translation process of the source sentence. For example, the word "track" in the English sentence "A man is performing a trick on a track" is an ambiguous word and could have at least two different translations in German – (1) "*Ein Mann führt einen Trick auf einer Strecke aus*", and (2) "*Ein Mann führt einen Trick auf einem Bahngleis aus*". Given the word "track", the context does not provide enough information to disambiguate and translate it correctly. Therefore, multimodal resources such as images can guide the

Proceedings of the 2022 Conference of the North American Chapter of the Association for Computational Linguistics: Human Language Technologies: Student Research Workshop, pages 89 - 95
July 10-15, 2022

translation system to select the correct sense based on the visual information. Word Sense Disambiguation (WSD) is widely studied in different natural language processing tasks. WSD analyses given the context of an ambiguous word to assign the correct sense based on a pre-defined sense net for words. Visual Sense Disambiguation (VSD) as a modified version of WSD use visual context instead of textual to disambiguate words. Although disambiguation of word sense can be done directly by Machine Translation models, research on Multimodal Machine Translation more focuses on analysing of contributions of each modality to disambiguate words in the translation process.

In this work, we focus on identifying ambiguous sentences and leverage therefore the WordNet hierarchical structure to calculate an ambiguity score for each sentence. This is then used to study a correlation between ambiguity and translation evaluation scores. Analysing the lexical ambiguity and translation quality allowed us to identify sentences that are more challenging in the translation process and most likely visual content can help the text-based NMT to translate sentences more accurate.

2 Related Work

Multimodal Machine Translation is a new trend in machine translation tasks that aims to create multimodal frameworks to use information from visual modality as well as text context (Specia et al., 2016). Different practices were used for the visual part of the MMT framework. The common approach is to extract visual information by using Convolutional Neural Networks (CNN) and then integrate this information with textual features (Yao and Wan, 2020). Many MMT models were developed based on the Transformer approach. The transformer approach extracts the relationships between words in the source and target sentences by using a multihead self-attention mechanism (Vaswani et al., 2017)

In some studies, the global image features are used in the encoder beside word sequences to use both types of features in the decoding stage (Huang et al., 2016) or used to initialise the hidden parameters of the encoder and decoder in RNN (Calixto and Liu, 2017). (Caglayan et al., 2017) use elementwise multiplication to initialise hidden states of encoder/decoder in the attention-based model. (Zhou et al., 2018) links visual and corresponding text semantically by using a visual attention mechanism.

Despite successfully using multimodal information in MMT, recent studies show that most of the information in the image is not related to the text while the translation process and when there is limited textual information, visual content plays more important for the translation model (Caglayan et al., 2019). The studies use visual features by focusing on relative importance among different modalities. (Lala et al., 2018) introduced a multimodal cross-lingual word sense disambiguation model based on Multimodal Lexical Translation Dataset (MLTD) (Lala and Specia, 2018) to generate contextually correct translations for the ambiguous words. MLTD includes a list of words of the source language with multiple translations in the training set of Multi30k. (Ive et al., 2019) introduced a translate-and-refine mechanism by using images in a second stage decoder to refine the text-based NMT model in the ambiguous words listed in MLT dataset. (Calixto et al., 2019) use a latent variable model to extract the multimodal relationships between modalities. Recent methods try to reduce the noise of visual information and select visual features related to the text. (Yao and Wan, 2020) use a multimodal transformer-based self-attention to encode relevant information in images. To capture various relationships, (Yin et al., 2020) propose a graph-based multimodal fusion encoder.

3 Experimental Setup

This section provides insights on the dataset used in this work, neural architectures and the translation evaluation metric BLEU.

3.1 Multi30K Dataset

Multi30K (Elliott et al., 2016) is an extended version of the Flickr30K dataset that includes images and paired descriptions expressed by one English sentence and translated sentences in multiple languages. Firstly, the German translation was added to the dataset (Young et al., 2014) and then it extended to French and Czech (Elliott et al., 2017) (Barrault et al., 2018). Many recent models in MNMT have focused on Multi30K as it provides an image for each sentence in English and three translation directions, i.e. in German, French and Czech. In this study, the evaluation dataset of Multi30k contains 1,000 instances.

3.2 Text-based NMT

OpenNMT (Klein et al., 2018) is used to train the text-based NMT model on a general En-De dataset. The model used a 6-layer transformer mechanism for both the encoder and decoder stage. We trained the model for 50,000 steps on a general dataset and set the parameters of the model to the original implementations of OpenNMT.

As the text-based NMT system cannot leverage the visual information, and to ensure a broad lexical and domain coverage of our text-based NMT system, we merged existing parallel for the English-German language pair from the OPUS web page[1] into one parallel corpus, i.e., Europarl (Koehn, 2005), DGT (Steinberger et al., 2014), EMEA, KDE4, OpenOffice (Tiedemann, 2009), OpenSubtitles2012 (Tiedemann, 2012), and randomly selected 10 million sentences for our training step.

3.3 Doubly-attentive MNMT

For the visual side, we used the model that proposed in (Zhao et al., 2020) to apply semantic image region features[2] for MNMT. This model is based on the Doubly-attentive mechanism (Calixto and Liu, 2017) to integrate visual and textual features by applying 100 semantic image features with a dimension of 2,048 at each time step. The hidden state dimension of the visual model is 500 for both 2-layer GRU encoder and 2-layer GRU decoder. The work also set the dimension of the source word embedding to 500, batch size to 400, beam size to 5, text dropout to 0.3, and image region dropout to 0.5. After training the model for 25 epochs using stochastic gradient descent with ADADELTA (Zeiler, 2012) and a learning rate of 0.002, the model of epoch 16 has been selected based on comparing BLEU scores of the final models.

3.4 Evaluation Metric

We report the automatic evaluation based on BLEU for the automatic evaluation. BLEU (Papineni et al., 2002) is calculated for individual translated segments (n-grams) by comparing them with a dataset of reference translations. For this work we use the *sacrebleu*[3] library (Post, 2018).

[1]`https://opus.nlpl.eu/`

[2]`https://github.com/Zhao-Yuting/MNMT-with-semantic-regions`

[3]`https://github.com/mjpost/sacrebleu`

3.5 Princeton WordNet

Princeton WordNet (Fellbaum, 1998) is a manually created resource that has been used in many different tasks and applications across linguistics and natural language processing. WordNet's hierarchical structure makes it a useful tool for many semantic applications and it also plays a vital role in various deep learning approaches (Rychalska et al., 2016).

3.6 Correlation Coefficients

The correlation coefficient is a measure to determine the relationship between two variables (Janse et al., 2021). In correlated data, the change in the magnitude of one variable leads to a change in the magnitude of another variable either in the same or in the opposite directions. Pearson product-moment correlation is a typical type of correlation for a linear relationship between two continuous variables. The range of the correlation coefficient is between -1 and +1, where 0 shows that there is no correlation between the two variables. The correlation coefficient near +1 and -1 shows a strong, same or opposite, correlation respectively. The equation for the correlation coefficient is:

$$Correl(X,Y) = \frac{\sum(x-\bar{x})(y-\bar{y})}{\sqrt{\sum(x-\bar{x})^2\sum(y-\bar{y})^2}}$$

where $\bar{x}$ and $\bar{y}$ are the sample means of array *X* and *Y* respectively.

4 Methodology

In this section, we explain our methodology to calculate the ambiguity scores for each sentence based on the hierarchical structure of WordNet. To find a meaningful relationship between ambiguity and translation quality, we analyse the correlation functions between different ambiguity scores and the translation evaluation metric BLEU. Our focus in this work is on the inherited structure of English nouns in WordNet. Each noun in WordNet can be defined as a set *W* of pairs *(w,s)* where *w* is a word in that language and a sense *s* is possible set of meanings (synonyms or *synsets*) for the word *w*. Table 1 shows all *synset* entries (11) for the noun *track* in WordNet. The inherited structure in WordNet is a hierarchical structure to organise the semantic relations of *synsets*. Furthermore, synsets in WordNet have different hierarchical structures from each other including *hyponymy* and *hypernymy*. Figure 1 shows the WordNet inherited structure of *synset* entries for the word *track*. *Entity*

path, track, course	a line or route along which something travels or moves
lead, track, trail	evidence pointing to a possible solution
track	a pair of parallel rails providing a runway for wheels
racetrack, racecourse, raceway, track	a course over which races are run
cut, track	a distinct selection of music from a recording or a compact disc
track, caterpillar track, caterpillar tread	an endless metal belt on which tracked vehicles move over the ground
track, data track	one of the circular magnetic paths on a magnetic disk that serve ... for writing and reading data
track	a groove on a phonograph recording
track, rail, rails, runway	a bar or pair of parallel bars of rolled steel making the railway along which railroad ... can roll
track, cart track, cartroad	any road or path affording passage especially a rough one
track, running	the act of participating in an athletic competition involving running on a track

Table 1: Synset entries (11) for the word *track* in the Princeton WordNet.

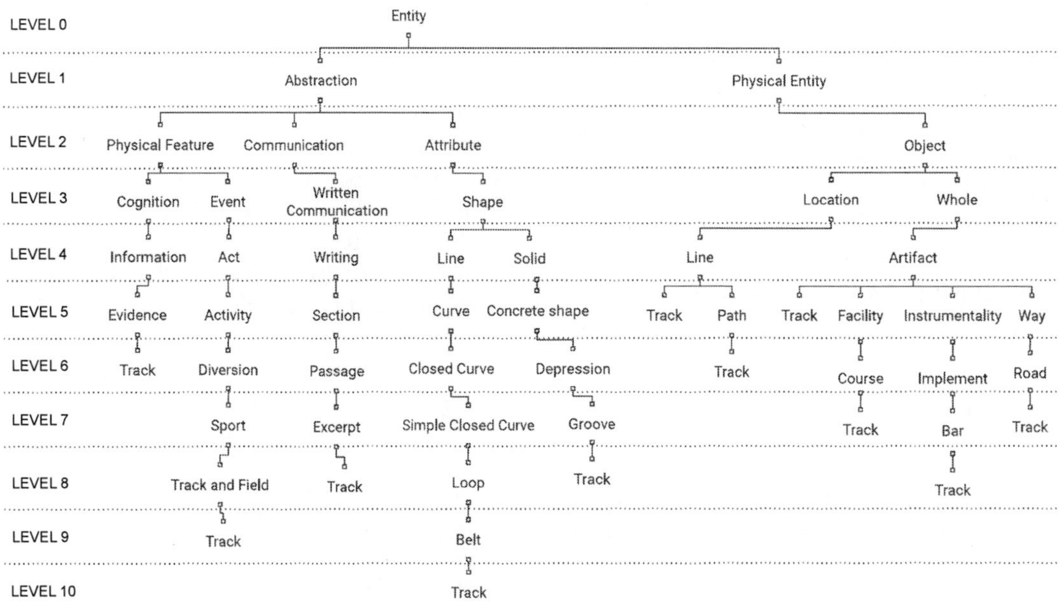

Figure 1: Hierarchical structure of the WordNet entry *track*.

(level 0), is the root node for all *synset* entries in WordNet. Each path between the root node and a *synset* entry has a different length that shows the different abstraction level. For example of the word *track*, `min_length` has a path length of 4, with six unique abstract concepts (*Information, Act, Writing, Line, Solid, Artifact*). On the other hand, `min_length-1` at the path length of 3, has six concepts as well, i.e. *Cognition, Event, Written Communication, Shape, Location, Whole*. The number of all *synsets* for *track* in WordNet is 11. After extracting this information for each word, we use the `sum` and `multiply` functions on all nouns of a sentence to calculate the overall ambiguity score (see example in Table 2 for the sentence *Dog runs at a track*). We normalised these scores by dividing them by the number of content words (nouns with more than one synset in WordNet) of the sentence to minimise the effect of sentence length on our experiments.

5 Results

This section provides the results of our experiments. After calculating ambiguity and BLEU scores (NMT, MNMT) for each sentence in the test set, we analysed the correlation coefficients between ambiguity and translation quality scores to find a meaningful relationship between them. To better analyse the correlation between the sentence ambiguity and translation quality, we grouped them into sets of 50 sentences (resulting in 20 groups) after ranking them by the ambiguity score. The corpus BLEU scores for NMT and MNMT on the evaluation dataset in En-De are 30.66 and 35.80 respectively.

Table 3 illustrates the correlation score (see Sec-

Approach	# of Concepts	# Nouns	Ambiguity
Sum(synsets)	7 + 11	2	9.0
Sum(min_length)	7 + 10	2	8.5
Sum(min_length-1)	6 + 6	2	6.0
Multiply(synsets)	7 * 11	2	38.5
Multiply(min_length)	7 * 10	2	35.0
Multiply(min_length-1)	6 * 6	2	18.0

Table 2: Examples of calculating the ambiguity score based on the number of concepts of each word, i.e. *dog* and *track*, at the certain hierarchical level, normalised with the set of nouns in the sentence.

Approach	NMT	MNMT
Sum(Synsets)	0.3987	0.3841
Sum(min_length)	0.2226	0.0445
Sum(min_length-1)	0.1017	-0.0453
Multiply(Synsets)	-0.5511	-0.6744
Multiply(min_length)	-0.5846	-0.6020
Multiply(min_length-1)	-0.5292	-0.6039

Table 3: Correlation between the calculated ambiguity scores and BLEU metric for NMT and MNMT on 20 groups.

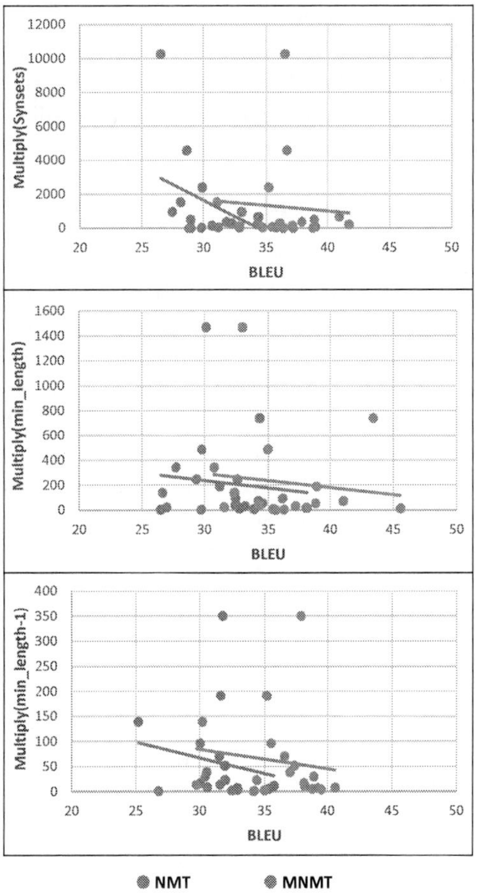

Figure 2: Correlation representation between the Multiply approach's ambiguity scores and the BLEU metric for NMT and MNMT on 20 groups.

tion 3.6), ambiguity scores and the BLEU evaluation metric for the approaches used to calculate the ambiguity scores of the sentences. As seen in the table, the best correlations for NMT and MNMT are obtained by the `Multiply(min_length)` and `Multiply(Synsets)` approaches respectively. Due to this, we focused on the `Multiply` approaches and provide graphs, which illustrate the correlation between the ambiguity and translation quality.

As seen in Figure 2 the ambiguity score calculated by the WordNet hierarchy correlates with the translation quality, i.e., if the ambiguity of a sentence is high, the translation quality in terms of BLEU is low. On the other hand, if the ambiguity of a sentence is low, the translation quality in terms of the BLEU metric improves. This can be seen for all methods used to calculate the ambiguity, i.e. `synsets`, `min_length`, `min_length-1`. In addition to that, the graphs also illustrate the better performance of the MNMT system (orange points) compared to the text-based NMT system (blue points).

6 Conclusion

Recent studies in Multimodal Machine Translation focused on using visual information to improve the quality of translation tasks. One of the main challenges for the translation systems is to find a correct translation in terms of the context used. Despite the progress of research in this area, the performance of multimodal translation systems is more related to the quality of visual content which is used along with textual dataset. In this study, we analysed different approaches to calculate the ambiguity of the sentence to find a correlation between sentence ambiguity and the translation quality in terms of the BLEU metric. We tested different approaches to calculate the ambiguity and observed that multiplying the number of entries at the minimum length level of the WordNet hierarchy for each noun provided the best correlation to the evaluation metric for each sentence. Within our future work, we plan to consider the frequency and further linguistic features of WordNet synsets. In addition to that, we plan to leverage the Polylingual Wordnet (Arcan et al., 2019), a large multilingual WordNet in more than 20 European languages, to calculate the lexical ambiguity beyond English. Furthermore, we plan the incorporation of ImageNet (Deng et al., 2009), which has an image dataset organised according to the WordNet hierarchy.

Acknowledgements

This publication has emanated from research conducted with the financial support of Science Foundation Ireland (SFI) under Grant Number SFI/12/RC/2289_P2, co-funded by the European Regional Development Fund. For the purpose of Open Access, the author has applied a CC BY public copyright licence to any Author Accepted Manuscript version arising from this submission. We would like to thank the anonymous reviewers for their insights on this work.

References

Mihael Arcan, John P. McCrae, and Paul Buitelaar. 2019. Polylingual wordnet. *CoRR*, abs/1903.01411.

Loïc Barrault, Fethi Bougares, Lucia Specia, Chiraag Lala, Desmond Elliott, and Stella Frank. 2018. Findings of the third shared task on multimodal machine translation. In *Proceedings of the Third Conference on Machine Translation: Shared Task Papers*, pages 304–323, Belgium, Brussels. Association for Computational Linguistics.

Ozan Caglayan, Walid Aransa, Adrien Bardet, Mercedes García-Martínez, Fethi Bougares, Loïc Barrault, Marc Masana, Luis Herranz, and Joost van de Weijer. 2017. LIUM-CVC submissions for WMT17 multimodal translation task. In *Proceedings of the Second Conference on Machine Translation*, pages 432–439, Copenhagen, Denmark. Association for Computational Linguistics.

Ozan Caglayan, Pranava Madhyastha, Lucia Specia, and Loïc Barrault. 2019. Probing the need for visual context in multimodal machine translation. In *Proceedings of the 2019 Conference of the North American Chapter of the Association for Computational Linguistics: Human Language Technologies, Volume 1 (Long and Short Papers)*, pages 4159–4170, Minneapolis, Minnesota. Association for Computational Linguistics.

Iacer Calixto and Qun Liu. 2017. Incorporating global visual features into attention-based neural machine translation. In *Proceedings of the 2017 Conference on Empirical Methods in Natural Language Processing*, pages 992–1003, Copenhagen, Denmark. Association for Computational Linguistics.

Iacer Calixto, Miguel Rios, and Wilker Aziz. 2019. Latent variable model for multi-modal translation. In *Proceedings of the 57th Annual Meeting of the Association for Computational Linguistics*, pages 6392–6405, Florence, Italy. Association for Computational Linguistics.

Jia Deng, Wei Dong, Richard Socher, Li-Jia Li, Kai Li, and Li Fei-Fei. 2009. Imagenet: A large-scale hierarchical image database. In *2009 IEEE Conference on Computer Vision and Pattern Recognition*, pages 248–255.

Desmond Elliott, Stella Frank, Loïc Barrault, Fethi Bougares, and Lucia Specia. 2017. Findings of the second shared task on multimodal machine translation and multilingual image description. In *Proceedings of the Second Conference on Machine Translation*, pages 215–233, Copenhagen, Denmark. Association for Computational Linguistics.

Desmond Elliott, Stella Frank, Khalil Sima'an, and Lucia Specia. 2016. Multi30K: Multilingual English-German image descriptions. In *Proceedings of the 5th Workshop on Vision and Language*, pages 70–74, Berlin, Germany. Association for Computational Linguistics.

Christiane Fellbaum. 1998. *WordNet: An Electronic Lexical Database*. Bradford Books.

Po-Yao Huang, Frederick Liu, Sz-Rung Shiang, Jean Oh, and Chris Dyer. 2016. Attention-based multimodal neural machine translation. In *Proceedings of the First Conference on Machine Translation: Volume 2, Shared Task Papers*, pages 639–645, Berlin, Germany. Association for Computational Linguistics.

Julia Ive, Pranava Madhyastha, and Lucia Specia. 2019. Distilling translations with visual awareness. In *Proceedings of the 57th Annual Meeting of the Association for Computational Linguistics*, pages 6525–6538, Florence, Italy. Association for Computational Linguistics.

Roemer J Janse, Tiny Hoekstra, Kitty J Jager, Carmine Zoccali, Giovanni Tripepi, Friedo W Dekker, and Merel van Diepen. 2021. Conducting correlation analysis: important limitations and pitfalls. *Clinical Kidney Journal*, 14(11):2332–2337.

Guillaume Klein, Yoon Kim, Yuntian Deng, Vincent Nguyen, Jean Senellart, and Alexander Rush. 2018. OpenNMT: Neural machine translation toolkit. In *Proceedings of the 13th Conference of the Association for Machine Translation in the Americas (Volume 1: Research Track)*, pages 177–184, Boston, MA. Association for Machine Translation in the Americas.

Philipp Koehn. 2005. Europarl: A Parallel Corpus for Statistical Machine Translation. In *Conference Proceedings: the tenth Machine Translation Summit*. AAMT.

Chiraag Lala, Pranava Swaroop Madhyastha, Carolina Scarton, and Lucia Specia. 2018. Sheffield submissions for WMT18 multimodal translation shared task. In *Proceedings of the Third Conference on Machine*

Translation: Shared Task Papers, pages 624–631, Belgium, Brussels. Association for Computational Linguistics.

Chiraag Lala and Lucia Specia. 2018. Multimodal lexical translation. In *Proceedings of the Eleventh International Conference on Language Resources and Evaluation (LREC 2018)*, Miyazaki, Japan. European Language Resources Association (ELRA).

Kishore Papineni, Salim Roukos, Todd Ward, and Wei-Jing Zhu. 2002. BLEU: a method for automatic evaluation of machine translation. In *Proceedings of the 40th Annual Meeting on Association for Computational Linguistics*, ACL '02, pages 311–318.

Matt Post. 2018. A call for clarity in reporting BLEU scores. In *Proceedings of the Third Conference on Machine Translation: Research Papers*, pages 186–191, Belgium, Brussels. Association for Computational Linguistics.

Barbara Rychalska, Katarzyna Pakulska, Krystyna Chodorowska, Wojciech Walczak, and Piotr Andruszkiewicz. 2016. Samsung Poland NLP team at SemEval-2016 task 1: Necessity for methods to measure semantic similarity. In *Proceedings of the 10th International Workshop on Semantic Evaluation*, pages 614–620.

Lucia Specia, Stella Frank, Khalil Sima'an, and Desmond Elliott. 2016. A shared task on multimodal machine translation and crosslingual image description. In *Proceedings of the First Conference on Machine Translation: Volume 2, Shared Task Papers*, pages 543–553, Berlin, Germany. Association for Computational Linguistics.

Ralf Steinberger, Mohamed Ebrahim, Alexandros Poulis, Manuel Carrasco-Benitez, Patrick Schlüter, Marek Przybyszewski, and Signe Gilbro. 2014. An overview of the european union's highly multilingual parallel corpora. *Language Resources and Evaluation*, 48(4):679–707.

Jorg Tiedemann. 2009. News from OPUS – A Collection of Multilingual Parallel Corpora with Tools and Interfaces. In *Advances in Natural Language Processing*, volume V, chapter V, pages 237–248. Borovets, Bulgaria.

Jörg Tiedemann. 2012. Character-based pivot translations for under-resourced languages and domains. In *Proceedings of the 13th Conference of the European Chapter of the Association for Computational Linguistics (EACL)*, pages 141–151, Avignon, France.

Ashish Vaswani, Noam Shazeer, Niki Parmar, Jakob Uszkoreit, Llion Jones, Aidan N Gomez, Ł ukasz Kaiser, and Illia Polosukhin. 2017. Attention is all you need. In *Advances in Neural Information Processing Systems*, volume 30. Curran Associates, Inc.

Shaowei Yao and Xiaojun Wan. 2020. Multimodal transformer for multimodal machine translation. In *Proceedings of the 58th Annual Meeting of the Association for Computational Linguistics*, pages 4346–4350, Online. Association for Computational Linguistics.

Yongjing Yin, Fandong Meng, Jinsong Su, Chulun Zhou, Zhengyuan Yang, Jie Zhou, and Jiebo Luo. 2020. A novel graph-based multi-modal fusion encoder for neural machine translation. In *ACL*.

Peter Young, Alice Lai, Micah Hodosh, and Julia Hockenmaier. 2014. From image descriptions to visual denotations: New similarity metrics for semantic inference over event descriptions. *Transactions of the Association for Computational Linguistics*, 2:67–78.

Matthew D. Zeiler. 2012. ADADELTA: an adaptive learning rate method. *CoRR*, abs/1212.5701.

Yuting Zhao, Mamoru Komachi, Tomoyuki Kajiwara, and Chenhui Chu. 2020. Double attention-based multimodal neural machine translation with semantic image regions. In *Proceedings of the 22nd Annual Conference of the European Association for Machine Translation*, pages 105–114, Lisboa, Portugal. European Association for Machine Translation.

Mingyang Zhou, Runxiang Cheng, Yong Jae Lee, and Zhou Yu. 2018. A visual attention grounding neural model for multimodal machine translation. In *Proceedings of the 2018 Conference on Empirical Methods in Natural Language Processing*, pages 3643–3653, Brussels, Belgium. Association for Computational Linguistics.

Building a Personalized Dialogue System with Prompt-Tuning

Tomohito Kasahara[1], Daisuke Kawahara[1], Nguyen Tung[2], Shengzhe Li[2], Kenta Shinzato[2], Toshinori Sato[2]
[1]Waseda University, [2]LINE Corporation
{tomo_k@ruri.,dkw@}waseda.jp
{tung.nguyen,shengzhe.li,kenta.shinzato,toshinori.sato}@linecorp.com

Abstract

Dialogue systems without consistent responses are not fascinating. In this study, we build a dialogue system that can respond based on a given character setting (persona) to bring consistency. Considering the trend of the rapidly increasing scale of language models, we propose an approach that uses prompt-tuning, which has low learning costs, on pre-trained large-scale language models. The results of automatic and manual evaluations in English and Japanese show that it is possible to build a dialogue system with more natural and personalized responses using less computational resources than fine-tuning.

1 Introduction

Large dialogue corpora used to train dialogue systems using neural network models contain utterances from various speakers. This has the disadvantage that the trained system is often inconsistent in the generated utterances (Li et al., 2016b). For example, after the system says, "I am from Tokyo," it might say, "I am from Kyoto."

We aim to build a dialogue system that can respond based on a persona to avoid inconsistent utterances. A simple method of giving a persona to a model can be to concatenate the persona to the model's input in natural language (Zhang et al., 2018). However, this method is not suitable because the more persona information is added, the longer the input text becomes. Therefore, we propose to freeze all parameters of a pre-trained language model and add a new fixed-length prompt before the input token sequence to embed the persona information. Specifically, only the embedding vectors of the added prompt are optimized using a dialogue corpus in which utterances are made based on the persona.

We conduct experiments on two languages: English and Japanese. Automatic and manual evaluations show that our method can build a dialogue system capable of natural responses based on a persona. Since our approach does not update the parameters of the pre-trained model, it can reduce the computational cost required for training. We also show that it is possible to build a personalized dialogue system with even a small dataset consisting of hundreds to thousands of utterance-response pairs.

2 Related Work

2.1 Prompt-Tuning

With the advent of pre-trained models such as BERT (Devlin et al., 2019) and T5 (Raffel et al., 2020), a method that adapts a pre-trained model to a target task by fine-tuning has become mainstream. However, as the scale of models grows and the cost of fine-tuning increases, methods for adapting a pre-trained model to a target task without updating their parameters are gaining attention.

Brown et al. (2020) proposed a zero/few-shot learning method based on language models with manually created task descriptions and zero/a few task examples (collectively called *prompt*). Although there are some studies on improving this method (Reynolds and McDonell, 2021; Zhao et al., 2021), they are inferior to fine-tuning in terms of accuracy.

Prompt-tuning is a method for automatically optimizing a prompt without creating it by manual labor. There are two kinds of methods in prompt-tuning: one is to select the best words from a discrete vocabulary (Shin et al., 2020), and the other is to optimize continuous embedding vectors (Qin and Eisner, 2021; Li and Liang, 2021; Lester et al., 2021; Liu et al., 2021; Vu et al., 2021). Prefix-tuning (Lester et al., 2021; Li and Liang, 2021) adds a sequence of tokens, called prefix tokens, to the beginning of the input and optimizes only their embedding vectors. There is also a study on multimodal prompt-tuning for images and natural

Proceedings of the 2022 Conference of the North American Chapter of the Association for Computational Linguistics: Human Language Technologies: Student Research Workshop, pages 96 - 105

language (Tsimpoukelli et al., 2021).

2.2 Persona-Based Dialogue Systems

According to Roller et al. (2021), for dialogue systems to interact more naturally with humans, it is essential to consider three perspectives: having a consistent personality, having knowledge, and having emotions and empathy for the interlocutor. Among these three perspectives, we focus on personality because we believe that it is the most important to generate consistent responses.

The Persona-Chat dataset (Zhang et al., 2018) is a dataset created with the goal of adding personality to a dialogue system. It consists of multi-turn dialogues between two crowdworkers, each of whom is given approximately five persona sentences, which describe their character settings. There are 1,155 personas in the Persona-Chat dataset. There are two types of persona sentences per persona: *original*, which the worker used in the dialogue, and *revised*, which is a paraphrased version of the original. In the experiments conducted by Zhang et al. (2018), models were trained using all the data in the Persona-Chat dataset, which contains utterances based on various personas. On the other hand, our method uses dialogue data uttered based on only one persona to train models. There is also a Japanese version of the Persona-Chat dataset, JPersonaChat (Sugiyama et al., 2021). Other dialogue corpora that contain speaker persona information include PersonalDialog (Zheng et al., 2019) and a corpus of dialogue data from Reddit (Mazaré et al., 2018). Zheng et al. (2019) proposed a method to add encoded persona information to the input before it is fed into a seq2seq model.

3 Method

This section describes our proposed method. The detailed setup for our experiments is described in Sections 4.1 and 4.2.

3.1 Proposed Model

We propose a Transformer-based model with an additional embedding layer for tokens that embed persona information. We refer to these tokens as *persona info tokens*. The architecture and input-output relation of the proposed model are shown in Figure 1.

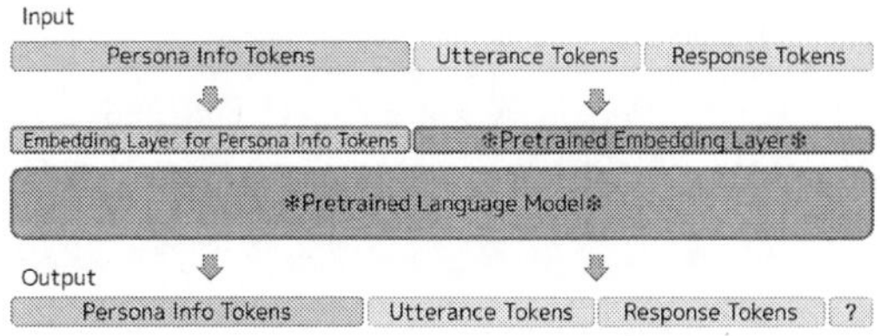

Figure 1: Architecture and input-output relation of the proposed model. All parameters of the pre-trained language model and its embedding layer are frozen. Only the newly added embedding layer for persona info tokens is tuned.

3.2 Datasets

Conversations in daily life are not always related to personal information (Song et al., 2021). To allow the model to generate not only utterances that are related to the persona but also utterances that are not related to the persona, we make a dialogue dataset that consists of two types of datasets. The first is a dialogue dataset where each utterance is based on the persona, and the second is a dialogue dataset that is not related to the persona.

3.3 Training

The newly added embedding layer embeds persona info tokens, and the embedding layer of the pre-trained language model embeds each pair of utterance and response (which consists of tokens already generated during training). These embedding vectors are combined and then input into the model. During training, the cross-entropy loss is calculated for the output tokens of the response sentence, and only the parameters of the embedding layer for the persona info tokens are updated.

The embedding layer for the persona info tokens is initialized with the persona sentences included in the Persona-Chat dataset. These sentences are embedded into vectors by the embedding layer of the pre-trained language model and then used for initialization. If the number of the tokens of the persona sentences is less than the length of the persona info tokens, the persona sentences are repeatedly arranged until the number is satisfied.

4 Experiments

Based on the method in Section 3, we build a personalized dialogue system. We used Hugging Face's Transformers to build the system and the NVIDIA A100 SXM4 GPU with a GPU memory size of 40 GB. The main experiments are conducted in English, and the results of additional experiments in Japanese are included at the end of this section.

4.1 Datasets Setup

We use the Persona-Chat dataset[1] and DailyDialog (Li et al., 2017)[2] for our experiments in English.

4.1.1 Training Datasets

First, the multi-turn dialogues in the Persona-Chat dataset are divided into two utterances of one round trip. We refer to this pair of two utterances as *a dialogue pair*. The dialogue pairs are aggregated according to the persona type given to the responder. There are 1,155 personas in the Persona-Chat dataset, but we use the three personas with the most dialogue pairs in our experiments. The reason for this is that we intend to experiment with a relatively large number of dialogue pairs even in the small dataset. The number of dialogue pairs based on these three personas is 185, 167, and 166, respectively. Three models corresponding to the three personas are trained and evaluated for each experimental setup. The aggregated dialogue pairs are divided into training and evaluation pairs in a ratio of 9:1.

The Persona-Chat dataset does not contain many short utterances or utterances unrelated to persona. To add utterances that are short and not related to persona to the dataset, we also use dialogue pairs contained in DailyDialog whose topic is Relationship,[3] which contains many such utterances. Among them, dialogue pairs in which the lengths of both the utterance and the response are less than 50 characters are mixed into the training datasets in a certain ratio. Based on the results of preliminary experiments, we determined the ratio of dialogue pairs added from DailyDialog to the number of those obtained from the Persona-Chat dataset as 1:1. We call this *the ratio of the training datasets*.

4.1.2 Evaluation Datasets

We made two datasets for evaluation: the persona eval dataset and the general eval dataset. The persona eval dataset is 10% of the 9:1 dataset described in Section 4.1.1. The general eval dataset consists of dialogue pairs obtained from DailyDialog under the same conditions as in Section 4.1.1, but not used for training.

[1]https://github.com/facebookresearch/ParlAI/tree/main/parlai/tasks/personachat

[2]https://aclanthology.org/I17-1099/

[3]Each dialogue is assigned a topic. There are ten topics: Attitude & Emotion, Culture & Education, Finance, Health, Ordinary Life, Politics, Relationship, School Life, Tourism, and Work.

Training Method	Model	Dist-1	Dist-2
Fine-Tuning (added)	GPT2-XL	0.199	0.526
Fine-Tuning (none)	GPT2-XL	0.210	0.568
Prompt-Tuning	GPT2-XL	0.177	0.494
Prompt-Tuning	GPT-J-6B	**0.213**	**0.595**

Table 1: Results of automatic evaluation by distinct-1, 2. The prompt-tuned GPT-J-6B model generates the most diverse responses. "Added" and "none" mean whether the persona sentences are added to the input sentence or not.

4.2 Model Setup

To compare our prompt-tuning model with fine-tuning, we use the datasets in Section 4.1 and tune the pre-trained models of GPT series. We use two model sizes: GPT2-XL (1.5B parameters) and GPT-J-6B (Wang and Komatsuzaki, 2021). Fine-tuning of the GPT-J-6B model is not tested due to the lack of GPU memory.

The hyperparameters for prompt-tuning are based on the settings of (Lester et al., 2021). The length of the persona info tokens was set to 200 based on the results of preliminary experiments. The strategy for generating the response sentences is the greedy search. The number of epochs was set to a value such that the loss during learning converges. For fine-tuning, we experimented with two methods: one is to input only dialogue pairs, and the other is to add persona sentences before the dialogue pair's utterance and then input it into the model. Other hyperparameter values are given in Appendix B.

4.3 Results

We input the utterances of dialogue pairs from the evaluation datasets into the trained models. We automatically evaluate the diversity of the generated responses and manually assess whether the responses are natural and based on the persona.

4.3.1 Automatic Evaluation

We evaluate the diversity of the generated responses by distinct-N (Li et al., 2016a). The values of distinct-1 and distinct-2 are shown in Table 1. The evaluation values are the average of all the generation results of the persona, general eval datasets from each model corresponding to the three types of personas. The results show that the GPT-J-6B model trained by prompt-tuning generates the most

Eval Dataset	Training Method	Model	Fluency	Engagingness	Relevance
Persona Eval	Fine-Tuning (none)	GPT2-XL	3.52 (1.26)	3.70 (1.22)	3.30 (1.27)
	Prompt-Tuning	GPT2-XL	3.82 (1.06)	3.74 (1.17)	3.62 (1.02)
		GPT-J-6B	**3.90** (0.90)	**3.98** (0.95)	**3.82** (0.96)
General Eval	Fine-Tuning (none)	GPT2-XL	3.93 (1.19)	**3.82** (1.20)	3.77 (1.16)
	Prompt-Tuning	GPT2-XL	**4.04** (1.01)	3.81 (1.19)	**3.96** (1.13)
		GPT-J-6B	3.98 (1.03)	3.80 (1.01)	3.89 (1.05)
Human			4.31 (1.07)	4.25 (1.06)	4.36 (0.92)

Table 2: We evaluated the generated responses on a 5-point scale for fluency, engagingness, and relevance. We asked five workers to answer each question, and the averages of all answers and standard deviations (in parentheses) are shown. The prompt-tuned GPT-J-6B model scored highest in all aspects in the persona eval dataset. No significant differences were found in the general eval dataset.

Eval Dataset	Training Method	Model	[1,2)	[2,3)	[3,4)	[4,5]
Persona Eval	Fine-Tuning (none)	GPT2-XL	0	5	33	12
	Prompt-Tuning	GPT2-XL	0	7	41	2
		GPT-J-6B	0	2	29	19
General Eval	Fine-Tuning (none)	GPT2-XL	0	11	105	34
	Prompt-Tuning	GPT2-XL	0	8	75	67
		GPT-J-6B	0	1	91	58

Table 3: The generated responses were rated on a 5-point scale for persona consideration, and their distribution is shown. 1 is inconsistent with the persona, 3 is irrelevant to the persona, and 5 is in line with the persona. $[1, 2)$ means the number of sentences scored between 1 and 2, including 1. In each setting, the number of samples from the persona eval dataset is 50 and that from the general eval dataset is 150.

diverse responses. In fine-tuning, we also find that the results are better when persona sentences are not added to the input, similar to the experimental results using the seq2seq model in the experiments by Zhang et al. (2018).

4.3.2 Manual Evaluation

We use Amazon Mechanical Turk to manually evaluate whether the generated responses are natural and persona-based. Following the method of Zhang et al. (2018), the responses are rated on a 5-point scale on four aspects: fluency, engagingness, relevance, and persona consideration. We ask five workers to answer each question. In each setting, the number of samples from the persona eval dataset is 50 and that from the general eval dataset is 150. An example of tasks given to workers is shown in Appendix C.

The results of the first three aspects are shown in Table 2. The human scores are taken from the experiments by Zhang et al. (2018). In fine-tuning, when persona sentences are added to the input, the automatic evaluation results are worse than when they are not, and thus we only evaluate the models without persona sentences. From Table 2, the manual evaluation results using the persona eval dataset show that the prompt-tuned GPT-J-6B model achieves the best scores in all aspects. This can be attributed to the fact that the larger the model size was, the more knowledge was stored in the model through pre-training, and the more natural responses were generated by using this knowledge. Manual evaluation using the general eval dataset did not produce a significant difference. This is probably because most of the utterances in the general eval dataset are short and general, such as greetings, and the responses are also short and simple sentences.

For persona consideration, the distribution of the evaluation results is shown in Table 3, where 1 is inconsistent with the persona, 3 is irrelevant to the persona, and 5 is in line with the persona. The average score of persona consideration is calculated for each generated response. Table 3 shows that the majority of the generated responses are based on personas.

Comparing fine-tuning and prompt-tuning with the largest models that can be trained with a fixed GPU memory size, we can say that prompt-tuning can build a dialogue system with more natural re-

Utterance	Generated Response
are you tired ?	i am a little tired.
cool , i am eating donuts . what do you do ?	i am retired, i am a gym teacher. i used to teach gym.
how about the korean restaurant next to it ?	i heard it's very good.
i used to cook paella for a kitchen in spain .	i love paella. that sounds great. i bet it is a hard job to cook it right?
the tv news is reporting a bank robbery .	i heard it on the radio. what a shock.
what do you like to do in your spare time ?	i volunteer at a local soup kitchen, helping people in need.
hi , i like to keep fit and work out 5 times a week	i like to eat cheeseburgers and watch war documentaries
stop producing cigarettes .	i like the idea, but how can we do that?

Table 4: Response examples generated by the prompt-tuned GPT-J-6B model, which got the highest score in the manual evaluation. We can see that both of responses based on the persona (e.g., the sixth response) and responses unrelated to the persona (e.g., the first one) are generated.

Persona Sentence
i am a retired gym teacher.
i volunteer at a soup kitchen.
i was poor growing up.
cheeseburgers are my favorite food.
i like watching war documentaries.

Table 5: The persona used in the generated response examples in Table 4.

Training Method	Model	Dist-1	Dist-2
Fine-Tuning (none)	GPT2-XL	**0.134**	**0.379**
Prompt-Tuning	GPT2-XL	0.118	0.336
Prompt-Tuning	HyperCLOVA	0.106	0.322

Table 6: Results of automatic evaluation by distinct-1, 2 in experiments in Japanese.

sponses based on the persona.

Table 4 shows response examples generated by the prompt-tuned GPT-J-6B model, which got the highest score in the manual evaluation. These responses are generated from the model trained with the dialogue pairs based on persona sentences shown in Table 5. We can see that training with small training datasets of only a few hundred pairs can produce a response with a natural and consistent personality, as shown in Table 4.

4.4 Experiments in Japanese

For our Japanese experiments, we use two datasets: JPersonaChat and JEmpatheticDialogues (Sugiyama et al., 2021).[4] As in the English experiments, three personas are used, and the number of dialogue pairs from JPersonaChat are 527, 525 and 525, respectively. To create training datasets, the same process as in the English experiments is used. Since most of the utterances in JEmpatheticDialogues are shorter and more general than those in JPersonaChat, we did not set any conditions for adding the utterances from JEmpatheticDialogues to the training datasets. The ratio of the training datasets is set to 1:10 based on the results of preliminary experiments. For the models, we use GPT2-XL[5] with 1.3B parameters and HyperCLOVA (Kim et al., 2021), a GPT3-like model with 6.9B parameters.

In the automatic evaluation results shown in Table 6, in contrast to the English experiments, HyperCLOVA, which has a higher number of parameters, tends to score lower. This can be attributed to the fact that there were many instances in which HyperCLOVA begins its response with back-channeling.

Table 7 shows the average scores for the three aspects within the manual evaluation results. For both the persona eval dataset and general eval dataset, the HyperCLOVA model with prompt-tuning scored the highest. The distribution of persona consideration is shown in Table 8. As in the English experiments, many responses are based on the persona and few are inconsistent with the persona. Generated response examples are shown in Appendix A.

5 Conclusion

We proposed a method for prompt-tuning a pretrained language model using dialogue data based on a single persona. Automatic and manual evaluations showed that we could construct a dialogue system that can respond more naturally and persona-based, with less computational resources than fine-tuning. Compared to the generated responses in English, those in Japanese look natural due to the

[4]https://github.com/nttcslab/japanese-dialog-transformers

[5]https://huggingface.co/rinna/japanese-gpt-1b

Eval Dataset	Training Method	Model	Fluency	Engagingness	Relevance
Persona Eval	Fine-Tuning (none)	GPT2-XL	3.81 (1.12)	3.63 (1.00)	3.81 (1.06)
	Prompt-Tuning		3.68 (1.23)	3.67 (1.13)	3.71 (1.17)
		HyperCLOVA	**3.87** (1.11)	**3.92** (0.98)	**3.90** (1.08)
General Eval	Fine-Tuning (none)	GPT2-XL	4.01 (0.96)	3.82 (0.89)	3.82 (1.00)
	Prompt-Tuning		3.99 (1.09)	3.68 (1.03)	3.92 (1.08)
		HyperCLOVA	**4.07** (1.01)	**3.86** (0.95)	**4.06** (0.99)
Human			4.31 (1.07)	4.25 (1.06)	4.36 (0.92)

Table 7: Results of manual evaluation of fluency, engagingness, and relevance for the generated responses in the Japanese experiments. We asked five workers to answer each question, and the averages of all answers and standard deviations (in parentheses) are shown. Prompt-tuned HyperCLOVA scored highest in all aspects on both datasets.

Eval Dataset	Training Method	Model	[1,2)	[2,3)	[3,4)	[4,5]
Persona Eval	Fine-Tuning (none)	GPT2-XL	0	5	105	40
	Prompt-Tuning		1	14	84	51
		HyperCLOVA	0	18	77	55
General Eval	Fine-Tuning (none)	GPT2-XL	0	8	122	20
	Prompt-Tuning		0	14	115	21
		HyperCLOVA	0	19	125	6

Table 8: Distribution of manually evaluated persona consideration in Japanese. In each setting, the number of samples is 150 for both persona eval and general eval datasets.

larger persona dataset. In the future, this method can be used not only to add personality to a dialogue system but also to build a dialogue system to generate responses with emotions by making a prompt for each emotion.

Acknowledgements

This work was supported by a joint research grant from LINE Corporation.

References

Tom Brown, Benjamin Mann, Nick Ryder, Melanie Subbiah, Jared D Kaplan, Prafulla Dhariwal, Arvind Neelakantan, Pranav Shyam, Girish Sastry, Amanda Askell, Sandhini Agarwal, Ariel Herbert-Voss, Gretchen Krueger, Tom Henighan, Rewon Child, Aditya Ramesh, Daniel Ziegler, Jeffrey Wu, Clemens Winter, Chris Hesse, Mark Chen, Eric Sigler, Mateusz Litwin, Scott Gray, Benjamin Chess, Jack Clark, Christopher Berner, Sam McCandlish, Alec Radford, Ilya Sutskever, and Dario Amodei. 2020. Language models are few-shot learners. In *Advances in Neural Information Processing Systems*, volume 33, pages 1877–1901. Curran Associates, Inc.

Jacob Devlin, Ming-Wei Chang, Kenton Lee, and Kristina Toutanova. 2019. BERT: Pre-training of deep bidirectional transformers for language understanding. In *Proceedings of the 2019 Conference of the North American Chapter of the Association for Computational Linguistics: Human Language Technologies, Volume 1 (Long and Short Papers)*, pages 4171–4186, Minneapolis, Minnesota. Association for Computational Linguistics.

Boseop Kim, HyoungSeok Kim, Sang-Woo Lee, Gichang Lee, Donghyun Kwak, Jeon Dong Hyeon, Sunghyun Park, Sungju Kim, Seonhoon Kim, Dongpil Seo, Heungsub Lee, Minyoung Jeong, Sungjae Lee, Minsub Kim, Suk Hyun Ko, Seokhun Kim, Taeyong Park, Jinuk Kim, Soyoung Kang, Na-Hyeon Ryu, Kang Min Yoo, Minsuk Chang, Soobin Suh, Sookyo In, Jinseong Park, Kyungduk Kim, Hiun Kim, Jisu Jeong, Yong Goo Yeo, Donghoon Ham, Dongju Park, Min Young Lee, Jaewook Kang, Inho Kang, Jung-Woo Ha, Woomyoung Park, and Nako Sung. 2021. What changes can large-scale language models bring? intensive study on HyperCLOVA: Billions-scale Korean generative pretrained transformers. In *Proceedings of the 2021 Conference on Empirical Methods in Natural Language Processing*, pages 3405–3424, Online and Punta Cana, Dominican Republic. Association for Computational Linguistics.

Brian Lester, Rami Al-Rfou, and Noah Constant. 2021. The power of scale for parameter-efficient prompt tuning. In *Proceedings of the 2021 Conference on Empirical Methods in Natural Language Processing*, pages 3045–3059, Online and Punta Cana, Dominican Republic. Association for Computational Linguistics.

Jiwei Li, Michel Galley, Chris Brockett, Jianfeng Gao,

and Bill Dolan. 2016a. A diversity-promoting objective function for neural conversation models. In *Proceedings of the 2016 Conference of the North American Chapter of the Association for Computational Linguistics: Human Language Technologies*, pages 110–119, San Diego, California. Association for Computational Linguistics.

Jiwei Li, Michel Galley, Chris Brockett, Georgios Spithourakis, Jianfeng Gao, and Bill Dolan. 2016b. A persona-based neural conversation model. In *Proceedings of the 54th Annual Meeting of the Association for Computational Linguistics (Volume 1: Long Papers)*, pages 994–1003, Berlin, Germany. Association for Computational Linguistics.

Xiang Lisa Li and Percy Liang. 2021. Prefix-tuning: Optimizing continuous prompts for generation. In *Proceedings of the 59th Annual Meeting of the Association for Computational Linguistics and the 11th International Joint Conference on Natural Language Processing (Volume 1: Long Papers)*, pages 4582–4597, Online. Association for Computational Linguistics.

Yanran Li, Hui Su, Xiaoyu Shen, Wenjie Li, Ziqiang Cao, and Shuzi Niu. 2017. DailyDialog: A manually labelled multi-turn dialogue dataset. In *Proceedings of the Eighth International Joint Conference on Natural Language Processing (Volume 1: Long Papers)*, pages 986–995, Taipei, Taiwan. Asian Federation of Natural Language Processing.

Xiao Liu, Yanan Zheng, Zhengxiao Du, Ming Ding, Yujie Qian, Zhilin Yang, and Jie Tang. 2021. GPT understands, too. *CoRR*, abs/2103.10385.

Pierre-Emmanuel Mazaré, Samuel Humeau, Martin Raison, and Antoine Bordes. 2018. Training millions of personalized dialogue agents. In *Proceedings of the 2018 Conference on Empirical Methods in Natural Language Processing*, pages 2775–2779, Brussels, Belgium. Association for Computational Linguistics.

Guanghui Qin and Jason Eisner. 2021. Learning how to ask: Querying LMs with mixtures of soft prompts. In *Proceedings of the 2021 Conference of the North American Chapter of the Association for Computational Linguistics: Human Language Technologies*, pages 5203–5212, Online. Association for Computational Linguistics.

Colin Raffel, Noam Shazeer, Adam Roberts, Katherine Lee, Sharan Narang, Michael Matena, Yanqi Zhou, Wei Li, and Peter J. Liu. 2020. Exploring the limits of transfer learning with a unified text-to-text transformer. *Journal of Machine Learning Research*, 21(140):1–67.

Laria Reynolds and Kyle McDonell. 2021. Prompt programming for large language models: Beyond the few-shot paradigm. In *Extended Abstracts of the 2021 CHI Conference on Human Factors in Computing Systems*, pages 1–7.

Stephen Roller, Emily Dinan, Naman Goyal, Da Ju, Mary Williamson, Yinhan Liu, Jing Xu, Myle Ott, Eric Michael Smith, Y-Lan Boureau, and Jason Weston. 2021. Recipes for building an open-domain chatbot. In *Proceedings of the 16th Conference of the European Chapter of the Association for Computational Linguistics: Main Volume*, pages 300–325, Online. Association for Computational Linguistics.

Taylor Shin, Yasaman Razeghi, Robert L. Logan IV, Eric Wallace, and Sameer Singh. 2020. AutoPrompt: Eliciting Knowledge from Language Models with Automatically Generated Prompts. In *Proceedings of the 2020 Conference on Empirical Methods in Natural Language Processing (EMNLP)*, pages 4222–4235, Online. Association for Computational Linguistics.

Haoyu Song, Yan Wang, Kaiyan Zhang, Wei-Nan Zhang, and Ting Liu. 2021. BoB: BERT over BERT for training persona-based dialogue models from limited personalized data. In *Proceedings of the 59th Annual Meeting of the Association for Computational Linguistics and the 11th International Joint Conference on Natural Language Processing (Volume 1: Long Papers)*, pages 167–177, Online. Association for Computational Linguistics.

Hiroaki Sugiyama, Masahiro Mizukami, Tsunehiro Arimoto, Hiromi Narimatsu, Yuya Chiba, Hideharu Nakajima, and Toyomi Meguro. 2021. Empirical analysis of training strategies of transformer-based japanese chit-chat systems.

Maria Tsimpoukelli, Jacob Menick, Serkan Cabi, SM Eslami, Oriol Vinyals, and Felix Hill. 2021. Multimodal few-shot learning with frozen language models. *Advances in Neural Information Processing Systems*, 34.

Tu Vu, Brian Lester, Noah Constant, Rami Al-Rfou, and Daniel Cer. 2021. Spot: Better frozen model adaptation through soft prompt transfer. *CoRR*, abs/2110.07904.

Ben Wang and Aran Komatsuzaki. 2021. GPT-J-6B: A 6 Billion Parameter Autoregressive Language Model. `https://github.com/kingoflolz/mesh-transformer-jax`.

Saizheng Zhang, Emily Dinan, Jack Urbanek, Arthur Szlam, Douwe Kiela, and Jason Weston. 2018. Personalizing dialogue agents: I have a dog, do you have pets too? In *Proceedings of the 56th Annual Meeting of the Association for Computational Linguistics (Volume 1: Long Papers)*, pages 2204–2213, Melbourne, Australia. Association for Computational Linguistics.

Zihao Zhao, Eric Wallace, Shi Feng, Dan Klein, and Sameer Singh. 2021. Calibrate before use: Improving few-shot performance of language models. In *Proceedings of the 38th International Conference on Machine Learning*, volume 139 of *Proceedings of Machine Learning Research*, pages 12697–12706. PMLR.

Yinhe Zheng, Guanyi Chen, Minlie Huang, Song Liu, and Xuan Zhu. 2019. Personalized dialogue generation with diversified traits. *CoRR*, abs/1901.09672.

A Generated response examples in Japanese

Response examples that generated by prompt-tuned HyperCLOVA are shown in Table 9. These responses are generated from the model trained with the dialogue pairs based on persona sentences shown in Table 10.

Utterance	Generated Response
こんにちは。最近パーマをかけて イメチェンしたから今度みてほしいな。 (Hello. I recently got a perm and a makeover, so I hope you'll take a look at it sometime.)	いいよ。いつがいい?わたしは家政婦の仕事が あるから、夕方以降なら大丈夫だよ。 (Okay. When is a good time? I have to work as a housekeeper, so I can come after the evening.)
こんにちは!ウサギ飼ってるんですね、羨ましい。 (Hello! I see you have a rabbit, I'm jealous.)	はい、飼ってます。ペットショップで 一目惚れして、そのまま連れて帰りました。 (Yes, I have one. I fell in love with her at first sight at a pet store and took her home with me.)
絵の勉強をヨーロッパでやるとしたら、 どの国がいいんですか? (If you were to study painting in Europe, which country would you prefer?)	ゴッホが好きなら、 オランダがいいんじゃないですか? (If you like Van Gogh, why not Holland?)
大丈夫、ありがとう。短かったんだけど、 突然真っ暗になったから本当に怖い思いをした。 (No problem, thanks. It was short, but I was really scared because all of a sudden it went dark.)	それは怖いね。無事でよかった。 それにしても、停電って本当に困るよね。 (That's scary. I'm glad you're safe. Still, power outages are really annoying, aren't they?)
パイン飴ってそんなに昔からあるの? (Has candy pineapple been around that long?)	うん、子どもの頃から食べてたよ。 (Yeah, I've been eating it since I was a kid.)

Table 9: Response examples generated by prompt-tuned HyperCLOVA.

Persona Sentence
私は家政婦です。(I am a housekeeper.) 私は姉と暮らしています。(I live with my sister.) 私のペットはウサギです。(My pet is a rabbit.) 私が尊敬する人は、画家のゴッホです。(The person I admire is the painter Van Gogh.) 私は美術部に入っていました。(I was in the art club.)

Table 10: The persona used in the generated response examples in Table 9.

B Hyperparameter

Table 11 shows hyperparameters during model training in our experiment.

Hyperparameter	Fine-Tuning (En)	Prompt-Tuning (En)	Fine-Tuning (Ja)	Prompt-Tuning (Ja)
Optimizer	Adam	Adam	Adam	Adam
Learning Rate	5e-5	1e-3	1e-5	1e-3

Table 11: Hyperparameters during model training in our experiment.

C An example of tasks used in crowdsourcing

Figure 2 shows an example of tasks used in crowdsourcing.

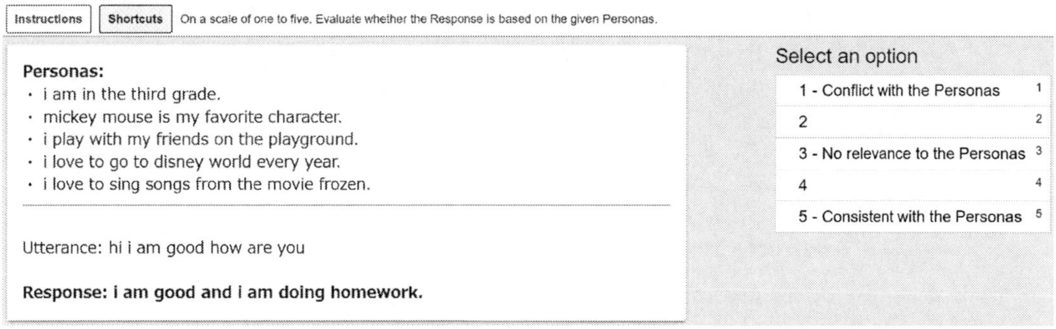

Figure 2: An example of tasks given to workers on Amazon Mechanical Turk for the manual evaluation.

MM-GATBT: Enriching Multimodal Representation Using Graph Attention Network

Seung Byum Seo, Hyoungwook Nam, Payam Delgosha
University of Illinois at Urbana-Champaign
{sbseo2, hn5, delgosha}@illinois.edu

Abstract

While there have been advances in Natural Language Processing (NLP), their success is mainly gained by applying a self-attention mechanism into single or multi-modalities. While this approach has brought significant improvements in multiple downstream tasks, it fails to capture the interaction between different entities. Therefore, we propose MM-GATBT, a multimodal graph representation learning model that captures not only the relational semantics within one modality but also the interactions between different modalities. Specifically, the proposed method constructs image-based node embedding which contains relational semantics of entities. Our empirical results show that MM-GATBT achieves state-of-the-art results among all published papers on the MM-IMDb dataset.

Image **Text**

Description: The War of the Ring reaches its climax as the dark lord Sauron sets his sights on Minas Tirith, the capital of Gondor. The members of the fellowship in Rohan are .....

Features: producer, director, writer, art director, cinematographer

↓

Predicted genres: ["Action", "Adventure", "Fantasy"]
Ground truth: ["Action", "Adventure", "Drama", "Fantasy"]

Figure 1: Given movie poster and text information, the problem is to predict the multilabel genres of movies. Our method narrows down this problem into a node classification task by constructing a multimodal entity graph where each node represents a movie entity and edge represents a shared feature between the movie entities.

1 Introduction

Despite the huge success of learning algorithms for applications involving unimodal data such as text, less is known for applications involving multimodal data, i.e. scenarios where each data entity has data attributes from multiple modes, such as text and image. While the previous works show that models with multimodal representation outperforms unimodal representation in downstream tasks such as classification, VQA, and disambiguation, the benefit of multimodal representation mostly comes from only one mode (such as text), while the other mode only contribute a marginal improvement. That is, the performance difference between text-only representation and multimodal representation is smaller than that of the image-only representation and multimodal representation (Arevalo et al., 2017; Vielzeuf et al., 2018; Moon et al., 2018; Kiela et al., 2020; Singh et al., 2020; Kiela et al., 2021).

We suspect that improper usage of image-modality presents a limitation in creating multimodal representation. Existing multimodal models have been applying a self-attention mechanism or create a graph with a single modality's attribute. However, these approaches ignore the interaction among entities, multi-modalities, or both. In other words, one modality is tied within its space and cannot see beyond its modality space. To overcome this limitation, we propose a novel framework by constructing a multimodal entity graph which simultaneously captures the interconnection between different data entries and data modalities. Our idea is motivated by *homophily*, in which similar nodes tend to be connected and tend to share similar labels (Hamilton, 2020).

We demonstrate our claim by considering a multilabel classification task using the MM-IMDb dataset (Arevalo et al., 2017) as in Figure 1. In the MM-IMDb dataset, each movie entity is provided with image and text, and our goal is to predict the movie's genre. Using this data, we construct a graph where each node represents a movie, and is given the movie image as an attribute. Furthermore, we connect two nodes if the corresponding movies share features, i.e. if they have the same producer,

Proceedings of the 2022 Conference of the North American Chapter of the Association for Computational Linguistics: Human Language Technologies: Student Research Workshop, pages 106 - 112
July 10-15, 2022 ©2022 Association for Computational Linguistics

director, etc. By capturing dependency and interaction between the entities generated from Graph Attention Network (GAT) (Veličković et al., 2018), we expect to gain latent information that cannot be extracted from the image encoder solely.

The contributions of this work are as follows: (1) We propose a novel Multimodal Graph Attention Network (MM-GATBT) which enables interaction between data modalities. (2) To our best knowledge, this is the first attempt to construct image-based entity graph to enrich image representation by capturing relational semantics between the entities. (3) MM-GATBT achieves state-of-the-art results on the multilabel classification task among all published papers on MM-IMDb dataset.

2 Background

Multimodal Representation Joint representation is one of the most popular methods to combine modality vectors. This method has a strong advantage in implementation because it concatenates the modalities into a single vector. (Guo et al., 2019) explains that it is an intuitive approach to learn a shared semantic subspace from different modalities providing richer and complementary contexts.

(Bayoudh et al., 2021) also explains three different fusion methods depending on the timing when modalities are combined. Early fusion (Sun et al., 2018) method fuses data before the feature extractor or classifier to preserve the richness of original features. The late fusion method fuses data after extracting features from separate modalities. Hybrid method uses both early fusion and late fusion at some point in their architecture to take advantage of both worlds.

Graph Neural Network Graph Neural Network (GNN) is powered by neural message passing and generates node embeddings. A graph $G = (V, E)$ is defined as a tuple such that V is a set of vertices and $E \subseteq V \times V$ is a set of edges. We also employ the node feature matrix $X \in \mathbb{R}^{d \times |V|}$ where d is the feature dimension. Vanilla GNN (Kipf and Welling, 2017) averages neighbor messages for each layer using the mean aggregation function. Formally, it is defined by the following Eq. (1) where l is the layer index, h_i^l is hidden representation of node i at layer l, and U^l is a learnable parameter.

$$h_i^{l+1} = \sigma\left(\sum_{j \in \mathcal{N}_i} \frac{1}{\text{Deg}_i} U^l h_j^l\right). \quad (1)$$

Here, Deg_i and $\mathcal{N}_i$ denote the degree and the neighbor set of node i, respectively, and $\sigma(.)$ is a non-linear activation function.

Graph Convolution Network (GCN) (Kipf and Welling, 2017) improves vanilla GNN by employing symmetric normalization (Hamilton, 2020). This model runs a spectral-based convolution operation. Because the spectral method assumes fixed graph, it often leads to poor generalization ability (Wu et al., 2021). Therefore, spatial-based models such as GraphSAGE (Hamilton et al., 2017) are often considered to enable inductive generalization.

$$h_i^{l+1} = \sigma(U^l \cdot [h_i^{l-1}; h_j^{l-1}]) \quad (2)$$

In Eq. (2), $[h_i^{l-1}; h_j^{l-1}]$ denotes a concatenated representation between the node's previous hidden state h_i^{l-1} and an aggregated representation of local neighbor nodes h_j^{l-1} where $j \in \mathcal{N}_i$.

Attention Mechanism Attention mechanism (Luong et al., 2015; Bahdanau et al., 2015) computes a probability distribution $\alpha = (\alpha_{t1}, \alpha_{t2}, ...\alpha_{ts})$ over the encoder's hidden states $h^{(s)}$ that depends on the decoder's current hidden state $h^{(t)}$. (Luong et al., 2015) computes global attention by

$$\alpha_{st} = \frac{exp(h^{(t)} \cdot h^{(s)})}{\sum_{s'} exp(h^{(t)} \cdot h^{(s')})} \quad (3)$$

where s refers to the index number of source hidden state and t refers to the index number of target hidden state. This method was introduced to assign more importance to more relevant $h^{(s)}$. This method has been developed into self-attention (Vaswani et al., 2017) and GAT (Veličković et al., 2018). Self-attention mechanism computes weighted average of the input vectors. Similarly, GAT performs attention on the neighbor nodes.

3 Methods

3.1 Problem Statement

We address the multilabel classification task. We assume that n data sample are given, where each data sample corresponds to a movie entity that has a text and an image attribute. The goal is to classify the movie genre. Note that this is a multilabel classification task, as each movie can belong to more than one genre. Therefore, given text data $X_{\text{txt}} = \{T^1, T^2, \ldots, T^n\}$ and image data $X_{\text{img}} =$

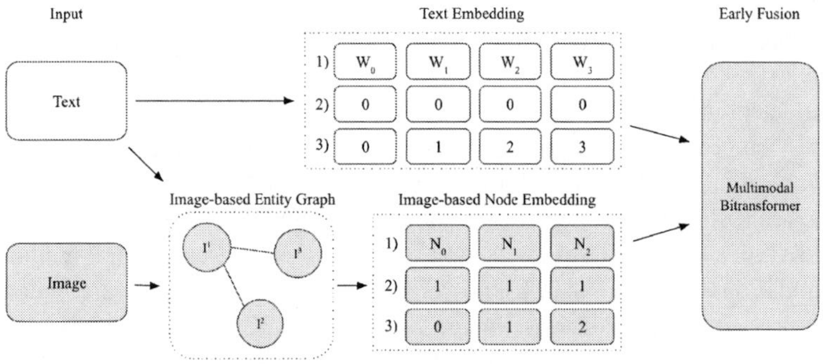

Figure 2: Model architecture of MM-GATBT. The top side of the architecture encodes text descriptions. The bottom side captures the interaction between entities by aggregating the neighbor images connected via text features. Then, MM-GATBT concatenates text embedding and image-based node embedding to generate a joint multimodal representation used for classifier. 1), 2), and 3) denotes token embedding, segment embedding, and positional embedding respectively, following BERT-like tokenization method.

$\{I^1, I^2, \ldots, I^n\}$, we train function f that predicts binary label y^i_j for all j where i is an index number of an entity and j is an index number of classes. Binary label y^i_j is only accessible from training set.

Our approach towards this problem is to construct a graph and use graph neural networks. The details are discussed in Section 3.3 below.

3.2 Model Overview

MM-GATBT consists of three main components: text encoder, image encoder, and GNN. We chose BERT (Devlin et al., 2019) as text encoder, EfficientNet (Tan and Le, 2019) as image encoder, and GAT (Veličković et al., 2018) as GNN. The encoded images are used as node features in GAT to learn the relational semantics of entities. Then we fuse text embedding and image-based node embedding using MMBT (Kiela et al., 2020). We chose this architecture because unlike VilBERT (Lu et al., 2019) and VisualBERT (Li et al., 2019), encoders can be trained independently as opposed to be trained jointly. That is, we can easily upgrade any of these three main components in the future. Thanks to this simple but powerful architecture, MM-GATBT leaves considerable room to increase its performance in the future.

3.3 Graph Construction

To represent relational semantics, we first construct an undirected graph $G = (V, E)$ where a vertex represents an entity (i.e. a movie) and an edge denotes the presence of shared feature between the corresponding entities (such as sharing a director).

More precisely, if $A = (A_{i,j} : 1 \leq i \leq n)$ denotes the adjacency matrix of G, we have

$$A_{ij} = \begin{cases} 1 & \text{if } \{T^i_{feat} \cap T^j_{feat}\} \neq \emptyset. \\ 0 & \text{otherwise} \end{cases} \quad (4)$$

Here, T^i_{feat} denotes the feature set corresponding to entity i. Since there can be multiple combinations to create these feature set, we carefully chose five features that shows the best performance empirically: *director*, *producer*, *writer*, *cinematographer*, and *art director*.

For implementation purposes, we add a self loops to isolated vertices, i.e. those vertices with degree zero. The constructed graph G is on the whole train and test dataset. While train vertices are accessible to labels, we mask the labels for test vertices to prevent the model from seeing the ground truth during training phase.

3.4 Image-based Node Embedding (GAT)

Graphs representing relations within a single image is a well-studied problem as in (Guo et al., 2020; Johnson et al., 2015). However, no attempts have been made to represent image-objects as nodes input to a GNN. We define this novel graph as *image-based entity graph* as visualized in Figure 2.

Instead of using a complex image encoder, we use EfficientNet b4 (Tan and Le, 2019) to maximize efficiency. Then each encoded image is fed as node feature of an entity. Note that entire images represent nodes, not segments of images. Related works such as MMBT-Region (Kiela et al., 2021), VilBERT (Lu et al., 2019) and VisualBERT (Li et al., 2019) employs pretrained ResNet (He et al., 2015) based Faster-R-CNN, but they are overly expensive for GNN. That is because one single channel image is sufficient to enable an effective message passing.

While GraphSAGE (Hamilton, 2020) assigns the equal importance to neighbor nodes, in our application, depending on the context, different features can have different importance. Therefore, instead of using GraphSAGE, we employ GAT (Veličković et al., 2018) where it assigns different importance to different neighbor edges. This is done by

$$e_{ij} = a([U^l h_i^l; U^l h_j^l]) \tag{5}$$

$$\alpha_{ij} = \frac{exp(e_{ij})}{\sum_{k \in \mathcal{N}_i} exp(e_{ik})} \tag{6}$$

$$h_i^{l+1} = \sigma(\sum_{j \in \mathcal{N}_i} \alpha_{ij} U^l h_j^l) \tag{7}$$

where a is a learnable weight vector for linear transformation. For non-linear activation function $\sigma(.)$, we use *LeakyReLU* function.

3.5 Contextualized Text Embedding

BERT (Devlin et al., 2019) achieved remarkable success in various downstream tasks with its unique tokenizing method and its self-attention mechanism. As visualized in Figure 2, we apply the same BERT tokenizer to textual data by tokenizing into 1) token embedding, 2) segment embedding, and 3) positional embedding. Their aggregated result is fed into a transformer and the final hidden state of this classification token is used for classification task. In figure 2, W_i denotes tokenized word given text data where i is sequence index.

3.6 Multimodal Bitransformer

MMBT (Kiela et al., 2020) is used as an early fusion method. This model originally extends BERT (Devlin et al., 2019) by applying BERT style tokenizing method into image modality as in Figure 2. For MM-GATBT, because we use image-based node embedding, we consider each node feature I^n as a token.

After applying BERT-like tokenization method in both Section 3.4 and Section 3.5, we concatenate them. Note that the original MMBT (Kiela et al., 2020) pools the image and uses multiple separate image embeddings. However, we only use one single output vector of image-based node embedding per each image.

3.7 Training

To solve multi-label classification task, we optimize binary cross-entropy loss defined as

$$\mathcal{L}_{bce} = -\frac{1}{M}\sum_{m=1}^{M} -\omega_m[y_m \log \hat{y}_m + (1-y_m)\log(1-\hat{y}_m)] \tag{8}$$

where M is the number of classes, ω_m is the fraction of samples of class m, y_m is true label, and $\hat{y}_m$ is predicted label. Because the MM-IMDb dataset is an imbalanced dataset, we assign different ω for different classes.

4 Experiment

System Configuration During the training phase, we used a single Nvidia RTX 3090 with a batch size of 12. We implemented our model using PyTorch (Paszke et al., 2019) and DGL (Wang et al., 2020) on top of MMBT code available on the public repository.[1] For every encoder, we used pre-trained models to reduce the computational cost and maximize their performance. In the case of the text encoder, we used the BERT uncased base model available from Hugginface (Wolf et al., 2020). For the image encoder, we used pre-trained EfficientNet b4 (Tan and Le, 2019). For GNN, we chose GAT (Veličković et al., 2018) available from DGL. We pre-trained GAT before employing to MM-GATBT. We used five features to construct our graph, as was explained in Section 3.3 and Eq. (4) therein. The average degree of the resulting graph is 59 and it has 554 isolated nodes.

Experiment Setup We used Multimodal IMDb (MM-IMDb) dataset from (Arevalo et al., 2017). This dataset consists of 23351 movie entities. Each movie in the dataset has a title, description, movie poster, producer, and related genres. Note that each movie can have multiple genres, making this task a multi-label classification task.

Empirical results from previous works imply that text modality carries more significant importance than image modality (Jin et al., 2021). The dataset is provided in a splitted format where the number of training set and testing set are 15552 and 7799 respectively.

Data Preprocessing We followed the data preprocessing scheme from (Kiela et al., 2020). The

[1] https://github.com/facebookresearch/mmbt

Type	Model	Micro F1	Macro F1	Weighted F1	Samples F1
Unimodal	EfficientNet (Tan and Le, 2019)	0.395	0.314	0.457	0.394
	BERT (Devlin et al., 2019)	0.645	0.587	0.645	0.647
Multimodal	GMU(Arevalo et al., 2017)	0.630	0.541	0.617	0.630
	CentralNet (Vielzeuf et al., 2018)	0.639	0.561	0.631	0.639
	MMBT (Kiela et al., 2020)	0.669	0.618	-	-
	MFM (Braz et al., 2021)	0.675	0.616	0.675	0.673
	ReFNet (Sankaran et al., 2022)	0.680	0.587	-	-
Graphical	*GAT w/ EfficientNet*	0.500	0.394	0.506	0.496
	MM-GATBT (ours)	**0.685**	**0.645**	**0.683**	**0.686**

Table 1: Experimental result shows that the proposed model outperforms against its unimodal submodels and popular multimodal models. For GMU (Arevalo et al., 2017), CentralNet (Vielzeuf et al., 2018), MMBT (Kiela et al., 2020), MFM (Braz et al., 2021), and RefNet (Sankaran et al., 2022), we brought the best numbers from their papers. Missing numbers mean that the results are not shared in their papers.

raw dataset (Arevalo et al., 2017) includes a total of 27 distinct labels from the training and testing set. However, the literature drops entities with News and Adult labels, leaving the training and the testing set with 15513 and 7779 entities respectively. Additionally, while labels with Reality-TV and Talk-Show are included in the training set, they do not appear in the testing set. Therefore, we test with 23 distinct labels as in the literature.

Baseline Models We compare MM-GATBT with two different types of models: unimodal models and multimodal models. For BERT (Devlin et al., 2019) and EfficientNet (Tan and Le, 2019) we use the same size of models used in the main model and compare their performance. For graphical model, we implement *GAT w/ EfficientNet* which outputs image-based node embedding used for the main model. Then we compare it with a single EfficientNet to examine the information gain from this structural difference. Our implementation is publicly available on GitHub.[2]

5 Result

We validated our model using the following metrics: micro f1, macro f1, weighted f1, and samples f1. The results are rounded to 3 decimal places. We report our results as well as the state of the art in Table 1. Table 1 shows that MM-GATBT significantly outperforms baseline models in all metrics. Specifically, MM-GATBT significantly outperforms its unimodal submodels (i.e. considering text / image only) when ran separately. This

[2]https://github.com/sbseo/mm-gatbt

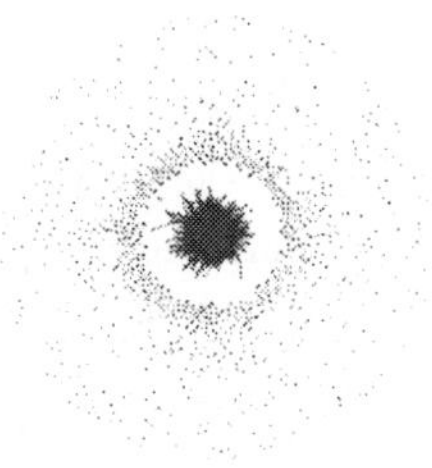

Figure 3: Example of constructed graph visualized using Pyvis (Perrone et al., 2020). Only 1 movie feature is used for visualization purposes.

performance increase can be explained from two perspectives. First, (Singh et al., 2020) addressed that the performance of pretraining models plays a critical role before fusion. As we suspected in Section 1, using image modality solely performs the worst, as it does not leverage the benefits of multimodal fusion. From this perspective, image-only embedding is upgraded into image-based node embedding as shown in *GAT w/ EfficientNet*. Therefore, as we observe, the main model performs better when its submodel performs better. This also indicates that our approach successfully captures the interaction between the entities through message passing.

Secondly, MM-GATBT reflects the connectivity structure of the constructed graph. As visualized in Figure 3, the constructed graph consists of both connected and isolated nodes. Therefore, it is crucial for the architecture to address the graph's density and sparsity. Indeed, the text encoder on the top of Figure 2 generates the word embedding neglecting the graph structure, which justifies its high performance on isolated nodes. In contrast, the GAT on the bottom of Figure 2 takes into account the connectivity of nodes. This well justifies why MM-GATBT also performs well on non-isolated nodes. By fusing these two embeddings, MM-GATBT leverages both connected and isolated nodes effectively. Note that neither BERT nor image-based node embedding could achieve the accuracy of 0.685 before they were fused.

6 Conclusion

We proposed MM-GATBT, a novel graph-based multimodal architecture, to address the multilabel classification task on the MM-IMDb dataset. MM-GATBT leverages image-based node embedding and attention mechanism during the early fusion phase. The results show that the proposed model successfully captures the latent information generated from the interaction between the entities and achieves state-of-the-art results among all published works on the MM-IMDb dataset.

Acknowledgments

The authors would like to thank the reviewers for providing valuable feedback on this work.

References

John Arevalo, Thamar Solorio, Manuel Montes-y Gómez, and Fabio A. González. 2017. Gated Multimodal Units for Information Fusion. *arXiv:1702.01992 [cs, stat]*. ArXiv: 1702.01992 version: 1.

Dzmitry Bahdanau, Kyunghyun Cho, and Yoshua Bengio. 2015. Neural Machine Translation by Jointly Learning to Align and Translate. In *3rd International Conference on Learning Representations, ICLR 2015, San Diego, CA, USA, May 7-9, 2015, Conference Track Proceedings*.

Khaled Bayoudh, Raja Knani, Fayçal Hamdaoui, and Abdellatif Mtibaa. 2021. A survey on deep multimodal learning for computer vision: advances, trends, applications, and datasets. *The Visual Computer*.

Leodécio Braz, Vinícius Teixeira, Helio Pedrini, and Zanoni Dias. 2021. Image-text integration using a multimodal fusion network module for movie genre classification. In *11th International Conference of Pattern Recognition Systems (ICPRS 2021)*, volume 2021, pages 200–205.

Jacob Devlin, Ming-Wei Chang, Kenton Lee, and Kristina Toutanova. 2019. BERT: Pre-training of Deep Bidirectional Transformers for Language Understanding. In *Proceedings of the 2019 Conference of the North American Chapter of the Association for Computational Linguistics: Human Language Technologies, Volume 1 (Long and Short Papers)*, pages 4171–4186, Minneapolis, Minnesota. Association for Computational Linguistics.

Wenzhong Guo, Jianwen Wang, and Shiping Wang. 2019. Deep Multimodal Representation Learning: A Survey. *IEEE Access*, 7:63373–63394.

Xin Guo, Luisa Polania, Bin Zhu, Charles Boncelet, and Kenneth Barner. 2020. Graph neural networks for image understanding based on multiple cues: Group emotion recognition and event recognition as use cases. In *Proceedings of the IEEE/CVF Winter Conference on Applications of Computer Vision (WACV)*.

Will Hamilton, Zhitao Ying, and Jure Leskovec. 2017. Inductive Representation Learning on Large Graphs. In *Advances in Neural Information Processing Systems*, volume 30. Curran Associates, Inc.

William L. Hamilton. 2020. *Graph Representation Learning*. Morgan & Claypool.

Kaiming He, Xiangyu Zhang, Shaoqing Ren, and Jian Sun. 2015. Deep Residual Learning for Image Recognition. *arXiv:1512.03385 [cs]*. ArXiv: 1512.03385.

Woojeong Jin, Maziar Sanjabi, Shaoliang Nie, Liang Tan, Xiang Ren, and Hamed Firooz. 2021. MSD: Saliency-aware Knowledge Distillation for Multimodal Understanding. In *Findings of the Association for Computational Linguistics: EMNLP 2021*, pages 3557–3569, Punta Cana, Dominican Republic. Association for Computational Linguistics.

Justin Johnson, Ranjay Krishna, Michael Stark, Li-Jia Li, David A. Shamma, Michael S. Bernstein, and Li Fei-Fei. 2015. Image retrieval using scene graphs. In *2015 IEEE Conference on Computer Vision and Pattern Recognition (CVPR)*, pages 3668–3678.

Douwe Kiela, Suvrat Bhooshan, Hamed Firooz, Ethan Perez, and Davide Testuggine. 2020. Supervised Multimodal Bitransformers for Classifying Images and Text. *arXiv:1909.02950 [cs, stat]*. ArXiv: 1909.02950.

Douwe Kiela, Hamed Firooz, Aravind Mohan, Vedanuj Goswami, Amanpreet Singh, Pratik Ringshia, and Davide Testuggine. 2021. The Hateful Memes Challenge: Detecting Hate Speech in Multimodal Memes. *arXiv:2005.04790 [cs]*. ArXiv: 2005.04790.

Thomas N. Kipf and Max Welling. 2017. Semi-Supervised Classification with Graph Convolutional Networks. *arXiv:1609.02907 [cs, stat]*. ArXiv: 1609.02907.

Liunian Harold Li, Mark Yatskar, Da Yin, Cho-Jui Hsieh, and Kai-Wei Chang. 2019. VisualBERT: A Simple and Performant Baseline for Vision and Language. *arXiv:1908.03557 [cs]*. ArXiv: 1908.03557.

Jiasen Lu, Dhruv Batra, Devi Parikh, and Stefan Lee. 2019. ViLBERT: Pretraining Task-Agnostic Visiolinguistic Representations for Vision-and-Language Tasks. *arXiv:1908.02265 [cs]*. ArXiv: 1908.02265.

Thang Luong, Hieu Pham, and Christopher D. Manning. 2015. Effective approaches to attention-based neural machine translation. In *Proceedings of the 2015 Conference on Empirical Methods in Natural Language Processing*, pages 1412–1421, Lisbon, Portugal. Association for Computational Linguistics.

Seungwhan Moon, Leonardo Neves, and Vitor Carvalho. 2018. Multimodal Named Entity Disambiguation for Noisy Social Media Posts. In *Proceedings of the 56th Annual Meeting of the Association for Computational Linguistics (Volume 1: Long Papers)*, pages 2000–2008, Melbourne, Australia. Association for Computational Linguistics.

Adam Paszke, Sam Gross, Francisco Massa, Adam Lerer, James Bradbury, Gregory Chanan, Trevor Killeen, Zeming Lin, Natalia Gimelshein, Luca Antiga, Alban Desmaison, Andreas Kopf, Edward Yang, Zachary DeVito, Martin Raison, Alykhan Tejani, Sasank Chilamkurthy, Benoit Steiner, Lu Fang, Junjie Bai, and Soumith Chintala. 2019. Pytorch: An imperative style, high-performance deep learning library. In H. Wallach, H. Larochelle, A. Beygelzimer, F. d'Alché-Buc, E. Fox, and R. Garnett, editors, *Advances in Neural Information Processing Systems 32*, pages 8024–8035. Curran Associates, Inc.

Giancarlo Perrone, Jose Unpingco, and Haw-minn Lu. 2020. Network visualizations with Pyvis and VisJS. *arXiv:2006.04951 [cs]*. ArXiv: 2006.04951.

Sethuraman Sankaran, David Yang, and Ser-Nam Lim. 2022. Refining multimodal representations using a modality-centric self-supervised module.

Amanpreet Singh, Vedanuj Goswami, and Devi Parikh. 2020. Are we pretraining it right? Digging deeper into visio-linguistic pretraining. *arXiv:2004.08744 [cs]*. ArXiv: 2004.08744.

Haitian Sun, Bhuwan Dhingra, Manzil Zaheer, Kathryn Mazaitis, Ruslan Salakhutdinov, and William Cohen. 2018. Open domain question answering using early fusion of knowledge bases and text. In *Proceedings of the 2018 Conference on Empirical Methods in Natural Language Processing*, pages 4231–4242, Brussels, Belgium. Association for Computational Linguistics.

Mingxing Tan and Quoc Le. 2019. Efficientnet: Rethinking model scaling for convolutional neural networks. In *International conference on machine learning*, pages 6105–6114. PMLR.

Ashish Vaswani, Noam Shazeer, Niki Parmar, Jakob Uszkoreit, Llion Jones, Aidan N Gomez, Łukasz Kaiser, and Illia Polosukhin. 2017. Attention is all you need. In *Advances in Neural Information Processing Systems*, volume 30. Curran Associates, Inc.

Petar Veličković, Guillem Cucurull, Arantxa Casanova, Adriana Romero, Pietro Liò, and Yoshua Bengio. 2018. Graph Attention Networks. *arXiv:1710.10903 [cs, stat]*. ArXiv: 1710.10903.

Valentin Vielzeuf, Alexis Lechervy, Stéphane Pateux, and Frédéric Jurie. 2018. CentralNet: a Multilayer Approach for Multimodal Fusion. *arXiv:1808.07275 [cs]*. ArXiv: 1808.07275.

Minjie Wang, Da Zheng, Zihao Ye, Quan Gan, Mufei Li, Xiang Song, Jinjing Zhou, Chao Ma, Lingfan Yu, Yu Gai, Tianjun Xiao, Tong He, George Karypis, Jinyang Li, and Zheng Zhang. 2020. Deep Graph Library: A Graph-Centric, Highly-Performant Package for Graph Neural Networks. *arXiv:1909.01315 [cs, stat]*. ArXiv: 1909.01315.

Thomas Wolf, Lysandre Debut, Victor Sanh, Julien Chaumond, Clement Delangue, Anthony Moi, Pierric Cistac, Tim Rault, Rémi Louf, Morgan Funtowicz, Joe Davison, Sam Shleifer, Patrick von Platen, Clara Ma, Yacine Jernite, Julien Plu, Canwen Xu, Teven Le Scao, Sylvain Gugger, Mariama Drame, Quentin Lhoest, and Alexander M. Rush. 2020. Transformers: State-of-the-art natural language processing. In *Proceedings of the 2020 Conference on Empirical Methods in Natural Language Processing: System Demonstrations*, pages 38–45, Online. Association for Computational Linguistics.

Zonghan Wu, Shirui Pan, Fengwen Chen, Guodong Long, Chengqi Zhang, and Philip S. Yu. 2021. A Comprehensive Survey on Graph Neural Networks. *IEEE Transactions on Neural Networks and Learning Systems*, 32(1):4–24. ArXiv: 1901.00596.

Simulating Feature Structures with Simple Types

Valentin D. Richard
LORIA, UMR 7503
Université de Lorraine, CNRS, Inria
54000 Nancy, France
valentin.richard@loria.fr

Abstract

Feature structures have been several times considered to enrich categorial grammars in order to build fine-grained grammars. Most attempts to unify both frameworks either model categorial types as feature structures or add feature structures on top of categorial types. We pursue a different approach: using feature structure as categorial atomic types. In this article, we present a procedure to create, from a simplified HPSG grammar, an equivalent abstract categorial grammar (ACG). We represent a feature structure by the enumeration of its totally well-typed upper bounds, so that unification can be simulated as intersection. We implement this idea as a meta-ACG preprocessor[1].

1 Introduction

Feature structures (FSs) (Carpenter, 1992) have been widely used to represent natural language syntax, particularly by HPSGs (*Head-driven Phrase Structure Grammars*, (Pollard and Sag, 1987, 1994)).

In the original ideas of categorial grammars (Ajdukiewicz, 1935; Bar-Hillel, 1953; Lambek, 1958), only a few number of atomic categories are taken, and complex categories are built on them as simple types. This approach makes it less flexible to capture fine-grained morpho-syntactic phenomena (e.g. agreement or case). Grammatical systems combining categorial and feature approaches have been developed, aiming at recovering these fine structures and grammatical interactions, but also allowing a better lexicon organization (e.g. hierarchy inheritance) (Moortgat, 1997).

According to Moortgat (1997), first generation hybrid systems (Zeevat, 1988; Bouma, 1988; Uszkoreit, 1986) encode categorial logic in feature logic.

By contrast, second generation hybrid systems (Dörre et al., 1996; Dörre and Manandhar, 1995) preserve the categorial inferential system by adding a layer of feature structures to categorial type atoms.[2]

While the general framework of feature logic may suffer from Turing-completeness when regarding time complexity of parsing (Carpenter, 1991), second generation hybrids bypass this issue by restricting feature structure power to subtyping (Buszkowski, 1988). However, this restriction forbids the latter to exploit structure-sharing (i.e. reentrancy).

More recent systems fall in either generation. Unification-based General Categorial grammars (Villavicencio, 2002; Baldridge, 2002) encode Combinatory Categorial Grammars (Steedman, 1988) as feature structures using asymmetric default unification. Extensions of Abstract Categorial Grammars (de Groote, 2001) to dependent product, variant types and records model feature logic inside type theory (de Groote and Maarek, 2007). However, these extensions make it undecidable (de Groote et al., 2007).

In this article, we advocate for a different, yet intuitive combination of categorial logic and feature logic: representing feature structures as atomic categorial types with no additional operation. Unification is not implemented, but simulated by set intersection. This proposal is based on two ideas:

1. Restrictions on appropriateness allows us to enumerate a representative set of any FS

2. The labor is divided into a preprocessor, handling FS combinatorics, and the grammar engine, performing categorial operations

This framework resembles second generation systems, because it creates a layer between feature

[1]Source code is available at https://doi.org/10.12763/VWKNSA

[2]Steedman (1990) and Muskens (2001) could also be put in the second generation. Moreover, we could mention Kraak (1995), who models FSs via modalities (Moortgat, 1996).

Proceedings of the 2022 Conference of the North American Chapter of the Association for Computational Linguistics: Human Language Technologies: Student Research Workshop, pages 113 - 122

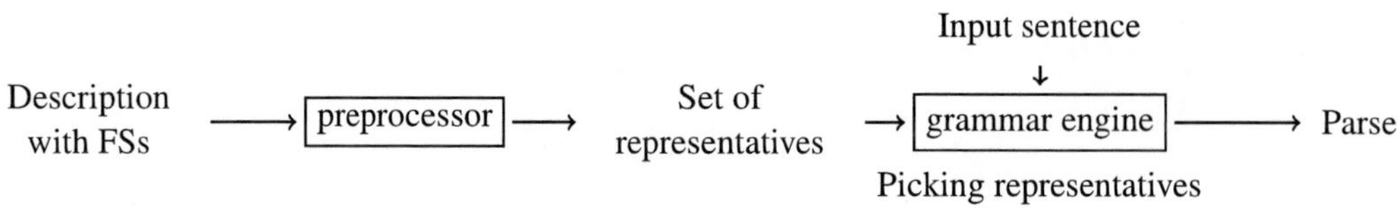

Figure 1: Division of labor between the preprocessor and the grammar engine

logic and categorial logic. However, there is no need to resort to unification, and it can deal with structure-sharing. Although it does not provide a different grammatical system, this solution has the advantage to be easier to implement.

We focus here on Abstract Categorial Grammars (ACGs). We present a first implementation of the preprocessor, called meta-ACG preprocessor. As feature structure are not yet implemented in ACGtk (Pogodalla, 2016), this program brings the possibility to work with ACGs and FSs. We also mention how it reduces labor when defining a grammar.

The motivation of this work is thus twofold:

1. Formalize a way to work with features structures and categorial logic, in particular ACGs
2. Improve ACGtk to be able to define feature structures and reduce some grammar design labor

In section 2, we present our system and its formal proof of work. We exemplify it by exhibiting a transformation from simplified HPSG grammars into ACG grammars. In section 3, we present the meta-ACG preprocessor.

2 Simulating feature structures

2.1 Feature structures as atoms

The idea of adding refinements of categorial atomic types goes back to Lambek (1958). He distinguishes third-person singular nouns n from third-person plural nouns n^*, and the verb *work* has two possible types: $n\backslash s$ and $n^*\backslash s$.

In systems where unification is not taken as granted, using FSs as atoms is a cheap solution: e.g. $\mathrm{PP_{to}}$ vs. $\mathrm{PP_{about}}$ in (Morrill et al., 2011), $NP\_NUM{=}PL$ in (Maršík, 2013), and *npe* (existentially quantified *np*) vs. *npu* (universally quantified) in (Amblard et al., 2021).

This technique relies on the grammar engine to select the right featured type when parsing. Therefore, no unification system has to be added. However, the main drawback is the combinatorial explosion due to the many possible values the attributes can take. For example, writing a grammar including all possible rules for *NP-VP* agreement would not only be long, but it also increases the risks of making typos. Maršík (2013) suggests to use meta-variables to, at least, present these rules more compactly.

We advocate for a more generic solution: automatizing the process of generation of constants and rules with FSs as atoms. For example, from a given description

$$\mathtt{np[AGR = x]} \to \mathtt{vp[AGR = x]} \to \mathtt{s}$$

we would like to generate

$$\begin{array}{c}\mathtt{np[AGR = [1, sg]]} \to \mathtt{vp[AGR = [1, sg]]} \to \mathtt{s}\\ \mathtt{np[AGR = [1, pl]]} \to \mathtt{vp[AGR = [1, pl]]} \to \mathtt{s}\\ \mathtt{np[AGR = [2, sg]]} \to \mathtt{vp[AGR = [2, sg]]} \to \mathtt{s}\\ \vdots\end{array} \quad (1)$$

where `np[AGR=[1,sg]]`,... are taken as atomic types.

The system we introduce works as depicted in Fig. 1. Given a set of descriptions, the preprocessor generates a set of representatives (like in (1)) out of any (underspecified) input FS. Then, the grammar engine can pick in this set when trying to parse a sentence.

In part 2.2 we define the set selected representatives are based on. Part 2.3 introduces ranked appropriateness, the hypothesis enabling this set to be enumerable. Finally, we present the transformation of simplified HPSG grammars into ACG grammars in part 2.4.

2.2 Set of representatives

We begin with some semi-formal reminders about feature structures.

Set $\langle \mathsf{T}, \sqsubseteq \rangle$ an inheritance hierarchy[3], and Att a finite set of attributes. By $\tau \sqsubseteq \sigma$, we mean that type τ is more general than type σ.

[3] Complementary formal definitions can be found in appendix B.

Type	Rank	Specification	Description
j-τ-list	0		list of at most j elements ($j \geq 0$)
j-τ-ne-list ($j \geq 1$)	$r(\tau) + 1$	HEAD : τ TAIL : $(j-1)$-*τ-list*	list of length between 1 and j

Table 1: Data structure simulating lists of at most m elements of type τ. 0-*τ-list* is the empty list (aka. *e-list*) The inheritance hierarchy is given in Fig. 2.

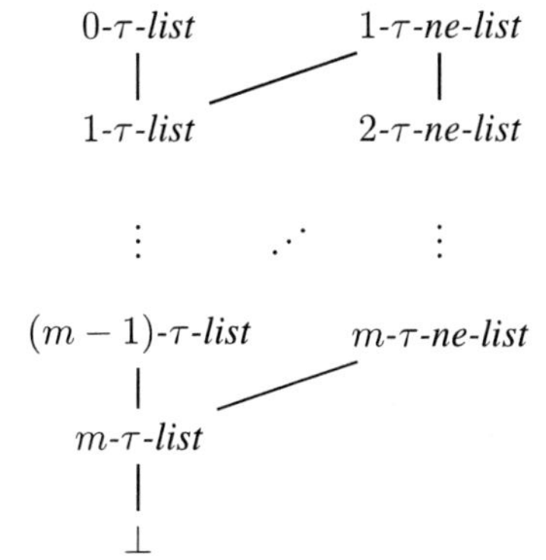

Figure 2: Inheritance hierarchy of types simulating lists of at most m elements of type τ. The appropriateness specification and ranks are given in Tab. 1.

Let us illustrate this here with *NP-VP* agreement, using $\mathsf{Att} = \{\text{P}, \text{N}\}$ and the following inheritance hierarchy:

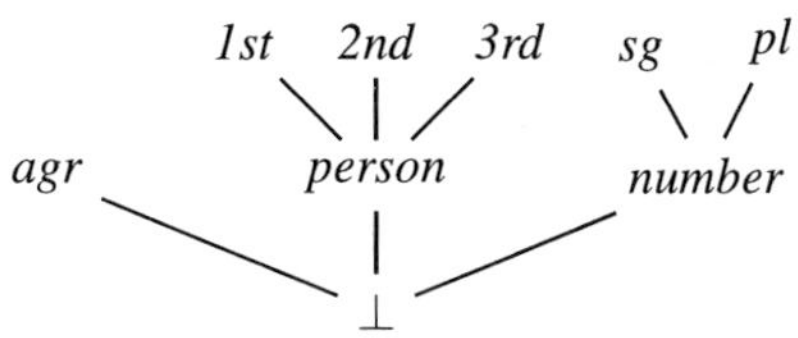

More general types are placed here at the bottom, e.g. *person* $\sqsubseteq$ *1st*. The most general type (i.e. the minimum) is $\bot$.

A feature structure (FS) is a pair of a type and a list of features. A feature is a pair of an attribute and a feature structure. We usually represent FSs as attribute-value matrices, like in (2). Subsumption $\sqsubseteq$ can be extended to FSs. The unification of two FSs F and G is the most general FS $F \sqcup G$ which is subsumed by F and G, if it exists. We only consider well-typed feature structures, i.e. having restrictions on the values a feature can take. These restrictions are expressed via an appropriateness specification.

By $X \nrightarrow Y$ we denote the set of partial functions f from X to Y, and we write $f(x)\downarrow$ if $x \in \mathsf{dom}\, f$, i.e. if x belongs to the definition domain of f.

Definition 1 (Appropriateness specification (Carpenter, 1992)). *An appropriateness specification is partial function* $\mathsf{Approp} : \mathsf{Att} \times \mathsf{T} \nrightarrow \mathsf{T}$ *such that*

Feature introduction: *For every* $\text{A} \in \mathsf{Att}$*, there exists* $\mathsf{Intro}(\text{A}) \in \mathsf{T}$ *s.t.* $\mathsf{Approp}(\text{A}, \mathsf{Intro}(\text{A}))\downarrow$

Monotonicity: *If* $\mathsf{Approp}(\text{A}, \sigma)\downarrow$ *and* $\sigma \sqsubseteq \tau$*, then* $\mathsf{Approp}(\text{A}, \tau)\downarrow$ *and* $\mathsf{Approp}(\text{A}, \sigma) \sqsubseteq \mathsf{Approp}(\text{A}, \tau)$

$\mathsf{Approp}(\text{A}, \tau) = \sigma$ means that a FS of type τ can have attribute A valued by a FS of type σ or more specific. The following notion of totally well-typed FSs allows us to talk about completely specified FSs.

Definition 2. *A feature structure is totally well-typed when all its appropriate attributes are valued.*

The appropriateness specification of our example is P : *person*, N : *number* for type *agr* (i.e. $\mathsf{Approp}(\text{P}, \mathit{agr}) = \mathit{person}$ and $\mathsf{Approp}(\text{N}, \mathit{agr}) = \mathit{number}$, and undefined elsewhere). For instance, both FSs below are well-typed, but only the one on the right is totally well-typed.

$$\begin{bmatrix} \mathit{agr} & \\ \text{P} & \mathit{1st} \end{bmatrix} \qquad \begin{bmatrix} \mathit{agr} & \\ \text{P} & \mathit{1st} \\ \text{N} & \mathit{number} \end{bmatrix} \tag{2}$$

First-order terms can be represented by their sets of subsumed ground terms. Similarly we could take, to represent a potentially underspecified FS in ACGs, its maximal (resp. or grounded) upper bounds. However, (Carpenter, 1992) points out that this fails because some feature structures can have the same set of maximal (resp. grounded) upper bounds, but still be different.

To solve this issue, we use totally well-typed (non-necessarily sort-resolved, grounded or maximal) upper bounds of a FS F to define the representative set of F.

Definition 3 (Totally well-typed upper-set)**.** *We call* $\mathcal{U}(F)$ *the set of totally well-typed upper bounds of* F.

This enables us to characterize unification as set intersection.

Proposition 1. *$F \sqcup G$ exists iff $\mathcal{U}(F) \cap \mathcal{U}(G) \neq \emptyset$, and in this case $\mathcal{U}(F \sqcup G) = \mathcal{U}(F) \cap \mathcal{U}(G)$.*

Proofs are given in appendix B.

2.3 Finite generation

We plan to model a feature structure F by adding a kind of copy of $\mathcal{U}(F)$ to an ACG grammar. The set $\mathcal{U}(F)$ has then to be finite. Therefore, we need FSs to be acyclic. Moreover, there must be no appropriateness (subsuming) loop, i.e. no type τ and path $\mathrm{W} \in \mathsf{Att}^*$ such that $\mathsf{Approp}(\mathrm{W}, \tau) \sqsubseteq \tau$. To enforce this, we require types to be ranked.

Definition 4. *Specification* Approp *is ranked if there exists a function $r : \mathsf{T} \to \mathbb{N}$ such that, for all $\tau \in \mathsf{T}$,*

1. *for all σ, if $\tau \sqsubseteq \sigma$ then $r(\tau) \leq r(\sigma)$*
2. *for all $\mathrm{A} \in \mathsf{Att}$ and σ, if $\mathsf{Approp}(\mathrm{A}, \tau) \sqsubseteq \sigma$, then $r(\tau) > r(\sigma)$*

$r(\tau)$ is the rank of τ.

Ranked appropriateness specifications allow us to proceed by induction on the set of well-typed feature structures.

Proposition 2. *If* Approp *is ranked, then the set of well-typed FSs is finite.*

A proof is given in appendix B.3.

Ranking restricts the expressive power of feature structures. However, we can still create a data structure resembling finite lists. Set τ a type and m an positive integer. We define τ-lists of at most m elements as in Tab. 1 and Fig. 2.

Ranking forbids potentially infinite elements, like lists of arbitrary length. This limit is actually not so restrictive because, supposing there is a reasonable maximal number of words a sentence can have, we could always resort to lists of a predefined maximal length.

2.4 Simple HPSG into ACG

The goal of this part is to illustrate our approach on a selected pair of language grammar formalisms based on feature structures and categorial types respectively.

We want to code a HPSG grammar $\mathcal{G}$ in an ACG grammar $\mathsf{ACG}(\mathcal{G})$. We focus on simple HPSG characteristics, following a context-free backbone. For simplicity, we do not take headedness and lexical rules into account. We also assume that the appropriateness specification of $\mathcal{G}$ is ranked (except for DTRS and PHON).

$$\frac{}{w \vdash \boxed{a} : \boxed{0}}\,(*)_{\boxed{a}}$$

$$\frac{u_1 \vdash \boxed{1'} : s_1 \quad \ldots \quad u_n \vdash \boxed{n'} : s_n}{u_1 \ldots u_n \vdash \boxed{c} : \boxed{0}}\,(**)_{\boxed{b}}$$

if there exists $\boxed{c} = \boxed{b} \sqcup \left[\text{DTRS} \quad \left\langle \boxed{1'}, \ldots, \boxed{n'} \right\rangle\right]$

for all $\boxed{a}$, $\boxed{b}$ in the grammar

Figure 3: Simplified HPSG deduction system

$$\frac{\mathsf{c}_F \in \mathcal{R}(\boxed{a})}{w \vdash \mathsf{c}_F : \boxed{0}}\,(*)_{\boxed{a},F}$$

$$\frac{u_1 \vdash M_1 : s_1 \quad \ldots \quad u_n \vdash M_n : s_n}{u_1 \ldots u_n \vdash \mathsf{c}_F\ M_1 \ldots M_n : \boxed{0}}\,(**)_{\boxed{b},F}$$

if $\mathsf{c}_F \in \mathcal{R}(\boxed{b})$ and $\mathsf{c}_F\ M_1 \ldots M_n : \mathsf{t}_{F_0}$ is well-typed

for all $\boxed{a}$, $\boxed{b}$ in the grammar and FS F

Figure 4: Image ACG deduction system. $\mathsf{c}_F\ M_1 \ldots M_n$ is λ-application.

We assume lexical items and phrases are of the form $(*)$ and $(**)$.

$$\boxed{a}\begin{bmatrix} \textit{word} & \\ \text{PHON} & w \\ \text{SYNSEM} & \boxed{0} \end{bmatrix} \qquad (*)$$

$$\boxed{b}\begin{bmatrix} \textit{phrase} & \\ \text{PHON} & u_1 \ldots u_n \\ \text{SYNSEM} & \boxed{0} \\ \text{DTRS} & \left\langle \boxed{1}\left[\text{PHON } u_1\right], \ldots, \boxed{n}\left[\text{PHON } u_n\right] \right\rangle \end{bmatrix} \qquad (**)$$

Feature structures of type *word* $(*)$ are lexical units. Attribute PHON specifies the phonological realization (here the spelling), and SYSSEM the syntactic and semantics properties.

Feature structures of type *phrase* $(**)$ represent phrases with contiguous daughters (DTRS) $\boxed{1}$,..., $\boxed{n}$. The concatenation of the phonological realizations of the daughters make up the PHON of the phrase. The syntactic and semantics properties of the phrase also depend on the ones of the daughters via structure sharing (i.e. reentrancy).

See appendix A for instance examples.

The constraints on HPSG parsing can be rephrased as the deduction system in Fig. 3 (using the notation of (∗) and (∗∗)).

We translate this system into the ACG deduction system in Fig. 4, using the representative sets defined in def. 5. Phrase FSs are represented by a set of second-order typed constants.

Definition 5. *Given a word* $\boxed{a}$ *as in* (∗) *or a phrase* $\boxed{b}$ *as in* (∗∗)*, its set of representatives is defined by induction on its rank, as the set of ACG typed constants:*

$$\begin{aligned} \mathcal{R}(\boxed{a}) = & \ \{c_F : t_F \mid F \in \mathcal{U}(\boxed{a})\} \\ \mathcal{R}(\boxed{b}) = & \ \{c_F : t_{F_1} \to \ldots \to t_{F_n} \to t_{F_0} \mid \\ & \quad F \in \mathcal{U}(\boxed{b}) \text{ consistent with} \\ & \quad F_i \in \mathcal{U}(\boxed{i}) \text{ for all } 0 \leq i \leq n\} \end{aligned} \quad (3)$$

using the same $\boxed{i}$*'s as in* (∗∗).

Fig. 4 presents an ACG grammar in the style of λ-grammars (Muskens, 2001). We give in appendix C an alternative presentation of this grammar using the format used by de Groote (de Groote, 2001).

Proposition 3. $\mathcal{G}$ *and* ACG($\mathcal{G}$) *have the same string language.*

A proof is given in appendix B.4. A derivation instance is displayed in appendix A.

A sample HPSG grammar modeling simple English questions in the meta-ACG language is provided in the `example` folder of the enclosed program.

3 Implementation

3.1 Meta-ACG preprocessor

ACGtk (Pogodalla, 2016) is a toolkit offering an environment to develop and test ACG grammars. Feature structures have not been implemented yet in this program.

We implement the preprocessor presented in part 2.1 as a python program called `macg`. Given an input file written in a specially designed language, called meta-ACG language, this program generates an ACG grammar. This output consists in tree files: deep syntax signature, surface syntax signature and surface lexicon (see definition 11).

The syntax of the meta-ACG language is greatly inspired by NLTK (Bird et al., 2009), except that variables are declared with `@`. See Fig. 5 for an example minimal code.

```
Type:  person < 1st, 2nd, 3rd
Type:  number < sg, pl
Type:  tense  < prst, past
Type:  agr
  P : person
  N : number
Type:  np
  AGR : agr       # agreement
  PRO : bool      # pronominal
Type:  vp
  AGR : agr
  T : tense
Type:  s
  T : tense
Constant:  Proper nouns
  Ash :  np[agr[3rd,sg],-PRO]
Constant:  Intransitive verbs
  sleeps :  vp[agr[3rd,sg],prst]
  slept  :  vp[past]
Rule:  Clause
  np[AGR=@a] -> vp[AGR=@a,T=@t] \
    -> s[T=@t]
```

Figure 5: Sample code in the meta-ACG language, exemplifying NP – VP agreement. Italics is put on comments. Boldface identifies control keywords. `bool` is the predefined type of booleans.

The meta-ACG preprocessor has two main goals:

1. Making it possible to develop and test ACG grammars with feature structures
2. Reducing the redundancy of ACGtk grammar design

Goal 1 is obtained through an iterator able to generate all unfolded totally well-typed upper bounds of a feature structure description. These upper bounds are written as distinct atomic types in the output files. For example, constant `slept` of Fig. 5 yields $4 \times 3 = 12$ deep syntax constant:

```
SLEPT_person_number_past  :  vp_person_number_past
SLEPT_person_sg_past      :  vp_person_sg_past
SLEPT_person_pl_past      :  vp_person_pl_past
SLEPT_1st_number_past     :  vp_1st_number_past
                          ⋮
SLEPT_3rd_pl_past         :  vp_3rd_pl_past
```

Similarly, rules are mapped to deep syntax constants of empty surface realization for every possible variable assignment. For example, the clause rule of Fig. 5 generates $(4 \times 3) \times 3 \times 3 = 108$ constants (i.e. every person, number, time, and pronominality type).

The ranking condition is ensured by the order in which the types and their appropriateness specifications are declared.

Goal 2 is obtained by two means. As a script language, the meta-ACG language aims at being light. The main contribution, however, revolves on the way ACG conventions are coded in the preprocessor. Even if ACGtk is able to handle a large variety of ACG grammars, most actually written test grammars follow the same pattern and code norms:

- a deep syntax constant in uppercase is mapped to its surface representation in lowercase
- the order in which the source types are declared is the same as the surface order of the respective arguments

This way, taking these conventions as default helps gain some time at the grammar design phase.

3.2 Limitations and future prospects

The `macg` program is still under development. We intend to add morphological rules and macros to facilitate even more the lexicon organization. Inequalities, default values and constraint equations could also be added in the future.

Although Tab. 1 gives an implementation of lists in our setting, the current meta-ACG language lacks primitives, like concatenation, to work with lists more easily. Technically, list concatenation can be written down by enumerating all element-wise operations as different rules. But this is not convenient. This also holds for sets, which are commonly used on LOCAL features in HPSG (e.g. SLASH).

Because of FS enumeration, there is an inevitable combinatorial explosion. This affects parsing time complexity exponentially in the number of attributes and the highest rank. In practice, we observe that our program actually runs slowly if complex type structures (e.g. lists as presented here) are involved. For instance, it took 1 hour to run `macg` on the very short `hpsg.macg` included example grammar, creating an intermediary grammar of several gigabytes. Therefore, this preprocessor approach might not be well suited for large-scale grammars. However, it offers a valuable tool for a quick development of experimental fragment grammars and prototypes.

Finally, we are planning to add the possibility to define a lexicon to type-theoretic semantics.

4 Conclusion

We introduced and formalized a novel way to include feature structures in categorial grammars. Our method consists in automatizing the idea of taking feature structures as categorial atomic types. The labor is divided into two separate modules: a preprocessor and a grammar engine. For every type with a feature structure, the preprocessor generates a representative set of categorial types. This creates an intermediary grammar given to the grammar engine. The latter works on these representative categorial types and just have to select right ones when parsing a sentence.

We proved that this approach of simulating feature structures by a set of representatives is sound and complete by showing that unification amounts to intersection of these representative sets. Having such a preprocessor avoids adding a unification module inside the grammar engine. It is modular and also easier to implement.

We evaluated this proposal by implementing a preprocessor for the grammar engine ACGtk working on abstract categorial grammars (ACG). This provides the first implementation of feature structures in an ACG toolkit. Example grammars show the well functioning of this method.

However, example grammars with a complex system of type hierarchy outlines the limits of the "enumeration-and-intersection" approach. Because of combinatorial explosion, the intermediary grammar can get really voluminous and take time to be created. This may restrict uses of such a preprocessor to toy ACG grammars only, waiting for a more efficient implementation of feature structures in ACGtk.

References

Kazimierz Ajdukiewicz. 1935. Die syntaktische Konnexität. *Studia Philosophica*, 1:1–27.

Maxime Amblard, Maria Boritchev, and Philippe de Groote. 2021. An inquisitive account of wh-questions through event semantics. In *LACL 2021 - Logical Aspects of Computational Linguistics*, Montpellier (online), France.

Jason Baldridge. 2002. *Lexically Specified Derivational Control in Combinatory Categorial Grammar*. Ph.D. thesis, Institute for Communicating and Collaborative Systems. University of Edinburgh.

Yehoshua Bar-Hillel. 1953. A Quasi-Arithmetical Notation for Syntactic Description. *Language*, 29(1):47–58.

Steven Bird, Ewan Klein, and Edward Loper. 2009. *Natural Language Processing with Python*. O'Reilly Media Inc.

Gosse Bouma. 1988. *Nonmonotonicity and Categorial Unification Grammar*. Ph.D. thesis, Rijksuniversiteit Groningen.

Wojciech Buszkowski. 1988. Generative Power of Categorial Grammars. In Richard T. Oehrle, Emmon Bach, and Deirdre Wheeler, editors, *Categorial Grammars and Natural Language Structures*, pages 69–94. Springer Netherlands, Dordrecht.

Bob Carpenter. 1991. The generative power of categorial grammars and head-driven phrase structure grammars with lexical rules. *Computational Linguistics*, 17(3):301–313.

Robert L. Carpenter. 1992. *The Logic of Typed Feature Structures: With Applications to Unification Grammars, Logic Programs and Constraint Resolution*. Cambridge Tracts in Theoretical Computer Science. Cambridge University Press, Cambridge.

Philippe de Groote. 2001. Towards abstract categorial grammars. In *Association for Computational Linguistics, 39th Annual Meeting and 10th Conference of the European Chapter*, pages 148–155, Toulouse, France.

Philippe de Groote and Sarah Maarek. 2007. Type-theoretic extensions of abstract categorial grammars. In *New Directions in Type-theoretic Grammars (NDTTG 2007). ESSLLI 2007 Workshop*, Dublin. Working paper or preprint.

Philippe de Groote, Sarah Maarek, and Ryo Yoshinaka. 2007. On Two Extensions of Abstract Categorial Grammars. In *Logic for Programming, Artificial Intelligence, and Reasoning*, Lecture Notes in Computer Science, pages 273–287, Berlin, Heidelberg. Springer.

Jochen Dörre, Esther König, and Dov Gabbay. 1996. Fibred Semantics for Feature-Based Grammar Logic. *Journal of Logic, Language, and Information*, 5(3/4):387–422.

Jochen Dörre and Suresh Manandhar. 1995. On Constraint-Based Lambek Calculi. In Patrick Blackburn and Marrten de Rijke, editors, *Logic, Structures and Syntax*. Reidel, Dordrecht.

Esther Kraak. 1995. French Clitics: A Categorial Perspective. Master's thesis, Universiteit Utrecht.

Joachim Lambek. 1958. The mathematics of sentence structure. *American Mathematical Monthly*, pages 154–170.

Jiří Maršík. 2013. Towards a Wide-Coverage Grammar : Graphical Abstract Categorical Grammars. Master's thesis, Université de Lorraine, June.

Michael Moortgat. 1996. Multimodal linguistic inference. *Journal of Logic, Language and Information*, 5(3/4):349–385.

Michael Moortgat. 1997. Categorial Type Logics. In Johan van Benthem and Alice ter Meulen, editors, *Handbook of Logic and Language*. Elsevier.

Glyn Morrill, Oriol Valentín, and Mario Fadda. 2011. The Displacement Calculus. *Journal of Logic, Language and Information*, 20(1):1–48.

Reinhard Muskens. 2001. Categorial Grammar and Lexical-Functional Grammar. In *Proceedings of the LFG01 Conference*, pages 259–279, University of Hong Kong.

Sylvain Pogodalla. 2016. ACGtk : un outil de développement et de test pour les grammaires catégorielles abstraites. In *Actes de la conférence conjointe JEP-TALN-RECITAL 2016. volume 5 : Démonstrations*, pages 1–2, Paris, France. AFCP - ATALA.

Carl Pollard and Ivan A. Sag. 1987. *Information-Based Syntax and Semantics, Vol. 1: Fundamentals*. The Center for the Study of Language and Information Publications, Stanford, CA.

Carl Pollard and Ivan A. Sag. 1994. *Head-Driven Phrase Structure Grammar*. University of Chicago Press, Chicago.

Mark Steedman. 1988. Combinators and Grammars. In Richard T. Oehrle, Emmon Bach, and Deirdre Wheeler, editors, *Categorial Grammars and Natural Language Structures*, pages 417–442. Springer Netherlands, Dordrecht.

Mark J. Steedman. 1990. Gapping as constituent coordination. *Linguistics and Philosophy*, 13(2):207–263.

Hans Uszkoreit. 1986. Categorial Unification Grammars. In *COLING 1986*, pages 187–194, Bonn.

Aline Villavicencio. 2002. *The Acquisition of a Unification-Based Generalised Categorial Grammar*. Ph.D. thesis, University of Cambridge, Cambridge.

Henk Zeevat. 1988. Combining Categorial Grammar and Unification. In U. Reyle and C. Rohrer, editors, *Natural Language Parsing and Linguistic Theories*, pages 202–229. Springer Netherlands, Dordrecht.

A Further examples

We provide here an example to illustrate section 2.4. By lack of space, let us consider a very simplified toy HPSG grammar able to parse the sentence "*Ash slept*". It is based on the example code given in Fig.5. This grammar includes the two word FSs $\boxed{1'}$ and $\boxed{2'}$ below, as well as the phrase FS $\boxed{b}$ (Fig. 6) used to create a basic sentence with *NP-VP* agreement.

$$\boxed{1'}\begin{bmatrix} word & \\ \text{PHON} & Ash \\ \text{SYNSEM} & \boxed{0_{1'}}\begin{bmatrix} np & \\ \text{AGR} & \begin{bmatrix} \text{P} & 3 \\ \text{N} & sg \end{bmatrix} \\ \text{PRO} & - \end{bmatrix} \end{bmatrix}$$

$$\boxed{2'}\begin{bmatrix} word & \\ \text{PHON} & slept \\ \text{SYNSEM} & \boxed{0_{2'}}\begin{bmatrix} vp & \\ \text{AGR} & agr \\ \text{T} & past \end{bmatrix} \end{bmatrix}$$

The derivation of "*Ash slept*" in the deduction system of Fig. 3 is given in (4). FS $\boxed{c}$ is like $\boxed{b}$ but with $\boxed{1}$ and $\boxed{2}$ unified with $\boxed{1'}$ and $\boxed{2'}$ respectively.

$$\dfrac{\dfrac{}{\text{Ash} \vdash \boxed{1'} : \boxed{0_{1'}}}(*)_{\boxed{1'}} \qquad \dfrac{}{\text{slept} \vdash \boxed{2'} : \boxed{0_{2'}}}(*)_{\boxed{2'}}}{\text{Ash slept} \vdash \boxed{c} : \boxed{0_c}}(**)_{\boxed{b}} \tag{4}$$

Its transformation in the ACG system of Fig. 4 as described by the proof of proposition 3 is written in (5).

$$\dfrac{\dfrac{}{\text{Ash} \vdash c_{\boxed{1'}} : \boxed{0_{1'}}}(*)_{\boxed{1'},\boxed{1'}} \qquad \dfrac{}{\text{slept} \vdash c_{\boxed{2'}} : \boxed{0_{2'}}}(*)_{\boxed{2'},\boxed{2'}}}{\text{Ash slept} \vdash c_{\boxed{b}}\, c_{\boxed{1'}}\, c_{\boxed{2'}} : \boxed{0_c}}(**)_{\boxed{b},\boxed{c}} \tag{5}$$

B Formal definitions and proofs

We provide here complementary formal definitions and proofs of the propositions stated in the main part.

B.1 Definitions

The following definitions are retrieved from Carpenter (1992).

Definition 6 (Inheritance hierarchy)**.** *An inheritance hierarchy* $\langle \mathsf{T}, \sqsubseteq \rangle$ *is a finite bounded complete partial order, i.e. a finite partial order such that every subset* $S \subseteq \mathsf{T}$ *having an upper bound has a least upper bound (aka. a join)* $\bigsqcup S \in \mathsf{T}$.

In particular, the empty set has a least upper bound noted $\bot$*, which is then the minimum of* T.

Definition 7 (Well-typed FS)**.** *A well-typed feature structure is a tuple* $F = \langle Q, \overline{q}, \theta, \delta \rangle$ *where*

- Q *is a finite non-empty tree of root* $\overline{q} \in Q$
- $\theta : Q \to \mathsf{T}$ *is a total node typing function*
- $\delta : \mathsf{Att} \times Q \nrightarrow Q$ *is a feature partial function*
- *for every* q, A *such that* $\delta(\text{A}, q)\downarrow$, *then* $\mathsf{Approp}(\text{A}, \theta(q))\downarrow$ *and*

$$\mathsf{Approp}(\text{A}, \theta(q)) \sqsubseteq \theta(\delta(\text{A}, q))$$

$\mathcal{TF}$ *is the set of well-typed feature structures.*

Here we only consider well-typed feature structures (FS), and up to alphabetic variance.

Subsumption $\sqsubseteq$ and unification $\sqcup$ can be extended to well-typed feature structures.

Definition 8 (Subsumption of FS)**.** $F = \langle Q, \overline{q}, \theta, \delta \rangle$ *subsumes* $F' = \langle Q', \overline{q}', \theta', \delta' \rangle$*, written* $F \sqsubseteq F'$*, if there exists a function* $h : Q \to Q'$ *called morphism meeting the following conditions*

- $h(\overline{q}) = \overline{q}'$
- *for every* $q \in Q$, $\theta(q) \sqsubseteq \theta'(h(q))$
- *for every* q, A*, if* $\delta(\text{A}, q)\downarrow$*, then* $h(\delta(\text{A}, q)) = \delta'(\text{A}, h(q))$

Subsumption is a partial ordering on $\mathcal{TF}$.

Definition 9 (Unification of FS)**.** *The unification of two well-typed FSs* F, F' *is, if it exists, the least upper bound of* F *and* F' *inside* $\mathcal{TF}$.

Here is the formal definition of totally well-typed FSs.

Definition 10 (Totally well-typed FS)**.** *A well-typed FS is totally well-typed if for all* $q \in Q$ *and* $\text{A} \in \mathsf{Att}$*, if* $\mathsf{Approp}(\text{A}, \theta(q))\downarrow$*, then* $\delta(\text{A}, q)\downarrow$.

B.2 Proof of proposition 1

Proof. Set two feature structures F and G.

• Suppose $F \sqcup G$ exists. As $\mathcal{U}$ is clearly antitonic, and $F, G \sqsubseteq F \sqcup G$, we have $\mathcal{U}(\mathcal{F} \sqcup G) \subseteq \mathcal{U}(F), \mathcal{U}(G)$, so

$$\mathcal{U}(\mathcal{F} \sqcup G) \subseteq \mathcal{U}(F) \cap \mathcal{U}(G)$$

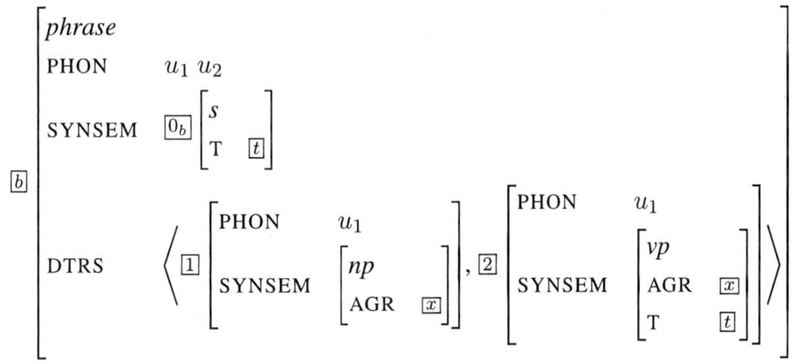

Figure 6: Feature structure for simple *NP-VP* phrase.

Moreover, by theorem 6.15 of Carpenter (1992), as Approp has no loop because of ranking, there exists at least one totally well-typed FS H such that $F \sqcup G \sqsubseteq H$. Therefore, $\mathcal{U}(\mathcal{F} \sqcup G) \neq \emptyset$, and so $\mathcal{U}(F) \cap \mathcal{U}(G) \neq \emptyset$.

• Now suppose there exists $H \in \mathcal{U}(F) \cap \mathcal{U}(G)$. As H is an upper bound of F and G, by theorem 6.9 of Carpenter (1992) they have a well-typed unification $\mathcal{F} \sqcup G$.

Moreover, we have $F \sqcup G \sqsubseteq H$ by minimality of the unification. As H is totally well-typed, H belongs to $\mathcal{U}(\mathcal{F} \sqcup G)$ too. Therefore

$$\mathcal{U}(F) \cap \mathcal{U}(G) \subseteq \mathcal{U}(\mathcal{F} \sqcup G)$$

In consequence, we proved that $\mathcal{F} \sqcup G$ exists iff $\mathcal{U}(F) \cap \mathcal{U}(G) \neq \emptyset$, and that in this case

$$\mathcal{U}(F) \cap \mathcal{U}(G) = \mathcal{U}(\mathcal{F} \sqcup G)$$

□

B.3 Proof of proposition 2

Proof. We write $\mathsf{T}_n = r^{-1}(n)$, which is finite because T is so.

By induction on $n \in \mathbb{N}$, let us prove that the set $\mathcal{TF}_n$ of FSs F of type $\tau \in \mathsf{T}_n$ is finite.

If $n = 0$, condition 2 of def. 4 implies that τ is appropriate for no attribute. As T_0 is finite, so is $\mathcal{TF}_0$.

If $n > 1$, then for all A such that $\delta(\mathrm{A}, \overline{q})\downarrow$, $\mathsf{Approp}(\mathrm{A}, \tau) \sqsubseteq \theta(\delta(\mathrm{A}, \overline{q}))$. Therefore

$$n = r(\tau) > r(\theta(\delta(\mathrm{A}, \overline{q})))$$

by condition 2 again.

So we can apply the induction hypothesis on $r(\theta(\delta(\mathrm{A}, \overline{q})))$. As Att is finite, so is the set of FSs of type τ. Then, as T_n is finite, so is $\mathcal{TF}_n$.

Since T is finite, there is a finite number of n such that $\mathsf{T}_n \neq \emptyset$. Therefore $\mathcal{TF} = \biguplus_{n \in \mathbb{N}} \mathcal{TF}_n$ is finite.

□

B.4 Proof of proposition 3

Proof. Let us begin with showing that

$$\mathcal{L}(\mathcal{G}) \subseteq \mathcal{L}(\mathsf{ACG}(\mathcal{G}))$$

$\boxed{\subseteq}$ Suppose string u is parsed by $\mathcal{G}$. There exists a derivation π of Fig. 3. We propagate the unification steps to the leaves and infer total type (Carpenter, 1992, thm. 6.15). From that, we construct a proof π' of Fig. 4 of same precedent and type, by induction on π:

If axiom $\pi = (*)_{\boxed{a}}$ exposes FS F, $F \in \mathcal{U}(\boxed{a})$. So we take $\pi' = (*)_{\boxed{a},F}$. This axioms has the same precedent w and type $\boxed{0}$ as π.

Suppose $\pi = (**)_{\boxed{b}}(\pi_1, ..., \pi_n)$ exposes FS F. Construct derivations $\pi'_1, ..., \pi'_n$ from $\pi_1, ..., \pi_n$ respectively, by induction hypothesis. We have $F \in \mathcal{U}(\boxed{c})$.

Moreover, from proposition 1 we deduce $\mathcal{U}(\boxed{c}) \subseteq \mathcal{U}(\boxed{b})$, because $\boxed{c} = \boxed{b} \sqcup \boxed{d}$ for some $\boxed{d}$. Therefore $F \in \mathcal{U}(\boxed{b})$.

As unification has been propagated, we have

$$F \left[\mathrm{DTRS} \quad \left\langle F_1 \,, ..., F_n \right\rangle \right]$$

where F_i is the FS exposed at π_i, and π'_i has term M_i.

We thus have $c_F : \mathsf{t}_{F_1} \to ... \to \mathsf{t}_{F_n} \to \mathsf{t}_{F_0}$ with $c_F \in \mathcal{R}(\boxed{b})$, therefore term $\mathsf{c}_F\ M_1\ ...\ M_n : \mathsf{t}_{F_0}$ is well-typed. As a result, the derivation $\pi' = (**)_{\boxed{b},F}(\pi'_1, ..., \pi'_n)$ is well-formed and has the same precedent $u_1 ... u_n$ and type $\boxed{0}$ as π.

As the root sequent of π is a finite sentence, its type is S, and so is the type of π'. Therefore $u \in \mathcal{L}(\mathsf{ACG}(\mathcal{G}))$.

Now let us show that

$$\mathcal{L}(\mathcal{G}) \supseteq \mathcal{L}(\mathsf{ACG}(\mathcal{G}))$$

$\boxed{\supseteq}$ Suppose string u is parsed by $\mathsf{ACG}(\mathcal{G})$. There exists a derivation π of Fig. 4 with precedent u. We construct a proof π' of Fig. 3 by induction on π by replacing axioms $(*)_{\boxed{a},F}$ by axioms $(*)_{\boxed{a}}$ and rules $(**)_{\boxed{b},F}$ by rules $(**)_{\boxed{b}}$. Each sequent $v \vdash M : s$ of π is mapped to $v \vdash \boxed{b} : s$ in π' with the λ-head c_F of M belonging to $\mathcal{R}(\boxed{b})$, so $F \in \mathcal{U}(\boxed{b})$. Therefore, π' is well-formed, has a sentence type, and thus $u \in \mathcal{L}(\mathcal{G})$.

□

C Alternative presentation of image ACG grammar

We give here an alternative presentation of the ACG grammar defined in Fig. 4 using the format used by de Groote (2001).

Definition 11. *Set Σ_1 the abstract signature where*

- *types are the* SYNSEM $\boxed{0}$ *of the word FSs and phrase FSs of $\mathcal{G}$*
- *constants are the representatives c_F of the word FSs or phrase FSs F of $\mathcal{G}$*
- *the type of c_F is the* SYNSEM *of F*

Set Σ_2 the signature of strings (de Groote, 2001, sec. 4), where constants are the phonological representations w of word FSs.

$$\begin{array}{c}\Sigma_1\\ \downarrow\mathcal{Y}\\ \Sigma_2\end{array}$$

We define the ACG grammar $\mathsf{ACG}(\mathcal{G}) = \langle \Sigma_1, \Sigma_2, \mathcal{Y}, S\rangle$ *with $\mathcal{Y} : \Sigma_1 \to \Sigma_2$ the lexicon mapping*

1. *$c_F \mapsto w$ if $F \in \mathcal{U}(\boxed{a})$ for some $\boxed{a}$ as in $(*)$*
2. *$c_F \mapsto \lambda x_1, ..., x_n.\ x_1 \ ...\ x_n$ if $F \in \mathcal{U}(\boxed{b})$ for some $\boxed{b}$ as in $(**)$*

and S is the feature structure of sentences[4] *(Pollard and Sag, 1994):*

$$\left[\text{LOC} \mid \text{CAT}\begin{bmatrix}\text{HEAD} & \textit{verb}\begin{bmatrix}\text{VFORM} & \textit{fin}\end{bmatrix}\\ \text{SUBCAT} & \textit{e-list}\end{bmatrix}\right]$$

As the appropriateness specification of $\mathcal{G}$ is ranked, $\mathsf{ACG}(\mathcal{G})$ is a well-defined ACG.

[4] Actually, there may be several FSs S of finite sentence (e.g. with different tenses). As the traditional definition of ACGs only allows one distinguished type, we could add a single extra abstract type s_d and abstract constants $T_S : S \to \mathsf{s}_d$ mapped to $\lambda x.\ x$ for every S.

Dr. Livingstone, I presume? Polishing of foreign character identification in literary texts

Aleksandra Konovalova
University of Turku
aleksandra.a.konovalova@utu.fi

Kristiina Taivalkoski-Shilov
University of Turku
kristiina.taivalkoski-shilov@utu.fi

Antonio Toral
University of Groningen
a.toral.ruiz@rug.nl

Abstract

Character identification is a key element for many narrative-related tasks. To implement it, the baseform of the name of the character (or lemma) needs to be identified, so different appearances of the same character in the narrative could be aligned. In this paper we tackle this problem in translated texts (English–Finnish translation direction), where the challenge regarding lemmatizing foreign names in an agglutinative language appears. To solve this problem, we present and compare several methods. The results show that the method based on a search for the shortest version of the name proves to be the easiest, best performing (83.4% F_1), and most resource-independent.

1 Introduction

Character identification is both a complex and a difficult task that can be solved using different methods, from manual (Declerck et al., 2012) to automatic (Goh et al., 2012). One of the necessary steps for character identification is to detect which exact character appears in the text (Labatut and Bost, 2019). For such detection, lemmatization is required.

Lemmatization is a process of assigning to a wordform its lemma (Kanerva et al., 2019). It is one of the important tasks in Natural Language Processing (henceforth NLP), since many other NLP methods require it during the preprocessing stage. For agglutinative languages, such as Finnish, correct lemmatization can turn out to be a difficult task because one word can have many wordforms (e.g. a Finnish word may have more than 50 wordforms. Consider an example for English name *Lizzy* in Finnish translation: *Lizzy*, *Lizzystä* (from / about Lizzy), *Lizzylle* (to Lizzy), *Lizzyn* (Lizzy's)). Current state-of-the-art models that use Neural Networks can help with solving this task. For example, such a lemmatization model is implemented as part of the Turku neural parser pipeline, which currently yields the best results for Finnish lemmatization (Kanerva et al., 2019). However, their accuracy, though close to 100%[1], is not perfect, so lemmatization may require further refinement which would help to enhance the end result for character identification.

In this paper we discuss enhancing foreign characters' identification for English characters in Finnish texts, via improving lemmatization of characters' names. The structure of the paper is as follows: first we provide an overview of the related work (Section 2), subsequently we describe our data (Section 3), after which we discuss the creation of the gold standard for our methods and a definition of character in the context of our research (Section 4). We continue the paper with describing the methods (Section 5) that we introduced and used. Finally, we present our results and analyze them (Section 6). We conclude our paper in Section 7. Code for the paper is available at https://github.com/AleksanKo/naacl2022.

2 Related work

Lemmatization for agglutinative languages, such as the one targeted in our study (Finnish), has been tackled from different perspectives. The first attempts to solve the problem for Finnish were the FINTWOL tool (Koskenniemi, 1983) and Morfo (Jäppinen and Ylilammi, 1986). Around three decades later one of the most known non-neural methods, Omorfi (Pirinen, 2015) was developed. Omorfi uses finite state transducers and can be used further for enhancing lemmatization (Silfverberg et al., 2016). The current state-of-the-art is represented by Turku neural parser pipeline (Kanerva et al., 2018), (Kanerva et al., 2019) that treats lemmatization as a sequence-to-sequence problem using the OpenNMT neural machine translation

[1] It ranges from 95.1% to 97.7%, depending on Finnish morphological annotation it is applied to (Kanerva et al., 2019).

Proceedings of the 2022 Conference of the North American Chapter of the Association for Computational Linguistics: Human Language Technologies: Student Research Workshop, pages 123 - 128
July 10-15, 2022 ©2022 Association for Computational Linguistics

toolkit (Klein et al., 2017) and yields 95%-97% accuracy.

In our research, we are focusing on retrieving canonical forms of foreign names. This may be challenging since foreign names are not typically expected by the lemmatizer, so it may be prone to errors. However, this step is necessary in case of agglutinative languages: otherwise one character may split into two or more characters (for example, instead of *Catherine*, we would have three entities: *Catherine*, *Catherinea* and *Catherinen*), which affects further the results for building character networks or narrative.

3 Data

The data used in our experiments is a corpus of Finnish translations made by Kersti Juva (a subcorpus of the *Classics of English and American Literature in Finnish* corpus, or *CEAL*[2]). The corpus consists of the short novel *Washingtonin Aukio*, 2003 ("Washington Square", 1880) by Henry James and the novels *Ylpeys ja ennakkoluulo*, 2013 ("Pride and Prejudice", 1813) by Jane Austen and *Kolea talo*, 2006 ("Bleak House", 1853) by Charles Dickens. The corpus is stored as text files, 3 files and 384,053 words in total.

4 Creation of gold standard

Before applying our methods (see Section 5), we had to choose a gold standard character names' list, so that we can evaluate our methods. To perform this task, we got the information from different internet sources that contain information about characters from the novels in our dataset (see Appendix A).

While creating a gold standard character names' list, we also faced many questions about characters, such as: what is a literary character? Who do we consider a character from the point of the narrative? Who do we consider a character from the point of character extraction where we are forced to filter the results of automatic Named Entity Recognition[3]? Do we take into consideration off-screen characters (characters that are only mentioned in the text and do not participate in the plot)? To answer these questions, we need to define what / who the character is.

[2]https://www.kielipankki.fi/corpora/ceal-2/

[3]This is part of the preprocessing used in our experiments, see Section 5.

The literary character can be seen as a construct whose definition and features depend on the study area (Margolin, 1990). Jannidis (2013) considered a character "a text- or media-based figure in a storyworld, usually human or human-like" or "an entity in a storyworld". Overall, characters are intertwined with narrative and storyworld, contributing to their development from many aspects.

We considered a literary character every figure that was relevant for the narrative development (thus, e.g. names of famous persons that are mentioned but do not appear in the novel were not included). So we decided to include both onscreen (entities that are actively participating in the storyworld) and off-screen (entities that are passively contributing to the construction of the storyworld) characters (e.g. in case of *Washington Square*, it was the mother of the main character that gets mentioned only twice). We also included all possible names that can be used for naming a certain character by splitting the full name (e.g. *Elizabeth Bennet* would also get versions *Elizabeth* and *Bennet*) and by analyzing possible versions (*Lizzy* for *Elizabeth Bennet*) that were mentioned in the internet sources (see Appendix A). So *Elizabeth Bennet* would get the following names: *Bennet*, *Eliza*, *Eliza Bennet*, *Elizabeth*, *Elizabeth Bennet*, *Lizzy*. The creating of the gold standard was carried out only by one annotator.

5 Methods

To apply our methods, we have to carry out the preprocessing first. This includes the following workflow:

1. Applying Named Entity Recognition on Finnish translations of English texts;
2. Filtering the named entities identified by label, removing all entities that are not persons;
3. Getting the lemmas for the remaining named entities.

For Named Entity Recognition on Finnish texts and further lemmatization, a Python library named Stanza (Qi et al., 2020) was used, because it provided a state-of-the-art level of Named Entity Recognition for this language. Finnish language models are represented in Stanza by Turku neural parser pipeline (Kanerva et al., 2019), so we will be using the Turku neural parser pipeline's lemmatizer (Kanerva et al., 2018) as a baseline.

We have used and compared three methods of finding correct names' lemmas. These methods were applied on the output of the preprocessing, i.e. lists of names that were results of applying Named Entity Recognition on Finnish translations, then filtering only person-type entities, and finally lemmatizing them. The methods were implemented using Python and are as follows:

1. *Method 1*: Check for the shortest version of the name. This method was based on two assumptions: 1) that the language is agglutinative, so the stem is modified a lot with the help of affixes, and 2) that a character name will appear many times, so not all its wordforms contain morphemes from the target language and there will be at least one occurrence of the correct lemma. Consider the following example: if we have the right lemma of the character name (*Catherine*) and wrong versions that were however recognized as lemmas by the lemmatizer (*Catherinen*, *Catherinea*), the right version is the shortest, so searching in the sorted list of names [*Catherine*, *Catherinea*, *Catherinen*] should yield the right result.

2. *Method 2.1* and *Method 2.2*: Check whether the name exists using Wikipedia[4] or Wiktionary,[5] respectively (in our case, the English version of these resources). This method requires that for most of the names there were articles in Wikipedia and in Wiktionary, and since we were using English versions of these resources, wrong forms that contained Finnish suffixes would be discarded. This assumption relied heavily on the genre of texts of the corpus, namely classic British and American literature, so the character's name was an actual name in the real world. If we consider the example from *Method 1*, *Catherine* would return an article from both Wikipedia and Wiktionary, while *Catherinen* and *Catherinea* would return an error which means that there was no such page, and, presumably, no such name in the English language.

3. *Method 3*: Check if the word occurrence contains suffixes (in our case, Finnish suffixes). In this implementation only suffixes corresponding to Finnish genitive and partitive cases were checked, since the lemmatizer usually made mistakes in such forms. For example, if we check for the words that end on *-a/ä* and *-n*, the wrongly lemmatized *Catherinen* and *Catherinea* would not be included in the end results.

[4]https://en.wikipedia.org/

[5]https://en.wiktionary.org/

6 Results

We evaluated the results of our methods and the baseline according to the following criteria:

- Precision (fraction of true positive instances among all extracted instances), recall (fraction of true positive instances that were retrieved) and F-score (harmonic mean of precision and recall).

- Language independence (whether the method depends on certain language features and / or language resources, such as corpora, or not).

- Need for external non-linguistic resources (whether the method requires external resources to perform checking or not).

The overall count of results can be found in Table 1. The *Gold standard* column contains the number of character names (number of true positive instances, or all possible versions that can be used for naming all the characters that appear in the novel), *Method 1* covers results for checking for the shortest version of the name, *Method 2.1 and Method 2.2* - for checking in Wikipedia / Wiktionary, and *Method 3* - for checking for suffixes.

In Table 2 and Table 3 we present the results for the precision and recall for each method and the baseline, respectively. The results for F-score were counted only on average level and can be seen in Table 4.

It is quite noticeable from Table 1 that Method 2.2. (search for a correct wordform using Wiktionary) usually retrieves less names than any of the other methods (it has the lowest count of names for *Bleak House*, and the second lowest for *Washington Square*). However, in terms of recall, which can be seen in Table 3, the results varied significantly for this method: from 46% to 92% (compared with other methods where recall did not go lower than 55%).

Method 1 performed well on both a short text (*Washington Square*) and a significantly longer novel (*Bleak House).* It reached 100% recall for

Work	Gold standard	Baseline	Method 1	Method 2.1	Method 2.2	Method 3
Washington Square	20	22	18	21	17	12
Pride and Prejudice	48	80	76	65	60	65
Bleak House	126	184	128	88	68	109

Table 1: Names count for the three methods and the baseline

Work	Baseline	Method 1	Method 2.1	Method 2.2.	Method 3
Washington Square	73%	89%	76%	88%	**92%**
Pride and Prejudice	59%	63%	69%	**73%**	65%
Bleak House	58%	84%	**85%**	**85%**	83%
Average precision	63.3%	78.7%	76.7%	**82.0%**	80.0%

Table 2: Precision of the three methods comparing to the baseline. Average precision is added for reference. Best result in each row shown in bold.

Work	Baseline	Method 1	Method 2.1	Method 2.2.	Method 3
Washington Square	**80%**	**80%**	80%	75%	55%
Pride and Prejudice	98%	**100%**	94%	92%	88%
Bleak House	85%	**86%**	60%	46%	72%
Average recall	87.7%	**88.7%**	78.0%	71.0%	71.7%

Table 3: Recall of the three methods comparing to the baseline. Average recall is added for reference. Best result in each row shown in bold.

Pride and Prejudice, but precision for this text was lower than for other two: 63%.

Both external sources that were used for Method 2 (Wikipedia and Wiktionary) showed the worst recall results on *Bleak House* (46% and 60%) but scored over 90% on *Pride and Prejudice*. In terms of precision, checking in Wiktionary (Method 2.2) performed better than using Wikipedia for both *Washington Square* and *Pride and Prejudice*, while the usage of both resources led to the same result for *Bleak House*. We assume that this result can be attributed to the difference between the names, surnames and nicknames used in these novels.

Method 3 achieved the second best precision overall (and the best precision for *Washington Square*), but did not show good results in terms of recall (worst for two texts out of three). While applying this method, we also noticed that, without applying additional checks, it seems to filter out a certain amount of true positive cases, since the suffixes in question (partitive and genitive) contain one or two letters and can easily be just parts of correct lemmas.

In Table 4 we present values for the aforementioned criteria of evaluation, i.e. language independence and need for other resources, as well as the average precision, recall and F-score.

Only one method can be considered language-independent: search for the shortest version of lemma (Method 1). It can also be considered the only method that does not require a lot of external sources of knowledge, since even searching for the suffixes requires knowledge of Finnish grammar. The only knowledge that is required for the first method is knowledge about the type of language (agglutinative / fusional), but since the problem with wrongly lemmatized names is mostly the problem of agglutinative languages, this knowledge can be considered basic.

It is worth noting that lemmatization and scrupulous study of extracted names has also shown changes in translation regarding the original text. Thus, there is no *Guster* (the servant of Mr. Snagsby and Mrs. Snagsby) in the Finnish version of Bleak House but *Molly*, due to the wordplay. Such changes made the creation of the gold standard more difficult since it was based on the original namings of characters. We suggest that

Criteria	Baseline	Method 1	Method 2.1 / Method 2.2	Method 3
Average precision	63.3%	78.7%	76.7% / **82.0%**	80.0%
Average recall	87.7%	**88.7%**	78.0% / 71.0%	71.7%
Average F-score	73%	**83.4%**	77.3% / 76.1%	75.6%
Language independence	-	partly yes	no	no
External resources	-	no	Yes, database	Yes, linguistic knowledge

Table 4: Comparison of the methods (also regarding the baseline). Best result in each row shown in bold.

word alignment with original texts could help find such cases automatically. However, word alignment would not solve the lemmatization in these cases, since the name in the original (English) and in the translation (Finnish) differ.

There were also some issues related to misprints in the Finnish translations (e.g. in the translation of Washington Square sometimes names *Lavinia* and *Catherine* were misprinted as *Lavina* and *Catherna*) which lead to additional wrong results. Such errors were fixed, so the final version of results contained only right versions of names.

7 Conclusion

Perhaps surprisingly, a rather simple method that searches for the shortest version of the character's name (Method 1) yielded one of the best results with average precision of 78.7%, the best overall recall (88.7%) as well as the best overall F_1 (83.4%).

Searching for a name in Wikipedia (Method 2.1) led to slightly lower precision (77.6%). Searching for a name in Wiktionary (Method 2.2) was overall slightly worse than Method 2.1 (F_1 76.1% vs 77.3%), but almost on the same level as checking if the name contains suffixes (Method 3): average precision for both was about 71%.

In addition, Method 1 did not require any additional resources and it was relatively language-independent which would allow it to be used without any modifications for other agglutinative languages. We suggest that a combination of these methods (for example, simple combination of Method 1 and Method 3 should help e.g. in case when the characters do not have common names in genres like fantasy or sci-fi) will further improve the search for the right lemmas for foreign names in texts written in agglutinative languages and thus enhance the character identification.

Acknowledgements

This research was supported by the TOP-Säätiö (*TOP Foundation*).

References

Thierry Declerck, Nikolina Koleva, and Hans-Ulrich Krieger. 2012. Ontology-based incremental annotation of characters in folktales. In *LaTeCH@EACL*.

Hui Ngo Goh, Lay Ki Soon, and Su Cheng Haw. 2012. Automatic identification of protagonist in fairy tales using verb. In *Advances in Knowledge Discovery and Data Mining - 16th Pacific-Asia Conference, PAKDD 2012, Proceedings*, number PART 2 in Lecture Notes in Computer Science (including subseries Lecture Notes in Artificial Intelligence and Lecture Notes in Bioinformatics), pages 395–406.

Fotis Jannidis. 2013. Character. In Peter Hühn et al., editor, *the living handbook of narratology*. Hamburg University, Hamburg.

Harri Jäppinen and Matti Ylilammi. 1986. Associative model of morphological analysis: An empirical inquiry. *Comput. Linguist.*, 12(4):257–272.

Jenna Kanerva, Filip Ginter, Niko Miekka, Akseli Leino, and Tapio Salakoski. 2018. Turku neural parser pipeline: An end-to-end system for the CoNLL 2018 shared task. In *Proceedings of the CoNLL 2018 Shared Task: Multilingual Parsing from Raw Text to Universal Dependencies*, pages 133–142, Brussels, Belgium. Association for Computational Linguistics.

Jenna Kanerva, Filip Ginter, and Tapio Salakoski. 2019. Universal lemmatizer: A sequence to sequence model for lemmatizing universal dependencies treebanks. *CoRR*, abs/1902.00972.

Guillaume Klein, Yoon Kim, Yuntian Deng, Jean Senellart, and Alexander Rush. 2017. OpenNMT: Open-source toolkit for neural machine translation. In *Proceedings of ACL 2017, System Demonstrations*, pages 67–72, Vancouver, Canada. Association for Computational Linguistics.

Kimmo Koskenniemi. 1983. *Two-Level Morphology: A General Computational Model for Word-Form Recognition and Production.* Number 11 in Publications.

University of Helsinki. Department of General Linguistics, Finland.

Vincent Labatut and Xavier Bost. 2019. Extraction and analysis of fictional character networks: A survey. *CoRR*, abs/1907.02704.

Uri Margolin. 1990. The what, the when, and the how of being a character in literary narrative. *Style*, 24:453–68.

Tommi A Pirinen. 2015. Development and use of computational morphology of finnish in the open source and open science era: Notes on experiences with omorfi development. *SKY Journal of Linguistics*, 28:381–393.

Peng Qi, Yuhao Zhang, Yuhui Zhang, Jason Bolton, and Christopher D. Manning. 2020. Stanza: A python natural language processing toolkit for many human languages. *CoRR*, abs/2003.07082.

Miikka Silfverberg, Teemu Ruokolainen, Krister Lindén, and Mikko Kurimo. 2016. Finnpos: an open-source morphological tagging and lemmatization toolkit for finnish. *LANGUAGE RESOURCES AND EVALUATION*, 50(4):863–878.

A Sources

1. The 5 Least Important Characters in Pride and Prejudice, accessed 09.01.2022. https://theseaofbooks.com/2016/04/29/the-5-least-important-characters-in-pride-and-prejudice/

2. Austenopedia, accessed 09.01.2022. http://austenopedia.blogspot.com/p/entry-number-1.html

3. Bleak House Characters | Course Hero, accessed 09.01.2022. https://www.coursehero.com/lit/Bleak-House/characters/

4. Washington Square Character Analysis | LitCharts, accessed 09.01.2022.https://www.litcharts.com/lit/washington-square/characters

Zuo Zhuan Ancient Chinese Dataset for Word Sense Disambiguation

Xiaomeng Pan, Hongfei Wang, Teruaki Oka, Mamoru Komachi
Tokyo Metropolitan University
pan-xiaomeng@ed.tmu.ac.jp, wang-hongfei@ed.tmu.ac.jp
teruaki-oka@tmu.ac.jp, komachi@tmu.ac.jp

Abstract

Word Sense Disambiguation (WSD) is a core task in Natural Language Processing (NLP). Ancient Chinese has rarely been used in WSD tasks, however, as no public dataset for ancient Chinese WSD tasks exists. Creation of an ancient Chinese dataset is considered a significant challenge because determining the most appropriate sense in a context is difficult and time-consuming owing to the different usages in ancient and modern Chinese. Actually, no public dataset for ancient Chinese WSD tasks exists. To solve the problem of ancient Chinese WSD, we annotate part of Pre-Qin (221 BC) text *Zuo Zhuan* using a copyright-free dictionary to create a public sense-tagged dataset. Then, we apply a simple Nearest Neighbors (k-NN) method using a pre-trained language model to the dataset. Our code and dataset will be available on GitHub[1].

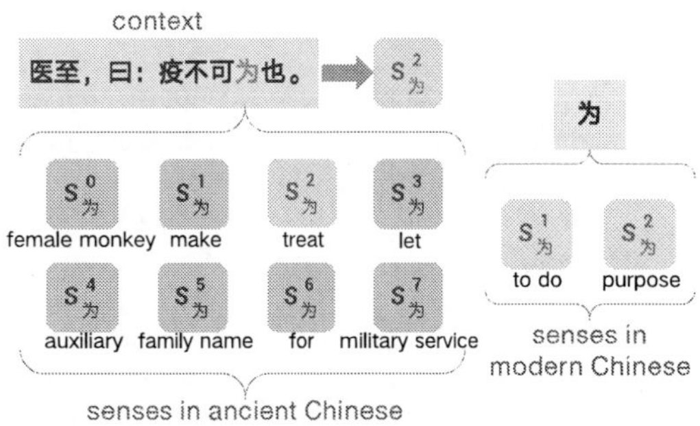

Figure 1: Illustration of choosing the right sense from the given context which means: *The doctor said that the disease could not be treated.* The senses of the target character "为" have different usages in ancient Chinese and modern Chinese. From the eight and two possible senses of the target character "为" in ancient and modern Chinese, the No. 2 sense in ancient Chinese, which denotes *"treat"* best fits the current context.

1 Introduction

Word sense disambiguation (WSD) is a crucial aspect of NLP, which identifies the sense of polysemous words that best fit the current context. Compared to some languages such as English, a character in Chinese, especially in ancient Chinese, usually has multiple and varying meanings, which greatly increases the difficulty of word sense disambiguation. At the present time, Dang et al. (2002); Li et al. (2005); Hou et al. (2020); Zheng et al. (2021) have made certain advances on modern Chinese WSD tasks. Nevertheless, unlike modern Chinese, ancient Chinese has hardly been explored in WSD tasks for lack of a dataset thus far. The main reason is that the smaller number of Chinese characters in the past led to even greater ambiguity in meaning than in modern Chinese. There are also fundamental differences in usage between ancient and modern Chinese. Figure 1 shows a context from *Zuo Zhuan*, a Pre-Qin Chinese book published late in the 4th century BC. The target character "为" has eight senses in ancient Chinese, differing from the two usual senses in modern Chinese. Without WSD, those unfamiliar with ancient Chinese have difficulty determining the correct senses. If WSD can be applied to ancient Chinese, it may contribute to the education of ancient Chinese and also many other tasks such as machine translation for ancient Chinese.

Previous researchers such as Yu et al. (2009); Chang et al. (2013) used few target characters and extracted the contexts to assemble an ancient Chinese lexical sample dataset for their WSD tasks. However, no public dataset for ancient Chinese WSD has yet been established. Consequently, researchers must create their own datasets to test their models for ancient Chinese WSD. Therefore, we choose to self-produce a public dataset for ancient Chinese WSD tasks.

In this study, we selected excerpts from *Zuo Zhuan* that includes approximately 200,000 char-

[1] https://github.com/pxm427/Ancient-Chinese-WSD

Proceedings of the 2022 Conference of the North American Chapter of the Association for Computational Linguistics: Human Language Technologies: Student Research Workshop, pages 129 - 135
July 10-15, 2022

acters (token). Then we annotated the texts with word senses from an open dictionary *Kangxi* to construct our dataset. In addition, we evaluated a supervised k-NN approach using a pre-trained model (Loureiro and Jorge, 2019) for ancient Chinese WSD tasks.

The main contributions of this paper are as follows:

1. We created a large public ancient Chinese WSD dataset for a lexical sampling task.

2. We applied a supervised k-NN approach using a pre-trained ancient Chinese language model to the ancient Chinese dataset.

2 Related Work

Word sense disambiguation is a task to predict the correct sense using an input word and its context. For example, "bank" has two meanings in English which refers to "a financial institution" and "sloping land". The ambiguity of word can cause noises in downstream tasks. Therefore, it is necessary to uniquely determine the meaning of a word. In Chinese, especially in ancient Chinese, one character usually has multiple and varying meanings. Hence, it adds more difficulties in distinguishing different meanings. Although there is the aforementioned educational aspect, WSD of ancient Chinese can improve machine translation (to modern-Chinese) and full-text search systems.

2.1 Chinese WSD Methods

Modern Chinese. Dang et al. (2002) adopted a maximum entropy method to investigate contextual features for Chinese. Li et al. (2005) used a naïve Bayes model based on local collocation and topical contextual features. Recently, Hou et al. (2020) used an unsupervised method based on HowNet (Dong et al., 2010) and made use of a pre-trained language model. Zheng et al. (2021) proposed FormBERT with word-formation for WSD and created a Chinese lexical sample dataset. All these approaches have performed effectively for Chinese WSD, but their target was modern, not ancient, Chinese.

Ancient Chinese. Yu et al. (2009) applied the CRF (Lafferty et al., 2001) model to tackle ancient Chinese WSD by using contextual words and linguistic features. They tested the model on six target characters with the best average F-score of 83.04% and proved that linguistic features can improve the WSD results for ancient Chinese. Chang et al. (2013) built a knowledge repository of ancient Chinese polysemous words and proposed an unsupervised method for ancient Chinese WSD based on a vector space model. They tested it on ten target characters and obtained an average accuracy of 79.5%. However, both were tested on limited numbers of characters and their datasets were non-public. In our study, we create a public ancient Chinese WSD dataset with 25 target characters, and then apply a k-NN approach using a pre-trained language model to our dataset.

2.2 Resources for Chinese WSD

HowNet is an online common-sense knowledge base including relationships between concepts and attributes with their English equivalents (Dong et al., 2010). It has been used on modern Chinese WSD task (Hou et al., 2020; Zhang et al., 2021), but cannot be applied to ancient Chinese because of the semantic diversity over 2000 years.

Zhang et al. (2012) used *Great Chinese Dictionary* as the knowledge resource and performed WSD of *Zuo Zhuan* by using a semi-supervised machine learning method. Owing to the copyright on the *Great Chinese Dictionary*, the authors have not made the corpus public. Unlike their approach, we used a public dictionary to annotate the word senses and thus can make our corpus publicly available.

Recently, the Pre-Qin Ancient Chinese WordNet (PQAC-WN), which contains 45,498 Pre-Qin basic words and 63,230 semantic classes was constructed by Xu et al. (2020). PQAC-WN organizes information based on semantic relationships and establishes lexical semantic mappings among Pre-Qin ancient Chinese, modern Chinese, and English. Nevertheless, it is not yet public. Therefore, we created an ancient Chinese WSD dataset that can be used freely for research purposes.

3 Construction of the *Zuo Zhuan* Ancient Chinese WSD Dataset

Since there is no public dataset for ancient Chinese WSD, we created the *Zuo Zhuan* Ancient Chinese WSD Dataset for ancient Chinese WSD. In this section, we describe the process of creating the dataset.

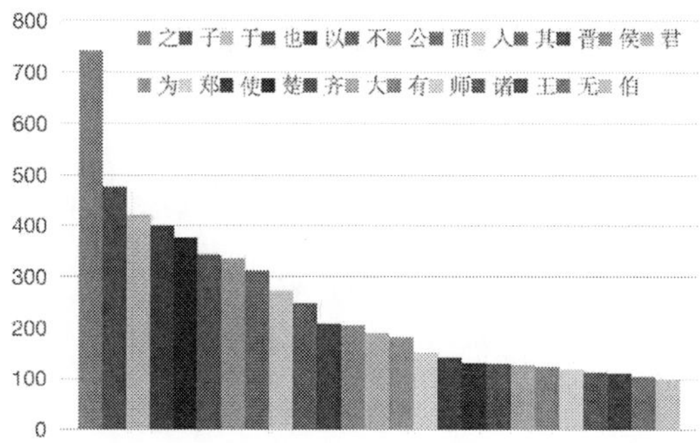

Figure 2: Data statistics. The figure shows the occurrences of 25 high-frequency characters. The vertical axis is the frequency of character, and the horizontal axis is the target characters of this study.

Problems	Examples
No Corresponding Notes	王为中君 → 率领 The king leads his army.
Multiple Similar Notes	晋人许之 → 语助词/他 The Jin promised (him).
Cannot Read	晋人以公为贰于楚 → ?

Figure 3: The three main problems encountered when annotating were termed: "No Corresponding Notes", "Multiple Similar Notes", and "Cannot Read".

3.1 Corpus

3.1.1 Data Selection

We used *Zuo Zhuan* following the previous study (Zhang et al., 2012). As one of the most famous ancient books, *Zuo Zhuan* is free from copyright restrictions, so that we can annotate and make it public. As shown in Figure 2, we selected those with a high-frequency as our target characters (approximately one hundred occurrences for each character) and ranked them from 1 to 25. We selected a total of 2,490 sentences containing the target characters from *Zuo Zhuan*, accounting for 12%. For each target character, we planned to select one hundred sample sentences randomly for annotation. However, the same target character may have appeared several times in the same context. Consequently, there are fewer than one hundred unique sentences for some characters. In such cases, we only chose the first target character to annotate for the context.

3.1.2 Annotation

We discerned the correct meaning of the target character in each context. To be more specific, first, we read every context including the target character and determined all the possible senses. Second, we selected the optimal meaning for the target character in the current context.

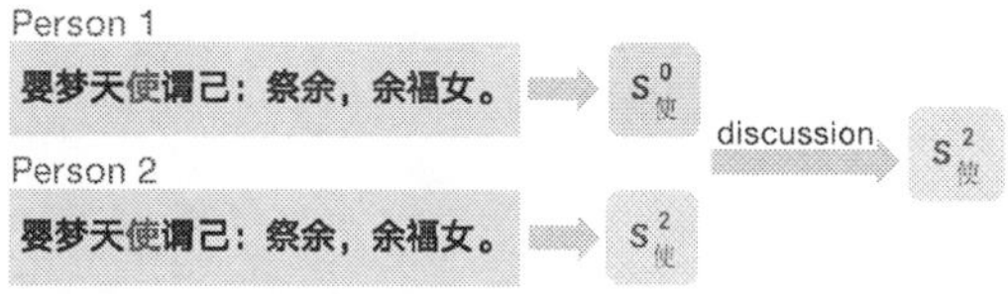

Figure 4: Two researchers annotated the same instance and discussed their readings for accuracy and reliability. Two senses are mentioned in the figure, No. 0 sense: *"make somebody do"* and No. 2 sense: *"Angel"*. This context means: *Zhao Ying dreamed that an angel said to him: Sacrifice me, and I will bless you.*

However, problems may be encountered when annotating. For example, the correct sense could sometimes not be found in the dictionary. As shown in Figure 3, the explanation of the first context is: *The king leads his army.* Here, the correct sense of character "为" is *"lead"* which can not be found in the dictionary. The second context can be translated into: *"The Jin promised."* by choosing the sense which refers to *"auxiliary word"*, or *"The Jin promised him."* by selecting the sense that means *"him"*. It is difficult to determine the most suitable one. In the third context, the correct sense is hard to choose because we could not accurately discern the meaning of the sentence. In such cases, we assigned a special tag *-1* to represent the undetermined sense.

Furthermore, to improve the accuracy and reliability of the annotation, two researchers, native Chinese PhD and master students majoring in NLP, annotated the same target characters separately and discussed them for final confirmation. As shown in Figure 4, occasionally situations arose where different senses were chosen by two researchers for the same instance. This may have been caused by different interpretations of the dictionary and the sentences.

We picked up one character for calculating the inter-annotator agreement of the dataset. For the character "使", the same one hundred sentences have been annotated separately by two researchers with two tags: No.0 and No.1. One researcher annotated 92 sentences with tag No.0 and 8 sentences with tag No.1, and the other researcher annotated 95 sentences with No.0 and 5 sentences with No.1. Using this data, the Cohen's kappa of two independent annotations was 0.75, which indicates moderate agreement (Carletta, 1996).

Fortunately, such consistency problems were

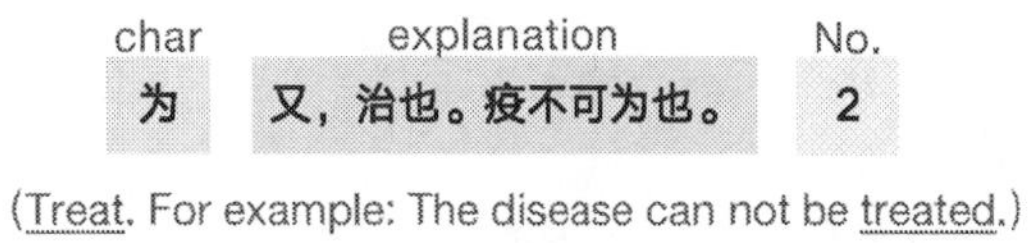

Figure 5: The structure of sense No. 2 for the "为" character from the dictionary. It consists of three parts: the target character, explanation, and sense number. The translation of the explanation part is shown below.

able to resolve after discussion. The consistency of annotation of the whole data (2,490 sentences) was 88% before discussion, but it finally increased to 100% after discussion and confirmation[2].

3.2 Dictionary

We chose *Kangxi* dictionary[3] compiled in 1716, which contains explanations for almost all the characters of the dynasties before the Qing Dynasty and is free of copyright. As shown in Figure 5, for the character "为", the explanation consists of three parts. The first part is the target character, the second part is the explanation of the particular sense, and the last part is the number of the sense.

4 k-Nearest Neighbors Method using a pre-trained language model for WSD

For this study, we applied the k-Nearest Neighbour classification (k-NN) using a pre-trained language model by following the approach from Loureiro and Jorge (2019). Specifically, we used *GuwenBert*, a pre-trained language model for ancient Chinese, to generate the embedding for WSD.

4.1 *GuwenBert*

GuwenBert-base is a RoBERTa (Liu et al., 2019) model pre-trained on ancient Chinese, which consists of 12 layers with 768 hidden units. The training data is from the daizhige dataset (殆知阁古代文献) that consists of 15,694 books in Classical Chinese, approximately 76% of which are punctuated. The total number of characters is 1.7B (1,743,337,673). All the traditional characters are converted to simplified characters.

It has been proved that *GuwenBert* was more effective than Chinese RoBERTa in Named Entity Recognition (NER) task on ancient Chinese[4], but it has not been used in any WSD tasks on ancient Chinese.

4.2 1-Nearest Neighbor

We applied 1-Nearest Neighbor classification by following the method from Loureiro and Jorge (2019). As shown in Figure 6, we combined sentence embedding E_s with gloss embedding E_g.

$$E = Combination(E_s, E_g) \tag{1}$$

Here, sense embedding E is the combination of sentence embedding and gloss embedding using concatenate or average. We compute the sentence embedding as follows:

$$E_s = \frac{1}{|D^{(t,s)}|} \sum_{c \in D^{(t,s)}} v^{(c,t)} \tag{2}$$

$$v^{(c,t)} = Embed(c)_t \tag{3}$$

where $v^{(c,t)}$ represents the embedding of the target character in the context from the dataset, $D^{(t,s)}$ is the set of contexts where target character t is associated with the sense s in the training data, respectively. Here, *c* and *t* are *context* from dataset and *target character*. $Embed(\cdot)_t$ returns the contextualized word embedding of the target character. Likewise, we calculate the gloss embedding as follows:

$$E_g = v^{(g,t)} = Embed(g)_t \tag{4}$$

where *g* means *gloss*, and $v^{(g,t)}$ represents the embedding of the target character in the gloss.

Finally, the similarity between combined sense embedding E and the target character embedding $v^{(c,t)}$ from test data[5] is calculated. We predicted the sense s as the one with the highest cosine similarity.

$$\hat{s} = \arg\max_{s} sim_{\cos}(v^{(c,t)}, E) \tag{5}$$

5 Experiments

5.1 Experimental Settings

Dataset. We first acquired contexts with same sense number for each sense. Then we split them into training data and test data in an 8:2 ratio. The statistics of the data are shown in Table 1.

[2]As the size of the dataset grows in the future, we are discussing and making a manual together so that the consistency will be as high as possible.

[3]https://www.kangxizidian.com

[4]https://github.com/ethan-yt/guwenbert

[5]When using concatenation to obtain E, the dimension of the combined embedding becomes twice as the sense embedding. Therefore, if we want to calculate the similarity, we need to concatenate the sense embedding $v^{(c,t)}$ itself from test data as well, so that the dimensions of both embeddings are identical.

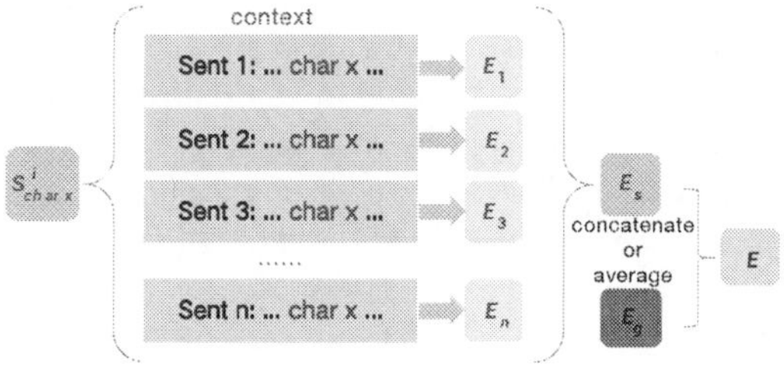

Figure 6: The process of obtaining the combined embedding.

Split	Characters	Sentences
Train	34,971	1,970
Test	9,648	520

Table 1: Statistics of training data and test data.

Baseline. The most frequent sense (MFS) baseline aims to find the sense which occurs most often in the annotated corpus. We selected the sense which appears most frequently in the training corpus for each character and calculated the accuracy.

k-NN As mentioned in Subsection 4.1, we chose *GuwenBert-base* as our model to obtain contextualized character embeddings in 1-NN classification. We only used it for obtaining the embeddings, so that no fine-tuning was required.

5.2 Results & Analysis

Table 2 shows the accuracy of 25 target characters on *Zuo Zhuan* Ancient Chinese WSD Dataset across MFS and 1-NN.

Dataset. As mentioned in 3.1.2, sometimes we cannot assign a definite sense number for a target character in certain contexts when annotating. Such cases account for 12% of the dataset. The cases for "No Corresponding Notes", "Multiple Similar Notes" and "Cannot Read" respectively account for 71%, 17%, 12% of these sentences. It is reasonable to assume that these cases arise mainly from missing explanations in the dictionary, uncertainties of the sentences themselves, and rare ancient usages.

We also find that the discussion improves the reliability of the dataset. The consistency increases from 84% to 100% after discussion and agreement between two researchers. So it is presumed that the dataset gains accuracy and credibility when annotated by more people.

Char	No.	QTY	MFS	Concat	Avg
之	3/8	11	**0.32**	0.23	0.27
子	-1	18	**0.41**	0.18	**0.41**
于	2	8	**1.00**	**1.00**	**1.00**
也	0	5	**1.00**	**1.00**	**1.00**
以	-1	6	**0.62**	0.24	0.29
不	0	12	**1.00**	**1.00**	**1.00**
公	3	17	**0.81**	0.00	0.10
而	6	10	**0.67**	0.14	0.24
人	0	8	0.77	0.00	**0.90**
其	0	9	0.68	**1.00**	**1.00**
晋	5	10	**1.00**	**1.00**	**1.00**
侯	0	11	0.95	**1.00**	**1.00**
君	0	18	0.73	0.00	**0.77**
为	1	8	0.52	0.52	**0.57**
郑	0	4	**1.00**	**1.00**	**1.00**
使	0	4	**0.90**	**0.90**	0.86
楚	6	14	**0.95**	0.00	**0.95**
齐	9	26	**0.95**	**0.95**	**0.95**
大	0	17	0.38	0.38	**0.48**
有	1	8	**0.86**	**0.86**	**0.86**
师	2	13	**0.86**	**0.86**	**0.86**
诸	6	22	**0.62**	**0.62**	**0.62**
王	0	16	**0.86**	**0.86**	0.82
无	0	15	**1.00**	0.90	0.90
伯	2	12	0.85	0.85	**0.90**
			0.79	0.62	0.75

Table 2: Accuracy results based on our dataset. **No.** means the sense number of the target character in the dictionary. **MFS** is the frequency of most frequent sense for each character from test data. **QTY** means the quantity of senses for each character in the dictionary. **concat** and **avg** mean the accuracy calculated by concatenate approach and average approach. Best results and median are shown in **bold** and underline. The last row of data is the average of the columns.

MFS baseline & 1-NN The MFS baseline assumes a sense annotated corpus from which the frequencies of individual senses are learned. Although this is a fairly naïve baseline without exploiting any contextual information, it has proven difficult to beat.

As shown in Table 2, the characters with low MFS accuracy also tend to be low in 1-NN. This may be related to the occurrence of the most frequently annotated senses. For example, the most frequently annotated sense of "于" appears in every context with an accuracy of 1. Therefore, it is more likely to have a higher 1-NN accuracy. In contrast,

"之" with an MFS accuracy of 0.32 can also be inferred to have a low 1-NN accuracy. Furthermore, we also observe that the sense distribution of the character with lower accuracy is more even. For example, in Table 2, "之" has the two most frequent senses with low accuracy.

The size and diversity of the dataset also affect the study. Since our dataset is relatively small, the distribution of senses is limited, and a larger and more comprehensive dataset would considerably improve the accuracy of the 1-NN model that can take advantage of contextualized word embeddings.

Combination strategy. Compared with the concatenate approach, the accuracy of the average approach is generally increased by about 13 points. The reason why the average method outperforms the concatenate method is likely because when using the concatenate approach, it is biased toward the training corpus since we copied the sense embedding from the test data, resulting in a smaller role for the dictionary. Conversely, the average method is more capable of combining the role of the training corpus and the dictionary. Table 2 shows that the accuracy is generally high when the known senses of characters appear in the sentence. In contrast, the appearance of unknown senses (a special tag *-1*) that do not exist in the dictionary cannot be predicted, consequently, resulting in a low accuracy.

Hard characters. It can be observed that the accuracy for the target characters which have unseen senses such as "以" is low in Table 2. The performance for the target characters with diverse senses such as "之" and "大" is also not high. Additionally, characters such as "公" and "而" are considered hard compared to the MFS. We leave improving the performance of these characters for future work.

6 Conclusion and Future Work

In this paper, we created the *Zuo Zhuan* Ancient Chinese WSD Dataset, and then evaluated a 1-NN approach using a pre-trained model *GuwenBert* on our dataset.

In future, we plan to increase the coverage of our dataset, explore whether this approach can detect unknown senses and improve the performance by adapting the pre-trained model to our dataset.

In addition, ancient Chinese and modern Chinese have changed greatly in word meanings and vocabulary. Among these, we would like to make a comparison of the two models for ancient Chinese and modern Chinese to address following questions: "How well do models optimized for modern language model perform in our dataset?" and "How well does the model for our ancient Chinese perform in the modern Chinese dataset?"

References

Jean Carletta. 1996. Assessing agreement on classification tasks: The kappa statistic. *Comput. Linguist.*, 22(2):249–254.

E Chang, Changxiu Zhang, Hanqing Hou, and Fuping Hui. 2013. Automatic word sense disambiguation of ancient Chinese based on vector space model. *Library and Information Service*, 057(002):114–118.

Hoa Trang Dang, Ching-yi Chia, Martha Palmer, and Fu-Dong Chiou. 2002. Simple features for Chinese word sense disambiguation. In *Proceedings of the 19th International Conference on Computational Linguistics*, pages 1–7, Taipei, Taiwan. International Committee on Computational Linguistics.

Zhendong Dong, Qiang Dong, and Changling Hao. 2010. HowNet and its computation of meaning. In *Proceedings of the 23rd International Conference on Computational Linguistics: Demonstrations*, pages 53–56. International Committee on Computational Linguistics.

Bairu Hou, Fanchao Qi, Yuan Zang, Xurui Zhang, Zhiyuan Liu, and Maosong Sun. 2020. Try to substitute: An unsupervised Chinese word sense disambiguation method based on HowNet. In *Proceedings of the 28th International Conference on Computational Linguistics*, pages 1752–1757, Barcelona, Spain (Online). International Committee on Computational Linguistics.

John Lafferty, Andrew Mccallum, and Fernando C. N. Pereira. 2001. Conditional random fields: Probabilistic models for segmenting and labeling sequence data. In *Proceedings of the Eighteenth International Conference on Machine Learning*, pages 282–289, Williamstown, MA, USA.

Wanyin Li, Qin Lu, and Wenjie Li. 2005. Integrating collocation features in Chinese word sense disambiguation. In *Proceedings of the Fourth SIGHAN Workshop on Chinese Language Processing*, pages 87–94, Jeju Island, Korea. Asian Federation of Natural Language Processing.

Yinhan Liu, Myle Ott, Naman Goyal, Jingfei Du, Mandar Joshi, Danqi Chen, Omer Levy, Mike Lewis, Luke Zettlemoyer, and Veselin Stoyanov. 2019. RoBERTa: A robustly optimized BERT pretraining approach. *CoRR*, abs/1907.11692.

Daniel Loureiro and Alípio Jorge. 2019. Language modelling makes sense: Propagating representations through WordNet for full-coverage word sense disambiguation. In *Proceedings of the 57th Annual Meeting of the Association for Computational Linguistics*, pages 5682–5691, Florence, Italy. Association for Computational Linguistics.

Huidan Xu, Siyu Chen, Jingjing Cai, Lin Cao, and Bin Li. 2020. The construction and statistical analysis of Pre-Qin ancient Chinese WordNet. *International Journal of Knowledge and Language Processing*, 11(3):48–61.

Lili Yu, Dexin Ding, Weiguang Qu, Xiaohe Chen, and Hui Li. 2009. Ancient Chinese word sense disambiguation based on CRF. *Microelectronics and Computers*, 26(10):4.

Minghao Zhang, Dongyu Zhang, and Hongfei Lin. 2021. Unsupervised Chinese verb metaphor recognition method based on HowNet. In *Proceedings of the 20th Chinese National Conference on Computational Linguistics*, pages 258–268, Huhhot, China. Chinese Information Processing Society of China.

Yingjie Zhang, Bin Li, Jiajun Chen, and Xiaohe Chen. 2012. A study in dictionary-based all-word word sense disambiguation for pre-Qin Chinese. *Journal of Chinese Information Processing*, 26(03):65–71.

Hua Zheng, Lei Li, Damai Dai, Deli Chen, Tianyu Liu, Xu Sun, and Yang Liu. 2021. Leveraging word-formation knowledge for Chinese word sense disambiguation. In *Findings of the Association for Computational Linguistics: EMNLP 2021*, pages 918–923, Punta Cana, Dominican Republic. Association for Computational Linguistics.

ViT5: Pretrained Text-to-Text Transformer for Vietnamese Language Generation

Long Phan[1,2], Hieu Tran[1], Hieu Nguyen[1,2], Trieu H. Trinh[1,3]
[1]VietAI Research
[2]Case Western Reserve University
[3]New York University
long.phan@case.edu

Abstract

We present ViT5, a pretrained Transformer-based encoder-decoder model for the Vietnamese language. With T5-style self-supervised pretraining, ViT5 is trained on a large corpus of high-quality and diverse Vietnamese texts. We benchmark ViT5 on two downstream text generation tasks, Abstractive Text Summarization and Named Entity Recognition. Although Abstractive Text Summarization has been widely studied for the English language thanks to its rich and large source of data, there has been minimal research into the same task in Vietnamese, a much lower resource language. In this work, we perform exhaustive experiments on both Vietnamese Abstractive Summarization and Named Entity Recognition, validating the performance of ViT5 against many other pretrained Transformer-based encoder-decoder models. Our experiments show that ViT5 significantly outperforms existing models and achieves state-of-the-art results on Vietnamese Text Summarization. On the task of Named Entity Recognition, ViT5 is competitive against previous best results from pretrained encoder-based Transformer models. Further analysis shows the importance of context length during the self-supervised pretraining on downstream performance across different settings.

1 Introduction

In recent years, Transformer-based architecture models and pretrained language models (LMs) have played a crucial role in the development of Natural Language Processing (NLP). Large pretrained models such as ELMo (Peters et al., 2018), GPT (Brown et al., 2020), BERT (Devlin et al., 2018) is trained on large corpora and have the ability to derive contextual representation of the language(s) in the training data. After pretraining is complete, these models achieved state-of-the-art results on a broad range of downstream tasks (Devlin et al., 2018). These self-supervised learning methods make use of learning objectives such as Masked Language Modeling (MLM) (Devlin et al., 2018) where random tokens in the input sequence are masked and the model attempts to predict the original tokens. The successes of pretrained models in English have inspired new research efforts to develop pretrained models in other languages such as Vietnamese (i.e., PhoBERT (Nguyen and Nguyen, 2020) and ViBERT (Bui et al., 2020)) and Italian (Sarti and Nissim, 2022). There are also ongoing efforts to develop multilingual pretrained models (mT5 (Xue et al., 2020), mBART (Liu et al., 2020)), in order to improve performance across multiple languages by learning both general and language-specific representations.

A short time ago, BARTpho (Tran et al., 2021), a large pretrained sequence-to-sequence model for Vietnamese inheriting BART style (Lewis et al., 2019), demonstrated the effectiveness of pretrained language models on Vietnamese abstractive summarization. Nevertheless, there are some past works that have shown that T5 architecture (Raffel et al., 2019) might outperform BART in some aspects (i.e., (Phan et al., 2021a)). Inspired by that, we propose ViT5, trained on the Vietnamese monolingual subset of CC100, following the architecture and training methodology in Raffel et al. (2019). We perform exhaustive comparisons on downstream performance to many different pretrained Transformer-based models (Nguyen et al., 2021; Tran et al., 2021; To et al., 2021). Specifically, we finetune the ViT5 on two summarization datasets, Wikilingua (Ladhak et al., 2020) and Vietnews (Nguyen et al., 2019), and one Named Entity Recognition dataset (PhoNER (Truong et al., 2021)).

Text summarization is an important downstream

Proceedings of the 2022 Conference of the North American Chapter of the Association for Computational Linguistics: Human Language Technologies: Student Research Workshop, pages 136 - 142

task whose input is a free-form text paragraph or document(s), and the output sequence is expected to be a short summarization of the input. ViT5 achieves state-of-the-art results on both two of the single-document summarization tasks. We also perform an analysis on the max-length hyperparameter for input and output sequences during self-supervised learning and showed that longer lengths that match the downstream document's length lead to better result.

For NER, we reformulated the per-token classification task into a generation task, where the decoder reconstructs the original input sentence with inserted Named Entity tags following each token (Phan et al., 2021b). This simple and straightforward formulation achieves competitive results in comparison to direct per-token classification done on encoder-only model (Nguyen and Nguyen, 2020).

2 Related Work

There are lots of abstractive summarization studies in English. In an early example, (Gehrmann et al., 2018) employed a bottom-up content selector (BottomUp) to determine which phrases in the source document should be part of the summary, and then a copy mechanism was applied only to pre-select phrases during decoding. Their experiments obtained significant improvements on ROUGE for some canonical summarization datasets.

In recent years, pretrained language models have been used to enhance performance on language generation tasks. (Liu and Lapata, 2019) developed a Transformer-based encoder-decoder model so that pretrained language models like BERT can be adopted for abstractive summarization. Here, the authors proposed a novel document-level BERT-based encoder (*BERTSum*) and a general framework encompassing both extractive and abstractive summarization tasks. Based on *BERTSum*, Dou et al. (2021) introduced *GSum* that effectively used different types of guidance signals as input in order to generate more suitable words and more accurate summaries. This model accomplished state-of-the-art performance on four popular English summarization datasets.

Meanwhile, there are a small number of studies on Vietnamese text summarization. Most of these focus on inspecting extractive summarization. The researchers (Nguyen et al., 2018) compared a wide range of extractive methods, including unsupervised ranking methods (e.g., LexRank, LSA, KL-divergence), supervised learning methods using TF-IDF and classifiers (e.g., Support Vector Machine, AdaBoost, Learning-2-rank), and deep learning methods (e.g., Convolutional Neural Network, Long-Short Term Memory). Similarly, the authors (Nguyen et al., 2019) also evaluated the extractive methods on their own dataset, which was released publicly as a benchmark for future studies.

Recent work (Quoc et al., 2021) investigated the combination of a pretrained BERT model and an unsupervised K-means clustering algorithm on extractive text summarization. The authors utilized multilingual and monolingual BERT models to encode sentence-level contextual information and then ranked this information using the K-means algorithm. Their report showed that monolingual models achieved better results compared when to multilingual models performing the same extractive summarization tasks. However, due to the lack of studies on Vietnamese abstractive summarization, we compare both multilingual and monolingual encoder-decoder models.

3 ViT5

In this section, we will explain our newly released ViT5 models, the vocabulary generation steps, the pretraining data, and the training setup.

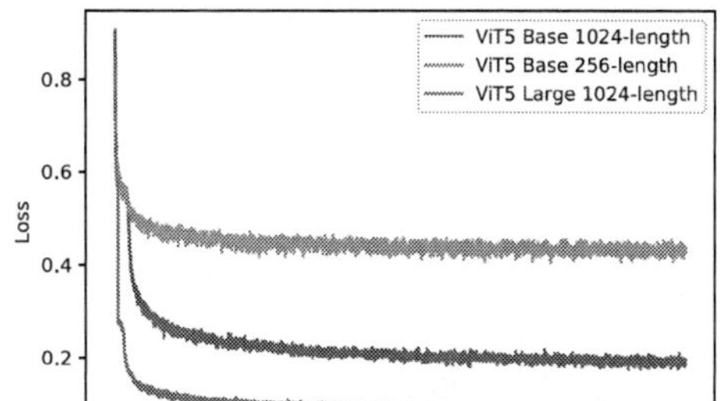

Figure 1: Loss curves for the masked span prediction task were used to pretrain the ViT5 models. Larger model with larger context optimizes much better, which leads to better downstream performance.

3.1 Model

ViT5 follows the encoder-decoder architecture proposed by Vaswani et al. (2017) and the T5

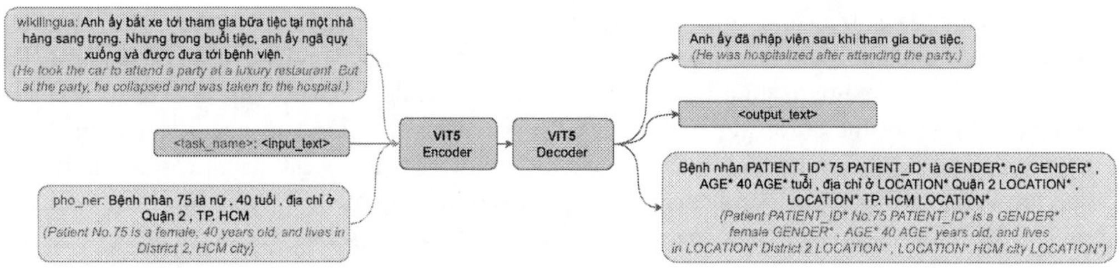

Figure 2: An overview of ViT5 encoder-decoder architecture, with input-output examples of two downstream tasks. For Named Entity Recognition, the decoder reconstructs the sentence with inserted Entity tags.

framework proposed by (Raffel et al., 2019). The original works of T5 proposed five different configs of model size: small, base, large, 3B, and 11B. For the purpose of practical study, we adapt the base (310M parameters) and large (866M parameters) models for ViT5 models and leave bigger models for future works.

We train ViT5 models with two different input and output lengths: 256 and 1024-length. We thoroughly experimented with these two models to have an insight into the importance of pretraining data length for summarization tasks. For the self-supervised training learning objectives, we use the span-corruption objective with a corruption rate of 15%. Figure 1 shows the computed loss during the self-supervised training stage for the three models.

3.2 Vocabulary

Different from some other current Vietnamese Transformer-based language models, we find that an effective vocabulary can contribute a significant improvement to our model performance. Therefore, we did pre-process on a 5GB subset of our pretraining corpus with care like normalizing punctuation and capitalization, splitting numbers. We fixed the size of vocabulary to 36K sub-words and trained SentencePiece (Kudo and Richardson, 2018) model on that dataset.

3.3 Pretraining Data

We use the CC100 Dataset (Monolingual Datasets from Web Crawl Data) (Wenzek et al., 2020; Conneau et al., 2020). The corpus contains monolingual data for over 100 languages. The corpus was constructed using the pipeline provided by (Wenzek et al., 2020) through processing January-December 2018 Commoncrawl snapshots. The total size for the Vietnamese Corpus is 138GB of raw text. We process and filter out 69GB of short paragraphs for 256-length model and 71GB of long paragraphs for 1024-length model.

Table 1: Input and Output Length of Finetuned Datasets

	Wikilingua	Vietnews
Train	13707	99134
Test	3916	22498
#avg body length	521	519
#avg abstract length	44	38

4 Abstractive Summarization

4.1 Wikilingua

Wikilingua (Ladhak et al., 2020) is a large-scale multilingual corpus for abstractive summarization tasks. The corpus consists of 18 languages, including Vietnamese. These article and summary pairs are extracted from WikiHow[1]. These articles have been reviewed by human authors to ensure quality. The Vietnamese articles are translated from the original English articles and have been reviewed by WikiHow's international translation team.

4.2 Vietnews

Vietnews (Nguyen et al., 2019) is a single-document abstractive summarization dataset including news data from reputable Vietnamese news website (*tuoitre.vn*, *vnexpress.net*, and *nguoiduatin.vn*). The authors of this work removed all articles related to questionnaires, analytical comments, and weather forecasts to ensure the quality of document summarization. The final released dataset only includes long document news events. The data consists of 150704 word-level news articles with a summary abstract and body text pairs. We follow the filtering pipeline by Tran et al. (2021) to deduplicate the train/dev/test dataset. The statistics after filtering are shown in Table 1.

[1]https://www.wikihow.com

Table 2: Test result on Wikilingua and Vietnews Summarization

Models	WikiLingua			Vietnews		
	ROUGE-1	ROUGE-2	ROUGE-L	ROUGE-1	ROUGE-2	ROUGE-L
Transformer (RND2RND)	46.25	16.57	29.82	57.56	24.25	35.53
PhoBERT2PhoBERT	50.4	19.88	32.49	60.37	29.12	39.44
mBERT2mBERT	52.82	20.57	31.55	59.67	27.36	36.73
mBART	55.21	25.69	37.33	59.81	28.28	38.71
mT5	55.27	27.63	38.30	58.05	26.76	37.38
BARTpho	57.16	31.18	40.89	61.14	30.31	40.15
ViT5$_{\text{base 256-length}}$	57.86	29.98	40.23	61.85	31.70	41.70
ViT5$_{\text{base 1024-length}}$	<u>58.61</u>	<u>31.46</u>	<u>41.45</u>	<u>62.77</u>	<u>33.16</u>	<u>42.75</u>
ViT5$_{\text{large 1024-length}}$	**60.22**	**33.12**	**43.08**	**63.37**	**34.24**	**43.55**

Notes: The best scores are in bold and second best scores are underlined. The scores in gray color are our experiments. Code and models for reproducing our experiments: https://github.com/vietai/ViT5

4.3 Baselines

In order to verify the effectiveness of our proposed methods, we compare ViT5 models with the Transformer models based on (Vaswani et al., 2017), the ViSum BERT2BERT models (Nguyen et al., 2021), multilingual encoder-decoder model (Xue et al., 2020; Liu et al., 2020), and Vietnamese encoder-decoder BARTpho model (Tran et al., 2021). The baseline transformer models (labeled RND) have a multi-head self-attention and a feed-forward network. RND models are initialized with random weights. For the BARTpho models, we follow the models set up and results released by (Tran et al., 2021). All finetuned ViT5 models are conducted with a sequence length of 1024.

4.4 Results

We report the results of the ViT5 models on two datasets: Wikilingua and Vietnews. We do experiments with two versions of pretraining ViT5: 256-length and 1024-length to have an insight into the importance of pretraining data's paragraph length for summarization in Vietnamese. We also compare the results of ViT5$_{\text{base}}$ and ViT5$_{\text{large}}$ models.

We use ROUGE (Recall-Oriented Understudy for Gisting Evaluation) as our benchmark metrics for both single document summarization datasets. The metric measures the overlap of n-grams and word sequences between two candidate and reference sequences. ROUGE-1, ROUGE-2, and ROUGE-L mean the overlap between unigram, bigram, and longest matching sequence, respectively.

4.4.1 Wikilingua

The results of our models on Wikilingua summarization dataset are shown in Table 2. ViT5 models outperform all of the experimented pretrained models, achieving state-of-the-art on all ROUGE metrics. There is also a significant increase in ROUGE scores when the models are pretrained on a longer input and output sequence (1024 compared to 256).

Both versions of ViT5$_{\text{1024-length}}$ achieve the highest results on Wikilingua summarization tasks across all ROUGE metrics with ViT5$_{\text{large 1024-length}}$ achieving state-of-the-art. There is a significant improvement in score between the base and large ViT5$_{\text{1024-length}}$ architectures (approximately 2% for ROUGE-1, ROUGE-2, and ROUGE-L). This is predictable as the number of parameters of ViT5$_{\text{large}}$ (866M) is approximately 2.8 times larger than ViT5$_{\text{base}}$ (310M).

There are interesting results when comparing the results of 256-length and 1024-length versions of ViT5$_{\text{base}}$. Although the finetuning settings are 1024-length for both ViT5$_{\text{base}}$ models, ViT5$_{\text{base 1024-length}}$ performs slightly better with 1% higher score for ROUGE-1, ROUGE-2, and ROUGE-L. These results are attributed to the longer sequences during self-supervised training. As reported in Table 1, the average words in an input body of Wikilingua corpus are more than 256 tokens, which can be considered long documents. For this reason, pretraining ViT5 on a 1024 sequence length corpus achieves better results on Wikilingua summarization task.

Two-out-of-three ViT5 models perform better

than the published BARTpho model in summarizing Wikilingua corpus. This can be the result of the quality of pretraining data. While BARTpho (and PhoBERT) was trained on 20GB of news data, ViT5 models are trained using CC100, which is a subset of Common Crawl data. CC100 corpus contains more diverse and general representation of the Vietnamese language than news data. Meanwhile, Wikilingua is more of an academic or instruction representation than news-like text.

4.4.2 Vietnews

The size of Vietnews corpus is much larger than Wikilingua corpus (with 7.7% for train and 5.8% for test set). The result of Vietnews abstractive summarization is in Table 2. Following the discussion of the need for an effective large pretrained encoder-decoder model in Section 1, we can see that there is a minimum increase in performance for the existing Vietnamese encoder-only model compared to the Transformer baseline. Pretraining on a large corpus of Vietnamese news, BARTpho still showed its limitation in the Vietnews summarization task with slightly better ROUGE scores than multilingual models (mBART and mT5).

Our ViT5 models still achieve state-of-the-art on Vietnews task for both 256 and 1024-length. For a more specific news-domain corpus, ViT5 models achieve notable results on the news domain although being trained on a more general Vietnamese natural language domain (CC100). This supports the assumption that our ViT5 models learn a better representation of the Vietnamese language even for more domain-specific summarization problems.

Similar to the results discussed in Section 4.4, ViT5$_{\text{base}}$ models when pretrained on a longer sequence corpus (1024-length) achieve better performance in summarizing compared to a short sequence corpus (256-length) across all ROUGE metrics. The average input length for Vietnews documents is approximately the same as in the Wikilingua task (more than 500 words). Therefore, the quality of long sequences during self-supervised training data also leads to a better summarizing in downstream Vietnews finetuned tasks.

5 Named Entity Recognition (NER)

Table 3: Test results on PhoNER_COVID19

Models	Micro-F1
XLM-R$_{\text{large}}$	93.8
PhoBERT$_{\text{base}}$	94.2
PhoBERT$_{\text{large}}$	**94.5**
ViT5$_{\text{base 256-length}}$	93.19
ViT5$_{\text{base 1024-length}}$	**94.5**
ViT5$_{\text{large 1024-length}}$	93.8

Notes: The best scores are in bold.

To verify the effectiveness of ViT5 on classification tasks, we test our models on PhoNER_COVID19 dataset (Truong et al., 2021). PhoNER is a dataset for recognizing named entities related to the COVID19 domain in Vietnamese. The dataset consists of 35,000 entities in over 10,000 sentences. The goal is to recognize 10 entity types related to the domain of COVID19 and epidemics topics. The dataset was released and benchmarked with PhoBERT (Nguyen and Nguyen, 2020).

We treat the NER classifications tasks as text-to-text generating tasks with tags of labels before and after an entity token (Phan et al., 2021b). An example of NER in text-to-text format is shown in Figure 2. The results are shown in Table 3.

The ViT5$_{\text{large 1024-length}}$ model, although effective in generating Vietnamese abstractive summarization, shows its limitation in classification tasks with lower F1 scores on NER task. On the other hand, our ViT5$_{\text{base 1024-length}}$ model still performs slightly better than PhoBERT$_{\text{base}}$ and competitively the same as the current state-of-the-art PhoBERT$_{\text{large}}$ on the PhoNER corpus.

6 Discussion

According to the results on both Wikilingua and Vietnews summarization tasks (Table 2 and Table 4.4.2), there is a steady increase in ROUGE scores going from the baseline Transformer, BERT2BERT related models (PhoBERT2PhoBERT and mBERT2mBERT), multilingual encoder-decoder models (mBART, mT5), to pretrained monolingual models (BARTpho and ViT5). For Vietnamese summarization tasks, monolingual encoder-decoder models noticeably outperform multilingual models, most likely thanks to their more focused and narrower pretraining stage.

Interestingly, a more general domain of pre-training texts can lead to a better domain-specific summarization performance. In Section 4.4.1, our ViT5 models while being trained on a more general corpus (CC100), outperform current models that are trained on news-related corpus. More technical domains such as laws, medicals, or engineering are not tested as we leave these domain-specific summarization tasks for future studies.

The slightly better performance of $\text{ViT5}_{\text{base 1024-length}}$ compared to $\text{ViT5}_{\text{base 256-length}}$ suggests that longer document summarization (more than 512 tokens) need a comparatively longer context length during the pretraining stage.

7 Conclusion

We introduce ViT5, a pretrained sequence-to-sequence Transformer model for the Vietnamese language. Leveraging the T5 self-supervised pre-training formulation on massive and high-quality Vietnamese corpora, we showed that finetuned ViT5 models are performant on both generation and classification tasks. We exhaustively compare ViT5 with other pretrained formulations on both multilingual and monolingual corpora. Our experiments show that ViT5 achieves state-of-the-art results on summarization in both Wikilingua and Vietnews corpus, and competitive results in generating Named Entity Recognition (NER) on the PhoNER_COVID19 dataset. We also analyze and discuss the importance of context length during the self-supervised pretraining stage, which strongly influences and positively leads to better downstream performance.

8 Acknowledgements

We would like to thank the Google TPU Research Cloud (TRC) program and VietAI for providing us with free access to TPU v3-8 to train and finetune large ViT5 models.

References

Tom B. Brown, Benjamin Mann, Nick Ryder, Melanie Subbiah, Jared Kaplan, Prafulla Dhariwal, Arvind Neelakantan, Pranav Shyam, Girish Sastry, Amanda Askell, Sandhini Agarwal, Ariel Herbert-Voss, Gretchen Krueger, Tom Henighan, Rewon Child, Aditya Ramesh, Daniel M. Ziegler, Jeffrey Wu, Clemens Winter, Christopher Hesse, Mark Chen, Eric Sigler, Mateusz Litwin, Scott Gray, Benjamin Chess, Jack Clark, Christopher Berner, Sam McCandlish, Alec Radford, Ilya Sutskever, and Dario Amodei. 2020. Language models are few-shot learners. *CoRR*, abs/2005.14165.

The Viet Bui, Oanh Thi Tran, and Phuong Le-Hong. 2020. Improving sequence tagging for vietnamese text using transformer-based neural models. *CoRR*, abs/2006.15994.

Alexis Conneau, Kartikay Khandelwal, Naman Goyal, Vishrav Chaudhary, Guillaume Wenzek, Francisco Guzmán, Edouard Grave, Myle Ott, Luke Zettlemoyer, and Veselin Stoyanov. 2020. Unsupervised cross-lingual representation learning at scale. In *Proceedings of the 58th Annual Meeting of the Association for Computational Linguistics*, pages 8440–8451, Online. Association for Computational Linguistics.

Jacob Devlin, Ming-Wei Chang, Kenton Lee, and Kristina Toutanova. 2018. BERT: pre-training of deep bidirectional transformers for language understanding. *CoRR*, abs/1810.04805.

Zi-Yi Dou, Pengfei Liu, Hiroaki Hayashi, Zhengbao Jiang, and Graham Neubig. 2021. Gsum: A general framework for guided neural abstractive summarization. In *Conference of the North American Chapter of the Association for Computational Linguistics (NAACL)*.

Sebastian Gehrmann, Yuntian Deng, and Alexander Rush. 2018. Bottom-up abstractive summarization. In *Proceedings of the 2018 Conference on Empirical Methods in Natural Language Processing*, pages 4098–4109, Brussels, Belgium. Association for Computational Linguistics.

Taku Kudo and John Richardson. 2018. Sentencepiece: A simple and language independent subword tokenizer and detokenizer for neural text processing. In *EMNLP*.

Faisal Ladhak, Esin Durmus, Claire Cardie, and Kathleen R. McKeown. 2020. Wikilingua: A new benchmark dataset for cross-lingual abstractive summarization. *CoRR*, abs/2010.03093.

Mike Lewis, Yinhan Liu, Naman Goyal, Marjan Ghazvininejad, Abdelrahman Mohamed, Omer Levy, Veselin Stoyanov, and Luke Zettlemoyer. 2019. BART: denoising sequence-to-sequence pre-training for natural language generation, translation, and comprehension. *CoRR*, abs/1910.13461.

Yang Liu and Mirella Lapata. 2019. Text summarization with pretrained encoders. In *EMNLP/IJCNLP*.

Yinhan Liu, Jiatao Gu, Naman Goyal, Xian Li, Sergey Edunov, Marjan Ghazvininejad, Mike Lewis, and Luke Zettlemoyer. 2020. Multilingual denoising pre-training for neural machine translation. *CoRR*, abs/2001.08210.

Dat Quoc Nguyen and Anh Tuan Nguyen. 2020. PhoBERT: Pre-trained language models for Vietnamese. In *Findings of the Association for Computational Linguistics: EMNLP 2020*, pages 1037–1042.

Hieu Nguyen, Long Phan, James Anibal, Alec Peltekian, and Hieu Tran. 2021. Viesum: How robust are transformer-based models on vietnamese summarization?

Minh-Tien Nguyen, Hoang-Diep Nguyen, Thi-Hai-Nang Nguyen, and Van-Hau Nguyen. 2018. Towards state-of-the-art baselines for vietnamese multi-document summarization. In *2018 10th International Conference on Knowledge and Systems Engineering (KSE)*, pages 85–90.

Van-Hau Nguyen, Thanh-Chinh Nguyen, Minh-Tien Nguyen, and Nguyen Hoai. 2019. Vnds: A vietnamese dataset for summarization. pages 375–380.

Matthew E. Peters, Mark Neumann, Mohit Iyyer, Matt Gardner, Christopher Clark, Kenton Lee, and Luke Zettlemoyer. 2018. Deep contextualized word representations. *CoRR*, abs/1802.05365.

Long Phan, Hieu Tran, Daniel Le, Hieu Nguyen, James Annibal, Alec Peltekian, and Yanfang Ye. 2021a. CoTexT: Multi-task learning with code-text transformer. In *Proceedings of the 1st Workshop on Natural Language Processing for Programming (NLP4Prog 2021)*, pages 40–47, Online. Association for Computational Linguistics.

Long N. Phan, James T. Anibal, Hieu Tran, Shaurya Chanana, Erol Bahadroglu, Alec Peltekian, and Grégoire Altan-Bonnet. 2021b. Scifive: a text-to-text transformer model for biomedical literature. *CoRR*, abs/2106.03598.

Huy To Quoc, Kiet Van Nguyen, Ngan Luu-Thuy Nguyen, and Anh Gia-Tuan Nguyen. 2021. Monolingual versus multilingual bertology for vietnamese extractive multi-document summarization.

Colin Raffel, Noam Shazeer, Adam Roberts, Katherine Lee, Sharan Narang, Michael Matena, Yanqi Zhou, Wei Li, and Peter J. Liu. 2019. Exploring the limits of transfer learning with a unified text-to-text transformer. *CoRR*, abs/1910.10683.

Gabriele Sarti and Malvina Nissim. 2022. It5: Large-scale text-to-text pretraining for italian language understanding and generation.

Huy Quoc To, Kiet Van Nguyen, Ngan Luu-Thuy Nguyen, and Anh Gia-Tuan Nguyen. 2021. Monolingual versus multilingual bertology for vietnamese extractive multi-document summarization.

Nguyen Luong Tran, Duong Minh Le, and Dat Quoc Nguyen. 2021. Bartpho: Pre-trained sequence-to-sequence models for vietnamese.

Thinh Hung Truong, Mai Hoang Dao, and Dat Quoc Nguyen. 2021. COVID-19 Named Entity Recognition for Vietnamese. In *Proceedings of the 2021 Conference of the North American Chapter of the Association for Computational Linguistics: Human Language Technologies*.

Ashish Vaswani, Noam Shazeer, Niki Parmar, Jakob Uszkoreit, Llion Jones, Aidan N. Gomez, Lukasz Kaiser, and Illia Polosukhin. 2017. Attention is all you need. *CoRR*, abs/1706.03762.

Guillaume Wenzek, Marie-Anne Lachaux, Alexis Conneau, Vishrav Chaudhary, Francisco Guzmán, Armand Joulin, and Edouard Grave. 2020. CCNet: Extracting high quality monolingual datasets from web crawl data. In *Proceedings of the 12th Language Resources and Evaluation Conference*, pages 4003–4012, Marseille, France. European Language Resources Association.

Linting Xue, Noah Constant, Adam Roberts, Mihir Kale, Rami Al-Rfou, Aditya Siddhant, Aditya Barua, and Colin Raffel. 2020. mt5: A massively multilingual pre-trained text-to-text transformer. *CoRR*, abs/2010.11934.

Compositional Generalization in Grounded Language Learning via Induced Model Sparsity

Sam Spilsbury and **Alexander Ilin**
Department of Computer Science
Aalto University
Espoo, Finland
{first.last}@aalto.fi

Abstract

We provide a study of how induced model sparsity can help achieve compositional generalization and better sample efficiency in grounded language learning problems. We consider simple language-conditioned navigation problems in a grid world environment with disentangled observations. We show that standard neural architectures do not always yield compositional generalization. To address this, we design an agent that contains a goal identification module that encourages sparse correlations between words in the instruction and attributes of objects, composing them together to find the goal.[1] The output of the goal identification module is the input to a value iteration network planner. Our agent maintains a high level of performance on goals containing novel combinations of properties even when learning from a handful of demonstrations. We examine the internal representations of our agent and find the correct correspondences between words in its dictionary and attributes in the environment.

1 Introduction

Ideally, when training an agent that acts upon natural language instructions, we want the agent to understand the meaning of the words, rather than overfitting to the training instructions. We expect that when an agent encounters an unfamiliar instruction made up of familiar terms, it should be able to complete the task. In this sense, the agent learns to leverage both *groundedness* of language; for example in English, tokens in the language map to observed attributes of objects or phenomena in its environment, as well as its *compositionality*; which enables the description of potentially infinite numbers of new phenomena from known components (Chomsky, 1965). Using language to express goals is potentially a way to approach task distribution shift and sample efficiency, key problems in reinforcement learning (Sodhani et al., 2021; Jang et al., 2021).

However, compositional generalization does not come automatically with standard architectures when using language combined with multi-modal inputs, as indicated by the mixed results of generalization performance in Goyal et al. (2021); Sodhani et al. (2021). Concurrently with Qiu et al. (2021), we show that the Transformer architecture can demonstrate generalization, but requires large amounts of data for training. In this work, we tackle sample inefficiency and retain generalization.

Our contributions are as follows. We propose a model and a training method that utilizes the inductive biases of *sparse interactions* and *factor compositionality* when finding relationships between words and disentangled attributes. We hypothesize that such sparsity in the *interactions* between object attributes and words (as opposed to just their representations) leads to a correct identification of what attributes the words actually correspond to, instead of what they are merely correlated with. We show in both quantitative and qualitative experiments that such sparsity and factor compositionality enable compositional generalization. To improve sample efficiency, we decouple the goal identification task (which requires language understanding) from the planning process (implemented with an extension of Value Iteration Networks).

2 Related Work

Compositional Generalization and Language Grounding There is a long line of work on learning to achieve language encoded instructions within interactive environments. Vision-Language Navigation environments typically require an agent to navigate to a requested goal object (for example, DeepMind Lab (Beattie et al., 2016), R2R (Anderson et al., 2018) and ALFRED (Shridhar et al., 2020)). Algorithmic and deep imitation learning approaches for autonomous agents in these environ-

[1] github.com/aalto-ai/sparse-compgen

Proceedings of the 2022 Conference of the North American Chapter of the Association for Computational Linguistics: Human Language Technologies: Student Research Workshop, pages 143 - 155

ments have been proposed, but room for improvement in both generalization performance and sample efficiency remains (Chen and Mooney, 2011; Bisk et al., 2016; Shridhar et al., 2021).

The generalization issue arises because there are many possible instructions or goals that could be expressed with language and a learner may not necessarily observe each one within its training distribution. Some are "out of distribution" and maintaining performance on them is not guaranteed; a problem well known the within reinforcement learning community (Kirk et al., 2021). However, a peculiar feature of language instructions is that language is *compositional* in nature. This has led to an interest in whether this aspect can be leveraged to get better generalization on unseen goals made up of familiar terms (Oh et al., 2017; Hermann et al., 2017). However, even in simple environments such as BabyAI (Chevalier-Boisvert et al., 2019), and gSCAN (Ruis et al., 2020) this can still be difficult problem.

Various approaches to leveraging compositionality have been proposed, including gated word-channel attention (Chaplot et al., 2018), hierarchical processing guided by parse-trees (Kuo et al., 2021), graph neural networks (Gao et al., 2020), neural module networks (Andreas et al., 2016), and extending agents with a boolean task algebra solver (Tasse et al., 2022). Closest to our approach are Heinze-Deml and Bouchacourt (2020); Hanjie et al. (2021) which use attention to identify goal states, Narasimhan et al. (2018); Ruis and Lake (2022), which decompose goal identification and planning modules, Bahdanau et al. (2019) which uses a discriminator to model reward for instructions and Buch et al. (2021) which factorizes object classification over components. We contribute a new approach of learning sparse attention over factored observations, then attaching that attention module to a learned planning module. This can be shown to solve the compositional generalization problem by learning the correct correspondences between words and factors without spurious correlation.

Representation Sparsity We hypothesize that sparsity is an important factor in the design of a compositional system because it can bias the optimization procedure towards solutions where relationships exist only between things that are actually related and not just weakly correlated. Previous work has shown that induced sparsity can improve both generalization (Zhao et al., 2021) and model interpretability (Wong et al., 2021). Induced sparsity has been applied both within the model weights (Jayakumar et al., 2020) and also within the attention computation (Zhang et al., 2019). In our work, we apply it in the space of all possible interactions between words in the language and attributes of objects in the environment.

Sample Efficiency In grounded language learning, improved sample efficiency may enable new use-cases, for example, the training of intelligent assistants by users who would not have the patience to give many demonstrations of a desired behavior (Tucker et al., 2020). Various tricks have been proposed to improve sample efficiency in reinforcement learning in general (Yu, 2018), including prioritized replay (Hessel et al., 2018), data augmentation (Laskin et al., 2020) and model based learning or replay buffers (van Hasselt et al., 2019; Kaiser et al., 2020). Limited work exists on explicitly addressing sample efficiency in the grounded language learning context (Chevalier-Boisvert et al., 2019; Hui et al., 2020; Qiu et al., 2021). In this work, sample efficiency is one of our primary objectives and we claim to achieve it using a functionally decomposed architecture and offline learning.

3 Experimental Setup

We study the performance of our proposed approach on the `GoToLocal` task of the BabyAI environment. A detailed description of the environment is given in Appendix A. The environment can be seen as a Goal-Conditioned Markov Decision Process, (formally defined in Kaelbling (1993)). Each episode is generated by a seed i and has an initial state $s_0^{(i)}$. To obtain a reward during an episode, the agent must successfully complete the language-encoded instruction (denoted g) that it is given. The language is simple and generated by the use of a templating system. `GoToLocal` consists only of statements "go to (a|the) (color) (object)". Each state is a fully observable 8-by-8 grid world and each cell (denoted c_{ij}) may contain an object, the agent, or nothing.

The information in each cell is *disentangled*; the object's color is in a separate channel to the object's type. We work with disentangled observations because they have been shown to improve the performance and sample-efficiency of attention-based models (see, e.g., Loynd et al., 2020). This disentanglement is preserved by embedding each component separately as factored embeddings q_a.

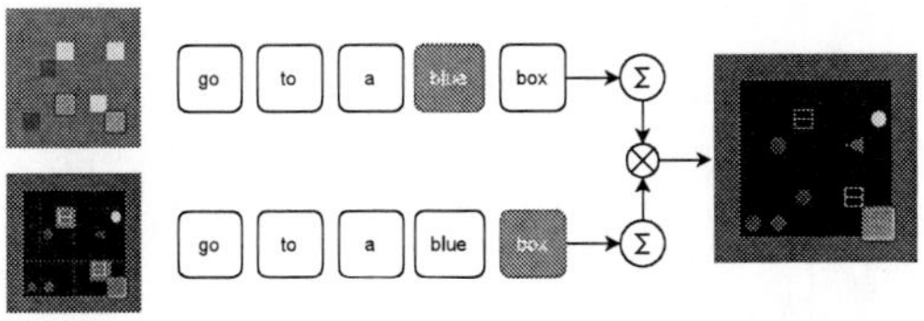

Figure 1: Attention over separate components of the input representation. The model is a single layer of query-key attention applied to each component individually, where queries are image attribute values for a given component, the keys are the words and values are a one-tensor. Performing an AND relation on the components means taking the product of each attention operation.

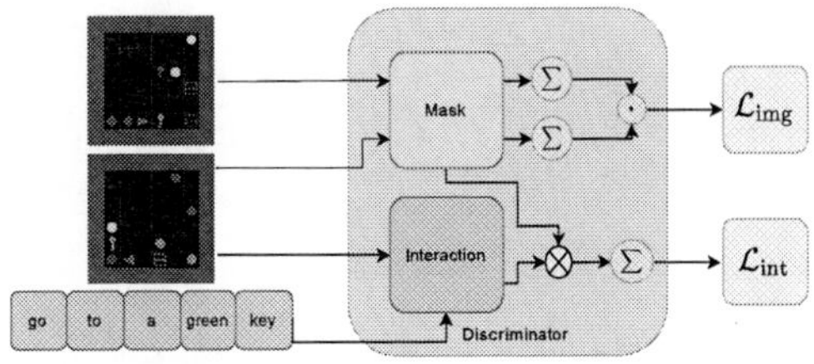

Figure 2: Discriminator training method. $\mathcal{L}_{\text{img}}$ is used to train the "mask" module. Because true examples are those where the agent is situated next to the same goal, an optimal mask module should select states the agent is facing. This can help with learning $S(s, g)$.

The environment also comes with an expert agent which can produce an optimal trajectory for a given initial state and goal $\tau^{(i)}|s_0, g$.

The key performance metric is *success rate*. A *success* happens if the agent completes the instruction within 64 steps. We study compositional generalization and sample efficiency.

By *compositional generalization* we mean maintaining performance when navigating to objects with attribute combinations not seen during training. To study this, we separate goals into $\mathcal{G}_{\text{ID}}$ and $\mathcal{G}_{\text{OOD}}$ following the principle of leaving one attribute combination out (shown in Table 1 and similar to the "visual" split in Ruis et al. (2020)). Then we create corresponding training and validation datasets, $\mathcal{D}_{\text{train}}$, $\mathcal{D}_{\text{v\_ID}}$ and $\mathcal{D}_{\text{v\_OOD}}$ each containing the same number of trajectories (10,000) per goal. Trajectories for each goal are generated in the same way, so we expect that a different split of $\mathcal{G}_{\text{ID}}$ and $\mathcal{G}_{\text{OOD}}$ following the same principle will cause similar behavior in both the baselines and our models. Finer details about the dataset construction are given in Appendix B.

	blue	red	green	yellow	purple	grey
box						
ball						
key						

Table 1: Split between $\mathcal{G}_{\text{ID}}$ and $\mathcal{G}_{\text{OOD}}$. Blue cells are object attributes appearing in the goals for $\mathcal{G}_{\text{ID}}$ and red cells correspond to those in $\mathcal{G}_{\text{OOD}}$.

By *sample efficiency* we mean achieving a high level of performance given a smaller number of samples than conventional methods might require. We denote N as the number of trajectories per goal that an agent has access to and study performance at different levels of N. We train various models using $\mathcal{D}_{\text{train}}$ and describe the training methodology and results in Section 5.1.

4 Designing a learning method

We now design a learning agent with Section 2 in mind. To complete an instruction, the agent needs to identify the goal and plan actions to reach it. The learning problem is decomposed into separate modules with separate training processes. Subsections 4.1 and 4.2 describe a sparse vision-language architecture and training process for identifying goal cells ($S(s, g) \in \mathbb{R}^{H \times W}$). Subsection 4.3 shows how to plan given that identification $\pi(a_t|S(s, g))$.

4.1 Sparse Factored Attention for Goal Identification

We hypothesize that learning to to match objects to descriptions by matching their factors to words individually is a process that generalizes more strongly than matching all at once. For example, the agent should match "red ball" to `red ball` because "red" matches factor `red` and "ball" matches `ball`. If the agent only learns that "red ball" means `red ball`, as a whole, then it may not learn what the meaning of the parts are. Standard architectures, which can mix information between all the words or factors of the observation might fall into the trap of doing the latter over the former. We propose two inductive biases to learn the former. The first bias is *factor compositionality*. As language is a descriptive tool, words should operate at the level of object properties and not entire objects. The second bias is *sparsity* in word/attribute relationships. A particular word should only match as many attributes as necessary.

From this intuition, we propose a "Sparse Factored Attention" architecture, pictured in Fig. 1. The words are the keys and attributes are the queries. However, a critical difference is that the attribute embeddings for each c_{jk} remain partitioned into separate components q_a corresponding to each factor. The normalized dot product $(\hat{c}_{jkq_a} \cdot \hat{g}_w)$ is computed separately between the instruction and

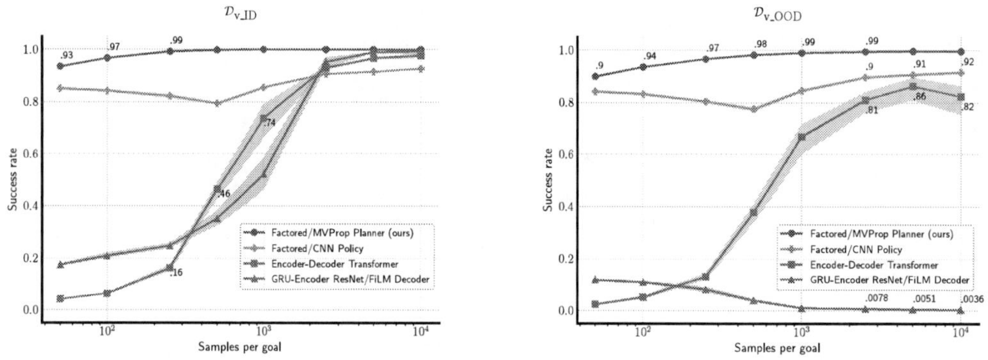

Figure 3: Success Rates on validation seeds. The x-axis is the log-scale number of samples per goal statement. Since there are 18 different goals in the training set, the total number of samples is $18 \times N$. Peak performance on within-distribution goals for prior methods in the same environment is typically reached at 2500 samples per goal, or 45,000 total samples. However, in the compositional generalization case ($\mathcal{D}_{\text{v\_OOD}}$), both baselines fail to maintain the same level of performance, although the Transformer baseline can provide a good amount of performance at a high number of samples. In comparison, Factored/MVProp (ours) reaches a comparable level of performance to peak performance of the baselines at 50 samples per goal, or 900 total samples, and maintains a consistent level of performance on the out-of-distribution validation set. Without a differentiable planner, Factored/CNN is still efficient but does not perform quite as well as Factored/MVProp.

the flattened observation cells for each factor, then the elementwise product is taken over each q_a:

$$S(s_t, g)_{jk} = \prod_{q_a} \sigma(\alpha(\sum_{w} \hat{c}_{jkq_a} \cdot \hat{g}_w) + \beta) \quad (1)$$

where α and β are a single weight and bias applied to all dot product scores and σ is the sigmoid activation function. In practice, exp-sum-log is used in place of $\prod_{q_a}$ for training stability. To encourage sparsity within the outer product, we add an L1 regularization penalty to the outer product of the normalized embedding spaces ($\lambda||\hat{E}_c \cdot \hat{E}_w{}^T||_1$) to the loss. This goes beyond just penalizing $S(s, g)$; it ensures that the system's entire knowledge base is sparse, which in turn assumes that no relationship exists between unseen pairs and is also not sensitive to imbalances in the dataset regarding how often different objects appear in the observations.

4.2 Training with a Discriminator

We found that performance of end-to-end learning by differentiating through the planner to our model was highly initialization sensitive. Instead we propose to learn goal-identification and planning separately. However, $\mathcal{D}$ does not have labels of which cells are goal cells, but only full observations of the environment at each step. To learn to identify the goals, we propose a self-supervised objective in the form of a state-goal discriminator architecture $\hat{D}(s, g)$ shown in Fig. 2, which is trained to match end-states to their corresponding goals.

The discriminator is defined as:

$$\hat{D}(s, g) = \sum_{HW} M(s) \cdot S(s, g) \quad (2)$$

where $S(s, g)$ is the trainable goal identification module and $M(s) \rightarrow \mathbb{R}^{H \times W}, \sum_{\text{HW}} M(s) = 1$ is a "Mask Module". The "Mask Module" is a convolutional neural network with no downsampling or pooling and returns a single-channel "spatial softmax" with the same spatial dimensions as s. Ideally the mask module should learn to identify the cell that the agent is facing. When $M(s)$ and $S(s, g)$ are correctly learned, then $\hat{D}(s, g)$ answers whether the agent is at the goal state. The training process for the discriminator uses a loss function similar to a triplet loss between positive, negative, and anchor samples. Positive and negative goals are sampled from the set of goals, then corresponding positive, anchor, and negative end-states. Finer details of this process are given in Appendix D.

4.3 Planning Module

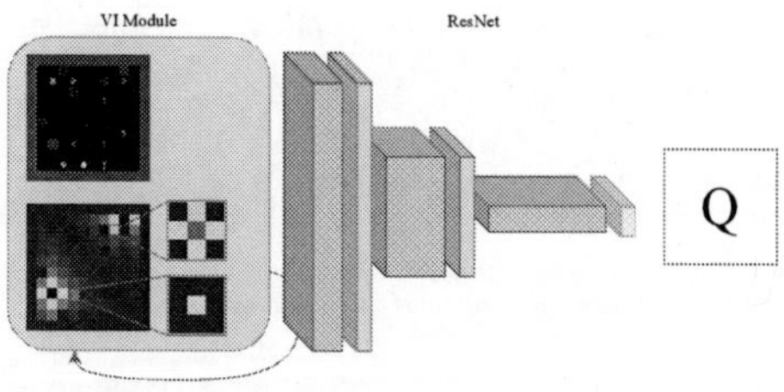

Figure 5: Using a Value Propagation Network (Nardelli et al., 2019) (VPN) to estimate the Q function. VPN is an extension of the Value Iteration Network (Tamar et al., 2017) which makes the convolutional filter propagating value from one cell to its neighbors conditional on its inputs. The Q function is estimated by concatenating the output of the VPN with the estimated rewards, visual features, and agent state, then processing it with a ResNet.

Once $S(s, g)$ is learned, with a knowledge of the connectivity between cells, full observability of the environment, and the assumption that each action

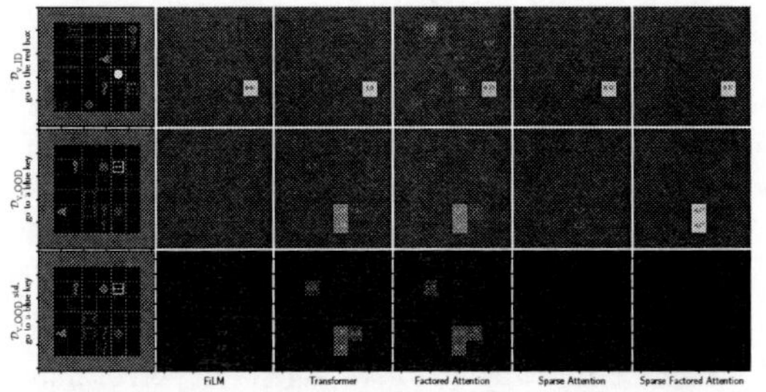

(**4a**) Qualitative evaluation of interaction networks on environment samples. The **top** row contains the mean activations a $\mathcal{D}_{\text{V\_ID}}$ sample, the **middle** and **bottom** rows are means and standard deviations on a $\mathcal{D}_{\text{V\_OOD}}$ sample. Other models either suffer from overfitting or high variance when predicting OOD goals.

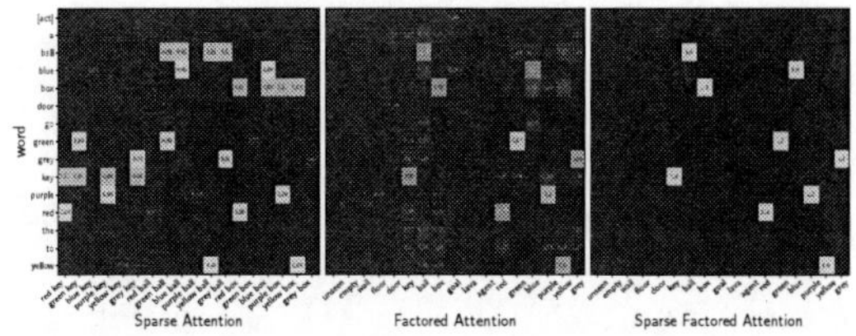

(**4b**) IQM of Embedding Internal Correlations for our method, showing the effect of applying L1 regularization to the embedding outer product. The horizontal axes correspond to factors and the vertical axes correspond to words. **Left:** when concatenating factor embeddings and applying sparse attention, unseen combinations such as `key/blue key` and `blue/blue key` are given little weight. **Middle:** without sparsity regularization, unrelated factors such as `box/yellow` are confused and less weight is given to the true correspondences. **Right:** ours, where the correspondences between words and factors are learned exactly and others are zero.

moves the agent to a either the same cell or an adjacent, learning to plan to reach a goal state becomes trivial. We extend Value Propagation Networks (Nardelli et al., 2019) for this purpose. Details of our implementation are given in Appendix E.

5 Experimental results

5.1 End-to-End performance on the benchmark task

We first examine performance and sample efficiency on both $\mathcal{D}_{\text{V\_ID}}$ and $\mathcal{D}_{\text{V\_OOD}}$ using the experimental setup described in Section 3. We train our approach and several baseline models for the same number (70,000) of training steps over many values of N and 10 random intializations. The models are briefly described as follows:

Factored/MVProp (blue circles, ours) Sparse Factored Attention is pre-trained with the Discriminator in Section 4.2 and frozen, then we only learn the planning and value networks in Section 4.3.

Factored/CNN (light orange plus marks) Ablation of our model with a skipped planning step; detected goals and observations are processed directly into a policy using a convolutional network.

Transformer (green squares) Standard encoder-decoder transformer, encoder inputs are position-encoded instruction word embeddings, decoder inputs are position-encoded flattened cells and a [CLS] token used to predict the policy.

GRU-Encoder ResNet/FiLM Decoder (red triangles) Process visual observation into policy with interleaved FiLM conditioning on the GRU-encoded instruction, similar to Hui et al. (2020).

The training objective is behavioral cloning of the expert policy. The model is evaluated is every 500 steps. Evaluation is performed in a running copy of the environment seeded using each of the stored seeds in the validation sets. To succeed the agent must solve the task - it is not enough to copy what the expert does on most steps. Further details are given in Appendices C and H.

In contrast to both baselines, our method in Fig. 3 attains a high level of performance on both $\mathcal{D}_{\text{V\_ID}}$ and $\mathcal{D}_{\text{V\_OOD}}$, even with a small number of samples, significantly outperforming both baselines even when those models have a greater number of samples available to learn from.

5.2 Examination of Interaction Module Architectures

We also examine what it is about our model architecture that explains its performance on the benchmark task. We perform an ablation study to examine the effectiveness of different architectures for $S(s,g)$. Performance is measured using a "soft F_1 score" against a ground truth on goal locations, as this is essentially an imbalanced classification problem. The metric is described in more detail in Appendix G

	$\mathcal{D}_{\text{V\_ID}}$	$\mathcal{D}_{\text{V\_OOD}}$
FiLM (Perez et al., 2018)	0.983 ± 0.000	0.015 ± 0.004
Transformer (Vaswani et al., 2017)	1.000 ± 0.000	0.799 ± 0.028
Sparse Attention	0.974 ± 0.000	0.069 ± 0.001
Factored Attention	0.891 ± 0.015	0.739 ± 0.028
Sparse Factored Attention	0.951 ± 0.000	0.951 ± 0.000

Table 2: Inter-quartile mean (IQM) of soft F1 scores (predicted goal location versus ground truth goal location) across seeds, dataset sizes, and checkpoints, with added 95% confidence intervals. Sparse Factored Attention scores consistently well on both datasets.

Each architecture for $S(s,g)$ was trained using $\mathcal{D}_{\text{train}}$ for 200,000 iterations with the parameters in Appendix F. The IQM and 95% confidence interval across seeds and top-10 checkpoints are reported in Table 2 using the package and method provided by (Agarwal et al., 2021). While not perfect, our Sparse Factored Attention model achieves high F_1 scores both $\mathcal{D}_{\text{v\_ID}}$ and $\mathcal{D}_{\text{v\_OOD}}$.

We also visualize mean model predictions and their variance across initializations on sample datapoints from both $\mathcal{D}_{\text{v\_ID}}$ and $\mathcal{D}_{\text{v\_OOD}}$ in Fig. 4a. The average is over instances with F_1 scores in the upper 75% range for their class. FiLM and Sparse Attention fail to identify the test-set goal, and the Transformer and Factored Attention models exhibit high variance on $\mathcal{D}_{\text{v\_OOD}}$ between initializations. Only our Sparse Factored Attention model reliably identifies the goal on both datasets.

5.3 Qualitative Evaluation of Model Weights

Since the Factored Attention model is very simple and its only parameters are the embeddings and single weight and bias, we can also visualize "what the model has learned" by taking the mean normalized outer product of both attribute E_c and word E_w embeddings for models shown in Fig. 4b. A perfect learner should learn a sparse correspondence between each attribute and its corresponding word; it should not confound attributes of different types. The heatmaps show the importance of sparsity regularization on the outer product of the embeddings. Without sparsity regularization, the mean correlation between a word and its correct attribute is weaker and not consistent across all initializations. There are also other "unwanted" confounding correlations, for example, between "box" and `blue`, which also appear more strongly in some initialization and data limit combinations as indicated by its high standard deviation. In contrast, the Sparse Factored Attention model displays an almost perfect correlation between each word and the corresponding attribute and very little variance between checkpoints (not pictured). In this sense, we can be much more confident that the Sparse Factored Attention model has *actually learned the symbol grounding* and the meaning of the words as they relate to cell attributes in the environment.

6 Conclusion

We studied the problem of compositional generalization and sample efficient grounded language learning for a vision-language navigation agent. We showed that even under strong assumptions on environment conditions such as full observability and disentanglement of inputs, compositional generalization and sample efficiency do not arise automatically with standard learning approaches. We demonstrate how such conditions can be leveraged by our Sparse Factored Attention model presented in Section 4.1. We demonstrate a method to learn goal identification without labels in Section 4.2 and planning Section 4.3 using a small number of offline trajectories. We further showed superior sample efficiency and generalization performance in Section 5.1 and perform a model analysis and ablation study in Section 5.2 to show how our proposed approach works the way we intended.

7 Limitations of this Work

Goal identification and planning The goal identification and planning methods proposed in Section 4.3 do not work over compound goals. The discriminator training method in Section 4.2 requires that $\mathcal{D}_{\text{train}}$ can be partitioned into subsets corresponding to each goal and that there is at most a many-to-one relationship between goal cell configurations and language statements.

Measuring sample efficiency Testing sample efficiency of gradient-based methods learned from off-policy datasets is not a well specified problem, since each training step could be used to improve the model performance by a small amount an arbitrary number of times. It was a qualitative judgment of the researchers of when to stop training, and we used the same upper bound on training steps for all models to ensure a fair comparison.

Further limitations of this work are discussed in Appendix I.

8 Responsible Research Statement

We also provide details regarding code and reproducibility in Appendix J and computational resource usage in Appendix K. We do not anticipate any special ethical issues to arise from this work as it is foundational in nature and uses a synthetically generated dataset. However, the methods presented in this work may be more amenable to analytic languages as opposed to synthetic ones.

9 Acknowledgements

We thank Yonatan Bisk for his valuable feedback and suggestions on this work. We also acknowledge the computational resources provided by the Aalto Science-IT project and the support within the Academy of Finland Flagship programme: Finnish Center for Artificial Intelligence (FCAI).

References

Rishabh Agarwal, Max Schwarzer, Pablo Samuel Castro, Aaron C Courville, and Marc Bellemare. 2021. Deep reinforcement learning at the edge of the statistical precipice. In *Advances in Neural Information Processing Systems 34: Annual Conference on Neural Information Processing Systems 2021, NeurIPS 2021*, pages 29304–29320.

Peter Anderson, Qi Wu, Damien Teney, Jake Bruce, Mark Johnson, Niko Sünderhauf, Ian Reid, Stephen Gould, and Anton van den Hengel. 2018. Vision-and-language navigation: Interpreting visually-grounded navigation instructions in real environments. In *2018 IEEE/CVF Conference on Computer Vision and Pattern Recognition*, pages 3674–3683.

Jacob Andreas, Marcus Rohrbach, Trevor Darrell, and Dan Klein. 2016. Neural module networks. In *2016 IEEE Conference on Computer Vision and Pattern Recognition (CVPR)*, pages 39–48.

Dzmitry Bahdanau, Felix Hill, Jan Leike, Edward Hughes, Seyed Arian Hosseini, Pushmeet Kohli, and Edward Grefenstette. 2019. Learning to understand goal specifications by modelling reward. In *7th International Conference on Learning Representations, ICLR 2019, New Orleans, LA, USA, May 6-9, 2019*.

Charles Beattie, Joel Z. Leibo, Denis Teplyashin, Tom Ward, Marcus Wainwright, Heinrich Küttler, Andrew Lefrancq, Simon Green, Víctor Valdés, Amir Sadik, Julian Schrittwieser, Keith Anderson, Sarah York, Max Cant, Adam Cain, Adrian Bolton, Stephen Gaffney, Helen King, Demis Hassabis, Shane Legg, and Stig Petersen. 2016. Deepmind lab. *arXiv:1612.03801*.

Richard Bellman. 1957. A Markovian Decision Process. In *Journal of Mathematics and Mechanics*, volume 6, pages 679–684.

Yonatan Bisk, Deniz Yuret, and Daniel Marcu. 2016. Natural language communication with robots. In *NAACL HLT 2016, The 2016 Conference of the North American Chapter of the Association for Computational Linguistics: Human Language Technologies, San Diego California, USA, June 12-17, 2016*, pages 751–761. The Association for Computational Linguistics.

Shyamal Buch, Li Fei-Fei, and Noah D. Goodman. 2021. Neural event semantics for grounded language understanding. *Transactions of the Association for Computational Linguistics*, 9:875–890.

Devendra Singh Chaplot, Kanthashree Mysore Sathyendra, Rama Kumar Pasumarthi, Dheeraj Rajagopal, and Ruslan Salakhutdinov. 2018. Gated-attention architectures for task-oriented language grounding. In *Proceedings of the Thirty-Second AAAI Conference on Artificial Intelligence, (AAAI-18), the 30th innovative Applications of Artificial Intelligence (IAAI-18), and the 8th AAAI Symposium on Educational Advances in Artificial Intelligence (EAAI-18), New Orleans, Louisiana, USA, February 2-7, 2018*, pages 2819–2826. AAAI Press.

David L. Chen and Raymond J. Mooney. 2011. Learning to interpret natural language navigation instructions from observations. In *Proceedings of the Twenty-Fifth AAAI Conference on Artificial Intelligence, AAAI 2011, San Francisco, California, USA, August 7-11, 2011*. AAAI Press.

Maxime Chevalier-Boisvert, Dzmitry Bahdanau, Salem Lahlou, Lucas Willems, Chitwan Saharia, Thien Huu Nguyen, and Yoshua Bengio. 2019. BabyAI: A platform to study the sample efficiency of grounded language learning. In *7th International Conference on Learning Representations, ICLR 2019, New Orleans, LA, USA, May 6-9, 2019*.

Maxime Chevalier-Boisvert, Lucas Willems, and Suman Pal. 2018. Minimalistic Gridworld Environment for OpenAI Gym. `https://github.com/maximecb/gym-minigrid`.

N. Chomsky. 1965. *Aspects of the Theory of Syntax*. MIT Press, Cambridge, MA.

Tong Gao, Qi Huang, and Raymond J. Mooney. 2020. Systematic generalization on gSCAN with language conditioned embedding. In *Proceedings of the 1st Conference of the Asia-Pacific Chapter of the Association for Computational Linguistics and the 10th International Joint Conference on Natural Language Processing, AACL/IJCNLP 2020, Suzhou, China, December 4-7, 2020*, pages 491–503. Association for Computational Linguistics.

Prasoon Goyal, Raymond J. Mooney, and Scott Niekum. 2021. Zero-shot task adaptation using natural language. *arXiv:2106.02972*.

Austin W. Hanjie, Victor Zhong, and Karthik Narasimhan. 2021. Grounding language to entities and dynamics for generalization in reinforcement learning. In *Proceedings of the 38th International Conference on Machine Learning, ICML 2021, 18-24 July 2021, Virtual Event*, volume 139, pages 4051–4062.

Christina Heinze-Deml and Diane Bouchacourt. 2020. Think before you act: A simple baseline for compositional generalization. *arXiv:2009.13962*, 2009.13962.

Karl Moritz Hermann, Felix Hill, Simon Green, Fumin Wang, Ryan Faulkner, Hubert Soyer, David Szepesvari, Wojciech Marian Czarnecki, Max Jaderberg, Denis Teplyashin, Marcus Wainwright, Chris Apps, Demis Hassabis, and Phil Blunsom. 2017. Grounded language learning in a simulated 3d world. *arXiv:1706.06551*.

Matteo Hessel, Joseph Modayil, Hado van Hasselt, Tom Schaul, Georg Ostrovski, Will Dabney, Dan Horgan, Bilal Piot, Mohammad Gheshlaghi Azar, and David Silver. 2018. Rainbow: Combining improvements in deep reinforcement learning. In *Proceedings of the*

Thirty-Second AAAI Conference on Artificial Intelligence, (AAAI-18), the 30th innovative Applications of Artificial Intelligence (IAAI-18), and the 8th AAAI Symposium on Educational Advances in Artificial Intelligence (EAAI-18), New Orleans, Louisiana, USA, February 2-7, 2018, pages 3215–3222. AAAI Press.

David Yu-Tung Hui, Maxime Chevalier-Boisvert, Dzmitry Bahdanau, and Yoshua Bengio. 2020. BabyAI 1.1. *arXiv:2007.12770*.

Eric Jang, Alex Irpan, Mohi Khansari, Daniel Kappler, Frederik Ebert, Corey Lynch, Sergey Levine, and Chelsea Finn. 2021. BC-Z: zero-shot task generalization with robotic imitation learning. In *5th Annual Conference on Robot Learning, 8-11 November 2021, London, UK*, pages 991–1002.

Siddhant M. Jayakumar, Razvan Pascanu, Jack W. Rae, Simon Osindero, and Erich Elsen. 2020. Top-KAST: Top-K always sparse training. In *Advances in Neural Information Processing Systems 33: Annual Conference on Neural Information Processing Systems 2020, NeurIPS 2020, December 6-12, 2020, Virtual Event.*

Leslie Pack Kaelbling. 1993. Learning to achieve goals. In *Proceedings of the 13th International Joint Conference on Artificial Intelligence. Chambéry, France, August 28 - September 3, 1993*, pages 1094–1099.

Lukasz Kaiser, Mohammad Babaeizadeh, Piotr Milos, Blazej Osinski, Roy H. Campbell, Konrad Czechowski, Dumitru Erhan, Chelsea Finn, Piotr Kozakowski, Sergey Levine, Afroz Mohiuddin, Ryan Sepassi, George Tucker, and Henryk Michalewski. 2020. Model based reinforcement learning for atari. In *8th International Conference on Learning Representations, ICLR 2020, Addis Ababa, Ethiopia, April 26-30, 2020.*

Robert Kirk, Amy Zhang, Edward Grefenstette, and Tim Rocktäschel. 2021. A survey of generalisation in deep reinforcement learning. *arXiv:2111.09794*.

Aviral Kumar, Aurick Zhou, George Tucker, and Sergey Levine. 2020. Conservative Q-learning for offline reinforcement learning. In *Advances in Neural Information Processing Systems 33: Annual Conference on Neural Information Processing Systems 2020, NeurIPS 2020, December 6-12, 2020, Virtual Event.*

Yen-Ling Kuo, Boris Katz, and Andrei Barbu. 2021. Compositional networks enable systematic generalization for grounded language understanding. In *Findings of the Association for Computational Linguistics: EMNLP 2021, Virtual Event / Punta Cana, Dominican Republic, 16-20 November, 2021*, pages 216–226. Association for Computational Linguistics.

Michael Laskin, Kimin Lee, Adam Stooke, Lerrel Pinto, Pieter Abbeel, and Aravind Srinivas. 2020. Reinforcement learning with augmented data. In *Advances in Neural Information Processing Systems 33: Annual Conference on Neural Information Processing Systems 2020, NeurIPS 2020, December 6-12, 2020, Virtual Event.*

Ricky Loynd, Roland Fernandez, Asli Celikyilmaz, Adith Swaminathan, and Matthew J. Hausknecht. 2020. Working memory graphs. In *Proceedings of the 37th International Conference on Machine Learning, ICML 2020, 13-18 July 2020, Virtual Event*, pages 6404–6414.

Karthik Narasimhan, Regina Barzilay, and Tommi S. Jaakkola. 2018. Grounding language for transfer in deep reinforcement learning. *J. Artif. Intell. Res.*, 63:849–874.

Nantas Nardelli, Gabriel Synnaeve, Zeming Lin, Pushmeet Kohli, Philip H. S. Torr, and Nicolas Usunier. 2019. Value propagation networks. In *7th International Conference on Learning Representations, ICLR 2019, New Orleans, LA, USA, May 6-9, 2019.*

Junhyuk Oh, Satinder P. Singh, Honglak Lee, and Pushmeet Kohli. 2017. Zero-shot task generalization with multi-task deep reinforcement learning. In *Proceedings of the 34th International Conference on Machine Learning, ICML 2017, Sydney, NSW, Australia, 6-11 August 2017*, pages 2661–2670.

Ethan Perez, Florian Strub, Harm de Vries, Vincent Dumoulin, and Aaron C. Courville. 2018. FiLM: Visual reasoning with a general conditioning layer. In *Proceedings of the Thirty-Second AAAI Conference on Artificial Intelligence, (AAAI-18), the 30th innovative Applications of Artificial Intelligence (IAAI-18), and the 8th AAAI Symposium on Educational Advances in Artificial Intelligence (EAAI-18), New Orleans, Louisiana, USA, February 2-7, 2018*, pages 3942–3951. AAAI Press.

Linlu Qiu, Hexiang Hu, Bowen Zhang, Peter Shaw, and Fei Sha. 2021. Systematic generalization on gSCAN: What is nearly solved and what is next? In *Proceedings of the 2021 Conference on Empirical Methods in Natural Language Processing, EMNLP 2021, Virtual Event / Punta Cana, Dominican Republic, 7-11 November, 2021*, pages 2180–2188. Association for Computational Linguistics.

Laura Ruis, Jacob Andreas, Marco Baroni, Diane Bouchacourt, and Brenden M. Lake. 2020. A benchmark for systematic generalization in grounded language understanding. In *Advances in Neural Information Processing Systems 33: Annual Conference on Neural Information Processing Systems 2020, NeurIPS 2020, December 6-12, 2020, Virtual Event.*

Laura Ruis and Brenden M. Lake. 2022. Improving systematic generalization through modularity and augmentation. *arXiv:2202.10745*.

Mohit Shridhar, Jesse Thomason, Daniel Gordon, Yonatan Bisk, Winson Han, Roozbeh Mottaghi, Luke Zettlemoyer, and Dieter Fox. 2020. ALFRED: A benchmark for interpreting grounded instructions for everyday tasks. In *2020 IEEE/CVF Conference on Computer Vision and Pattern Recognition, CVPR 2020, Seattle, WA, USA, June 13-19, 2020*, pages 10737–10746. Computer Vision Foundation / IEEE.

Mohit Shridhar, Xingdi Yuan, Marc-Alexandre Côté, Yonatan Bisk, Adam Trischler, and Matthew J. Hausknecht. 2021. ALFWorld: Aligning text and embodied environments for interactive learning. In *9th International Conference on Learning Representations, ICLR 2021, Virtual Event, Austria, May 3-7, 2021*.

Shagun Sodhani, Amy Zhang, and Joelle Pineau. 2021. Multi-task reinforcement learning with context-based representations. In *Proceedings of the 38th International Conference on Machine Learning, ICML 2021, 18-24 July 2021, Virtual Event*, pages 9767–9779.

Aviv Tamar, Yi Wu, Garrett Thomas, Sergey Levine, and Pieter Abbeel. 2017. Value iteration networks. In *Proceedings of the Twenty-Sixth International Joint Conference on Artificial Intelligence, IJCAI 2017, Melbourne, Australia, August 19-25, 2017*, pages 4949–4953.

Geraud Nangue Tasse, Steven James, and Benjamin Rosman. 2022. Generalisation in lifelong reinforcement learning through logical composition. In *10th International Conference on Learning Representations, ICLR 2022, Virtual Event.*

Aaron D. Tucker, Markus Anderljung, and Allan Dafoe. 2020. Social and governance implications of improved data efficiency. In *AIES '20: AAAI/ACM Conference on AI, Ethics, and Society, New York, NY, USA, February 7-8, 2020*, pages 378–384. ACM.

Hado van Hasselt, Matteo Hessel, and John Aslanides. 2019. When to use parametric models in reinforcement learning? In *Advances in Neural Information Processing Systems 32: Annual Conference on Neural Information Processing Systems 2019, NeurIPS 2019, December 8-14, 2019, Vancouver, BC, Canada*, pages 14322–14333.

Ashish Vaswani, Noam Shazeer, Niki Parmar, Jakob Uszkoreit, Llion Jones, Aidan N. Gomez, Lukasz Kaiser, and Illia Polosukhin. 2017. Attention is all you need. In *Advances in Neural Information Processing Systems 30: Annual Conference on Neural Information Processing Systems 2017, December 4-9, 2017, Long Beach, CA, USA*, pages 5998–6008.

Eric Wong, Shibani Santurkar, and Aleksander Madry. 2021. Leveraging sparse linear layers for debuggable deep networks. In *Proceedings of the 38th International Conference on Machine Learning, ICML 2021, 18-24 July 2021, Virtual Event*, pages 11205–11216.

Yang Yu. 2018. Towards sample efficient reinforcement learning. In *Proceedings of the Twenty-Seventh International Joint Conference on Artificial Intelligence, IJCAI 2018, July 13-19, 2018, Stockholm, Sweden*, pages 5739–5743.

Jiajun Zhang, Yang Zhao, Haoran Li, and Chengqing Zong. 2019. Attention with sparsity regularization for neural machine translation and summarization. *IEEE ACM Trans. Audio Speech Lang. Process.*, 27(3):507–518.

Mingde Zhao, Zhen Liu, Sitao Luan, Shuyuan Zhang, Doina Precup, and Yoshua Bengio. 2021. A consciousness-inspired planning agent for model-based reinforcement learning. In *Advances in Neural Information Processing Systems 34: Annual Conference on Neural Information Processing Systems 2021, NeurIPS 2021, December 6-14, 2021, Virtual Event.*

A Details of the BabyAI Environment

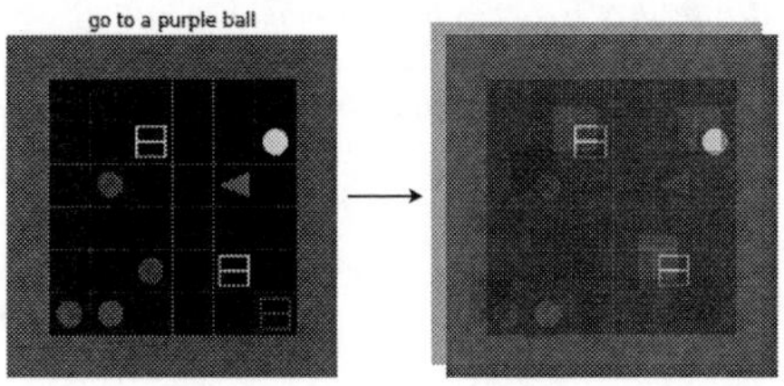

Figure 6: An illustration of the integer-encoded inputs provided by the BabyAI environment. Color and shape information are encoded in separate channels and are independent from each other.

BabyAI is a simple grid world-like environment based on Minigrid (Chevalier-Boisvert et al., 2018). chose to use this environment for this project due to its simplicity, ease of generating expert trajectories, and input representation characteristics. In the environment, the agent is given instructions to complete in a sythetically generated language that is a subset of English. The seed for the environment, i, determines its initial state s_0 and goal g, which comes from the set $\mathcal{G}$ for a given level. Within the environment, there are a few different object types (`ball`, `box`, `key`) each of which may be one of six different colors (`red`, `blue`, `green`, `grey`, `purple`, `yellow`). The agent can face one of four different directions. There are seven actions available to the agent: `turn left`, `turn right`, `go forward`, `open`, `pick up`, `put down` and `signal done`. The original implementation provides partial observations, however we modify the environment to make the state space fully observable due to the inherent difficulty planning over unobservable states.[2] The observations are subdivided into cells as explained in Section 3. Each cell is a disentangled vector of integers of comprised of three components, the first corresponding to the object type, the second corresponding to the color and the third corresponding to the object that the agent is holding.

The goals g come in the form of simple language statements such as "go to a red box". BabyAI comes in several "levels". Each level requires the agent to demonstrate competency at a certain subset of "skills", summarized in Table 1 of the original by Chevalier-Boisvert et al. (2019).

[2]We also reproduce the relevant experiments in (Chevalier-Boisvert et al., 2019) using this fully-observable state space for fair comparison in Section 5.1 of this work.

In this work, we focus on the `GoToLocal` task, where the agent must learn to reach the goal object indicated in the language-encoded instruction by navigating to the correct location in an 8×8 grid world and then performing the `signal done` action within a fixed number of steps. Performing `signal done` facing the wrong cell terminates the episode with a reward of zero. Requiring the `signal done` action precludes the trivial solution of ignoring g and visiting every object until successful. Other objects may exist in the grid as *distractors*; non-goal objects that the agent must learn to ignore and navigate around depending on the goal.

B Collecting Trajectories for the Dataset

In the `GoToLocal` task there are 36 possible goal statements. Each statement begins with "go to", followed by "the" or "a", then color and object terms. To collect the seeds to generate each environment and their corresponding solutions $\tau_i | s_0, g$, we iterate consecutively through random seeds starting from zero and reset the environment using each seed. The environment is "solved" using the provided `BotAgent`, which implements an optimal policy. We do not want our measurements or training to be biased by imbalances in the dataset, so we want to ensure that each goal has the same number of samples in $\mathcal{D}$. 10,000 state-action trajectories with a length of at least 7 are stored for each goal g. A trajectory τ is a tuple $(x, (s_0, ..., s_t), (a_0, ..., a_t), (r_0, ..., r_t), g)$, consisting of (respectively), the seed, state trajectory, action trajectory, rewards and goal.

We split the data into training, "in-distribution" and "combinatorial generalization" (out of distribution) validation sets. To make these splits, we first split the goals into "in-distribution" goals $\mathcal{G}_{\text{ID}}$ and "combinatorial generalization" goals $\mathcal{G}_{\text{OOD}}$. One color and object combination is omitted from $\mathcal{G}_{\text{ID}}$ for each color and placed in $\mathcal{G}_{\text{OOD}}$, specifically, goals containing `red ball`, `green box`, `blue key`, `purple ball`, `grey box` and `yellow key`. The "in-distribution" validation set $\mathcal{D}_{\text{v\_ID}}$ consists of the last 20 trajectories in $\mathcal{D}$ corresponding to each $g \in \mathcal{G}_{\text{ID}}$. The "combinatorial generalization" set $\mathcal{D}_{\text{v\_OOD}}$ is defined similarly with the last 40 trajectories in $\mathcal{G}_{\text{OOD}}$.[3] The training

[3]The reason for using the last 40 trajectories is to ensure that both validation datasets have the same number trajectories in total; since there are twice as many goals covered in $\mathcal{D}_{\text{v\_ID}}$

set $\mathcal{D}$ consists of all trajectories corresponding to $g \in \mathcal{G}_{\text{ID}}$, excluding those in $\mathcal{D}_{\text{v\_ID}}$.

C Details of the Baselines

The first baseline is similar to the architecture used in (Hui et al., 2020); featuring a GRU to encode g, a ResNet to encode s and the use of FiLM layers (Perez et al., 2018) to modulate feature maps according to the encoded g, which in turn is flattened and concatenated with an embedding corresponding to the agent's current direction to produce a hidden representation z. The policy π is estimated using an MLP from z. The only difference to (Hui et al., 2020) is that the memory module used to handle partial observability and exploration is removed, since the environment is fully observable.

The second baseline is an encoder-decoder Transformer model (Vaswani et al., 2017), where the input sequence is the individual words in g added with their 1D positional encodings, and the output sequence is the 2D encoded observation s added with their 2D positional encodings. A classification token is appended to the end of the output sequence, which uses a linear prediction head to estimate π in the same way as above. 10000 steps of learning rate warmup followed by subsequent logarithmic decay in the learning rate are used when training the Transformer.

For all models, an embedding dimension of 32 is used for both the words in g and each attribute in c_{jk}, implying that the total embedding dimension is 96 after each embedded attribute is concatenated together. The batch size and learning rate for Adam used during training are 32 and 10^{-4} respectively.

D Training the Discriminator

Two goals, g_+, g_- are sampled without replacement uniformly from the set of all known goals $\mathcal{G}_{\text{v\_ID}}$. Two trajectories are sampled without replacement from $\{\mathcal{D}_{\text{train}} | g = g_+\}$, τ_1^{g+}, τ_2^{g+} and one trajectory is sampled from $\{\mathcal{D}_{\text{train}} | g = g_-\}$, τ^{g-}. s_r is assumed to be the rewarding states for all three trajectories and are denoted $(s_r^{g+})_1, (s_r^{g+})_2, (s_r^{g-})_1$. With probability $\frac{1}{|\mathcal{G}|}$, $(s_r^{g-})_1$ is replaced with a random state in $\tau_{0:T-1}^{g-}$, so that the discriminator also sees states that are not rewarding for any goal. The discriminator's inputs and labels are tuples (s_1, s_2, g, y). In this tuple, s_1 is an "anchor" state, s_2 is a comparison state, g is the goal and y is the label. The tuple $((s_r^{g+})_1, (s_r^{g+})_2, g_+, 1)$ is a "true" example and the tuple $((s_r^{g+})_1, (s_r^{g-})_1, g_+, 0)$ is a "false" example. True and false examples are sampled consecutively.

We define the loss for the discriminator as:

$$\mathcal{L}_D(s_1, s_2, g, y) = \mathcal{L}_{\text{int}}(s_2, g, y) + \mathcal{L}_{\text{img}}(s_1, s_2, y) \quad (3)$$

The "interaction loss" $\mathcal{L}_{\text{int}}$ is used to optimize $S(s, g)$. As S classifies whether a given s is a rewarding state for g, the loss is a binary-cross-entropy loss, where the outputs of S are logits:

$$\mathcal{L}_{\text{int}}(s_2, g, y) = y \log D(s_2, g) + (1 - y) \log(1 - D(s_2, g)) \quad (4)$$

The image-matching loss $\mathcal{L}_{\text{img}}$ is used to resolve the ambiguity of whether a high loss value in $\mathcal{L}_{\text{int}}$ was caused by an incorrect parameterization of $M(s)$ or $S(s, g)$. Define the *mask-weighted image* as $I(s) = \sum_{\text{HW}} M(s) \odot s$ and the *normalized mask-weighted image* as $\hat{I}(s) = \frac{I(s)}{||I(s)||_2^2}$ Then the normalized image-matching loss L_{img} is given by:[4]

$$\mathcal{L}_{\text{img}}(s_1, s_2, y) = ||(\hat{I}(s_1) \cdot \hat{I}(s_2)) - y||_2^2 \quad (5)$$

E Planning with Value Iteration

Value-based differentiable planning networks assume the existence of a function $r(s, g)$: $\mathbb{R}^{H \times W \times A}$ which returns the cell-action combinations in s that give a reward for being reached by an agent. In this case, r is modelling a reward function for goal g in terms of c_{jk}. Knowing both this function and the dynamics $p(s_{t+1}|s, a_t)$ with a discrete state space enables using *Value Iteration* (Bellman, 1957) to solve for the *optimal value function* V^*, which induces an *optimal policy*:

$$\pi^* = \max_a Q(s, a) = \max_a \sum_{a \in |\mathcal{A}} r(s, a) + \gamma p(s_{t+1}|s, a_t) V(s_{t+1}) \quad (6)$$

In this case, we do not know the dynamics exactly, but we have a prior that we can start from, which is that all neighboring cells to a given cell are uniformly reachable from the current cell by any action $p(c_{j+l,k+m}|a_t, c_{jk}), l, m \in [-1, 1], a \in \mathcal{A}$. In this problem, the agent's occupancy of a cell c_{jk} corresponds to a state s given the initialization s_0, so a mapping exists from values of cells to values

[4]We use mean-squared error as opposed to binary cross entropy loss for the the image-matching loss as we found that in practice it was less sensitive to label noise, which was present in this problem, since goals such as "go to a red key" and "go to the red key" involve the same object color combination but are nevertheless treated as separate goals by the discriminator.

of states up to the agent's rotation given an initialization $V(c_{jk}) \rightarrow V(s|s_0)$.

To refine our estimate of the the dynamics $p(s_{t+1}|s, a_t)$ and improve our estimate of $Q(s, a_t, g)$, we can use the above assumptions and a differentiable planning method known as a *Value Iteration Network* (VIN) (Tamar et al., 2017). Starting with $V_0(c_{jk}) = r(c_{jk}, g)$, VIN re-expresses value-iteration as a form of *convolution* performed recursively K times:

$$V_{k+1}(c_{jk}, g) = \max \begin{cases} V_k(c_{jk}, g), \\ \max_{a \in \mathcal{A}} \sum_{l,m \in \mathcal{N}(c_{jk})} \mathbf{P}_{a,l-j,m-k} V_k(c_{lm}, g) \end{cases} \quad (7)$$

where $\mathcal{N}(c_{jk})$ are the neighbors of a cell and $\mathbf{P}$ is a learnable linear estimate of the dynamics (the transition probabilities to neighboring cells for each action). In reality, the dynamics are dependent on what the neighboring cells actually contain. *Max Value Propagation Networks* (MVProp) (Nardelli et al., 2019) extend on VIN by replacing $\mathbf{P}$ with a scalar *propagation weight* conditioned on the current cell $\phi(c_{jk})$, where ϕ is any learnable function with non-negative output. In that sense, we learn to model how value *propagates* around the cells. Using the dataset $\mathcal{D}$ we can generate traces of returns from trajectories using an optimal planner with discount factor γ. Then learning $Q(s, a_t, g)$ is done by minimizing the empirical risk with respect to some loss function $\mathcal{L}$:

$$\arg\min_{Q_\theta} \mathbb{E}_{s,a_t \sim \mathcal{D}_{\text{tr}}} \mathcal{L}(Q(s, a_t, g), R(s, a_t))) \quad (8)$$

In the MVProp framework, it is the responsibility of the consumer of $V_K(s, g)$ to map neighboring values of a cell to Q values for actions. Both Tamar et al. (2017) and Nardelli et al. (2019) resolve this problem by including the cell that the agent is currently occupying as part of the state. However, this information is not available to us in $\mathcal{D}$ as we have only the state s and action observation a_t. In practice, this problem turns out not to be insurmountable and good performance can be achieved by simply concatenating as additional channels $V_0(s, g)$ and $V_k(s, g)$ to the initial encoding of s and using a Convolutional Neural Network to encode the image into a single vector of which represents the vector-valued output $Q(s, g) \rightarrow \mathbb{R}^{|\mathcal{A}|}$, eg the action-value function for all actions.

Finally, there is the question of which loss function to use to learn $Q(s, a_t, g)$. We observed that simply using mean-squared error loss between $R(s, a_t)$ and $Q(s, a_t, g)$ led to over-optimistic estimates of Q-values for non-chosen actions. To fix this problem, we added an additional term penalizing any non-zero value for those actions: similar to Conservative Q Learning (Kumar et al., 2020):

$$\begin{aligned} \mathcal{L}_{\text{VIN}}(s, a_t, g) = ||R(s, a_t, g) - Q(s, a_t, g)||_2^2 + \\ \lambda||Q(s, a_-, g), a_- \in \{\mathcal{A} \setminus a_t\}||_2^2 \end{aligned} \quad (9)$$

F Training Parameters of $S(s, g)$

$S(s, g)$ is trained for 200,000 steps, using a learning rate of 10^{-5}, a batch size of 1024 and 16-bit mixed precision used for the model weights and embeddings. During training, models were evaluated both $\mathcal{D}_{\text{v\_ID}}$ and $\mathcal{D}_{\text{v\_OOD}}$ every 20 training steps. The top-10 performing model checkpoints by F_1 score on $\mathcal{D}_{\text{v\_ID}}$ were stored, along with their F_1 score on $\mathcal{D}_{\text{v\_OOD}}$.

G Soft F1 Score

The problem in Section 4.2 is unbalanced; there are a small number of goal states and a large number of non-goal states. Therefore, we propose to use a metric that is robust to the class imbalance, but also takes into account the weight of the predictions as this will be used as the reward model in the planner. The metric is a "soft F1 score" is defined as the harmonic mean of soft-precision and soft-recall, for a single trajectory i (with indexes omitted for brevity):

$$\begin{aligned} P &= \frac{\sum_{\text{HW}}^{jk} y_{jk} S(s, g)_{jk}}{\sum_{\text{HW}}^{jk} (y_{jk} S(s, g)_{jk} + (1 - y_{jk}) S(s, g)_{jk})} \\ R &= \sum_{\text{HW}}^{jk} y_{jk} S(s, g)_{jk} / \sum_{\text{HW}}^{jk} (y_{jk}) \\ F_1 &= 2PR/(P + R) \end{aligned} \quad (10)$$

A high value of soft-F_1 indicates that both precision *and* recall are high.

H End-to-end usage our proposed model

The model is trained in two phases; first, the Sparse Factored Attention model in Section 4.1 is trained using the discriminator task in Section 4.2 for 200,000 steps with a learning rate of $10e^{-5}$ and batch size of 1024. Then, the weights at the end of training (for the corresponding initialization seed and $\mathcal{D}_N$ are frozen and used as the initialization for the VIN model described in Section 4.3. The training parameters and setup used otherwise is the same as is described in Appendix C.

I Additional Limitations

Controlled Environment We used the `GoToLocal` task on BabyAI as the sole reference environment for this study. A fully observable state space, knowledge of the state-space connectivity, and disentangled factors on cell states are very strong assumptions that are leveraged to achieve the results that we present.

Computational resources Sample efficiency does not imply computational efficiency. In particular, we found that training the discriminator in Section 4.2 requires large batch sizes and a large number of samples generated from $\mathcal{D}_N$ to converge.

J Reproducibility of this work

We kept the importance of reproducible research in mind when designing our experimental method. We provide the source code for our approach and seeds used to generate each environment and trajectory in $\mathcal{D}$.

We are unable to provide pre-trained models or log files due to space constraints.

K Computational Resource usage of this work

The person responsible for developing the method took about one year to do so and used a workstation with a single NVIDIA RTX2060 GPU with 6GB of GPU memory to test different approaches. Because the methods that we present in this paper may be sensitive to different weight initializations, we believed it was necessary to show trained model performance using different initialization random initializations, using the methods in (Agarwal et al., 2021) for a more reliable presentation of results. To conduct the experiments using the final version of our methods, we used our SLURM compute cluster with an array of shared NVIDIA Tesla V100 GPUs. We ran 6 different versions of the discriminator experiment, over five different models, ten dataset sizes, ten random initializations, each one taking up to 8 hours to complete, making for 24,000 hours of GPU time used. We ran 3 different versions of the end-to-end experiments over 4 different models, with the same number of dataset sizes and random initializations each one taking up to 12 hours, making for an additional 19,200 hours.

How do people talk about images? A study on open-domain conversations with images.

Yi-Pei Chen
The University of Tokyo
ypc@g.ecc.u-tokyo.ac.jp

Nobuyuki Shimizu
Yahoo Japan
nobushim@yahoo-corp.jp

Takashi Miyazaki
Yahoo Japan
takmiyaz@yahoo-corp.jp

Hideki Nakayama
The University of Tokyo
nakayama@ci.i.u-tokyo.ac.jp

Abstract

This paper explores how humans conduct conversations with images by investigating an open-domain image conversation dataset, ImageChat. We examined the conversations with images from the perspectives of *image relevancy* and *image information*.We found that utterances/conversations are not always related to the given image, and conversation topics diverge within three turns about half of the time. Besides image objects, more comprehensive non-object image information is also indispensable. After inspecting the causes, we suggested that understanding the overall scenario of image and connecting objects based on their high-level attributes might be very helpful to generate more engaging open-domain conversations when an image is presented. We proposed enriching the image information with image caption and object tags based on our analysis. With our proposed *image*$^+$ features, we improved automatic metrics including BLEU and Bert Score, and increased the diversity and image-relevancy of generated responses to the strong SOTA baseline. The result verifies that our analysis provides valuable insights and could facilitate future research on open-domain conversations with images.

1 Introduction

A picture is worth a thousand words. Human communication often involves both text and images. Understanding the image content and chatting about it is crucial for a chatbot to interact with people. Current multimodal dialogue systems often equip with an object detector, and adapt similar architecture as text-based dialogue systems, except fusing text and image modalities through concatenation (Shuster et al., 2020b,c) or an attention mechanism (Ju et al., 2019).

To investigate whether an additional object detector is enough, and to understand what factors direct the conversation content when an image exists, we conducted a deep analysis of the ImageChat dataset (Shuster et al., 2020a). We aimed to answer the following questions: (1) How is a conversation with image different from an open-domain conversation? Is the image necessary or supplemental? How related is the image to the conversation topic? (2) Does the topic of the three-turns conversation always be on the image? How does the transfer happen if the conversation topic transits from the image to others? Can we predict the shift from the image? (3) What types of image information are used in the conversation? More specifically, we want to know how helpful image objects are in the conversation since baseline models usually use an object detection model as the image encoder.

We addressed the questions by sampling and analyzing ImageChat dataset from the aspects of *image relevancy* and *image information*, which are independent but intertwined. The former labels whether the given image is relevant to the conversation theme, and the latter marks the type of image information in utterances. The annotation results show that about 31% of utterances are not on the image-related theme, i.e., the utterances do not describe or could be generated without the image. In terms of the conversation, people transit conversation topics 54% of the time within three utterances, and surprisingly 7% of conversations entirely consist of non-image-related utterances. In these conversations where the image is optional, the topic often derived from attributes of one of image objects. We also discovered that 45% of utterances contain image objects, 23.7% have non-object image information such as the description of events in the image, and 31.3% do not have any image information at all. This result hints that including comprehensive descriptions of the image beyond image objects could benefit the generation of utterances with image information.

Based on our analysis, we propose to enhance the generation of image-dependent response by augmenting image features from image caption

Proceedings of the 2022 Conference of the North American Chapter of the Association for Computational Linguistics: Human Language Technologies: Student Research Workshop, pages 156 - 162
July 10-15, 2022 ©2022 Association for Computational Linguistics

Image	Style	Utterance	Related
	*Cowardly:*	Never had this food before and not sure if I'm ready to try it today.	✔
	Grateful:	I am always up to trying new things. It looks like a lot of effort went into this food and I plan to enjoy every bite.	✔
	Cowardly:	I don't know, it looks like it might be too much.	✔
	*Extraordinary:*	What an unusual place! The colors of the train really bounce off the grey backdrop of the city.	✔
	Narcissistic:	Well, of course this is a fantastic picture, since it was MY magnificent photographic skills that produced it!	✔
	Extraordinary:	I had no idea you have such talent!	✘
	*Spontaneous:*	That's it, I going to Vegas tomorrow. Who's coming with me?	✘
	Morbid:	Someone died in that Vegas spot.	✘
	Spontaneous:	Lets go on a vegas trip this weekend!	✘

Table 1: Examples of conversation themes are related and unrelated to the given image.

and object tags, and using the text information explicitly rather than fusing image captioning and object detection models to the text-based conversation model. Our model with enhanced image features outperforms the strong SOTA model Multimodal BlenderBot (MMB) (Shuster et al., 2020c) on BLEU and BertScore. In addition, we also generate more image-related and more diverse responses than MMB.

2 Analysis of Conversations on Image

2.1 ImageChat Dataset

We analyzed the ImageChat dataset (Shuster et al., 2020a), which is so far the only dialogue dataset that focuses on *open-domain conversations on images*, to the best of our knowledge. Each conversation is paired with one image from YFCC 100M (Thomee et al., 2016) and consists of three turn utterances from two speakers with assigned speaking styles. There are total 215 style types, such as sympathetic or optimistic. The images are highly diverse ones across multiple domains. We obtained the object tags by Scene Graph Benchmark (Han et al., 2021) implementation of Faster R-CNN (Ren et al., 2016), which is also the image encoder used in the baseline model MMB. We also generated the caption of each image using the SOTA language-vision pretrained model VinVL (Zhang et al., 2021).

2.2 Annotation

We randomly sampled 300 utterances (100 conversations) from the validation set and annotated each utterance for its image relevancy and what image information it contains.

2.2.1 Image Relevance to Dialogue Theme

We first asked whether the *conversation theme* is always related to the image, and if not, how often is each utterance directly related to the image. We defined *image relevancy* as a binary classification of whether the given image is necessary for generating each utterance. If one could generate the utterance without the given image, the utterance is labeled as unrelated. Examples of image-related and unrelated utterances are shown in Table 1.

2.2.2 Image Information in the Dialogue

Based on our observation of the data, we categorized each utterance into one of the 8 classes, indicating the type of image information mentioned in the utterance. Classes start with **O** mean image objects are mentioned in the utterance; classes start with **R** mean there are non-object image related information mentioned in the utterance; and **NI** class means there is no image information in the utterance at all. See Table 2 for the details and examples of each category.

Class	Explanation	Utterance (U) I Object Tags (T)
O	Words in utterance **exactly match** object tags	U: I guess this is an interesting **building**. T: ['cloud', 'window', 'sky', **'building'**]
OS	**Synonyms** of object tags in the utterance, including hyponym/hypernym pairs, e.g. "seagull" in U and "bird" in T.	U: I'd like to party with that **guy**! T:['watch', **'man'**, 'phone', 'guitar', ...]
OP	**Pronoun** is used to refer to image objects.	U: Would **she** shut up already? T: ['book', 'jacket', 'tree', **'woman'**, ...]
OF	Words in the utterance refer to image objects but have no overlap with object tags, probably due to **false object detection** results.	U: The **aluminum** art was different. T: ['rock', 'ground', 'foil']
R	Words in the utterance referring to **non-object image information**, e.g., the scene of the image.	U: It's obviously a **festival**. T: ['sunglasses', 'hat', 'balloon', ...]
RI	The utterance is about the **image itself**, not the content of the image.	U: A **screenshot** by definition does not die. T: ['man', 'hat', 'photo', 'glass']
RP	**Pronoun** is used to refer to image-related information in the utterance.	U: **It**'s beautiful! I would love to visit. T: ['leaf', 'flower', 'branch', 'tree']
NI	**No image-related** information mentioned in the utterance.	U: yeah sure does. T: ['sunglasses', 'hat', 'man', 'light', ...]

Table 2: Classes of image information in the utterance.

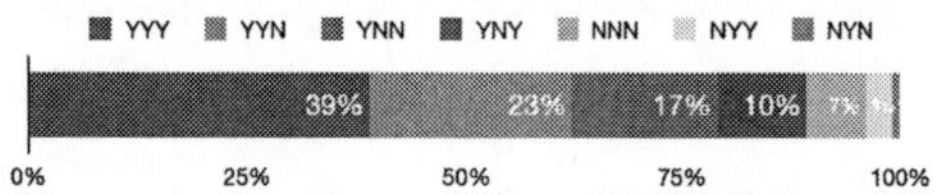

Figure 1: Different combination of image-related utterances in 3-turns dialogues. Y: image-related utterance; N: non-related utterance. Green hue indicates the dialogue is more image-dependent, and the red family suggests the opposite.

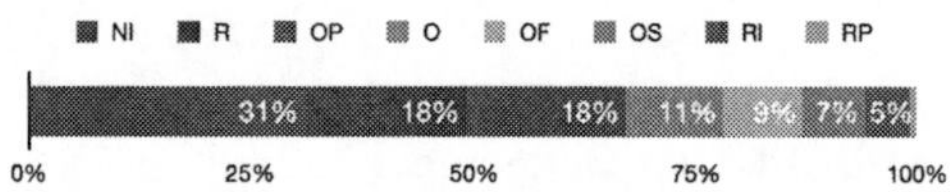

Figure 2: Classes of image information in utterances. Green hue refers to image objects, blue hue refers to non-object image information, and red means there is no image information at all.

2.3 Analysis Result and Finding

2.3.1 Image Relevancy

We found that conversation themes of ImageChat dialogues are not always about the image. In fact, the conversation often goes back and forth between image-related to non-related topics even within only three conversation turns. Figure 1 illustrates such a phenomenon with dialogues of different combinations of the image-relevance utterances. While an image-related utterance is labeled as 'Y' and non-image-related utterance is labeled as 'N', 'YYY' means all three turns in a dialogue are image-related utterances and 'YYN' means the conversation diverse from image-related topics to other domain not related to the given image.

Further investigating the combination of image-related and non-related utterances in a dialogue, we could roughly classify them into two schemas: (1) One speaker responds to the other, and if one extends out of the image-related topic, the following conversation is diverse, and vice versa. 'YNN', 'YYN', 'NYY' are in this category. The transition between 'Y' and 'N' may result from the mention of an object related to objects in the image but not related to the image itself. In this case, the related object often links to the image object with some high-level attributes, such as the object's category, shape, or material. Alternatively, the 'N' utterance might be a general non-informative response or an invented non-image-related scenario. (2) Some dialogues seem unnatural because one of the speakers continues their previous (self-)expression and does not respond to the other's utterance. 'YNY' and 'NYN' usually belong to this schema. Note that there is no combination of 'NNY,' showing that it is less likely to talk about the image after chatting on off-image topics.

We found that about 7% of dialogues are non-image-related ('NNN'), although most utterances are still image-related (Y: 69% vs. N:31%). Investigating the reason, we noticed that many of the non-image-related dialogues are stimulated by attributes of one of objects in the image. For example, a conversation about fighting in a ring is given an image with a ring-shaped object. This observation suggests that capturing attributes of objects and linking objects to much broader scenarios are essential directions to generate natural utterances.

2.3.2 Image Information

Figure 2 shows the distribution of image information classes. The green hue represents the utterances with image objects (Ox, 45.0%). Among them, a great portion of utterances have objects referred by a pronoun (OP, 17.7%), 11.3% of utterances have the exact match of image objects (O), 9.3% contain objects not in the tag set (OF), and the rest of 6.7% have objects mentioned in synonyms (OS). While many objects are indicated by pronouns, linking the objects and their attributes to mentions in the utterance becomes a vital task for utterance generation.

On the other hand, the blue hue refers to the utterances with non-object image information (Rx, 23.7%), which usually describes the event, action, or scenario in the image. Thus, knowing the scene beyond the given objects is also important.

The rest of 31.3% of utterances represents in red are the class NI without any image information. These utterances are usually on the off-image theme and the only hint to reconstruct such utterances is from their conversational context.

3 Augmenting Image Information

Our analysis suggests the importance of the non-object image information, which is often the scene in the image. Therefore, we augmented the image feature by image caption to capture the scenario. We also found that explicitly using texts of objects tags and captions works better than fusing the latent vectors from captioning and object detection models. Given object tags, we replace the single full-image feature in the baseline model with several image region features to facilitate the extraction of image object information.

3.1 Experiments

3.1.1 Settings

We ran our experiments on the ImageChat dataset (Shuster et al., 2020a) which is described in Sec 2.1. All our experiments are conducted using the ParlAI (Miller et al., 2017) framework. We compared with the SOTA multimodal dialogue system: Multimodal Blenderbot (MMB) (Shuster et al., 2020c).

We obtain image tags from Scene Graph Benchmark (Han et al., 2021) and the image caption from pretrained VinVL model (Zhang et al., 2021). The image feature dimension is set to 2054, with additional 6-dim image information such as weight and height to the 2048-dim FasterRCNN feature in the original model. Each image is paired with 1 to 10 unique tags, an image caption with maximum 12 tokens, and at most 32 image object features. All models are finetuned from the Reddit pretrained model, following the instruction from MMB[1].

Following previous works, we reported the number of perplexity (PPL), Rouge-L, BLEU-4, and F1 score. As existing research has reported that these numbers are not highly correlated with human evaluation (Liu et al., 2016; Li et al., 2016), we also reported Bert Score (rescale) (Zhang* et al., 2020), which reflects the semantics similarity instead of the token-wised matching. To show how relevant the generated response is to the image, we ran the image-text retrieval task using VinVL (Zhang et al., 2021). We also reported the number of average length, unique vocabularies, and Distinct-1 (Li et al., 2015) to show the diversity of utterances.

3.2 Results and Analysis

Table 3 demonstrates that our enhanced image features improve the strong baseline without training on many additional datasets. This result implies that *image*$^+$ provides much more useful information that neither additional text-only dialogue datasets (BST+) nor image captioning pretraining is needed. Besides, the result also suggests that a pipeline approach of explicitly adding image caption to the input is better than end-to-end training on the additional image captioning task.

[1]https://github.com/facebookresearch/ParlAI/blob/main/parlai/zoo/multimodal_blenderbot/README.md

Model	Datasets	PPL	Rouge	BLEU	F1	Bert Score P	Bert Score R	Bert Score F1
MMB	R,I,C,B	13.60	12.40	0.386	12.94	33.81	25.21	29.49
MMB	R,I,C	15.00	11.35	0.278	11.81	31.73	23.52	27.61
MMB	R,I	12.89	13.04	0.419	13.52	32.58	24.23	28.39
MMB + *image*$^+$	R,I,C,B	**12.63**	**13.36**	0.447	13.75	34.76	26.36	30.54
MMB + *image*$^+$	R,I	12.76	13.29	**0.461**	**13.82**	**35.36**	**26.38**	**30.85**

Table 3: We compare models pretrained on Reddit (R) (Baumgartner et al., 2020) and finetuned on different datasets such as COCO Captioning (C) (Chen et al., 2015), text-only dialogue datasets BST+(B) (Smith et al., 2020; Dinan et al., 2019a,b; Rashkin et al., 2019), and ImageChat (I). *image*$^+$ refers to our proposed enhanced image features (image caption and object tags).

Model	Image-to-Text R@1	Image-to-Text R@10	Text-to-Image R@1	Text-to-Image R@10	Length	Vocabs	Distinct-1
Gold	0.02	0.14	0.03	0.32	**9.90**	**9,431**	**0.064**
MMB	**0.04**	0.16	0.03	0.29	7.87	3,436	0.029
MMB + *image*$^+$	**0.04**	**0.26**	**0.04**	**0.35**	8.04	3,865	0.032

Table 4: We evaluate how much the utterance is related to the image by image-text retrieval task. We also show the average length, vocabulary size, and diversity of utterances in the validation set. Gold refers to the reference utterances by human.

Feature	PPL	R	B	BS
Tags	13.9	12.26	0.325	30.29
Caption	13.8	12.33	0.373	30.20
Both	12.8	13.29	0.461	30.85

Table 5: Ablation results of MMB + *image*$^+$ trained on Reddit and ImageChat datasets. PPL: perplexity, R: Rouge, B: BLEU, BS: Bert Score

We also found that the Reddit pretraining is essential for dialogue generation. Without pretraining, the perplexity would boost to about 34, and all other metrics get much worse based on our empirical results. In fact, the perplexity is already around 26 at the very beginning of the training when finetuning on the Reddit pretrained model.

Our ablation experiment (Table 5) shows that the model with the caption feature has better Rouge and BLEU scores compared with the model only with tags, but the Bert Score is about the same. The result suggests that both tags and the caption can generate semantically equivalent utterances.

As shown in Table 4, we demonstrated our model's superiority in generating more diverse and image-relevant responses. We got the best retrieval result in both image-to-text and text-to-image retrieval, which even outperforms the human reference, showing that our generated responses are the most relevant to the given image. We also generated longer sentences with more diverse vocabularies than the MMB baseline. We provided some example outputs from MMB and our MMB + *image*$^+$ in the Appendix.

4 Conclusions

In this paper, we analyzed the factors that influence open-domain conversations with images, from aspects of (a) image relevancy to the conversation theme and (b) image information in the conversation. According to our observations, open-domain conversations with images often branch off from one topic to another even within only three turns. The relation between the attributes of objects is the key to linking utterances with different themes. From the dynamics of image-relevancy, it is also interesting to notice that some conversation is a solo play where people just express themselves without responding. Moreover, a comprehensive view of the whole image and the understanding of the image scene are also critical image information in utterances, besides image objects. Therefore, we proposed incorporating image captions that could capture the overall image semantics beyond objects and may provide some hints to the links to other objects. We also found empirically that explicitly using texts of caption and object tags work better than incorporating captioning and object detection models in latent space. With our enhanced image features *image*$^+$, we outperformed MMB on BLEU, F1, and Bert Score, and generated more image-related and diverse conversation responses, confirming the effectiveness of our findings. We believe that our in-depth analysis and proposed findings would benefit the future research on the open-domain conversations with images.

Acknowledgements

We thank Hong Chen, Minh-Duc Vo, Noriki Nishida, and the anonymous reviewers for their valuable comments on this work.

References

Jason Baumgartner, Savvas Zannettou, Brian Keegan, Megan Squire, and Jeremy Blackburn. 2020. The pushshift reddit dataset. In *Proceedings of the international AAAI conference on web and social media*, volume 14, pages 830–839.

Xinlei Chen, Hao Fang, Tsung-Yi Lin, Ramakrishna Vedantam, Saurabh Gupta, Piotr Dollár, and C Lawrence Zitnick. 2015. Microsoft coco captions: Data collection and evaluation server. *arXiv preprint arXiv:1504.00325*.

Emily Dinan, Varvara Logacheva, Valentin Malykh, Alexander Miller, Kurt Shuster, Jack Urbanek, Douwe Kiela, Arthur Szlam, Iulian Serban, Ryan Lowe, et al. 2019a. The second conversational intelligence challenge (convai2). *arXiv preprint arXiv:1902.00098*.

Emily Dinan, Stephen Roller, Kurt Shuster, Angela Fan, Michael Auli, and J. Weston. 2019b. Wizard of wikipedia: Knowledge-powered conversational agents. *ArXiv*, abs/1811.01241.

Xiaotian Han, Jianwei Yang, Houdong Hu, Lei Zhang, Jianfeng Gao, and Pengchuan Zhang. 2021. Image scene graph generation (sgg) benchmark.

Da Ju, Kurt Shuster, Y-Lan Boureau, and J. Weston. 2019. All-in-one image-grounded conversational agents. *ArXiv*, abs/1912.12394.

Jiwei Li, Michel Galley, Chris Brockett, Jianfeng Gao, and Bill Dolan. 2015. A diversity-promoting objective function for neural conversation models. *arXiv preprint arXiv:1510.03055*.

Jiwei Li, Will Monroe, Alan Ritter, Michel Galley, Jianfeng Gao, and Dan Jurafsky. 2016. Deep reinforcement learning for dialogue generation. *arXiv preprint arXiv:1606.01541*.

Chia-Wei Liu, Ryan Lowe, Iulian V Serban, Michael Noseworthy, Laurent Charlin, and Joelle Pineau. 2016. How not to evaluate your dialogue system: An empirical study of unsupervised evaluation metrics for dialogue response generation. *arXiv preprint arXiv:1603.08023*.

A. H. Miller, W. Feng, A. Fisch, J. Lu, D. Batra, A. Bordes, D. Parikh, and J. Weston. 2017. Parlai: A dialog research software platform. *arXiv preprint arXiv:1705.06476*.

Hannah Rashkin, Eric Michael Smith, Margaret Li, and Y-Lan Boureau. 2019. Towards empathetic open-domain conversation models: A new benchmark and dataset. In *Proceedings of the 57th Annual Meeting of the Association for Computational Linguistics*, pages 5370–5381, Florence, Italy. Association for Computational Linguistics.

Shaoqing Ren, Kaiming He, Ross Girshick, and Jian Sun. 2016. Faster r-cnn: towards real-time object detection with region proposal networks. *IEEE transactions on pattern analysis and machine intelligence*, 39(6):1137–1149.

Kurt Shuster, Samuel Humeau, Antoine Bordes, and Jason Weston. 2020a. Image-chat: Engaging grounded conversations. In *Proceedings of the 58th Annual Meeting of the Association for Computational Linguistics*, pages 2414–2429, Online. Association for Computational Linguistics.

Kurt Shuster, Da Ju, Stephen Roller, Emily Dinan, Y-Lan Boureau, and J. Weston. 2020b. The dialogue dodecathlon: Open-domain knowledge and image grounded conversational agents. *ArXiv*, abs/1911.03768.

Kurt Shuster, Eric Michael Smith, Da Ju, and Jason Weston. 2020c. Multi-modal open-domain dialogue. *arXiv preprint arXiv:2010.01082*.

Eric Michael Smith, Mary Williamson, Kurt Shuster, Jason Weston, and Y-Lan Boureau. 2020. Can you put it all together: Evaluating conversational agents' ability to blend skills. *arXiv preprint arXiv:2004.08449*.

Bart Thomee, David A Shamma, Gerald Friedland, Benjamin Elizalde, Karl Ni, Douglas Poland, Damian Borth, and Li-Jia Li. 2016. Yfcc100m: The new data in multimedia research. *Communications of the ACM*, 59(2):64–73.

Pengchuan Zhang, Xiujun Li, Xiaowei Hu, Jianwei Yang, Lei Zhang, Lijuan Wang, Yejin Choi, and Jianfeng Gao. 2021. Vinvl: Making visual representations matter in vision-language models. *CVPR 2021*.

Tianyi Zhang*, Varsha Kishore*, Felix Wu*, Kilian Q. Weinberger, and Yoav Artzi. 2020. Bertscore: Evaluating text generation with bert. In *International Conference on Learning Representations*.

A Example Outputs

	[1st Turn]		
Curious:	What did they have to do to help support cancer? Fundraisers always intrigue me.	Irrational:	Is she doing a backflip twist?
MMB:	What is that kid doing?	MMB:	I don't think she's going to catch the ball
Ours:	**I wonder what they are doing.**	Ours:	**I bet they are going to fall and hurt themselves.**
	[2nd Turn]		
Patriotic:	Maybe they donated. All Americans should donate to show that we are a proud and caring country.	Obnoxious:	I don't think so. I think she is passing gas.
MMB:	They are fighting for our country.	MMB:	She is doing a back flip.
Ours:	**They are supporting their country by raising money for cancer research.**	Ours:	**I hope she falls and breaks her neck.**
	[3rd Turn]		
Curious:	They don't look american, I wonder if this is somewhere else?	Irrational:	She needs to find a restroom quick!
MMB:	I wonder what they did to help.	MMB:	She is definitely not passing gas.
Ours:	**I wonder what they did to help.**	Ours:	**I think she is trying to fly.**

Table 6: Example conversations. The 1st row in each turn is the ground truth speaking style and utterance, 2nd and 3rd rows are utterances generated by MMB (underlined) and our MMB + *image*$^{+}$ (bold), given the speaking style, image, and ground truth utterance(s) in previous turn(s).

Text Style Transfer for Bias Mitigation using Masked Language Modeling

Ewoenam Kwaku Tokpo
Department of Computer Science
University of Antwerp

Toon Calders
Department of Computer Science
University of Antwerp

Abstract

It is well known that textual data on the internet and other digital platforms contain significant levels of bias and stereotypes. Various research findings have concluded that biased texts have significant effects on target demographic groups. For instance, masculine-worded job advertisements tend to be less appealing to female applicants. In this paper, we present a text-style transfer model that can be trained on non-parallel data and be used to automatically mitigate bias in textual data. Our style transfer model improves on the limitations of many existing text style transfer techniques such as the loss of content information. Our model solves such issues by combining latent content encoding with explicit keyword replacement. We will show that this technique produces better content preservation whilst maintaining good style transfer accuracy.

1 Introduction

Authors such as Bolukbasi et al. (2016) and May et al. (2019) have drawn attention to some fairness problems in the NLP domain. In a post on Buzz-Feed (Subbaraman, 2017) with the title, "Scientists Taught A Robot Language. It Immediately Turned Racist", the author reports how various automated language systems are disturbingly learning discriminatory patterns from data. Another prominent example of bias in NLP is Amazon's AI recruitment tool which turned out to be biased against female applicants (Dastin, 2018). Mitigating bias in textual data before training can be an important preprocessing step in training fair language systems like chatbots, language translation systems, and search engines, but a more direct need for mitigating bias in textual data has been pointed out by various researchers (Gaucher et al., 2011; Tang et al., 2017; Hodel et al., 2017) who have uncovered the worrying issue of bias in job advertisements. This can have significant implications on the job recruitment process. As a matter of fact, Gaucher et al. (Gaucher et al., 2011) explored the effect of biased job advertisements on participants of a survey. They found that changing the wording of a job advertisement to favor a particular gender group considerably reduced the appeal of the job to applicants not belonging to that gender, regardless of the gender stereotype traditionally associated with the job. Consequent to such findings, a few tools and models have been developed to detect and mitigate biases in job advertisements. Some of these tools include text editors like Textio which has been successfully used by companies such as Atlassian to increase diversity in their workforce (Daugherty et al., 2019).

Another area of impact, regarding biased texts, is in news publications; Kiesel et al. (2019) explore the issue of hyperpartisan news from an extreme left or right-wing perspective. Again, with the prevalence of hate speech and microaggression perpetuated on various social media platforms, there have been growing concerns about fairness in such areas.

A machine learning technique that can be employed to mitigate bias in text documents is *style transfer*. Style transfer is a technique that involves converting text or image instances from one domain to another, such that the content and meaning of the instance largely remain the same but the style changes. However, a problem that has challenged research in text style transfer is the relative unavailability of parallel data that would ideally be required to train such models (Rao and Tetreault, 2018; Fu et al., 2018; Shen et al., 2017). Training with parallel data makes it possible to directly map training instances from one domain to the other, hence, facilitating the learning process. Due to this, most style transfer systems mainly employ training techniques that fall under two categories: keyword replacement and auto-encoder sequence-to-sequence techniques. In the case of keyword replacement, biased words are deleted

Proceedings of the 2022 Conference of the North American Chapter of the Association for Computational Linguistics: Human Language Technologies: Student Research Workshop, pages 163 - 171

and replaced with alternative words. In the case of the auto-encoder sequence-to-sequence generative approach, the input text is directly encoded by an encoder to get a latent representation of the text, which is subsequently decoded by a decoder.

The main contributions of this work include:

1. The development of an end-to-end text bias mitigation model that can convert a piece of biased text to a neutral version [1] whilst maintaining significant content information. For example, given the female-biased text, *"The event was kid-friendly for all the* ***mothers*** *working in the company"*, our task is to transform this text into a gender-neutral version like *"The event was kid-friendly for all the* ***parents*** *working in the company"*. Our model is trained exclusively on nonparallel data. Since parallel corpora are relatively hard to obtain, training with only non-parallel data is of great importance.

2. A novel way of improving content preservation and fluency in text style transfer by combining keyword replacement and latent content information. Some other key novelties in our work include our approach to generating latent content representation and our approach to identifying attribute tokens.

We make the code and data used in this work available [2].

2 Style transfer

Style transfer has been widely explored in computer vision to convert images from one style to another (Gatys et al., 2016; Huang and Belongie, 2017; Johnson et al., 2016). However, directly applying image style transfer techniques for text is problematic because of the unique characteristics of both domains. For instance, in text, style and content are more tightly coupled and harder to separate (Hu et al., 2020). In addition to that, the non-differentiability of discrete words causes optimization problems (Yang et al., 2018; Lample et al., 2018).

In NLP, style transfer has mostly been explored in areas such as sentiment analysis (Li et al., 2018; Fu et al., 2018; Zhang et al., 2018) and machine translation (Lample et al., 2017). A few style transfer learning techniques use parallel data for training. Hu et al. (2020) give an elaborate survey on such models. In this paper, we will only focus on models that are trained on non-parallel data, some of which we will review in the following subsection.

2.1 Auto-encoder sequence-to-sequence models

Auto-encoder sequence-to-sequence models basically consist of an encoder that encodes the given text into a latent representation which is then decoded by a decoder. Many of these models adopt an adversarial approach to learn to remove any style attribute from the latent representation. The resulting disentangled latent representation is decoded by the decoder in a sequential generative manner.

Shen et al. (2017) propose two models for text style transfer based on the auto-encoder sequence-to-sequence technique: an aligned auto-encoder model and a variant of that, called the cross-aligned auto-encoder model. Prabhumoye et al. (2018) propose a style transfer model using back-translation. This is based on prior research that suggests that language translation retains the meaning of a text but not the stylistic features (Rabinovich et al., 2017).

An issue with Auto-encoder sequence-to-sequence models, in general, is the loss of information due to compression when encoding. Furthermore, Wu et al. (2019) note that sequence-to-sequence models for style transfer often have limited abilities to produce high-quality hidden representations and are unable to generate long meaningful sentences. Nonetheless, sequence-to-sequence generative models can prove more effective in applications where the text needs to be considerably rephrased (eg. from informal style to a formal style).

2.2 Explicit Style Keyword Replacement

These methods follow the general approach of identifying attribute markers, deleting these markers, and predicting appropriate replacements for these markers which conform to the target style. Li et al. (2018) propose the DeleteOnly and the Delete&Retrieve, which use a three-step Delete, Retrieve, and Generate approach. Sudhakar et al. (2019) introduce Blind Generative Style Transformer (B-GST) and Guided Generative Style Transformer (G-GST) as improvements on DeleteOnly and the Delete&Retrieve from (Li et al., 2018).

[1] See Section 7 for discussion on how we define bias.

[2] https://github.com/EwoeT/MLM-style-transfer

Since Explicit Style Keyword Replacement methods only delete a small portion of the input text, they preserve much more information. These systems on the other hand are unable to properly capture information of the deleted tokens (Sudhakar et al., 2019), leading to examples such as *"The event was kid-friendly for all the **mothers** working in the company"* → *"The event was kid-friendly for all the **children** working in the company"*.

3 Methodology

The goal of our model is to transform any piece of biased text into a neutral version. If we take the two style attributes s_a and s_b to represent neutral style and biased style respectively, given a text sample x_b that belongs to s_b, our goal is to convert x_b to x_a, such that x_a belongs to style s_a but has the same semantic content as x_b except for style information.

Our model is composed of four main components, as illustrated in Fig 1. We also illustrate the process with an example in Fig. 2.

3.1 Attribute Masker

The Attribute Masker identifies the attribute words (words responsible for bias in a text) and masks these words with a special *[MASK]* symbol. The resultant text is fed as input to the Token Embedder.

We use LIME (Ribeiro et al., 2016), a model agnostic explainer that can be used on textual data, to identify attribute tokens. Although very effective, using LIME can increase computational time, especially for long text sequences. Some Explicit Style Keyword Replacement models use relatively simple techniques to identify attribute words. Li et al. (2018) use the relative frequency of words in the source style. Others like Sudhakar et al. (2019) employ more advanced methods like using attention weights. However, using techniques like attention weights to identify attribute tokens has been proven to not be very effective (Jain and Wallace, 2019).

To use LIME to detect attribute words, we first need to train a text classifier *f* that predicts whether a given text is biased. We fine-tune BERT (Devlin et al., 2019), a pretrained language model, as a text classifier by training it on a labeled corpus containing both biased and neutral texts. Lime linearly approximates the local decision boundary of *f* and assigns weights to tokens based on their influence on the classification outcome. With these weights (scores), we set a threshold value μ to select words to be masked. These words are replaced by a special *[MASK]* token.

3.2 Token Embedder

The Token Embedder is responsible for generating token embeddings for the masked tokens. To do this, we train a BERT model for masked language modeling on a corpus of unbiased texts. The Token Embedder outputs a set of all token embeddings $W = \{w_1, ..., w_n\} \in R^{n \times d}$. Following the convention used by Devlin et al. (2019), we take the size of every embedding to be $d = 768$ throughout this paper.

3.3 Latent-content Encoder

The Latent-content Encoder takes the original (unmasked) text as input and encodes it into a latent content representation. An important part of this stage is our approach to disentangle the resulting latent content representation from the biased style.

The Latent-content Encoder is responsible for generating a latent content representation of the input sentence. For this, we train a BERT embedding model that takes as input the original text (unmasked) x_b and generates a target latent representation $\hat{z}$.

When x_b is given as an input, the Latent-content Encoder first generates token embeddings $v_i \in R^d$ for each token $t_i \in x_b$. The set of token embeddings $V = \{v_1, ..., v_n\} \in R^{n \times d}$ is mean-pooled to generate $\hat{z} \in R^d$. Since we want $\hat{z}$ to have the same content as x_b but not the bias that exists in x_b, we use a dual objective training to debias $\hat{z}$.

Both the Latent-content Encoder and the Source Content Encoder take x_b as input. The Latent-content Encoder generates output $\hat{z}$ whereas the Source Content Encoder generates z. Firstly, the goal is to make $\hat{z}$ and z have the same content, hence, we want them to be as similar as possible. We use the cosine-similarity to quantify this similarity. The similarity loss is minimized using mean-squared error; defined as:

$$\mathcal{L}_{sim} = \frac{1}{N} \sum_{j=1}^{N} (cosine\_similarity(\hat{z}_j, z_j) - 1)^2$$

Secondly, a bias detector takes $\hat{z}$ as input and returns the class probabilities of $\hat{z}$. Because we want $\hat{z}$ to belong to the neutral class, the Latent-content Encoder has to learn to generate $\hat{z}$ that is always classified as neutral. This is achieved by minimizing the cross-entropy loss:

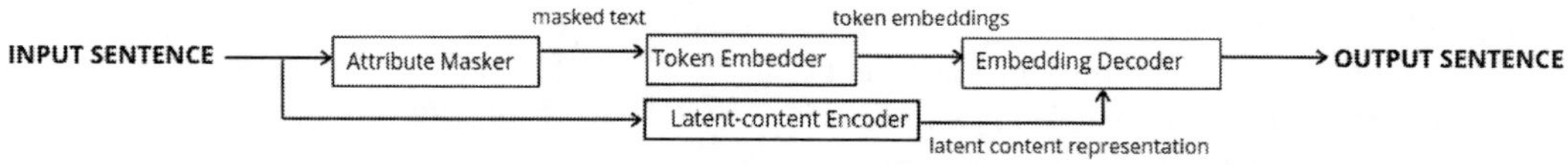

Figure 1: The architecture of our proposed model. The model consists of four main components. The arrows show the flow of information within the model, and how the various components interact with each other.

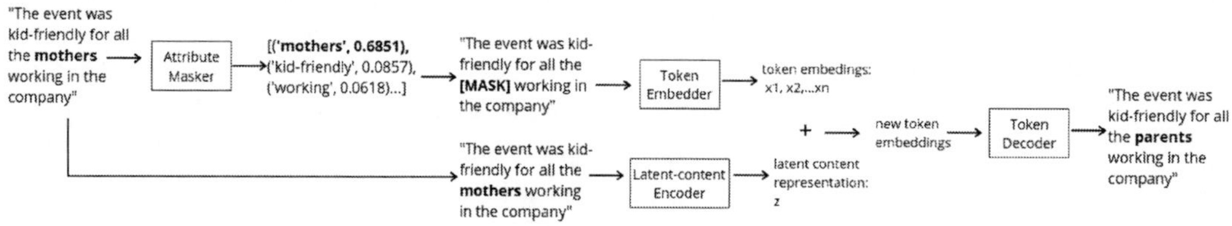

Figure 2: An example to illustrate the end-to-end bias mitigation process. This demonstrates the operation of each component of the model. In the case of multiple attribute words, these attribute words are all masked and replaced simultaneously. The Latent-content Encoder aims to remove traces of gender information from sentence-level semantic content before being added to the token embeddings.

$\mathcal{L}_{acc_{\hat{z}_j}} = -\sum_{j=1}^{N} logP(s_a|\hat{z}_j)$

$P(s_a|\hat{z}_j)$ is the classifier's prediction of the probability of $\hat{z}$ being neutral.

Combining both losses we get the dual objective: $LCE\_loss = (1-\lambda)\mathcal{L}_{sim} + \lambda\mathcal{L}_{acc_{\hat{z}_j}}$

3.4 Token Decoder

The Token Decoder computes the average of each token embedding and the latent content representation to generate new token embeddings. The Token Decoder uses these embeddings to predict the correct tokens.

The Token Decoder first adds latent content information to word embeddings. To do this, the Token Decoder takes as inputs both W from the Token Embedder and $\hat{z}$ from the Latent-content Encoder. For each $w_i \in W$, a new token embedding $\hat{w}_i \in R^d$ is generated by computing the weighted average of $w_i \in R^d$ and $\hat{z} \in R^d$. After generating $\hat{w}_i$, the Token Decoder uses it to predict the right token by computing the probability distribution over all the tokens in the vocabulary. We compute the decoding loss as: $\mathcal{L}_{dec} = -\sum_{i=1;t_{\pi_i}\in T_\Pi}^{n} logP(t_{\pi_i}|\hat{w}_{i\Pi})$

To augment this process, we use a pretrained classifier to ensure that the output sentence x_a is always neutral. A dual objective is again used in this process: $TD\_loss = (1-\gamma)\mathcal{L}_{dec} + \gamma\mathcal{L}_{acc_{x_a}}$. Where $\mathcal{L}_{acc_{x_a}}$ is the loss from the classifier. Because x_a is made up of discrete tokens (one-hot encodings) which are non-differentiable during back-propagation, we use a soft sampling approach as was done in (Wu et al., 2019; Prabhumoye et al., 2018): $t_{\pi_i} \sim softmax(\mathbf{o}_t/\tau)$

4 Experiments

For our experiments, we focus on gender bias (we limit our work to a binary definition of gender) [3]. The use of gender is motivated by the relative availability of resources such as datasets. Nonetheless, we believe that our work is adaptable to other forms of biases such as racial bias since the technique is not dependent on the domain (only neutral and bias examples are needed). To show our technique's applicability in different domains, we experiment on gender obfuscation, where instead of mitigating the bias, we try to convert female-authored texts to "look like" male-authored texts. We arbitrarily chose to convert from female to male just for the sake of experiment; the same technique can be applied for male to female as well.

All experiments are conducted using English language corpus. In the future, we hope to extend our work to cover other languages as well. We discuss the details of our experiments in the following subsections.

4.1 Dataset

We run our experiments [4] on two datasets discussed below. Some statistics of the datasets are given in A Table 3

[3]See Section 7

[4]All experiments are run on a Tesla V100-SXM3 GPU with 32Gb memory.

4.1.1 Jigsaw dataset:

The Jigsaw datasets[5] consists of comments that are labeled by humans with regard to bias towards or against particular demographics. Using the value 0.5 as a threshold, we extract all texts with gender (male or female) label ≥ 0.5 as the gender-biased class of texts and extract a complementary set with gender labels < 0.5 as the neutral class.

4.1.2 Yelp dataset:

We extract this dataset from the preprocessed Yelp dataset used by (Prabhumoye et al., 2018; Reddy and Knight, 2016a). This dataset contains short single sentences which we use for author gender obfuscation.

4.2 Evaluation models and metrics

To evaluate the performance of our model, we compare it to six other models; Delete-only, Delete-and-retrieve (Li et al., 2018), B-GST, G-GST (Sudhakar et al., 2019), CAE (Shen et al., 2017) and BST (Prabhumoye et al., 2018).

The evaluation is based on three automated evaluation metrics for style transfer discussed by Hu et al. (2020); *style transfer accuracy* (Transfer strength), *content preservation*, and *fluency*.

Style transfer accuracy: This gives the percentage of texts that were successfully flipped from the source style (bias style) to the target style (neutral style) by our model. To predict whether a text was successfully flipped, we use a trained BERT classifier different from the one used to train the respective models.

Content preservation: We measure content preservation by computing the similarity between the generated text and the original text. Similar to Fu et al. (2018), we use the cosine similarity between the original text embedding and the transferred text embedding to measure the content preservation. To make this more effective, we generate text embeddings with SBERT (Reimers and Gurevych, 2019), a modified version of pre-trained BERT that generates semantically meaningful sentence embeddings for sentences so that similar sentences have similar sentence embeddings, that can be compared using cosine-similarity.

Fluency: Similar to (Subramanian et al., 2018), we measure the fluency of the generated text using the *perplexity* produced by a Kneser–Ney smoothing 5-gram language model, KenLM (Heafield, 2011) trained on the respective datasets.

[5]https://www.kaggle.com/c/Jigsaw-unintended-bias-in-toxicity-classification/data

Table 1: **Jigsaw dataset-** Transfer strength and Content preservation scores for the models on all three datasets. **C.P.**: Content preservation, **PPL**: Fluency (Perplexity), **Accuracy**: Style transfer accuracy, **Original*:** refers to the original input text. For A.C., C.P.and Agg, higher values are better. For PPL, lower values are better

	C.P.	PPL	AC%
Original*	100.00	12.51	0.08
Del	97.47	363.64	**92.30**
Del&ret	97.50	242.33	71.70
B-GST	96.73	1166.4	10.10
G-GST	99.11	621.50	38.80
CAE	95.60	795.58	83.70
Our model	**99.71**	**76.75**	88.10

Table 2: **Yelp dataset-** Transfer strength and Content preservation scores for the models for the . **C.P.**: Content preservation, **PPL**: Fluency (Perplexity), **Accuracy**: Style transfer accuracy, **Original*:** refers to the original input text. . For A.C., C.P.and Agg, higher values are better. For PPL, lower values are better

	C.P.	PPL	AC%
Original*	100.00	11.39	17.80
Del	98.70	**41.03**	33.79
Del&ret	98.25	57.73	30.90
B-GST	95.94	141.81	23.90
G-GST	97.28	70.24	21.00
CAE	98.48	43.78	32.09
BST	95.49	63.33	**68.80**
Our model	**99.05**	45.17	43.20

4.3 Results and discussion

From Table 1, as we expected from the compared models, the models that perform considerably well in one metric suffer significantly in other metrics. For instance, Delete-Only (Del) produces the best transfer accuracy but lags behind other models in content preservation and fluency. For content preservation and fluency, our model produces improved results over all the other models. This result is consistent with our expectation of improving content preservation with our techniques. Again, the accuracy score (second highest) produced by our model confirms the claim that our model preserves content information without a significant drop in transfer accuracy.

From Table 2, the same observation is made for gender obfuscation; models that perform very well in one metric fall short in other metrics. BST produces the best style transfer accuracy but at the same time has the worst content preservation score.

From the results from both datasets, one key observation is that models that perform very well in one metric tend to fall short in other metrics. This goes to show the difficulty for style transfer models to preserve content information whilst maintaining a strong transfer accuracy. This observation is confirmed by previous works (Li et al., 2018; Wu et al., 2019; Hu et al., 2020) which mention the general trade-off between style transfer accuracy and content preservation. Our model shows good results in maintaining a good balance across all metrics. Some text samples from our experiments are shown in Appendix A Table 4. Also, in Appendix A, Table 5 and Table 6 show the results from an ablation analysis on the Yelp dataset, where we strip off components of our model to analyze the effect. Text samples from the ablation study are also provided in Appendix A, Table 7 and Table 8.

5 Related work

He et al. (2021) propose DePen, a Detect and Perturb approach to neutralize biased texts, using graduate school admissions as a case study. Sun et al. (2021) propose a method that aims to rewrite English texts with gender-neutral English (in particular, the use of singular *they* for gender pronouns) using a combination of regular expressions, a dependency parser, and GPT-2 (Radford et al., 2019) model. Nogueira dos Santos et al. (2018) propose an RNN-based auto-encoder model to neutralize offensive language on social media, using a combination of classification loss and reconstruction loss to ensure style transfer and to improve text generation. In a different but related context, Reddy and Knight (2016b) propose a gender obfuscation technique to disguise or change the gender of an author of a text as a means of privacy protection or for the prevention of inadvertent discrimination against the author. Their method is a word substitution technique based on word2vec (Mikolov et al., 2013).

6 Conclusion

In this work, we introduce a style transfer model that can be used to mitigate bias in textual data. We show that explicit keyword replacement can be effectively combined with latent content representation to improve the content preservation of text style transfer models.

As part of our future work, we intend to expand this work to other languages, we plan to explore possible improvements to the model such as adversarial learning, and also to include human evaluators for qualitative evaluation. Again, we intend to investigate other forms of attributes beyond tokens, such as sentence length, and how that affects bias in textual data. We also plan to apply our model as a preprocessing technique to train fair language models. We believe this could significantly reduce biases found in automated language systems.

7 Ethical considerations

Works like Dev et al. (2021) have drawn attention to gender exclusivity and issues relating to non-binary representation in NLP, particularly in the English language. For practical constraints such as the limited availability of non-binary gender data and/or the significant under-representation of non-binary gender identities in available datasets, we limit this study to a binary definition of gender. For the same reasons stated above, our definition of gender is analogous to female and male definitions of sex (Walker and Cook, 1998). Although this is an obvious limitation to our work, we believe this work opens the door to extensively explore similar issues in non-binary gender settings, which need a more expansive discussion.

Since the definition of a biased text is highly domain, context, and task dependent, especially when it relates to the use of language (English in this case), our approach identifies "biased" and "neutral" texts as per how they are defined or annotated in the training data for a specific task. Hence, the labels (fair or biased) assigned to certain text examples may not be perceived accordingly in other settings and tasks. We also note that, although the use of explicit gender terms in certain domains may be deemed to introduce biases (in some recruitment scenarios for instance), this practice may be acceptable or even encouraged in other domains such as in text discussions about diversity and sexism.

Acknowledgements

This research was supported by the Flemish Government under the "Onderzoeksprogramma Artificiële Intelligentie (AI) Vlaanderen" programme.

References

Tolga Bolukbasi, Kai-Wei Chang, James Zou, Venkatesh Saligrama, and Adam Kalai. 2016. Man is to computer programmer as woman is to homemaker? debiasing word embeddings. NIPS'16, page 4356–4364, Red Hook, NY, USA. Curran Associates Inc.

Jeffrey Dastin. 2018. Amazon scraps secret ai recruiting tool that showed bias against women. `https://www.reuters.com/article/us-amazon-com-jobs-automation-insight/amazon-scraps-secret-ai-recruiting-tool-that-showed-bias-against-women-idUSKCN1MK08G`. Accessed: 2021-08-21.

Paul R Daugherty, H James Wilson, and Rumman Chowdhury. 2019. Using artificial intelligence to promote diversity. *MIT Sloan Management Review*, 60(2):1.

Sunipa Dev, Masoud Monajatipoor, Anaelia Ovalle, Arjun Subramonian, Jeff Phillips, and Kai-Wei Chang. 2021. Harms of gender exclusivity and challenges in non-binary representation in language technologies. In *Proceedings of the 2021 Conference on Empirical Methods in Natural Language Processing*, pages 1968–1994, Online and Punta Cana, Dominican Republic. Association for Computational Linguistics.

Jacob Devlin, Ming-Wei Chang, Kenton Lee, and Kristina Toutanova. 2019. BERT: pre-training of deep bidirectional transformers for language understanding. In *Proceedings of the 2019 Conference of the North American Chapter of the Association for Computational Linguistics: Human Language Technologies, NAACL-HLT 2019, Minneapolis, MN, USA, June 2-7, 2019, Volume 1 (Long and Short Papers)*, pages 4171–4186. Association for Computational Linguistics.

Zhenxin Fu, Xiaoye Tan, Nanyun Peng, Dongyan Zhao, and Rui Yan. 2018. Style transfer in text: Exploration and evaluation. In *Proceedings of the AAAI Conference on Artificial Intelligence*, volume 32.

Leon A Gatys, Alexander S Ecker, and Matthias Bethge. 2016. Image style transfer using convolutional neural networks. In *Proceedings of the IEEE conference on computer vision and pattern recognition*, pages 2414–2423.

Danielle Gaucher, Justin Friesen, and Aaron C Kay. 2011. Evidence that gendered wording in job advertisements exists and sustains gender inequality. *Journal of personality and social psychology*, 101(1):109.

Zexue He, Bodhisattwa Prasad Majumder, and Julian McAuley. 2021. Detect and perturb: Neutral rewriting of biased and sensitive text via gradient-based decoding. In *Findings of the Association for Computational Linguistics: EMNLP 2021*, pages 4173–4181, Punta Cana, Dominican Republic. Association for Computational Linguistics.

Kenneth Heafield. 2011. KenLM: Faster and smaller language model queries. In *Proceedings of the Sixth Workshop on Statistical Machine Translation*, pages 187–197, Edinburgh, Scotland. Association for Computational Linguistics.

Lea Hodel, Magdalena Formanowicz, Sabine Sczesny, Jana Valdrová, and Lisa von Stockhausen. 2017. Gender-fair language in job advertisements: A cross-linguistic and cross-cultural analysis. *Journal of Cross-Cultural Psychology*, 48(3):384–401.

Zhiqiang Hu, Roy Ka-Wei Lee, and Charu C Aggarwal. 2020. Text style transfer: A review and experiment evaluation.

Xun Huang and Serge Belongie. 2017. Arbitrary style transfer in real-time with adaptive instance normalization. In *Proceedings of the IEEE International Conference on Computer Vision*, pages 1501–1510.

Sarthak Jain and Byron C. Wallace. 2019. Attention is not Explanation. In *Proceedings of the 2019 Conference of the North American Chapter of the Association for Computational Linguistics: Human Language Technologies, Volume 1 (Long and Short Papers)*, pages 3543–3556, Minneapolis, Minnesota. Association for Computational Linguistics.

Justin Johnson, Alexandre Alahi, and Li Fei-Fei. 2016. Perceptual losses for real-time style transfer and super-resolution. In *European conference on computer vision*, pages 694–711. Springer.

Johannes Kiesel, Maria Mestre, Rishabh Shukla, Emmanuel Vincent, Payam Adineh, David Corney, Benno Stein, and Martin Potthast. 2019. Semeval-2019 task 4: Hyperpartisan news detection. In *Proceedings of the 13th International Workshop on Semantic Evaluation*, pages 829–839.

Guillaume Lample, Alexis Conneau, Ludovic Denoyer, and Marc'Aurelio Ranzato. 2017. Unsupervised machine translation using monolingual corpora only.

Guillaume Lample, Sandeep Subramanian, Eric Smith, Ludovic Denoyer, Marc'Aurelio Ranzato, and Y-Lan Boureau. 2018. Multiple-attribute text rewriting. In *International Conference on Learning Representations*.

Juncen Li, Robin Jia, He He, and Percy Liang. 2018. Delete, retrieve, generate: a simple approach to sentiment and style transfer. In *Proceedings of the 2018 Conference of the North American Chapter of the Association for Computational Linguistics: Human Language Technologies, Volume 1 (Long Papers)*, pages 1865–1874, New Orleans, Louisiana. Association for Computational Linguistics.

Chandler May, Alex Wang, Shikha Bordia, Samuel R. Bowman, and Rachel Rudinger. 2019. On measuring social biases in sentence encoders. In *Proceedings of the 2019 Conference of the North American Chapter of the Association for Computational Linguistics: Human Language Technologies, Volume 1 (Long and*

Short Papers), pages 622–628, Minneapolis, Minnesota. Association for Computational Linguistics.

Tomas Mikolov, Kai Chen, Greg Corrado, and Jeffrey Dean. 2013. Efficient estimation of word representations in vector space. *arXiv preprint arXiv:1301.3781*.

Cicero Nogueira dos Santos, Igor Melnyk, and Inkit Padhi. 2018. Fighting offensive language on social media with unsupervised text style transfer. In *Proceedings of the 56th Annual Meeting of the Association for Computational Linguistics (Volume 2: Short Papers)*, pages 189–194, Melbourne, Australia. Association for Computational Linguistics.

Shrimai Prabhumoye, Yulia Tsvetkov, Ruslan Salakhutdinov, and Alan W Black. 2018. Style transfer through back-translation. In *Proceedings of the 56th Annual Meeting of the Association for Computational Linguistics (Volume 1: Long Papers)*, pages 866–876, Melbourne, Australia. Association for Computational Linguistics.

Ella Rabinovich, Raj Nath Patel, Shachar Mirkin, Lucia Specia, and Shuly Wintner. 2017. Personalized machine translation: Preserving original author traits. In *Proceedings of the 15th Conference of the European Chapter of the Association for Computational Linguistics: Volume 1, Long Papers*, pages 1074–1084, Valencia, Spain. Association for Computational Linguistics.

Alec Radford, Jeffrey Wu, Rewon Child, David Luan, Dario Amodei, Ilya Sutskever, et al. 2019. Language models are unsupervised multitask learners. *OpenAI blog*, 1(8):9.

Sudha Rao and Joel Tetreault. 2018. Dear sir or madam, may I introduce the GYAFC dataset: Corpus, benchmarks and metrics for formality style transfer. In *Proceedings of the 2018 Conference of the North American Chapter of the Association for Computational Linguistics: Human Language Technologies, Volume 1 (Long Papers)*, pages 129–140, New Orleans, Louisiana. Association for Computational Linguistics.

Sravana Reddy and Kevin Knight. 2016a. Obfuscating gender in social media writing. In *Proceedings of the First Workshop on NLP and Computational Social Science*, pages 17–26.

Sravana Reddy and Kevin Knight. 2016b. Obfuscating gender in social media writing. In *Proceedings of the First Workshop on NLP and Computational Social Science*, pages 17–26, Austin, Texas. Association for Computational Linguistics.

Nils Reimers and Iryna Gurevych. 2019. Sentence-bert: Sentence embeddings using siamese bert-networks.

Marco Tulio Ribeiro, Sameer Singh, and Carlos Guestrin. 2016. " why should i trust you?" explaining the predictions of any classifier. In *Proceedings of the 22nd ACM SIGKDD international conference on knowledge discovery and data mining*, pages 1135–1144.

Tianxiao Shen, Tao Lei, Regina Barzilay, and Tommi Jaakkola. 2017. Style transfer from non-parallel text by cross-alignment. In *Proceedings of the 31st International Conference on Neural Information Processing Systems*, NIPS'17, page 6833–6844, Red Hook, NY, USA. Curran Associates Inc.

Nidhi Subbaraman. 2017. Scientists taught a robot language. it immediately turned racist. `https://www.buzzfeednews.com/article/nidhisubbaraman/robot-racism-through-language`. Accessed: 2021-08-22.

Sandeep Subramanian, Guillaume Lample, Eric Michael Smith, Ludovic Denoyer, Marc'Aurelio Ranzato, and Y-Lan Boureau. 2018. Multiple-attribute text style transfer.

Akhilesh Sudhakar, Bhargav Upadhyay, and Arjun Maheswaran. 2019. "transforming" delete, retrieve, generate approach for controlled text style transfer. In *Proceedings of the 2019 Conference on Empirical Methods in Natural Language Processing and the 9th International Joint Conference on Natural Language Processing, EMNLP-IJCNLP 2019, Hong Kong, China, November 3-7, 2019*, pages 3267–3277. Association for Computational Linguistics.

Tony Sun, Kellie Webster, Apu Shah, William Yang Wang, and Melvin Johnson. 2021. They, them, theirs: Rewriting with gender-neutral english. *arXiv preprint arXiv:2102.06788*.

Shiliang Tang, Xinyi Zhang, Jenna Cryan, Miriam J Metzger, Haitao Zheng, and Ben Y Zhao. 2017. Gender bias in the job market: A longitudinal analysis. volume 1, pages 1–19. ACM New York, NY, USA.

Phillip L Walker and Della Collins Cook. 1998. Brief communication: Gender and sex: Vive la difference. *American Journal of Physical Anthropology: The Official Publication of the American Association of Physical Anthropologists*, 106(2):255–259.

Xing Wu, Tao Zhang, Liangjun Zang, Jizhong Han, and Songlin Hu. 2019. Mask and infill: Applying masked language model for sentiment transfer. In *Proceedings of the Twenty-Eighth International Joint Conference on Artificial Intelligence, IJCAI-19*, pages 5271–5277. International Joint Conferences on Artificial Intelligence Organization.

Zichao Yang, Zhiting Hu, Chris Dyer, Eric P. Xing, and Taylor Berg-Kirkpatrick. 2018. Unsupervised text style transfer using language models as discriminators. NIPS'18, page 7298–7309, Red Hook, NY, USA. Curran Associates Inc.

Zhirui Zhang, Shuo Ren, Shujie Liu, Jianyong Wang, Peng Chen, Mu Li, Ming Zhou, and Enhong Chen. 2018. Style transfer as unsupervised machine translation.

A Appendix

Table 3: Dataset statistics

Dataset	Attributes	Classifier	Train	Dev	Test
Jigsaw	Sexist	24K	32K	1K	1K
	Neutral	24K	92K	3K	3K
Yelp	Male	100K	100K	1K	1K
	Female	100K	100K	1K	1K

Table 4: Sample text outputs from experiments

Gender bias mitigation (biased → neutral): Jigsaw	
input text	i hope the *man* learned his lesson to slow down and buckle up .
our model	i hope the *driver* learned his lesson to slow down and buckle up .
input text	i married a wonderful mature , loyal and dedicated foreign *women* while working abroad ...
our model	i married a wonderful mature , loyal and dedicated foreign *person* while working abroad ...
Gender obfuscation (female → male): Yelp	
input text	overall , worth the *extra* money to *stay* here .
our model	overall , worth the *damn* money to *eat* here .
input text	i had prosecco and my *boyfriend* ordered a beer .
our model	i had prosecco and my *wife* ordered a beer .

Table 5: Ablation study of our model on the **Jigsaw gender dataset**. **Without-LR**: model with soft sampling (class constraint) but no latent content representation, **Without-LR&SS**: model with no class constraint and no latent content representation

	C.P	PPL	ACC%
Our model	**99.71**	**76.75**	88.10
Without-LR	99.69	98.87	**93.44**
Without-LR&SS	99.70	98.68	93.44

Table 6: Ablation study of our model on the **Yelp dataset**. **Without-LR**: model with soft sampling (class constraint) but no latent content representation, **Without-LR&SS**: model with no class constraint and no latent content representation. Although Without-LR has a very high accuracy score, as can be seen from the example in 8, many of the Without-LR texts are unable to preserve content information

	C.P	PPL	ACC%
Our model	**99.05**	45.17	43.20
Without-LR	96.62	45.72	**84.20**
Without-LR&SS	96.89	**41.84**	41.00

Table 7: Sample text outputs from ablation study from Jigsaw dataset

Gender bias mitigation (biased → neutral): Jigsaw	
input text	if there was an article disparaging *women* as idiots there would be a protest and a parade .
our model	if there was an article disparaging *them* as idiots there would be a protest and a parade .
Without-LR	if there was an article disparaging *muslims* as idiots there would be a protest and a parade .
Without-LR&SS	if there was an article disparaging *muslims* as idiots there would be a protest and a parade .

Table 8: Sample text outputs from ablation study Yelp dataset

Gender obfuscation (female → male): Yelp	
input text	i did not buy extra insurance !
our model	i did not buy auto insurance !
Without-LR	i did not buy life insurance !
Without-LR&SS	i did not buy the pistol !

Differentially Private Instance Encoding against Privacy Attacks

Shangyu Xie
Illinois Institute of Technology
sxie14@hawk.iit.edu

Yuan Hong
Illinois Institute of Technology
yuan.hong@iit.edu

Abstract

TextHide was proposed to protect the training data via instance encoding in the natural language domain. Due to the lack of theoretic privacy guarantee, such instance encoding scheme has been shown to be vulnerable to privacy attacks, e.g., reconstruction attacks. To address such limitation, we integrate differential privacy into the instance encoding scheme, and thus provide a provable guarantee against privacy attacks. The experimental results also show that the proposed scheme can defend against privacy attacks while ensuring learning utility (as a trade-off).

1 Introduction

Machine learning models have been widely deployed in a wide range of applications/domains, such as speech recognition (Zhang et al., 2018b), computer vision (Guo et al., 2020) and natural language processing (Chen et al., 2019; Radford et al., 2019; Brown et al., 2020). Meanwhile, the privacy issues have also aroused more and more attention as machine learning-based systems usually aggressively collect large amounts of data for better performance, which could contain user's personal information and thus jeopardize user's privacy. For instance, the hospital admission information and diagnosis report can be processed by language models to predict the readmission rate of a patient (Lehman et al., 2021). Another example is that the prediction of keyboard input would require personal users' daily input texts for better accuracy (Chen et al., 2019). This may not only lose customer trust, but also violate some data regulations or laws, e.g., GDPR (Wachter et al., 2017).

The privacy-enhancing technologies (PETs) (Gentry, 2009; Chaudhuri et al., 2011; Mohassel and Zhang, 2017; Cabrero-Holgueras and Pastrana, 2021) have been widely studied to ensure the data privacy in the machine learning, which mainly include two foundations of theory as following. First, the cryptographic protocols (Mohassel and Zhang, 2017; Mohassel and Rindal, 2018) can help to securely train the model with the private data (in encrypted format), and the privacy of data depends on the hard mathematical problems (Paillier, 1999). Although the cryptographic protocol-based schemes provide good data privacy, these also arouse high computational overheads due to the computation on encrypted data and other complicated building blocks.

Second, differential privacy (DP) (Dwork et al., 2006b, 2014) provides a lightweight way to protect the data against the adversaries with arbitrary information during the training, which can obtain quantifiable privacy guarantees. For example, the widely used DP-SGD (Bassily et al., 2014; Abadi et al., 2016) ensures the privacy of training data sample by clipping the gradients and adding DP noise (e.g., Gaussian mechanism) with the model updates. The introduction of DP noise enables the limited effect of one individual data on the trained model (and thus achieving the privacy guarantee). Additionally, another category of work is to add DP noise into the dataset following the method of DP synthetic data release and then train a model on such private data (Vaidya et al., 2013; Mohammady et al., 2020). Yet, the differential privacy-based learning schemes could cause great accuracy loss.

Alternatively, a private learning scheme called instance encoding (Huang et al., 2020a,b) has been proposed to obtain both privacy and utility for model training, which encodes the private data into "encrypted" data via mixup (Zhang et al., 2018a). While the privacy is claimed to be guaranteed by the encoding scheme, the data utility can be maintained by mixup scheme, only causing minor accuracy loss. However, it has been shown that such instance encoding scheme cannot provide strong privacy guarantee as cryptographic protocols (Mohassel and Rindal, 2018) or differential privacy (Dwork et al., 2014) against privacy attacks empiri-

Proceedings of the 2022 Conference of the North American Chapter of the Association for Computational Linguistics: Human Language Technologies: Student Research Workshop, pages 172 - 180

cally (Carlini et al., 2020a). That is, well-designed privacy attacks (Carlini et al., 2020b; Xie and Hong, 2021) can break the instance encoding scheme to reconstruct the original data from the encoded data with high success rates. To address the privacy issue, we improve the TextHide with differential privacy and prove the improved scheme ensures theoretical privacy guarantee under the differential privacy framework. Besides, the experimental results validate the performance of proposed scheme.

2 Background & Related Work

2.1 TextHide

TextHide (Huang et al., 2020a) was proposed to protect the privacy of an individual's training data in the distributed learning by mixing up multiple raw training data. First, it utilizes a transformer encoder model, e.g., BERT (Devlin et al., 2019) as feature extractor to convert the raw training text into feature vectors. Second, TextHide designs an instance encoding method to mix up the original input feature vector with some randomly selected feature vectors from the training set (the corresponding data labels are also mixed up as well). Such mixed feature vectors with labels will be further utilized as training dataset for various down-stream language tasks, e.g., sentence classification (Cohan et al., 2019) and other natural language inference tasks (e.g., sentence similarity (Cer et al., 2017)).

More formally, we denote the language feature extractor as $\phi(\cdot)$, and the raw text data/label as x_i/y_i. Then we get the feature vector $v_i = \phi(x_i)$. Given the number of mix-up data points K, one private encoded vector $\widetilde{v}$ and corresponding mix-up label $\widetilde{y}$ can be computed as following:

$$\widetilde{v} = \sigma \circ \sum_{i=1}^{K} \lambda_i v_i, \quad \widetilde{y} = \sum_{i=1}^{K} \lambda_i y_i \tag{1}$$

where λ_i is chosen uniformly at random such that $\sum_i^K \lambda_i = 1$, the sign-flipping mask $\sigma \in \{-1, 1\}^d$ is also chosen uniformly at random, and d denotes the dimension of the input vector. $\circ$ represents the Hardamard multiplication. For each training batch, K data points will be randomly selected to generate the private encoded vector per Equation 1. Besides, TextHide also sets another parameter m as the size of mask pool to improve the security. This formalizes the (m, K)-TextHide scheme (Algorithm 1 in (Huang et al., 2020a)). The privacy notion of TextHide was based on a *k-vector subset sum* (Abboud and Lewi, 2013) oracle with mixup, which would require $O(n^{k/2})$ efforts to break as original claim in (Huang et al., 2020a).

2.2 Privacy Attacks in ML

Privacy attacks against machine learning mainly consist of two categories: 1) membership inference attacks (MIA) (Shokri et al., 2017; Salem et al., 2018; Song and Mittal, 2021); 2) data reconstruction or extraction attacks. On the one hand, membership inference attacks (MIA) (Shokri et al., 2017; Song and Raghunathan, 2020; Hisamoto et al., 2020) have worked as state-of-the-art attack scheme due to its simpleness and effectiveness, where an attacker can determine whether a data point was used to train the ML model or not. Such MIAs have been commonly used for auditing training dataset privacy (Carlini et al., 2021).

On the other hand, as a stronger attack primitive, data reconstruction attacks (Fredrikson et al., 2015; Wu et al., 2016; Zhu et al., 2019; Carlini et al., 2020a) usually refer to the attacks that could utilize auxiliary information (e.g., background knowledge) and counter measures to reconstruct or extract the original private data. For example, model inversion attacks (Song and Raghunathan, 2020) or data extraction by memorization (Carlini et al., 2020c) could extract private information of training dataset by querying the target model without access to dataset. Another example is that the attacker can utilize gradients to recover data (Zhu et al., 2019; Geiping et al., 2020).

2.3 Privacy-Enhancing Technologies (PETs)

As data privacy risks become an emerging issue, there have been a number of research works, namely, privacy-enhancing technologies (PETs) focusing on the data protection in the machine learning (Mohassel and Rindal, 2018; Chaudhuri et al., 2011), including the two main directions as following: 1) designing secure computation protocols with cryptographic building blocks to secure the data-in-use (Bonawitz et al., 2016; Mohassel and Zhang, 2017; Mohassel and Rindal, 2018), which could achieve "perfect" secrecy but bring both extra computational and communication costs; 2) improving the privacy of machine learning algorithm with differential privacy (Vaidya et al., 2013; Abadi et al., 2016). For example, a Naïve Bayes classifier can be trained by applying Laplace noise on the dataset by computing proper sensitivity (Vaidya et al., 2013), which will be further utilized to add

Laplace noise to satisfy DP notion. Another popular but different scheme, DP-SGD (Abadi et al., 2016) applies the Gaussian noise into the gradients of a single data sample during the model training, which aims to bound the influence of such one individual data sample under the paradigm of differential privacy. It is worth noting that there have been recent works in NLP (Kerrigan et al., 2020; Yu et al., 2021; Li et al., 2021; Dupuy et al., 2022), which aim to empirically train/fine-tune language models to satisfy DP notion. We will further discuss such related literature in Section 2.4.

Both categories of privacy-enhancing schemes above can provide provable privacy guarantee for the training data. However, the instance encoding scheme may not obtain such privacy guarantee. As mentioned earlier in Section 2.1, the instance encoding scheme (Huang et al., 2020a,b) was proposed to protect the training data's privacy by mixing up input data (Zhang et al., 2018a). The paper claims that such scheme can preserve data privacy while maintaining good data utility. However, recent data reconstruction attacks (Carlini et al., 2020a) have shown that instance encoding lacks provable privacy guarantee. That is, the "indistinguishability" definition of privately encoded data is rather spurious, which does not comply with the concept of indistinguishability in either cryptography or DP. For example, the security of asymmetric encryption scheme could be theoretically proven by a security game (defined as IND-CPA (Goldreich, 2009)) where no adversary can win the game with significantly greater probability than an adversary with random guessing. Similarly, differential privacy (Dwork et al., 2006b; Abadi et al., 2016) also presents the individual data with deniability that attacker cannot differentiate it with some probability bound. Considering that TextHide fails to provide such privacy guarantee, it can be broken by the carefully designed attacks and leak the private data (Carlini et al., 2020a; Xie and Hong, 2021).

In this work, we focus on integrating the instance encoding scheme with differential privacy to address the privacy risks of the instance encoding scheme presenting with privacy attacks, which would obtain provable privacy under the paradigm of differential privacy as shown in Section 4.

2.4 Differentially Private Learning in NLP

Differentially Private Stochastic Gradient Descent (DP-SGD) (Abadi et al., 2016) has been a gold standard for preserving data privacy in machine learning. There have been various DP-related works in the language domain (Hoory et al., 2021; Yu et al., 2021; Li et al., 2021; Mireshghallah et al., 2021; Anil et al., 2021; Dupuy et al., 2022). For example, public pretraining has been shown to be helpful for the downstream DP fine-tuning (Kerrigan et al., 2020). Hoory et al. (Hoory et al., 2021) pretained a differentially private BERT model with DP optimization and identified the existence of memory issues with large batch size for high performance. Dupuy et al. (Dupuy et al., 2022) have also proposed an efficient DP-SGD training for large transformer model with GPU architecture. Mireshghallah et al. (Mireshghallah et al., 2021) utilized the adversarial and privacy regularization to ensure uniform treatment of under-represented subgroups in language model training. However, the previous works usually struggle with greatly decreased performance as the added DP noise needs to be scaled with large model parameters (resulting in high noise levels).

Recently, Li et al. (Li et al., 2021) and Yu et al. (Yu et al., 2021) have both demonstrated that the large pre-trained language models can be effectively and efficiently fine-tuned for various downstream tasks with very few privacy leakage. For example, Yu et al. proposed to use ghost clipping to reduce the memory costs of gradient clipping in DP-SGD. Besides, they also showed that there is no explicit relationship between the dimensionality of gradient updates and private fine-tuning performance (Yu et al., 2021).

It is worth noting that our work is orthogonal to all the DP-SGD-based works above in language domain in two main folds. First, the threat models are different. Specifically, DP-SGD considers a trusted authority to train on the private dataset. It aims to convert the learning algorithm with differential privacy, and thus get the trained model to defend against a "weak" adversary for "distinguishing" data, e.g., membership inference attacks (Shokri et al., 2017). In this work, we consider a stronger attack based on the scenario of instance encoding, i.e., the attacker could have access to the instance encoded data and try to reconstruct the original data by reconstruction attacks (Carlini et al., 2020b).

Second, the privacy protection methods are different. To address the risk of data reconstruction attacks, we follow the notion of conventional data publishing with differential privacy, i.e., adding noise on the training data directly (integrated in the instance encoding scheme) while DP-SGD is to add noise on the gradient updates during the learning process (Abadi et al., 2016).

3 Preliminaries of Differential Privacy

As one main category of privacy-enhancing technologies, differential privacy (DP) (Dwork et al., 2006b, 2014) has been widely used as a de facto standard notion in protecting individual's data privacy for data collection and analysis (Dwork and Smith, 2010), especially in machine learning applications (Vaidya et al., 2013; Abadi et al., 2016).

The principle of the differential privacy (Dwork et al., 2006b, 2014) is that an individual's data point x in one dataset D will not arouse significant change to the outcome of a randomized mechanism or algorithm applied to the D. Thus, the attacker cannot make difference with such a specific data point x by observing the outputs of D by the randomized mechanism, which thus provides deniability for the existence of x (ensuring data privacy).

Formally, to define individual's privacy, we first define the neighboring datasets, i.e., D, $D' \in \mathcal{D}$ are the neighbors if they only differs in one data point, denoted as $D \sim D'$. Then we define the DP notation as following:

Definition 1 (Differential Privacy (Dwork et al., 2006b, 2014)). *For any two neighboring datasets, $D, D' \in \mathcal{D}$, a randomized mechanism $\mathcal{M}$ is said to be (ϵ, δ)-differentially private if it satisfies the following equation:*

$$Pr(\mathcal{M}(D) \in \mathcal{O}) \leq e^{\epsilon}\, Pr(\mathcal{M}(D') \in \mathcal{O}) + \delta \quad (2)$$

where $\mathcal{O}$ denote all the events in the output space of $\mathcal{M}$. If $\delta = 0$, $\mathcal{M}$ is ϵ-differentially private.

In this work, we will utilize the Laplace and Gaussian mechanisms to guarantee (ϵ, δ)-DP.

The Laplace mechanism (Dwork et al., 2006b) adds the noise from Laplace distribution with mean zero and scale parameter b, denoted as Lap(b) with density function $\frac{1}{2b}\exp^{\frac{-|x|}{b}}$. Formally, we have the following theorem:

Theorem 1 (Laplace Mechanism (Dwork et al., 2006b, 2014)). *Given any function $f : \mathcal{D} \rightarrow \mathbb{R}^d$, the Laplace mechanism is defined as $\mathcal{M}_L(D, f, \epsilon) = f(D) + N$, where N is the random noise drawn from Laplace distribution Lap$(\frac{\Delta f}{\epsilon})$, and Δf is ℓ_1 sensitivity. Laplace mechanism satisfies $(\epsilon, 0)$-DP.*

Theorem 2 (Gaussian Mechanism (Dwork et al., 2006a, 2014)). *Given any function $f : \mathcal{D} \rightarrow \mathbb{R}^d$, the Gaussian mechanism is defined as $\mathcal{M}_G(D, f, \epsilon) = f(D) + N$, where N is the random noise drawn from Gaussian Distribution $\mathcal{N}(0, \sigma^2 I_d)$ with $\sigma \geq \Delta f \sqrt{2\ln(1.25/\delta)}/\epsilon$. Δf is the ℓ_2 sensitivity of function f, i.e., $\ell_2 = \sup_{D \sim D'} ||f(D) - f(D')||_2$. Guassian mechanism satisfies (ϵ, δ)-DP.*

4 DP Instance Encoding

Given a training batch of data samples of size M $\mathcal{B} = \{(x_1, y_1), (x_2, y_2), \cdots, (x_i, y_i)\}, i \in [1, M]$, which is randomly sampled from the training set. TextHide will first encode every sample into a feature vector of dimension size d by a pretrained feature extractor $\phi(\cdot)$, i.e., $v_i = \phi(x_i)$. Then we can get the corresponding batch of encoded feature vectors $\mathcal{B}_e = \{(v_1, y_1), (v_2, y_2), \cdots, (v_N, y_N)\}$. For original instance encoding, TextHide would mixup such set of size k vectors to generate private encoded vectors as training data per Equation 1. To address the privacy issue, we apply the differential private mechanism to such mixup process. Algorithm 1 demonstrates the details.

Algorithm 1: DP Instance Encoding

Input: Batch of encoded vectors $\mathcal{B}_e$,
Number of mixed data samples k,
clip bound for encoder vectors C
DP Noise $\mathcal{M}$: Laplace, Gaussian

Output: Differentially private encoded vector set $\mathcal{B}_{dp}$ of size $|\mathcal{B}_{dp}|$

Initialize DP mechanism $\mathcal{M} = \{\mathcal{M}_L, \mathcal{M}_G\}$
Randomly sample K mixup coefficients:
  $\Sigma_i^K \lambda_i = 1, \lambda_i \in \mathcal{N}(0, I)$
// Instance Encoding by mixup
Randomly sample K data samples from $\mathcal{B}_e$
for $i \rightarrow 1$ *to* $|\mathcal{B}_e|$ **do**
  // Clip Input Vector
  $v_i \leftarrow v_i \cdot \min(1, \frac{C}{||v_i||_2})$
if $\mathcal{M}_G$ **then**
  $N \leftarrow^{s} \mathcal{N}(0, \sigma^2 I_d)$
else
  $N \leftarrow^{s} \frac{\epsilon}{4C}\exp^{\frac{-\epsilon|x|}{2C}}$
for $j \rightarrow 1$ *to* $|\mathcal{B}_{dp}|$ **do**
  $\widetilde{v}_j \leftarrow \sum_{i=1}^{K} \lambda_i v_i + N$
  $\widetilde{y}_j \leftarrow \sum_{i=1}^{K} \lambda_i y_i$
return $|\mathcal{B}_{dp}|$ private encoded data vectors

Theorem 3. *The DP Instance Encoding revised with Laplace noise satisfies $(\epsilon, 0)$-DP, where the added noise N_L is draw from Laplace distribution as following:*

$$N_L = \frac{\epsilon}{4C}\exp^{\frac{-\epsilon|x|}{2C}} \quad (3)$$

Proof. The proof complies with the original proof of Laplace mechanism (Dwork et al., 2006b, 2014). The instance encoding scheme with clipping works as the function f. The ℓ_1 sensitivity here is $2C$ since the maximum ℓ_1 norm difference of two vectors are $2C$ (viewed as a hyper-sphere of radius C). Then replacing Δf with $2C$ in Laplace distribution, we get the Equation 3. It has shown that adding Laplace noise sampled from Eq. 3 satisfies ϵ-DP (Dwork et al., 2006b), i.e., the DP instance encoding with $\mathcal{M}_L$ satisfies $(\epsilon, 0)$-DP. □

Theorem 4. *The DP Instance Encoding revised with Gaussian noise satisfies* (ϵ, δ)*-DP.*

Proof. Similar to the previous proof for Laplace, we choose the Gaussian distribution $\mathcal{N}(0, \sigma^2)$ with mean zero and standard deviation $\sigma^2 = (\frac{1+\sqrt{2\log(1/\delta)}}{\epsilon})^2 C^2$, where the ℓ_2 sensitivity is C. Note that the input vectors are multi-dimensional, and the noise added will be drawn independently from $\mathcal{M}_G$. Then we can derive that DP instance encoding with $\mathcal{M}_G$ satisfies (ϵ, δ)-DP. □

5 Experimental Evaluation

For experiments, we would like to evaluate both utility and privacy of the proposed scheme as the following: 1) utility of the private instance encoding scheme, i.e., the performance (accuracy) of model trained on the private dataset; 2) privacy guarantee of the scheme against reconstruction attacks, i.e., the attack success rate (the percentage of reconstructed private vectors).

5.1 Experimental Setup

Dataset. We consider the sentence classification task with two popular datasets: 1) Corpus of Linguistic Acceptability (CoLA) (Warstadt et al., 2019) (about 8500 training samples) for acceptability; 2) Stanford Sentiment Treebank (SST-2) (Socher et al., 2013) (about 67000 samples) for sentiment analysis.

Model Implementation. We use the pre-trained BERT model (Devlin et al., 2019) as the language feature extractor to generate the text representation vectors (the dimensionality d is 768). Note that TextHide will encode such representation vectors into the training vectors for downstream tasks. For downstream task training, we follow TextHide to choose a multilayer perceptron of hidden-layer size $(768, 768, 768)$ since we take TextHide as baseline.

Utility Evaluation. We will apply our scheme (including Gaussian and Laplace mechanism, denoted as "DP-IE Gaussian" and "DP-IE Laplace", respectively) and TextHide to the two datasets during training, and then report the model accuracy, respectively. In addition, we will also demonstrate the accuracy of the raw dataset (without any privacy protection scheme) for better utility comparison.

Privacy Evaluation. To fully evaluate the proposed DP instance encoding scheme, we also utilize a privacy reconstruction attack (Xie and Hong, 2021) on instance encoding scheme. Specifically, we first construct a set of private vectors generated by our proposed scheme and TextHide (as baseline), respectively. We report the final attack success rate (the percentage of reconstructed data vectors out of the original set) by implementing reconstruction attack on the generated vectors above.

5.2 Utility Evaluation

For our proposed scheme, we set the privacy parameter $\epsilon = \{0.1, 1, 2, 4, 8, 10, 15, 20\}$. For Gaussian mechanism, we set δ to be 10^{-5}. Then we evaluate the model accuracy with varied ϵ for both Laplace and Gaussian mechanism on the two datasets as depicted above. For TextHide, we select $(m = 16, k = 4)$ as its own privacy parameters. We also evaluate the base case (without any privacy-protection scheme). We report the final model accuracy (the testing performance of trained model on the private dataset).

Figure 1 demonstrates the results. From the figure, we can observe that the model accuracy increases as the private parameter ϵ increases for both Gaussian and Laplace. This is reasonable since the privacy parameter ϵ of the DP schemes works as the privacy budget to determine the privacy-protection level for the dataset. That is, the larger the privacy budget, the smaller the noise added to the original data vectors (the privacy-protection would be weaker). As a result, the utility of the training set would not be affected too much. In addition, we can also observe that the model accuracy can approach the base case as ϵ increases, which will cause the compromise of privacy to some extent (as shown in the privacy evaluation).

5.3 Privacy Attack Evaluation

We follow the attack model setting (Carlini et al., 2020a; Xie and Hong, 2021) that the attacker could obtain the background knowledge of the private

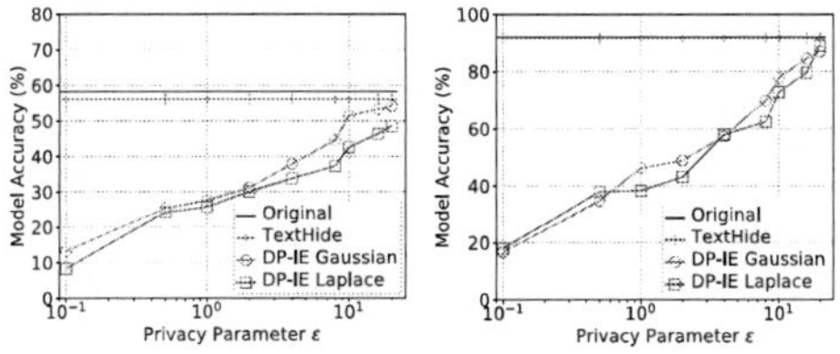

(a) CoLA (b) SST-2

Figure 1: Accuracy (learning utility) on the two datasets with DP-IE schemes.

dataset but be unaware of the specific data for training, which would utilize any auxiliary information to reconstruct the vectors (as a strong attack). We reproduce the attack scheme following the attack proposed in (Xie and Hong, 2021). More specifically, we randomly select 100 data points and generate 5000 encoded data by our DP schemes for each dataset, respectively. We measure the attack results with varying values of the privacy parameter $\epsilon = \{0.1, 1, 2, 4, 8, 10, 15, 20\}$ (referring to different levels for privacy-protection). For example, $\epsilon = 0.1$ is the strong protection and 20 is a weak protection. We repeat the same process for TextHide using the same privacy parameter as the previous utility evaluation.

Figure 2 demonstrates the final attack results. First, we can observe that the TextHide cannot ensure data privacy against privacy attacks, i.e., the privacy attack can recover around 85% of the original data vectors for both CoLA and SST-2 dataset. This also conforms to the previous works. Second, the results show that our proposed DP scheme can defend against such privacy attack from reconstructing the data. Take Figure 2(a) as an example, the overall attack success rate is lower than the baseline's. Besides, the attack success rate increases as the privacy parameter ϵ increases, which indicates that a higher privacy budget will lead weaker protection by differential privacy. Such results also validate the previous DP theorems. Again, it should be noted that DP cannot prevent leakage of the dataset completely. Instead, we would like to achieve a proper utility-privacy trade-off while applying differential privacy to the machine learning applications. For example, some privacy-sensitive applications, e.g., on-device input prediction, could require strong privacy guarantee while tolerating a fair utility loss. We can also improve our instance encoding scheme with other techniques, e.g., Federated Learning (Konečný et al., 2016) or optimize the privacy budget to get a better utility accordingly.

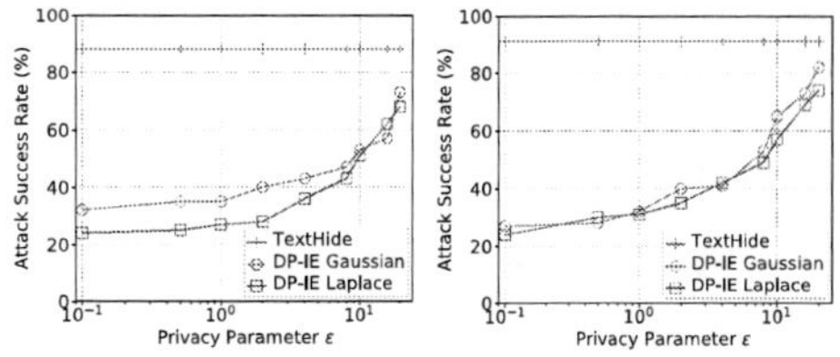

(a) CoLA (b) SST-2

Figure 2: Attack success rate on the two datasets with DP-IE schemes.

6 Conclusion & Future Work

In this paper, we facilitate the instance encoding scheme with differential privacy. We have theoretically proven that the revised instance encoding with DP mechanism could provide good privacy guarantee under differential privacy framework. Experimental results have shown that the proposed differentially private scheme can obtain good utility for downstream learning tasks, e.g., text classification. Besides, we also evaluate the proposed DP scheme against privacy attacks and the results show that the scheme can ensure the privacy of dataset while presenting with attacks.

For the future work, we would like to further revise current DP instance encoding with another differential privacy notion, i.e., Rényi differential privacy (Mironov, 2017), which generalizes the concept of differential privacy based on the Rényi divergence. That is, revising the instance encoding scheme with Rényi DP would derive a tighter privacy bound and thus achieve better privacy-protection. Besides, another potential direction is to rescale the text vectors (generated by language feature extractor model) to a lower dimension vector by an extra MLP model or auto-encoder (Liou et al., 2014). We can utilize composition theorem (Dwork et al., 2014) in DP to theoretically find a better guarantee for various downstream tasks.

Acknowledgements

The authors would like to thank the anonymous reviewers for their helpful feedback and suggestions. This work is partially supported by the NSF under the Grants No. CNS-2046335 and CNS-2034870, and the Cisco Research Award.

References

Martin Abadi, Andy Chu, Ian Goodfellow, H Brendan McMahan, Ilya Mironov, Kunal Talwar, and Li Zhang. 2016. Deep learning with differential privacy. In *Proceedings of the 2016 ACM SIGSAC conference on computer and communications security*, pages 308–318.

Amir Abboud and Kevin Lewi. 2013. Exact weight subgraphs and the k-sum conjecture. In *International Colloquium on Automata, Languages, and Programming*, pages 1–12. Springer.

Rohan Anil, Badih Ghazi, Vineet Gupta, Ravi Kumar, and Pasin Manurangsi. 2021. Large-scale differentially private bert. *arXiv preprint arXiv:2108.01624.*

Raef Bassily, Adam Smith, and Abhradeep Thakurta. 2014. Private empirical risk minimization: Efficient algorithms and tight error bounds. In *2014 IEEE 55th Annual Symposium on Foundations of Computer Science*, pages 464–473. IEEE.

Keith Bonawitz, Vladimir Ivanov, Ben Kreuter, Antonio Marcedone, H Brendan McMahan, Sarvar Patel, Daniel Ramage, Aaron Segal, and Karn Seth. 2016. Practical secure aggregation for federated learning on user-held data. *arXiv preprint arXiv:1611.04482.*

Tom Brown, Benjamin Mann, Nick Ryder, Melanie Subbiah, Jared D Kaplan, Prafulla Dhariwal, Arvind Neelakantan, Pranav Shyam, Girish Sastry, Amanda Askell, et al. 2020. Language models are few-shot learners. *Advances in neural information processing systems*, 33:1877–1901.

José Cabrero-Holgueras and Sergio Pastrana. 2021. Sok: Privacy-preserving computation techniques for deep learning. *Proceedings on Privacy Enhancing Technologies*, 2021(4):139–162.

Nicholas Carlini, Steve Chien, Milad Nasr, Shuang Song, Andreas Terzis, and Florian Tramer. 2021. Membership inference attacks from first principles. *arXiv preprint arXiv:2112.03570.*

Nicholas Carlini, Samuel Deng, Sanjam Garg, Somesh Jha, Saeed Mahloujifar, Mohammad Mahmoody, Shuang Song, Abhradeep Thakurta, and Florian Tramer. 2020a. An attack on instahide: Is private learning possible with instance encoding? *arXiv preprint arXiv:2011.05315.*

Nicholas Carlini, Samuel Deng, Sanjam Garg, Somesh Jha, Saeed Mahloujifar, Mohammad Mahmoody, Shuang Song, Abhradeep Thakurta, and Florian Tramer. 2020b. Is private learning possible with instance encoding? *arXiv preprint arXiv:2011.05315.*

Nicholas Carlini, Florian Tramer, Eric Wallace, Matthew Jagielski, Ariel Herbert-Voss, Katherine Lee, Adam Roberts, Tom Brown, Dawn Song, Ulfar Erlingsson, et al. 2020c. Extracting training data from large language models. *arXiv preprint arXiv:2012.07805.*

Daniel Cer, Mona Diab, Eneko Agirre, Iñigo Lopez-Gazpio, and Lucia Specia. 2017. SemEval-2017 task 1: Semantic textual similarity multilingual and crosslingual focused evaluation. In *Proceedings of the 11th International Workshop on Semantic Evaluation (SemEval-2017)*, pages 1–14, Vancouver, Canada. Association for Computational Linguistics.

Kamalika Chaudhuri, Claire Monteleoni, and Anand D Sarwate. 2011. Differentially private empirical risk minimization. *Journal of Machine Learning Research*, 12(3).

M. Chen, B. Lee, Gagan Bansal, Yuan Cao, Shuyuan Zhang, Justin Y. Lu, Jackie Tsay, Yinan Wang, Andrew M. Dai, Z. Chen, Timothy Sohn, and Yonghui Wu. 2019. Gmail smart compose: Real-time assisted writing. *Proceedings of the 25th ACM SIGKDD International Conference on Knowledge Discovery & Data Mining.*

Arman Cohan, Iz Beltagy, Daniel King, Bhavana Dalvi, and Dan Weld. 2019. Pretrained language models for sequential sentence classification. In *Proceedings of the 2019 Conference on Empirical Methods in Natural Language Processing and the 9th International Joint Conference on Natural Language Processing (EMNLP-IJCNLP)*, pages 3693–3699, Hong Kong, China. Association for Computational Linguistics.

Jacob Devlin, Ming-Wei Chang, Kenton Lee, and Kristina Toutanova. 2019. BERT: Pre-training of deep bidirectional transformers for language understanding. In *Proceedings of the 2019 Conference of the North American Chapter of the Association for Computational Linguistics: Human Language Technologies, Volume 1 (Long and Short Papers)*, pages 4171–4186, Minneapolis, Minnesota. Association for Computational Linguistics.

Christophe Dupuy, Radhika Arava, Rahul Gupta, and Anna Rumshisky. 2022. An efficient dp-sgd mechanism for large scale nlu models. In *ICASSP 2022-2022 IEEE International Conference on Acoustics, Speech and Signal Processing (ICASSP)*, pages 4118–4122. IEEE.

Cynthia Dwork, Krishnaram Kenthapadi, Frank McSherry, Ilya Mironov, and Moni Naor. 2006a. Our data, ourselves: Privacy via distributed noise generation. In *Annual international conference on the theory and applications of cryptographic techniques*, pages 486–503. Springer.

Cynthia Dwork, Frank McSherry, Kobbi Nissim, and Adam Smith. 2006b. Calibrating noise to sensitivity in private data analysis. In *Theory of cryptography conference*, pages 265–284. Springer.

Cynthia Dwork, Aaron Roth, et al. 2014. The algorithmic foundations of differential privacy. *Found. Trends Theor. Comput. Sci.*, 9(3-4):211–407.

Cynthia Dwork and Adam Smith. 2010. Differential privacy for statistics: What we know and what we want to learn. *Journal of Privacy and Confidentiality*, 1(2).

Matt Fredrikson, Somesh Jha, and Thomas Ristenpart. 2015. Model inversion attacks that exploit confidence information and basic countermeasures. In *Proceedings of the 22nd ACM SIGSAC Conference on Computer and Communications Security*, CCS '15, page 1322–1333, New York, NY, USA. Association for Computing Machinery.

Jonas Geiping, Hartmut Bauermeister, Hannah Dröge, and Michael Moeller. 2020. Inverting gradients-how easy is it to break privacy in federated learning? *Advances in Neural Information Processing Systems*, 33:16937–16947.

Craig Gentry. 2009. Fully homomorphic encryption using ideal lattices. In *Proceedings of the forty-first annual ACM symposium on Theory of computing*, pages 169–178.

Oded Goldreich. 2009. *Foundations of cryptography: volume 2, basic applications*. Cambridge university press.

Jian Guo, He He, Tong He, Leonard Lausen, Mu Li, Haibin Lin, Xingjian Shi, Chenguang Wang, Junyuan Xie, Sheng Zha, et al. 2020. Gluoncv and gluonnlp: deep learning in computer vision and natural language processing. *J. Mach. Learn. Res.*, 21(23):1–7.

Sorami Hisamoto, Matt Post, and Kevin Duh. 2020. Membership inference attacks on sequence-to-sequence models: Is my data in your machine translation system? *Transactions of the Association for Computational Linguistics*, 8:49–63.

Shlomo Hoory, Amir Feder, Avichai Tendler, Sofia Erell, Alon Peled-Cohen, Itay Laish, Hootan Nakhost, Uri Stemmer, Ayelet Benjamini, Avinatan Hassidim, and Yossi Matias. 2021. Learning and evaluating a differentially private pre-trained language model. In *Findings of the Association for Computational Linguistics: EMNLP 2021*, pages 1178–1189, Punta Cana, Dominican Republic. Association for Computational Linguistics.

Yangsibo Huang, Zhao Song, Danqi Chen, Kai Li, and Sanjeev Arora. 2020a. TextHide: Tackling data privacy in language understanding tasks. In *Findings of the Association for Computational Linguistics: EMNLP 2020*, pages 1368–1382, Online. Association for Computational Linguistics.

Yangsibo Huang, Zhao Song, Kai Li, and Sanjeev Arora. 2020b. InstaHide: Instance-hiding schemes for private distributed learning. In *Proceedings of the 37th International Conference on Machine Learning*, volume 119 of *Proceedings of Machine Learning Research*, pages 4507–4518. PMLR.

Gavin Kerrigan, Dylan Slack, and Jens Tuyls. 2020. Differentially private language models benefit from public pre-training. In *Proceedings of the Second Workshop on Privacy in NLP*, pages 39–45, Online. Association for Computational Linguistics.

Jakub Konečný, H Brendan McMahan, Felix X Yu, Peter Richtárik, Ananda Theertha Suresh, and Dave Bacon. 2016. Federated learning: Strategies for improving communication efficiency. *arXiv preprint arXiv:1610.05492*.

Eric Lehman, Sarthak Jain, Karl Pichotta, Yoav Goldberg, and Byron Wallace. 2021. Does BERT pretrained on clinical notes reveal sensitive data? In *Proceedings of the 2021 Conference of the North American Chapter of the Association for Computational Linguistics: Human Language Technologies*, pages 946–959, Online. Association for Computational Linguistics.

Xuechen Li, Florian Tramer, Percy Liang, and Tatsunori Hashimoto. 2021. Large language models can be strong differentially private learners. *arXiv preprint arXiv:2110.05679*.

Cheng-Yuan Liou, Wei-Chen Cheng, Jiun-Wei Liou, and Daw-Ran Liou. 2014. Autoencoder for words. *Neurocomputing*, 139:84–96.

Fatemehsadat Mireshghallah, Huseyin Inan, Marcello Hasegawa, Victor Rühle, Taylor Berg-Kirkpatrick, and Robert Sim. 2021. Privacy regularization: Joint privacy-utility optimization in LanguageModels. In *Proceedings of the 2021 Conference of the North American Chapter of the Association for Computational Linguistics: Human Language Technologies*, pages 3799–3807, Online. Association for Computational Linguistics.

Ilya Mironov. 2017. Rényi differential privacy. In *2017 IEEE 30th computer security foundations symposium (CSF)*, pages 263–275. IEEE.

Meisam Mohammady, Shangyu Xie, Yuan Hong, Mengyuan Zhang, Lingyu Wang, Makan Pourzandi, and Mourad Debbabi. 2020. R2dp: A universal and automated approach to optimizing the randomization mechanisms of differential privacy for utility metrics with no known optimal distributions. In *Proceedings of the 2020 ACM SIGSAC Conference on Computer and Communications Security*, CCS '20, page 677–696, New York, NY, USA. Association for Computing Machinery.

Payman Mohassel and Peter Rindal. 2018. Aby3: A mixed protocol framework for machine learning. In *Proceedings of the 2018 ACM SIGSAC Conference on Computer and Communications Security*, pages 35–52.

Payman Mohassel and Yupeng Zhang. 2017. Secureml: A system for scalable privacy-preserving machine learning. In *2017 IEEE Symposium on Security and Privacy (SP)*, pages 19–38.

Pascal Paillier. 1999. Public-key cryptosystems based on composite degree residuosity classes. In *International conference on the theory and applications of cryptographic techniques*, pages 223–238. Springer.

Alec Radford, Jeffrey Wu, Rewon Child, David Luan, Dario Amodei, Ilya Sutskever, et al. 2019. Language models are unsupervised multitask learners. *OpenAI blog*, 1(8):9.

Ahmed Salem, Yang Zhang, Mathias Humbert, Pascal Berrang, Mario Fritz, and Michael Backes. 2018. Ml-leaks: Model and data independent membership inference attacks and defenses on machine learning models. *arXiv preprint arXiv:1806.01246*.

Reza Shokri, Marco Stronati, Congzheng Song, and Vitaly Shmatikov. 2017. Membership inference attacks against machine learning models. In *2017 IEEE symposium on security and privacy (SP)*, pages 3–18. IEEE.

Richard Socher, Alex Perelygin, Jean Wu, Jason Chuang, Christopher D. Manning, Andrew Ng, and Christopher Potts. 2013. Recursive deep models for semantic compositionality over a sentiment treebank. In *Proceedings of the 2013 Conference on Empirical Methods in Natural Language Processing*, pages 1631–1642, Seattle, Washington, USA. Association for Computational Linguistics.

Congzheng Song and Ananth Raghunathan. 2020. Information leakage in embedding models. In *Proceedings of the 2020 ACM SIGSAC Conference on Computer and Communications Security*, pages 377–390.

Liwei Song and Prateek Mittal. 2021. Systematic evaluation of privacy risks of machine learning models. In *30th USENIX Security Symposium (USENIX Security 21)*, pages 2615–2632.

Jaideep Vaidya, Basit Shafiq, Anirban Basu, and Yuan Hong. 2013. Differentially private naive bayes classification. In *2013 IEEE/WIC/ACM International Joint Conferences on Web Intelligence (WI) and Intelligent Agent Technologies (IAT)*, volume 1, pages 571–576. IEEE.

Sandra Wachter, Brent Mittelstadt, and Chris Russell. 2017. Counterfactual explanations without opening the black box: Automated decisions and the gdpr. *Harv. JL & Tech.*, 31:841.

Alex Warstadt, Amanpreet Singh, and Samuel R. Bowman. 2019. Neural network acceptability judgments. *Transactions of the Association for Computational Linguistics*, 7:625–641.

Xi Wu, Matthew Fredrikson, Somesh Jha, and Jeffrey F Naughton. 2016. A methodology for formalizing model-inversion attacks. In *2016 IEEE 29th Computer Security Foundations Symposium (CSF)*, pages 355–370. IEEE.

Shangyu Xie and Yuan Hong. 2021. Reconstruction attack on instance encoding for language understanding. In *Proceedings of the 2021 Conference on Empirical Methods in Natural Language Processing*, pages 2038–2044, Online and Punta Cana, Dominican Republic. Association for Computational Linguistics.

Da Yu, Saurabh Naik, Arturs Backurs, Sivakanth Gopi, Huseyin A Inan, Gautam Kamath, Janardhan Kulkarni, Yin Tat Lee, Andre Manoel, Lukas Wutschitz, et al. 2021. Differentially private fine-tuning of language models. *arXiv preprint arXiv:2110.06500*.

Hongyi Zhang, Moustapha Cisse, Yann N. Dauphin, and David Lopez-Paz. 2018a. mixup: Beyond empirical risk minimization. In *International Conference on Learning Representations*.

Zixing Zhang, Jürgen Geiger, Jouni Pohjalainen, Amr El-Desoky Mousa, Wenyu Jin, and Björn Schuller. 2018b. Deep learning for environmentally robust speech recognition: An overview of recent developments. *ACM Transactions on Intelligent Systems and Technology (TIST)*, 9(5):1–28.

Ligeng Zhu, Zhijian Liu, and Song Han. 2019. Deep leakage from gradients. In *Advances in Neural Information Processing Systems*, volume 32. Curran Associates, Inc.

A Simple Approach to Jointly Rank Passages and Select Relevant Sentences in the OBQA Context

Anonymous ACL submission

Abstract

In the open book question answering (OBQA) task, selecting the relevant passages and sentences from distracting information is crucial to reason the answer to a question. HotpotQA dataset is designed to teach and evaluate systems to do both passage ranking and sentence selection. Many existing frameworks use separate models to select relevant passages and sentences respectively. Such systems not only have high complexity in terms of the parameters of models but also fail to take the advantage of training these two tasks together since one task can be beneficial for the other one. In this work, we present a simple yet effective framework to address these limitations by jointly ranking passages and selecting sentences. Furthermore, we propose consistency and similarity constraints to promote the correlation and interaction between passage ranking and sentence selection.The experiments demonstrate that our framework can achieve competitive results with previous systems and outperform the baseline by 28% in terms of exact matching of relevant sentences on the HotpotQA dataset.

Question: The football manager who recruited David Beckham managed Manchester United during what timeframe?

Passage1, 1995–96 Manchester United F.C. season: The1995-96 season was Manchester United's fourth season in the Premier League, and their 21st consecutive season in the top division of English football. United finished the season by becoming the first English team to win the Double (league title and FA Cup) twice. *Their triumph was made all the more remarkable by the fact that Alex Ferguson had sold experienced players Paul Ince, Mark Hughes and Andrei Kanchelskis before the start of the season, and not made any major signings.Instead, he had drafted in young players like Nicky Butt, David Beckham, Paul Scholes and the Neville brothers, Gary and Phil.*

passage2, Alex Ferguson: *Sir Alexander Chapman Ferguson,CBE (born 31 December 1941) is a Scottish former football manager and player who managed Manchester United from1986 to 2013.* He is regarded by many players, managers and analysts to be one of the greatest and most successful managers of all time.

Answer: from 1986 to 2013

Supporting facts: [["1995-96 Manchester United F.C.season",2],["1995-96 Manchester United F.C. season",3],["AlexFerguson",0]]

Figure 1: An example from the HotpotQA dataset, where the question should be answered by combining supporting facts(SP) from two passages. In the SP, the first string refers to the title of passage, and the second integer means the index of the sentence.

1 Introduction

Open book question answering (OBQA) requires a system to find the relevant documents to reason the answer to a question. It has wide and practical Natural Language Processing (NLP) applications such as search engines (Kwiatkowski et al., 2019) and dialogue systems (Reddy et al., 2019; Choi et al., 2018). Among several OBQA datasets (Dhingra et al., 2017; Mihaylov et al., 2018; Khot et al., 2020), HotpotQA (Yang et al., 2018) is more challenging because it requires a system not only to find the relevant passages from large corpus but also find the relevant sentences in the passage which eventually reach to the answer. Such a task also increases the interpretability of the systems.

To address this challenge, most of the previous work (Nie et al., 2019; Fang et al., 2020; Tu et al., 2019; Groeneveld et al., 2020) use two-step pipeline: identify the most relevant passage by one model and then match each question with a single sentence in the corresponding passage by another model. Such systems are heavy in terms of the size of the models which requires long training and inference time. Green AI has recently been advocated to against the trend of building large models which are both environmentally unfriendly and expensive, raising barriers to participation in NLP research (Schwartz et al., 2020). Apparently, systems using multiple models to solve HotpotQA task do not belong to the family of Green AI. Furthermore, the benefits of learning from passage ranking

Proceedings of the 2022 Conference of the North American Chapter of the Association for Computational Linguistics: Human Language Technologies: Student Research Workshop, pages 181 - 187
July 10-15, 2022 ©2022 Association for Computational Linguistics

and selecting relevant sentences are not well utilized by these systems. Intuitively, if a passage is ranked high, then some sentences in the passage should be selected as relevant. On the other hand, if a passage is ranked low, then all sentences in the passage should be classified as irrelevant.

To build a Green AI system and take advantage of multi-task learning, we introduce a Two-in-One model, a simple model trained on passage ranking and sentence selection jointly. More specifically, our model generates passage representations and sentence representations simultaneously, which are then fed to a passage ranker and sentence classifier respectively. Then we promote the interaction between passage ranking and sentence classification using consistency and similarity constraints. The consistency constraint is to enforce that the relevant passage includes relevant sentences, while the similarity constraint ensures the model to generate the representation of relevant passages more closer to the representations for relevant sentences than irrelevant ones. The experiments conducted on the HotpotQA datasets demonstrate that our simple model achieves competitive results with previous systems and outperforms the baselines by 28%.

2 Related Work

HotpotQA Systems A straightforward way to solve the HotpotQA challenge is to build a hierarchical system (Nie et al., 2019), meaning a system first ranks relevant passages and then identifies relevant sentences from the selected passages. Such a hierarchical system involves multiple models thus requires long inference time. More importantly, such a system only leverages the impact of passage ranking on sentence selection but ignores the influence of the sentence selection on the passage ranking. Our framework achieves these two tasks by one model and facilitates the interaction by two constraints. Groeneveld et al. (2020) proposes a pipeline based on three BERT models (Devlin et al., 2019) to solve the HotpotQA challenge. The system first selects relevant sentences and then detects the answer span, finally, identifies the relevant sentences according to the answer span. Though the pipeline is strong, the way it solves the problem is opposite to human beings. We, humans, identify the relevant sentences, and then give the answer span. Many existing works demonstrate the effectiveness of graph neural networks(GNN) on HotpotQA challenge (Fang et al., 2020; Tu et al., 2019). Since GNN is out of the scope of this work, we do not compare it with these frameworks.

Joint Model for QA Joint learning has been studied in Question Answering Tasks. Deng et al. (2020) proposes a joint model to tackle community question answering such that the model can simultaneously select the set of correct answers from candidates and generate an abstractive summary for each selected answer. Sun et al. (2019) proposes a generative collaborative network to answer questions and generate questions. The main difference between our work and previous ones are in two sense (1) our proposed model uses the shared encoder to tackle two classification tasks (2) besides the loss function to optimize individual tasks, we also propose two constraints that utilize the relation between these two tasks.

3 HotpotQA Dataset

HotpotQA dataset (Yang et al., 2018) is designed for multi-hop reasoning question answering tasks, i.e. to reason over multiple documents and answer questions (see Figure 1). Particularly, HotpotQA challenge requires reasoning over two passages. Furthermore, to guide the system to perform meaningful and explainable reasoning, the dataset also provides supporting facts (SP) that reach the answer to the question. HotpotQA provide two challenging settings: in **Fullwiki setting**, a system needs to rank passage from the entire wiki corpus; in **Distractor setting**, 10 distracting passages (including relevant ones) are given for each question. In this work, we mainly focus on the latter setting. From the training set, we find that 70.4% questions have exactly two supporting facts (SP), and 60.0% of SP are the first sentence of passages.

4 Method

We aim to jointly conduct two tasks, passage ranking and supporting facts selection for HotpotQA. Given a question Q, the goal is to simultaneously rank the set of candidates A = $\{a_1, ..., a_i\}$ and identify the supporting facts for the TopK[1] passages.

4.1 Model: Two-in-One Framework

We introduce the proposed joint model for passage ranking and support fact selection, Two-in-One, which uses state-of-the-art transformer-based

[1] The value of K depends on the task, and for HotpotQA, K is 2.

model (Vaswani et al., 2017) to encode questions and contexts. In this work, we use RoBERTa (Liu et al., 2019), however, any other variants like ELECTRA (Clark et al., 2020) can be applied in this framework. The model architecture is given in Figure 2. On top of the encoder, there are two MLP layers to score passages and sentences respectively. In details, given a question and a passage, we firstly create an input to feed through RoBERTa (Liu et al., 2019) by concatenating the question and the passage as follows, $\langle s\rangle Q\langle /s\rangle S_1\langle /s\rangle S_2...\langle /s\rangle S_k\langle /s\rangle$ where $\langle s\rangle$ and $\langle /s\rangle$ are special tokens in RoBERTa, S_i is the ith sentence from a passage. We take $\langle s\rangle$ as the contextual representation for passage ranking and the $\langle /s\rangle$ in front of each sentence for sentence selection. The passage ranker and the sentence classifier have identical structure (two-layer Multiple-Layer Perceptron(MLP)) but different weights.

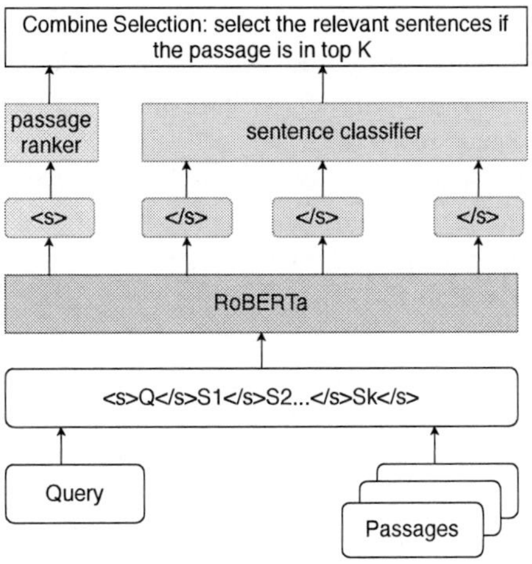

Figure 2: The architecture of Two-in-One model for passage ranking and relevant sentence selection. For HotpotQA dataset, K is two.

The model is jointly trained by passage loss and sentence loss. In detail, during the training time, we assign the relevant passages and sentences with ground truth score 1 while irrelevant passages and sentences with ground truth score -1. Then, Mean Square Error(MSE) loss is applied to calculate the passage and sentence loss as follows,

$$\begin{aligned}\mathcal{L}^{pass} &= (\hat{y} - y)^2,\\ \mathcal{L}^{sent} &= \sum_{i=1}^{K}(\hat{x_i} - x_i)^2, \qquad (1)\\ \mathcal{L}^{joint} &= \mathcal{L}^{pass} + \mathcal{L}^{sent},\end{aligned}$$

where $\hat{y}$ is the predicted passage score, y is the ground truth score of the passage, $\hat{x_i}$ and x_i are the predicted sentence score and ground truth score of S_i, respectively, and K is the total number of sentences in the passage. We simply sum up the passage loss and sentence loss to jointly update model parameters.

During the inference time, passages are ranked based on the logits given by the passage ranker. For the sentence classification, we take 0[2] as the threshold to classify the relevance of each sentence: if the score given by the sentence classifier is larger than 0, then it is relevant; otherwise, irrelevant.

Next, we introduce two constraints to facilitate the interaction between these two tasks.

4.2 Consistency Constraint

Intuitively, if a passage is relevant to the question, then there are some sentences from the passages that are relevant; on the other hand, if a passage is not relevant to the answer, then there should not be relevant sentences inside the passage. Thus, we propose a consistency constraint over the passage ranker and sentence classifier to minimize the gap between the passage score and the maximum sentence score. The loss function is as follows:

$$\mathcal{L}^{con} = (\hat{y} - max(\mathbf{x}))^2, \qquad (2)$$

where $\mathbf{x} = [\hat{x}_1 \dots \hat{x}_n]$ denotes a stack of predicted sentence scores.

4.3 Similarity Constraint

As we have shown at the beginning of this section, token $\langle s\rangle$ is used to get the passage score, and each token $\langle /s\rangle$ is used to get the sentence score. Intuitively, the similarity between token $\langle s\rangle$ of a relevant passage is more close to token $\langle /s\rangle$ of a relevant sentence than to $\langle /s\rangle$ of any irrelevant sentence. To enforce this constraint, we use triplet as follows:

$$\begin{aligned}\mathcal{L}^{sim} = \frac{1}{N \cdot M}\sum_{i=1}^{N}\sum_{j=1}^{M}(max\{d(v^p, v_i^r)\\ - d(v^p, v_j^n) + m, 0\}),\end{aligned} \qquad (3)$$

where $d(\cdot,\cdot)$ is the Euclidian similarity, N is the number of relevant sentences, M is the number of irrelevant sentences, v^p, v^r, v^n is the vector representation of the relevant passage, relevant sentence,

[2]The reason for threshold "0" is that it is the middle value of 1 and -1, which are labels for relevant and irrelevant sentences in the training time.

and irrelevant sentence respectively. Equation 3 enforces that all the relevant sentences should have higher similarity with the passage than all the irrelevant sentences by a margin m; otherwise, the model would be penalized. In practice, we set the margin m at 1 and find optimum results. We train our model in an end-to-end fashion by combining $\mathcal{L}^{joint}$, $\mathcal{L}^{con}$ and $\mathcal{L}^{dis}$.

5 Experiment

In this section, we first describe the training setup, and then introduce two baselines. We evaluate the two baselines and our proposed joint model on the HotpotQA dataset. Yang et al. (2018) provides two metrics for supporting facts evaluation, exact matching (EM) and F1 score. We also present the precision and recall of SP, and the exact matching of passages for detailed comparison. Meanwhile, we compare our model with the QUARK system (Groeneveld et al., 2020). Lastly, we conduct an ablation study to show the effectiveness of the proposed similarity loss and consistent loss.

5.1 Experiment Setup

We use Huggingface (Wolf et al., 2020) and Pytorch (Paszke et al., 2019) libraries to implement each model. We use 4 TX1080 and V100 NVIDIA to train models in 5 epochs with a learning rate of 1e-5, batch size of 32. We set the maximum input length in training to be 512.

5.2 Baseline

To have comparable size of the model, two baselines have similar structure as our Two-in-One model. Our model has two classification heads, whereas each of the baselines has one classification head. One baseline is to select relevant sentences, and the other one is to rank passages.

Sentence Selection Baseline The first baseline is to select relevant sentence, and particularly, we use a RoBERTa-large with an additional MLP trained on question and a single sentence: $\langle s\rangle Q\langle/s\rangle S\langle/s\rangle$, where Q is a question and S is a sentence. Although this model can not predict the relevant passage directly, based on the assumption that relevant passages include relevant sentences, we pick up two relevant passages based on the top2 sentence scores. When the top1 and the top2 sentences are from the same passage, we continue searching based on the ranking sentence scores until the second document comes up. Then the supporting facts are those sentences from the relevant documents with a score larger than 0.

Passage Selection Baseline In the second baseline, again, we use RoBERTa-large but with the goal of passage selection. The input to the model is a question and a passage: $\langle s\rangle Q\langle/s\rangle P\langle/s\rangle$. Since such a model can not predict sentence relevancy score, based on the statistic of HotpotQA that majority of training set has two supporting facts and the most of them are the first sentences in a paragraph (see Section 3), we select supporting facts by the first sentence of the top1 and top2 passages.

5.3 Result

As we see from Table 1, Two-in-One framework outperforms two baselines with large-margin improvement in all metrics, especially we see a significant improvement on the EM of SP. Our framework outperforms the Sentence Selection Baseline by 20% and 4.5% improvement on the precision and recall of SP, respectively, which demonstrates that jointly learning is beneficial for sentence classification. Also, jointly learning benefits for the passage ranking by comparing Two-in-One with Passage Selection Baseline on the EM of passage. Besides, we also compare Two-in-One with QUARK (Groeneveld et al., 2020), a framework involving three BERT models, (roughly three times larger than ours). Two-in-One achieves comparable results in terms of F1 and EM of SP regardless of much less parameters in our system. Notice that we do not have the other three values because they are not presented in their original paper.

5.4 Ablation

To evaluate the impacts of the consistency constraint and the similarity constraint, we conduct experiments with and without constraints. From Table 2, we see that both consistency constraint and similarity constraint improve F1 and EM of SP and the similarity constraint also improves the EM of passages. We found that without any constraint, though the model can rank the passages well, it suffers from distinguishing between close sentences. The similarity constraint addresses this issue in some sense by maximizing the distance between relevant and irrelevant sentences.

To better understand the impact of consistency constraint, we analyze the consistency between the passage score and the sentence score. The predic-

Model	# Parameters	SP Precision	SP Recall	SP F1	SP EM	Passage EM
Sentence Selection Baseline	∼330M	67.96	81.05	72.02	28.12	69.70
Passage Selection Baseline	∼330M	66.43	56.55	60.20	27.30	90.44
Two-in-One + sim (Ours)	∼330M	**88.06**	**85.68**	**85.82**	**59.17**	**91.11**
QUARK	∼1020M*	N/A	N/A	86.97	60.72	N/A
SAE(RoBERTa)	∼660M+*	N/A	N/A	87.38	**63.30**	N/A
HGN(RoBERTa)	∼330M+*	N/A	N/A	**87.93**	N/A	N/A

Table 1: The Results for two baselines and Two-in-One model with similarity constraint on dev set of HotpotQA distracting dataset. SP stands for supporting facts and EM for Exact Match. * refers to estimation. The bottom systems have much larger model size than our method, where QUARK (Groeneveld et al., 2020), is the result of a framework with 3 BERT models, SAE (Tu et al., 2019) uses two large language models and an GNN model, and HGN (Fang et al., 2020) uses a large language model, a GNN model and other reasoning layers.

Model	SP F1	SP EM	Passage EM
Two-in-One	85.52	58.67	90.93
Two-in-One + con	85.55	58.98	90.29
Two-in-One + sim	**85.82**	**59.17**	**91.11**
Two-in-One + con + sim	85.63	58.74	90.78

Table 2: The results for Two-in-One model with or without consistency and similarity constraints.

tion of a model is consistent if the passage score agrees with the sentence scores and the agreement can be measured by the gap between the passage score and the maximum sentence score among all sentences in that passage. We observe that by adding the consistency constraint, the gap between the passage score and the sentence score is much smaller than without the consistency constraint, i.e. 0.03 v.s. 0.11. It demonstrates that the constraint is beneficial for consistent prediction.

6 Future Work

While in this work, we show the initial and promising results of the Two-in-One model on one single dataset, there are a couple of directions we can explore in the future such as those discussed below.

Model Architecture It is easy to extend the Two-in-One model to Three-in-One model such that besides the passage ranking and sentence selection modules, a third module can predict the answer span. Like the simple extractive QA model based on RoBERTa, where a linear layer or an MLP can predict the start and end position of the answer span. A restricted inference procedure can be enforced that the answer span should be predicted from the selected sentence given by the previous model. One benefit is to reduce the difficulty for the answer selection model since less sentences will be seen by the model and the second benefit is to increase the interpretability of the model. On the other hand, if the sentence selection model makes mistakes, then such errors will carry to the answer span model which yields the wrong answer eventually.

Passage and Sentence Representation We use the contextual vector of a special token in front of each sentence to represent the sentence; we can also try to use the average pooling of every token in the sentence to get the representation of a sentence. Similar for the passage representation.

Evaluate on More Dataset To show that the generalization of the proposed model, it can also evaluate on more datasets, such as NaturalQuestion (NQ) dataset (Kwiatkowski et al., 2019). Although the NQ dataset does not have annotated support sentences, the sentence which contains the answer can be taken as the support sentence to train the sentence selection model. It is worth mentioning that in the HotpotQA dataset, there are multiple support sentences while the NQ only has one, thus, if the Two-in-One model is trained on a single dataset, then one model might not generalize well to other dataset. A simple solution might be to train the Two-in-One model on multi-datasets.

Zero-shot Testing It is also interesting to see if Two-in-One model can generalize better to unseen domains than simple baselines without any fine-tuning. To verify this, we can compare the Two-in-One model and baselines models trained on the HotpotQA dataset to other datasets.

7 Conclusion

In this work, we present a simple model, Two-in-One, to rank passage and classify sentence together. By jointly training with passage ranking and sentence selection, the model is capable of capturing the correlation between passages and sentences. We show the effectiveness of our proposed framework by evaluating the model performance on the HotpotQA datasets, concluding that jointly modeling passage ranking and sentence selection is beneficial for the task of OBQA. Compared to the existing QA systems, our model, with fewer parameters and more green than previous models, can achieve competitive results. We also propose multiple future directions to improve our model such as exploring the relationship among passages, supporting sentences, and answers in modeling and generalizing our method on more datasets.

References

Eunsol Choi, He He, Mohit Iyyer, Mark Yatskar, Wen-tau Yih, Yejin Choi, Percy Liang, and Luke Zettlemoyer. 2018. QuAC: Question answering in context. In *Proceedings of the 2018 Conference on Empirical Methods in Natural Language Processing*, pages 2174–2184, Brussels, Belgium. Association for Computational Linguistics.

Kevin Clark, Minh-Thang Luong, Quoc V. Le, and Christopher D. Manning. 2020. ELECTRA: pre-training text encoders as discriminators rather than generators. In *8th International Conference on Learning Representations, ICLR 2020, Addis Ababa, Ethiopia, April 26-30, 2020*. OpenReview.net.

Yang Deng, Wai Lam, Yuexiang Xie, Daoyuan Chen, Yaliang Li, Min Yang, and Ying Shen. 2020. Joint learning of answer selection and answer summary generation in community question answering. In *The Thirty-Fourth AAAI Conference on Artificial Intelligence, AAAI 2020, The Thirty-Second Innovative Applications of Artificial Intelligence Conference, IAAI 2020, The Tenth AAAI Symposium on Educational Advances in Artificial Intelligence, EAAI 2020, New York, NY, USA, February 7-12, 2020*, pages 7651–7658. AAAI Press.

Jacob Devlin, Ming-Wei Chang, Kenton Lee, and Kristina Toutanova. 2019. BERT: Pre-training of deep bidirectional transformers for language understanding. In *Proceedings of the 2019 Conference of the North American Chapter of the Association for Computational Linguistics: Human Language Technologies, Volume 1 (Long and Short Papers)*, pages 4171–4186, Minneapolis, Minnesota. Association for Computational Linguistics.

Bhuwan Dhingra, Kathryn Mazaitis, and William W. Cohen. 2017. Quasar: Datasets for question answering by search and reading. *ArXiv preprint*, abs/1707.03904.

Yuwei Fang, Siqi Sun, Zhe Gan, Rohit Pillai, Shuohang Wang, and Jingjing Liu. 2020. Hierarchical graph network for multi-hop question answering. In *Proceedings of the 2020 Conference on Empirical Methods in Natural Language Processing (EMNLP)*, pages 8823–8838, Online. Association for Computational Linguistics.

Dirk Groeneveld, Tushar Khot, Mausam, and Ashish Sabharwal. 2020. A simple yet strong pipeline for HotpotQA. In *Proceedings of the 2020 Conference on Empirical Methods in Natural Language Processing (EMNLP)*, pages 8839–8845, Online. Association for Computational Linguistics.

Tushar Khot, Peter Clark, Michal Guerquin, Peter Jansen, and Ashish Sabharwal. 2020. QASC: A dataset for question answering via sentence composition. In *The Thirty-Fourth AAAI Conference on Artificial Intelligence, AAAI 2020, The Thirty-Second Innovative Applications of Artificial Intelligence Conference, IAAI 2020, The Tenth AAAI Symposium on Educational Advances in Artificial Intelligence, EAAI 2020, New York, NY, USA, February 7-12, 2020*, pages 8082–8090. AAAI Press.

Tom Kwiatkowski, Jennimaria Palomaki, Olivia Redfield, Michael Collins, Ankur Parikh, Chris Alberti, Danielle Epstein, Illia Polosukhin, Jacob Devlin, Kenton Lee, Kristina Toutanova, Llion Jones, Matthew Kelcey, Ming-Wei Chang, Andrew M. Dai, Jakob Uszkoreit, Quoc Le, and Slav Petrov. 2019. Natural questions: A benchmark for question answering research. *Transactions of the Association for Computational Linguistics*, 7:452–466.

Yinhan Liu, Myle Ott, Naman Goyal, Jingfei Du, Mandar Joshi, Danqi Chen, Omer Levy, Mike Lewis, Luke Zettlemoyer, and Veselin Stoyanov. 2019. Roberta: A robustly optimized bert pretraining approach. *ArXiv preprint*, abs/1907.11692.

Todor Mihaylov, Peter Clark, Tushar Khot, and Ashish Sabharwal. 2018. Can a suit of armor conduct electricity? a new dataset for open book question answering. In *Proceedings of the 2018 Conference on Empirical Methods in Natural Language Processing*, pages 2381–2391, Brussels, Belgium. Association for Computational Linguistics.

Yixin Nie, Songhe Wang, and Mohit Bansal. 2019. Revealing the importance of semantic retrieval for machine reading at scale. In *Proceedings of the 2019 Conference on Empirical Methods in Natural Language Processing and the 9th International Joint Conference on Natural Language Processing (EMNLP-IJCNLP)*, pages 2553–2566, Hong Kong, China. Association for Computational Linguistics.

Adam Paszke, Sam Gross, Francisco Massa, Adam Lerer, James Bradbury, Gregory Chanan, Trevor Killeen, Zeming Lin, Natalia Gimelshein, Luca Antiga, Alban Desmaison, Andreas Köpf, Edward Yang, Zachary DeVito, Martin Raison, Alykhan Tejani, Sasank Chilamkurthy, Benoit Steiner, Lu Fang, Junjie Bai, and Soumith Chintala. 2019. Pytorch: An imperative style, high-performance deep learning library. In *Advances in Neural Information Processing Systems 32: Annual Conference on Neural Information Processing Systems 2019, NeurIPS 2019, December 8-14, 2019, Vancouver, BC, Canada*, pages 8024–8035.

Siva Reddy, Danqi Chen, and Christopher D. Manning. 2019. CoQA: A conversational question answering challenge. *Transactions of the Association for Computational Linguistics*, 7:249–266.

Roy Schwartz, Jesse Dodge, Noah A Smith, and Oren Etzioni. 2020. Green ai. *Communications of the ACM*, 63(12):54–63.

Yibo Sun, Duyu Tang, Nan Duan, Tao Qin, Shujie Liu, Zhao Yan, Ming Zhou, Yuanhua Lv, Wenpeng Yin, Xiaocheng Feng, et al. 2019. Joint learning of question answering and question generation. *IEEE Transactions on Knowledge and Data Engineering*, 32(5):971–982.

Ming Tu, Kevin Huang, Guangtao Wang, Jing Huang, X. He, and Bowen Zhou. 2019. Select, answer and explain: Interpretable multi-hop reading comprehension over multiple documents. *ArXiv preprint*, abs/1911.00484.

Ashish Vaswani, Noam Shazeer, Niki Parmar, Jakob Uszkoreit, Llion Jones, Aidan N. Gomez, Lukasz Kaiser, and Illia Polosukhin. 2017. Attention is all you need. In *Advances in Neural Information Processing Systems 30: Annual Conference on Neural Information Processing Systems 2017, December 4-9, 2017, Long Beach, CA, USA*, pages 5998–6008.

Thomas Wolf, Lysandre Debut, Victor Sanh, Julien Chaumond, Clement Delangue, Anthony Moi, Pierric Cistac, Tim Rault, Remi Louf, Morgan Funtowicz, Joe Davison, Sam Shleifer, Patrick von Platen, Clara Ma, Yacine Jernite, Julien Plu, Canwen Xu, Teven Le Scao, Sylvain Gugger, Mariama Drame, Quentin Lhoest, and Alexander Rush. 2020. Transformers: State-of-the-art natural language processing. In *Proceedings of the 2020 Conference on Empirical Methods in Natural Language Processing: System Demonstrations*, pages 38–45, Online. Association for Computational Linguistics.

Zhilin Yang, Peng Qi, Saizheng Zhang, Yoshua Bengio, William Cohen, Ruslan Salakhutdinov, and Christopher D. Manning. 2018. HotpotQA: A dataset for diverse, explainable multi-hop question answering. In *Proceedings of the 2018 Conference on Empirical Methods in Natural Language Processing*, pages 2369–2380, Brussels, Belgium. Association for Computational Linguistics.

Multimodal Modeling of Task-Mediated Confusion

Camille Mince
Pomona College
cima2018@mymail.pomona.edu

Skye Rhomberg
Colby College
sorhom22@colby.edu

Cecilia O. Alm **Reynold Bailey** **Alexander Ororbia**
Rochester Institute of Technology
{coagla, rjbvcs, agovcs}@rit.edu

Abstract

In order to build more human-like cognitive agents, systems capable of detecting various human emotions must be designed to respond appropriately. Confusion, the combination of an emotional and cognitive state, is under-explored. In this paper, we build upon prior work to develop models that detect confusion from three modalities: video (facial features), audio (prosodic features), and text (transcribed speech features). Our research improves the data collection process by allowing for continuous (as opposed to discrete) annotation of confusion levels. We also craft models based on recurrent neural networks (RNNs) given their ability to predict sequential data. In our experiments, we find that text and video modalities are the most important in predicting confusion while the explored audio features are relatively unimportant predictors of confusion in our data.

1 Introduction

Humans are adept at recognizing the emotions of others. They can identify whether another person has positive, negative, neutral, or more nuanced emotions by considering their facial expressions, voice, and words. To construct more human-like cognitive systems, it is important that, just as humans do, computational systems can infer emotions of the users that they interact with. Modeling confusion is relatively under-explored and can be difficult to detect computationally. Confusion can occur when someone does not know how to proceed with a task or when reconciling old beliefs with confounding information. The American Psychological Association's Dictionary of Psychology defines confusion as "a mental disturbance characterized by bewilderment, inability to think clearly or act decisively, and disorientation for time, place, and person" (Association, 2021). Potential applications of a confusion-detecting agent include task-driven dialogue chat-bots and detecting a learner's confusion in online learning environments.

We present models that leverage data across several modalities - facial expressions, speech signals with prosody, and transcribed spoken language - that not only can be used to predictively model confusion but also to extract insights with respect to which features of which modalities are clearer indicators of confusion. In this work, we answer the following research questions:

RQ1 How can we improve upon prior data collection methods to obtain a more precise multimodal dataset with confusion labels?

RQ2 How accurate of a model can we construct that classifies the degree of confusion at different points within a task?

RQ3 What facial, audio, and language features serve as good predictors of confusion (or a lack thereof)?

2 Related Work

Detecting confusion has mostly been explored in educational settings to discern students' confusion. As MOOCs (Massively Open Online Courses) have become more prevalent, researchers have focused on building models that accurately detect students' confusion. Defining a learner's confusion as "an individual state of bewilderment and uncertainty as to how to move forward," Atapattu et al. (2020) found that linguistic-only features were highly accurate predictors of confusion. Using a dataset of nearly 30,000 anonymous posts from Stanford's MOOC discussion forum, they used natural language processing resources, e.g., sentiment analysis, and a MANOVA test to extract feature importance. While Atapattu et al. (2020) focused on linguistic-only features, Shi et al. (2019) analyzed facial expressions to classify learners' confusion. They used statistical learning models that leveraged a combination of histogram of oriented gradients (HOG) features and local binary patterns (LBPs)

Proceedings of the 2022 Conference of the North American Chapter of the Association for Computational Linguistics: Human Language Technologies: Student Research Workshop, pages 188 - 194

in tandem with a prediction system, composed of a support-vector machine (SVM) and a convolutional neural network (CNN). The CNN-SVM had the best performance, indicating that facial expressions can be good predictors of confusion.

Our research differs from these past experiments in that we aim to create a multimodal model. Furthermore, we incorporate additional speech analysis to craft a more richly informed predictor of confusion. The study most closely related with our own is Kaushik et al. (2021), which experimented with a random forest classification scheme applied over discrete time intervals extracted from two-person interactions. Notably, this work considered interpretable metrics such as disfluencies (like *um*), questions, and pauses, although these were less correlated with confusion than the best-correlated facial expressions. We expand upon the study by Kaushik et al. (2021), repeating the human subject set-up of two people collaboratively solving a task over Zoom. While that study had participants label their level of confusion across a 30-second interval, our research explores continuous annotation instead of discrete spans. We expect that continuous confusion labels will enable more useful reference data for classification.

3 Methodology

3.1 Data Collection

In this IRB-approved study, subjects were recruited through email to participate in a "conversational behavior study." We did not debrief participants until after the study was complete that the true aim was to analyze confusion. Participants were paired by availability to work together through a series of three confusion-evoking tasks. We had participants complete the tasks in pairs to elicit intuitive and meaningful interactions. Our goal was to construct a dataset of multimodal text, speech audio, and video-based facial expression features with confusion-inducing tasks. Additionally, we sought to improve upon the prior research of Kaushik et al. (2021) by supporting continuous annotation of confusion levels by participants. The first and third tasks were adapted from Kaushik et al. (2021); in the first task, participants were given four minutes to find a 30 minute meeting time given two calendars which actually had no overlapping availability (see Figure 1).

The second and third tasks were logic puzzles (one was the widely known puzzle titled "Cheryl's

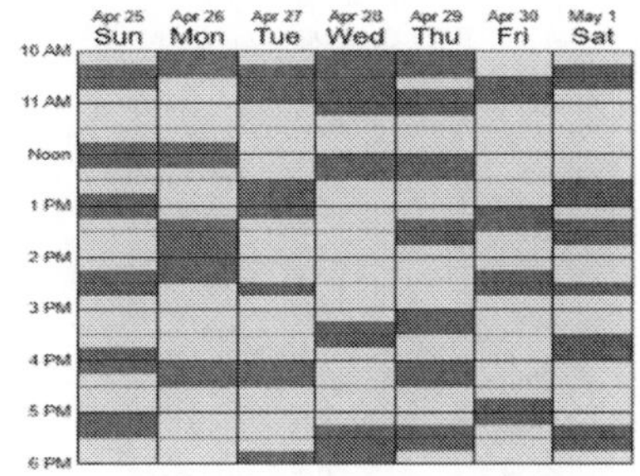

Figure 1: In one task, participants were given two calendars without overlapping availability. They were asked to find a 30 minute meeting time at which they were both available.

Figure 2: In our continuous confusion annotation, participants were instructed to use the four radio buttons to continuously annotate their confusion levels. They were instructed to change the radio button whenever they noticed a change in their own confusion level.

Birthday"). Given a list of potential birthdays and clues about which of those dates could not have been Cheryl's birthday, participants were asked to reason through hints, rule out dates, and determine Cheryl's true birthday.[1] Participants were given four to seven minutes to solve the riddles with periodic hints sent via Zoom chat. After participants completed the three tasks, they were then told that the true purpose of the experiment and asked to annotate their confusion levels throughout each task utilizing our website: the *Confuse-o-Meter*. The website displayed the playback of the participants solving the task on top of a set of radio buttons with the following labels: *Not Confused, Slightly Confused, Very Confused,* and *Extremely Confused.*

[1]https://en.wikipedia.org/wiki/Cheryl%27s_Birthday

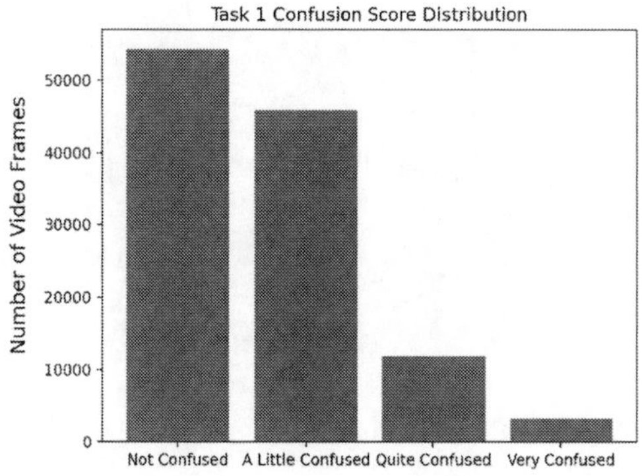

Figure 3: Our method for continuous annotation allowed for us to label each video frame with the participant's indicated confusion level. Above is the distribution of labels for each video frame. Task 1 was the least confusing task, as shown by the fact that the majority of the labels appear in the *Not Confused* state.

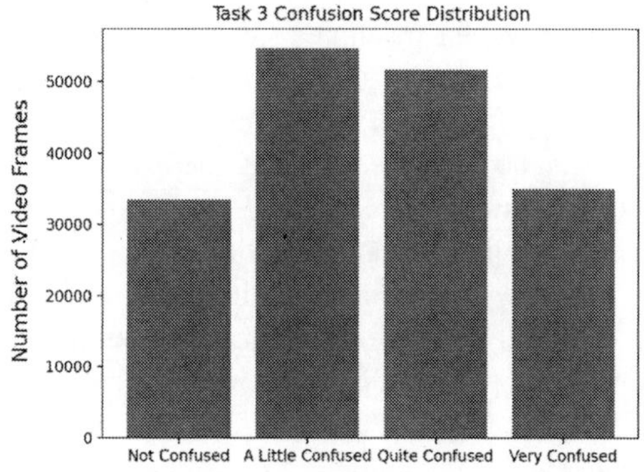

Figure 4: Task 3 was the most confusing task. Although the majority of the labels fall under *A Little Confused,* there are a considerable number of video frames labeled as *Quite Confused* and *Very Confused.*

As seen in Figure 2, participants were instructed to click on the appropriate radio button whenever they noticed a change in their confusion level. From the website, we obtained data in the following form: [(timestamp of change, new confusion label), (timestamp of next change, new confusion label),. . .]. We used this encoding to produce confusion labels for every time-step of data. This approach allowed us to generate a dataset in which every time-step of data was accurately labeled with the participant's confusion level.

Some tasks were harder than others. We intended for the tasks to progress in difficulty so that we could collect ample *Not Confused* and *Confused* data. The distribution of the participants' confusion ratings in the first and last task are shown in Figures 3 and 4, respectively. It is clear that the participants found the first task to be less confusing, with the majority of the labels being in the *Not Confused* state. A higher proportion of the labels fall in the *Quite Confused* and *Very Confused* categories for tasks 2 and 3.

3.2 Feature Extraction

The *OpenFace* (Baltrušaitis et al., 2015, 2018) software package was used to extract 17 different Ekman and Friesen (1976) facial action units (FACs) defined by per video frame. Audeering's *openSMILE* (Schuller et al., 2009; Eyben et al., 2010) toolkit was used to extract 34 different audio features, including pitch, intensity, speech rate, and MFCCs per frame. Finally, Amazon Transcribe was used to transcribe speech and *deep-disfluency* Hough and Schlangen (April, 2017) was used to extract disfluent words in the form of transcribed text. Similar to Kaushik et al. (2021), disfluencies like edits, repair, reparandum, and interregnum word tokens were further identified.

Table 1: Text Encoding Feature Descriptions

Feature	Type	Description
$is\_question$	bool	token is part of question
is_pause	bool	token is $\geq 0.398s$ pause within utterance
$curr\_sentence\_length$	int	number of words in current sentence
$speech\_rate$	float	words/min. of current sentence
is_edit_word $is\_reparandum$ $is\_interregnum$ is_repair	bool	generated by Deep Disfluency

Using the output of Amazon Transcribe, each participant's text was divided into a sequential list of tokens, where a token could be a spoken word or a period of silence. For each token, we extracted 8 features, as shown in Table 1.

Since Amazon Transcribe's output was tagged with timestamps, we were able to align the text, audio, and video features. With missing data eliminated or smoothed out by inserting the averages of data in nearby frames, the audio and visual feature vectors for each word token were then taken to be the averages of all the frames within the token's given time-span. Participant confusion labels over each time-span were finally collapsed to the most-occurring label for each word/token. Participant confusion labels were "smeared" (or duplicated) over frames according to their time-step, such that each frame was associated with the confusion label that the participant had selected at that time marker.

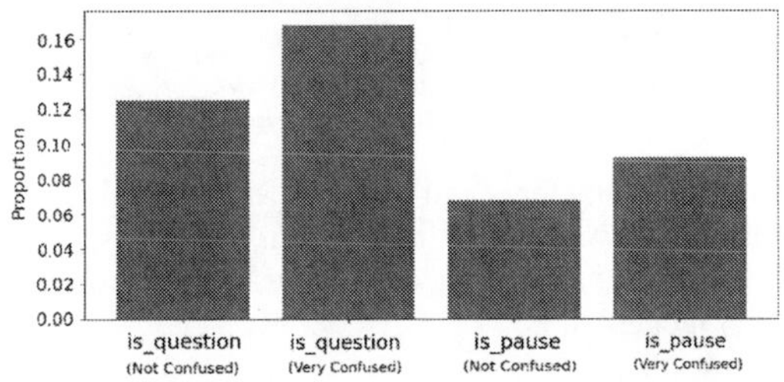

Figure 5: **Text Features:** The y-axis is the proportion of tokens that were: (a) a part of a spoken question, or (b) a distinct pause in the participant's speech. Observe that a higher proportion of tokens are part of a question or a pause when the participant is highly confused.

3.3 Exploration of Hidden Markov Models

We explored Hidden Markov Models (HMMs) because of their interpretability and applicability to sequential data. The HMM relies on the Markov assumption, which means that the state of the system at time step i is only dependent on the state of the system at time step $i-1$. Experimenting with different temporal increments based on video frames or word tokens, our model was unable to accurately predict confusion. This left us with a trade-off: either use all our frame-by-frame data and have the time increment be so small that the HMM yields a diagonal-heavy transition matrix or have longer increments but make our dataset prohibitively small by averaging over longer intervals.

3.4 The Neural Modeling Approach

We designed recurrent neural networks (RNNs) given their ability to extract temporal dependencies inherent to sequences (Schäfer and Zimmermann, 2006; Ororbia II et al., 2017). In essence, RNNs are stateful ANNs that "remember" information in prior time-steps $< t$ when processing data at t.

While taking a neural engineering approach offers a great deal of flexibility in terms of the type of architecture that one might design to process streams of different modalities (meaning there are many possible model designs we could craft), in this work, we take a simple approach. For each data modality, we crafted one RNN modality-processing model that specifically implements $p(y_t|\mathbf{x}^m_0, \mathbf{x}^m_1, ..., \mathbf{x}^m_t; \Theta_m) = f^m(\mathbf{x}^m_t; \Theta_m)$ where y_t is the (integer) confusion label[2] at time t and $\mathbf{x}_t \in \mathcal{R}^{O\times 1}$ is the specific feature vector (with O feature values) for modality m, where $m = \{\text{vis, aud, txt}\}$ (*vis* means visual, *aud* means audio, and *txt* means text/symbols) and Θ_m contains all of the learnable weight parameters. Concretely, any modality-processing RNN with H hidden neurons is specified by the dynamics:

$$\mathbf{h}_t = \phi_h(\mathbf{W}^m \cdot \mathbf{x}^m_t + \mathbf{V}^m \cdot \mathbf{h}_{t-1} + \mathbf{b}^m) \quad (1)$$

$$\hat{\mathbf{y}}_t = \phi_o(\mathbf{U}^m \cdot \mathbf{h}_t + \mathbf{c}^m) \quad (2)$$

where $\phi(v) = \max(0, v)$ is the linear rectifier used for the hidden layer activation function, $\phi(\mathbf{o}) = \exp(\mathbf{o})/\sum_j \exp(\mathbf{o})[j]$ is the softmax used for the output layer, $\cdot$ denotes matrix-vector multiplication, and $\odot$ denotes the Hadamard product.

$\mathbf{W}^m \in \mathcal{R}^{H\times O}$ is the input-to-hidden weight matrix, $\mathbf{V}^m \in \mathcal{R}^{H\times H}$ is the recurrent weight matrix, and $\mathbf{U}^m \in \mathcal{R}^{O\times H}$ is the output/feature emission matrix while $\mathbf{b}^m \in \mathcal{R}^{H\times 1}$ and $\mathbf{c}^m \in \mathcal{R}^{O\times 1}$ are bias vectors. The RNN weight parameters $\Theta_m = \{\mathbf{W}^m, \mathbf{V}^m, \mathbf{U}^m, \mathbf{b}^m, \mathbf{c}^m\}$ are initialized using a scaled, centered Gaussian distribution and parameters are fit data using backpropagation through time to calculate the gradients of the cost function $\mathcal{L}(\hat{\mathbf{y}}_t, \mathbf{y}_t) = \sum_{t=1}^{T} -\sum_j (\mathbf{y}_t \odot \log(\hat{\mathbf{y}}_t))[j]$. The resulting $\frac{\partial \mathcal{L}(\hat{\mathbf{y}}_t, \mathbf{y}_t)}{\partial \Theta^m}$ (the partial derivatives) is used to adjust Θ using stochastic gradient descent based on the Adam update rule (Kingma and Ba, 2014).

Given the three modality-processing RNNs we trained, i.e., $f^{vis}(\mathbf{x}^{vis}_t, \Theta_{vis})$, $f^{aud}(\mathbf{x}^{aud}_t, \Theta_{aud})$, $f^{txt}(\mathbf{x}^{txt}_t, \Theta_{txt})$, final label predictions were made using a late-fusion aggregation scheme (Snoek et al., 2005). In other words, we computed the final predicted label y_t as follows: $y_t = \arg\max(\alpha_{vis}\mathbf{y}^{vis}_t + \alpha_{aud}\mathbf{y}^{aud}_t + \alpha_{txt}\mathbf{y}^{txt}_t)$, which returns the index of class within the average of the three modal probability distributions. Importance weights α_{vis}, α_{aud}, and α_{txt} were set to 1.0, which means we assume equal weight per modality.

4 Results

4.1 Recurrent Neural Modeling Results

Our RNN modality-processing system was trained only on single modalities, with the final predicted

[2]We further encode this as a one-of-C binary vector $\mathbf{y}_t \in \mathcal{R}^{C\times 1}$, where C is the number of confusion levels/classes.

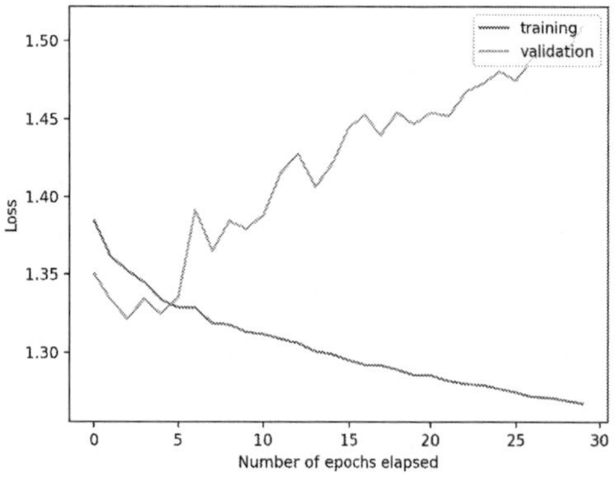

Figure 6: Training and validation loss (for the video modality) of the RNN system. It is evident that after 5 epochs, the model begins to severely overfit the training data, as the training loss continues to decrease while the validation loss begins to increase.

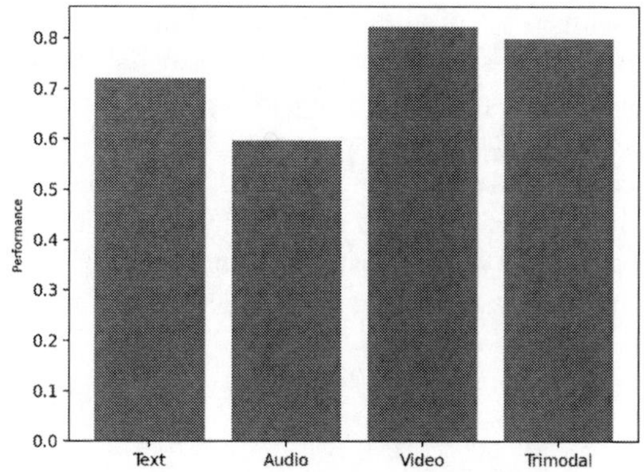

Figure 7: Unimodal and trimodal RNN model performance: the video-only model performs the best, followed by the trimodal late-fusion, text-only, and audio-only models.

label y_t aggregated through the late-fusion scheme described above. We had 20 participants and held out one randomly selected female and male participant to validate model performance. In Figure 6, we present training and validation loss curves (total loss value plotted against epoch of training) for the model trained on video features only. This model performed better than the unimodal text and audio models, as well as the late-fusion trimodal model.

An RNN trained on only video features was able to achieve the lowest loss and best accuracy performance, suggesting video data conveyed the most meaningful knowledge about the confusion state. However, this model begins to overfit the training data around epoch 5 (Figure 6), at which point the training loss continues to decrease while the validation loss begins to increase. Changing parameters like the number of hidden neurons did not reduce the model overfitting though future work will investigate regularization schemes. Given our small dataset, the model appears to struggle to generalize to the two unseen participants. When we early-stop the training after 5 epochs to combat overfitting, we obtain the validation accuracy values for each uni-modal model shown in Figure 7.

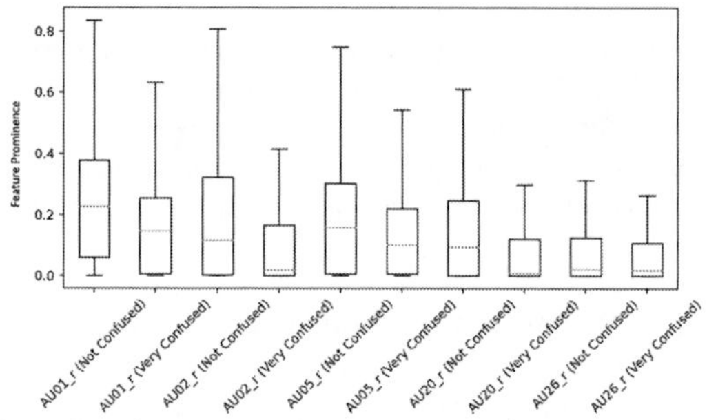

Figure 8: Box plots for select video features where the y-axis is the facial action unit reading produced by OpenFace: a 0-1 scale quantifies how heavily a facial action unit is being produced by a participant.

AU01	Inner brow raiser
AU02	Outer brow raiser
AU05	Upper lid raiser
AU20	Lip stretcher
AU26	Jaw drop

Table 2: The facial action units displayed in Figure 8.

4.2 Modality-Based Data Analysis

To inspect which features were possible predictors of confusion, we created box plots and bar charts to examine the distribution of feature values from participants while in the *Not Confused* state versus the *Very Confused State*. The features examined in this analysis were selected based on which had the highest difference in median value between the *Not Confused* and *Very Confused* states. In Figure 5, observe that some results make sense: participants are more likely to pause and ask questions when they are very confused versus when they are not confused at all. The facial action units are shown in Figure 8 and in Table 2. Intuitively, it makes sense that these facial action units are tied to confusion.

Some analysis results, in contrast, are more surprising: we found nearly no difference between the distributions of the audio features extracted in the *Not Confused* versus the *Very Confused* states. This suggests that prosodic features are potentially less effective predictors of confusion in this study.

5 Discussion

Given the results of the previous section, we discuss the contributions of our work driven by our initially presented questions. Specifically, we make the following contributions which we next state as answers to our original research questions:

RQ 1: The annotation method used by Kaushik et al. (2021) involved participants marking their confusion level for every 30-second block. We improved upon this approach by implementing the *Confuse-o-Meter* website, which allowed participants to continuously annotate their confusion levels. This method for annotation was found to provide a richer dataset in which we were able to obtain confusion labels for every time-step of data.

RQ 2: The RNN results showed that we were able to build a model that could relatively accurately classify confusion in the test set participants.

RQ 3: There were inconclusive results on which facial, audio, and language features were the best predictors of confusion because different methods yielded conflicting results. However, based on our limited results, we reason that the following features may be linked with confusion: text disfluencies, pauses, questions, AU01 (inner brow raiser), AU02 (outer brow raiser), AU05 (upper lid raiser), AU17 (lid tighten), AU20 (lip stretcher), AU23 (lip tighten), and AU26 (jaw drop).

The main limitation of our work is the size of the collected dataset – with only 20 participants, it makes sense that our models, particularly the highly nonlinear RNN system, overfit to the training samples. For any choice of two participants, it is unlikely that a model trained on 18 other participants would generalize to the test participants since confusion is a complicated emotion and not all humans display it the same way. It would take a larger dataset in order to generalize to the broader population. Additionally, our models predicted the *Not Confused* states more often than the *Confused* states. The distribution of our confusion dataset is similarly unbalanced, as seen in Figure 9.

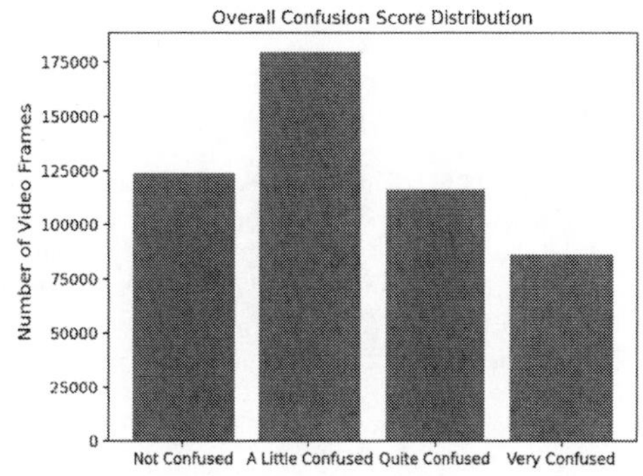

Figure 9: The confusion label distribution indicates that participants generally spent more time in the not confused states as opposed to the confused states.

6 Conclusions

In this study, our goal was to build a model that was capable of accurately predicting confusion and to understand which text, audio, and video features were accurate predictors of confusion. Given that the RNN has low interpretability, we utilized statistical methods to accomplish the latter half of this goal. Furthermore, we improved upon previous methods of data collection to allow for continuous annotation of confusion states. This design choice provided us with a more precise multimodal dataset with rich confusion reference labels across time. To computationally model the predictive label distributions and perform confusion classification, we constructed a computational model based on recurrent neural networks (RNNs), which lack interpretability but proved to be reasonably accurate even with our limited data. Future work will include generalizing our RNN computational model further to better handle the different modalities (in an intermediate modality fusion scheme as in Ororbia et al. (2019)) found within our dataset, as opposed to our current method of taking the (late-fusion) weighted consensus of three separately trained modality-processing RNNs. In addition, another future next step would be to repeat our study to collect a larger dataset that better represents the general population. This may also reduce the overfitting observed in our predictive confusion models. Additional research could investigate dimensionality reduction techniques and alternative forms of statistical analysis to explore measured features in our data.

Acknowledgements

This material is based upon work supported by the National Science Foundation under Award No. IIS-1851591 and DGE-2125362. Any opinions, findings, and conclusions or recommendations expressed in this material are those of the author(s) and do not necessarily reflect the views of the National Science Foundation.

References

American Psychology Association. 2021. Confusion. https://dictionary.apa.org/confusion.

Thushari Atapattu, Katrina Falkner, Menasha Thilakaratne, Lavendini Sivaneasharajah, and Rangana Jayashanka. 2020. What do linguistic expressions tell us about learners' confusion? a domain-independent analysis in moocs. *IEEE Transactions on Learning Technologies*, 13(4):878–888.

Tadas Baltrušaitis, Marwa Mahmoud, and Peter Robinson. 2015. Cross-dataset learning and person-specific normalisation for automatic action unit detection. In *Facial Expression Recognition and Analysis Challenge, IEEE International Conference on Automatic Face and Gesture Recognition.*

Tadas Baltrušaitis, Amir Zadeh, Yao Chong Lim, , and Louis-Philippe Morency. 2018. Openface 2.0: Facial behavior analysis toolkit. In *IEEE International Conference on Automatic Face and Gesture Recognition.*

Paul Ekman and Wallace V. Friesen. 1976. Measuring facial movement. *Environmental Psychology and Nonverbal Behavior*, 1(1):56–75.

Florian Eyben, Martin Wöllmer, and Björn Schuller. 2010. opensmile – the munich versatile and fast open-source audio feature extractor. In *MM'10 - Proceedings of the ACM Multimedia 2010 International Conference*, pages 1459–1462.

Julian Hough and David Schlangen. April, 2017. Joint, incremental disfluency detection and utterance segmentation from speech. In *EACL 2017*, Valencia, Spain.

Nikhil Kaushik, Reynold J. Bailey, Alexander G. Ororbia, and Cecilia O. Alm. 2021. Elicitation of confusion in online conversational tasks. In *Interspeech 2021, 22nd Annual Conference of the International Speech Communication Association*, Brno, Czech Republic.

Diederik P Kingma and Jimmy Ba. 2014. Adam: A method for stochastic optimization. *arXiv preprint arXiv:1412.6980.*

Alexander Ororbia, Ankur Mali, Matthew Kelly, and David Reitter. 2019. Like a baby: Visually situated neural language acquisition. In *Proceedings of the 57th Annual Meeting of the Association for Computational Linguistics*, pages 5127–5136.

Alexander G Ororbia II, Tomas Mikolov, and David Reitter. 2017. Learning simpler language models with the differential state framework. *Neural computation*, 29(12):3327–3352.

Anton Maximilian Schäfer and Hans Georg Zimmermann. 2006. Recurrent neural networks are universal approximators. In *International Conference on Artificial Neural Networks*, pages 632–640. Springer.

Björn Schuller, S. Steidl, and Anton Batliner. 2009. The interspeech 2009 emotion challenge. In *Interspeech 2009, 10th Annual Conference of the International Speech Communication Association*, Brighton, UK.

Zheng Shi, Ya Zhang, Cunling Bian, and Weigang Lu. 2019. Automatic academic confusion recognition in online learning based on facial expressions. In *2019 14th International Conference on Computer Science Education (ICCSE)*, pages 528–532.

Cees GM Snoek, Marcel Worring, and Arnold WM Smeulders. 2005. Early versus late fusion in semantic video analysis. In *Proceedings of the 13th annual ACM international conference on Multimedia*, pages 399–402.

Probe-Less Probing of BERT's Layer-Wise Linguistic Knowledge with Masked Word Prediction

Tatsuya Aoyama
Georgetown University
ta571@georgetown.edu

Nathan Schneider
Georgetown University
nathan.schneider@georgetown.edu

Abstract

The current study quantitatively (and qualitatively for an illustrative purpose) analyzes BERT's layer-wise masked word prediction on an English corpus, and finds that (1) the layer-wise localization of linguistic knowledge primarily shown in probing studies is replicated in a behavior-based design and (2) that syntactic and semantic information is encoded at different layers for words of different syntactic categories. Hypothesizing that the above results are correlated with the number of likely potential candidates of the masked word prediction, we also investigate how the results differ for tokens within multiword expressions.

1 Introduction

The attention mechanism of Transformers (Vaswani et al., 2017) has enabled language models (LMs) to effectively incorporate contextual information into word representation. One such model, BERT (Devlin et al., 2019), has been shown particularly useful in a wide range of downstream tasks, outperforming the state-of-the-art benchmarks in many cases. However, it is yet to be clear what exactly such LMs learn, and what information is encoded in their contextual word representations (CWRs). For this reason, much work has been devoted to answering these questions, often referred to as BERTology (see Rogers et al., 2020 for a comprehensive review).

Among such studies, of particular interest is the localization of linguistic knowledge. As BERT consists of multiple layers (12 layers for `bert-base` and 24 layers for `bert-large`), it is crucial to understand what information is encoded in each layer, and how it differs from one another. However, the methodologies employed in such studies differ substantially from each other (§2): some directly utilize the internal structure of such models by training probing classifiers, while others study the behaviors of such models at inference time. Structure-based probes have often been successful at assigning particular domains of linguistic knowledge to local regions, yet the reliance on probing classifiers (and the introduction of extra parameters) makes it unclear if such linguistic knowledge is just an artifact of the classifier or is truly encoded in the model. Behavior-based probes do not rely on external classifiers, but tend to focus on qualitative analyses of the outputs from the final layer, whereas quantitative analysis of layer-wise output remains understudied in the behavioral paradigm.

In this study, we explore layer localization with behavioral probing. Specifically, we mask out tokens one at a time and check whether BERT predicts the same word, another word with the same part of speech, or neither (3). By using different layers for the prediction, we can determine which parts of the network correspond to higher or lower rates of congruent predictions. Along with generally confirming some of the main observations of the structure-based probing studies, we find considerable variation by part of speech and some effect of multiword expression status, and discuss possible interpretations of these findings (§4).

2 Previous Work

2.1 Structure-Based

Since the advent of BERT (Devlin et al., 2019), much work has been devoted to revealing what linguistic knowledge it has. Among such studies, Tenney et al. (2019a) observed that one line of work is behavior-based, while the other directly investigates the structure of the CWRs. Whereas the former focuses on the qualitative error analyses of BERT's predictions on certain controlled tasks, the latter directly probes the internal structure of the model. Building on the latter line of the work, Tenney et al. (2019a) apply a probing method called *edge probing* (Tenney et al., 2019b), which allow them to infer what sentence-level in-

Proceedings of the 2022 Conference of the North American Chapter of the Association for Computational Linguistics: Human Language Technologies: Student Research Workshop, pages 195 - 201

formation BERT encodes based on a given span by restricting the input to the probing classifier. They find that BERT's layer-wise linguistic knowledge resembles classical NLP pipelines; in other words, lower layers are more responsible for syntactic knowledge and higher layers for semantic knowledge, although syntactic knowledge is more localizable at lower layers whereas semantic knowledge is rather spread across the layers.

Jawahar et al. (2019) make similar observations, based on a suite of probing tasks developed by Conneau et al. (2018). They find that the lowest layer is most successful at phrase detection, and the performance degrades until layer 8, beyond which it reaches a plateau. In another set of experiments, they find that lower, middle, and higher layers are responsible for surface, syntactic, and semantic information, respectively. Corroborating this result, Hewitt and Manning (2019) employ a novel method called a structural probe to retrieve a syntactic tree from contextualized word embeddings, and find that the representation from middle layers have better performance in the tree retrieval task.

With an increasing number of studies employing probing classifiers, in their comprehensive review of BERTology, Rogers et al. (2020) raise a warning that such probing may not provide us with a full picture of what BERT is: "If a more complex probe recovers more information, to what extent are we still relying on the original model?" Indeed, while some studies use a linear classifier as a probe to limit the number of newly introduced parameters (e.g., part of Liu et al., 2019), others use more complex models, such as multi-layer perceptron (MLP), obscuring the source of success on probing tasks. Hewitt and Liang (2019) suggested a metric called *selectivity* to measure how well a probe reflects the actual linguistic knowledge encoded in the CWRs in question, as opposed to learning the task independently of such CWRs.

2.2 Behavior-Based

Complementing such limitation of probing studies, more recent works have attempted to avoid introducing new parameters through creative probing methodologies, such as contextual word embedding (CWE) similarity ranking (Gessler and Schneider, 2021), and direct probe (Zhou and Srikumar, 2021).

In fact, the other line of work, which Tenney et al. (2019a) described as behavior-based, which usually relies on qualitative (error) analyses of BERT's predictions on controlled tasks, is parameter-free and utilizes BERT's behaviors at inference time, and Rogers et al. (2020) also argue for the importance of this line of work. Such work includes investigation of semantic knowledge (Ettinger, 2020; Marvin and Linzen, 2018) and syntactic knowledge (Goldberg, 2019; Poliak et al., 2018).

For example, analyzing BERT's masked word prediction output on controlled tasks developed in psycholinguistic studies, Ettinger (2020) finds that BERT struggles with common sense and pragmatics, role-based event prediction, and negation. Goldberg (2019) also studies BERT's masked word prediction outputs on both naturally occurring sentences and manually crafted stimuli, finding that BERT is sensitive to subject-verb agreement.

While these studies have revealed a great deal about BERT's linguistic knowledge, they have primarily focused on (1) content words, such as verbs and nouns, and (2) the output from the final layer. Although the data used in the current study are not manually crafted or controlled in any way similar to the above-mentioned studies, it attempts to add to the existing body of literature by (1) extending the analyses to all syntactic categories and (2) analyzing how BERT's predictions differ across layers. In light of all this, we ask the following questions:

1. Can the layer-wise linguistic knowledge found in structure studies be replicated with a behavior-based approach, namely, layer-wise masked word prediction analyses (§4.1.1)?
2. Do the results vary by syntactic category (§4.1.2)?

3 Experimental Setup

We used STREUSLE 4.4 (Schneider et al., 2018; Schneider and Smith, 2015), a corpus of web reviews written in English. This corpus contains 723 documents, 3,813 sentences, and 55,590 tokens in total with rich annotation of various syntactic and lexical-semantic information (e.g., annotation of 3,013 strong multiword expressions). The BERT's prediction data were prepared in the following way:

1. For each sentence, create n variants, where n is the number of tokens in the sentence, by replacing one token by [MASK] token.
2. For each variant (where one word is repalced with [MASK] in step 1) of each sentence, run vanilla BERT to generate a prediction from each layer $\ell \in L$.
3. For each of the n variants of each sentence,

where [MASK] is now replaced by a predicted token in step 2, POS-tag the predicted token to identify its syntactic category.

For the BERT model, we use `bert-base-uncased` because `bert-base` and `bert-large` have similar distributions of layers, which Rogers et al. (2020) call "stretch effect", although they do sometimes exhibit heterogeneous behaviors, such as responses to perturbation in word prediction (Ettinger, 2020). The model was retrieved from the PyTorch implementation of BERT by `huggingface` (Wolf et al., 2020).

For POS, the tag set of 17 POSs from Universal Dependencies (UD) v2 (Nivre et al., 2020) was used, and Stanza (Qi et al., 2020) was used for the automatic tagging of predicted tokens.

The above experiment resulted in the prediction of, and the tagging of, $L \times S \times N = 722,670$ masked tokens, where L, S, and N are the number of layers, the number of sentences, and the (mean) length of the sentences, respectively. In addition to analyzing the descriptive statistics, in order to quantify the relative contribution of each layer to POS match and word match, differential scores at each task (POS match or word match) for each layer $\Delta_T^{(\ell)}$ were obtained by computing the incremental gain from the previous layer (Equation 3 of Tenney et al., 2019a):

$$\Delta_T^{(\ell)} = Score_T^{(\ell)} - Score_T^{(\ell-1)} \quad (1)$$

As a summary statistic of these scores, (pseudo) expectation of differential scores (Equation 4 of Tenney et al., 2019a) was also calculated:

$$\bar{E}_\Delta[\ell] = \frac{\sum_{\ell=1}^{L} l \cdot \Delta_T^{(\ell)}}{\sum_{\ell=1}^{L} \Delta_T^{(\ell)}} \quad (2)$$

This is an "expected layer", at which the gain scores are centered around. If the differential scores were uniformly distributed, the expected layer would simply be the middle layer, which is layer 6. If the contribution of lower layers were higher (i.e., differential scores were higher at lower layers), then the expected layer would be lower than 6, and vice versa.

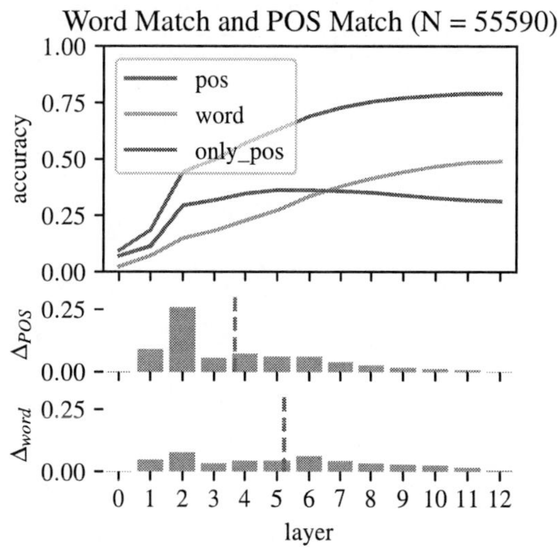

Figure 1: Layer-wise Accuracy of POS Match, Word Match, and POS Match without Word Match

4 Results

4.1 Quantitative Results

4.1.1 Overall

The top graph in Figure 1 illustrates the accuracy score[1] of POS match, word match, and POS match without word match (i.e., the predicted word is not the same as the original word, but is the same POS). Notably, POS match tends to increase at lower layers and approaches plateau towards the middle to high layers, whereas word match tends to increase linearly from lower to higher layers. Consequently, the proportion of the tokens with only POS match peaks at around layers 5 and 6 and starts declining beyond that point.

The middle and bottom graphs in Figure 1 illustrate the differential scores of POS match and word match, respectively. The vertical red dotted lines represent the expected layer defined in §3. The differential scores for POS match are clearly centered around lower layers followed by a sharp decline beyond middle layer, with the expected layer of 3.68. In contrast, the differential scores for word match are relatively more uniformly distributed across layers, and the expected layer is 5.22. This supports the findings from previous work that syntactic knowledge is more localizable at lower to middle

[1] Accuracy was chosen here for direct comparability; the proportion of the top predictions that are of the same POS as the original token, the proportion of the top predictions that are of the same word as the original token, and the proportion of the top predictions that are of the same POS but different word as the original token.

		N	POS	POS_M	word	$word_M$
open	ADJ	3169	4.04	4.24	6.45	6.35
	ADV	3080	3.42	3.76	5.74	5.30
	INTJ	108	3.48	9.33	7.13	8.75
	NOUN	7265	3.98	4.48	7.53	6.99
	PROPN	1406	**6.68**	6.11	**8.05**	7.88
	VERB	5328	3.96	3.68	6.73	6.38
closed	ADP	3368	3.16	3.52	5.01	5.18
	AUX	2950	3.10	4.43	5.14	5.08
	CCONJ	1803	5.48	5.32	5.88	4.74
	DET	3525	2.16	2.54	3.11	3.43
	NUM	555	5.70	6.81	6.73	7.23
	PART	1314	<u>1.80</u>	<u>1.31</u>	<u>2.08</u>	<u>1.40</u>
	PRON	5264	3.91	4.61	6.76	5.96
	SCONJ	808	5.05	4.45	5.71	5.45

Table 1: Expected Layer by UPOS. POS_M and $word_M$ stand for POS_{MWE} and $word_{MWE}$, respectively.

layers (Tenney et al., 2019a; Liu et al., 2019) and that semantic knowledge is spread across layers (Tenney et al., 2019a).

4.1.2 By Syntactic Category

Table 1 summarizes the expected layers for POS match and word match for all tokens, as well as for tokens that are part of multiword expressions (MWEs), by UPOS.[2] In this section, we will focus on the former. First, in general, the expected layers for POS match and word match differ substantially by syntactic category. Whereas lower layers contribute much more for POS match for PART ($\bar{E}_\Delta[\ell] = 1.80$), middle to higher layers contribute more for POS match for PROPN ($\bar{E}_\Delta[\ell] = 6.68$). A similar observation is made for word match: on the one hand, lower layers contribute more for PART($\bar{E}_\Delta[\ell] = 2.08$), and higher layers contribute more for PROPN ($\bar{E}_\Delta[\ell] = 8.05$) on the other hand.

Although no straightforward generalizations can be made, for word match, we observe a tendency that expected layers tend to be higher when the original tokens are in open class, such as PROPN ($\bar{E}_\Delta[\ell] = 8.05$) and NOUN ($\bar{E}_\Delta[\ell] = 7.53$), whereas they tend to be lower when the original tokens are in closed class, such as PART ($\bar{E}_\Delta[\ell] = 2.08$) and DET ($\bar{E}_\Delta[\ell] = 3.11$).[3] This seems to suggest that higher layers tend to contribute more to word match for tokens in syntactic categories with more word types (i.e., open class), and that lower layers tend to contribute more for tokens in syntactic categories with fewer word types (i.e., closed class).

[2] Miscellaneous tags, i.e. PUNCT, SYM, and X, are excluded from the analysis.

[3] Open and closed classes are based on the classification by UD project's (Nivre et al., 2020) website: `https://universaldependencies.org/u/pos/index.html`

However, notable exceptions from closed class include NUM ($\bar{E}_\Delta[\ell] = 6.73$) and PRON ($\bar{E}_\Delta[\ell] = 6.76$). The former belongs to closed class because its atomic elements are finite (i.e., 0-9); however, with the infinite number of combinations of such elements, this class may be behaving similarly to open class. This is clearly not the case for the latter—PRON has a finite number of word types, which are fewer than the ones in open class. One plausible explanation is that identifying a correct pronoun requires a resolution of subject-verb agreement, which is shown to be handled well by BERT (Goldberg, 2019; van Schijndel et al., 2019) especially at layers 8 and 9 (Jawahar et al., 2019). However, upon closer examination, expected layers for personal pronouns in accusative case ($\bar{E}_\Delta[\ell] = 8.19$) or those in (in)direct object positions ($\bar{E}_\Delta[\ell] = 8.08$) are found to be much higher than those in nominative case ($\bar{E}_\Delta[\ell] = 6.34$) or in subject positions ($\bar{E}_\Delta[\ell] = 6.29$), although the latter should benefit from the subject-verb agreement resolution at higher layers. Given this observation, it may be the case that personal pronouns in accusative case or (in)direct object positions are more likely to necessitate long-distance coreference resolution in English, and such long-distance dependencies are shown to be handled better at higher layers (Jawahar et al., 2019). However, this hypothesis remains inconclusive (see §4.2 for more discussion).

4.1.3 Multiword Expressions

As an additional analysis of the effect of the number of potential candidates on expected layer, we calculate the expected layer only for tokens that are part of MWEs, based on the annotation of strong MWE in STREUSLE (Schneider et al., 2018; Schneider and Smith, 2015). Although the strong MWEs in STREUSLE consist of heterogeneous sets of expressions, such as idioms, light verb constructions, and noun compounds, we assume that, overall, this linguistic environment is more constrained and has fewer potential candidates for masked word prediction.

The POS_M and $word_M$ columns in Table 1 represent the expected layers of POS match and word match only for the tokens that are part of MWEs, respectively. The expected layers are colored in red if they are higher for MWEs than for all tokens, and in blue if they are lower for MWEs than for all tokens. In general, on the one hand, for word match, they are lower for MWEs than for all tokens, which is congruent with the hypothesis from

ℓ	**prediction**
3	*to, a, him, me, them, her, the, us, one, people*
6	*him, me, her, them, us, to, people, everyone, it, you*
12	*us, her, me, we, them, everyone, our, him, it, stephanie*

Context: Stephanie's knowledge of the market and properties in our price range, made [MASK] (original: us) feel secure in our decision to buy when we did. (*reviews-341397-0002*)

Table 2: Selected Example 1 from STREUSLE

ℓ	**prediction**
3	*own, new, prison, personal, old, back, hospital, private, usual, current*
6	*own, private, bedroom, parking, damn, front, hotel, hospital, office, kitchen*
12	*car, garage, front, apartment, bedroom, office, cell, back, truck, elevator*

Context: they fixed my [MASK] (original: garage) doors in literally less than an hour. (*reviews-341397-0002*)

Table 3: Selected Example 2 from STREUSLE

§4.1.2 that lower layers contribute more when the number of potential candidates is relatively small. On the other hand, however, the expected layers for POS match tend to be higher for MWEs than for all tokens. The precise reason why this was the case is left for future work; however, we provide a potential account for these observations below.

One possible explanation for the higher expected layers of POS match is that semantic information plays an important role in predicting certain sequences of POSs observed in MWEs. For example, the common occurrences of noun compounds could be a contributing factor to the higher expected layer for POS match only for NOUNs that are part of MWE ($\bar{E}_\Delta[\ell] = 4.48$) compared to that of all NOUNs ($\bar{E}_\Delta[\ell] = 3.98$). Given that the meaning of the second token (the head of the compound) is crucial in detecting its (dis)preference on forming a compound, it may require more semantic information for BERT to correctly identify that the first token is NOUN rather than ADJ, resulting in a higher expected layer. Indeed, for all NOUNs that are part of MWE, the most common incorrect prediction was ADJ at all layers from layer 2 through 12, which was not the case for NOUNs that are not part of MWE (see §4.2 for an example).

4.2 Qualitative Results

In this section, we present a set of selected examples from the STREUSLE corpus to illustrate the observations made in §4.1.

Table 2 illustrates the identification of a personal pronoun at each layer of BERT (only showing layers 3, 6, and 9). From lower to higher layers, it is clear that the ranking of the correct pronoun *us* is steadily promoted. In fact, it is not until layer 11 that the correct pronoun *us* receives the highest prediction probability. In §4.1.2, one hypothesis that can potentially account for the higher expected layer of PRON (personal pronouns in object positions or in accusative case in particular) was the long-distance dependency. In Table 2, pronouns *our* and *we* are readily available in relatively close proximity, but the correct pronoun *us* is not identified until layer 11. This seems to suggest that pronouns that are ACC-marked or in object positions pose unique challenges not explicable only by the distance of the dependency.

Table 3 illustrates BERT's predictions of the first token of a noun compound *garage doors*. As discussed in §4.1.3, at layer 3, many of the predictions are generic adjectives (e.g., *own, new, old, private, usual, current*), although the meaning of the word *door* seems to be captured to some extent, as we can see from some of the predictions (e.g., *prison, back, hospital*). At layer 6, such prediction of nouns that are specific to the meaning of the word *door* becomes more dominant. This is even more so at layer 12, where such nouns occupy most of the predictions despite the presence of a cue, *my*, which strongly collocates with *own*. This supports our observation that, for some syntactic categories including NOUN, MWE's production of certain sequences of POSs necessitates more semantic information to restore the POS of the original word, resulting in a higher expected layer.

5 Conclusion

In this study, we set out to investigate if (1) the layer-wise linguistic knowledge found in structure studies can be replicated with a behavior-based design and if (2) the results vary by syntactic category. By analyzing BERT's layer-wise masked word prediction, we have shown that the localization of linguistic knowledge found in various probing studies was indeed replicated; more specifically, syntactic knowledge was encoded primarily in lower layers, whereas semantic knowledge was spread across the 12 layers.

We also observed that the contribution of particular layers on syntactic and semantic information varied substantially, depending on the syntactic category (i.e., UPOS) and on the syntactic class (i.e., open vs. closed class) more generally, of the original token. Hypothesizing that the number of potential candidates is one of the contributing factors to this difference, we showed that, in general, the expected layers were higher for POS match and lower for word match for the tokens that are part of MWEs (a supposedly more constrained environment).

Our contribution is twofold. First, by leveraging BERT's layer-wise outputs, we confirmed the previous studies without relying on external probing classifiers or introducing extra parameters that can potentially obfuscate the locus of the observed linguistic knowledge (i.e., language model vs. probing classifier). Second, by extending the analyses to all open and closed class categories rather than limiting the scope to popular content-words, such as verb, noun, and adjective, we show that the encoding of syntactic and semantic knowledge about words of different UPOS varies substantially.

Lastly, we acknowledge that this study has a few limitations. First, the layer-wise masked word prediction essentially feeds intermediate layers directly to the classification layer, thereby inferring the linguistic information encoded in the intermediate layers. However, this is not what BERT is trained for; that is to say, arguably, only the final layer is optimized for the masked word prediction task, and other layers are not. Hence, the intermediate layers' lower POS and word match accuracy may not be due to the "absence" of syntactic or semantic knowledge encoded in those layers; rather, they may simply suggest that those intermediate layers are not trained for such tasks.

Second, although we provided a possible explanation for our observations and showed a few examples that seem to support our hypotheses, these are highly speculative and not meant to prove anything. We consider this a limitation of our approach, and a more controlled experiment is needed to make stronger claims or to test our hypotheses, and this is left for future work.

Acknowledgements

We thank the three anonymous reviewers for their insightful and constructive feedback. We also thank Dr. Ellie Pavlick and others at Mid-Atlantic Student Colloquium on Speech, Language and Learning (MASC-SLL) for their helpful comments.

References

Alexis Conneau, German Kruszewski, Guillaume Lample, Loïc Barrault, and Marco Baroni. 2018. What you can cram into a single $&!#* vector: Probing sentence embeddings for linguistic properties. In *Proceedings of the 56th Annual Meeting of the Association for Computational Linguistics (Volume 1: Long Papers)*, pages 2126–2136, Melbourne, Australia. Association for Computational Linguistics.

Jacob Devlin, Ming-Wei Chang, Kenton Lee, and Kristina Toutanova. 2019. BERT: Pre-training of deep bidirectional transformers for language understanding. In *Proceedings of the 2019 Conference of the North American Chapter of the Association for Computational Linguistics: Human Language Technologies, Volume 1 (Long and Short Papers)*, pages 4171–4186, Minneapolis, Minnesota. Association for Computational Linguistics.

Allyson Ettinger. 2020. What bert is not: Lessons from a new suite of psycholinguistic diagnostics for language models. *Transactions of the Association for Computational Linguistics*, 8:34–48.

Luke Gessler and Nathan Schneider. 2021. BERT has uncommon sense: Similarity ranking for word sense BERTology. In *Proceedings of the Fourth BlackboxNLP Workshop on Analyzing and Interpreting Neural Networks for NLP*, pages 539–547, Punta Cana, Dominican Republic. Association for Computational Linguistics.

Yoav Goldberg. 2019. Assessing bert's syntactic abilities. *arXiv preprint arXiv:1901.05287*.

John Hewitt and Percy Liang. 2019. Designing and interpreting probes with control tasks. In *Proceedings of the 2019 Conference on Empirical Methods in Natural Language Processing and the 9th International Joint Conference on Natural Language Processing (EMNLP-IJCNLP)*, pages 2733–2743, Hong Kong, China. Association for Computational Linguistics.

John Hewitt and Christopher D. Manning. 2019. A structural probe for finding syntax in word representations. In *Proceedings of the 2019 Conference of the North American Chapter of the Association for Computational Linguistics: Human Language Technologies, Volume 1 (Long and Short Papers)*, pages 4129–4138, Minneapolis, Minnesota. Association for Computational Linguistics.

Ganesh Jawahar, Benoît Sagot, and Djamé Seddah. 2019. What does BERT learn about the structure of language? In *Proceedings of the 57th Annual Meeting of the Association for Computational Linguistics*, pages 3651–3657, Florence, Italy. Association for Computational Linguistics.

Nelson F. Liu, Matt Gardner, Yonatan Belinkov, Matthew E. Peters, and Noah A. Smith. 2019. Linguistic knowledge and transferability of contextual representations. In *Proceedings of the 2019 Conference of the North American Chapter of the Association for Computational Linguistics: Human Language Technologies, Volume 1 (Long and Short Papers)*, pages 1073–1094, Minneapolis, Minnesota. Association for Computational Linguistics.

Rebecca Marvin and Tal Linzen. 2018. Targeted syntactic evaluation of language models. In *Proceedings of the 2018 Conference on Empirical Methods in Natural Language Processing*, pages 1192–1202, Brussels, Belgium. Association for Computational Linguistics.

Joakim Nivre, Marie-Catherine de Marneffe, Filip Ginter, Jan Hajič, Christopher D. Manning, Sampo Pyysalo, Sebastian Schuster, Francis Tyers, and Daniel Zeman. 2020. Universal dependencies v2: An evergrowing multilingual treebank collection.

Adam Poliak, Aparajita Haldar, Rachel Rudinger, J. Edward Hu, Ellie Pavlick, Aaron Steven White, and Benjamin Van Durme. 2018. Collecting diverse natural language inference problems for sentence representation evaluation. In *Proceedings of the 2018 Conference on Empirical Methods in Natural Language Processing*, pages 67–81, Brussels, Belgium. Association for Computational Linguistics.

Peng Qi, Yuhao Zhang, Yuhui Zhang, Jason Bolton, and Christopher D. Manning. 2020. Stanza: A Python natural language processing toolkit for many human languages. In *Proceedings of the 58th Annual Meeting of the Association for Computational Linguistics: System Demonstrations*.

Anna Rogers, Olga Kovaleva, and Anna Rumshisky. 2020. A primer in BERTology: What we know about how BERT works. *Transactions of the Association for Computational Linguistics*, 8:842–866.

Nathan Schneider, Jena D. Hwang, Vivek Srikumar, Jakob Prange, Austin Blodgett, Sarah R. Moeller, Aviram Stern, Adi Bitan, and Omri Abend. 2018. Comprehensive supersense disambiguation of English prepositions and possessives. In *Proceedings of the 56th Annual Meeting of the Association for Computational Linguistics (Volume 1: Long Papers)*, pages 185–196, Melbourne, Australia. Association for Computational Linguistics.

Nathan Schneider and Noah A. Smith. 2015. A corpus and model integrating multiword expressions and supersenses. In *Proceedings of the 2015 Conference of the North American Chapter of the Association for Computational Linguistics: Human Language Technologies*, pages 1537–1547, Denver, Colorado. Association for Computational Linguistics.

Ian Tenney, Dipanjan Das, and Ellie Pavlick. 2019a. BERT rediscovers the classical NLP pipeline. In *Proceedings of the 57th Annual Meeting of the Association for Computational Linguistics*, pages 4593–4601, Florence, Italy. Association for Computational Linguistics.

Ian Tenney, Patrick Xia, Berlin Chen, Alex Wang, Adam Poliak, R Thomas McCoy, Najoung Kim, Benjamin Van Durme, Sam Bowman, Dipanjan Das, and Ellie Pavlick. 2019b. What do you learn from context? probing for sentence structure in contextualized word representations. In *International Conference on Learning Representations*.

Marten van Schijndel, Aaron Mueller, and Tal Linzen. 2019. Quantity doesn't buy quality syntax with neural language models. In *Proceedings of the 2019 Conference on Empirical Methods in Natural Language Processing and the 9th International Joint Conference on Natural Language Processing (EMNLP-IJCNLP)*, pages 5831–5837, Hong Kong, China. Association for Computational Linguistics.

Ashish Vaswani, Noam Shazeer, Niki Parmar, Jakob Uszkoreit, Llion Jones, Aidan N. Gomez, Lukasz Kaiser, and Illia Polosukhin. 2017. Attention is all you need.

Thomas Wolf, Lysandre Debut, Victor Sanh, Julien Chaumond, Clement Delangue, Anthony Moi, Pierric Cistac, Tim Rault, Remi Louf, Morgan Funtowicz, Joe Davison, Sam Shleifer, Patrick von Platen, Clara Ma, Yacine Jernite, Julien Plu, Canwen Xu, Teven Le Scao, Sylvain Gugger, Mariama Drame, Quentin Lhoest, and Alexander Rush. 2020. Transformers: State-of-the-art natural language processing. In *Proceedings of the 2020 Conference on Empirical Methods in Natural Language Processing: System Demonstrations*, pages 38–45, Online. Association for Computational Linguistics.

Yichu Zhou and Vivek Srikumar. 2021. DirectProbe: Studying representations without classifiers. In *Proceedings of the 2021 Conference of the North American Chapter of the Association for Computational Linguistics: Human Language Technologies*, pages 5070–5083, Online. Association for Computational Linguistics.

Multimodal large language models for inclusive collaboration learning tasks

Armanda Lewis
New York University
726 Broadway
New York, NY 10003
al861@nyu.edu

Abstract

This PhD project leverages advancements in multimodal large language models to build an inclusive collaboration feedback loop, in order to facilitate the automated detection, modeling, and feedback for participants developing general collaboration skills. This topic is important given the role of collaboration as an essential 21st century skill, the potential to ground large language models within learning theory and real-world practice, and the expressive potential of transformer models to support equity and inclusion. We address some concerns of integrating advances in natural language processing into downstream tasks such as the learning analytics feedback loop.

1 Introduction

Collaboration, a coordinated process involving two or more individuals participating in a task in an interdependent way, is an important topic of study given its importance as a major 21st century skill (Lai et al., 2017; Council, 2011; Rios et al., 2020). Though collaboration as a general term is viewed as a learnable competency, notable distinctions emerge when examining how collaboration surfaces within relevant research. One semantic distinction is that the term collaboration is not explicitly defined, or is used interchangeably with concepts such as group collaboration, teamwork, collective problem solving, cooperation, and more (OECD, 2015). These inconsistencies in meaning make it challenging to connect various research agendas that purport the advantages of collaboration. Another distinction to note is modality-related. Some research does not make any modality distinctions when reporting the impacts of results, though much has viewed collaboration via online/computer-mediated interactions, both synchronous and asynchronous, while other research has examined co-located collaborative acts that happen face-to-face. Despite semantic, modality, and other distinctions, various fields have advanced what we know about collaboration, specifically collaboration as a language-mediated process.

Scholars within the fields of NLP, cognitive science, and educational research have focused separately on verbal and written aspects of collaborative exchanges - speech, text-based outputs, and audio such as non-linguistic pauses - to better understand aspects of collaboration. Recent NLP research, for example, has explored neural models equipped with dynamic knowledge graph embeddings, the use of large language models to model real world speech, and the development of collaboration datasets (Ekstedt and Skantze, 2020; He et al., 2017; Lee et al., 2022), while cognitive science has explored general modeling approaches for collaborative behavior and large language models as knowledge sources for intelligent agents (Goldstone and Gureckis, 2009; Huang et al., 2022; Wray et al., 2021). Learning analytics, a subset of educational research that extracts diverse datastreams from the learning process to improve learning, has developed automated multimodal approaches to detect, model and provide feedback about collaborative learning exchanges (Dowell et al., 2019; Pugh et al., 2022; Worsley and Ochoa, 2020). Though these studies differ in their disciplinary perspectives, they view language as essential to individuals' application of collaborative behavior and researchers' understanding of said behavior.

2 Purpose of Research Project

Because language is grounded in experience (Bisk et al., 2020), and collaboration is mediated through language, collaboration is an appropriate skill to be learned, practiced, and analyzed through language-mediated experiences and techniques. This dissertation project, situated at the intersection of NLP, cognitive science, and learning analytics, focuses on how we may support people in their development of complex, dynamic collaborative language

Proceedings of the 2022 Conference of the North American Chapter of the Association for Computational Linguistics: Human Language Technologies: Student Research Workshop, pages 202 - 210

skills. The project extends prior research, but also introduces unexplored areas such as multimodal language modeling and inclusive collaboration. Therefore, the aim is to contribute to several open research questions related to how we may foster collaborative language, a proxy for overall collaboration skills, in people as an explicit act of learning. This project examines these critical gaps in current research to explore the ultimate question of: How can we use multimodal large language models to detect, model, and provide feedback on inclusive collaboration behavior? Sub-questions include:

- How may a multimodal framework offer improved collaborative language detection over and above unimodal language modeling?;
- What are possibilities for detecting and modeling inclusive collaboration language among a group of diverse participants?, and
- How may we leverage multimodal large language modeling in the service of learning to collaborate through automated and feedback mechanisms?

This study explores the potentials of adopting multimodal NLP techniques within a learning analytics lens. Multimodal NLP is an emerging area within NLP that stems from the development of the large language model, a massive-parameter pretrained model. Large language models are an active area of development within NLP, and one set of researchers have demonstrated impressive semantic and generative capabilities (Kaplan et al., 2020; Tay et al., 2021), while others pose ethical, environmental, and interpretability concerns about unbounded scaling of model size (Bender et al., 2021; Strubell et al., 2020; Weidinger et al., 2021). We focus on the potential of multimodal NLP, large language models that integrate multimodal (acoustic, image, tactile, and/or video) data beyond text-based language, and explore potentials of multimodal NLP for automated, fine-grained detection of collaborative processes that will support learners within and across experiences, an important downstream application of the technology (Bommasani et al., 2021; Brown et al., 2020; Islam and Iqbal, 2021; Rahman et al., 2020). We also contribute to current critiques of performance-first modeling that may overlook important opportunities to create real world NLP models that reduce bias. This project operationalizes an inclusive collaboration index with the goal of general equity and inclusion over identity-specific bias mitigation.

3 Integrating Inclusion into Downstream NLP Collaboration Tasks

Within learning analytics (Holstein and Doroudi, 2021), NLP (Blodgett et al., 2020; Tsvetkov et al., 2018), and general machine learning/AI applications (Doshi-Velez and Kim, 2017; Dwork et al., 2012), researchers have made arguments for more equitable, fair, and inclusive practices. This includes verifying that the research approach is informed by ethical and human-centered principles, developing research methods that detect/mitigate unethical outcomes, and/or our aim of proposing that research methods should translate ethically when used in real-world contexts.

With the recent focus on equity and inclusion across our fields of interest, formal inclusion theories are stated as important to integrate as a future idealized goal, though we lack blueprints for what forms these integrations may take. Within research across learning analytics, NLP, and machine learning, formal experiments provide empirical support for those methods with the most promise for identifying and reducing unwanted societal bias, ambiguity, and exclusion in datasets and models (Caliskan et al., 2017; Dinan et al., 2020; Hutchinson et al., 2020; Sap et al., 2020), though there is less support for what works as an embedded practice within downstream tasks that utilize these algorithms, datasets, and platforms. This study considers ethical research approaches and outcomes, but primarily focuses on the stated areas of potential development - the ethical deployment of our NLP and learning analytics research methods in downstream tasks situated within actual learning settings by detecting lack of inclusion and intervening. Our focus is not yet to identify any causal relationship between one or more social identities and collaboration quality, but rather to detect inclusive collaboration of individuals and groups, and in the process identify any disparities in collaboration quality among individuals and within the group as a whole.

In this sense, our work advances the concept of inclusion (Mor-Barak and Cherin, 1998; Young, 1995), defined as the degree to which diverse individuals demonstrate that they are part of the collaborative process. We recognize that this study falls short of addressing equity since equity examines outcomes at the societal rather than individual or group level, though we highlight that inclusion is an integral step on the way to equity and ethical treatment within collaborative experiences (Bernstein et al., 2020).

4 Methodology

We have sub-divided the planned methodology into multiple tasks as: Due to the multidisciplinary nature of collaboration, this study will incorporate methods that stem from four distinct fields - learning analytics, cognitive science, natural language processing, and inclusion theory - to create an inclusive view of learning to collaborate. From learning analytics, we get a roadmap for developing an automated feedback loop necessary for learning to collaborate, and a variety of methods for detecting collaborative behaviors and operationalizing them into signals for model building. From cognitive science, we have an example for linking psychological theory, model, and real world behaviors, as well as ongoing research on intelligent agents as used for understanding learning and adaptation through feedback. From natural language processing, we have access to the ability of large language models to parse and generate human language, as well as approaches for addressing inclusion in language model building. Lastly, we operationalize tenets of inclusion theory in order to build a learning to collaborate model that detects linguistic bias, thus working towards a more inclusive collaboration environment.

All aspects involving human subjects, including Phase 1 data collected via Amazon Mechanical Turk, Phase 2 large language modeling, and Phase 3 interventions will receive full approval of the University's Institutional Review Board (IRB) prior to launching the study. Datasets are either open for research use and cited, or collected and stored as part of the IRB approval process and regulations.

4.1 Phase 1: Multimodal collaboration detection and dataset creation

As part of Phase 1 (multimodal collaboration detection and dataset creation), we will (a) develop a rubric for inclusive collaboration; (b) finalize the process of capturing and preprocessing multimodal data (video and transcribed audio) from collaborative exchanges, and (c) create an evaluation dataset. The inclusive collaboration rubric pulls from existing research on collaboration quality that identifies four collaboration indicators (information sharing, reciprocal interaction, shared understanding, and inclusion) from participants' audio, text, and video data (Cukurova et al., 2018; Praharaj et al., 2021), and the technical feat of capturing and preprocessing collaborative exchanges is informed by previous scholarship in Multimodal Learning Analytics research (Ochoa et al., 2013; Worsley and Blikstein, 2015). Automatic distillation of raw data into collaboration features would include: automatic speech recognition, computational linguistic methods to clean, parse, and analyze transcribed dialogue (eg. word counts, duration, general content analysis, inclusive content analysis), detection of non-linguistic audio (speech prosody), and video signal filtering to detect person placement and basic gestures.

Following the general dataset collection procedures described in He et al. (2017), we will gather human annotations according to our collaboration rubric of transcribed audio at the sentence-level and video portions at the frame-level that is captured for collaborative exchanges. We will use representative samples of open source collaboration datasets and datasets collected as part of an approved IRB protocol that contain text-based dialogue, spoken dialogue, and/or video of multi-person collaborative exchanges, including the AMI Meeting Corpus (Carletta et al., 2006), D64 Multimodal Conversation Corpus (Oertel et al., 2013) How2 Dataset for Multimodal Language Understanding (Sanabria et al., 2018), Pragmatic Framework for Collaboration (Boothe et al., 2022), and MutualFriends Corpus (He et al., 2017). In addition to annotation of the four dimensions of interest, we also have annotators evaluate along the modality (text, image, and video). We integrate recent NLP crowdsourcing research findings (Nangia et al., 2021) by collecting expert annotations that will then inform guidance for generally skilled Amazon Mechanical Turk (MTurk) workers, and and will use the process outlined in Bowman et al. (2015), and the Fair Work tool (Whiting et al., 2019) to ensure a fair payment structure.

The contributions of Phase 1 are multiple: to expand beyond research that analyzes collaborative language at the surface level, such as looking at word counts or temporal durations, and support deeper content-level analysis (Praharaj et al., 2021); to map current trends in large language modeling to theoretically-sound learning and inclusion frameworks that extend past pure performance measures and support responsible downstream usage of such models.

4.2 Phase 2: Multimodal large language models for measuring collaboration quality

Phase 2 focuses on formalizing the task specification for inclusive collaboration, a process in which we operationalize human-supplied descriptions into an inclusive collaboration quality classification model. Specifically, we will conduct finetuning experiments with large transformer models to detect collaborative language and behaviors of individual members of a 3-person group.

We will utilize several pretrained large language models accessible through HuggingFace ((Wolf et al., 2020)), including BERT-base (Sanh et al., 2020), GPT-2 (Radford and Narasimhan, 2018), GPT-J, the open source version of GPT-3 (Brown et al., 2020), and FLAVA (Singh et al., 2022), a recent multimodal language model pretrained on visual and linguistic data. We will also integrate lessons learned from education-specific research utilizing large language models (Clavié and Gal, 2019; Shen et al., 2021; Suresh et al., 2021). These pretrained models will be finetuned on a random sample of the multimodal collaboration data (audio, text, and/or video frames) that has been held out of the evaluation dataset step. We will generate finetuned models with unimodal and multimodal collaborative data, and learning rates and batch sizes will be determined according to standard task settings, and we follow the training-test splits and standards articulated by Guo et al. (2020) and Minaee et al. (2021). For this study, we will limit our datasets and modeling experiments to English-language text and dialogue datasets to supplement those pre-trained models primarily trained on English-language data.

We compare the performance of our finetuned models in terms of classification accuracy of our expert and general crowdworker classification scores on the 4 collaboration dimensions. The area under the receiver operating characteristic curve (AUROC) metric is used for each dimension. Following Pugh et al. (2022), we report the chance baseline as a random shuffling of labels within each collaborative session and thus computing accuracy. Comparing different unimodal and multimodal finetuned model performance will serve as an ablation approach to examine the role of additional data modalities in terms of overall model performance, as well as a comparison between unimodal and multimodal models (Singh et al., 2022). Additionally, we conduct an analysis of random examples to determine points of synergy with, divergence from, and bias markers that differ from human classification. This will serve as essential future directions to frame the use of automated collaboration detection using large language models.

Following the design-based protocol outlined in (Praharaj et al., 2018), we will complete a pilot study within a real classroom. Small groups (of 3 people) conduct a general collaborative task and we use the detection setup established in Phase 1 to detect multimodal signals (eg. speaking duration, pauses, large language model features) correlated to collaboration quality and use our multimodal models to assess quality. We will conduct an additional automated and human evaluation on this real-life scenario.

There are two novel aspects of this modeling of collaborative quality. One involves using the large language model to provide a nuanced view of collaborative linguistic exchanges at the content level. According to Praharaj et al. (2021) note that very few studies integrate an analysis of "verbal audio indicators or the content of the audio for the analysis of [in-person] collaboration quality" (pg. 2). We leverage the large language model to explore improvements in supervised dialogue detection tasks, and also unsupervised training strategies to explore emergent and content-specific cases of collaboration so that the model can learn without direct supervision. Additionally, we propose a measure on inclusive collaboration and evaluate its association on overall collaboration quality.

4.3 Phase 3: Language generation to support collaboration learning

Since we are ultimately concerned with learning to collaborate, we build a learning analytics cycle with the development of a robust feedback loop. The feedback system will take the form of an intelligent agent that can monitor and detect aspects of the collaboration process, focusing on the measurement of collaboration quality. The key behavior is for our model to detect differences in collaboration, in order to pinpoint disparities in inclusion. The inclusive collaboration models created by generative language models will drive generative behavior of the intelligent agent, which will produce select audio-based feedback during the collaboration exchange based on detected features.

The study will take on an experimental setup for higher education course recitations that engage in collaborative problem solving. The three groups - the no feedback control group (i.e. those randomly assigned as the control group with no intervention), the manual feedback experimental group (i.e. those randomly assigned as the manual feedback group which entails an instructor offering general, preparatory guidance on quality collaboration), and the automated feedback experimental group (i.e. those randomly assigned as the automated feedback group) - will engage in a series of four collaborative sessions. During session 1, we will record collaboration exchanges between the randomly assigned groups in order to capture multimodal baseline collaboration data. During sessions 2 and 3, the control group will collaborate in the absence of any explicit feedback, the manual feedback group will collaborate with initial collaboration guidance by the instructor, and the automated feedback group will collaborate while the intelligent agent interjects in real time. Session 4 will record collaboration exchanges between the three groups in the absence of any intervention. The goal is to assess how well all groups perform on inclusive collaboration quality.

This study hypothesizes that feedback loops built on top of multimodal large language models will capture the most relevant information associated with collaboration due to their scaled representational qualities. We will extend progress - finetuning; masked language model prompting; contextual prompting; and case-based prompting - made in extracting relevant information from language models to serve as knowledge sources for cognitive agents, and identify the method that maps to encouraging collaboration quality (Huang et al., 2022; Wray et al., 2021; Yousfi-Monod and Prince, 2007). The development of the agent will use language and simple feedback to offer corrective and encouraging input to students.

5 Initial Results

An initial pilot focused on the language modeling portion, and uses IRB-approved data that takes place within recitations of a large, STEM class. Groups of 3 students participated in small group work for the duration of the 75 minute period, and were tasked with solving problems related to the lecture and readings. Audio and video recordings were captured, cleaned, and processed. Transcripts were generated by an Automated Speech Recognition (ASR) software and corrected by hand, and were then paired with video frames. A random sampling of the text-based dialogue and video frames were generated and then mapped to the inclusive collaboration framework by 2 expert annotators and an additional 5 general skill annotators. These data will serve as the evaluation set. BERT-base and GPT-2 were finetuned on a randomized sample (80%) of the AMI collaboration dataset, as well as dialogue (text-based) portions of the Multi-party Collaboration corpus. Results indicate some marginal improvement between the finetuned models, and between BERT and the larger GPT-2 model, but additional analysis and more thorough data preparation and testing are needed. The finetuned GPT-2 model performed better than chance on all except for the inclusion dimension. We anticipate that more thorough finetuning and integration of multimodal finetuning data should improve performance on multimodal classification tasks.

6 Conclusion

As an essential 21st century skill, our aim is to utilize the potentials of multimodal large language models to advance our ability to detect and model collaborative behaviors, with the ultimate goal being to offer feedback to learners as they develop these important skills. Importantly, we focus on the tenets of inclusive collaboration, so that collaborators are encouraged to have equitable and inclusive exchanges as they work with each other. This doctoral research project builds an automated end-to-end inclusive collaboration feedback loop, relying on advancements in large language modeling as it is used in downstream tasks, and grounding machine learning methods within theory and real-world practice.

References

Emily M. Bender, Timnit Gebru, Angelina McMillan-Major, and Shmargaret Shmitchell. 2021. On the Dangers of Stochastic Parrots: Can Language Models Be Too Big? 🦜. In *Proceedings of the 2021 ACM Conference on Fairness, Accountability, and Transparency*, FAccT '21, pages 610–623, Virtual Event, Canada. Association for Computing Machinery.

Dimension	BERT	BERT*	GPT-2	GPT-2*	Shuffled
Info sharing	.43	.51	.52	.59	.56
Reciprocity	.41	.49	.55	.61	.54
Understanding	.47	.49	.59	.64	.52
Inclusion	.37	.43	.45	.50	.53

Table 1: Mean AUROC score across 5 iterations on 4 collaboration dimensions. Asterisk indicates models finetuned on dialogue data only.

Ruth Sessler Bernstein, Morgan Bulger, Paul Salipante, and Judith Y. Weisinger. 2020. From Diversity to Inclusion to Equity: A Theory of Generative Interactions. *Journal of Business Ethics*, 167(3):395–410.

Yonatan Bisk, Ari Holtzman, Jesse Thomason, Jacob Andreas, Yoshua Bengio, Joyce Chai, Mirella Lapata, Angeliki Lazaridou, Jonathan May, Aleksandr Nisnevich, Nicolas Pinto, and Joseph Turian. 2020. Experience Grounds Language. *arXiv:2004.10151 [cs]*. ArXiv: 2004.10151.

Su Lin Blodgett, Solon Barocas, Hal Daumé III, and Hanna Wallach. 2020. Language (Technology) is Power: A Critical Survey of "Bias" in NLP. *arXiv:2005.14050 [cs]*. ArXiv: 2005.14050.

Rishi Bommasani, Drew A. Hudson, Ehsan Adeli, Russ Altman, Simran Arora, Sydney von Arx, Michael S. Bernstein, Jeannette Bohg, Antoine Bosselut, Emma Brunskill, Erik Brynjolfsson, Shyamal Buch, Dallas Card, Rodrigo Castellon, Niladri Chatterji, Annie Chen, Kathleen Creel, Jared Quincy Davis, Dora Demszky, Chris Donahue, Moussa Doumbouya, Esin Durmus, Stefano Ermon, John Etchemendy, Kawin Ethayarajh, Li Fei-Fei, Chelsea Finn, Trevor Gale, Lauren Gillespie, Karan Goel, Noah Goodman, Shelby Grossman, Neel Guha, Tatsunori Hashimoto, Peter Henderson, John Hewitt, Daniel E. Ho, Jenny Hong, Kyle Hsu, Jing Huang, Thomas Icard, Saahil Jain, Dan Jurafsky, Pratyusha Kalluri, Siddharth Karamcheti, Geoff Keeling, Fereshte Khani, Omar Khattab, Pang Wei Kohd, Mark Krass, Ranjay Krishna, Rohith Kuditipudi, Ananya Kumar, Faisal Ladhak, Mina Lee, Tony Lee, Jure Leskovec, Isabelle Levent, Xiang Lisa Li, Xuechen Li, Tengyu Ma, Ali Malik, Christopher D. Manning, Suvir Mirchandani, Eric Mitchell, Zanele Munyikwa, Suraj Nair, Avanika Narayan, Deepak Narayanan, Ben Newman, Allen Nie, Juan Carlos Niebles, Hamed Nilforoshan, Julian Nyarko, Giray Ogut, Laurel Orr, Isabel Papadimitriou, Joon Sung Park, Chris Piech, Eva Portelance, Christopher Potts, Aditi Raghunathan, Rob Reich, Hongyu Ren, Frieda Rong, Yusuf Roohani, Camilo Ruiz, Jack Ryan, Christopher Ré, Dorsa Sadigh, Shiori Sagawa, Keshav Santhanam, Andy Shih, Krishnan Srinivasan, Alex Tamkin, Rohan Taori, Armin W. Thomas, Florian Tramèr, Rose E. Wang, William Wang, Bohan Wu, Jiajun Wu, Yuhuai Wu, Sang Michael Xie, Michihiro Yasunaga, Jiaxuan You, Matei Zaharia, Michael Zhang, Tianyi Zhang, Xikun Zhang, Yuhui Zhang, Lucia Zheng, Kaitlyn Zhou, and Percy Liang. 2021. On the Opportunities and Risks of Foundation Models. *arXiv:2108.07258 [cs]*. ArXiv: 2108.07258.

Maurice Boothe, Collin Yu, Armanda Lewis, and Xavier Ochoa. 2022. Towards a Pragmatic and Theory-Driven Framework for Multimodal Collaboration Feedback. In *LAK22: 12th International Learning Analytics and Knowledge Conference*, LAK22, pages 507–513, New York, NY, USA. Association for Computing Machinery.

Samuel R. Bowman, Gabor Angeli, Christopher Potts, and Christopher D. Manning. 2015. A large annotated corpus for learning natural language inference. *arXiv:1508.05326 [cs]*. ArXiv: 1508.05326.

Tom B. Brown, Benjamin Mann, Nick Ryder, Melanie Subbiah, Jared Kaplan, Prafulla Dhariwal, Arvind Neelakantan, Pranav Shyam, Girish Sastry, Amanda Askell, Sandhini Agarwal, Ariel Herbert-Voss, Gretchen Krueger, Tom Henighan, Rewon Child, Aditya Ramesh, Daniel M. Ziegler, Jeffrey Wu, Clemens Winter, Christopher Hesse, Mark Chen, Eric Sigler, Mateusz Litwin, Scott Gray, Benjamin Chess, Jack Clark, Christopher Berner, Sam McCandlish, Alec Radford, Ilya Sutskever, and Dario Amodei. 2020. Language Models are Few-Shot Learners. *arXiv:2005.14165 [cs]*. ArXiv: 2005.14165.

Aylin Caliskan, Joanna J. Bryson, and Arvind Narayanan. 2017. Semantics derived automatically from language corpora contain human-like biases. *Science*, 356(6334):183–186.

Jean Carletta, Simone Ashby, Sebastien Bourban, Mike Flynn, Mael Guillemot, Thomas Hain, Jaroslav Kadlec, Vasilis Karaiskos, Wessel Kraaij, Melissa Kronenthal, Guillaume Lathoud, Mike Lincoln, Agnes Lisowska, Iain McCowan, Wilfried Post, Dennis Reidsma, and Pierre Wellner. 2006. The AMI Meeting Corpus: A Pre-announcement. In Steve Renals and Samy Bengio, editors, *Machine Learning for Multimodal Interaction*, volume 3869, pages 28–39. Springer Berlin Heidelberg, Berlin, Heidelberg.

Benjamin Clavié and Kobi Gal. 2019. EduBERT: Pretrained Deep Language Models for Learning Analytics. *arXiv:1912.00690 [cs]*. ArXiv: 1912.00690.

National Research Council. 2011. *Assessing 21st Century Skills: Summary of a Workshop*. National Academies Press, Washington, D.C.

Mutlu Cukurova, Rose Luckin, Eva Millán, and Manolis Mavrikis. 2018. The NISPI framework: Analysing collaborative problem-solving from students' physical interactions. *Computers & Education*, 116:93–109.

Emily Dinan, Angela Fan, Ledell Wu, Jason Weston, Douwe Kiela, and Adina Williams. 2020. Multi-Dimensional Gender Bias Classification. pages 314–331.

Finale Doshi-Velez and Been Kim. 2017. Towards A Rigorous Science of Interpretable Machine Learning. *arXiv:1702.08608 [cs, stat]*. ArXiv: 1702.08608.

Nia Dowell, Yiwen Lin, Andrew Godfrey, and Christopher Brooks. 2019. Promoting Inclusivity Through Time-Dynamic Discourse Analysis in Digitally-Mediated Collaborative Learning. In *Artificial Intelligence in Education*, Lecture Notes in Computer Science, pages 207–219, Cham. Springer International Publishing.

Cynthia Dwork, Moritz Hardt, Toniann Pitassi, Omer Reingold, and Rich Zemel. 2012. Fairness through Awareness. In *Proceedings of the 3rd innovations in theoretical computer science conference*, pages 214–226. ACM.

Erik Ekstedt and Gabriel Skantze. 2020. TurnGPT: a Transformer-based Language Model for Predicting Turn-taking in Spoken Dialog. *Findings of the Association for Computational Linguistics: EMNLP 2020*, pages 2981–2990. ArXiv: 2010.10874.

Robert L. Goldstone and Todd M. Gureckis. 2009. Collective Behavior. *Topics in Cognitive Science*, 1(3):412–438.

Mandy Guo, Yinfei Yang, Daniel Cer, Qinlan Shen, and Noah Constant. 2020. MultiReQA: A Cross-Domain Evaluation for Retrieval Question Answering Models. *arXiv:2005.02507 [cs]*. ArXiv: 2005.02507.

He He, Anusha Balakrishnan, Mihail Eric, and Percy Liang. 2017. Learning Symmetric Collaborative Dialogue Agents with Dynamic Knowledge Graph Embeddings. *arXiv:1704.07130 [cs]*. ArXiv: 1704.07130.

Kenneth Holstein and Shayan Doroudi. 2021. Equity and Artificial Intelligence in Education: Will "AIEd" Amplify or Alleviate Inequities in Education? *arXiv:2104.12920 [cs]*. ArXiv: 2104.12920.

Wenlong Huang, Pieter Abbeel, Deepak Pathak, and Igor Mordatch. 2022. Language Models as Zero-Shot Planners: Extracting Actionable Knowledge for Embodied Agents. *arXiv:2201.07207 [cs]*. ArXiv: 2201.07207.

Ben Hutchinson, Vinodkumar Prabhakaran, Emily Denton, Kellie Webster, Yu Zhong, and Stephen Denuyl. 2020. Social Biases in NLP Models as Barriers for Persons with Disabilities. *arXiv:2005.00813 [cs]*. ArXiv: 2005.00813.

Md Mofijul Islam and Tariq Iqbal. 2021. Multi-GAT: A Graphical Attention-Based Hierarchical Multimodal Representation Learning Approach for Human Activity Recognition. *IEEE Robotics and Automation Letters*, 6(2):1729–1736.

Jared Kaplan, Sam McCandlish, Tom Henighan, Tom B. Brown, Benjamin Chess, Rewon Child, Scott Gray, Alec Radford, Jeffrey Wu, and Dario Amodei. 2020. Scaling Laws for Neural Language Models. *arXiv:2001.08361 [cs, stat]*. ArXiv: 2001.08361.

Emily Lai, Kristen DiCerbo, and Peter Foltz. 2017. *Skills for Today: What We Know about Teaching and Assessing Collaboration*. Pearson.

Mina Lee, Percy Liang, and Qian Yang. 2022. CoAuthor: Designing a Human-AI Collaborative Writing Dataset for Exploring Language Model Capabilities. *arXiv:2201.06796 [cs]*. ArXiv: 2201.06796.

Shervin Minaee, Nal Kalchbrenner, Erik Cambria, Narjes Nikzad, Meysam Chenaghlu, and Jianfeng Gao. 2021. Deep Learning Based Text Classification: A Comprehensive Review. *arXiv:2004.03705 [cs, stat]*. ArXiv: 2004.03705.

Michal E. Mor-Barak and David A. Cherin. 1998. A Tool to Expand Organizational Understanding of Workforce Diversity. *Administration in Social Work*, 22(1):47–64.

Nikita Nangia, Saku Sugawara, Harsh Trivedi, Alex Warstadt, Clara Vania, and Samuel R. Bowman. 2021. What Ingredients Make for an Effective Crowdsourcing Protocol for Difficult NLU Data Collection Tasks? In *Proceedings of the 59th Annual Meeting of the Association for Computational Linguistics and the 11th International Joint Conference on Natural Language Processing (Volume 1: Long Papers)*, pages 1221–1235, Online. Association for Computational Linguistics.

Xavier Ochoa, Katherine Chiluiza, Gonzalo Méndez, Gonzalo Luzardo, Bruno Guamán, and James Castells. 2013. Expertise estimation based on simple multimodal features. In *Proceedings of the 15th ACM on International conference on multimodal interaction*, ICMI '13, pages 583–590, Sydney, Australia. Association for Computing Machinery.

OECD. 2015. PISA 2015 Assessment and Analytical Framework: Science, Reading, Mathematic, Financial Literacy and Collaborative Problem Solving.

Catharine Oertel, Fred Cummins, Jens Edlund, Petra Wagner, and Nick Campbell. 2013. D64: a corpus of richly recorded conversational interaction. *Journal on Multimodal User Interfaces*, 7(1-2):19–28.

Sambit Praharaj, Maren Scheffel, Hendrik Drachsler, and Marcus Specht. 2018. MULTIFOCUS - MULTImodal Learning Analytics FOr Co-located Collaboration Understanding and Support. *Proceedings of the 13th EC-TEL Doctoral Consortium co-located with 13th European Conference on Technology Enhanced*

Learning (EC-TEL 2018), Leeds, UK, September 3rd, 2018.

Sambit Praharaj, Maren Scheffel, Marcel Schmitz, Marcus Specht, and Hendrik Drachsler. 2021. Towards Automatic Collaboration Analytics for Group Speech Data Using Learning Analytics. *Sensors*, 21(9):3156.

Samuel L. Pugh, Arjun Rao, Angela E.B. Stewart, and Sidney K. D'Mello. 2022. Do Speech-Based Collaboration Analytics Generalize Across Task Contexts? In *LAK22: 12th International Learning Analytics and Knowledge Conference*, pages 208–218, Online USA. ACM.

Alec Radford and Karthik Narasimhan. 2018. Improving Language Understanding by Generative Pre-Training. *undefined*.

Wasifur Rahman, Md Kamrul Hasan, Sangwu Lee, Amir Zadeh, Chengfeng Mao, Louis-Philippe Morency, and Ehsan Hoque. 2020. Integrating Multimodal Information in Large Pretrained Transformers. *arXiv:1908.05787 [cs, stat]*. ArXiv: 1908.05787.

Joseph A. Rios, Guangming Ling, Robert Pugh, Dovid Becker, and Adam Bacall. 2020. Identifying Critical 21st-Century Skills for Workplace Success: A Content Analysis of Job Advertisements. *Educational Researcher*, 49(2):80–89.

Ramon Sanabria, Ozan Caglayan, Shruti Palaskar, Desmond Elliott, Loïc Barrault, Lucia Specia, and Florian Metze. 2018. How2: A Large-scale Dataset for Multimodal Language Understanding. *arXiv:1811.00347 [cs]*. ArXiv: 1811.00347.

Victor Sanh, Lysandre Debut, Julien Chaumond, and Thomas Wolf. 2020. DistilBERT, a distilled version of BERT: smaller, faster, cheaper and lighter. *arXiv:1910.01108 [cs]*. ArXiv: 1910.01108.

Maarten Sap, Saadia Gabriel, Lianhui Qin, Dan Jurafsky, Noah A. Smith, and Yejin Choi. 2020. Social Bias Frames: Reasoning about Social and Power Implications of Language. pages 5477–5490.

Jia Tracy Shen, Michiharu Yamashita, Ethan Prihar, Neil Heffernan, Xintao Wu, Ben Graff, and Dongwon Lee. 2021. MathBERT: A Pre-trained Language Model for General NLP Tasks in Mathematics Education. *arXiv:2106.07340 [cs]*. ArXiv: 2106.07340.

Amanpreet Singh, Ronghang Hu, Vedanuj Goswami, Guillaume Couairon, Wojciech Galuba, Marcus Rohrbach, and Douwe Kiela. 2022. FLAVA: A Foundational Language And Vision Alignment Model. *arXiv:2112.04482 [cs]*. ArXiv: 2112.04482.

Emma Strubell, Ananya Ganesh, and Andrew McCallum. 2020. Energy and Policy Considerations for Modern Deep Learning Research. *Proceedings of the AAAI Conference on Artificial Intelligence*, 34(09):13693–13696.

Abhijit Suresh, Jennifer Jacobs, Vivian Lai, Chenhao Tan, Wayne Ward, James H. Martin, and Tamara Sumner. 2021. Using Transformers to Provide Teachers with Personalized Feedback on their Classroom Discourse: The TalkMoves Application. *arXiv:2105.07949 [cs]*. ArXiv: 2105.07949.

Yi Tay, Mostafa Dehghani, Jinfeng Rao, William Fedus, Samira Abnar, Hyung Won Chung, Sharan Narang, Dani Yogatama, Ashish Vaswani, and Donald Metzler. 2021. Scale Efficiently: Insights from Pre-training and Fine-tuning Transformers. *arXiv:2109.10686 [cs]*. ArXiv: 2109.10686.

Yulia Tsvetkov, Vinodkumar Prabhakaran, and Rob Voigt. 2018. Socially Responsible NLP. In *Proceedings of the 2018 Conference of the North American Chapter of the Association for Computational Linguistics: Tutorial Abstracts*, pages 24–26, New Orleans, Louisiana. Association for Computational Linguistics.

Laura Weidinger, John Mellor, Maribeth Rauth, Conor Griffin, Jonathan Uesato, Po-Sen Huang, Myra Cheng, Mia Glaese, Borja Balle, Atoosa Kasirzadeh, Zac Kenton, Sarah Brown, Will Hawkins, Tom Stepleton, Courtney Biles, Abeba Birhane, Julia Haas, Laura Rimell, Lisa Anne Hendricks, William Isaac, Sean Legassick, Geoffrey Irving, and Iason Gabriel. 2021. Ethical and social risks of harm from Language Models. Technical report, DeepMind.

Mark E. Whiting, Grant Hugh, and Michael S. Bernstein. 2019. Fair Work: Crowd Work Minimum Wage with One Line of Code. *Proceedings of the AAAI Conference on Human Computation and Crowdsourcing*, 7:197–206.

Thomas Wolf, Lysandre Debut, Victor Sanh, Julien Chaumond, Clement Delangue, Anthony Moi, Pierric Cistac, Tim Rault, Rémi Louf, Morgan Funtowicz, Joe Davison, Sam Shleifer, Patrick von Platen, Clara Ma, Yacine Jernite, Julien Plu, Canwen Xu, Teven Le Scao, Sylvain Gugger, Mariama Drame, Quentin Lhoest, and Alexander M. Rush. 2020. HuggingFace's Transformers: State-of-the-art Natural Language Processing. *arXiv:1910.03771 [cs]*. ArXiv: 1910.03771.

Marcelo Worsley and Paulo Blikstein. 2015. Leveraging multimodal learning analytics to differentiate student learning strategies. In *Proceedings of the Fifth International Conference on Learning Analytics And Knowledge*, LAK '15, pages 360–367, Poughkeepsie, New York. Association for Computing Machinery.

Marcelo Worsley and Xavier Ochoa. 2020. Towards collaboration literacy development through multimodal learning analytics. In *Companion Proceedings 10th International Conference on Learning Analytics & Knowledge (LAK20)*, volume 2610, pages 53–63.

I. I. I. Wray, James R. Kirk, and John E. Laird. 2021. Language Models as a Knowledge Source for Cognitive Agents. *arXiv:2109.08270 [cs]*. ArXiv: 2109.08270.

H. Peyton Young. 1995. *Equity: in theory and practice*, 1. princeton paperback printing edition. A Russell Sage Foundation book. Princeton Univ. Press, Princeton, NJ.

Mehdi Yousfi-Monod and Violaine Prince. 2007. Knowledge Acquisition Modeling through Dialog Between Cognitive Agents. *International Journal of Intelligent Information Technologies (IJIIT)*, 3(1):060.

Neural Networks in a Product of Hyperbolic Spaces

Jun Takeuchi[1], **Noriki Nishida**[2], **and Hideki Nakayama**[1]

[1,3]The University of Tokyo
[2]RIKEN
{takeuchi, nakayama}@nlab.ci.i.u-tokyo.ac.jp
noriki.nishida@riken.jp

Abstract

Machine learning in hyperbolic spaces has attracted much attention in natural language processing and many other fields. In particular, Hyperbolic Neural Networks (HNNs) have improved a wide variety of tasks, from machine translation to knowledge graph embedding. Although some studies have reported the effectiveness of embedding into the product of multiple hyperbolic spaces, HNNs have mainly been constructed in a single hyperbolic space, and their extension to product spaces has not been sufficiently studied. Therefore, we propose a novel method to extend a given HNN in a single space to a product of hyperbolic spaces. We apply our method to Hyperbolic Graph Convolutional Networks (HGCNs), extending several HNNs. Our model improved the graph node classification accuracy especially on datasets with tree-like structures. The results suggest that neural networks in a product of hyperbolic spaces can be more effective than in a single space in representing structural data.

1 Introduction

Machine learning that utilizes the properties of non-euclidean spaces has attracted much attention in recent years (Bronstein et al., 2017). In representation learning on natural language and graphs, where hierarchical data appear, hyperbolic spaces have recently been shown to be effective. In natural language processing (NLP), hyperbolic spaces have been applied to a variety of tasks such as word embedding (Nickel and Kiela, 2017; Tifrea et al., 2018), document embedding (Zhu et al., 2020b), natural language inference (Ganea et al., 2018), and machine translation (Gulcehre et al., 2018; Shimizu et al., 2021). Hyperbolic spaces have also been shown to be effective in graph embedding (Chamberlain et al., 2017; Sala et al., 2018; Chami et al., 2019), which is helpful for NLP models to utilize external knowledge graphs (Chami et al., 2020).

Recent progress in the use of hyperbolic space is supported by the development of hyperbolic neural networks (HNNs) (Tifrea et al., 2018), which consist of components such as linear and attention layers that are appropriately extended to hyperbolic spaces. How to define linear operations in hyperbolic space is non-trivial, and several different methods have been proposed (Shimizu et al., 2021; Chen et al., 2021).

Unlike Euclidean spaces, a product space of non-Euclidean spaces is geometrically different from a single space of the same dimension, and some studies have reported that using the product of small hyperbolic spaces improves the performance in graph and word embedding (Tifrea et al., 2018; Gu et al., 2019). In addition, Shimizu et al. observed that the superiority of their hyperbolic machine translation model over the Euclidean counterpart is lost as the dimensionality of word features increases, and they proposed using a product of multiple small hyperbolic spaces as a possible solution. However, existing HNN frameworks are defined in a single hyperbolic space, and how to extend HNNs to product spaces is still an open question.

Therefore, this paper proposes a novel method to extend a given HNN in a single space to a product of hyperbolic spaces. More specifically, we construct a general method to extend a hyperbolic matrix-vector multiplication, a major factor that distinguishes HNN variants, to a product space.

We apply our method to Hyperbolic Graph Convolutional Networks (HGCNs) (Chami et al., 2019) and show that our method outperforms the baselines especially on datasets with tree-like structures, suggesting that neural networks in a product of hyperbolic spaces are more effective for representing structural data than neural networks in a single hyperbolic space.

Proceedings of the 2022 Conference of the North American Chapter of the Association for Computational Linguistics: Human Language Technologies: Student Research Workshop, pages 211 - 221
July 10-15, 2022 ©2022 Association for Computational Linguistics

Contribution to NLP community

Single-space HNNs have already been applied to a variety of NLP tasks, and our method is applicable to most of them, with the potential to improve performance. As a start, we extended HNN++ (Shimizu et al., 2021), a recently proposed HNN variant, and applied it to machine translation tasks. The preliminary experimental results show that our method performs better, at least on small datasets. We plan to conduct experiments on large datasets soon.

2 Preliminaries

2.1 Riemannian Geometry

An n-dimensional manifold $\mathcal{M} = \mathcal{M}^n$ is an n-dimensional space locally approximated to an n-dimensional Euclidean tangent space $T_{\boldsymbol{x}}\mathcal{M}$ at each point $\boldsymbol{x} \in \mathcal{M}^n$. A Riemannian manifold is a differentiable manifold with a metric tensor $\mathfrak{g}$. The exponential map $\exp_{\boldsymbol{x}} : T_{\boldsymbol{x}}\mathcal{M} \to \mathcal{M}$ and its inverse function $\log_{\boldsymbol{x}}$ are bijections defined locally around $\mathbf{0} \in T_{\boldsymbol{x}}\mathcal{M}$. For more details, please refer to Petersen et al. (2006).

2.2 Hyperbolic Space

A hyperbolic space $\mathbb{H} = \mathbb{H}_c^n$ is an n-dimensional Riemannian manifold with a constant negative curvature $-c$ $(c > 0)$. There are several equivalent models to represent a hyperbolic space. In the Poincaré Ball model $\mathbb{B}$, a hyperbolic space is represented as a ball of radius $\frac{1}{\sqrt{c}}$. Other models like the hyperboloid model and the equivalence between all models are detailed in Cannon et al. (1997).

2.3 Hyperbolic Neural Networks

Hyperbolic spaces have a structure similar to that of linear spaces called Gyrovector spaces (Ungar, 2008). The hyperbolic versions of addition and scalar multiplication are called Möbius Addition $\oplus$ [1] and Möbius Scalar Multiplication $\otimes$.

The matrix multiplication in hyperbolic space was proposed by Ganea et al. (2018). First, they showed that $\exp_0$ and $\log_0$ correspondence between hyperbolic space and its tangent space at origin are globally extended. Then Möbius Matrix Multiplication $\otimes$ between a matrix M and $\boldsymbol{x}$ is defined through tangent space approximation:

$$M \otimes_c \boldsymbol{x} := \exp_0(M \cdot \log_0(\boldsymbol{x})). \tag{1}$$

Hyperbolic version $\sigma^{\otimes_c}$ of any activation function σ in Euclidean space is defined in the same way:

$$\sigma^{\otimes_c}(\boldsymbol{x}) := \exp_0(\sigma(\log_0(\boldsymbol{x}))). \tag{2}$$

Shimizu et al. (2021) pointed out that the approximation using the tangent space at the origin (Eq. 1) produces distortions. They proposed a new hyperbolic affine transformation layer (Poincaré FC layer) and used it to construct a novel HNN framework, HNN++ (Shimizu et al., 2021).

3 Proposed Method

Neural network layers can be considered to be composed of basic operations: vector addition, scalar-vector multiplication, matrix-vector multiplication, and nonlinear activation functions. In this section, we introduce how to extend the basic operations in hyperbolic neural networks to the product space of m hyperbolic spaces, $\mathbf{P} = \mathbb{H}^{n_1} \times \cdots \times \mathbb{H}^{n_m}$. Here we will treat the case where $\mathbb{H}$ is $\mathbb{B}$ (Poincaré Ball model), and all the curvatures are the same.

3.1 Addition and Scalar Multiplication in a Product of Hyperbolic Spaces

In Euclidean space, addition $+$ and scalar multiplication $\times$ are element-wise operations, and there is no need to consider the interaction across different elements. Therefore, we define alternatives to these operations in $\mathbf{P}$ as element-wise Möbius operations:

$$\boldsymbol{x} \oplus_{\mathbf{P}} \boldsymbol{y} := (\boldsymbol{x}_1 \oplus \boldsymbol{y}_1, \ldots, \boldsymbol{x}_m \oplus \boldsymbol{y}_m), \tag{3}$$

$$r \otimes_{\mathbf{P}} \boldsymbol{y} := (r \otimes \boldsymbol{y}_1, \ldots, r \otimes \boldsymbol{y}_m), \tag{4}$$

where $\boldsymbol{x} = (\boldsymbol{x}_1, \ldots, \boldsymbol{x}_m)$ and $\boldsymbol{y} = (\boldsymbol{y}_1, \ldots, \boldsymbol{y}_m)$ are tuples of points in the product space $\mathbf{P}$, and $r \in \mathbb{R}$ is a scalar value. Each point $\boldsymbol{x}_i$ (or $\boldsymbol{y}_i$) is a vector in an n_i-dimensional hyperbolic space. $\oplus$ and $\otimes$ on the right-hand side are the Möbius operations in a single hyperbolic space.

3.2 Matrix Multiplication in a Product of Hyperbolic spaces

Matrix multiplication involves interactions between different elements. Therefore, the extension of Möbius matrix multiplication to product spaces

[1] For $\boldsymbol{x}, \boldsymbol{y} \in \mathbb{B}$, Möbius Addition is defined as:

$$\boldsymbol{x} \oplus_c \boldsymbol{y} := \frac{(1 + 2c\langle \boldsymbol{x}, \boldsymbol{y}\rangle + c\|\boldsymbol{y}\|^2)\boldsymbol{x} + (1 - c\|\boldsymbol{x}\|^2)\boldsymbol{y}}{1 + 2c\langle \boldsymbol{x}, \boldsymbol{y}\rangle + c^2\|\boldsymbol{x}\|^2\|\boldsymbol{y}\|^2}.$$

See Appendix A for explicit representation of other operations.

should take into account the interaction between any two hyperbolic spaces.

Let $\mathbf{P}' = \mathbb{H}^{n'_1} \times \cdots \times \mathbb{H}^{n'_{m'}}$ be the target product space of m' hyperbolic spaces of a total dimensionality $n' = n'_1 + \cdots + n'_{m'}$. Inspired by the block matrix multiplication in Euclidean space, we define Möbius matrix multiplication in $\mathbf{P}$ as follows:

$$M \otimes_{\mathbf{P}} \boldsymbol{x} = \begin{pmatrix} M_{11} & \cdots & M_{1m} \\ \vdots & \ddots & \vdots \\ M_{m'1} & \cdots & M_{m'm} \end{pmatrix} \otimes_{\mathbf{P}} \begin{pmatrix} \boldsymbol{x}_1 \\ \vdots \\ \boldsymbol{x}_m \end{pmatrix}$$
$$:= \begin{pmatrix} M_{11} \otimes \boldsymbol{x}_1 \oplus \cdots \oplus M_{1m} \otimes \boldsymbol{x}_m \\ \vdots \\ M_{m'1} \otimes \boldsymbol{x}_1 \oplus \cdots \oplus M_{m'm} \otimes \boldsymbol{x}_m \end{pmatrix}, \quad (5)$$

where $M \in \mathbb{R}^{n' \times n}$ is a matrix, and $M_{ij} \in \mathbb{R}^{n'_i \times n_j}$ is a submatrix block of M. The off-diagonal blocks correspond to interactions between two different hyperbolic component spaces.

It is worth noting that Eq. (5) can be used to extend an arbitrary hyperbolic linear layer to a product space. For example, Shimizu et al. (2021) and Chen et al. (2021) defined hyperbolic linear layers $\mathcal{F}$ using a matrix parameter M, i.e., $\mathcal{F} = \mathcal{F}(M)$.[2] We can extend the hyperbolic linear layers $\mathcal{F}$ to the product space as follows:

$$\mathcal{F}_{\mathbf{P}}(M)(\boldsymbol{x}) :=$$
$$\begin{pmatrix} \mathcal{F}(M_{11})(\boldsymbol{x}_1) \oplus \cdots \oplus \mathcal{F}(M_{1m})(\boldsymbol{x}_m) \\ \vdots \\ \mathcal{F}(M_{m'1})(\boldsymbol{x}_1) \oplus \cdots \oplus \mathcal{F}(M_{m'm})(\boldsymbol{x}_m) \end{pmatrix}.$$

3.3 Activation Function in a Product of Hyperbolic spaces

In Euclidean space, activation functions are also element-wise operations. Activation functions in product of hyperbolic spaces can be defined as:

$$\sigma^{\otimes_{\mathbf{P}}}(\boldsymbol{y}) := (\sigma^{\otimes}(\boldsymbol{y}_1), \ldots, \sigma^{\otimes}(\boldsymbol{y}_m)). \quad (6)$$

3.4 HHGCN

HGCN (Chami et al., 2020) is a Hyperbolic version of Graph Convolutional Network (GCN) (Kipf and Welling, 2017), a widely used Graph Neural Network (GNN) architecture. First, in HGCN, each node's representation in the $(l-1)$-th layer, $\boldsymbol{x}_i^{l-1}$, is linearly transformed, i.e.,

$$\boldsymbol{h}_i^l = (W^l \otimes \boldsymbol{x}_i^{l-1}) \oplus \boldsymbol{b}. \quad (7)$$

[2]We omit the bias parameters b for simplicity.

Then, attention-based neighborhood aggregation is performed for each node through tangent space:

$$\boldsymbol{y}_i^l = \mathrm{Agg}(\boldsymbol{h}^l)_i$$
$$:= \exp_{\boldsymbol{h}_i^l}\left(\sum_{j \in N(i)} (w_{ij}^l \log_{\boldsymbol{h}_i^l}(\boldsymbol{h}_j^l))\right). \quad (8)$$

$N(i)$ denotes the set of neighboring nodes of the i-th node, and $\boldsymbol{h}^l = \{\boldsymbol{h}_j^l\}_j$ represents all the feature vectors at the l-th layer. w_{ij}^l is an attention weight calculated in tangent space:

$$w_{ij}^l = \mathrm{Softmax}_{j \in N(i)}(\mathrm{MLP}(\log_0(\boldsymbol{h}_i^l), \log_0(\boldsymbol{h}_j^l))).$$

Finally, a non-linear activation function is applied to each node:

$$\boldsymbol{x}_i^l = \sigma^{\otimes}(\boldsymbol{y}_i^l). \quad (9)$$

Now, we describe how to extend the HGCN architecture to a product space using the operations defined above: $\oplus_{\mathbf{P}}$, $\otimes_{\mathbf{P}}$, and $\sigma^{\otimes_{\mathbf{P}}}$. Here, we focus on the simplest case where the product space consists of two Hyperbolic spaces of the same dimension in each layer. We denote the extended model in $\mathbb{H} \times \mathbb{H}$ as **HHGCN**.

In HHGCN, each node's feature vector represents a tuple of points in the product space $\mathbf{P} = \mathbb{H} \times \mathbb{H}$. Let $\boldsymbol{x}_i^{l,\mathbf{P}} = (\boldsymbol{x}_i^{l,1}, \boldsymbol{x}_i^{l,2})$ $(\boldsymbol{x}_i^{l,k} \in \mathbb{H}, k = 1, 2)$ be the feature vector of the i-th node in the l-th layer. The product-space version of Eq. (7) is defined as follows:

$$\boldsymbol{h}_i^{l,\mathbf{P}} = (W^l \otimes_{\mathbf{P}} \boldsymbol{x}_i^{l-1,\mathbb{P}}) \oplus_{\mathbf{P}} \boldsymbol{b}. \quad (10)$$

Then, we perform neighborhood aggregation for each single hyperbolic space $\mathbb{H}$, i.e., for $k \in \{1, 2\}$,

$$\boldsymbol{y}_i^{l,k} = \mathrm{Agg}(\boldsymbol{h}^{l,k})_i. \quad (11)$$

Finally, we apply a non-linear activation function:

$$\boldsymbol{x}_i^{l,\mathbf{P}} = \sigma^{\otimes_{\mathbf{P}}}(\boldsymbol{y}_i^{l,\mathbf{P}}). \quad (12)$$

Note that the above extension can be applied to a product of any number of hyperbolic spaces.

3.5 Task-Specific Prediction Using HHGCN

As described in Section 3.4, HHGCN outputs embeddings $\boldsymbol{x}_i^{L,\mathbf{P}} \in \mathbf{P}$ for each node i, where L denotes the last layer. In downstream tasks such as node classification, we first project the node embeddings into a single hyperbolic space using the beta concatenation proposed in HNN++ (Shimizu et al., 2021), and then apply an appropriate task-specific decoder to the projected representation. For example, in the link prediction task, we utilize the Fermi-Dirac decoder (Krioukov et al., 2010; Nickel and Kiela, 2017) to calculate the probability score for each edge. In the node classification task, we project the representations to tangent space by $\log_0$, then perform Euclidean multinomial logistic regression, following HGCN (Chami et al., 2019).

3.6 HEGCN

We also attempt a combination of Hyperbolic space $\mathbb{H}$ and Euclidean space $\mathbb{E}$, which is expected to show high performance for less-hyperbolic datasets. We can define the linear layer like Eq. (5):

$$\begin{aligned} M \otimes \boldsymbol{x} &= \begin{pmatrix} M_{11} & M_{12} \\ M_{21} & M_{22} \end{pmatrix} \otimes \begin{pmatrix} \boldsymbol{x}_1 \\ \boldsymbol{x}_2 \end{pmatrix} \\ &:= \begin{pmatrix} M_{11} \otimes \boldsymbol{x}_1 \oplus M_{12} \otimes \exp_0(\boldsymbol{x}_2) \\ M_{21}\log_0(\boldsymbol{x}_1) + M_{22}\boldsymbol{x}_2 \end{pmatrix}, \end{aligned} \tag{13}$$

where M denotes a matrix, and $\boldsymbol{x} = (\boldsymbol{x}_1, \boldsymbol{x}_2)$ is a point of the product space $\mathbb{H} \times \mathbb{E}$. We can extend the GCN for this product space $\mathbb{H} \times \mathbb{E}$ in a similar way to Section 3.4 and call this model **HEGCN**.

4 Experiments

4.1 Setup

Following the previous studies on Hyperbolic GCNs (Chami et al., 2019; Chen et al., 2021), we evaluate our method in two tasks: node classification (NC) and link prediction (LP). We use four network embedding datasets: Disease and Airport (Chami et al., 2019), PubMed (Namata et al., 2012), and Cora (Sen et al., 2008). For each dataset, we show the Gromov's δ-hyperbolicity (Adcock et al., 2013; Narayan and Saniee, 2011; Jonckheere et al., 2008) calculated by Chami et al. (2019) with the results. Lower δ means higher tree-likeness, and thus hyperbolic architectures are expected to show higher performance.

To test the effectiveness of our method and neural networks in a product space of hyperbolic spaces, we adopt HGCN and the following Euclidean GNNs as the baselines: GCN (Kipf and Welling, 2017), GAT (Velickovic et al., 2018), SAGE (Hamilton et al., 2017), and SGC (Wu et al., 2019).

We also test the effectiveness of our method using different hyperbolic space representations: hyperboloid and Poincaré ball: HHGCN_h and HEGCN_h use hyperboloid, while HHGCN_p and HEGCN_p use Poincaré ball as the hyperbolic space. The difference changes the explicit formula of the Möbius operations used in HNN and may change computational stability. Note that HGCN uses the hyperboloid model.

We mainly follow the training setups of previous studies (Chami et al., 2019; Chen et al., 2021). The dimensions are all set to $n = 16 = 8 + 8$ for fair comparison. We use Riemannian Adam (rAdam) optimizer (Becigneul and Ganea, 2019) for hyperbolic parameters. Curvatures of hyperbolic space are set to -1 for our product-space models. Please refer to Appendix D for detailed information.

4.2 Results and Discussion

Table 1 shows the performance of the proposed and baseline models.

HHGCN vs. HGCN, GCN

For the tree-like datasets with lower δ (Disease, Airport), HHGCNs show higher performance than the baselines especially in the node classification task. Particularly, HHGCN_h shows comparable or better results than the baselines on every task in these datasets and yields significant improvement in Disease. In contrast, for the datasets with higher δ (PubMed, Cora), HHGCNs consistently underperform HGCN. These results suggest that HHGCN is more effective than the single-space counterparts especially in hyperbolic datasets.

HHGCN vs. HEGCN

Table 1 demonstrates that HHGCN outperforms HEGCN on the datasets with lower δ and slightly underperform with lower δ. These results suggest that HEGCN is less specialized to tree-like datasets than HHGCN due to the incorporation of Euclidean space. On the other hand, unexpectedly, the performance of HEGCN in Pubmed and Cora is worse than those of HGCN, even though HGCN uses only hyperbolic space. These results may suggest that Eq. (13) for HEGCN is insufficient to represent the interaction between spaces with different properties.

Hyperboloid vs. Poincaré ball

We can observe that HHGCN_h and HEGCN_h show stable performance, while HHGCN_p and HEGCN_p show performance degradation in the Disease dataset in the LP task. These results may

Dataset Hyperbolicity	Disease $\delta = 0$		Airport $\delta = 1$		PubMed $\delta = 3.5$		Cora $\delta = 11$	
Method	LP	NC	LP	NC	LP	NC	LP	NC
GCN (2017)	$64.7_{\pm 0.5}$	$69.7_{\pm 0.4}$	$89.3_{\pm 0.4}$	$81.4_{\pm 0.6}$	$91.1_{\pm 0.5}$	$78.1_{\pm 0.2}$	$90.4_{\pm 0.2}$	$81.3_{\pm 0.3}$
GAT (2018)	$69.8_{\pm 0.3}$	$70.4_{\pm 0.4}$	$90.5_{\pm 0.3}$	$81.5_{\pm 0.3}$	$91.2_{\pm 0.1}$	$79.0_{\pm 0.3}$	$\mathbf{93.7}_{\pm 0.1}$	$\mathbf{83.0}_{\pm 0.7}$
SAGE (2017)	$65.9_{\pm 0.3}$	$69.1_{\pm 0.6}$	$90.4_{\pm 0.5}$	$82.1_{\pm 0.5}$	$86.2_{\pm 1.0}$	$77.4_{\pm 2.2}$	$85.5_{\pm 0.6}$	$77.9_{\pm 2.4}$
SGC (2019)	$65.1_{\pm 0.2}$	$69.5_{\pm 0.2}$	$89.8_{\pm 0.3}$	$80.6_{\pm 0.1}$	$94.1_{\pm 0.0}$	$78.9_{\pm 0.0}$	$91.5_{\pm 0.1}$	$81.0_{\pm 0.1}$
HGCN (2019)	$90.8_{\pm 0.3}$	$74.5_{\pm 0.9}$	$96.4_{\pm 0.1}$	$90.6_{\pm 0.2}$	$\mathbf{96.3}_{\pm 0.0}$	$\mathbf{80.3}_{\pm 0.3}$	$92.9_{\pm 0.1}$	$79.9_{\pm 0.2}$
HHGCN_h	$\underline{\mathbf{96.1}}_{\pm 0.8}$	$\underline{94.0}_{\pm 1.2}$	$\underline{\mathbf{96.7}}_{\pm 0.3}$	$\underline{90.9}_{\pm 2.3}$	$93.4_{\pm 1.6}$	$76.0_{\pm 1.1}$	$92.8_{\pm 2.1}$	$77.2_{\pm 1.7}$
HHGCN_p	$89.9_{\pm 5.6}$	$\underline{\mathbf{94.7}}_{\pm 1.3}$	$94.9_{\pm 1.3}$	$\underline{\mathbf{93.8}}_{\pm 0.8}$	$93.2_{\pm 1.9}$	$75.9_{\pm 0.4}$	$91.8_{\pm 3.0}$	$78.4_{\pm 1.3}$
HEGCN_h	$\underline{93.6}_{\pm 1.9}$	$\underline{94.0}_{\pm 0.8}$	$94.0_{\pm 0.3}$	$\underline{91.5}_{\pm 1.6}$	$94.8_{\pm 0.8}$	$76.1_{\pm 0.6}$	$\underline{93.2}_{\pm 1.4}$	$78.3_{\pm 1.2}$
HEGCN_p	$86.4_{\pm 2.0}$	$\underline{94.1}_{\pm 1.1}$	$95.7_{\pm 1.0}$	$\underline{92.9}_{\pm 1.1}$	$95.0_{\pm 1.7}$	$76.2_{\pm 0.5}$	$\underline{93.2}_{\pm 1.2}$	$78.{}_{\pm 1.1}3$

Table 1: ROC AUC (%) for the link prediction (LP) task and F1 scores (%) for the node classification (NC) task. The best scores for each column are shown in bold. We underline the scores of HHGCN and HEGCN if the scores are higher than the baselines' scores.

be due to the learning instability of the Poincaré ball model mentioned by Nickel and Kiela (2018).

HHGCN with HNNs Variants

Recently, Shimizu et al. (2021) proposed HNN++, which introduced a novel linear transformation in Poincaré ball with less distortion than the tangent space approximation Eq. (5). However, to the best of our knowledge, HNN++ has not been applied to the HGCN even in a single space. Thus, we apply the HNN++ to HGCN and HHGCN by replacing the hyperbolic transformation in Eq. (7) and further compare these models. We call the extensions HGCN_{++} and HHGCN_{++} , respectively. We also extend HyboNet (Chen et al., 2021), a novel HNN architecture in the Lorentz model, to HHGCN. We denote this extension as HHGCN_{HN} .

Table 2 shows the results. HHGCN_{++} yields higher or comparable performance than HGCN_{++} in the NC task. In contrast, in the LP task on the Disease dataset, HHGCN_{++} shows performance degradation. On the other hand, HHGCN_{HN} underperforms HyboNet in most cases except for the NC task on the Airport dataset.

These results suggest that certain HNN variants are not effective in extending to the product space. We leave more in-depth investigation to future work.

5 Preliminary Experiments on Machine Translation

5.1 Setup

We also tested the applicability of our method to machine translation tasks.

In the paper proposing HNN++, Shimizu et al. constructed a hyperbolic version of the convolutional sequence-to-sequence (ConvSeq2Seq) model (Gehring et al., 2017) by replacing various operations with the new hyperbolic operations they proposed, and applied it to machine translation. We extended their model to the product of two hyperbolic spaces using the operations proposed in Section 3.

They used WMT'17 English-German (Bojar et al., 2017) dataset containing 4M sentence pairs as training data. We extract 40K sentence pairs as a training dataset from it for the preliminary experiments. We train several scaled-down models with Riemannian Adam for 5K iterations. For more implementation details, please refer to Appendix E.

5.2 Results and Discussion

Table 3 shows that our model outperformed HNN++, albeit with lower overall performance due to the small size of the training data. All models show a significant performance drop at D=256. This may be due to the models being too large for the training data. Shimizu et al. suggested that the reason why the Euclidean model performs better

Dataset	Disease		Airport		PubMed		Cora	
Method	LP	NC	LP	NC	LP	NC	LP	NC
HGCN_{++}	$89.1_{\pm 1.3}$	$88.0_{\pm 4.3}$	$96.8_{\pm 0.2}$	$86.8_{\pm 2.5}$	$93.0_{\pm 0.2}$	$75.2_{\pm 1.7}$	$89.2_{\pm 0.6}$	$80.1_{\pm 0.6}$
HHGCN_{++}	$84.3_{\pm 1.9}$	$\underline{90.6}_{\pm 3.3}$	$96.3_{\pm 0.6}$	$\underline{91.4}_{\pm 1.1}$	$92.8_{\pm 0.2}$	$\underline{75.9}_{\pm 0.9}$	$\underline{89.3}_{\pm 1.2}$	$79_{\pm 0.4}$
HyboNet (2021)	$96.3_{\pm 0.3}$	$94.5_{\pm 0.8}$	$97.0_{\pm 0.2}$	$92.5_{\pm 0.9}$	$96.4_{\pm 0.1}$	$77.9_{\pm 1.0}$	$94.3_{\pm 0.3}$	$81.3_{\pm 0.9}$
HHGCN_{HN}	$92.6_{\pm 1.7}$	$94.4_{\pm 3.9}$	$94.1_{\pm 0.9}$	$\underline{93.6}_{\pm 0.8}$	$94.1_{\pm 0.8}$	$74.8_{\pm 0.9}$	$88.0_{\pm 1.3}$	$74.3_{\pm 1.6}$

Table 2: Results of the extension of HNN variants to a product space. We underline the scores of HHGCN_{++} and HHGCN_{HN} if these models outperform the corresponding single-space counterparts.

than the Hyperbolic model as the dimensionality increases is that sufficient computational complexity can be obtained through optimization. The fact that the Euclidean ConvSeq2Seq has the lowest results for D=256 may be due to its complexity resulting in overfitting. Comparative experiments with larger data sets are still needed, which we plan to do in the near future.

6 Related Work

GCN in a Product Space

κ-GCN with learnable curvature κ was proposed by Bachmann et al. (2020). They also attempted learning on the product of two constant curvature spaces. Unlike our results, HGCN showed better performance than their product space model in the Airport node classification task. It suggests that our proposed method is more suited to datasets with tree-like structures.

Hyperbolic-Euclidean Hybrid Model

Graph embedding in $\mathbb{H} \times \mathbb{E}$ considering the interaction between $\mathbb{H}$ and $\mathbb{E}$ has been done by GIL (Zhu et al., 2020a). While GIL is specialized for graphs, our method (Eq. 13) is applicable to general neural networks in $\mathbb{H} \times \mathbb{E}$ not limited to GNNs.

7 Conclusion

We proposed a general method to extend existing single-space HNN architectures to a product Space. We applied our method to HGCN and conducted experiments across several graph datasets and HNN architectures. The results show that models using a product of hyperbolic spaces perform better on tree-like datasets than models using a single hyperbolic space especially in the node classification task.

Future Work

We applied our method to the several HNN variants and found that our method was effective with some HNN types but not with others. The theoretical explanation for this difference will be a future issue.

We plan to conduct machine translation experiments using the entire WMT'17 Endlish-German training data and to apply our method to Transformer-based machine translation models in the near future. We are also going to investigate the effectiveness and limitations of our method on other NLP tasks such as natural language inference and document classification.

Acknowledgements

These research results were obtained from the commissioned research (No. 225) by National Institute of Information and Communications Technology (NICT), Japan. This work was also supported by JSPS KAKENHI Grant Number JP19H04166.

References

Aaron B. Adcock, Blair D. Sullivan, and Michael W. Mahoney. 2013. Tree-like structure in large social and information networks. In *2013 IEEE 13th International Conference on Data Mining*, pages 1–10.

Roy M. Anderson and Robert M. (Robert McCredie) May. 1991. *Infectious diseases of humans : dynamics and control*. Oxford University Press.

Gregor Bachmann, Gary Bécigneul, and Octavian-Eugen Ganea. 2020. Constant curvature graph convolutional networks.

Gary Becigneul and Octavian-Eugen Ganea. 2019. Riemannian adaptive optimization methods. In *International Conference on Learning Representations*.

Ondřej Bojar, Rajen Chatterjee, Christian Federmann, Yvette Graham, Barry Haddow, Shujian Huang, Matthias Huck, Philipp Koehn, Qun Liu, Varvara

Model	D=16	D=64	D=256
ConvSeq2Seq (Gehring et al., 2017)	1.30	**2.47**	0.0
HNN++ (Shimizu et al., 2021)	1.41	1.29	0.86
Ours	**1.94**	2.17	**0.87**

Table 3: BLEU-4 (Papineni et al., 2002) scores for the machine translation using the small dataset we extracted from WMT'17 English-German dataset. D denotes the dimensions of token embeddings.

Logacheva, Christof Monz, Matteo Negri, Matt Post, Raphael Rubino, Lucia Specia, and Marco Turchi. 2017. Findings of the 2017 conference on machine translation (WMT17). In *Proceedings of the Second Conference on Machine Translation*, pages 169–214, Copenhagen, Denmark. Association for Computational Linguistics.

Michael M. Bronstein, Joan Bruna, Yann LeCun, Arthur Szlam, and Pierre Vandergheynst. 2017. Geometric deep learning: Going beyond euclidean data. *IEEE Signal Processing Magazine*, 34(4):18–42.

James W Cannon, William J Floyd, Richard Kenyon, Walter R Parry, et al. 1997. Hyperbolic geometry. *Flavors of geometry*, 31(59-115):2.

Benjamin Paul Chamberlain, James Clough, and Marc Peter Deisenroth. 2017. Neural embeddings of graphs in hyperbolic space.

Ines Chami, Adva Wolf, Da-Cheng Juan, Frederic Sala, Sujith Ravi, and Christopher Ré. 2020. Low-dimensional hyperbolic knowledge graph embeddings. In *Proceedings of the 58th Annual Meeting of the Association for Computational Linguistics*, pages 6901–6914, Online. Association for Computational Linguistics.

Ines Chami, Zhitao Ying, Christopher Ré, and Jure Leskovec. 2019. Hyperbolic graph convolutional neural networks. In *Advances in Neural Information Processing Systems 32: Annual Conference on Neural Information Processing Systems 2019, NeurIPS 2019, December 8-14, 2019, Vancouver, BC, Canada*, pages 4869–4880.

Weize Chen, Xu Han, Yankai Lin, Hexu Zhao, Zhiyuan Liu, Peng Li, Maosong Sun, and Jie Zhou. 2021. Fully hyperbolic neural networks. *CoRR*, abs/2105.14686.

Octavian-Eugen Ganea, Gary Bécigneul, and Thomas Hofmann. 2018. Hyperbolic neural networks.

Jonas Gehring, Michael Auli, David Grangier, Denis Yarats, and Yann N. Dauphin. 2017. Convolutional sequence to sequence learning. In *Proceedings of the 34th International Conference on Machine Learning, ICML 2017, Sydney, NSW, Australia, 6-11 August 2017*, volume 70 of *Proceedings of Machine Learning Research*, pages 1243–1252. PMLR.

Albert Gu, Frederic Sala, Beliz Gunel, and Christopher Ré. 2019. Learning mixed-curvature representations in product spaces. In *International Conference on Learning Representations*.

Caglar Gulcehre, Misha Denil, Mateusz Malinowski, Ali Razavi, Razvan Pascanu, Karl Moritz Hermann, Peter Battaglia, Victor Bapst, David Raposo, Adam Santoro, and Nando de Freitas. 2018. Hyperbolic attention networks.

William L. Hamilton, Zhitao Ying, and Jure Leskovec. 2017. Inductive representation learning on large graphs. In *Advances in Neural Information Processing Systems 30: Annual Conference on Neural Information Processing Systems 2017, December 4-9, 2017, Long Beach, CA, USA*, pages 1024–1034.

Edmond Jonckheere, Poonsuk Lohsoonthorn, and Francis Bonahon. 2008. Scaled gromov hyperbolic graphs. *Journal of Graph Theory*, 57(2):157–180.

Thomas N. Kipf and Max Welling. 2017. Semi-supervised classification with graph convolutional networks. In *5th International Conference on Learning Representations, ICLR 2017, Toulon, France, April 24-26, 2017, Conference Track Proceedings*. OpenReview.net.

Max Kochurov, Rasul Karimov, and Serge Kozlukov. 2020. Geoopt: Riemannian optimization in pytorch.

Dmitri Krioukov, Fragkiskos Papadopoulos, Maksim Kitsak, Amin Vahdat, and Marián Boguñá. 2010. Hyperbolic geometry of complex networks. *Phys. Rev. E*, 82:036106.

Galileo Namata, Ben London, Lise Getoor, and Bert Huang. 2012. Query-driven active surveying for collective classification. In *ICML Workshop on MLG*.

Onuttom Narayan and Iraj Saniee. 2011. Large-scale curvature of networks. *Phys. Rev. E*, 84:066108.

Maximilian Nickel and Douwe Kiela. 2017. Poincaré embeddings for learning hierarchical representations.

Maximilian Nickel and Douwe Kiela. 2018. Learning continuous hierarchies in the lorentz model of hyperbolic geometry. In *Proceedings of the 35th International Conference on Machine Learning, ICML 2018, Stockholmsmässan, Stockholm, Sweden, July 10-15, 2018*, volume 80 of *Proceedings of Machine Learning Research*, pages 3776–3785. PMLR.

Kishore Papineni, Salim Roukos, Todd Ward, and Wei-Jing Zhu. 2002. Bleu: a method for automatic evaluation of machine translation. In *Proceedings of the 40th Annual Meeting of the Association for Computational Linguistics*, pages 311–318, Philadelphia, Pennsylvania, USA. Association for Computational Linguistics.

Peter Petersen, S Axler, and KA Ribet. 2006. *Riemannian geometry*, volume 171. Springer.

Frederic Sala, Chris De Sa, Albert Gu, and Christopher Re. 2018. Representation tradeoffs for hyperbolic embeddings. In *Proceedings of the 35th International Conference on Machine Learning*, volume 80 of *Proceedings of Machine Learning Research*, pages 4460–4469. PMLR.

Prithviraj Sen, Galileo Namata, Mustafa Bilgic, Lise Getoor, Brian Galligher, and Tina Eliassi-Rad. 2008. Collective classification in network data. *AI Magazine*, 29(3):93.

Ryohei Shimizu, YUSUKE Mukuta, and Tatsuya Harada. 2021. Hyperbolic neural networks++. In *International Conference on Learning Representations*.

Alexandru Tifrea, Gary Bécigneul, and Octavian-Eugen Ganea. 2018. Poincaré glove: Hyperbolic word embeddings.

Abraham Albert Ungar. 2008. A gyrovector space approach to hyperbolic geometry. *Synthesis Lectures on Mathematics and Statistics*, 1(1):1–194.

Petar Velickovic, Guillem Cucurull, Arantxa Casanova, Adriana Romero, Pietro Liò, and Yoshua Bengio. 2018. Graph attention networks. In *6th International Conference on Learning Representations, ICLR 2018, Vancouver, BC, Canada, April 30 - May 3, 2018, Conference Track Proceedings*. OpenReview.net.

Felix Wu, Amauri Souza, Tianyi Zhang, Christopher Fifty, Tao Yu, and Kilian Weinberger. 2019. Simplifying graph convolutional networks. In *Proceedings of the 36th International Conference on Machine Learning*, volume 97 of *Proceedings of Machine Learning Research*, pages 6861–6871. PMLR.

Shichao Zhu, Shirui Pan, Chuan Zhou, Jia Wu, Yanan Cao, and Bin Wang. 2020a. Graph geometry interaction learning. In *Advances in Neural Information Processing Systems 33: Annual Conference on Neural Information Processing Systems 2020, NeurIPS 2020, December 6-12, 2020, virtual*.

Yudong Zhu, Di Zhou, Jinghui Xiao, Xin Jiang, Xiao Chen, and Qun Liu. 2020b. HyperText: Endowing FastText with hyperbolic geometry. In *Findings of the Association for Computational Linguistics: EMNLP 2020*, pages 1166–1171, Online. Association for Computational Linguistics.

A Operations in hyperbolic space

Möbius Addition $\oplus$ and Möbius Scalar Multiplication $\otimes$ in the Poincaré Ball model

The hyperbolic versions of addition(Möbius Addition $\oplus$) and scalar multiplication (Möbius Scalar Multiplication $\otimes$) are defined as follows:

$$\boldsymbol{x} \oplus_c \boldsymbol{y} := \frac{(1 + 2c\langle \boldsymbol{x}, \boldsymbol{y}\rangle + c\|\boldsymbol{y}\|^2)\boldsymbol{x} + (1 - c\|\boldsymbol{x}\|^2)\boldsymbol{y}}{1 + 2c\langle \boldsymbol{x}, \boldsymbol{y}\rangle + c^2\|\boldsymbol{x}\|^2\|\boldsymbol{y}\|^2},$$

$$r \otimes_c \boldsymbol{x} := \frac{1}{\sqrt{c}} \tanh(r \tanh^{-1}(\sqrt{c}\|\boldsymbol{x}\|)) \frac{\boldsymbol{x}}{\|\boldsymbol{x}\|},$$

where $\boldsymbol{x}, \boldsymbol{y}$ are points in a hyperbolic space $\mathbb{B}$ and $r \in \mathbb{R}$ is scalar value.

These were first introduced in the context of Einstein's special theory of relativity in order to successfully describe the composite law of velocities such that the absolute value does not exceed the speed of light (Ungar, 2008).

Exp and Log Maps in the Poincaré Ball model

For $\boldsymbol{v} \in T_0\mathbb{B}_c^n \setminus \{0\}$ and $\boldsymbol{y} \in \mathbb{B}_c^n \setminus \{0\}$,

$$\exp_0^c(\boldsymbol{v}) = \tanh(\sqrt{c}\|\boldsymbol{v}\|) \frac{\boldsymbol{v}}{\sqrt{c}\|\boldsymbol{v}\|},$$

$$\log_0^c(\boldsymbol{y}) = \tanh^{-1}(\sqrt{c}\|\boldsymbol{y}\|) \frac{\boldsymbol{y}}{\sqrt{c}\|\boldsymbol{y}\|}.$$

Attention Mechanism in Hyperbolic Space

In order to realize the attention mechanism, centroid (weighted sum) in hyperbolic space had several definitions depending on the model, but Shimizu et al. (2021) showed that they are equivalent to Möbius gyromidpoint. For the Poincaré Ball model, the Möbius gyromidpoint $\boldsymbol{m}$ of hyperbolic vectors $\{\boldsymbol{b}_i \in \mathbb{B}_c^n\}_{i=1}^N$ with the scalar weights $\{\nu_i \in \mathbb{R}\}_{i=1}^N$ is defined as:

$$\boldsymbol{m} = \mathsf{Centroid}(\{\nu_i \in \mathbb{R}\}_{i=1}^N, \{\boldsymbol{b}_i \in \mathbb{B}_c^n\}_{i=1}^N) := \frac{1}{2} \otimes_c \left(\frac{\sum_{i=1}^N \nu_i \quad \lambda_{\boldsymbol{b}_i}^c \boldsymbol{b}_i}{\sum_{i=1}^N |\nu_i|(\lambda_{\boldsymbol{b}_i}^c - 1)} \right). \tag{14}$$

B Decoding Mechanism

B.1 Beta Concatenation

We utilized beta concatetenation proposed in HNN++ (Shimizu et al., 2021) to project product-space representations into a single hyperbolic space:

$$\boldsymbol{x}_i^{\text{out}} = \exp_0(\frac{\beta_n}{\beta_{n_1}} \log_0(\boldsymbol{x}_i^{L,1}), \frac{\beta_n}{\beta_{n_2}} \log_0(\boldsymbol{x}_i^{L,2})). \tag{15}$$

Where n is the overall dimension, and n_i is the dimension of i-th space (here $n_1 = n_2 = \frac{n}{2}$). Inside the $\exp_0$ parentheses, the usual concatenation of two Euclidean vectors is performed. $\beta_N := B(\frac{N}{2}, \frac{1}{2})$ (B : beta function) are the scaling factors to preserve the expectation of the norm.

B.2 Fermi-Dirac Decoder

For link prediction task, we utilize the Fermi-Dirac decoder (Krioukov et al., 2010; Nickel and Kiela, 2017), a generalization of sigmoid, to calculate the probability score for edges:

$$p(i, j) = [e^{(d_{\mathbb{H}}(\boldsymbol{x}_i^{\text{out}}, \boldsymbol{x}_j^{\text{out}}) - r)/t}]^{-1}. \tag{16}$$

where $r, t > 0$ are hyperparameters and $d_{\mathbb{H}}$ is distance function of hyperbolic space $\mathbb{H}$.

C Dataset Description

We use four network embedding datasets, Disease (Chami et al., 2019), Airport (Chami et al., 2019), PubMed (Namata et al., 2012), and Cora (Sen et al., 2008) following Chami et al. (2019); Chen et al. (2021). PubMed and Cora are standard benchmarks, where nodes are scientific papers, edges are citations between them, and node labels represent the academic domains of the papers. The first two datasets are constructed by Chami et al. (2019). Disease is a tree dataset built by simulating SIR disease spread model (Anderson and May, 1991), and Airport is a graph dataset consisting of airports and air routes obtained from OpenFlights.org [3].

The four datasets are preprocessed by Chami et al. (2019) and published in their code repository.[4] We show statistics of the datasets in table 4. For more information, please refer to the paper (Chami et al., 2019).

D Details on Network Embedding Experiments

We utilize Geoopt (Kochurov et al., 2020) and Riemannian Adam (rAdam) optimizer (Becigneul and Ganea, 2019) for hyperbolic parameters. For each dataset and model, we conduct hyper-parameter

[3] https://openflights.org

[4] https://github.com/HazyResearch/hgcn

Name	Nodes	Edges	Classes	Node features
Disease	1044	1043	2	1000
Airport	3188	18631	4	4
PubMed	19717	88651	3	500
Cora	2708	5429	7	1433

Table 4: Datasets' statistics.

search over Dropout $\in \{0, 0.1, 0.3, 0.7, 0.9\}$, Weight-Decay $\in \{0, 0.01, 0.1, 0.2, 0.4\}$. The performance is evaluated using five different random seeds for each condition. We fixed curvatures of hyperbolic spaces to -1. This is because learnable curvature sometimes showed instability. Some hyper-parameters, such as the initial learning rate and the number of layers, are fixed as shown in table 5, with reference to the previous study (Chen et al., 2021).

E Machine Translation Experiments

Following the setting of HNN++ (Shimizu et al., 2021), each model is the encoder-decoder model, both of which are composed of five convolutional layers with a kernel size of three and a channel size of D, five convolutional layers with a kernel size of three and a channel size of 2D, and two convolutional layers with a kernel size of one and a channel size of 4D. In each layer of our model, the hyperbolic affine transformation of HNN++ is replaced by its extension to the product of two hyperbolic spaces.

For training and optimization, we mainly follow the setting of HNN++. The main differences are the size of the dataset and iteration numbers. We extract (40K, 10K, 1K) sentences from the entire WMT'17 English-German dataset consisting of (4M, 40K, 3K) sentences for (training, validation, test). We trained models for 5K iterations instead of 100K iterations.

We use the same parameter as HNN++ for the Riemannian Adam optimizer; $\beta_1 = 0.9, \beta_2 = 0.98$ and $\epsilon = 10^{-9}$. The warm-up period was set as the first 400 iteration instead of 4000 iteration.

Dataset	Disease		Airport		PubMed		Cora	
Task	LP	NC	LP	NC	LP	NC	LP	NC
Layers	2	4	2	6	2	3	2	3
Initial Learning Rate	0.005	0.005	0.01	0.02	0.008	0.02	0.02	0.02
Max Grad Norm	None	0.5	0.5	1	0.5	0.5	0.5	1

Table 5: Hyper-parameters for each task.

Explicit Use of Topicality in Dialogue Response Generation

Takumi Yoshikoshi Hayato Atarashi Takashi Kodama Sadao Kurohashi
Kyoto University, Japan
{takumiyoshiko, atarashi, kodama}@nlp.ist.i.kyoto-u.ac.jp
kuro@i.kyoto-u.ac.jp

Abstract

The current chat dialogue systems implicitly consider the topic given the context, but not explicitly. As a result, these systems often generate inconsistent responses with the topic of the moment. In this study, we propose a dialogue system that responds appropriately following the topic by selecting the entity with the highest "topicality." In topicality estimation, the model is trained through self-supervised learning that regards entities appearing in both context and response as the topic entities. In response generation, the model is trained to generate topic-relevant responses based on the estimated topicality. Experimental results show that our proposed system can follow the topic more than the existing dialogue system that considers only the context.

1 Introduction

In recent years, end-to-end chat dialogue systems have been developed remarkably, making it possible to generate rich and flexible responses. However, such current chat dialogue systems only implicitly consider the topic given the context as it is, but do not explicitly consider it (Adiwardana et al., 2020; Roller et al., 2021). As a result, these systems often generate inconsistent responses with the topic (Sugiyama et al., 2021).

In this study, we propose a dialogue system that selects the next dialogue topic and responds using the selected topic explicitly. Our system selects the next topic entity based on **topicality** (Givón, 1983). Here, we define the entity as a noun or compound nouns, and topicality as the degree of speaker awareness directed toward each entity in the dialogue context. In addition, we call the entity with the highest topicality in the context **topic entity**. In the response generation part, our system generates responses based on the estimated topic entity as well as the context.

We propose the **Two-Stage** model, which learns topicality estimation and response generation in two stages, and the **End-to-End** model, which learns in the end-to-end method.

Due to the lack of dialogue corpus with the topic annotated, we use a self-supervised learning method to train our proposed models. Specifically, we extract triples of <*context*, *response*, *labeled topic entity candidates*> from the unannotated dialogue corpus.

For labeling, we regard topic entity candidates (= entities in the context) in the response as topic entities and assign labels to them. This procedure assumes that the entity in the response can be considered the topic entity. Furthermore, zero anaphora resolution is applied to restore those omitted words when assigning labels because word omission is pervasive in actual dialogue (especially in Japanese).

The automatic and human evaluation results show that our proposed system can follow the topic more than the existing dialogue system that considers only the context.

2 Related Work

2.1 Dialogue Systems that Consider only Context

Existing dialogue systems that consider only the dialogue context sometimes generate dull responses for elevating a naturalness of response (Vinyals and Le, 2015; Shang et al., 2015). To solve this issue, dialogue systems based on the Transformer (Vaswani et al., 2017), such as Meena (Adiwardana et al., 2020) and BlenderBot (Roller et al., 2021), have been proposed. These dialogue systems generate diverse and engaging responses with large dialogue data and model parameters.

However, the above dialogue systems, which only consider the context, do not consider the topic explicitly and may generate inconsistent responses with the topic (Sugiyama et al., 2021). In this study, we construct dialogue systems that explicitly con-

Proceedings of the 2022 Conference of the North American Chapter of the Association for Computational Linguistics: Human Language Technologies: Student Research Workshop, pages 222 - 228
July 10-15, 2022

	# of dialogues	# of utterances	# of triples w/o ZAR	# of triples w/ ZAR
Twitter corpus	250M	670M	-	-
JPersonaChat	5,000	61,794	23,217 / 147,166	27,809 / 176,122
JEmpatheticDialogues	20,000	80,000	16,269 / 64,999	31,466 / 114,888
KUHCC	5,114	86,192	21,503 / 120,770	35,467 / 199,094

Table 1: Statistics for each dialogue corpus. ZAR stands for Zero Anaphora Resolution. The left sides of columns "w/o ZAR" and "w/o ZAR" show the number of triples with the positive label, and the right side shows the number of triples with the negative label.

sider topicality to generate responses following the topic.

2.2 Dialogue Systems that Explicitly Consider the Topic

There are two purposes for explicitly considering the topic: generating informative responses and generating responses following the topic.

To generate informative responses, Xing et al. (2017) proposed a dialogue system considering the topic explicitly. This system predicts topic words that are highly relevant to words in the context by a pretrained Twitter LDA model (Zhao et al., 2011) and generates responses based on the predicted topic words. Mou et al. (2016) proposed a system that selects the noun with the highest PMI (Church and Hanks, 1990) against words in the context and generates responses that contains the noun.

To generate responses following the topic, Zhang et al. (2020) attempts to generate topic-relevant responses by learning examples in which entities in the dialogue context continue to appear in the response as the topic. However, in actual dialogues, the topic entity is omitted more frequently than other words (Givón, 1983). The method of Zhang et al. (2020) does not consider this omission problem, but we consider it by restoring the omitted entities.

3 Dataset Construction

We construct the dataset for self-supervised training of the proposed model. The dataset is constructed based on the assumption that entities that appear in both context and response are the topic entities. Considering the pervasiveness of word omission in actual dialogue, the omitted words are restored by zero anaphora resolution.

3.1 Dialogue Corpora

All models used in this study are pre-trained by the Twitter Corpus and then fine-tuned by JPersonaChat (Sugiyama et al., 2021), JEmpatheticDialogues (Sugiyama et al., 2021), and Kyoto University Hobby Chat Corpus (KUHCC). The size of each corpus is shown in Table 1.

JPersonaChat (Sugiyama et al., 2021) is a dialogue corpus between two Japanese speakers with specific personas based on PesonaChat (Zhang et al., 2018). JEmpatheticDialogues (Sugiyama et al., 2021) is a dialogue corpus between two Japanese speakers talking about an event based on diverse emotional expressions referring to EmpatheticDialogues (Rashkin et al., 2019).

In addition to these two existing corpora, we collect a chat dialogue corpus about hobbies, KUHCC, which is collected by crowdsourcing[1]. For dialogue collection, we use existing dialogue collection framework [2]. In this framework, when workers access the specified URL for dialogue collection, pair-matching is performed automatically, and a chat room is created for the workers to interact in real-time. It is challenging to get the workers to chat completely freely, therefore, paired workers are assigned different roles: one is the speaker, and the other is the listener. The speaker talks about their hobbies, and the listener listens while asking questions about the speaker's hobbies.

3.2 Method

We extract triples of <*context*, *response*, *labeled topic entity candidates*> from dialogue corpora by the self-supervised method.

For each context-response pair, up to 8 recently used nouns are extracted from the context and used as topic entity candidates. Personal pronouns and interrogatives are removed, and consecutive nouns in the same clause are extracted together as compound nouns. If an entity appears multiple times in a context, only the last entity is extracted. Juman++ (Tolmachev et al., 2018) and BERTKNP[3]

[1] `https://crowdsourcing.yahoo.co.jp/`

[2] `https://github.com/ku-nlp/ChatCollectionFramework`

[3] `https://github.com/ku-nlp/bertknp`

were used in this process.

In order to restore the word omissions in the response, we applied zero anaphora resolution using the Cohesion Analysis model (Ueda et al., 2020). This model was trained with multiple Japanese semantic relation analysis tasks: predicate-argument structure analysis, bridging anaphora resolution, and coreference resolution.

The topic entity candidates that appear in the response, including the restored one, are then assigned the "positive" label, which indicates that the entity is the topic entity. On the contrary, we assign the "negative" label, which indicates that the entity is not the topic entity, to the topic entity candidates that do not appear in the response. If there is more than one positive label in the context, only the last entity in the context is assigned the positive label[4].

3.3 Statistics

The models do not learn topicality estimation[5] in pre-training, hence we only extract context-response pairs from the Twitter Corpus. For fine-tuning, we extract triples from each of the three corpora, using the method described in Section 3.2. Table 1 shows the statistics of the constructed dataset. By restoring omitted words, we can obtain 33,548 more triples for JPersonaChat, 65,086 for JEmpatheticDialogues, and 92,288 for KUHCC.

4 Model

In this section, we describe the Two-Stage model, in which topicality estimation and response generation are learned in two stages (Section 4.1), and the End-to-End model, in which they are learned in the end-to-end method (Section 4.2).

4.1 Two-Stage Model

The Two-Stage model generates responses in two stages: Stage 1 and Stage 2 (Figure 1). In Stage 1 (topicality estimation), the model selects a topic entity from topic entity candidates based on the dialogue context. In Stage 2 (response generation), the model generates the response based on the context and the topic entity selected in Stage 1. Note that the gold topic entity is used during the training phase.

[4]In our preliminary experiments, the method, in which all topic entity candidates in the response are considered to be positive, did not get good results.

[5]The method for learning topicality estimation using Twitter corpus did not yield good results in preliminary experiments.

4.1.1 Model Architecture

We use BERT (Devlin et al., 2019) as the topicality estimation model in Stage 1. The input to the model is a topic entity candidate and the utterances in the context in sequence across [SEP] tokens. All topic entity candidates are input in the same way, and the topic entity candidate with the highest output for each [CLS] token is selected as the topic entity.

We use the encoder-decoder model with BERT as the encoder and Transformer (Vaswani et al., 2017) as the decoder in Stage 2. The encoders encode the context and the topic entity separately and then concatenate them. The parameters of these encoders are shared. In the decoder, we additionally use the rewarding mechanism (Takebayashi et al., 2018) to increase the generation probability of topic entities and attempt to generate responses that reflect topic entities.

4.1.2 Loss Function

In Stage 1, the topicality estimation model is trained by minimizing the cross-entropy loss between the probability distribution of the prediction and the gold label.

In Stage 2, the encoder-decoder model is trained by minimizing the following loss function $\mathcal{L}_{nll}$:

$$\mathcal{L}_{nll} = -\sum_{t=1}^{T'} \log p(y_t | y_{<t}, \mathbf{x}, \mathbf{e}), \quad (1)$$

where T' is the length of the target response, $y_{<t}$ is previously generated sequence, $\mathbf{x}$ is the context, and $\mathbf{e}$ is the topic entity.

4.2 End-to-End Model

The End-to-End model learns topicality estimation and response generation simultaneously (Figure 1). The topicality is estimated using the hidden states of topic entity candidates extracted from the encoded context. The response is generated based on the topic vector calculated based on topicality and the context vector.

4.2.1 Model Architecture

We use BERT as the encoder. The input to the encoder is the contexts split by [SEP] token. We additionally insert a special token [NO_ENTITY] at the beginning of the contexts. The encoder outputs the context vectors: $\mathbf{x} = [\mathbf{x}_1, ..., \mathbf{x}_M]^T \in \mathbf{R}^{M \times d}$ (M is the length of the context).

We then obtain the entity vectors: $\mathbf{e} = [\mathbf{e}_1, ..., \mathbf{e}_{N+1}]^T \in \mathbf{R}^{(N+1) \times d}$ (N is the number

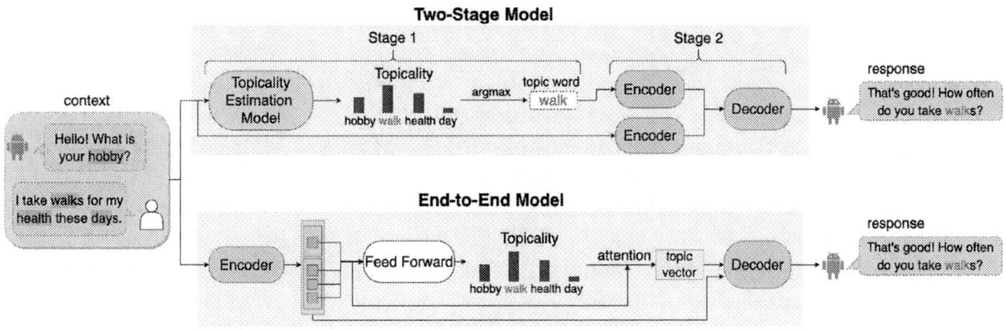

Figure 1: Overview of our proposed models. The Two-Stage model is trained in two stages, Stage 1 (topicality estimation) and Stage 2 (response generation). The End-to-End model learns topicality estimation and response generation simultaneously.

of topic entity candidates) by extracting and concatenating the corresponding vectors of each topic entity candidate in the the context vectors. In the case of a multi-token entity, we take the average of context vectors of the corresponding tokens. Given $\mathbf{e}$ as input, topicality is formulated as follows:

$$P_{topic}(\mathbf{e}) = softmax(\mathbf{e}\mathbf{W}_{topic}) \in \mathbb{R}^{(N+1)\times 1}, \tag{2}$$

where $\mathbf{W}_{topic} \in \mathbb{R}^{d\times 1}$ is a learnable linear layer. The topic vector is calculated using dot-product attention between $P_{topic}(\mathbf{e})$ and $\mathbf{e}$.

The input to the decoder is the concatenated vector of $\mathbf{x}$ and $\mathbf{v}_{topic}$. Similar to the Two-Stage model, the rewarding mechanism is incorporated in the decoder process.

4.2.2 Loss Function

We combine the negative log-likelihood loss for response generation $\mathcal{L}_{nll}$ and the cross-entropy loss for topicality estimation $\mathcal{L}_{topic}$ modulated by a weight by α, which is the hyperparameter. The overall loss function $\mathcal{L}$ is:

$$\mathcal{L} = (1-\alpha)\mathcal{L}_{nll} + \alpha\mathcal{L}_{topic} \tag{3}$$

Note that $\mathcal{L}_{nll}$ is the same as in equation (1), and in the loss function for the topicality estimation, the parameters are not updated if the corresponding label is negative (= the topic entity candidate is not in the response.)

5 Experiment

5.1 Experimental Settings

We use the Japanese pre-trained BERT Large model with whole word maskifng[6] as the encoder. For the decoder, we use a 12-layer Transfomer decoder (Vaswani et al., 2017) in all models.

For the dataset construction method, we compare the method without zero anaphora resolution (**w/o ZAR**) and the one with zero anaphora resolution (**w/ ZAR**). For the decoder type, we compare the standard Transformer decoder and the one with a rewarding mechanism (**+ reward**).

For comparison, we use the response generation model that considers only the context as the Baseline. The Baseline model selects the topic entity using a heuristic method that regards the last entity in the context as the topic entity.

In decoding, we use sample-and-rank decoding (Adiwardana et al., 2020) for all models, including the Baseline. Each parameter is set at temperature T=1.0 and the number of response candidates N=50. For random sampling, top-k sampling and top-p sampling are applied, with k=40 and p=0.9. We also apply the bigram penalty (Paulus et al., 2018; Klein et al., 2017).

5.2 Evaluation Method

5.2.1 Topicality Estimation

We create the evaluation data for assessing topicality estimation using crowdsourcing.[7] First, we randomly select 57 dialogues from the test data of KUHCC and then extract 4,702 topic entity candidates along with the context using the method as in Section 3.2. Crowdworkers are shown the context and the topic entity candidates, and asked to select appropriate entities as the next topic from provided topic entity candidates (multiple choice is allowed).

[6] https://nlp.ist.i.kyoto-u.ac.jp/?ku_bert_japanese

[7] https://crowdsourcing.yahoo.co.jp/

	topicality estimation			response generation			
	P@1	R@1	R@3	PPL	BLEU-2/4	Natural	Topic
Baseline	0.561	0.440	0.777	24.40	7.14/0.88	2.46	2.52
Two-Stage w/o ZAR	0.625	0.491	0.803	**21.73**	7.22/**1.03**	2.33	2.52
Two-Stage w/o ZAR + reward	0.625	0.491	0.803	21.86	7.35/0.94	2.51	2.65
Two-Stage w/ ZAR	**0.658**	**0.523**	**0.838**	23.14	7.29/1.01	**2.75**	2.79
Two-Stage w/ ZAR + reward	**0.658**	**0.523**	**0.838**	23.14	**7.44**/1.01	2.71	**2.82**
End-to-End w/o ZAR	0.477	0.363	0.747	21.82	6.84/0.91	2.42	2.40
End-to-End w/o ZAR + reward	0.446	0.310	0.691	**21.73**	7.08/0.85	2.45	2.56
End-to-End w/ ZAR	0.580	0.449	0.776	21.86	6.87/0.91	2.56	2.59
End-to-End w/ ZAR + reward	0.605	0.479	0.801	21.87	7.11/0.82	2.45	2.63

Table 2: Results of evaluation of topicality estimation and response generation

All the entities selected by five or more workers are used as positive examples (= topic entities), and the rest are used as negative ones. Note that we remove the pairs of the context and the topic entity candidates for which no positive examples exist from the evaluation data. As a result, we obtained 741 positive examples and 3,219 negative examples as evaluation data.

We evaluate the models using the created evaluation data. We use P@1 and R@k as evaluation metrics. P@1 is the top-1 precision, and R@k is the top-k recall (k=1,3 in this paper).

5.2.2 Response Generation

We evaluate the models using both automatic metrics and human evaluations. For automatic metrics, we calculate perplexity (PPL) and BLEU-2/4 (Papineni et al., 2002) for test data of three corpora for fine-tuning. Perplexity measures the fluency of generated responses, and BLEU metrics measure the accuracy of generated responses in terms of lexical overlap with references.

In human evaluations, crowdworkers evaluate responses by their degree of agreement to the following questions referring to the method of Zhang et al. (2020), on a five-point Likert scale (1: completely disagree, 5: completely agree).

- **Naturalness (Natural)**: "Do you think the given response is natural as Japanese?"
- **Topic-Following (Topic)**: "Do you think the given responses follows the topic in the context?"

The crowdworkers are shown pairs of a context and a response. The input to the models for generating responses is 100 contexts randomly extracted from the test data of KUHCC, Each pair of context and response is rated by five crowdworkers.

5.3 Results and Analysis

5.3.1 Topicality Estimation

Table 2 shows the evaluation results of the topicality estimation. Two-Stage w/ ZAR achieves the best scores on both precision and recall.

For the dataset construction method, w/ ZAR is better than w/o ZAR for both Two-Stage and End-to-End models. These results suggest that restoring the word omissions help improve the accuracy of topicality estimation.

As for the decoder type, the Two-Stage model outperforms the End-to-End model on the whole. This may be because the Two-Stage model directly optimizes the topicality estimation, whereas the End-to-End model does both the topicality estimation and response generation.

5.3.2 Response Generation

The results of the automatic evaluation for the response generation are shown in Table 2. The Two-Stage and End-to-End models we proposed in this paper show lower perplexity than the Baseline. For BLEU metrics, Two-Stage outperforms Baseline for both BLEU-2/4, although End-to-End shows no improvement. This result suggests that while topicality estimation helps improve response generation, multi-task learning of topicality estimation and response generation does not improve response generation.

The results of the human evaluation for the response generation are also shown in Table 2. In terms of restoring omission of words, both Two-Stage w/ ZAR and End-to-End w/ ZAR achieve better Topic-Following score compared to the Baseline. This improvement indicates that restoring the omission of entities helps generate the topic-following responses. In addition, the Topic-

Following score further improves by adding a rewarding mechanism, which is the method to increase the generation probability of the topic entity.

As for the decoder type, the Two-Stage model is better than the End-to-End model in both Naturalness and Topic-Following. This difference may be due to the fact that the End-to-End did not learn well to reflect on the topic entity because only about 50% of all context-response pairs are labeled with some topic entities.

6 Conclusion

We proposed dialogue systems that explicitly consider topicality to generate responses following the topic. Both automatic and human evaluation results confirmed that the proposed Two-Stage model could generate more topic-following responses than the dialogue system that only considers context. In addition, by restoring the word omission in the response by zero anaphora resolution, topicality estimation was further improved, and it was also confirmed that the generated responses can better capture the topic.

On the other hand, the Naturalness score of the generated responses tends to be low overall in the human evaluation, and there is still room for improvement. We will work to improve the quality of the response generation part by using some pretraining models as future work.

References

Daniel Adiwardana, Minh-Thang Luong, David R. So, Jamie Hall, Noah Fiedel, Romal Thoppilan, Zi Yang, Apoorv Kulshreshtha, Gaurav Nemade, Yifeng Lu, and Quoc V. Le. 2020. Towards a human-like open-domain chatbot. *CoRR*, abs/2001.09977.

Kenneth Ward Church and Patrick Hanks. 1990. Word Association Norms, Mutual Information, and Lexicography. *Computational Linguistics*, 16(1):22–29.

Jacob Devlin, Ming-Wei Chang, Kenton Lee, and Kristina Toutanova. 2019. BERT: Pre-training of Deep Bidirectional Transformers for Language Understanding. In *Proceedings of the 2019 Conference of the North American Chapter of the Association for Computational Linguistics: Human Language Technologies, Volume 1 (Long and Short Papers)*, pages 4171–4186, Minneapolis, Minnesota. Association for Computational Linguistics.

Thomas Givón. 1983. *Topic Continuity in Discourse: A quantitative cross-language study*, volume 3. John Benjamins Publishing Company.

Guillaume Klein, Yoon Kim, Yuntian Deng, Jean Senellart, and Alexander Rush. 2017. OpenNMT: Open-Source Toolkit for Neural Machine Translation. In *Proceedings of ACL 2017, System Demonstrations*, pages 67–72, Vancouver, Canada. Association for Computational Linguistics.

Lili Mou, Yiping Song, Rui Yan, Ge Li, Lu Zhang, and Zhi Jin. 2016. Sequence to backward and forward sequences: A content-introducing approach to generative short-text conversation. In *Proceedings of COLING 2016, the 26th International Conference on Computational Linguistics: Technical Papers*, pages 3349–3358, Osaka, Japan. The COLING 2016 Organizing Committee.

Kishore Papineni, Salim Roukos, Todd Ward, and Wei-Jing Zhu. 2002. Bleu: a Method for Automatic Evaluation of Machine Translation. In *Proceedings of the 40th Annual Meeting of the Association for Computational Linguistics*, pages 311–318, Philadelphia, Pennsylvania, USA. Association for Computational Linguistics.

Romain Paulus, Caiming Xiong, and Richard Socher. 2018. A Deep Reinforced Model for Abstractive Summarization. In *In Proceedings of the 6th International Conference on Learning Representations*, Vancouver, BC, Canada.

Hannah Rashkin, Eric Michael Smith, Margaret Li, and Y-Lan Boureau. 2019. Towards Empathetic Open-domain Conversation Models: a New Benchmark and Dataset.

Stephen Roller, Emily Dinan, Naman Goyal, Da Ju, Mary Williamson, Yinhan Liu, Jing Xu, Myle Ott, Eric Michael Smith, Y-Lan Boureau, and Jason Weston. 2021. Recipes for building an open-domain chatbot. In *Proceedings of the 16th Conference of the European Chapter of the Association for Computational Linguistics: Main Volume*, pages 300–325, Online. Association for Computational Linguistics.

Lifeng Shang, Zhengdong Lu, and Hang Li. 2015. Neural Responding Machine for Short-Text Conversation. In *Proceedings of the 53rd Annual Meeting of the Association for Computational Linguistics and the 7th International Joint Conference on Natural Language Processing (Volume 1: Long Papers)*, pages 1577–1586, Beijing, China. Association for Computational Linguistics.

Hiroaki Sugiyama, Masahiro Mizukami, Tsunehiro Arimoto, Hiromi Narimatsu, Yuya Chiba, Hideharu Nakajima, and Toyomi Meguro. 2021. Empirical analysis of training strategies of transformer-based japanese chit-chat systems. *CoRR*, abs/2109.05217.

Yuto Takebayashi, Chu Chenhui, Yuki Arase†, and Masaaki Nagata. 2018. Word rewarding for adequate neural machine translation. In *Proceedings of the 15th International Conference on Spoken Language Translation*, pages 14–22, Brussels. International Conference on Spoken Language Translation.

Arseny Tolmachev, Daisuke Kawahara, and Sadao Kurohashi. 2018. Juman++: A Morphological Analysis Toolkit for Scriptio Continua. In *Proceedings of the 2018 Conference on Empirical Methods in Natural Language Processing: System Demonstrations*, pages 54–59, Brussels, Belgium. Association for Computational Linguistics.

Nobuhiro Ueda, Daisuke Kawahara, and Sadao Kurohashi. 2020. BERT-based Cohesion Analysis of Japanese Texts. In *Proceedings of the 28th International Conference on Computational Linguistics*, pages 1323–1333, Barcelona, Spain (Online). International Committee on Computational Linguistics.

Ashish Vaswani, Noam Shazeer, Niki Parmar, Jakob Uszkoreit, Llion Jones, Aidan N Gomez, Ł ukasz Kaiser, and Illia Polosukhin. 2017. Attention is All you Need. In *Advances in Neural Information Processing Systems*, volume 30, pages 5998–6008. Curran Associates, Inc.

Oriol Vinyals and Quoc V. Le. 2015. A Neural Conversational Model. In *Proceedings of the International Conference on Machine Learning, Deep Learning Workshop*.

Chen Xing, Wei Wu, Yu Wu, Jie Liu, Yalou Huang, Ming Zhou, and Wei-Ying Ma. 2017. Topic Aware Neural Response Generation. In *Proceedings of the Thirty-First AAAI Conference on Artificial Intelligence*, AAAI'17, page 3351–3357. AAAI Press.

Saizheng Zhang, Emily Dinan, Jack Urbanek, Arthur Szlam, Douwe Kiela, and Jason Weston. 2018. Personalizing Dialogue Agents: I have a dog, do you have pets too? In *Proceedings of the 56th Annual Meeting of the Association for Computational Linguistics (Volume 1: Long Papers)*, pages 2204–2213, Melbourne, Australia. Association for Computational Linguistics.

Shuying Zhang, Tianyu Zhao, and Tatsuya Kawahara. 2020. Topic-relevant Response Generation using Optimal Transport for an Open-domain Dialog System. In *Proceedings of the 28th International Conference on Computational Linguistics*, pages 4067–4077, Barcelona, Spain (Online). International Committee on Computational Linguistics.

Wayne Zhao, Jing Jiang, Js Weng, Jing He, Ee-Peng Lim, Hongfei Yan, and Xiaoming Li. 2011. Comparing Twitter and Traditional Media Using Topic Models. volume 6611/2011, pages 338–349.

Automating Human Evaluation of Dialogue Systems

Sujan Reddy
Department of Information Technology
National Institute of Technology Karnataka, Surathkal
Mangalore, India
sujanreddy242@gmail.com

Abstract

Automated metrics to evaluate dialogue systems like BLEU, METEOR, etc., weakly correlate with human judgments. Thus, human evaluation is often used to supplement these metrics for system evaluation. However, human evaluation is time-consuming as well as expensive. This paper provides an alternative approach to human evaluation with respect to three aspects: naturalness, informativeness, and quality in dialogue systems. I propose an approach based on fine-tuning the BERT model with three prediction heads, to predict whether the system-generated output is natural, fluent and informative. I observe that the proposed model achieves an average accuracy of around 77% over these 3 labels. I also design a baseline approach that uses three different BERT models to make the predictions. Based on experimental analysis, I find that using a shared model to compute the three labels performs better than three separate models.

1 Introduction

The evaluation of Natural Language Generation (NLG) systems has generally been carried out by using automatic metrics such as BLEU (Papineni et al., 2002), METEOR (Banerjee and Lavie, 2005), ROUGE (Lin, 2004), etc. However, previous work Novikova et al. (2017) demonstrated that these metrics only weakly reflect human judgments of these NLG systems' output, and some form of human evaluation is required to better measure the quality of such NLG systems. Human annotators are generally asked three questions to evaluate whether a system-generated reference is acceptable or not . These questions, along with the corresponding aspects, are:

1. **Naturalness**- Could the utterance have been produced by a native speaker?
2. **Quality**- Is the utterance grammatically correct and fluent?
3. **Informativeness**- Does the utterance provide all the useful information from the meaning representation?

Since human evaluations can be expensive and time-consuming, an automated approach to flag such instances could make it easier for system designers to garner insights into the kind of instances the system is failing to generate good text for. In this paper, I propose a BERT-based model trained to predict answers to questions pertaining to the three aspects: naturalness, quality, and informativeness, with a "YES" (label=1) or a "NO" (label=0). The proposed model automatically flags system-generated references that are not up to a predefined standard. To the best of my knowledge, this is the first attempt to develop an automated model for predicting scores pertaining to multiple aspects of a system-generated reference.

The major contributions of this work can be summarized as follows : First, I propose a binarization scheme to binarize the human judgment scores in the dataset as these scores tend to be very subjective. A threshold is set, and all scores above the threshold are assigned a label and the scores below the threshold are assigned another label. Second, the BERT-based model is fine-tuned to predict three labels, answering the questions corresponding to the three aspects of the system-generated reference. I also perform an ablation study where three separate BERT-models are trained independently, each of which predicts a label.

The remainder of this paper is structured as follows: Section 2 talks about the recent works in the same domain. Section 3 discusses about the BERT-model that is used for the experiments. In section 4, I discuss about the dataset, pre-processing required, hyper-parameters as well as the baseline model's design. In section 5, I discuss about the performance of the proposed apporach in comparison with the baseline model. Finally in 6, I draw conclusions and outline future works.

Proceedings of the 2022 Conference of the North American Chapter of the Association for Computational Linguistics: Human Language Technologies: Student Research Workshop, pages 229 - 234

2 Related Work

Several works have been proposed in recent years which focus on fine-tuning BERT (Devlin et al., 2018) and its variants to evaluate the quality of a system-generated text. These approaches tend to correlate much better with human assessments. BERTScore (Zhang et al., 2019) compares the similarity of each token in the system generated reference with each token in the original reference using contextual embeddings rather than exact matching. This metric was observed to relate very closely to human judgments for image captioning systems. MoverScore (Zhao et al., 2019) is another metric that combines contextualized representations with distance measures. This metric was observed to generalize well across various tasks like summarization, machine translation, image captioning, and data-to-text generation. BLEURT (Sellam et al., 2020) is a BERT-based model that was pretrained on a large amount of synthetic data. This model can then be fine-tuned on a relatively small number of human judgments. It was observed to be very effective when the training data is scarce and imbalanced. COMET (Rei et al., 2020) is another neural framework that is used for training multi-lingual machine translation quality evaluation models.

All these works evaluate only the quality of the system-generated reference. While quality is correlated with the other aspects of the utterance, it might not be sufficient to capture all insights about an incorrectly generated text with just a single aspect. A grammatically correct text could lack some vital information that was present in the original reference (informativeness) or may not capture the natural speech patterns of a native speaker (naturalness).

Liu et al. (2021) proposed an automatic method for evaluating the naturalness of generated text in dialogue systems by fine-tuning a BERT-based model. The proposed model predicts a score between 1 and 6, indicating how natural the system-generated utterance is. However, this work does not consider that human judgments tend to be subjective. The data being fed to the model is therefore ambiguous in nature. In addition, the best model proposed in this paper uses human judgments on other related aspects like quality and informativeness by leveraging the positive correlation between these three aspects. However, this paper proposes a solution that eliminates human evaluation at inference time. Human annotations are used only for training the model. After training, the model can mimic/replace human annotators. Given the success of BERT-based models for system evaluation, I also use pre-trained BERT in my approach.

3 Method

BERT stands for Bidirectional Encoder Representation Transformer. The architecture of BERT was based on the encoder part of Transformers (Vaswani et al., 2017). BERT uses attention mechanism (Bahdanau et al., 2014) to convert the input representation into a better representation that takes context into account (Devlin et al., 2018). BERT makes use of fine-tuning to leverage the knowledge gained from pre-training. This means that BERT is pretrained on a relatively generic task, and the same architecture is fine-tuned on similar downstream tasks.

In this paper, I use the uncased BERT-Base model. that consists of 12 layers, 768 hidden states, and 12 attention heads. We will be leveraging the pre-training knowledge gained from NSP more than MLM. A [CLS] token is added to the system-generated reference's beginning. A [SEP] token is then added to the system-generated reference, followed by the original human-written reference. This is again followed by a [SEP] token. The tokens fed as input are tokenized using WordPiece embeddings. Sequence embeddings are also passed as input which stores information about which sentence the token belongs to. Positional embeddings from the Transfomer model are added to the input word embeddings along with sequence embeddings. So the model takes in two sentences as the input and predicts whether the second sentence follows the first sentence or not. The encoded representation of the [CLS] token contains information about the representation of the entire sequence. This is called pooled output. The pooled output is passed through a linear layer which is then followed by the output layer with 3 nodes having sigmoid activation. The final output is three values indicating the probability that the system reference is natural, fluent, and informative, respectively (see Fig 1).

4 Experimental Setup

4.1 Dataset

I consider the "Human Ratings of Natural Language Generation Outputs" (Novikova et al., 2017)

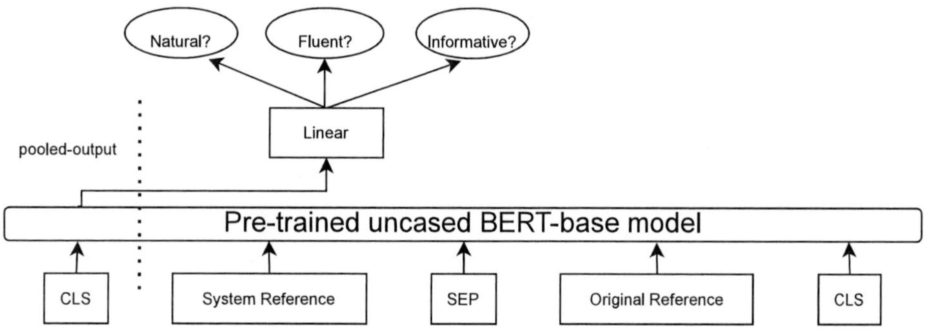

Figure 1: Fine-tuning BERT architecture

dataset in this paper. The dataset contains textual dialogue response from RNNLG[1], TGen[2] and LOLs[3]. These are data-driven natural language generation systems that were applied on 3 different but closely related domains- **SF hotel, SF restaurant** (Wen et al., 2015) and **BAGEL** (Mairesse et al., 2010) respectively. SF hotel and SF restaurant are based on information regarding hotels and restaurants in San Francisco, while BAGEL has information about restaurants in Cambridge. For every NLG system-generated reference, there is also a human-written reference in the dataset. The dataset also contains scores from 3 different human annotators for the system-generated reference's naturalness, quality, and informativeness. These scores were provided on the 6-point Likert-Scale with the lowest score being one and the highest being six. Table 1 contains an example of an instance from the dataset. Here judge refers to the label of the human annotators. Since there are three human annotators, the three labels are 1,2, and 3. The table also presents the BLEU , rouge-L and Meteor scores for the system generated output. These metrics are on higher side, which might indicate that the system-generated output is good. However, the human judge allots low scores for all three aspects for this instance.

Table 2 contains the distribution of the median of the scores from the three annotators over 11,122 instances. For some instances, I observed that more than one NLG system generated the same text. In such cases, the median of all such scores obtained from different NLG systems over the three human judges was considered. If the median is not a whole number, I consider the ceiling of the median score. The higher scores are due to the fact that the dataset considers state-of-the-art NLG systems.

Scores	naturalness	quality	informativeness
1	426	403	153
2	348	501	405
3	801	1071	320
4	1876	1930	1040
5	3383	3531	3427
6	4288	3686	5777

Table 2: Distribution of the median scores

Human annotations on naturalness, quality, and informativeness tend to be subjective. In fact, all three human annotators give the same naturalness score for only 1351 instances, identical quality scores for 1180 instances, and identical informativeness scores for 1772 instances.

Hence, to remove this ambiguity in the dataset, I decided to binarize the dataset by defining a fixed threshold. Novikova et al. (2017) classify all the ratings with scores greater than or equal to 5 as good ratings. Hence, I chose 5 as the threshold. All the instances with median scores below five are assigned a label of '0' and are considered bad utterances. All instances with median scores greater than or equal to 5 are assigned a label of '1' and considered good utterances.

Class	naturalness	quality	informativeness
0	3450	3904	1920
1	7672	7218	9202

Table 3: Distribution of the binarized scores

[1]https://github.com/shawnwun/RNNLG

[2]https://github.com/UFAL-DSG/tgen

[3]https://github.com/glampouras/JLOLS

Field	Value
System Generated Output	x is a french and restaurant near x..
Original Reference	x is a restaurant serving french food, near x
Judge	3
Informativeness	2
Naturalness	2
Quality	2
BLEU-1	0.875
BLEU-2	0.790569415
BLEU-3	0.678604404
BLEU-4	0.5
rouge-L	0.944690265
meteor	0.540778542

Table 1: Example of an instance from the dataset.

Table 3 shows the new distribution after binarizing the dataset. It can be observed that judgments are still skewed towards the higher scores. The ratios of positive (greater than or equal to 5-points) for the three aspects are 68:32, 64:36, and 82:18, respectively. The dataset (11122 instances) is randomly split into train, validation, and test with an 80:10:10 ratio.

4.2 Baseline

To test the performance of the proposed architecture, I use another approach that involves fine-tuning BERT. In this approach, I use three different BERT models, each fine-tuned to predict one of the aspects pertaining to the system-generated utterance. This approach is computationally less efficient than my proposed approach because it takes more time to train and get inferences from 3 different models. Also, this approach utilizes close to three times the memory used by my approach.

4.3 Experimental Setting

The BERT-base model contains 12 layers, 768 hidden states, and 12 attention heads. The pooled output is fed to a linear layer that contains 768 nodes. For all the experiments, I set the batch size to 16. I use the Adam optimizer and set the learning rate to 3e-4. All the models were run for five epochs. Since I use the BERT-Base model, the linear layer has dimension 768.

To deal with the class imbalance problem, I use the balanced cross-entropy function (L) (see equation 1) where $\hat{y}$ refers to the model output and y refers to the ground truth.

$$L = -\beta y log(\hat{y}) - (1-\beta)(1-y)(log(1-\hat{y})) \quad (1)$$

This loss function penalizes the model by a greater factor when it misclassifies an instance with a negative label than a positive label. I tune the parameter β using grid-search for the approach that uses 3 different BERT models. Zhou et al. (2017) suggests utilizing the ratio of negative instances to the total number instances as this factor. So I perform a grid search over values 5%, 10%, 15%, 20%, and 25% lesser as well as greater than this ratio. I observe that the optimal parameters obtained from grid search to be 0.3535, 0.3130, and 0.1454 for naturalness, quality, and informativeness, respectively. I use the same parameter for my approach with a single BERT model with three prediction heads.

5 Results and Discussion

Table 4 reports the comparison of the accuracies between both of my approaches. Given that the data is imbalanced, I also compare the f-1 scores of both of my approaches in Table 5. The tables report the mean and standard deviation of each metric computed over five iterations, each iteration having a different random seed. In Table 4 and Table 5, 3-BERT indicates three separate BERT models, and shared-BERT indicates a single BERT model with three prediction heads. The accuracy and f-1 scores suggest that shared-BERT outperforms 3-BERTs with respect to both measures for naturalness and informativeness. Since the prediction for all three aspects would require similarly encoded input representations, having a shared model instead of 3 individual models can significantly reduce the memory needed. Shared weights act as a regularizer and lessen the chances of over-fitting.

Aspect	3-BERT	shared-BERT
naturalness	76.19 (±1.00)	**77.98*** (±1.99)
quality	**67.66** (±3.14)	66.01 (±1.69)
informativeness	86.48 (±2.31)	**89.04*** (±0.79)

Table 4: Comparison of accuracies of predicting labels for system evaluation. * indicates that the difference is statistically significant with $p < 0.05$.

Aspect	3-BERT	shared-BERT
naturalness	81.81 (±1.60)	**84.63*** (±1.44)
quality	**73.87** (±3.27)	73.17 (±1.90)
informativeness	91.78 (±1.55)	**93.53*** (±0.48)

Table 5: Comparison of f-1 scores of predicting labels for system evaluation. * indicates that the difference is statistically significant with $p < 0.05$

Also, such a model can generalize well on new aspects that can be added in the future. The results suggest that both models can model the data well despite the class imbalance. This can be attributed to the balanced cross-entropy loss function.

I use the ANOVA test (Girden, 1992) to test the statistical significance of the difference in the f-1 scores and accuracies between both approaches. I set the significance level to 0.05. I observe that the results are statistically significant for naturalness and informativeness, which clearly demonstrates that the shared BERT model outperforms the 3-BERT model on these two aspects. For the aspect of quality, 3-BERT shows better performance. However, the gain in performance is not statistically significant. Further, in terms of model complexity, shared-BERT has only 2304 (768x3) learnable parameters more than a single BERT model, and the 3-BERT approach has three times the number of learnable parameters compared to a single BERT model. Hence, shared-BERT is a more efficient model in terms of memory occupied and computational complexity.

Qualitative example: I consider the example instance from Table 1. The scores from the automated evaluation metrics suggest that the system-generated output is a good one. However, the human annotator assigned low scores for this instance. Table 6 presents the scores obtained from both my approaches for this instance. These low probabilities indicate that the system-generated output is not natural, not informative and not fluent. This is an example of an instance which demonstrates the significance of having human annotations, and how the proposed models can mimic human annotators.

Aspect	3-BERT	shared-BERT
naturalness	0.15	0.12
quality	0.28	0.19
informativeness	0.33	0.22

Table 6: Model Output for considered example

6 Conclusion and Future Work

In this paper, I proposed an automated approach to evaluate three aspects of a system-generated sentence : naturalness, quality, and informativeness. I experiment with two BERT-based model approaches. Experimental validation suggests that the proposed approach that uses a single BERT model with three prediction heads is more efficient than three different BERT models with a single prediction head each.

The goal of this paper is to reduce the load on human annotators and automate the evaluation of dialogue systems. I hope that this work will motivate researchers to realize that this process can be automated and be made more reliable with the collection of additional relevant data. Further, aspects other than the three considered in this paper can yield some more insights into the performance of a dialogue system. As an extension of this work, I will verify the performance of my approach on other NLG systems like image captioning, question answering, machine translation, etc.

References

Dzmitry Bahdanau, Kyunghyun Cho, and Yoshua Bengio. 2014. Neural machine translation by jointly learning to align and translate. *arXiv preprint arXiv:1409.0473*.

Satanjeev Banerjee and Alon Lavie. 2005. Meteor: An automatic metric for mt evaluation with improved correlation with human judgments. In *Proceedings of the acl workshop on intrinsic and extrinsic evaluation measures for machine translation and/or summarization*, pages 65–72.

Jacob Devlin, Ming-Wei Chang, Kenton Lee, and Kristina Toutanova. 2018. Bert: Pre-training of deep bidirectional transformers for language understanding. *arXiv preprint arXiv:1810.04805*.

Ellen R Girden. 1992. *ANOVA: Repeated measures*. 84. sage.

Chin-Yew Lin. 2004. Rouge: A package for automatic evaluation of summaries. In *Text summarization branches out*, pages 74–81.

Ye Liu, Wolfgang Maier, Wolfgang Minker, and Stefan Ultes. 2021. Naturalness evaluation of natural language generation in task-oriented dialogues using bert. *arXiv preprint arXiv:2109.02938*.

François Mairesse, Milica Gasic, Filip Jurcicek, Simon Keizer, Blaise Thomson, Kai Yu, and Steve Young. 2010. Phrase-based statistical language generation using graphical models and active learning. In *Proceedings of the 48th Annual Meeting of the Association for Computational Linguistics*, pages 1552–1561.

Jekaterina Novikova, Ondřej Dušek, Amanda Cercas Curry, and Verena Rieser. 2017. Why we need new evaluation metrics for nlg. *arXiv preprint arXiv:1707.06875*.

Kishore Papineni, Salim Roukos, Todd Ward, and Wei-Jing Zhu. 2002. Bleu: a method for automatic evaluation of machine translation. In *Proceedings of the 40th annual meeting of the Association for Computational Linguistics*, pages 311–318.

Ricardo Rei, Craig Stewart, Ana C Farinha, and Alon Lavie. 2020. Comet: A neural framework for mt evaluation. *arXiv preprint arXiv:2009.09025*.

Thibault Sellam, Dipanjan Das, and Ankur P Parikh. 2020. Bleurt: Learning robust metrics for text generation. *arXiv preprint arXiv:2004.04696*.

Ashish Vaswani, Noam Shazeer, Niki Parmar, Jakob Uszkoreit, Llion Jones, Aidan N Gomez, Łukasz Kaiser, and Illia Polosukhin. 2017. Attention is all you need. *Advances in neural information processing systems*, 30.

Tsung-Hsien Wen, Milica Gasic, Nikola Mrksic, Pei-Hao Su, David Vandyke, and Steve Young. 2015. Semantically conditioned lstm-based natural language generation for spoken dialogue systems. *arXiv preprint arXiv:1508.01745*.

Tianyi Zhang, Varsha Kishore, Felix Wu, Kilian Q Weinberger, and Yoav Artzi. 2019. Bertscore: Evaluating text generation with bert. *arXiv preprint arXiv:1904.09675*.

Wei Zhao, Maxime Peyrard, Fei Liu, Yang Gao, Christian M Meyer, and Steffen Eger. 2019. Moverscore: Text generation evaluating with contextualized embeddings and earth mover distance. *arXiv preprint arXiv:1909.02622*.

Xinyu Zhou, Cong Yao, He Wen, Yuzhi Wang, Shuchang Zhou, Weiran He, and Jiajun Liang. 2017. East: an efficient and accurate scene text detector. In *Proceedings of the IEEE conference on Computer Vision and Pattern Recognition*, pages 5551–5560.

Strong Heuristics for Named Entity Linking

Marko Čuljak,[‡*] Andreas Spitz,[§] Robert West,[¶] Akhil Arora[¶†]
[‡]University of Zagreb, [§]University of Konstanz, [¶]EPFL
marko.culjak@fer.hr, andreas.spitz@uni-konstanz.de
robert.west@epfl.ch, akhil.arora@epfl.ch

Abstract

Named entity linking (NEL) in news is a challenging endeavour due to the frequency of unseen and emerging entities, which necessitates the use of unsupervised or zero-shot methods. However, such methods tend to come with caveats, such as no integration of suitable knowledge bases (like Wikidata) for emerging entities, a lack of scalability, and poor interpretability. Here, we consider person disambiguation in QUOTEBANK, a massive corpus of speaker-attributed quotations from the news, and investigate the suitability of intuitive, lightweight, and scalable heuristics for NEL in web-scale corpora. Our best performing heuristic disambiguates 94% and 63% of the mentions on QUOTEBANK and the AIDA-CoNLL benchmark, respectively. Additionally, the proposed heuristics compare favourably to the state-of-the-art unsupervised and zero-shot methods, EIGENTHEMES and mGENRE, respectively, thereby serving as strong baselines for unsupervised and zero-shot entity linking.

1 Introduction

While many of the most famous historic quotes are wise irrespective of their origin, this is less true for the majority of contemporary quotes in the news, which require speaker attribution to be useful in journalism or the social and political sciences. This observation is the motivation behind the construction of QUOTEBANK, a corpus of 178 million unique quotations that are attributed to speaker mentions and were extracted from 162 million news articles published between 2008 and 2020 (Vaucher et al., 2021). However, given the ambiguity of names, attributing quotes to mentions is insufficient for proper attribution, and thus, named entity disambiguation is required, a feature which QUOTEBANK lacks.

To tackle this shortcoming and investigate the disambiguation of person mentions in QUOTEBANK as a prototypical example of a web-scale corpus, we explore the suitability of scalable named entity linking (NEL) heuristics, which map mentions of entity names in the text to a unique identifier in a referent knowledge base (KB) and thus, resolve the ambiguity. NEL is an established task and solutions have been used for a variety of applications such as KB population (Dredze et al., 2010) or information extraction (Hoffart et al., 2011), yet the frequency of emerging and unseen entities in news data renders the adaptation of supervised NEL approaches difficult and tends to require unsupervised or zero-shot methods.

While such unsupervised methods (Le and Titov, 2019; Arora et al., 2021) and zero-short methods (Logeswaran et al., 2019; Cao et al., 2021) have been developed in recent years, scalability is an issue. For example, fully disambiguating QUOTEBANK with the state-of-the-art zero-shot NEL method, mGENRE (De Cao et al., 2022), would require approximately 37 years on a single GPU according to our experimental estimates. Therefore, we investigate the suitability of heuristic NEL methods that rely on signals that are simple to extract from mention contexts or entity entries in a KB. In contrast to mGENRE, we find that our best-performing heuristics can solve the same task in 108 days on a single CPU core, i.e., orders of magnitude faster and on cheaper hardware, while achieving comparable performance.

Contributions. To address the need for NEL in web-scale corpora, we investigate the disambiguation performance of simple, interpretable, scalable, and lightweight heuristics and compare them to state-of-the-art zero-shot and unsupervised NEL methods. Our experiments on QUOTEBANK and the AIDA-CoNLL benchmark demonstrate the competitiveness of these heuristics.

*Research done while at EPFL.
†Corresponding author.

Proceedings of the 2022 Conference of the North American Chapter of the Association for Computational Linguistics: Human Language Technologies: Student Research Workshop, pages 235 - 246
July 10-15, 2022 ©2022 Association for Computational Linguistics

2 Related Work

Viable learning-based methods for NEL in settings without available training data can be classified into *zero-shot* and *unsupervised* learning.

Zero-shot NEL was introduced by Logeswaran et al. (2019) with the objective of linking mentions to entities that were unseen during training. Later, Wu et al. (2020) proposed a BERT-based model for this task. Finally, Cao et al. (2021) proposed GENRE, a supervised NEL method that leverages BART to retrieve entities by generating their unique names autoregressively, conditioned on the context by employing beam search. While GENRE uses Wikipedia as its referent KB and is not directly compatible with our setting, we compare our methods to mGENRE (De Cao et al., 2022), a multilingual adaptation of GENRE using Wikidata.

Unsupervised NEL. Le and Titov (2019) proposed τMIL-ND, a BiLSTM model trained on noisy labels, which are generated via a heuristic that ranks the candidate entities of a mention based on matching words in a mention and candidate labels. Similarly, Fan et al. (2015) experiment with distant learning for NEL and create training data by merging Freebase with Wikipedia. Recently, Arora et al. (2021) proposed EIGENTHEMES, which is based on the observation that vector representations of gold entities lie in a low-rank subspace of the full embedding space. These low-rank subspaces are used to perform collective entity disambiguation.

While powerful, the aforementioned methods are designed for general domains and multiple entity types, and thus, cannot capitalize on domain- and entity-specific signals. In the following, we investigate the suitability of unsupervised NEL heuristics for person disambiguation in the domain of news quotes in comparison to these methods.

3 Problem Formalization

The input to our NEL system are articles $a \in \mathscr{A}$ from the set $\mathscr{A}$ of all articles in QUOTEBANK. In each article a, a set of entity mentions $\mathscr{M}_a$ is annotated. Each such mention $m \in \mathscr{M}_a$ can be mapped to a set of candidate Wikidata entities $\mathscr{E}_m$, which are uniquely identified by their Wikidata QID identifier (for further details regarding Wikidata, see Appendix D). If multiple entity candidates are available for a mention, we refer to this mention as *ambiguous*. Conversely, *unambiguous* mentions have only a single candidate entity. Given an article $a \in \mathscr{A}$, an ambiguous mention $m \in \mathscr{M}_a$, and all candidate entities $\mathscr{E}_m$, the task of NEL is to identify the entity $e \in \mathscr{E}_m$ to which m refers.

We assume that NEL methods assign a rank $r(e,m)$ to each candidate entity $e \in \mathscr{E}_m$ by ranking candidates according to the score provided by the method, which corresponds to the likelihood that e is the correct entity for m. Consequently, we assume that methods cannot identify cases in which the entity does not exist in the KB or is not contained in the list of candidates (i.e., out-of-KB or NIL predictions). Thus, our focus is on the evaluation of methods in cases where at least one candidate is available.

4 Scoring Methods

We consider three main signals for entity candidate ranking methods: *entity popularity*, *entity-content similarity*, and *entity-entity similarity*. Implementation details are provided in Appendix B.

4.1 Entity Popularity

Entity popularity is an important signal for disambiguating entities in news articles as popular entities are more likely to appear in the news (Shen et al., 2015). Since popularity cannot be measured directly, we utilize 4 proxies derived from Wikidata, some of which have also been used previously as features for supervised NEL (Delpeuch, 2020).

Number of properties (NP). Based on the assumption that Wikidata contains more information for popular entities, we use the number of Wikidata properties to approximate entity popularity.

Number of site links (NS). Similar to NP, a more popular entity is likely connected to more Wikimedia pages. We thus use the number of site links to estimate entity popularity.

PageRank (PR) is a graph centrality metric that was originally developed for web search as a part of Google's search engine (Page et al., 1999). We experiment with two PageRank scores computed on the Wikidata graph (PR_{WD}) and the Wikipedia graph (PR_{WP}) and report their results separately.

Lowest QID (LQID). The Wikidata QID is an auto-incremented integer identifier. Intuitively, well-known entities are added to Wikidata early and their QIDs are low. Therefore, we simply select the candidate with the lowest QID value.

4.2 Entity-Content Similarity

In addition to entity-centric information, we consider the mention context and attempt to match it to the attributes of candidate entities in the KB. Consider the following example from QUOTEBANK:

*"Professor **Tim Wheeler, Vice-Chancellor of the University of Chester**, said: "The university is dedicated to educating the very best nurses [...]"*

Tim Wheeler's title, *Vice-Chancellor of the University of Chester*, exactly matches the short description of a Wikidata entity with QID Q2434362. Therefore, it stands to reason that we can leverage content similarity metrics for entity linking.

Intersection score (IScore). The IScore captures word overlap between mention context and entity descriptions. Let $\mathscr{W}_a$ be a set of lowercased words occurring in article a, let $\mathscr{W}_e$ be a set of words occurring in the textual representation of an entity in Wikidata, and let $\mathscr{W}_{sw}$ be a set of English stopwords. We then compute the IScore of an entity e with respect to article a as

$$\text{IScore}(a,e) = |(\mathscr{W}_a \cap \mathscr{W}_e) \setminus \mathscr{W}_{sw}| \quad (1)$$

While we could normalize the score by $|\mathscr{W}_a \cup \mathscr{W}_e|$ to obtain a Jaccard similarity, we intentionally bias the IScore towards entities with more substantial descriptions, thereby implicitly incorporating entity popularity information. We use the Porter stemmer (Porter, 1980) for stemming words before matching (please see Appendix E for experiments with IScore using raw input words or lemmatization).

Narrow IScore (NIScore). For a more focused context representation, we also compute a version of the IScore with a narrow context that only contains the sentences in which a mention of the given entity occurs. For further experiments with the selection of mention contexts, see Appendix E.

Cosine similarity of embeddings (CSE). Following a baseline from Arora et al. (2021), to capitalize on the effectiveness of transformer models for NLP tasks, we leverage contextualized language models to create embeddings of article contents and candidate entity descriptions, which are then compared. We employ $\text{BART}_{\text{BASE}}$ (Lewis et al., 2020) to generate embeddings and then compute cosine similarity scores. For details, see Appendix B.

Narrow CSE (NCSE). Similar to the NIScore, we consider a narrow context around entity mentions for computing the CSE by restricting the context that is used for the creation of embeddings to sentences in which the entity occurs.

4.3 Entity-Entity Similarity

Since many mentions of entities can be expected to be unambiguous, we may use such mentions as anchors and leverage their relations to ambiguous mentions for the purpose of disambiguation. Similar to the entity-content similarity methods described above, we experiment with metrics that use intersections of entity occurrences and embedding similarities of attribute values from Wikidata.

Entity-entity IScore (EEIScore). Following the above intuition, the EEIScore utilizes the information that is contained in relations between ambiguous and unambiguous mentions. Let $\mathscr{U}_a$ be the set of all entities that can be mapped to unambiguous mentions in an article a (i.e., mentions that can be trivially disambiguated). Let $\mathscr{S}_e$ be the set of all statements that occur in the Wikidata entry corresponding to an entity e. We define $\mathscr{S}_{\mathscr{U}_a} := \bigcup_{e \in \mathscr{U}_a} \mathscr{S}_e$. Using this set of all statements of unambiguous entities, we then compute the EEIScore of a candidate entity e for an ambiguous mention as:

$$\text{EEIScore}(e, \mathscr{U}_a) = |\mathscr{S}_e \cap \mathscr{S}_{\mathscr{U}_a}| \quad (2)$$

Cosine similarity of statement value embeddings (CSSVE). We refine the idea behind the intersection score of entity relations by using embeddings of Wikidata statement values and property types (i.e., relations in Wikidata). For each entity e, Wikidata contains a set of statements $s_e = (p_e, v_e)$, consisting of a property p_e and a value v_e. Using this data, we first create embeddings $\varepsilon(v)$ of the values for all statements $s \in \mathscr{S}_{\mathscr{U}_a} \cup \mathscr{S}_e$. We then compute CSSVE as the sum of cosine similarities of statement value embeddings between all pairs of statements of the candidate entity and statements of unambiguous mentions in the article that have matching property types (i.e., describe the same type of relation):

$$\text{CSSVE}(e, \mathscr{U}_a) = \sum_{\substack{(s_u, s_e) \in (\mathscr{S}_{\mathscr{U}_a} \times \mathscr{S}_e) \\ p_u = p_e}} \frac{\varepsilon(v_u) \cdot \varepsilon(v_e)}{\|\varepsilon(v_u)\| \|\varepsilon(v_e)\|} \quad (3)$$

4.4 Composite Scores

We also use two composite scores in our evaluation: **UIScore** refers to the weighted sum of IScore, NIScore, and EEIScore, while **UCSE** refers to the weighted sum of CSE, NCSE, and CSSVE. Since

CSE and NCSE are cosine similarities, their outputs are constrained to the $[-1, 1]$ interval, while CSSVE is unbounded. To ensure similar magnitudes we map all scores to the $[0, 1]$ interval by applying the transformation $f(x) = \frac{1}{2}(x+1)$ to CSE and NCSE, and additive smoothing to CSSVE.

5 Data

We focus on QUOTEBANK data, but also investigate the performance on AIDA-CoNLL as a benchmark. Similar to Arora et al. 2021, Raiman and Raiman 2018, and Guo and Barbosa 2018 we label the mentions as either *'easy'* or *'hard'*. In QUOTEBANK, we deem a mention easy if it can be correctly disambiguated using NS and hard otherwise, while in AIDA-CoNLL we use the definition proposed by Arora et al. 2021. In Table 1 we present the statistics for easy and hard mentions in the datasets.

QUOTEBANK is a collection of quotes that were extracted from 127 million news articles and attributed to one of 575 million speaker mentions (Vaucher et al., 2021), out of which 75% are unambiguous. For our evaluation, we use a randomly sampled subset of 300 articles that are manually annotated with 1,866 disambiguated person mentions. 70% of these mentions are unambiguous. Out of the ambiguous mentions, it was possible to determine ground truth labels for 310 (57%), which we use in our evaluation. We split the ground truth into 245 mentions (79%) for evaluation and 65 mentions (21%) for parameter tuning. For a more thorough description of the QUOTEBANK ground truth, see Appendix A.

AIDA-CoNLL. To assess whether the proposed methods can be used for unsupervised NEL in general, we also evaluate their performance on the AIDA-CoNLL benchmark (Hoffart et al., 2011), which is based on the CoNLL 2003 shared task (Sang and Meulder, 2003). We use the same setup as Arora et al. 2021 and use the validation set for hyperparameter optimization. The differences between the evaluation setups of QUOTEBANK and AIDA-CoNLL are explained in Appendix C.

6 Evaluation

All the resources (code, datasets, etc.) required to reproduce the experiments in this paper are available at `https://github.com/epfl-dlab/nelight`.

Table 1: The number of mentions in different difficulty categories. The definitions of *Easy* and *Hard* mentions are presented in § 6.2. On AIDA-CoNLL, #Easy + #Hard $\neq$ #Overall because for some mentions, the gold-entity was not contained in the candidate set.

Dataset	#Easy	#Hard	#Overall
QUOTEBANK	203	42	245
AIDA-CoNLL	2555	1136	4478

6.1 Evaluation Setup

We use *micro* precision at one (P@1) and mean reciprocal rank (MRR) as the evaluation metrics. The metrics are aggregated over all ambiguous mentions for which ground truth data is available. Performance is reported with 95% bootstrapped confidence intervals (CIs) over 10,000 bootstrap samples. To identify optimal weight parameters for the composite metrics, we perform a grid search over the range $[0, 1]$. For the QUOTEBANK data, the best performance is obtained for weights $(1, 1, 1)$ for UIScore and $(0.45, 0.9, 0.2)$ for UCSE. For the AIDA-CoNLL data, we perform the parameter optimization on the official validation set, where the best performance is obtained for weights $(0.9, 0, 1)$ and $(0, 1, 1)$ for UIScore and UCSE, respectively.

Tie breaking. Several ranking methods introduce ties, which we break by using popularity heuristics. Among the popularity heuristics, only LQID is injective and always outputs distinct scores for different entities. In our experiments, we, therefore, use LQID to break ties if they remain after using other tie-breakers. A full breakdown of the tie-breaking performance for all popularity-based methods can be found in Appendix E.3.

6.2 Results

We report P@1 for all the methods in Table 2, and MRR in Appendix G. For comparison, we present the analytically computed performance of a random baseline, which picks one of the entity candidates uniformly at random.

QUOTEBANK. Among the popularity-based metrics, the best results are achieved by NS. However, considering the confidence intervals, the performance gains of NS over PR_{WP} and NP are not significant. LQID and PR_{WD} perform poorly in comparison to the other methods. All popularity methods outperform the random baseline, confirming their usefulness as a prior for NEL.

Table 2: P@1 of the methods on QUOTEBANK and AIDA-CoNLL. Eigen (IScore) refers to EIGENTHEMES weighted by IScore. Eigen on QUOTEBANK is weighted by NS, while On AIDA, it denotes the results obtained by Arora et al. 2021. The best obtained P@1 in each column is highlighted **bold**.

	QUOTEBANK			AIDA-CoNLL		
Method	**Easy**	**Hard**	**Overall**	**Easy**	**Hard**	**Overall**
Random	0.374 ± 0.017	0.260 ± 0.045	0.354 ± 0.024	0.267 ± 0.014	0.066 ± 0.004	0.169 ± 0.009
LQID	0.828 ± 0.054	0.238 ± 0.140	0.727 ± 0.056	0.856 ± 0.014	0.259 ± 0.029	0.554 ± 0.016
NP	0.921 ± 0.040	0.143 ± 0.120	0.788 ± 0.052	0.856 ± 0.014	0.190 ± 0.023	0.536 ± 0.015
NS	$\mathbf{1.000 \pm 0.000}$	0.000 ± 0.000	0.829 ± 0.048	0.908 ± 0.012	0.275 ± 0.026	0.588 ± 0.014
PR_{WD}	0.768 ± 0.059	0.214 ± 0.132	0.673 ± 0.061	0.838 ± 0.014	0.155 ± 0.021	0.517 ± 0.015
PR_{WP}	0.926 ± 0.040	0.333 ± 0.140	0.824 ± 0.048	$\mathbf{0.938 \pm 0.010}$	0.282 ± 0.027	0.607 ± 0.014
IScore	0.956 ± 0.030	0.762 ± 0.134	0.922 ± 0.034	0.863 ± 0.014	0.549 ± 0.029	0.632 ± 0.015
NIScore	0.966 ± 0.030	0.571 ± 0.151	0.851 ± 0.014	0.851 ± 0.014	0.407 ± 0.028	0.562 ± 0.015
CSE	0.901 ± 0.044	0.500 ± 0.159	0.833 ± 0.047	0.386 ± 0.019	0.276 ± 0.026	0.290 ± 0.014
EEIScore	0.951 ± 0.034	0.690 ± 0.143	0.906 ± 0.036	0.815 ± 0.016	0.382 ± 0.031	0.562 ± 0.015
CSSVE	0.872 ± 0.049	0.357 ± 0.155	0.784 ± 0.051	0.712 ± 0.017	0.256 ± 0.026	0.471 ± 0.015
UIScore	0.966 ± 0.030	$\mathbf{0.833 \pm 0.123}$	0.943 ± 0.029	0.833 ± 0.014	0.577 ± 0.028	0.621 ± 0.014
UCSE	0.941 ± 0.034	0.595 ± 0.156	0.882 ± 0.042	0.465 ± 0.019	0.386 ± 0.029	0.363 ± 0.014
Eigen	0.995 ± 0.010	0.238 ± 0.134	0.865 ± 0.044	0.859 ± 0.014	0.500 ± 0.030	0.617 ± 0.015
Eigen (IScore)	0.956 ± 0.030	0.714 ± 0.147	0.914 ± 0.037	0.794 ± 0.015	$\mathbf{0.702 \pm 0.029}^{\dagger}$	0.631 ± 0.014
mGENRE	0.995 ± 0.010	0.810 ± 0.143	$\mathbf{0.963 \pm 0.025}$	0.925 ± 0.011	0.610 ± 0.028	$\mathbf{0.682 \pm 0.014}^{\dagger}$

† Indicates statistical significance ($p < 0.05$) between the best and the second-best method using bootstrapped 95% CIs.

Table 3: P@1 of representative methods on various entity types in the AIDA-CoNLL dataset. In the evaluation dataset, there are 1016 PER, 1345 ORG, 1575 LOC, and 542 MISC mentions. The best P@1 in each column is highlighted **bold**.

Method	**PER**	**ORG**	**LOC**	**MISC**
NS	0.687 ± 0.030	0.410 ± 0.027	0.777 ± 0.021	0.292 ± 0.039
PR_{WP}	0.719 ± 0.029	0.477 ± 0.026	0.752 ± 0.023	$\mathbf{0.293 \pm 0.042}$
IScore	0.786 ± 0.026	0.597 ± 0.026	0.694 ± 0.022	0.245 ± 0.035
UIScore	$\mathbf{0.789 \pm 0.026}$	0.601 ± 0.026	0.664 ± 0.023	0.232 ± 0.035
mGENRE	0.720 ± 0.027	0.608 ± 0.027	$\mathbf{0.858 \pm 0.018}$	0.284 ± 0.039
Eigen (IScore)	0.760 ± 0.026	$\mathbf{0.732 \pm 0.025}$	0.608 ± 0.024	0.205 ± 0.035
Eigen	0.696 ± 0.028	0.671 ± 0.026	0.655 ± 0.023	0.223 ± 0.035

The performances of entity-entity similarity methods are similar to their entity-content similarity counterparts. This is in line with the hypothesis that the gold entities mentioned in the same article are more closely related than the other subsets of entity candidates (Arora et al., 2021). Generally, combining the entity-content similarity methods with their entity-entity similarity counterparts leads to performance gain, as seen from the example of UIScore and UCSE. Considering the overall performance, UIScore outperforms CSE and all entity popularity methods. The performance of CSE is similar to the performance of NS, which is considerably simpler. Finally, the performance of UIScore is comparable to mGENRE, achieving a slightly higher P@1 on hard mentions.

AIDA-CoNLL. In the AIDA-CoNLL data, IScore and UIScore achieve a comparable performance to the current state-of-the-art in unsupervised entity linking, EIGENTHEMES (Arora et al., 2021), but lag slightly behind mGENRE (De Cao et al., 2022), the state-of-the-art zero-shot method. In contrast to QUOTEBANK, we do not observe performance gains as a result of combining different heuristics as UIScore fails to outperform IScore. EIGENTHEMES weighted by IScore achieves by far the strongest performance on the hard mentions, despite a relatively poor performance on easy mentions. Overall, the performance makes an encouraging case for the heuristics to be used as strong baselines for entity linking in general, and on large data sets in particular.

AIDA-CoNLL entity type analysis. The results of the analysis with respect to the entity types available in the original CoNLL 2003 dataset (Sang and Meulder, 2003) are shown in Table 3. In CoNLL 2003, there are four entity types: person (PER), organization (ORG), location (LOC), and miscellaneous (MISC).

The UIScore heuristic achieves the best performance on PER mentions, outperforming even mGENRE. As described in Subsection 4.2, persons that are mentioned in the news are usually introduced by a simple description of their background or current occupation even if they are well known. Since the heuristics proposed for person disambiguation in QUOTEBANK are based on this assumption, this explains a relatively strong performance of the UIScore heuristic on PER type entities in AIDA-CoNLL.

Despite superior performance on PER mentions, UIScore lags behind mGENRE and EIGENTHEMES on other types. We attribute this to a lack of introductory context in comparison to PER mentions (e.g., a mention of "China" in an article would typically not be followed by "a state in East Asia"). Furthermore, non-person named entities are frequently used as metonyms (e.g., "Kremlin" is a frequent metonym for the Russian government, but it can also refer to the Kremlin building). Depending on the context, a simple heuristic such as IScore may thus struggle to properly link candidates.

Computational performance. While mGENRE achieves the best performance on both QUOTEBANK and on AIDA-CoNLL, it is a transformer model and takes *substantially* longer to run in comparison to UIScore. Disambiguating a single mention with mGENRE takes approximately 533 times longer than with UIScore, and approximately 533K times longer than with NS, thereby rendering it infeasible for speaker disambiguation in QUOTEBANK, which contains millions of news articles. For a detailed breakdown of inference times per mention, see Appendix F.

7 Discussion

Overall, the results highlight the practicality of the proposed heuristics. Our simple heuristics outperform those based on word embeddings and are competitive in comparison to mGENRE.

7.1 Error analysis

To take a closer at avenues for improvement, we show a manual error analysis for UIScore in Table 4. In 6 cases, the predicted entity and the gold entity have a matching domain (e.g., both are sportsmen). In 4 cases, the key property by which a human could determine the correct entity was only implicitly mentioned in the context, which caused a failure in string matching. For 3 articles, a key property of the gold entity was not listed in Wikidata, even though it could be found in external sources such as Wikipedia. The remaining error stems from the presence of a "decoy" entity, i.e, an influential but unrelated entity that induced spurious matches. For a thorough description and illustration of the error categories, see Appendix H.

7.2 Limitations

Since UIScore is the most promising of our heuristics, we focus on it and its components.

Table 4: Error sources for UIScore.

Error source	**#Mentions**
Similar domain	6 (42.9%)
Key property implicit in the text	4 (28.6%)
Key property not in Wikidata	3 (21.4%)
Decoy mention	1 (7.1%)

The biggest limitation of IScore is imposed by the equal importance that is assigned to words in the context, which could be improved by re-ranking important words for given entities. Similarly, Wikidata properties for EEIScore and CSSVE could be ranked or filtered (for example, the property *date of birth* is likely to cause spurious matches, while *occupation* is likely useful).

Regarding tie-breaking, the use of LQID is intuitive for persons in the news domain, but may fail for other entity types and other domains, and is dependent on Wikidata. Finally, in our focus on QUOTEBANK data, we are reliant on the authors' method for candidate generation, which could be improved for better performance in the future.

8 Conclusions and Future Work

We tackled the problem of entity linking in QUOTEBANK by employing heuristics that rely on simple signals in the context of mentions and the referent KB. The solid overall performance of the proposed heuristics on QUOTEBANK, their low computational complexity, and competitive performance on the AIDA-CoNLL benchmark suggest that they can be used as strong baselines for unsupervised entity linking in large datasets.

Future work. We plan to experiment with weighting schemes that account for word importance, utilize additional signals from the KB, and include improved candidate generation methods. Finally, we aim to provide a disambiguated version of QUOTEBANK to the community.

Acknowledgements

We would like to thank Vincent Ng for providing insightful feedback during the pre-submission mentorship phase. This project was partly funded by the Swiss National Science Foundation (grant 200021_185043), the European Union (TAILOR, grant 952215), the Microsoft Swiss Joint Research Center, and the University of Konstanz Zukunftskolleg. We also acknowledge generous gifts from Facebook and Google supporting West's lab.

References

Akhil Arora, Alberto García-Durán, and Robert West. 2021. Low-rank subspaces for unsupervised entity linking. In *Proceedings of the 2021 Conference on Empirical Methods in Natural Language Processing*.

Nicola De Cao, Gautier Izacard, Sebastian Riedel, and Fabio Petroni. 2021. Autoregressive entity retrieval. In *9th International Conference on Learning Representations*.

Nicola De Cao, Ledell Wu, Kashyap Popat, Mikel Artetxe, Naman Goyal, Mikhail Plekhanov, Luke Zettlemoyer, Nicola Cancedda, Sebastian Riedel, and Fabio Petroni. 2022. Multilingual Autoregressive Entity Linking. *Transactions of the Association for Computational Linguistics*, 10:274–290.

Antonin Delpeuch. 2020. Opentapioca: Lightweight entity linking for wikidata. In *Proceedings of the 1st Wikidata Workshop (Wikidata 2020) co-located with the 19th International Semantic Web Conference*.

Mark Dredze, Paul McNamee, Delip Rao, Adam Gerber, and Tim Finin. 2010. Entity disambiguation for knowledge base population. In *Proceedings of the 23rd International Conference on Computational Linguistics*.

Miao Fan, Qiang Zhou, and Thomas Fang Zheng. 2015. Distant supervision for entity linking. In *Proceedings of the 29th Pacific Asia Conference on Language, Information and Computation*.

Zhaochen Guo and Denilson Barbosa. 2018. Robust named entity disambiguation with random walks. *Semantic Web*, 9:459–479.

Johannes Hoffart, Mohamed Amir Yosef, Ilaria Bordino, Hagen Fürstenau, Manfred Pinkal, Marc Spaniol, Bilyana Taneva, Stefan Thater, and Gerhard Weikum. 2011. Robust disambiguation of named entities in text. In *Proceedings of the 2011 Conference on Empirical Methods in Natural Language Processing*.

Phong Le and Ivan Titov. 2019. Distant learning for entity linking with automatic noise detection. In *Proceedings of the 57th Conference of the Association for Computational Linguistics*.

Mike Lewis, Yinhan Liu, Naman Goyal, Marjan Ghazvininejad, Abdelrahman Mohamed, Omer Levy, Veselin Stoyanov, and Luke Zettlemoyer. 2020. BART: Denoising sequence-to-sequence pre-training for natural language generation, translation, and comprehension. In *Proceedings of the 58th Annual Meeting of the Association for Computational Linguistics*.

Yinhan Liu, Jiatao Gu, Naman Goyal, Xian Li, Sergey Edunov, Marjan Ghazvininejad, Mike Lewis, and Luke Zettlemoyer. 2020. Multilingual denoising pre-training for neural machine translation. *Transactions of the Association for Computational Linguistics*, 8:726–742.

Lajanugen Logeswaran, Ming-Wei Chang, Kenton Lee, Kristina Toutanova, Jacob Devlin, and Honglak Lee. 2019. Zero-shot entity linking by reading entity descriptions. In *Proceedings of the 57th Annual Meeting of the Association for Computational Linguistics*.

George A. Miller. 1995. Wordnet: A lexical database for english. *Commun. ACM*, 38(11):39–41.

Lawrence Page, Sergey Brin, Rajeev Motwani, and Terry Winograd. 1999. The pagerank citation ranking: Bringing order to the web. Technical Report 1999-66, Stanford InfoLab. Previous number = SIDL-WP-1999-0120.

Dario Pavllo, Tiziano Piccardi, and Robert West. 2018. Quootstrap: Scalable unsupervised extraction of quotation-speaker pairs from large news corpora via bootstrapping. In *Proceedings of the Twelfth International Conference on Web and Social Media*.

Martin F Porter. 1980. An algorithm for suffix stripping. *Program*, 14(3):130–137.

Jonathan Raiman and Olivier Raiman. 2018. Deeptype: Multilingual entity linking by neural type system evolution. In *Proceedings of the Thirty-Second AAAI Conference on Artificial Intelligence*.

Erik F. Tjong Kim Sang and Fien De Meulder. 2003. Introduction to the conll-2003 shared task: Language-independent named entity recognition. In *Proceedings of the Seventh Conference on Natural Language Learning*.

Wei Shen, Jianyong Wang, and Jiawei Han. 2015. Entity linking with a knowledge base: Issues, techniques, and solutions. *TKDE*, 27(2).

Timoté Vaucher, Andreas Spitz, Michele Catasta, and Robert West. 2021. Quotebank: A corpus of quotations from a decade of news. In *Proceedings of the 14th ACM International Conference on Web Search and Data Mining*.

Ledell Wu, Fabio Petroni, Martin Josifoski, Sebastian Riedel, and Luke Zettlemoyer. 2020. Scalable zero-shot entity linking with dense entity retrieval. In *Proceedings of the 2020 Conference on Empirical Methods in Natural Language Processing*.

Appendix

A Ground Truth Data

For the method evaluation, we randomly sample 300 articles from QUOTEBANK. The ground truth for 160 articles is determined by the author, while the remaining 140 articles are annotated by the author's colleagues. The annotators were provided with article content, article title, publication date, article URL, a list of ambiguous named entity mentions, and for each ambiguous mention, a candidate set of QIDs as listed in QUOTEBANK. The annotators had to either select the correct QID from the candidate set or select one of the following categories if the correct QID is not listed:

- *The mention does not refer to a person.* Sometimes, buildings and other artifacts named after some person are identified as a person. We ignore such mentions in the evaluation.
- *The correct QID does not exist in Wikidata.* This means that a person is likely not significant enough to have a Wikidata item. For example, sometimes a journalist or a photographer of a newspaper where the article is published shares the name of a famous person and is therefore listed as a speaker candidate.
- *The correct QID exists in Wikidata but is not listed.* This can happen if the correct QID is added to Wikidata after the candidate entities were generated.
- *Impossible to determine.* Some articles are either too noisy or do not contain enough information for disambiguation to be feasible.

In Table 5, we present the distribution of person mentions in the evaluation data with respect to different categories. We observe that more than 70% of the 1866 mentions are unambiguous. For 310 (57%) of the ambiguous mentions, it was possible to determine the ground truth based on the given candidate sets. For the majority of the remaining 43% of ambiguous mentions no correct entity was available in Wikidata.

The main drawback of the QUOTEBANK evaluation dataset is its small size. Since all articles were annotated by only one annotator, there is no data on the inter-annotator agreement. In the future, we aim to create a more sophisticated benchmark dataset via crowdsourcing.

Table 5: Distribution of mentions in the ground truth data with respect to ambiguity and availability of ground truth.

Category		**#Mentions**
Unambiguous		1322 (70.8%)
Ambiguous	Gold entity exists	310 (16.6%)
	No correct QID in Wikidata	151 (8.1%)
	Impossible	37 (2.0%)
	Correct QID not listed	24 (1.3%)
	Not a person	22 (1.2%)
Total		1866

B Implementation Details of the Scoring Methods

B.1 IScore

To calculate the IScore, we first obtain labels of Wikidata statement values listed for e. We then tokenize the content of a using the tagset of the Penn Treebank Tokenizer. We use the computed tokens to create sets $\mathscr{W}_a$ and $\mathscr{W}_e$. Then, we apply the formula given in equation 1 and compute the IScore based on $\mathscr{W}_a$, $\mathscr{W}_e$, and a predefined set of English stopwords $\mathscr{W}_{sw}$[1].

B.2 CSE

To embed an article, we follow the standard transformer model preprocessing procedure. We tokenize the article content using the model-specific tokenizer, respecting BART's 1024 token limit by simply truncating the input if the limit is exceeded. We then feed the obtained tokens to BART and average the last hidden state of the model output. Since truncation leads to loss of information in comparison to other methods, we experimented with chunking the input into chunks of at most 1024 tokens, computing token embeddings in each chunk separately, and aggregating the obtained token embeddings. However, this did not improve performance on QUOTEBANK (0.698 P@1 and 0.818 MRR), while all articles from AIDA-CoNLL are within the token limit so we report the results of the first approach.

Embedding the entity is slightly more challenging. Following the same procedure as for the computation of the article content embeddings, we compute the embedding the the first paragraph in an entity's Wikipedia page if such a page is available. Otherwise, we compute the embeddings of the short description, and each statement value la-

[1]https://gist.github.com/sebleier/554280

Table 6: Results of the IScore ablation study with respect to word normalization and inclusion of different Wikidata features. In each row, we report P@1 and MRR of IScore method for the combinations of the following Wikidata features: short description (D), Wikipedia first paragraph (P), statement value labels (S), and statement value labels and aliases (S_A) for a setting without word normalization, as well as for settings with stemming and lemmatization. The best results in each column are in bold. Since S_A is essentially a superset of S, we omit the combinations where both S and S_A appear. All the experiments were run with NS as a tie-breaker.

	No normalization		**Lemmatization**		**Stemming**	
Combination	**P@1**	**MRR**	**P@1**	**MRR**	**P@1**	**MRR**
D	0.869 ± 0.044	0.921 ± 0.027	0.890 ± 0.040	0.930 ± 0.026	0.894 ± 0.039	0.934 ± 0.026
P	0.832 ± 0.049	0.903 ± 0.030	0.816 ± 0.051	0.895 ± 0.029	0.832 ± 0.047	0.902 ± 0.029
S	0.894 ± 0.040	0.936 ± 0.026	0.898 ± 0.039	0.940 ± 0.024	0.906 ± 0.038	0.944 ± 0.024
S_A	0.886 ± 0.041	0.932 ± 0.025	0.890 ± 0.042	0.935 ± 0.025	0.898 ± 0.039	0.939 ± 0.024
D + P	0.841 ± 0.046	0.907 ± 0.028	0.820 ± 0.050	0.898 ± 0.030	0.841 ± 0.047	0.906 ± 0.028
D + S	**0.902 ± 0.039**	**0.943 ± 0.024**	**0.906 ± 0.038**	0.945 ± 0.022	**0.918 ± 0.035**	**0.952 ± 0.021**
D + S_A	0.890 ± 0.041	0.937 ± 0.023	**0.906 ± 0.038**	**0.947 ± 0.022**	0.914 ± 0.037	0.950 ± 0.022
P + S	0.861 ± 0.044	0.919 ± 0.028	0.861 ± 0.045	0.920 ± 0.028	0.873 ± 0.044	0.925 ± 0.026
P + S_A	0.878 ± 0.042	0.928 ± 0.025	0.882 ± 0.041	0.931 ± 0.025	0.882 ± 0.042	0.930 ± 0.025
D + P + S	0.861 ± 0.045	0.921 ± 0.026	0.861 ± 0.045	0.920 ± 0.027	0.873 ± 0.042	0.926 ± 0.026
D + P + S_A	0.886 ± 0.042	0.934 ± 0.025	0.886 ± 0.041	0.934 ± 0.025	0.882 ± 0.042	0.930 ± 0.026

Table 7: Comparison of performances of CSE and IScore when considering different context sizes. Ensemble refers to the sum of the scores obtained considering the narrow and entire context of the article, respectively. The best results for each scoring method are in bold. All the experiments were run with NS as a tie-breaker.

Method	Context	P@1	MRR
CSE	Narrow	0.751 ± 0.055	0.857 ± 0.033
	Entire	0.833 ± 0.050	0.902 ± 0.029
	Ensemble	**0.857 ± 0.044**	**0.921 ± 0.025**
IScore	Narrow	0.898 ± 0.039	0.941 ± 0.023
	Entire	0.918 ± 0.035	0.952 ± 0.021
	Ensemble	**0.922 ± 0.036**	**0.954 ± 0.022**

bel listed for an entity in Wikidata, and aggregate them via arithmetic mean.

B.3 mGENRE

We use mGENRE in a similar setup as De Cao et al. (2022). Suppose that we want to disambiguate entity mention m occurring in an article a. We first enclose m with special tokens `[START]` and `[END]` that correspond to the start and the end of a mention span. We then take at most t mBART (Liu et al., 2020) tokens from either side. As the input for mGENRE, we use a string consisting of the left context, the mention enclosed with the special tokens, and the right context. mGENRE then outputs the top k entity QIDs and their respective scores, where k is the beam size. For entities in $\mathcal{Q}_m$ that are not retrieved by mGENRE, we simply assign 0 as a score. Note that mGENRE outputs the scores corresponding to the negative log-likelihood of the resulting sequence. Thus, in order for 0 to be the smallest possible score, we exponentiate the scores obtained from mGENRE. In the QUOTEBANK setup, we also perform one additional step: since each speaker candidate can be mentioned multiple times in the text, we run mGENRE for each of the speaker candidate mentions and sum the scores obtained for each of the candidate Wikidata entities.

Table 8: Performances of mGENRE for different context sizes. The best result in each column is highlighted **bold**.

	QUOTEBANK		**AIDA-CoNLL**	
t	**P@1**	**MRR**	**P@1**	**MRR**
64	0.951 ± 0.029	0.968 ± 0.018	0.664 ± 0.013	0.713 ± 0.012
128	**0.963 ± 0.025**	**0.976 ± 0.017**	0.675 ± 0.014	0.723 ± 0.013
256	0.959 ± 0.026	0.972 ± 0.021	**0.682 ± 0.014**	**0.730 ± 0.013**

In Table 8, we present the performances of mGENRE on both QUOTEBANK and AIDA-CoNLL for different values of t, while in Table 2 we report only the best obtained P@1. In all our experiments with mGENRE, we set the beam size k to 10.

C Evaluation Setup Details

QUOTEBANK. The QUOTEBANK data exclusively contains annotations of person mentions. Before training a model that attributes the quotations to their respective speakers, the quotations and speaker candidates are identified in the article text

(Vaucher et al., 2021). The extraction of speaker candidates is explained in detail by Pavllo et al. (2018). Although a speaker candidate can appear in an article multiple times, the quotations are not attributed to specific mentions but rather to the most likely speaker candidate. Thus, we evaluate our methods on QUOTEBANK on a speaker candidate level and refer to speaker candidates as mentions to ensure that our method and result descriptions are consistent with the standard nomenclature.

AIDA-CoNLL. When evaluating our methods on the AIDA-CoNLL benchmark, we do not ignore the mentions for which the gold entity either cannot be determined or is not retrieved by the candidate generator. As a consequence, the resulting P@1 and MRR reported on AIDA-CoNLL are significantly lower in comparison to the QUOTEBANK results as they are bounded by the recall of the candidate generator. We use the same candidate generator as Arora et al. (2021), which imposes an upper bound of 0.824 to P@1 and MRR. Additionally, to ensure a fair comparison with Arora et al. (2021), we break ties by selecting the first speaker candidate with the same score and use the same definition of the easy and hard mentions when reporting the method performances.

D Wikidata

Wikidata is a large community-driven KB. It boasts more than 96 million data items as of January 2022, out of which 6 million are humans. Each Wikidata item is identified by a unique positive integer prefixed with the upper-case letter Q, also known as QID (e.g. Earth (Q2), Mahatma Gandhi (Q1001)). Obligatory data fields of items are a label and a description. Labels and descriptions need not be unique, but each item is uniquely identified by a combination of a label and a short description. Therefore, each QID is linked to the label-description combination. Optionally, some items consist of aliases (alternative names for an entity) and statements. Statements provide additional information about an item and they consist of at least one property-value pair. A property is a pre-defined data type, identified by a unique positive integer, but unlike items, it is prefixed with the upper-case letter P (e.g. occupation (P106), sex or gender (P21)). The value of a statement may take on many types, such as Wikidata items, strings, numbers, or media files. Some items also have a list of site links that connect them to the corresponding page of the entity in other Wikimedia projects, such as Wikipedia or Wikibooks. The methods we propose in Section 4 leverage the described information to link the named entity mentions in the news articles to their respective Wikidata entities.

E Additional Experiments

E.1 Wikidata Features and Word Normalization Ablation for IScore

In Table 6, we show the results of an ablation study that aims to assess the effect of the inclusion of different Wikidata entity features on the performance of IScore and word normalization methods. The features we consider are short descriptions, statement value labels with and without aliases, and Wikipedia first paragraphs. We obtain the best results by leveraging short descriptions and Wikidata statement values. When using only Wikipedia first paragraphs, we obtain a performance similar to NS, a simple entity popularity metric. Seemingly, the inclusion of aliases does not improve the performance. Additionally, we observe that lemmatization (using the WordNet lemmatizer (Miller, 1995)) and stemming (using the Porter stemmer (Porter, 1980)) improve IScore performance by a small margin. Furthermore, we observe a slight performance gain of stemming over lemmatization. This is especially important considering the volume of the data and the inefficiency of lemmatization when compared to stemming.

E.2 Context Size

As shown in Table 7, narrowing down the context has a negative impact on the performances of both the CSE and IScore scoring methods. However, we hypothesize that the words that occur close to the entity mention are more important than those in a broader context. Therefore, we also experiment with the linear combination of the respective scores for each context size. In both cases, the optimal weights obtained through grid search optimization are $(1, 1)$. We observe a slight performance gain for the ensemble of both scoring methods.

E.3 Tie breakers

In Table 6, we present the results of the experiment with various tiebreakers. Seemingly, all the tie-breakers are a reasonable choice since no tie-breaker clearly outperforms the others.

Table 9: P@1 of different popularity metrics as tiebreakers. Rows correspond to scoring methods and columns to tiebreakers. CSE and UCSE are omitted from the table because their performance remains the same irrespective of the tiebreaker. The best P@1 in each row is highlighted **bold**.

	NS	NP	PR WP	PR WD	LQID
IScore	0.918 ± 0.036	$\mathbf{0.922 \pm 0.035}$	0.918 ± 0.036	0.918 ± 0.036	0.906 ± 0.038
EEIScore	0.898 ± 0.039	0.894 ± 0.039	$\mathbf{0.906 \pm 0.037}$	0.878 ± 0.042	0.873 ± 0.042
CSSVE	$\mathbf{0.784 \pm 0.052}$	0.780 ± 0.054	$\mathbf{0.784 \pm 0.053}$	$\mathbf{0.784 \pm 0.051}$	$\mathbf{0.784 \pm 0.052}$
UIScore	0.939 ± 0.032	0.939 ± 0.032	$\mathbf{0.942 \pm 0.031}$	0.935 ± 0.033	0.931 ± 0.033

Table 10: Estimated per-mention inference times of the selected methods. mGENRE is run on Nvidia GeForce GTX TITAN X, while UIScore and NS were executed on a single 2.5 GHz core of Intel Xeon E5-2680 processor.

	Inference time	
Method	QUOTEBANK	AIDA-CoNLL
mGENRE	8.0 s	1.9 s
NS	15 μs	26 μs
IScore	7.9 ms	67 ms
UIScore	15 ms	135 ms
Eigen	11 ms	39 ms

F Inference Time

In Table 10, we present the inference times of mGENRE, EIGENTHEMES, our best-performing methods on QUOTEBANK and AIDA-CoNLL: UIScore and IScore, respectively, and the well-performing entity popularity metric NS. EIGENTHEMES and the selected heuristics are significantly more efficient than mGENRE. The differences in inference times on Quotebank and AIDA-CoNLL are due to the setup differences (see C). Additionally, the inference times of NS, IScore, UIScore, and EIGENTHEMES largely depend on the number of candidates per mention. Thus, since on average, the number of candidate entities per mention on AIDA-CoNLL (approx. 18) is substantially larger than in QUOTEBANK (approx. 5), their inference times on AIDA-CoNLL are longer. Note that our best methods do not require GPU, making them easily parallelizable on CPU cores.

G Mean reciprocal rank of the methods

As an extension of Table 2, in Table 11 we present the MRR of the methods. MRR follows similar trends as P@1.

H Error Source Descriptions

Similar domain. If the gold entity and the system output have similar backgrounds or occupations, their Wikidata items tend to contain similar statements. For example, in one of the articles, the gold entity for Shawn Williams was Q7491485 (lacrosse player), while the output of the model was Q13064143 (American football player, defensive back). Shawn Williams first appears in the following sentence:

*Canada head coach Randy Mearns kept his No. 51 warm-up shirt - honoring Tucker Williams, the son of NLL star **Shawn Williams** of the Buffalo Bandits who is currently undergoing the treatment for Burkitt's Lymphoma - on throughout the game.*

Earlier in the article, *lacrosse* was mentioned directly, which in addition to the mention of *NLL* (National Lacrosse League) made it clear that Q7491485 is the gold entity. However, the UIScore of Q13064143 was just 1 point higher than the UIScore of Q7491485, which led to the erroneous prediction.

Key property not in Wikidata. In some cases, the Wikidata item does not contain the key information that is used to describe the entity in the article. Such cases are difficult even for humans as they require background knowledge stored in multiple sources. An example of this is John Prendergast (Q6253345), who was described in one article as the *co-founder of Enough.* This property is not listed in the Wikidata item of Q6253345 but can be found in external sources. The output of the model was Q6253343, a late British Army officer who served in World War II. The article in which Prendergast was mentioned was about violent events in Congo and was thus rich in war-related terms. Most importantly, World War II was mentioned in the article, leading to three spuriously matched words in Q6253343's Wikidata item. The final scores of Q6253345 and Q6253343 were 8 and 12

Table 11: MRR of the methods on QUOTEBANK and AIDA-CoNLL. Eigen and Eigen (IScore) have the same definition as in Table 2. The best obtained MRR in each column is highlighted **bold**.

	QUOTEBANK			AIDA-CoNLL		
	Easy	**Hard**	**Overall**	**Easy**	**Hard**	**Overall**
Random	0.622 ± 0.022	0.484 ± 0.058	0.597 ± 0.030	0.387 ± 0.013	0.205 ± 0.006	0.273 ± 0.009
LQID	0.904 ± 0.030	0.505 ± 0.094	0.836 ± 0.036	0.912 ± 0.009	0.451 ± 0.021	0.635 ± 0.013
NP	0.959 ± 0.021	0.457 ± 0.082	0.873 ± 0.034	0.901 ± 0.010	0.352 ± 0.021	0.603 ± 0.013
NS	$\mathbf{1.000 \pm 0.000}$	0.389 ± 0.044	0.895 ± 0.031	0.943 ± 0.007	0.485 ± 0.020	0.661 ± 0.012
PR_{WD}	0.873 ± 0.032	0.453 ± 0.098	0.801 ± 0.039	0.903 ± 0.009	0.336 ± 0.019	0.601 ± 0.013
PR_{WP}	0.962 ± 0.020	0.561 ± 0.101	0.893 ± 0.031	$\mathbf{0.966 \pm 0.005}$	0.491 ± 0.020	0.676 ± 0.012
IScore	0.977 ± 0.016	0.842 ± 0.096	0.954 ± 0.022	0.908 ± 0.009	0.686 ± 0.021	0.692 ± 0.013
NIScore	0.980 ± 0.016	0.750 ± 0.093	0.941 ± 0.023	0.903 ± 0.010	0.538 ± 0.024	0.651 ± 0.013
CSE	0.947 ± 0.023	0.682 ± 0.099	0.902 ± 0.029	0.871 ± 0.011	0.455 ± 0.024	0.612 ± 0.013
EEIScore	0.972 ± 0.018	0.801 ± 0.097	0.943 ± 0.023	0.555 ± 0.016	0.467 ± 0.022	0.435 ± 0.011
CSSVE	0.930 ± 0.027	0.586 ± 0.100	0.871 ± 0.033	0.796 ± 0.013	0.412 ± 0.023	0.559 ± 0.013
UIScore	0.980 ± 0.015	$\mathbf{0.891 \pm 0.080}$	0.965 ± 0.019	0.888 ± 0.010	0.718 ± 0.020	0.689 ± 0.013
UCSE	0.970 ± 0.018	0.743 ± 0.099	0.931 ± 0.025	0.874 ± 0.011	0.630 ± 0.021	0.659 ± 0.013
Eigen (IScore)	0.974 ± 0.018	0.817 ± 0.092	0.947 ± 0.024	0.864 ± 0.011	$\mathbf{0.804 \pm 0.020}^{\dagger}$	0.697 ± 0.013
Eigen	0.998 ± 0.005	0.529 ± 0.090	0.917 ± 0.027	0.910 ± 0.009	0.674 ± 0.019	0.690 ± 0.012
mGENRE	0.998 ± 0.005	0.869 ± 0.089	$\mathbf{0.976 \pm 0.017}$	0.959 ± 0.006	0.720 ± 0.022	$\mathbf{0.730 \pm 0.012}^{\dagger}$

† Indicates statistical significance ($p < 0.05$) between the best and the second-best method using bootstrapped 95% CIs.

respectively. If *co-founder of Enough* was listed in Wikidata and if *World War II* was treated as a single noun phrase, the UIScore of the gold entity, Q6253345, would beat the score of Q6253343.

Key property implicit in text. Some errors occur when enough information is provided in the article and in Wikidata, but the key properties are not mentioned in the text explicitly. For example, professional golfer Will Mackenzie (Q8002946) was mentioned in an article that was clearly about golf. However, golf was not mentioned at all in the article, yet Mackenzie's profession could be inferred from other terms related to golf, such as PGA Tour, which does not appear in the Wikidata item of Q8002946. The output of the method was Q4019878 (actor and director). Although there were other golfers mentioned in the article (leading to an EEIScore of 4 for Q8002946), its item matched no stems in text, while Q4019878 matched two stems that were completely unrelated to the article: *provid* (He was born in Providence which shares the same stem as provide) and *televis* (he was a television actor). Furthermore, Q4019878 matched citizenship, spoken language, and gender with other unambiguous mentions in the article. As a result, Q4019878 was the predicted label. This indicates the need for assigning weights to Wikidata properties to avoid irrelevant matches.

Decoy mention. To illustrate the decoy mention error source, we consider the following example:

*"Amazon will debut five new comedy drama pilots in 2014, including "The After", from **Chris Carter** ("The X-Files"); "Bosch", based on book series by Michael Conelly; "Mozart in the Jungle", from Roman Coppola ("The Darjeeling Limited"); "The Rebels" from former New York Giants football player **Michael Strahan**; and "Transparent" from Jill Soloway ("Six Feet Under")."*

Suppose that we want to disambiguate Chris Carter. Clearly, the correct entity corresponding to Chris Carter is the movie producer who created the science-fiction drama "The X-Files" (Q437267). However, the appearance of Michael Strahan increased the IScore of sportsmen named Chris Carter that played for a New York team (due to the appearance of the words "player", "New", and "York"). Note that a limitation of IScore is that it treats the words New and York separately, although they should be treated as a single noun phrase.

Static and Dynamic Speaker Modeling based on Graph Neural Network for Emotion Recognition in Conversation

Anonymous ACL submission

Abstract

Each person has a unique personality which affects how they feel and convey emotions. Hence, speaker modeling is important for the task of emotion recognition in conversation (ERC). In this paper, we propose a novel graph-based ERC model which considers both conversational context and speaker personality. We model the internal state of the speaker (personality) as *Static* and *Dynamic* speaker state, where the *Dynamic* speaker state is modeled with a graph neural network based encoder. Experiments on benchmark dataset shows the effectiveness of our model. Our model outperforms baseline and other graph-based methods. Analysis of results also show the importance of explicit speaker modeling.

1 Introduction

Emotion recognition in conversation (ERC) is a task within the sphere of emotion recognition. ERC aims to predict the emotion of each utterance in a conversation. With the recent advances of dialogue research, ERC has gained popularity due to its potential to support downstream applications such as affective dialog systems (Majumder et al., 2020) and opinion mining from social media chats (Chatterjee et al., 2019).

The emotion of an utterance depends on many factors including surrounding context and speaker personality. Previous studies show that the same utterance can express different emotions under different contexts (Poria et al., 2019b). On the other hand, the speaker's personality and background should be considered when we interpret the emotion of an utterance. For example, in Figure 1, the utterance "This is great!" can carry the emotion of *anger* (sarcastic person) or *joy* (not sarcastic). This difference can be attributed to the different personalities of the speakers.

In speaker modeling, we aim to model the internal state of the speaker. Moreover, we distinguish

Figure 1: The emotion conveyed by the phrase "This is great" can either be *anger* (sarcasm) or *joy* (in the case that the person ordered the wrong item). This example is taken from (Poria et al., 2019b).

between the *Static* and *Dynamic* states of a speaker. The *Static* speaker state refers to the average state of a person that remains unchanged over a long period of time. On the other hand, the *Dynamic* speaker state refers to the deviation from the *Static* state in presence of external stimuli. External stimuli can dictate and change the speaker's internal state, which in turn affects the emotion displayed by an individual, hence modeling the *Dynamic* state of a speaker is important for ERC.

In the past few years, Graph Neural Networks (GNNs) have been used increasingly for ERC. GNNs provide an intuitive way to model conversations (Shen et al., 2021) given the inherent structural flexibility of the graph. The graph structure can be used to capture the dependency between utterances and speakers.

Recent works such as DialogGCN (Ghosal et al., 2019), RGAT (Ishiwatari et al., 2020), EmoBERTa (Kim and Vossen, 2021) and DAG-ERC (Shen et al., 2021) have modelled conversational contexts using various methods, however they do not model speaker state explicitly. Whereas ConGCN (Zhang et al., 2019) and MMGCN (Hu et al., 2021) models the speaker state explicitly, however, they use random embedding for initialization and model just the *Static* aspect.

In this study, we propose a novel graph-based ERC model which considers both *Static* and *Dynamic* aspects of speaker state. We utilize a graph

Proceedings of the 2022 Conference of the North American Chapter of the Association for Computational Linguistics: Human Language Technologies: Student Research Workshop, pages 247 - 253
July 10-15, 2022

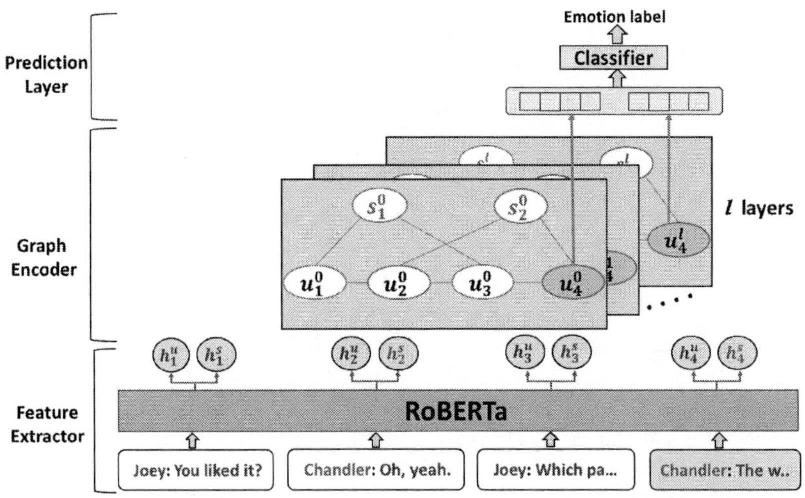

Figure 2: Model overview. The target utterance is denoted in yellow color.

which includes past utterance nodes and explicit speaker nodes to model the interactions between utterances and speakers in the dialogue. Experimental results on the benchmark MELD dataset (Poria et al., 2019a) verified the effectiveness of our model regarding both context and speaker modeling.

2 Related Work

DialogGCN (Ghosal et al., 2019) was the first paper to use GNN to model dialogues. Given an input dialogue, a complete graph within a fixed context (past and future) window is built. Since graph-based neural networks do not take sequential information into account, RGAT (Ishiwatari et al., 2020) uses relational positional encodings to improve upon DialogGCN. DAG-ERC (Shen et al., 2021) built a more intuitive graph structure by considering local and remote information, without using any future utterance.
EmoBERTa (Kim and Vossen, 2021) modeled the speaker state and context by prepending the speaker names to utterances and inserting separation tokens between the utterances in a dialogue, and feeding it to RoBERTa. ConGCN (Zhang et al., 2019) explicitly used speaker nodes, which were initialized randomly. MMGCN (Hu et al., 2021) also incorporated randomly initialized speaking embeddings in their model.

3 Methodology

Our model consists of three components: Feature extractor, Graph encoder, and Prediction layer. Figure 2 shows an overview of our proposed model. We will give a detailed explanation of our model in this section.

3.1 Problem Definition

In ERC, a dialogue is defined as a sequence of utterances $\{U_1, U_2, ..., U_N\}$, where N is the number of utterances. Each utterance U_i is spoken by a speaker S_i and has an emotion label Y_i. The goal of ERC is to predict the emotion label Y_t for a given U_t and S_t .

3.2 Feature Extractor

We use pretrained RoBERTa (Liu et al., 2019) as our feature extractor. Inspired by EmoBERTa (Kim and Vossen, 2021), we feed the following sequence to RoBERTa for each utterance U_i with speaker S_i (as shown in Figure 2):

$$[CLS]S_i : U_i[SEP] \quad (1)$$

For each utterance U_i, we take the output vector of RoBERTa corresponding to the [CLS] token as the **utterance embedding** h_i^u. In addition, we extract the RoBERTa output vector corresponding to the speaker token[1] S_i as the **speaker embedding** h_i^s. This component is responsible for the *Static* speaker state modeling and h_i^s represents the *Static* speaker state.

3.3 Graph Encoder

In this section, we introduce the construction of a dialogue graph and the details of the graph encoder.

[1]In the case when speaker name is a multi-token entity, we consider the first token for the speaker embedding.

3.3.1 Graph Construction

For a target utterance U_t in the dialogue, we build a graph $G = (V, E)$ to model the surrounding context and speaker information, where V denotes the set of nodes and E is the set of edges.

The graph G contains two types of nodes:

- *Utterance node:* We consider the target utterance U_t and up to w utterances preceding U_t as past utterances.
- *Speaker node:* We consider the unique speakers of the target and past utterances.

The set of nodes can be represented as:

$$V = \{U_i\}_{i=t-w}^{i=t} \cup \text{Uniq}(\{S_i\}_{i=t-w}^{i=t}) \quad (2)$$

where the function Uniq() returns all the unique elements in a set.

Our graph contains two types of edges:

- *Utterance-Utterance Edge:* We connect each utterance to its previous utterance. These model the effect of past utterance on the present utterance. These are given by $E_{uu} = \{(U_{i-1}, U_i)\}_{i=t-w+1}^{i=t}$
- *Utterance-Speaker Edge:* We connect each utterance U_i to its corresponding speaker S_j. The set of utterance-speaker edges are denoted as $E_{us} = \{(U_i, S_j)\}_{i=t-w}^{i=t}$. These edges model the effect of speakers on the utterances.

The set of edges can be given by:

$$E = E_{uu} \cup E_{us}, \quad (3)$$

Figure 2 (Graph Encoder part) illustrates an example of the constructed graph with a target utterance U_4 (colored in yellow) and 3 past utterances. U_1 and U_3 are spoken by a unique speaker S_1, while U_2 and U_4 are spoken by another unique speaker S_2. (Note that the subscripts of the speakers reflects the indices after Uniq().)

3.3.2 Node Initialization

We initialize the Utterance and Speaker nodes as follows:

- *Utterance node* : $u_i^0 = h_i^u \quad \forall i \in [t-w, t]$
- *Speaker node* : $s_j^0 = avg(h_i^s) \quad \forall i$ spoken by S_j.

Since there is only one speaker node for each unique speaker, we use the averaged speaker embeddings to initialize the Speaker node.

3.3.3 GNN-Based Graph Encoding Layers

After constructing and initializing the graph, we feed it to the GNN-based encoding layers, which update node representations considering the graph structure. This component is responsible for the *Dynamic* speaker state modeling.

We use l-layered GNN to get the updated node representations based on the graph structure of G. For k^{th} layer, all the nodes (Speaker and Utterance nodes) are updated considering each of their direct neighbours:

$$(\{u_i^k\}, \{s_j^k\}) = GNN^k(\{u_i^{k-1}\}, \{s_j^{k-1}\}) \quad (4)$$

After being updated by l layers, the *Static* speaker state, s_j^0, is updated to s_j^l, which represents the *Dynamic* speaker state. Similarly, the initial utterance embedding u_i^0 is updated to final utterance embedding u_i^l.

3.4 Emotion Classification

Finally, we concatenate the initial and the final utterance embeddings of target utterance and feed it through a feed-forward network to classify emotions.

$$P_t = \text{softmax}(FFN(u_t^0 || u_t^l)), \quad (5)$$

$$Y_t^* = \text{argmax}(P_t), \quad (6)$$

Here, $||$ denotes the concatenation operation, FFN is the feed-forward neural network layer, and P_t is the probability distribution for the predicted emotion.

3.5 Training Objective

We use the standard cross-entropy along with L2-regularization as the loss ($\mathcal{L}$):

$$\mathcal{L} = -\sum_{x=1}^{M}\sum_{t=1}^{N_x} \log P_{x,t}[Y_{x,t}] + \lambda||\theta||_2, \quad (7)$$

Here, M is the total number of training dialogues, N_x is the number of utterances in the xth dialogue, $P_{x,t}$ and $Y_{x,t}$ are the predicted probability distribution of emotion labels and the truth label respectively for utterance t of the dialogue x. λ is the L2-regularization weight, and θ is the set of all trainable parameters.

	Train	Dev	Test
# Utterance	9,989	1,109	2,610
# Dialogue	1,039	114	280

Table 1: Statistics for the MELD dataset.

4 Experiments and Results

Experiments on the benchmark dataset shows the effectiveness of our model. Details of experiments and analysis are given in this section.

4.1 Dataset

We evaluate our model on the benchmark Multimodal EmotionLines Dataset (MELD) dataset (Poria et al., 2019a). MELD is a multi-modal dataset collected from the TV show Friends. There are 7 emotion labels: neutral, happiness, surprise, sadness, anger, disgust, and fear. Since this is an imbalanced dataset, weighted-F1 is used as the evaluation metric. More than 85% of the utterances in MELD are spoken by 6 main speakers, this high utterance per speaker is useful for modeling the speaker state. The statistics of MELD are shown in Table 1.

4.2 Experimental Settings

The feature extractor used is the pre-trained RoBERTa-large (Liu et al., 2019). The size of all the hidden features is 1024. We experiment with Graph Convolutional Network(GCN) (Kipf and Welling, 2017) and Graph Attention Network(GAT) (Veličković et al., 2018) as the GNN-based graph encoding layers. For the GCN based model, the past context is set to be 3 utterances and the number of GNN layers was set to be 2. For the GAT based model, the past context is set to be 5 utterances and the number of GNN layers was set to be 3. GAT model also has three attention heads in addition to the above settings.

The models are trained for 10 epochs, batch size is set to be 8, and the learning rate is set to 1e-6. The model with the highest weighted-F1 on the validation set is selected for evaluation. Due to the stochastic nature of the model, we report the averaged score of 3 random runs on the test set.

4.3 Evaluation

Compared Methods and Results: We compare our proposed model with baselines and previous works. The results are reported in Table 2.

First, we establish two baselines: *RoBERTa (no context)* and *RoBERTa (w/ modified input)*. In the *RoBERTa (no context)* utterance alone is used as input to the pre-trained RoBERTa model. In the *RoBERTa (w/ modified input)* we use a modified input as given by Equation 1. Our proposed method outperforms both RoBERTa baselines by F1 scores of 2.4 and 1.8, respectively. This shows the advantage of using the graph encoding mechanism.

Next, we compare our model with other GNN-based models: *DAG-ERC*, *DialogGCN* and *RGAT*. For fair comparison, we use the models which use RoBERTa-large as the feature extractor[2]. Our model outperforms all these models, proving the advantage of using explicit speaker nodes to model conversations.

Finally, we compare our results with the *EmoBERTa* model[3]. Our model with GCN encoder performs slightly worse than EmoBERTa. However, our model with GAT encoder outperforms EmoBERTa. Hence, we can state that the performance of our model and EmoBERTa is comparable. Note that EmoBERTa uses both past and future utterances as context, whereas we only use the past utterances as context, which is more natural as conversations proceed with time and future utterances cannot be used for real-time applications. Under the condition that only the past utterances are allowed, both our proposed models outperform *EmoBERTa (wo/ future context)*.

GCN vs. GAT: In our experiments, models which utilize GAT as graph encoders outperformed the GCN ones. The edge weights for all edges in our GCN models were set to be 1. On the other hand, the edge weights for GAT models were learned and optimized during the training of our model due to the explicit attention heads of the GAT based models.

We speculate that since the utterance-utterance edge and speaker-utterance edge are different in nature so their edge weight should be different, hence GAT outperformed GCN and has the ability to better represent the relations between nodes.

Since, GAT based model performs superior to GCN based one, we use GAT based models for further analysis.

[2]The authors of DAG-ERC re-implement DialogGCN and RGAT using RoBERTa-large as feature extractor, we include the scores reported by the DAG-ERC paper.

[3]EmoBERTa was the SOTA model while this research was conducted, the new SOTA model is EmotionFlow. (https://github.com/fpcsong/emotionflow/blob/master/EmotionFlow.pdf)

Model	Weighted-F1
RoBERTa (no context)	0.635
RoBERTa (w/ modified input)	0.641
DAG-ERC	0.636
RGAT (+RoBERTa)	0.628
DialogueGCN (+RoBERTa)	0.630
EmoBERTa	0.656
EmoBERTa (wo/ future context)	0.646
Proposed (GCN)	0.652
Proposed (GAT)	**0.659**

Table 2: Experimental results on MELD.

Method	Weighted-F1
Proposed (Static + Dynamic)	**0.658**
Proposed (wo/ speaker) (Static)	0.646
Proposed (random init. speaker)	0.638

Table 3: Impact of speaker modeling.

4.4 Analysis

In this section, we conduct various analysis of our proposed model.

4.4.1 Impact of Speaker Modeling

To investigated the impact of the speaker modeling on the performance, we evaluated our model by removing speaker nodes, *Proposed (wo/ speaker)*, and by randomly initializing speaker nodes, *Proposed (random init. speaker)*. The results are shown in Table 3. These results are with three past context and two GAT layer model.

Removing speaker nodes reduces the weighted-F1 score by 1.2. The significant decrease indicates the importance of speaker modeling to the ERC task. Whereas, randomly initializing speaker nodes results in a performance drop of 2.0 points. Moreover, the score with random speaker initialization is lower than the score of the model without any speaker nodes. We hypothesize that the random embeddings create noise and hinder the performance.

4.4.2 Impact of Context Window Size and the Number of GAT layers

To analyze the impact of context window size, we varied the past context window size from 1 to 5. The results are reported for two and three GAT layers in Figure 3. The model performs worst when we use only one past context, which illustrates the necessity to model sufficient context. Moreover, we also find out that the optimal number of past context varied for different number of GNN layers (3 context for 2 layers and 5 context for 3 layers).

Next, we investigated the effect of changing the number of layers on the performance. One layer of graph encoder updates a node considering all the one-hop neighbours. The scores for the number of layers from two to five for a past context of size five is given in the Figure 4. The score is highest for three layers. Our graph structure allows information to be aggregated from the last context utterance in few hops due to utterances being connected by speaker nodes, so the performance does not change greatly by changing the number of layers.

4.4.3 Case Study

We performed a qualitative analysis for our model. We used the model with five past contexts and three GAT layers. We manually inspected ten test samples that were predicted correctly and ten instances that were predicted incorrectly.

We found that utterances with speakers other than the six main speakers have a higher chance of being predicted incorrectly (six out of ten incorrectly predicted test samples contained at least one speaker other than the main speakers). We speculate that this can be attributed to the fact that we only modeled the main six speakers, and for the case of other speakers, we did not construct any speaker nodes. In the first sample given in Table 4 it is noted that a non-main speaker (Steve) accounts for a considerable part of the dialogue and our system predicts the emotion incorrectly.

However, in the cases in which the main speakers make up the majority of the past context, the emotion of utterances of other speakers can be predicted correctly. The second sample in Table 4 shows this, where the emotion label for the dialogue of a non-main speaker (Fireman #1) is predicted correctly. The reason might be that the speaker nodes of the main speakers assist the model in predicting the emotion label.

5 Conclusion

We proposed a novel graph-based method to model speaker states explicitly for the task of ERC. Experiments showed that our model outperforms baselines and other graph-based models. We analyse the impact of speaker modeling and show that both *Static* speaker state and *Dynamic* speaker state modeling are important for the accurate prediction of emotions in ERC. In addition, we investigate the

Dialogue	Predicted	Gold
Steve: Oh, okay, I get it. Ross : No wait, look. Look! I'm sorry, it's just I've never even Steve: Howard's the, Ross: Yes but too me he's just, man. *Steve : Okay, fine, whatever. Welcome to the building.*	**neutral**	**anger**
Phoebe: Oh! Rachel : My God! Joey: Hey buddy, do you think I can borrow your uniform this Thursday? *Fireman #1: Excuse me?*	**surprise**	**surprise**

Table 4: Case study. The target utterance is shown in italics.

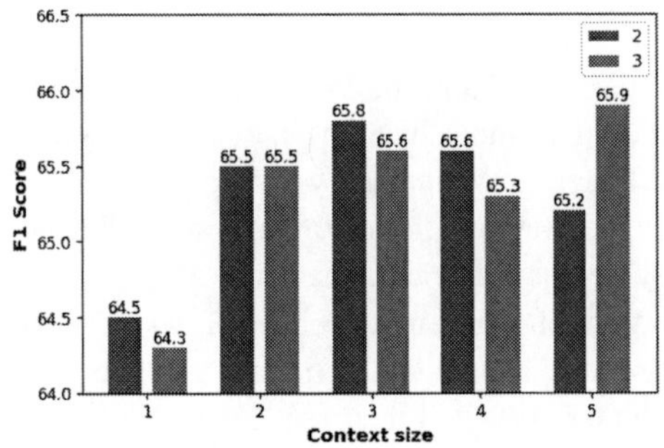

Figure 3: Impact of past context size with two and three GAT layers.

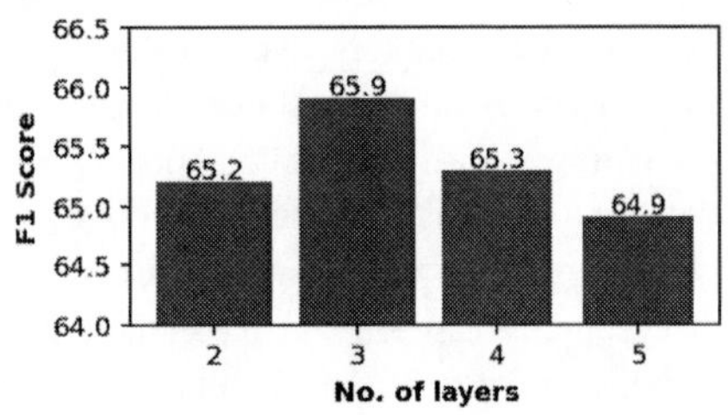

Figure 4: Impact of number of GAT layers. Context window is of size 5.

effect of changing the number of GNN layers and the past context on the performance of our model.

References

Ankush Chatterjee, Kedhar Nath Narahari, Meghana Joshi, and Puneet Agrawal. 2019. SemEval-2019 task 3: EmoContext contextual emotion detection in text. In *Proceedings of the 13th International Workshop on Semantic Evaluation*, pages 39–48, Minneapolis, Minnesota, USA. Association for Computational Linguistics.

Deepanway Ghosal, Navonil Majumder, Soujanya Poria, Niyati Chhaya, and Alexander Gelbukh. 2019. DialogueGCN: A graph convolutional neural network for emotion recognition in conversation. In *Proceedings of the 2019 Conference on Empirical Methods in Natural Language Processing and the 9th International Joint Conference on Natural Language Processing (EMNLP-IJCNLP)*, pages 154–164, Hong Kong, China. Association for Computational Linguistics.

Jingwen Hu, Yuchen Liu, Jinming Zhao, and Qin Jin. 2021. MMGCN: Multimodal fusion via deep graph convolution network for emotion recognition in conversation. In *Proceedings of the 59th Annual Meeting of the Association for Computational Linguistics and the 11th International Joint Conference on Natural Language Processing (Volume 1: Long Papers)*, pages 5666–5675, Online. Association for Computational Linguistics.

Taichi Ishiwatari, Yuki Yasuda, Taro Miyazaki, and Jun Goto. 2020. Relation-aware graph attention networks with relational position encodings for emotion recognition in conversations. In *Proceedings of the 2020 Conference on Empirical Methods in Natural Language Processing (EMNLP)*, pages 7360–7370, Online. Association for Computational Linguistics.

Taewoon Kim and Piek Vossen. 2021. Emoberta: Speaker-aware emotion recognition in conversation with roberta.

Thomas N. Kipf and Max Welling. 2017. Semi-supervised classification with graph convolutional networks.

Yinhan Liu, Myle Ott, Naman Goyal, Jingfei Du, Mandar Joshi, Danqi Chen, Omer Levy, Mike Lewis, Luke Zettlemoyer, and Veselin Stoyanov. 2019. Roberta: A robustly optimized bert pretraining approach.

Navonil Majumder, Pengfei Hong, Shanshan Peng, Jiankun Lu, Deepanway Ghosal, Alexander Gelbukh, Rada Mihalcea, and Soujanya Poria. 2020. MIME: MIMicking emotions for empathetic response generation. In *Proceedings of the 2020 Conference on Empirical Methods in Natural Language Processing (EMNLP)*, pages 8968–8979, Online. Association for Computational Linguistics.

Soujanya Poria, Devamanyu Hazarika, Navonil Majumder, Gautam Naik, Erik Cambria, and Rada Mihalcea. 2019a. MELD: A multimodal multi-party dataset for emotion recognition in conversations. In *Proceedings of the 57th Annual Meeting of the Association for Computational Linguistics*, pages 527–536, Florence, Italy. Association for Computational Linguistics.

Soujanya Poria, Navonil Majumder, Rada Mihalcea, and Eduard Hovy. 2019b. Emotion recognition in conversation: Research challenges, datasets, and recent advances. *IEEE Access*, 7:100943–100953.

Weizhou Shen, Siyue Wu, Yunyi Yang, and Xiaojun Quan. 2021. Directed acyclic graph network for conversational emotion recognition. In *Proceedings of the 59th Annual Meeting of the Association for Computational Linguistics and the 11th International Joint Conference on Natural Language Processing (Volume 1: Long Papers)*, pages 1551–1560, Online. Association for Computational Linguistics.

Petar Veličković, Guillem Cucurull, Arantxa Casanova, Adriana Romero, Pietro Liò, and Yoshua Bengio. 2018. Graph attention networks.

Dong Zhang, Liangqing Wu, Changlong Sun, Shoushan Li, Qiaoming Zhu, and Guodong Zhou. 2019. Modeling both context- and speaker-sensitive dependence for emotion detection in multi-speaker conversations. In *Proceedings of the Twenty-Eighth International Joint Conference on Artificial Intelligence, IJCAI-19*, pages 5415–5421. International Joint Conferences on Artificial Intelligence Organization.

Few-Shot Fine-Tuning SOTA Summarization Models for Medical Dialogues

David Fraile Navarro[1], Mark Dras[2], Shlomo Berkovsky[1]

[1]Centre for Health Informatics, Australian Institute of Health Innovation, Macquarie University, Sydney, Australia
[2]Department of Computing, Macquarie University, Sydney, Australia
david.frailenavarro@hdr.mq.edu.au, {mark.dras, shlomo.berkovsky}@mq.edu.au

Abstract

Abstractive summarization of medical dialogues presents a challenge for standard training approaches given the paucity of suitable datasets. We explore the performance of state-of-the-art models with zero-shot and few-shot learning strategies and measure the impact of pre-training with general domain and dialogue specific text on the summarization performance.

1 Introduction

Clinical dialogues between patients and health professionals are among the core elements of the clinical encounter, containing most of the initial anamnesis questions, diagnostic information, treatment options, patient advice and counselling. Doctors usually summarize the content of these conversations into clinical notes, after each clinical visit or make use of expensive human medical scribes. As recent speech-recognition technologies show increasingly good performance (Chung et al., 2021; Zhang et al., 2020b), capturing these dialogues and generating abstractive summaries would help to reduce clinician load and improve patient care (Coiera et al., 2018).

Abstractive summarization has been one of the main challenges for NLP (Gupta and Gupta, 2019). The accuracy of abstractive summarization has improved over the past years due to the use of transformer-based, sequence to sequence (seq2seq) models (Aghajanyan et al., 2021; Raffel et al., 2019), larger training datasets and denser neural networks. Although several general-purpose datasets such as XSum (Narayan et al., 2018), CNN-DailyMail (Hermann et al., 2015), and SAMSUM (Gliwa et al., 2019) have been used for their training and development, few corpora exist that could be applied to the health scenario, medical terminology rich dialogues, with frequent interjections, ellipsis, and logical connections between semantic units (e.g., drug Y *treats* condition Z and not vice versa).

We fine-tuned several state-of-the-art (SOTA) models in a newly created medical dialogue dataset of 143 snippets, based on 27 general practice conversations paired with their respective summaries. We tested 10 transformer models to assess their performance in abstractive summarization of these dialogues. We learned that models pre-trained on general dialogues outperform baseline models. BART-based models were found to achieve the highest scores, although medical inconsistencies persisted in the generated summaries. In the future, we plan to perform further evaluations as the need for metrics that highlight inconsistencies in medical summaries remains unresolved.

2 Background

Training and fine-tuning NLP models for medical tasks has been a challenge, given the paucity of high-quality training data, although several initiatives such as MIMIC (Johnson et al., 2016) and n2c2 challenges (Henry et al., 2020) have advanced the field. Strategies to reduce dependence on large training datasets, such as transfer learning, have been explored (Fabbri et al., 2021a) to improve the model performance. Transformer-based models and their various implementations are well suited for transfer learning and fine-tuning with sparse datasets.

Proceedings of the 2022 Conference of the North American Chapter of the Association for Computational Linguistics: Human Language Technologies: Student Research Workshop, pages 254 - 266
July 10-15, 2022 ©2022 Association for Computational Linguistics

Additionally, zero-shot and few-shot approaches may help strike the balance between the model's

Dialogue: Doctor: Okay. Thank you for seeing Jane Doe. Jane is a student here. She gives a history of intermittent ear pain, both ears, isn't it? Jane: Yeah, both ears. Doctor: Bilateral ear pains at night? Jane: Yep, and occasionally throughout the day. Doctor: Oh okay? Jane: Yeah. Not like the pain, just the pulsing. Doctor: Oh okay? Jane: Sorry, I mean. Doctor: For several years and also, mainly in your right ear, isn't it? Jane: The pulsing is in the right ear. The pain is in the left ear. Doctor: Oh, pain in your left? Jane: Sorry. I'm just thinking about it now. Doctor: Sorry. I thought. Doctor: It was both ears? Jane: I'm noticing, when I think about it, sorry, the pulsing is definitely more in the right ear. Doctor: Left ear pain and also right ear pulsing? Jane: But I don't know how else to describe it. Like that's. Doctor: No, no. We know exactly what you mean? Jane: It, yeah, like a. Doctor: A throbbing? Jane: It's like a, yeah, throbbing. Like a blood rush sort of. Doctor: Pulsation? Jane: Sensation. But not. Doctor: Okay. With throbbing? Jane: Obviously blood rush. Doctor: Throbbing in, for up to six months, maybe six months? Jane: Yeah. About, up to six months. Doctor: She looks very well, looks very well. Nil to find today, today. BP, what was it? I think it was 104. Doctor: Okay.
Summary: Jane has a history of bilateral ear pains at night in her left ear and pulsing, throbbing sensation in her right ear, like a blood rush, for

Box 1: Dialogue-summary example

performance, training time and training data requirements. Several recent developments have shown the effect of few-shot strategies in medical abstractive summarization (Goodwin et al., 2020) as well as in online medical dialogues (Nair et al., 2021).

Although few-shot and pre-training strategies have been studied separately, none have experimentally compared how these two interact in the medical dialogue domain and how different seq2seq models perform under these circumstances. In this work, we study how different few-shot strategies and pre-trained models affect the performance of abstractive summarization in medical dialogues.

3 Methods

3.1 Dataset

Our dataset consisted of 27 recorded conversations between general practitioners and patients collected by (Quiroz et al., 2020), where the data was used to characterize the structure and content of primary care consultations. These recordings took place at Primary Care facilities at Macquarie Health Clinics, Sydney, Australia. The conversations were professionally transcribed and anonymized. The conversations included in the dataset exceeded the token limit for existing language models (either 512 or 1024 tokens). Thus, we pre-processed the dataset by slicing the conversations into 400-word snippets. They were further processed to ensure that they contained semantically sound pairs of clinician-patient interactions, e.g., Doctor asks questions and Patient answers. A small number of snippets (less than 5%) were removed as they did not contain relevant medical information, such that the final dataset consisted of 143 snippets, containing 56,158 words. Box 1 shows a sample snippet. The dataset was partitioned using an 80-20 train-evaluation split. The training split was then subsequently split into further incremental few-shot sub-samples.

3.2 Annotation

A trained primary care physician with over 7 years of practical experience created summaries for all the snippets maintaining the following clinical information: medical information, medical advice, prescriptions, and general patient information. Annotation was performed by a single person; therefore, no inter-annotator agreement was calculated. Summaries varied in length between 17 and 158 words, as some snippets were more informative than others, with an average length of 68 words.

3.3 Models

Transformer-based models are currently the SOTA in several summarization benchmarks (Aghajanyan et al., 2020). We included the BART (Lewis et al., 2019), PEGASUS (Zhang et al., 2020a), and T5 (Raffel et al., 2019) families of models in our evaluation.

Among the various fine-tuned variants of these models, we included those having a fine-tuned version of the base model trained on the SAMSUM dialogue dataset (Gliwa et al., 2019). This dataset contains dialogues from various online chats, and it is one of the freely available dialogue summarization datasets. We harnessed the 'large' versions of these models. To explore medical transfer learning, we also included one model fine-tuned for PubMed summarization (Gupta et al., 2021). All the models included are available at HuggingFace[1]. Overall, 10 models were included in our evaluation: T5, T5$_{SAMSUM}$, BART, BART$_{SAMSUM}$, BART$_{CNN\text{-}Dailymail}$, BART$_{CNN\text{-}SAMSUM}$, PEGASUS, PEGASUS$_{CNN\text{-}Dailymail}$ PEGASUS$_{CNN\text{-}Dailymail\text{-}SAMSUM}$, and PEGASUS$_{PUBMED}$. The complete training strategy and best-fine-tuned models are available in our GitHub repository [2] and on the HuggingFace platform[3].

3.4 Fine-tuning strategy

We used the HuggingFace implementation of transformers and adapted their default fine-tuning scripts[4]. The default fine-tuning strategy consisted of training models for 3 epochs without further adjustments. Given the small size of the dataset, the evaluation split was only used at the end of the training and was not used to adjust the learning rate, which was set to the default value for each model. Initial analysis also showed that the loss value increased with additional training epochs. Therefore, to avoid overfitting, no further rounds of training were performed.

We implemented an incremental few-shot learning (FSL) strategy evaluating the models at zero-shot, and then incrementally fine-tuning pre-trained models with 10-shot, 20-shot, 50-shot, and the full dataset.

3.5 Metrics and evaluation

We quantitatively evaluated the summaries using the ROUGE scores (ROUGE-1, ROUGE-2, ROUGE-L, ROUGE-L-sum) (Lin, 2004) for each model and FSL strategy. These were calculated immediately after training with the provided script in the 20% (29 snippets) that were held out for evaluation. We also computed the improvement over zero-shot learning (ZSL) for each model with each incremental FSL step.

For the qualitative evaluation, a small sample of 7 generated snippets was inspected by a clinician, aiming to analyse the semantic and medical accuracy of the generated summaries according to the following aspects: (1) assertion (e.g., information is correctly affirmed or negated); (2) major (e.g., symptom, diagnosis or treatment) or minor medical information missing; (3) medical coherence (e.g., wrong cause-and-effect relationship); and (4) contradicting advice (e.g., stop treatment instead of start treatment).

4 Results

4.1 Quantitative evaluation

All the models pre-trained with dialogues outperformed their base counterparts both in ZSL and across all the FSL steps, irrespective of the underlying model (T5, BART or PEGASUS). Table 1 shows the ZSL performance of the base models and dialogue *(SAMSUM)* pre-trained models. The best-performing model within each family is highlighted for each metric. Table 2 shows the performance of the models pre-trained with the full dataset of 114 snippets. Figure 1 shows ROUGE-1 score for all models being incrementally trained with 0, 10, 20, and 50 shots, and the full dataset.

Overall, BART-based models outperformed both T5 and PEGASUS, both for ZSL and 10, 20, and 50 FSL steps. Training on the full dataset, BART$_{\text{-}CNN\text{-}SAMSUM}$ scored highest for ROUGE-1 and ROUGE-2, but T5$_{\text{-}SAMSUM}$ outperformed it for the ROUGE-L and ROUGE-L-sum scores. Appendix A shows the full results across the FSL steps for all models.

Baseline	**R-1**	**R-2**	**R-L**	**R-L-Sum**
T5	30.93	11.40	22.44	28.59
T5-SAMSUM	**35.74**	**13.99**	**24.63**	**33.76**
BART	32.70	9.69	19.74	30.78
BART-CNN	36.72	11.90	22.46	34.73
BART-SAMSUM	37.38	15.88	26.11	35.40
BART-CNN-SAMSUM	**40.82**	**16.00**	**27.26**	**38.78**
PEGASUS	**35.23**	11.46	22.95	**32.83**
PEGASUS CNN	34.36	12.06	23.66	29.68
PEGASUS CNN-SAMSUM	33.69	**13.63**	**24.79**	31.79
PEGASUS -PUBMED	15.31	1.00	10.41	13.99

Table 1: Zero-shot ROUGE scores

[1] https://huggingface.co/models

[2] https://github.com/dafraile/Clinical-Dialogue-Summarization

[3] https://huggingface.co/dafraile

[4] https://github.com/huggingface/transformers/tree/master/examples/pytorch/summarization

Full training (n=114)	R-1	R-2	R-L	R-L-Sum
T5	51.79	23.77	37.54	49.41
T5$_{\text{-SAMSUM}}$	**54.91**	**26.64**	**40.46**	**52.37**
BART	52.31	23.66	34.18	49.34
BART$_{\text{-CNN}}$	53.59	25.07	37.72	50.96
BART$_{\text{-SAMSUM}}$	52.99	24.88	37.22	50.87
BART$_{\text{-CNN-SAMSUM}}$	**55.32**	**27.12**	**39.67**	**52.22**
PEGASUS-	39.51	15.74	27.57	37.22
PEGASUS$_{\text{-CNN}}$	**50.94**	23.30	36.40	48.52
PEGASUS$_{\text{-CNN-SAMSUM}}$	50.89	**24.54**	**37.25**	**48.92**
PEGASUS$_{\text{-PUBMED}}$	30.87	11.13	21.05	28.30

Table 2 ROUGE scores for the full dataset training

Table 3 shows the average (across multiple models) relative improvement obtained for ZSL to FSL with 10, 20, and 50 shots, and the full dataset. This is further broken down into the baseline and dialogue-trained models. The performance of the models consistently improved with FSL increasing steadily up to 50-shot and further to the full dataset. The largest improvements were observed from baseline to 10-shot, and from 20-shot to 50-shot. Appendix B presents all the increments observed across FSL.

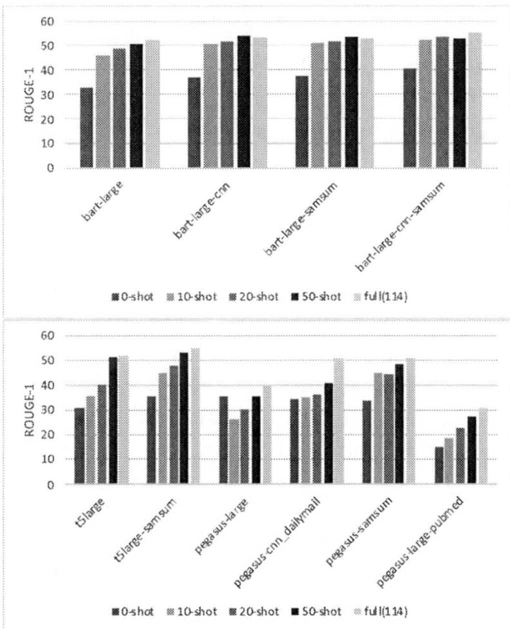

Figure 1: ROUGE-1 scores for each model for ZSL, FSL step, and the full dataset

Base Models	***ΔR-1***	***ΔR-2***	***ΔR-L***	***ΔR-Lsum***
10-shot	13.45	32.23	13.94	15.07
20-shot	22.70	49.71	23.60	26.13
50-shot	37.50	82.56	43.13	41.81
Full dataset	46.74	98.81	56.48	51.35
Dialogue Pre-Trained	***ΔR-1***	***ΔR-2***	***ΔR-L***	***ΔR-Lsum***
10-shot	30.69	52.52	35.32	31.43
20-shot	33.37	49.04	33.64	33.44
50-shot	41.43	67.31	46.20	43.38
Full dataset	45.49	74.17	50.65	46.83

Table 3: Average relative (%) improvement for the 4 ROUGE metrics and incremental FSL strategy

4.2 Qualitative evaluation

We focused our evaluation on the three best performing models of each family with respect to ROUGE scores: BART$_{\text{CNN-SAMSUM}}$, T5$_{\text{SAMSUM}}$, and PEGASUS$_{\text{-CNN-SAMSUM}}$. We detected several inconsistencies, incorrect advice, and missing information across the produced summaries. Box 2 shows a sample of the generated summaries, where the Doctor explores irritated tonsils caused by acid reflux and provides advice and treatment (Mylanta®).

PEGASUS$_{\text{-CNN-SAMSUM}}$
She is *coughing but not coughing*. Her tonsils are still swollen. If it is acid coming up, it can give her irritation in the throat. She hasn't lost a lot of weight, but she has lost one kilo. It is common to have acid problems related to spicy food, coffee, chocolate, alcohol and acidic food. (Missing: **no blood in bowel motions or vomiting, treatment advice, weight is missing**)

BART$_{\text{-CNN-SAMSUM}}$
No coughing, but the tonsils are still swollen. Acid can give you irritation in the throat. She hasn't lost a lot of weight. Fifty-four point three is one kilo less. There is no blood in bowel motions or vomiting blood. Sometimes it can be related to the food you eat spicy or acidic. You don't want to eat a huge amount of food in one sitting because it puts pressure on the stomach. **At night is pain at 11 when drinking hot milk.** ~~Tablets can also be bought from chemist Mylanta from Cambodia.~~

T5$_{\text{-SAMSUM}}$
Tonsils are still swollen and she is not coughing. Acid can give irritation in the throat. She hasn't lost a lot of weight. One kilo less. No blood in bowel motions or vomiting blood. Sometimes it can be related to spicy food, coffee, chocolate, alcohol or food that is very acidic. Trying to avoid certain foods. Drinking hot milk can sometimes help. There are tablets and also Mylanta liquid that she can drink. (Missing: 54.3 kg is the actual weight)

Human
No coughing but tonsils are still swollen. Acid coming up can irritate the lining of the throat. Weights 54.3 kilos and has lost a kilo. No blood in the bowel motions or when vomiting. Acid can relate to food you eat like spicy, coffee, chocolate, or alcohol. Sometimes a cup of hot milk helps. You can also buy Mylanta from the chemist.

Box 2: Sample of generated summaries and their evaluation. Legend: **Bold** – contradicting advice, *Italic* – medical incoherence, Underlined – missing information (*minor* or ***major***), ~~Strikethrough~~ – incorrect affirmation

Snippet evaluation (n=7)	T5-samsum	Pegasus-cnn-samsum	Bart-cnn-samsum
Missing information major	2	5	1
Missing information minor	2	2	1
Contradicting advice	0	0	1
Medical incoherencies	0	3	1
Assertion confused	1	3	0

Table 4: Qualitative examination of summaries

In the above examples, the best performing model, $BART_{CNN\text{-}SAMSUM}$ offered contradicting advice and incorrectly pointed out that the medicine needed to be bought in Cambodia (the country appeared in the text, but the meaning was confused). $PEGASUS_{CNN\text{-}SAMSUM}$ missed completely the medical advice given. $T5_{SAMSUM}$ did not produce incoherencies but failed to capture the actual patient weight. Table 4 shows the number of issues detected across the 7 examined snippets. Appendix C contains all the generated snippets and highlights additional issues.

5 Discussion

Our experiment shows that fine-tuning pre-trained models with few-shot learning offers a reliable strategy to improve summarization scores with small training data, making it appropriate for fine-tuning transformer models in domain-specific contexts, such as medical dialogues. By contrast, pre-training on medical literature did not improve results and showed poorer performance than the baseline models. BART based models achieve the highest ROUGE scores across all the FSL steps, with a relatively smaller footprint in terms of the required training time and the number of examples compared to both T5 and PEGASUS. Our experiment confirms previous findings that BART based models outperformed PEGASUS and T5 for summarization (Aghajanyan et al., 2020) and with few-shot strategies (Fabbri et al., 2021a). However, we observe that T5 gets higher ROUGE-L and ROUGE-L-sum results when trained on the full dataset. Although we obtain differences in the ROUGE scores across the best performing models, a limited qualitative analysis did not show a clear difference for T5 vs. BART. Our preliminary qualitative evaluation shows that T5 produced usable summaries (with no contradicting advice and no medical incoherencies) although further evaluation is required. This may reflect that relevant medical information may be situated at longer than 1-gram or 2-gram distances, suggesting that the longest common subsequence metric (ROUGE-L) can be more important for the quality of conversation summaries.

Moreover, we focus our analysis on the ROUGE score metrics, although this family of metrics alone is often insufficient to computationally appraise the quality of the summarization (Suleiman and Awajan, 2020). For instance, character n-gram F-score (chrF) (Popović, 2015), when evaluated for summarization tasks (Fabbri et al., 2021b) shows a higher correlation with the coherency of produced summaries than the ROUGE metrics. Further research is needed to establish the most apt metrics for evaluating the quality of medical summaries, especially as the need for maximizing factual correctness is critical for practical summarization applications in the medical domain.

An important limitation of our study is the small number of snippets and size of the medical dialogue dataset. Given the sensitive nature of medical conversations, this is a pervasive problem facing the development of NLP medical models. It is unlikely that medical dialogue conversations can be easily recorded, transcribed, and released as a public dataset given that they are likely to contain highly sensitive information. However, our experimental design focuses on this pervasive issue in medical NLP by exploring how FSL and pre-training may be leveraged to overcome the scarcity of large datasets.

In this work, we focus on a single document abstractive summarization. Given the length and complexity of medical dialogues, further experiments exploring multi-document summarization, aimed at producing full-dialogue summaries, would be necessary. Previous strategies for long-text summarization, such as global encoding seq2seq approach (Xi et al., 2020) or a globalized BERT architecture using a hierarchical propagation layer (Grail et al., 2021), may prove successful for summarizing long medical dialogues. Further model development, as well as refined training and fine-tuning strategies (e.g., adjusting transformer's structure, learning rate optimizations, and optimizing for additional metrics) or domain-specific dialogue datasets, may help further improve performance. Medical knowledge embeddings may also be a suitable strategy to improve performance and prevent medical incoherencies illustrated above.

Additional evaluations involving multiple clinicians and creating a more encompassing taxonomy of medical summarization errors would be needed for a thorough qualitative evaluation and proper appraisal of the model output quality. Establishing additional contrasts between qualitative and quantitative analysis may help to identify metrics that reliably capture important medical qualitative differences, potentially informing the development of new metrics, and quantifying the issues identified in our evaluation.

6 Conclusions and future work

Summarization of medical dialogues with FSL using pre-trained models is a feasible strategy for model development. Future research needs to focus on uncovering the most adequate set of metrics for capturing medically relevant and factually correct information in medical summaries. Additional qualitative evaluation may shed light on these issues and inform either the selection or development of the right metrics.

References

Armen Aghajanyan, Anchit Gupta, Akshat Shrivastava, Xilun Chen, Luke Zettlemoyer, and Sonal Gupta. 2021. Muppet: Massive Multi-task Representations with Pre-Finetuning. In *Proceedings of the 2021 Conference on Empirical Methods in Natural Language Processing*, pages 5799–5811, Online and Punta Cana, Dominican Republic, November. Association for Computational Linguistics.

Armen Aghajanyan, Akshat Shrivastava, Anchit Gupta, Naman Goyal, Luke Zettlemoyer, and Sonal Gupta. 2020. Better fine-tuning by reducing representational collapse. *arXiv preprint arXiv:2008.03156*.

Yu-An Chung, Yu Zhang, Wei Han, Chung-Cheng Chiu, James Qin, Ruoming Pang, and Yonghui Wu. 2021. W2v-BERT: Combining Contrastive Learning and Masked Language Modeling for Self-Supervised Speech Pre-Training. *arXiv:2108.06209 [cs, eess]*, September. arXiv: 2108.06209.

Enrico Coiera, Baki Kocaballi, John Halamka, and Liliana Laranjo. 2018. The digital scribe. *NPJ digital medicine*, 1(1):1–5.

Alexander R. Fabbri, Simeng Han, Haoyuan Li, Haoran Li, Marjan Ghazvininejad, Shafiq Joty, Dragomir Radev, and Yashar Mehdad. 2021a. Improving Zero and Few-Shot Abstractive Summarization with Intermediate Fine-tuning and Data Augmentation. *arXiv:2010.12836 [cs]*, April. arXiv: 2010.12836.

Alexander R Fabbri, Wojciech Kryściński, Bryan McCann, Caiming Xiong, Richard Socher, and Dragomir Radev. 2021b. Summeval: Re-evaluating summarization evaluation. *Transactions of the Association for Computational Linguistics*, 9:391–409.

Bogdan Gliwa, Iwona Mochol, Maciej Biesek, and Aleksander Wawer. 2019. SAMSum corpus: A human-annotated dialogue dataset for abstractive summarization. *arXiv preprint arXiv:1911.12237*.

Travis R. Goodwin, Max E. Savery, and Dina Demner-Fushman. 2020. Flight of the PEGASUS? Comparing Transformers on Few-Shot and Zero-Shot Multi-document Abstractive Summarization. *Proceedings of COLING. International Conference on Computational Linguistics*, 2020:5640–5646, December.

Quentin Grail, Julien Perez, and Eric Gaussier. 2021. Globalizing BERT-based transformer architectures for long document summarization. In pages 1792–1810.

Som Gupta and S. K Gupta. 2019. Abstractive summarization: An overview of the state of the art. *Expert Systems with Applications*, 121:49–65, May.

Vivek Gupta, Prerna Bharti, Pegah Nokhiz, and Harish Karnick. 2021. SUMPUBMED: Summarization Dataset of PubMed Scientific Articles. In pages 292–303.

Sam Henry, Kevin Buchan, Michele Filannino, Amber Stubbs, and Ozlem Uzuner. 2020. 2018 n2c2 shared task on adverse drug events and medication extraction in electronic health records. *Journal of the American Medical Informatics Association*, 27(1):3–12.

Karl Moritz Hermann, Tomas Kocisky, Edward Grefenstette, Lasse Espeholt, Will Kay, Mustafa Suleyman, and Phil Blunsom. 2015. Teaching Machines to Read and Comprehend. In *Advances in Neural Information Processing Systems*, volume 28. Curran Associates, Inc.

Alistair EW Johnson, Tom J Pollard, Lu Shen, Li-wei H Lehman, Mengling Feng, Mohammad Ghassemi, Benjamin Moody, Peter Szolovits, Leo Anthony Celi, and Roger G Mark. 2016. MIMIC-III, a freely accessible critical care database. *Scientific data*, 3(1):1–9.

Mike Lewis, Yinhan Liu, Naman Goyal, Marjan Ghazvininejad, Abdelrahman Mohamed, Omer Levy, Ves Stoyanov, and Luke Zettlemoyer. 2019. Bart: Denoising sequence-to-sequence pre-training for natural language generation, translation, and comprehension. *arXiv preprint arXiv:1910.13461*.

Chin-Yew Lin. 2004. ROUGE: A Package for Automatic Evaluation of Summaries. In *Text Summarization Branches Out*, pages 74–81, Barcelona, Spain, July. Association for Computational Linguistics.

Varun Nair, Namit Katariya, Xavier Amatriain, Ilya Valmianski, and Anitha Kannan. 2021. Adding more data does not always help: A study in medical conversation summarization with PEGASUS. *arXiv:2111.07564 [cs]*, November. arXiv: 2111.07564.

Shashi Narayan, Shay B. Cohen, and Mirella Lapata. 2018. Don't Give Me the Details, Just the Summary! Topic-Aware Convolutional Neural Networks for Extreme Summarization. *arXiv:1808.08745 [cs]*, August. arXiv: 1808.08745.

Maja Popović. 2015. chrF: character n-gram F-score for automatic MT evaluation. In *Proceedings of the Tenth Workshop on Statistical Machine Translation*, pages 392–395, Lisbon, Portugal, September. Association for Computational Linguistics.

Juan C Quiroz, Liliana Laranjo, Ahmet Baki Kocaballi, Agustina Briatore, Shlomo Berkovsky, Dana Rezazadegan, and Enrico Coiera. 2020. Identifying relevant information in medical conversations to summarize a clinician-patient encounter. *Health Informatics Journal*, 26(4):2906–2914.

Colin Raffel, Noam Shazeer, Adam Roberts, Katherine Lee, Sharan Narang, Michael Matena, Yanqi Zhou, Wei Li, and Peter J Liu. 2019. Exploring the limits of transfer learning with a unified text-to-text transformer. *arXiv preprint arXiv:1910.10683*.

Dima Suleiman and Arafat Awajan. 2020. Deep learning based abstractive text summarization: approaches, datasets, evaluation measures, and challenges. *Mathematical problems in engineering*, 2020.

Xuefeng Xi, Zhou Pi, and Guodong Zhou. 2020. Global encoding for long chinese text summarization. *ACM Transactions on Asian and Low-Resource Language Information Processing (TALLIP)*, 19(6):1–17.

Jingqing Zhang, Yao Zhao, Mohammad Saleh, and Peter Liu. 2020a. PEGASUS: Pre-training with Extracted Gap-sentences for Abstractive Summarization. In *Proceedings of the 37th International Conference on Machine Learning*, pages 11328–11339. PMLR, November.

Yu Zhang, James Qin, Daniel S. Park, Wei Han, Chung-Cheng Chiu, Ruoming Pang, Quoc V. Le, and Yonghui Wu. 2020b. Pushing the Limits of Semi-Supervised Learning for Automatic Speech Recognition. *arXiv:2010.10504 [cs, eess]*, October. arXiv: 2010.10504.

Appendices

Appendix A: Results for 10, 20, and 50 few-shot strategies

Baseline(ZSL)	loss	rouge-1	rouge-2	rouge-L	rouge-Lsum
t5large	2.78	30.93	11.40	22.44	28.59
t5-large-samsum	2.26	35.74	13.99	24.63	33.76
bart-large	3.26	32.70	9.69	19.74	30.78
bart-large-cnn	2.15	36.72	11.90	22.46	34.73
bart-large-samsum	2.18	37.38	15.88	26.11	35.40
bart-large-cnn-samsum	2.00	40.82	16.00	27.26	38.78
pegasus-large	3.15	35.23	11.46	22.95	32.83
pegasus-large-cnn_dailymail	2.65	34.36	12.06	23.66	29.68
pegasus-large-cnn-samsum	2.20	33.69	13.63	24.79	31.79
pegasus-large-pubmed	6.93	15.31	1.00	10.41	13.99
10 shot	loss	rouge-1	rouge-2	rouge-L	rouge-Lsum
t5large	1.94	35.31	11.58	24.38	33.29
t5-large-samsum	1.79	44.81	20.05	33.55	42.73
bart-large	2.23	45.66	19.63	25.36	42.73
bart-large-cnn	1.95	50.79	23.22	34.90	48.17
bart-large-samsum	2.27	51.23	25.61	35.63	48.76
bart-large-cnn-samsum	1.97	52.28	26.18	37.84	49.65
pegasus-large	2.28	25.95	7.53	19.03	23.43
pegasus-large-cnn_dailymail	2.19	34.88	11.57	22.30	32.65
pegasus-large-cnn-samsum	1.93	44.56	19.33	32.19	42.41
pegasus-large-pubmed	4.99	18.81	2.74	13.22	17.20
20shot	loss	rouge-1	rouge-2	rouge-L	rouge-Lsum
t5large	1.68	40.37	15.46	29.05	38.17
t5-large-samsum	1.55	47.47	20.54	33.83	45.29
bart-large	2.20	48.89	22.05	27.17	47.01
bart-large-cnn	1.96	51.88	23.37	35.30	49.39
bart-large-samsum	2.22	51.65	24.21	34.79	49.11
bart-large-cnn-samsum	2.02	53.32	24.93	36.99	49.97
pegasus-large	2.09	30.49	9.82	20.94	28.52
pegasus-large-cnn_dailymail	2.05	36.31	12.44	24.23	34.22
pegasus-large-cnn-samsum	1.89	44.42	19.21	31.82	41.98
pegasus-large-pubmed	4.63	22.67	4.58	16.67	20.92
50shot	loss	rouge-1	rouge-2	rouge-L	rouge-Lsum
t5large	1.47	51.03	23.15	36.77	48.46
t5-large-samsum	1.43	53.19	25.02	38.98	51.07
bart-large	1.98	50.76	22.26	28.96	48.39
bart-large-cnn	2.11	54.06	26.80	39.18	51.79
bart-large-samsum	2.29	53.63	26.40	36.54	51.38
bart-large-cnn-samsum	2.10	53.15	25.19	38.99	51.11
pegasus-large	1.89	35.74	13.14	24.59	33.25
pegasus-large-cnn_dailymail	1.89	40.76	16.87	29.22	39.15
pegasus-large-cnn-samsum	1.81	48.27	22.71	35.60	46.20
pegasus-large-pubmed	4.07	27.29	8.69	18.56	24.85

all(114 shot)	loss	rouge-1	rouge-2	rouge-L	rouge-Lsum
t5large	1.39	51.79	23.77	37.54	49.41
t5-large-samsum	1.39	54.91	26.64	40.46	52.37
bart-large	1.86	52.31	23.66	34.18	49.34
bart-large-cnn	2.05	53.59	25.07	37.72	50.96
bart-large-samsum	2.05	52.99	24.88	37.22	50.87
bart-large-cnn-samsum	2.04	55.32	27.12	39.67	52.22
pegasus-large	1.78	39.51	15.74	27.57	37.22
pegasus-large-cnn_dailymail	1.81	50.94	23.30	36.40	48.52
pegasus-large-cnn-samsum	1.76	50.89	24.54	37.25	48.92
pegasus-large-pubmed	3.66	30.87	11.13	21.05	28.30

Appendix B: Relative (%) increase by training strategy for all models with 10, 20, 50 and full dataset

Model (10 shot % increase)	loss	rouge-1	rouge-2	rouge-L	rouge-Lsum
t5large	-30.08%	14.17%	1.60%	8.63%	16.44%
t5-large-samsum	-20.84%	25.38%	43.32%	36.19%	26.58%
bart-large	-31.42%	39.62%	102.71%	28.51%	38.84%
bart-large-cnn	-9.59%	38.31%	95.23%	55.42%	38.68%
bart-large-samsum	4.06%	37.05%	61.25%	36.47%	37.74%
bart-large-cnn-samsum	-1.62%	28.06%	63.65%	38.78%	28.03%
pegasus-large	-27.59%	-26.34%	-34.31%	-17.09%	-28.63%
pegasus-large-cnn_dailymail	-17.57%	1.52%	-4.06%	-5.76%	10.01%
pegasus-large-cnn-samsum	-12.25%	32.29%	41.87%	29.84%	33.39%
pegasus-large-pubmed	-27.97%	22.85%	173.45%	27.04%	22.89%
20 shot % increase	loss	rouge-1	rouge-2	rouge-L	rouge-Lsum
t5large	-39.51%	30.54%	35.64%	29.44%	33.50%
t5-large-samsum	-31.51%	32.81%	46.84%	37.31%	34.14%
bart-large	-32.34%	49.49%	127.63%	37.68%	52.73%
bart-large-cnn	-9.22%	41.27%	96.48%	57.21%	42.20%
bart-large-samsum	2.03%	38.18%	52.46%	33.26%	38.73%
bart-large-cnn-samsum	1.04%	30.61%	55.84%	35.66%	28.84%
pegasus-large	-33.62%	-13.45%	-14.33%	-8.76%	-13.11%
pegasus-large-cnn_dailymail	-22.60%	5.65%	3.15%	2.44%	15.31%
pegasus-large-cnn-samsum	-14.42%	31.88%	41.00%	28.32%	32.06%
pegasus-large-pubmed	-33.11%	48.09%	357.35%	60.19%	49.51%
50 shot % increase	loss	rouge-1	rouge-2	rouge-L	rouge-Lsum
t5large	-46.98%	65.00%	103.14%	63.84%	69.47%
t5-large-samsum	-36.83%	48.80%	78.88%	58.22%	51.28%
bart-large	-39.35%	55.20%	129.81%	46.72%	57.24%
bart-large-cnn	-2.16%	47.22%	125.27%	74.46%	49.09%
bart-large-samsum	5.15%	43.46%	66.26%	39.97%	45.15%
bart-large-cnn-samsum	5.20%	30.18%	57.43%	43.01%	31.79%
pegasus-large	-39.86%	1.46%	14.67%	7.12%	1.31%
pegasus-large-cnn_dailymail	-28.62%	18.62%	39.93%	23.51%	31.92%
pegasus-large-cnn-samsum	-17.79%	43.29%	66.69%	43.61%	45.30%
pegasus-large-pubmed	-41.32%	78.25%	767.70%	78.32%	77.56%
full dataset % increase	loss	rouge-1	rouge-2	rouge-L	rouge-Lsum
t5large	-49.78%	67.46%	108.51%	67.30%	72.81%
t5-large-samsum	-38.30%	53.61%	90.42%	64.25%	55.11%
bart-large	-42.90%	59.93%	144.22%	73.15%	60.32%
bart-large-cnn	-5.06%	45.92%	110.73%	67.97%	46.71%
bart-large-samsum	-5.96%	41.76%	56.65%	42.58%	43.70%
bart-large-cnn-samsum	1.79%	35.51%	69.54%	45.51%	34.64%
pegasus-large	-43.53%	12.16%	37.36%	20.12%	13.40%
pegasus-large-cnn_dailymail	-31.89%	48.24%	93.25%	53.88%	63.50%
pegasus-large-cnn-samsum	-20.00%	51.06%	80.05%	50.26%	53.86%
pegasus-large-pubmed	-47.18%	101.67%	1010.81%	102.24%	102.21%

9 Appendix C: Evaluation snippets and human summary.

model prediction_t5	model_prediction_pegasus	model_prediction_bart	human_summary
She was on Yas before and didn't get different headaches. She has not noticed a real difference in her headache since then. Sometimes hormones and migraines are related. Do you get worse when you are having your period or just before? Sometimes dehydration might trigger them. It is just the heat and if it rains it changes. A starting point would be to keep some sort of headache diary.	She didn't get more, different headaches on Yas or Estelle. It would have been nine months. Sometimes hormones and migraines are related. She does not get headaches worse when she is having a period or just before. On Sunday it was really hot and she was feeling basically dead.	She was on Yas before and didn't like it. She hasn't noticed any difference in headaches since then. Sometimes hormones and migraines are related. Not related to her period. Keep a headache calendar to see if there is a pattern. Try different treatments and also writing down the days and mark when periods are and exams are. Has no neck issues.	She was on Yas before, but she didn't liked it. She has been nine months on Estelle. She has not noticed a difference in headaches since then. She does not get worse headaches when having a period. She does not keep a calendar. On Sunday it was terrible, and it was really hot. A starting point is to keep a headache diary to see if there is a pattern. She does not have neck issues or pains.
She is in the boot still. She fractured one of the metatarsals and has avascular new necrosis on her talus. It took ages to figure it out because everyone thought it was the fracture that was painful.	She fractured one of the metatarsals and she has avascular new, new necrosis on her talus. She has been in the boot for 11 weeks and has an appointment with the orthopaedic surgeon in two weeks.	She fractured her toe and fractured one of the metatarsals. She has avascular new necrosis on her talus and has been in the boot for 11 weeks. Has an appointment with the orthopaedic surgeon in two weeks to check it out. Had a pelvic exam before. Is studying clinical science at Macquarie for two years. It is not covered by HECS.	Doing the swabs involves a pelvic exam and having a look at the external skin. She fractured her toe and is in the boot still. She fractured one of the metatarsals and have an avascular necrosis of the talus. She has been on the boot for 11 weeks. She has an appointment with the orthopaedic surgeon in two weeks. She studies clinical science at Macquarie. She does not know what she will do next.
He is coughing for two weeks. He feels itchy inside and there are sticky things in his throat. When he coughs it feels like a dry cough but it is not coming out. Breathing feels normal sometimes. Has asthma or chest problems. Used to use puffers. Had asthma four years ago and coughed all the winter. Have allergies to some food like yellow beans, beans and flour or some plant or seafood.	He has been coughing for two weeks. itchy inside of here and annoying sticky things in his throat. It feels like there is a bit of stuff there but it is not coming out. Has a history of asthma or chest problems. He used to have puffers but they are a long time ago. There was no fever or sore throat and nothing else. After he had ice cream he coughed a runny nose.	Cough has been two weeks. Apart from the cough he feels itchy. There are annoying sticky things in his throat. It feels like there is a bit of stuff there, but it is not coming out. Breathing feels normal sometimes. He had a history of asthma and chest problems in China and used to take puffers. Nothing else besides cough. No fever, sore throat, or runny nose. Cough reminds him of a cough a few years ago that didn't stop. Has allergies to some food but not heavy. Some kind of plant or seafood.	Cough for two weeks, feeling itchy inside and having stuff that is not coming out. Sometimes having difficulty breathing. Four years ago, had an asthma episode in China and used a puffer. No fever or sore throat. No runny nose. This cough reminds of the previous one. He says it start after a cold drink or ice-cream especially in winter. He has mild allergies to some food, usually pimples on the skin, but not affecting breathing.

Nothing like that. He is generally healthy. At night he coughs more but still has good sleep. Before this two weeks, if you are running or exercising, you get breathing problems or cough. Two weeks ago was in China and will start coughing after two ice creams. Temperature can sometimes have an effect on breathing. It could be that you picked up some sort of infection that has triggered the cough, but it is more like asthma. They will listen to his chest and use a puffer. There is no one around him.	He is generally healthy. He coughs more at night but has good sleep. If he is running or exercising he gets breathing problems or cough. Two weeks ago he was in China and had a cough one day before leaving. It doesn't sound like he has had the runny nose or sore throat.	He is generally healthy. He coughs more at night but still gets good sleep. Usually, he doesn't exercise or run. Two weeks ago he was in China and ate two ice creams. Temperature can have an effect on breathing but not like weeks of cough. It doesn't sound like he had a runny nose or sore throat. There are a lot of sticky things in the chest but it does not come out. They will have a listen to his chest and check his throat and ears and temperature. He may need to use a puffer for a while. Nobody else has a cough	He is healthy. Coughing more at night but still sleeping. He will cough when running for a train or bus or when exerting. He felt the cough was starting after eating an ice cream. Temperature can have an effect but won't give weeks of cough. He just has sticky things that doesn't come out. It could be some infection that triggered the cough. No one around him has cough.
It is difficult to breathe. She feels a little bit painful in the food pipe. Her digestion system is not functioning well. The intestine is fine. When she is hungry the acid level goes up and up. Last year she used to have that but she had some medicine to reduce the level in Cambodia. It helped when she took the medicine. Sometimes we do an endoscopy to look down with the camera. There is no vomiting or other stomach symptoms. No runny nose.	It feels like difficult to breathe. She feels pain in the food pipe. Her digestion system is not functioning well, so she thought it might be the stomach. The stomach is fine. Last year she used to have some medicine to reduce the acid level and it improved. It was prescribed in Cambodia.	It is difficult to breathe when breathing and a bit painful in the food pipe. The first time she met you said it was about the windpipe but because her digestion system is not functioning well, she thought it might be the front. There is nothing down here. She feels very hungry high up in her tummy and acid levels go up and up. Last year she used to have acid reflux but then she took some medicine to reduce acid level and it improved. It was prescribed in Cambodia. Taking the medicine helped. Sometimes we trial some treatment and if it responds it can be done with an endoscopy. Has not vomited or had a fever or runny nose.	It feels like is difficult to breathe and sometimes a little painful in the food pipe. Intestines and tummy feel fine. Feels uncomfortable when very hungry and that the acid is coming up. Used to have it last year but improved with medicine to reduce acid. It was prescribed in Cambodia. Sometimes we trial treatments, we don't rush in and do an endoscopy if not necessary. Felt tired. No vomiting, fever or runny nose.
Tonsils are still swollen and she is not coughing. Acid can give irritation in the throat. She hasn't lost a lot of weight. One kilo less. No blood in bowel motions or vomiting blood. Sometimes it can be related to spicy food, coffee, chocolate, alcohol or food that is very acidic. Trying to	She is coughing but not coughing. Her tonsils are still swollen. If it is acid coming up, it can give her irritation in the throat. She hasn't lost a lot of weight, but she has lost one kilo. It is common to have acid problems related to spicy food, coffee, chocolate, alcohol and acidic food.	No coughing, but the tonsils are still swollen. Acid can give you irritation in the throat. She hasn't lost a lot of weight. Fifty-four point three is one kilo less. There is no blood in bowel motions or vomiting blood. Sometimes it can be related to the food you eat spicy or acidic. You don't want to eat a huge amount of food in one sitting because it puts pressure on	No coughing but tonsils are still swollen. Acid coming up can irritate the lining of the throat. Weights 54.3 kilos and has lost a kilo. No blood in the bowel motions or when vomiting. Acid can relate to food you eat like spicy, coffee, chocolate, or alcohol. Sometimes a cup of hot

avoid certain foods. Drinking hot milk can sometimes help. There are tablets and also Mylanta liquid that she can drink.		the stomach. At night is pain at 11 when drinking hot milk. Tablets can also be bought from chemist Mylanta from Cambodia.	milk helps. You can also buy Mylanta from the chemist.
She had a miscarriage and gave some test on Tuesday. She started vaginal bleeding on last Wednesday and she was not here on Thursday. They gave her an ultrasound and they couldn't hear the heartbeat. The baby did not grow much.	She had a miscarriage. She was in study notes and couldn't do the test on time. Before last Wednesday she started bleeding, vaginal bleeding. On the Thursday she came to see the doctor and told them. They appointed her to Lucy and gave her ultrasound. The first ultrasound was 153 heartbeat. Then on the same day they could not find heartbeat and the baby didn't grow much.	She had a miscarriage. She was given a test on Tuesday and couldn't do it on time. Before last Wednesday she started bleeding, vaginal bleeding. They couldn't hear the heartbeat and she was about 13 weeks pregnant. The baby didn't grow much, about seven or eight weeks growth.	Lucy had a miscarriage. She started a vaginal bleeding last Wednesday. They did an emergency ultrasound and could not hear a heartbeat. First ultrasound was normal. She was 13 weeks pregnant. The first ultrasound showed it wasn't growing.

10

Unifying Parsing and Tree-Structured Models for Generating Sentence Semantic Representations

Antoine Simoulin[1,2] **Benoît Crabbé**[1]
[1]University of Paris, LLF [2]Quantmetry
asimoulin@quantmetry.com
benoit.crabbe@u-paris.fr

Abstract

We introduce a novel tree-based model that learns its composition function together with its structure. The architecture produces sentence embeddings by composing words according to an induced syntactic tree. The parsing and the composition functions are explicitly connected and, therefore, learned jointly. As a result, the sentence embedding is computed according to an interpretable linguistic pattern and may be used on any downstream task. We evaluate our encoder on downstream tasks, and we observe that it outperforms tree-based models relying on external parsers. In some configurations, it is even competitive with BERT base model. Our model is capable of supporting multiple parser architectures. We exploit this property to conduct an ablation study by comparing different parser initializations. We explore to which extent the trees produced by our model compare with linguistic structures and how this initialization impacts downstream performance. We empirically observe that downstream supervision troubles producing stable parses and preserving linguistically relevant structures.

1 Introduction

Computing sentence semantic representations traditionally calls for a recursive compositional function whose structure is tree-shaped. There is a strong intuition in natural language processing that language has a recursive structure (Chomsky, 1956; Shen et al., 2019). Tree-based models should thus mimic the compositional effect of language and enable better generalization and abstraction.

Yet, tree-based models need carefully hand-annotated data to be trained. Alternative methods such as recurrent neural network (Hochreiter and Schmidhuber, 1997; Cho et al., 2014) or BERT (Devlin et al., 2019) have gained increased popularity as they only require raw text as input. On the other hand, as many results suggest (Linzen et al., 2016; Jawahar et al., 2019; Clark et al., 2019), these new models acquire some sort of tree structure.

Another line of work, called *latent tree learning*, induces trees from raw text and computes semantic representations along with the inferred structure (Socher et al., 2011; Bowman et al., 2016; Dyer et al., 2016; Maillard et al., 2019; Yogatama et al., 2017; Kim et al., 2019). Such methods preserve explicit recursive computation and produce intelligible tree structures. Moreover, the parser and composition function are learned jointly and are specific to a given task or domain. Choi et al. (2018) propose the closest approach to ours by composing a tree using the Gumbel-Softmax estimator. The method is fully differentiable, produces a discrete tree, and does not require training the parser using an auxiliary task. However, Williams et al. (2018) show the method does not produce meaningful syntactic representations and that trees are inconsistent across initializations. Moreover, Choi et al. (2018) produces trees by selecting and merging adjacent nodes. Therefore, it cannot directly use architectures designed for standard parsing formalisms such as dependency structures.

We propose a unified architecture, which infers an explicit tree structure and recursively trains a sentence embedding model. Our method is fully differentiable and relies on existing and well-known components. We use a standard dependency parsing structure, obtained using a graph-based biaffine dependency parser (Dozat and Manning, 2017). However, our model is not limited to a particular parser architecture as long as it is differentiable.

We organize our paper as follows: we present our model in section 2. In section 3, we evaluate our model on textual entailment and semantic similarity tasks. We then conduct an ablation study and analyze the impact of the parser initialization. We compare the learned structures across initializations and with interpretable annotations (4.1) and we study how latent structures impact performance on downstream tasks (4.2).

Proceedings of the 2022 Conference of the North American Chapter of the Association for Computational Linguistics: Human Language Technologies: Student Research Workshop, pages 267 - 276

2 Model

Our model jointly performs sentence parsing and the prediction of a sentence embedding. The sentence embedding is predicted by a weighted TREE-LSTM whose tree structure is provided by a dependency parser. The TREE-LSTM recursive composition function crucially uses a weighted sum of the child representations whose weights are provided by the parser edges, hence linking the parser outputs to the TREE-LSTM recursion. Figure 1 illustrates the architecture detailed in Eq. 1 to 10.

Parsing model The parser is a standard graph based biaffine dependency parser[1] (Dozat and Manning, 2017). It is formalized in two steps. First, Eq. 1 and 2 compute a weight matrix that is interpreted as a weighted directed graph whose nodes are the sentence tokens:

$$a_k^{(dep)} = \mathrm{MLP}(h_k), \quad a_j^{(head)} = \mathrm{MLP}(h_j) \quad (1)$$

$$s_{kj}^{(arc)} = (a_k^{(dep)} \oplus 1)^\top U^{(b)} a_j^{(head)} + b^{(b)} \quad (2)$$

With $h_k \in \mathbb{R}^d$ the hidden state associated with the word at index k in the input sentence and in Eq. 2, $U^{(b)} \in \mathbb{R}^{(d+1)\times d}$ and $b^{(b)} \in \mathbb{R}$. The symbol $\oplus$ denotes vector concatenation and MLP in Eq. 1 are single-layer perceptron networks.

The second step performs parsing by computing a maximum spanning tree from the graph. As in Dozat and Manning (2017), we use the Max Spanning Tree (MST) algorithm to ensure the well-formedness of the tree (Chu, 1965; Edmonds et al., 1967):

$$\alpha_{kj} = \mathbb{1}_{\mathrm{mst}(s_{kj}^{(arc)})} s_{kj}^{(arc)} \quad (3)$$

Where α_{kj} is the probability of the edge linking node j to node k. For a given node k, there is at most one non-zero edge leading to its governor j.

Compositionally weighted tree LSTM Given a predicted tree structure, we recursively encode the sentence using a variant of the Child Sum Tree model from Tai et al. (2015). The recursion follows the predicted structure: from the leaves to the root. At each step j, the transition function takes as input the word vector representation x_j of the head node j and the previously computed hidden states h_k from all its children.

[1]We give hyper-parameter details for the biaffine parser in Appendix A.3.

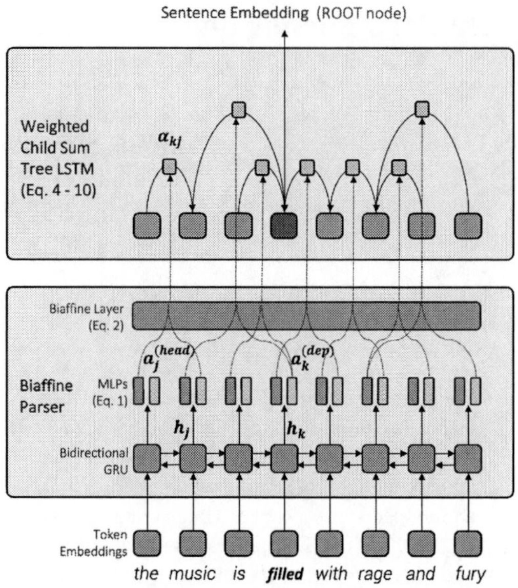

Figure 1: We illustrate the architecture detailed in Eq. 1 to 10. The Biaffine parser provides the sentence structure from which the TREE-LSTM computes sentence embeddings. The full pipeline is differentiable as the TREE-LSTM weights are given by the parser.

$$\tilde{h}_j = \sum_{k \in C(j)} \alpha_{kj} h_k, \quad (4)$$

$$i_j = \sigma\left(W^{(i)} x_j + U^{(i)} \tilde{h}_j + b^{(i)}\right), \quad (5)$$

$$o_j = \sigma\left(W^{(o)} x_j + U^{(o)} \tilde{h}_j + b^{(o)}\right), \quad (6)$$

$$u_j = \tanh\left(W^{(u)} x_j + U^{(u)} \tilde{h}_j + b^{(u)}\right), \quad (7)$$

$$f_{jk} = \sigma\left(W^{(f)} x_j + U^{(f)} h_k + b^{(f)}\right), \quad (8)$$

$$c_j = i_j \odot u_j + \sum_{k \in C(j)} f_{jk} \odot c_k, \quad (9)$$

$$h_j = o_j \odot \tanh(c_j), \quad (10)$$

Where x_j and h_j are respectively the word vector representation and hidden state associated with the head node j. In Eq. 4, $C(j)$ denotes the set of children of node j. σ denotes the logistic sigmoid function and $\odot$ denotes elementwise multiplication. Crucially, in our case, Eq. 4 is a weighted sum rather than a standard sum and the weights are those α_{kj} provided by the parser.

We use the embedding computed by the weighted TREE-LSTM at the root of the tree as the sentence embedding. The tree shape and the edge weights are given by the best prediction of a graph parser. The parsing model is linked to the TREE-LSTM by the weights α_{kj}. This architecture allows us to jointly update the parser and the TREE-LSTM weights using only the downstream task loss. The supervision comes only from the objective of the downstream task, and no intermediate structure target is required. Our model is fully differentiable and preserves the discreteness of the tree composition process. It relies on a dependency parsing formalism and could accommodate any differentiable parser.

3 Evaluation

Our architecture primarily aims to produce relevant embeddings for downstream tasks. To this end, we compare our setup with other models from the literature on various tasks. For this comparison, we first pre-train the parsing submodel on human-annotated sentences from the Penn Tree Bank (PTB) (Marcus et al., 1993) converted to Stanford dependencies. We then fine-tune the parser's parameters on the task while training the full model[2].

3.1 Semantic textual similarity (STS)

We first evaluate our model on the SICK-R downstream task (Marelli et al., 2014), which is dedicated to assessing models' compositional properties. The dataset comprises 9,927 sentence pairs, distributed in a 4,500/500/4,927 train/dev/test split, annotated for semantic similarity on a 1 to 5 real range. It includes specific examples of variations on passive and active forms, quantifier and modifier switches, or negations[3].

We use a similar training procedure as in Tai et al. (2015). We transform the target y from the SICK-R task into the distribution p defined by:

$$p_i = \begin{cases} y - \lfloor y \rfloor, & i = \lfloor y \rfloor + 1 \\ \lfloor y \rfloor - y + 1, & i = \lfloor y \rfloor \\ 0 & \text{otherwise} \end{cases}$$

We use a dedicated architecture to predict the similarity distribution from a pair of sentences. The similarity module takes as input a pair of sentence vectors h_L and h_R and computes their component-wise product $h_L \odot h_R$ and their absolute difference $|h_L - h_R|$. Given these features, we compute the probability distribution $\hat{p}_\theta$ using a two-layer perceptron network (MLP):

$$\begin{aligned} h_\times &= h_L \odot h_R, \quad h_+ = |h_L - h_R|, \\ h_s &= \sigma(W^{(\times)} h_\times + W^{(+)} h_+ + b^{(h)}), \\ \hat{p}_\theta &= \text{softmax}(W^{(p)} h_s + b^{(p)}), \end{aligned} \tag{11}$$

We use the KL-divergence between the prediction $\hat{p}_\theta$ and the ground truth p as training objective:

$$J(\theta) = \frac{1}{N} \sum_{k=1}^{N} \text{KL}(p^{(k)} || \hat{p}_\theta^{(k)}) + \lambda ||\theta||_2^2 \tag{12}$$

Finally during inference, the similarity score $\hat{y}$ is computed as $\hat{y} = r^\top \hat{p}_\theta$ with $r^\top = [1, \ldots, 5]$.

Encoder	r
BOW†	78.2 (1.1)
LSTM†	84.6 (0.4)
Bidirectional LSTM†	85.1 (0.4)
N-ary TREE-LSTM† (Tai et al., 2015)	85.3 (0.7)
Childsum TREE-LSTM† (Tai et al., 2015)	86.5 (0.4)
BERT-base (Devlin et al., 2019)	87.3 (0.9)
Unified TREE-LSTM† (Our model)	87.0 (0.3)

Table 1: Evaluation on the SICK-R task: we pre-train our parsing module on the PTB and continue to update the full model on the SICK-R task. We compare with BERT and models relying on sequential and tree structures. We report Pearson correlation on the test set, by convention as $r \times 100$ (avg. and std. from 5 runs). † indicates models that we trained. All models are trained following the same procedure detailed in Appendix A.1.

Table 1 reports the results from the test set. As expected, structured models perform better than models using weaker underlying structures. We also observe that our model is competitive with a BERT-base upper-line. It is essential to note that BERT models are heavily pre-trained on vast corpora, whereas our structured models are trained only on the SICK-R and PTB data.

3.2 Textual entailment

We also test our model on the Stanford Natural Language Inference (SNLI) task (Bowman et al., 2015), which includes 570k pairs of sentences with

[2]In this configuration, we observe pre-training the parser may cause weights α to become too large in Eq. 3. This leads to poor downstream performance. We correct this with a multiplicative parameter τ whose value is estimated during training. It means we replace Eq. 3 with: $\alpha_{kj} = \tau \cdot \mathbb{1}_{mst(s_{kj}^{(arc)})} s_{kj}^{(arc)}$ for tree weights computation.

[3]Appendix A.1 details the hyper-parameters and training infrastructure.

the labels entailment, contradiction, and neutral, distributed in a 550k/10k/10k train/dev/test split[4].

We use a similar training procedure as in Choi et al. (2018). A dedicated architecture is used to predict the similarity distribution from a pair of sentences. The similarity module takes as input a pair of sentence vectors h_L and h_R and computes their componentwise product $h_L \odot h_R$ and their absolute difference $|h_L - h_R|$. Given these features, we compute the probability distribution $\hat{p}_\theta$ using a three-layer perceptron network (MLP):

$$\begin{aligned} h_\times &= h_L \odot h_R, \quad h_+ = |h_L - h_R|, \\ h_s &= h_\times \oplus h_+ \oplus h_L \oplus h_R \\ h_s &= \text{ReLU}(W^{(1)} h_s + b^{(1)}), \\ h_s &= \text{ReLU}(W^{(2)} h_s + b^{(2)}), \\ \hat{p}_\theta &= \text{softmax}(W^{(p)} h_s + b^{(p)}), \end{aligned} \tag{13}$$

We use the cross entropy loss between the prediction $\hat{p}_\theta$ and the ground truth p as training objective:

$$J(\theta) = -\frac{1}{N} \sum_{k=1}^{N} p^{(k)} \log \hat{p}_\theta^{(k)} + \lambda ||\theta||_2^2 \tag{14}$$

Encoder	Test Acc.
SPINN \w Reinforce (Yogatama et al., 2017)	80.5
CYK and TREE-LSTM (Maillard et al., 2019)	81.6
SPINN (Bowman et al., 2016)	83.2
ST-Gumbel (Choi et al., 2018)	86.0
Structured Alignment (Liu et al., 2018)	86.3
BERT-base (Zhang et al., 2020)	90.7
Unified TREE-LSTM (Our model)	85.0 (0.2)

Table 2: Evaluation on the SNLI-R task: We pre-train our parsing module on the PTB and continue to update the full model on the SNLI task. We compare with BERT and latent tree learning models. We report the accuracy on the test set (avg. and std. from 2 runs).

We report the results in Table 2. Our results are close to Choi et al. (2018), which also compute semantic representations along to discrete tree structures but relies on a distinct syntactic formalism. In models from Liu et al. (2018) and Zhang et al. (2020) sentences are encoded with direct interaction using an attention mechanism. These architectures relying on cross sentence attention outperform those without. We hypothesize that, on this textual entailment task, the final prediction cannot be directly deduced from both sentence embeddings. In this case, BERT and the structured alignment model have a clear advantage since they encode interactions between both sentences.

[4]Appendix A.2 details the hyper-parameters and training infrastructure.

4 Impact of the parser initialization

Our framework primarily aims to be a structured sentence encoder. Accordingly, we have demonstrated in the previous section that our architecture is competitive with comparable approaches and might even be competitive with BERT-based models. We are also interested in interpreting the structures the model actually learns and how such structures impact downstream performance.

In the previous section, we pre-trained the parser on human annotated data. However, the optimal structure might differ from the task. Moreover, for computational reasons, it might even differ significantly from linguistic insights. In this section we perform an ablation study to better understand how the initialization of the parser impacts the resulting structures (4.1) and the final downstream performance (4.2). We define two initialization scenarios below. In both, we either continue to update the parser when fine-tuning the model on downstream tasks or freeze the parser and only train the TREE-LSTM. These two configurations are indicated with respectively ✓ and × symbols.

Linguistic annotations Tree-structured models traditionally rely on linguistic structures obtained by parsers (Tai et al., 2015). For languages such as English, linguistic resources are available; it is technically possible to pre-train the parser. However, resources such as the PTB are not available in all languages. To better quantify the benefits of using linguistic annotations, we propose the following configurations, using various proportions of the PTB to initialize the parser:

- In the **PTB-All** configuration, the parser is previously pre-trained on the PTB. This configuration is the same as in section 3.
- In the **PTB-∅** configuration, the parser parameters are randomly initialized
- We also consider an initialization with only a small proportion of the **PTB** and train a parser by only using 100 randomly selected samples. This configuration is referred as **PTB-100**.

Unsupervised structures Many lines of work investigate if attention matrices from large pre-trained models reflect syntactic structures (Jawahar et al., 2019; Clark et al., 2019; Ravishankar et al., 2021) or if tree structures can be integrated into transformers (Wang et al., 2019; Bai et al., 2021).

Since our model is not specific to any parser architecture. It is possible to use the internal representations from BERT to infer sentence structure.

BERT relies upon the self-attention mechanism. Inside each layer, tokens are computed as a weighted combination from each other. For each token x, a query and key vector are computed using a linear transformation detailed in Eq 15. Given these vector tuples, the attention weights s are computed following Eq 16 in which N refers to the dimension of the query and key vectors.

$$q_j, k_j = W^{(q,k)} x_j + b^{(q,k)} \tag{15}$$

$$s_{kj} = \text{softmax}\left(\frac{k_k \cdot q_j}{\sqrt{N}}\right) \tag{16}$$

We induce a tree structure following a procedure close from Ravishankar et al. (2021). We interpret the combination weights s as a weighted graph whose nodes are tokens. We then apply Eq 2 to induce a maximum spanning tree from the attention matrix as detailed in section 2. We make use of the last layer and induce a tree for each attention head taken separately[5]. Given the tree structure induced from BERT, we apply our TREE-LSTM model detailed in Eq. 4 to 10. In this configuration, we only use BERT as an unsupervised parser to infer a sentence structure. The semantic composition along with the structure to produce a sentence embedding is solely computed by the weighted TREE-LSTM.

4.1 Impact on parses

This section analyzes to which extent the structures generated by our model are comparable with meaningful linguistic annotations. We compare the parses generated by two distinct models differing by their initialization on the development set of both tasks. Our reference is the silver parses from the PTB-All configuration, where the parser is previously pre-trained on the full PTB and not updated during training.

Table 3 measures the Unlabeled Attachment Score (UAS) between the two parsers, that is, the ratio from the number of common arcs between two parses by the total number of arcs[6].

Parser 1	Parser 2	SICK-R (dev UAS)	SNLI (dev UAS)
Impact of parser fine-tuning			
PTB-100 (✓)	PTB-100 (×)	85.2 (1.5)	5.6 (1.9)
PTB-All (✓)	PTB-All (×)	98.4 (0.1)	11.7 (0.9)
Impact of the PTB sample size			
PTB-100 (✓)	PTB-∅ (✓)	6.3 (0.0)	10.1 (10.7)
PTB-All (✓)	PTB-∅ (✓)	10.1 (0.0)	15.1 (15.4)
PTB-All (✓)	PTB-100 (✓)	76.9 (0.7)	0.3 (0.2)
Unsupervised parser			
BERT (×)	PTB-All (×)	—	13.0 (4.9)
BERT (✓)	PTB-All (×)	—	13.7 (2.7)

Table 3: Impact of the parser initialization on parses: we compare the parses from the SICK-R and SNLI development sets using different parser initializations. We obtained the PTB parses with the graph parser initialized on a given proportion of the PTB (section 2). Regarding BERT , we inferred the structures from the pattern learn by the pre-trained model (section 4). We either continue to update the parser (✓) when fine-tuning the model on downstream tasks or freeze the parser (×) and only train the TREE-LSTM. UAS corresponds to the mean pairwise comparison of two configurations between two runs (std. in parentheses).

We observed distinct behaviors given both tasks. We believe this effect is due to the differences between training configurations. In particular, we use the Adagrad optimizer for the SICK-R task and Adam for the SNLI task.

For the SICK-R task, the UAS between PTB-∅ and PTB-All are very low. This reveals that the parses obtained with only downstream task supervision have few in common with gold linguistic parses. In this regard, we share the observation from Williams et al. (2018) that latent trees obtained from sole downstream supervision are not meaningful in syntax. However, PTB-All and PTB-100 are remarkably close; only a few PTB samples are needed to obtain intelligible linguistic parses with our setup. Regarding the PTB-100 configuration, we note an evolution of the parses when fine-tuning on the downstream task. We hypothesize that the model can adapt to the dataset's specificity.

For the SNLI task, fine-tuning the parser deeply impacts the shape of the parses. Depending from the initialization, parses will converge to distinct structures. Indeed, the UAS between all configura-

[5]We give details about the hyper-parameters in Appendix A.4.

[6]We present some parse tree examples in Appendix A.5.

tions is very low. Moreover, when using a random initialization (PTB-∅), the standard deviation between UAS from various runs is very high: without fixed initialization, parses become unstable.

For the initialization with an unsupervised structure, we only evaluate our setup on the SNLI task, which has more training samples. We compare the structures obtained with BERT with the silver trees from the PTB-All-× configuration. We present the mean UAS over the trees obtained for all attention heads. The standard deviation is relatively high, pointing underlying structures differ given the attention head. Nonetheless, self-supervised structures do not align well with linguistic insights. When updating BERT together with the TREE-LSTM, the UAS increases while the standard deviation decreases. As BERT is fine-tuned, structures tend to become more standard and present slightly more similarities with linguistic patterns.

4.2 Impact on downstream tasks

We observed in previous section 4.1 that the initialization and the training configuration of the parser component deeply impact the resulting parses. We now study the impact of the parser initialization on downstream performance.

PTB sample size	Parser fine-tuning	SICK-R (r)	SNLI (Acc.)
Linguistic annotations			
PTB-∅	✓	85.6 (85.6)	84.6 (85.5)
PTB-100	×	86.4 (86.6)	84.5 (85.5)
PTB-100	✓	86.5 (86.9)	84.9 (85.8)
PTB-All	×	86.8 (87.2)	85.0 (85.8)
PTB-All	✓	87.0 (87.5)	85.0 (85.5)
Unsupervised parser			
BERT	×	—	84.4 (85.3)
BERT	✓	—	84.6 (85.1)

Table 4: Impact of the parser initialization on downstream task performance: We pre-train the parser module with a given sample size from the PTB. We either freeze (×) or update (✓) the parser during the fine-tuning. We report the average test score set from 5 runs for SICK-R and 2 runs for SNLI (the score from the development set are in parentheses). We report Pearson correlation by convention as $r \times 100$.

Table 4 compares the impact of the different initializations for both tasks. We report the Pearson correlation on the test set of the SICK-R task and the accuracy on the test set from the SNLI task.

We either freeze the parser component or continue to update it, given the downstream loss for each initialization. Fine-tuning the parser on the task generally leads to an improvement of the downstream results. In that regard, we share the observation from other latent tree learning methods (Maillard et al., 2019; Choi et al., 2018); models jointly learning the parsing and composition function outperform those with a fixed structure.

Models using the full or partial annotated data outperform models relying on the sole downstream supervision (PTB-∅), in particular on the SICK-R task. We previously observed that fine-tuning the parser can lead to tree structure diverging from linguistic patterns. Nonetheless, regarding the downstream performance, human annotation appears as a good initialization for our model.

Models relying on linguistic-driven structures seem to achieve better performance. Nonetheless, the difference is thin, and we present here an average score across trees obtained from all attention heads. Therefore some attention heads might present structures as efficient as linguistic patterns.

5 Conclusion and future work

We investigate the relevance of incorporating tree-like structural bias in the context of sentence semantic inference. To this end, we formulate an original model for learning tree structure with distant downstream supervision. Our model is based on well-known components and could therefore accommodate a variety of parsing architectures such as graph parsers or attention matrices from BERT.

We evaluate our model on textual entailment and semantic similarity tasks and outperform sequential models and tree-structured models relying on external parsers. Moreover, when initialized on human-annotated structures, our model improves inference close to BERT base performance on the semantic similarity task.

We then conduct an ablation study to quantify the impact of the parser initialization on the resulting structures and downstream performance. We corroborate that the sole use of downstream supervision is insufficient to produce parses that are easy to interpret. To encourage convergence towards readable linguistic structures, we examine a number of initialization setups. Our structures often converge toward trivial branching patterns, which have few in common with gold linguistic parses. Yet, regarding downstream performance, linguistic insights appear as a relevant initialization.

References

Jiangang Bai, Yujing Wang, Yiren Chen, Yaming Yang, Jing Bai, Jing Yu, and Yunhai Tong. 2021. Syntax-bert: Improving pre-trained transformers with syntax trees. In *Proceedings of the 16th Conference of the European Chapter of the Association for Computational Linguistics: Main Volume, EACL 2021, Online, April 19 - 23, 2021*, pages 3011–3020. Association for Computational Linguistics.

Samuel R. Bowman, Gabor Angeli, Christopher Potts, and Christopher D. Manning. 2015. A large annotated corpus for learning natural language inference. In *Proceedings of the 2015 Conference on Empirical Methods in Natural Language Processing, EMNLP 2015, Lisbon, Portugal, September 17-21, 2015*, pages 632–642. The Association for Computational Linguistics.

Samuel R. Bowman, Jon Gauthier, Abhinav Rastogi, Raghav Gupta, Christopher D. Manning, and Christopher Potts. 2016. A fast unified model for parsing and sentence understanding. In *Proceedings of the 54th Annual Meeting of the Association for Computational Linguistics, ACL 2016, August 7-12, 2016, Berlin, Germany, Volume 1: Long Papers*. The Association for Computer Linguistics.

Kyunghyun Cho, Bart van Merrienboer, Çaglar Gülçehre, Dzmitry Bahdanau, Fethi Bougares, Holger Schwenk, and Yoshua Bengio. 2014. Learning phrase representations using RNN encoder-decoder for statistical machine translation. In *Proceedings of the 2014 Conference on Empirical Methods in Natural Language Processing, EMNLP 2014, October 25-29, 2014, Doha, Qatar, A meeting of SIGDAT, a Special Interest Group of the ACL*, pages 1724–1734.

Jihun Choi, Kang Min Yoo, and Sang-goo Lee. 2018. Learning to compose task-specific tree structures. In *Proceedings of the Thirty-Second AAAI Conference on Artificial Intelligence, (AAAI-18), the 30th innovative Applications of Artificial Intelligence (IAAI-18), and the 8th AAAI Symposium on Educational Advances in Artificial Intelligence (EAAI-18), New Orleans, Louisiana, USA, February 2-7, 2018*, pages 5094–5101. AAAI Press.

Noam Chomsky. 1956. Three models for the description of language. *IRE Trans. Inf. Theory*, 2(3):113–124.

Yoeng-Jin Chu. 1965. On the shortest arborescence of a directed graph. *Scientia Sinica*, 14:1396–1400.

Kevin Clark, Urvashi Khandelwal, Omer Levy, and Christopher D. Manning. 2019. What does BERT look at? an analysis of bert's attention. In *Proceedings of the 2019 ACL Workshop BlackboxNLP: Analyzing and Interpreting Neural Networks for NLP, BlackboxNLP@ACL 2019, Florence, Italy, August 1, 2019*, pages 276–286. Association for Computational Linguistics.

Jacob Devlin, Ming-Wei Chang, Kenton Lee, and Kristina Toutanova. 2019. BERT: pre-training of deep bidirectional transformers for language understanding. In *Proceedings of the 2019 Conference of the North American Chapter of the Association for Computational Linguistics: Human Language Technologies, NAACL-HLT 2019, Minneapolis, MN, USA, June 2-7, 2019, Volume 1 (Long and Short Papers)*, pages 4171–4186. Association for Computational Linguistics.

Timothy Dozat and Christopher D. Manning. 2017. Deep biaffine attention for neural dependency parsing. In *5th International Conference on Learning Representations, ICLR 2017, Toulon, France, April 24-26, 2017, Conference Track Proceedings*. OpenReview.net.

Chris Dyer, Adhiguna Kuncoro, Miguel Ballesteros, and Noah A. Smith. 2016. Recurrent neural network grammars. In *NAACL HLT 2016, The 2016 Conference of the North American Chapter of the Association for Computational Linguistics: Human Language Technologies, San Diego California, USA, June 12-17, 2016*, pages 199–209. The Association for Computational Linguistics.

Jack Edmonds et al. 1967. Optimum branchings. *Journal of Research of the national Bureau of Standards B*, 71(4):233–240.

Sepp Hochreiter and Jürgen Schmidhuber. 1997. Long short-term memory. *Neural Computation*, 9(8):1735–1780.

Ganesh Jawahar, Benoît Sagot, and Djamé Seddah. 2019. What does BERT learn about the structure of language? In *Proceedings of the 57th Conference of the Association for Computational Linguistics, ACL 2019, Florence, Italy, July 28- August 2, 2019, Volume 1: Long Papers*, pages 3651–3657. Association for Computational Linguistics.

Yoon Kim, Alexander M. Rush, Lei Yu, Adhiguna Kuncoro, Chris Dyer, and Gábor Melis. 2019. Unsupervised recurrent neural network grammars. In *Proceedings of the 2019 Conference of the North American Chapter of the Association for Computational Linguistics: Human Language Technologies, NAACL-HLT 2019, Minneapolis, MN, USA, June 2-7, 2019, Volume 1 (Long and Short Papers)*, pages 1105–1117. Association for Computational Linguistics.

Tal Linzen, Emmanuel Dupoux, and Yoav Goldberg. 2016. Assessing the ability of lstms to learn syntax-sensitive dependencies. *Trans. Assoc. Comput. Linguistics*, 4:521–535.

Yang Liu, Matt Gardner, and Mirella Lapata. 2018. Structured alignment networks for matching sentences. In *Proceedings of the 2018 Conference on Empirical Methods in Natural Language Processing, Brussels, Belgium, October 31 - November 4, 2018*, pages 1554–1564. Association for Computational Linguistics.

Jean Maillard, Stephen Clark, and Dani Yogatama. 2019. Jointly learning sentence embeddings and syntax with unsupervised tree-lstms. *Nat. Lang. Eng.*, 25(4):433–449.

Mitchell P. Marcus, Beatrice Santorini, and Mary Ann Marcinkiewicz. 1993. Building a large annotated corpus of english: The penn treebank. *Computational Linguistics*, 19(2):313–330.

Marco Marelli, Stefano Menini, Marco Baroni, Luisa Bentivogli, Raffaella Bernardi, and Roberto Zamparelli. 2014. A SICK cure for the evaluation of compositional distributional semantic models. In *Proceedings of the Ninth International Conference on Language Resources and Evaluation, LREC 2014, Reykjavik, Iceland, May 26-31, 2014*, pages 216–223. European Language Resources Association (ELRA).

Vinit Ravishankar, Artur Kulmizev, Mostafa Abdou, Anders Søgaard, and Joakim Nivre. 2021. Attention can reflect syntactic structure (if you let it). In *Proceedings of the 16th Conference of the European Chapter of the Association for Computational Linguistics: Main Volume, EACL 2021, Online, April 19 - 23, 2021*, pages 3031–3045. Association for Computational Linguistics.

Yikang Shen, Shawn Tan, Alessandro Sordoni, and Aaron C. Courville. 2019. Ordered neurons: Integrating tree structures into recurrent neural networks. In *7th International Conference on Learning Representations, ICLR 2019, New Orleans, LA, USA, May 6-9, 2019*. OpenReview.net.

Haoyue Shi, Hao Zhou, Jiaze Chen, and Lei Li. 2018. On tree-based neural sentence modeling. In *Proceedings of the 2018 Conference on Empirical Methods in Natural Language Processing, Brussels, Belgium, October 31 - November 4, 2018*, pages 4631–4641. Association for Computational Linguistics.

Richard Socher, Jeffrey Pennington, Eric H. Huang, Andrew Y. Ng, and Christopher D. Manning. 2011. Semi-supervised recursive autoencoders for predicting sentiment distributions. In *Proceedings of the 2011 Conference on Empirical Methods in Natural Language Processing, EMNLP 2011, 27-31 July 2011, John McIntyre Conference Centre, Edinburgh, UK, A meeting of SIGDAT, a Special Interest Group of the ACL*, pages 151–161. ACL.

Kai Sheng Tai, Richard Socher, and Christopher D. Manning. 2015. Improved semantic representations from tree-structured long short-term memory networks. In *Proceedings of the 53rd Annual Meeting of the Association for Computational Linguistics and the 7th International Joint Conference on Natural Language Processing of the Asian Federation of Natural Language Processing, ACL 2015, July 26-31, 2015, Beijing, China, Volume 1: Long Papers*, pages 1556–1566. The Association for Computer Linguistics.

Yau-Shian Wang, Hung-yi Lee, and Yun-Nung Chen. 2019. Tree transformer: Integrating tree structures into self-attention. In *Proceedings of the 2019 Conference on Empirical Methods in Natural Language Processing and the 9th International Joint Conference on Natural Language Processing, EMNLP-IJCNLP 2019, Hong Kong, China, November 3-7, 2019*, pages 1061–1070. Association for Computational Linguistics.

Adina Williams, Andrew Drozdov, and Samuel R. Bowman. 2018. Do latent tree learning models identify meaningful structure in sentences? *Trans. Assoc. Comput. Linguistics*, 6:253–267.

Dani Yogatama, Phil Blunsom, Chris Dyer, Edward Grefenstette, and Wang Ling. 2017. Learning to compose words into sentences with reinforcement learning. In *5th International Conference on Learning Representations, ICLR 2017, Toulon, France, April 24-26, 2017, Conference Track Proceedings*. OpenReview.net.

Zhuosheng Zhang, Yuwei Wu, Hai Zhao, Zuchao Li, Shuailiang Zhang, Xi Zhou, and Xiang Zhou. 2020. Semantics-aware BERT for language understanding. In *The Thirty-Fourth AAAI Conference on Artificial Intelligence, AAAI 2020, The Thirty-Second Innovative Applications of Artificial Intelligence Conference, IAAI 2020, The Tenth AAAI Symposium on Educational Advances in Artificial Intelligence, EAAI 2020, New York, NY, USA, February 7-12, 2020*, pages 9628–9635. AAAI Press.

A Appendices

A.1 SICK-R training configuration

Hyper-parameters We set the hyperparameters given literature on the domain, in particular regarding choices made in Tai et al. (2015). For all experiments detailed in the current section, the batch size is fixed to 25, weight decay to $1e^{-4}$ and gradient clipping set to 5.0. The learning rate is set to 0.025 for the TREE-LSTM parameters. When using a pre-training procedure for the parser, we set the learning rate to $5e^{-3}$ and use the following warm-up: for the first epoch, the parser is frozen. For the following epochs, all parameters are trained. At each epoch, the parser learning rate is divided by a factor of two. Without pre-training, the learning rate is set to $5e^{-4}$ for the parser. All model weights are initialized with a Xavier distribution. The hidden size of the similarity architecture is set to 50. The TREE-LSTM hidden size is set to 150. We use the Adagrad optimizer. We do not apply any dropout. We perform training for a maximum of 20 epochs and stop when no improvement was observed on the development set for 3 consecutive epochs. Regarding the vocabulary, we limit the size to 20,000 words and initialize the embeddings layer with 300-dimensional GloVe embeddings[7]. The embeddings are not updated during training.

Training infrastructure We trained all models on a single 1080 Ti Nvidia GPU. Training time for each epoch is approximately 1 minute. The model counts 13.7M parameters. Data can be downloaded using the SentEval package[8].

A.2 SNLI training configuration

Hyper-parameters We set the hyper-parameters given literature on the domain, in particular regarding choices made in Choi et al. (2018). For all experiments detailed in section 3.2, the batch size is fixed to 128, weight decay to 0, and gradient clipping set to 5.0. The learning rate is set to $1e^{-3}$ for the TREE-LSTM and the parser. The hidden size of the similarity architecture is set to 1,024. The TREE-LSTM hidden size is set to 600. We use the Adam optimizer. We apply a 0.2 dropout within the similarity architecture. We perform training for a maximum of 20 epochs and stop when no improvement was observed on the development set for 3 consecutive epochs. Regarding the vocabulary, we limit the size to 100,000 words and initialize the embeddings layer with 300-dimensional GloVe embeddings. The embeddings are not updated during training.

Training infrastructure We trained all models on a single 1080 Ti Nvidia GPU. Training time for each epoch is approximately 2h30 hours. The model counts 13.7M parameters. Data can be downloaded using the SentEval package[9].

A.3 Model Architecture

Regarding the biaffine parser, all parameters are chosen given Dozat and Manning (2017) recommendations. We use a hidden size of 150 for the MLPs layers and 100 for the biaffine layer. The dropout rate is fixed to 0.33. We use an open-source implementation of the parser and replace the pos-tags features with character level features. Therefore we don't need pos-tags annotations to parse our corpus[10]. We encode words using 100-dimensional GloVe embedding and a character embedding size of 50. Word vectors are then fed to a bidirectional LSTM with 3 layers of size 400.

A.4 BERT unsupervised parsing

When using BERT to perform unsupervised parsing, we use the implementation of BERT-base model from the Transformers library[11]. When fine-tuning the parser component, we set the learning rate to $2e^{-5}$ When fine-tuning BERT parser, each epoch takes around 5 hours on the SNLI. Without fine-tuning, this time is reduced to 90 minutes.

A.5 Visualization of the parses

We illustrate the effect summarize on Table 3 on some random examples. Figures from the first column (2a, 2c and 2e) show the parses obtained without updating the parser component on the downstream task. Figures from the second column(2b, 2d and 2f) show the evolution of the parses for the same initialization but after fine-tuning the parser on the SNLI task. Figures from the first row (2a and 2b) are initialized using the full PTB, the second row (2c and 2d) is initialized using 100 PTB

[7] `https://nlp.stanford.edu/projects/glove/`

[8] `https://github.com/facebookresearch/SentEval`

[9] `https://github.com/facebookresearch/SentEval`

[10] `https://github.com/yzhangcs/biaffine-parser`

[11] `https://huggingface.co/transformers/model_doc/bert.html`

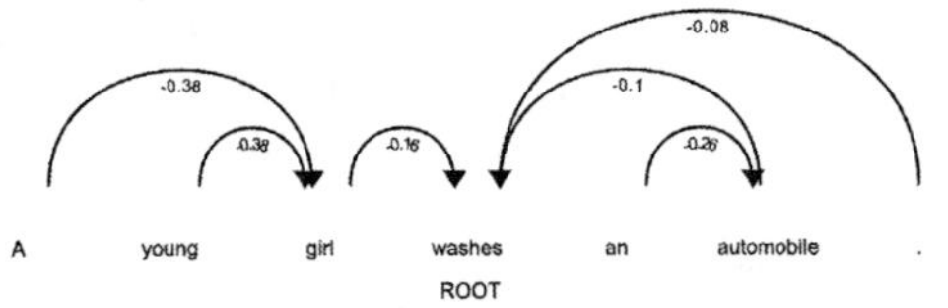

(a) Parse obtained using the the PTB-All (×) configuration.

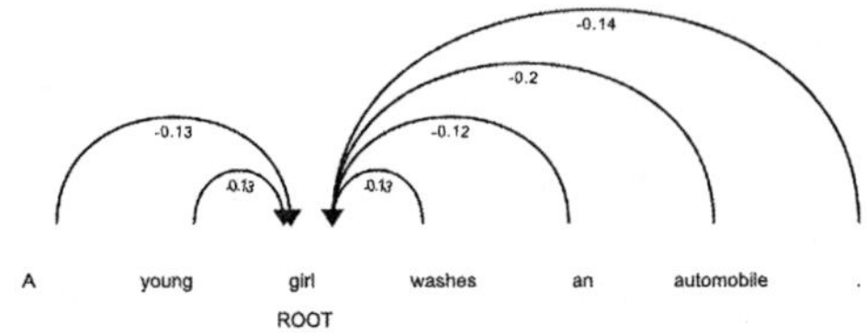

(b) Parse obtained using the the PTB-All (✓) configuration.

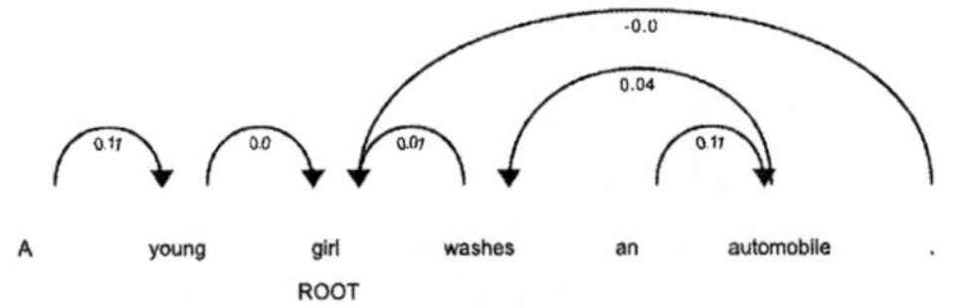

(c) Parse obtained using the the PTB-100 (×) configuration.

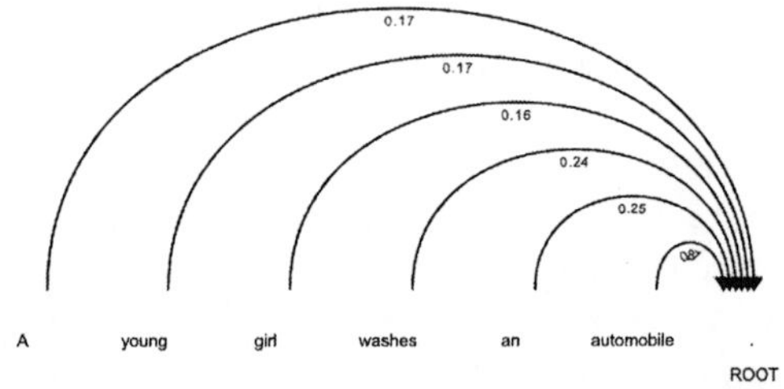

(d) Parse obtained using the the PTB-100 (✓) configuration.

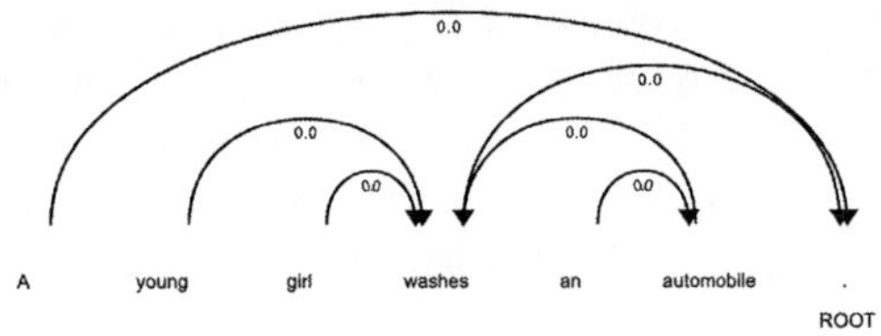

(e) Parse obtained using the attention head #1 and without updating BERT.

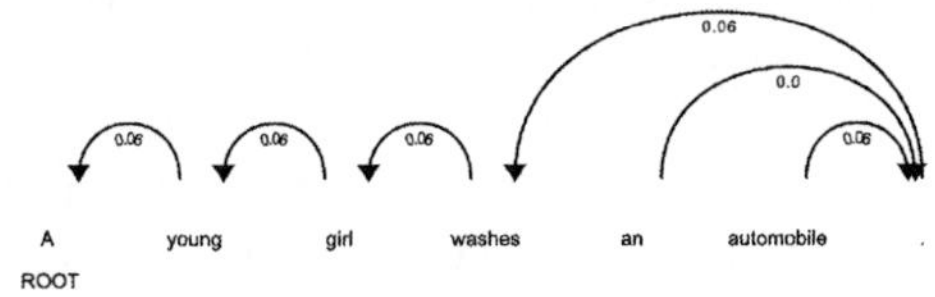

(f) Parse obtained using the attention head #1 and updating BERT.

Figure 2: Example of parse obtained using various configurations from our model. The parser component is initialized on PTB-All (2a, 2b), PTB-100 (2c, 2d) or BERT (2e, 2f). We either freeze (×) or update (✓) the parser during the fine tuning on the SNLI. We include the weights α produced from the parser. We report the accuracy from a single run on the test set.

samples while the one from the last row (2e and 2f) are initialized using unsupervised patterns.

For the initialization with the PTB, we observe the fine-tuning makes the tree evolve to trivial structures and tend to connect every node to an arbitrary root. We hypothesize, such trivial structures present advantages from a computational point of view. As observed in Shi et al. (2018), trivial trees without syntax properties might lead to surprisingly good results. Shi et al. (2018) hypothesize that trivial trees gain might benefit from shallow and balanced properties.

For BERT parser initialization, we observe the fine-tuning produces rather sequential patterns, with words connected to direct neighbors. Some isolated groups of words also present inner connections.

Multiformer: A Head-Configurable Transformer-Based Model for Direct Speech Translation

Gerard Sant, Gerard I. Gállego, Belen Alastruey and **Marta R. Costa-Jussà**
TALP Research Center, Universitat Politècnica de Catalunya, Barcelona
gerard.muniesa@estudiantat.upc.edu
{gerard.ion.gallego, belen.alastruey, marta.ruiz}@upc.edu

Abstract

Transformer-based models have been achieving state-of-the-art results in several fields of Natural Language Processing. However, its direct application to speech tasks is not trivial. The nature of this sequences carries problems such as long sequence lengths and redundancy between adjacent tokens. Therefore, we believe that regular self-attention mechanism might not be well suited for it.

Different approaches have been proposed to overcome these problems, such as the use of efficient attention mechanisms. However, the use of these methods usually comes with a cost, which is a performance reduction caused by information loss. In this study, we present the Multiformer, a Transformer-based model which allows the use of different attention mechanisms on each head. By doing this, the model is able to bias the self-attention towards the extraction of more diverse token interactions, and the information loss is reduced. Finally, we perform an analysis of the head contributions, and we observe that those architectures where all heads relevance is uniformly distributed obtain better results. Our results show that mixing attention patterns along the different heads and layers outperforms our baseline by up to 0.7 BLEU.

1 Introduction

Conventionally, Speech-to-text Translation (ST) task has been addressed through cascade approaches (Ney, 1999), which consists of the concatenation of an Automatic Speech Recognition block (ASR), for the audio transcription, with another Machine Translation block (MT), for the translation of such transcription into the desired language. However, this approach ignores some information present in the audio, since it translates from the audio transcript, and is also vulnerable to error propagation, since an error in the ASR block automatically causes a mistranslation (Sperber and Paulik, 2020; Bentivogli et al., 2021). Consequently, end-to-end alternatives based on an encoder-decoder structure and attention mechanisms have become increasingly popular in recent years (Anastasopoulos et al., 2016; Duong et al., 2016; Weiss et al., 2017). These are capable of translating the audio without the explicit need for transcription, thus avoiding the problems of the cascade approach and allowing unified optimization of the training parameters.

The advent of the Transformer (Vaswani et al., 2017) revolutionized the MT field, enabling models based on this architecture to achieve the state-of-the-art results. Nowadays, Transformer-based models are used to process all types of data, such as images (Parmar et al., 2018) or speech (Dong et al., 2018; Di Gangi et al., 2019a). However, due to its self-attention mechanism, the vanilla Transformer scales quadratically with the input sequence length, which makes it extremely inefficient when processing long sequences.

In speech tasks, it is common to extract audio features every 10 ms to build the input sequences, which causes them to be considerably longer than text sequences. Moreover, since the representation of a single phoneme requires several tokens (Igras et al., 2013; Ma et al., 2021), the presence of redundancy among the audio tokens is inferred. Therefore, state-of-the-art architectures propose the implementation of down sampling strategies prior to the model collapsing adjacent vectors in a fixed way (Bérard et al., 2018; Di Gangi et al., 2019b; Wang et al., 2020a). Similarly, some studies propose to extract more informative sequences using pre-trained compression modules (Salesky et al., 2019; Zhang et al., 2020; Gaido et al., 2021), obtaining considerable translation quality gains. While these achieve good results, we propose another approach, questioning the use of multi-head self-attention (MHSA), originally proposed for text, for the information extraction from speech sequences.

Proceedings of the 2022 Conference of the North American Chapter of the Association for Computational Linguistics: Human Language Technologies: Student Research Workshop, pages 277 - 284
July 10-15, 2022 ©2022 Association for Computational Linguistics

The closest work to ours was done by Alastruey et al. (2021), who used Longformer's (Beltagy et al., 2020) local attention pattern as an efficient alternative to self-attention for speech processing. However, they observed that, due to the scarcity of global context in the encoder output, the quality of the translations was slightly hindered. Recently, inspired by Linformer's (Wang et al., 2020b) attention, Papi et al. (2021) proposed ConvAttention as an attention mechanism that, by compressing keys and values, is more efficient and therefore able to directly process long sequences. However, this mechanism is not used as a replacement of the encoder self-attention, but as an extra input processing before a CTC-based compression module (Gaido et al., 2021).

Our contribution to ST field is a new Transformer variant, the Multiformer, an architecture based on the S2T Transformer by Wang et al. (2020a). Our architecture enables the use of different attention mechanisms in the same encoder layer, by configuring individually the pattern of each head. With this approach, the Multiformer is able to apply efficient attention mechanisms, while maintaining the ability to learn both local and global content from speech sequences. This diversity among heads in a layer is also meant to stimulate a more varied information extraction and, therefore, reduce the presence of low-relevant heads (Voita et al., 2019; Michel et al., 2019; Bian et al., 2021; Zhang et al., 2021). Furthermore, we explore the use of different head configurations for each encoder layer. This could help to adapt the attention mechanisms to the needs of each layer. To the best of our knowledge, this is the first study that allows this kind of head-wise configuration.

2 Model

In this section, we first introduce a new self-attention module that allows the use of multiple attention mechanisms in parallel (§2.1). Next, we explain the Multiformer (§2.2), which replaces the Transformer encoder MHSA by the new proposed module.

2.1 Multi-head Multi-attention

An increasing number of studies have observed the presence of redundant heads in multi-head self-attention (Michel et al., 2019; Bian et al., 2021; Zhang et al., 2021). Moreover, Voita et al. (2019) even tried to prune them, and observed that the quality of the translations (in MT) was almost not affected. This suggests that the model does not exploit the full potential present in the use of attention heads. In addition, the quadratic time and memory complexity of Self-Attention with respect to the input sequence length makes it impossible to use it directly in Speech tasks. To address this challenge, end-to-end ST models are based on reducing the length of speech sequences, usually by a factor of 4, through compression techniques, so that they can be processed by the Transformer (Di Gangi et al., 2019b; Wang et al., 2020a). However, after this compression, the resulting sequences are still considerably longer and more redundant than their text counterparts. Alastruey et al. (2021) proposed the use of efficient Transformers for ST, but, as observed in different tasks by Tay et al. (2021), they suffer from a drop in performance quality. The main reason for this deterioration is that most efficient Transformers propose strategies that deprive the model of the ability to learn all types of content from the input stream.[1]

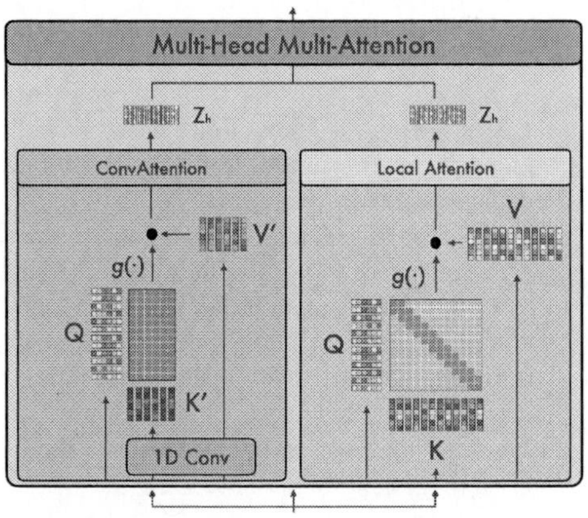

Figure 1: Scheme of the MHMA with the representation of each of the attention mechanisms it incorporates. The function $g()$ denotes the downscaling and computation of the $softmax()$ function.

To solve the aforementioned problems, we propose multi-head multi-attention (MHMA) (Figure 1) which, using heads with different attention mechanisms, is meant to force a more diversified learning, thus (i) hindering the presence of irrelevant heads and (ii) allowing the model to learn both local and global content from the input sequence,

[1]In efficient Transformers that approximate the $softmax()$ function (Choromanski et al., 2021) or the attention matrix (Wang et al., 2020b), the quality drop can be attributed to an imperfection in these approximations.

while applying efficient attention mechanisms. The MHMA module is manually set by selecting the type of attention mechanism for each head in each layer within the following ones:

ConvAttention. Efficient attention mechanism proposed by Papi et al. (2021). The ConvAttention compresses the keys and values by means of a convolutional layer, decreasing the size of the attention matrix by a factor of χ, to reduce the original complexity to $O((\frac{n}{\chi})^2)$. By not compressing the queries, they manage to maintain the dimensions of the input sequence at the output.

Local Attention. Attention mechanism with a sliding window pattern (Beltagy et al., 2020). It only computes the product between queries and keys of nearby tokens within the same input sequence, so it is more efficient than the regular Self-Attention. In particular, given a fixed window size w, each token attends to $\frac{w}{2}$ tokens on each side, achieving a linear scaling ($O(n \times w)$) of the module complexity. As in Alastruey et al. (2021), this attention pattern is intended to force the learning of local relations, while being more efficient.

2.2 Multiformer

The Multiformer is a Transformer-based architecture inspired by Wang et al. (2020a). The original model consists on a regular Transformer, preceded by two 1D convolutional layers, that help to tackle speech-specific problems such as a longer sequence length or information redundancy in adjacent tokens. The Multiformer proposes to modify the self-attention module on each encoder layer by a MHMA, since we believe that this module could be helpful to deal with speech.

The introduction of MHMA allows the model to learn from different representational and contextual levels. This enables the construction of architectures capable of extracting different kinds of information from the input sequence, while performing more efficient attention mechanisms. In addition, the model is biased towards learning different types of token interactions, hindering the presence of irrelevant heads.

However, the generation of attention diversity at the head level does not address the presence of redundancy between layers noted by Dalvi et al. (2020), who, using linear Center Kernel Alignment (Kornblith et al., 2019), observed that, except for the last two layers, layer redundancy increases throughout the encoder. Moreover, the information

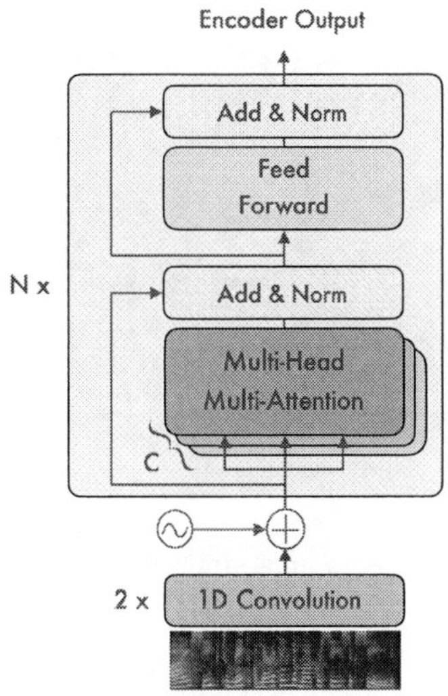

Figure 2: Diagram of the Multiformer encoder. It comprises N layers, each one with C heads that can use different attention mechanisms.

processed by each layer differs, hence using the same MHMA configuration in all encoder layers may not be the optimal.

Therefore, the Multiformer (Figure 2) allows the use of different MHMA configurations, which is meant to create architectures that process the speech sequence in a more progressive manner. This approach emphasizes the learning of different content along the encoder layers, while hampering information redundancy.

3 Heads Contribution Analysis

MHMA allows the use of different attention mechanisms in parallel, therefore we wanted to evaluate the head contribution in each of the encoder layers.

In general, given an input sequence of n tokens $\{\mathbf{x_1}, ..., \mathbf{x_n}\} \in \mathbb{R}^{n \times d}$ and a model with an embeddings dimension d (head dimension d_h), the output of each attention-head $\mathbf{z_i^h} \in \mathbb{R}^{d_h}$ is:

$$\mathbf{z}_i^h = \sum_j^N \mathbf{A}_{i,j}^h \mathbf{W}\mathbf{v}^h \, \mathbf{x}_j \quad (1)$$

where $\mathbf{A}_{i,j}^h$ is the attention weight of token j on token i and $\mathbf{W}\mathbf{v}^h \in \mathbb{R}^{d_h \times d}$ is the learned projection matrix of the values. The final output representation of the attention module $\mathbf{y_i} \in \mathbb{R}^d$ is:

$$\mathbf{y}_i = \mathbf{Wo} \text{ Concat}\{\mathbf{z}_i^1, ..., \mathbf{z}_i^H\} + \mathbf{b}_o \quad (2)$$

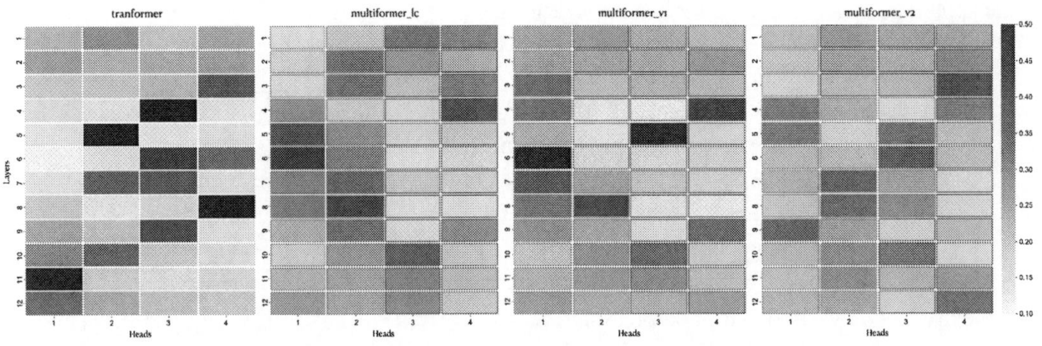

Figure 3: Head relevance for each layer of the proposed models. They have been computed using the median of n contributions (equation 4) from 500 random samples of the en-de training partition. Heads marked in orange use Local Attention while those in purple are using ConvAttention.

with $\mathbf{Wo} \in \mathbb{R}^{d \times H \cdot d_h}$ as the output projection matrix trained jointly with the model, and $\mathbf{b}_o \in \mathbb{R}^d$ referring to the bias. As previously done for interpretability research (Kobayashi et al., 2020), the above expression (equation 2) can be rewritten as follows:

$$\mathbf{y}_i = \sum_{h}^{H} \mathbf{Wo}^h \, \mathbf{z}_i^h + \mathbf{b}_o \tag{3}$$

where $\mathbf{Wo}^h \in \mathbb{R}^{d \times d_h}$ is the part of the output projection matrix corresponding to each head. Note that from this last expression, it can be defined $\xi_i^h = \mathbf{Wo}^h \mathbf{z}_i^h \in \mathbb{R}^d$ as the projected output vector of a head.

Inspired by Kobayashi et al. (2020), for each layer, we define the contribution of each head to the attention output $\mathbf{y}_i$ as the Euclidean norm of the projected output vector of heads:

$$c_{i,h} = ||\xi_i^h||_2 \tag{4}$$

4 Experiments

In this section we first explain the training details (§4.1) in order to ensure reproducibility of experiments.[2] Then we briefly describe Multiformer architectures and the procedure we followed (§4.2).

4.1 Experimental Settings

The Multiformer architectures have been trained on 3 different language directions of the MuST-C dataset (Cattoni et al., 2021). This corpus consists of audio, transcriptions, and translations of TED talks in English. MuST-C provides 8 language directions ranging in size from 385 (Portuguese) to 504 (Spanish) hours of transcribed and translated speech.

To ensure a faithful comparison with the baseline model, the small architecture of the S2T Transformer in Fairseq (Wang et al., 2020a), all our models consist of 12 encoder layers, 6 decoder layers and 4 heads in each attention layer. The embedding dimension of the model is 256. Moreover, following the baseline architecture, we have kept the convolutional layers with downsampling prior to the model.

For the ConvAttention, we use a kernel size of 5 and a stride of 2, reducing the length of keys and values to the half. Regarding the Local Attention, as in Alastruey et al. (2021) we have chosen a window size of 64 tokens. These hyperparameters have been employed in all Multiformer architectures. For a detailed description of training parameters, see appendix A.

4.2 Experiments Description

First, we trained two architectures based on a single attention mechanism (Local or ConvAttention), in order to obtain a comparison between models with and without diversity.

After this, we trained the first Multiformer architecture, the $multiformer\_lc$. It has a configuration of the MHMA with 2 heads of ConvAttention and 2 heads of Local Attention for all encoder layers. Then, we analyzed the contribution of each head following the methodology described in §3. This allowed us to better understand the needs of each layer, and to propose architectures based on this. From Figure 3, it can be seen that in the first 3 layers, the $multiformer\_lc$ assigns low rele-

[2]Code available: `https://github.com/mt-upc/fairseq/tree/multiformer`

Model	en-de			en-fr			en-es			Avg($\Delta\%$)
	BLEU	ΔBLEU	$\Delta\%$	BLEU	ΔBLEU	$\Delta\%$	BLEU	ΔBLEU	$\Delta\%$	
baseline	22.65	-	-	32.97	-	-	26.99	-	-	-
local_attention	22.69	+0.04	+0.17	33.00	+0.03	+0.09	27.10	+0.11	+0.41	+0.22
conv_attention	22.45	−0.20	−0.88	33.07	+0.10	+0.30	26.96	−0.04	−0.15	−0.73
multiformer_lc	22.80	+0.15	+0.66	33.25	+0.28	+0.85	27.56	+0.57	+2.11	+1.21
multiformer_v1	**23.16**	**+0.51**	**+2.25**	33.10	+0.13	+0.39	**27.68**	**+0.69**	**+2.56**	**+1.73**
multiformer_v2	22.98	+0.33	+1.46	**33.26**	**+0.29**	**+0.88**	27.44	+0.45	+1.67	+1.34

Table 1: BLEU results in 3 different language directions of the MuST-C dataset, English→German (en-de), English→French (en-fr) and English→Spanish (en-es). Relative improvements are calculated with respect to the baseline (Wang et al., 2020a).

vance to the representations extracted by one of the Local Attention heads, which could indicate the prioritization of the global context in the first layers. In the middle layers, a change in this trend is observed, with Local Attention heads acquiring more importance. As for the last layers, we see an equal relevance distribution between heads of both mechanisms.

These observations have motivated the training of the $multiformer\_v1$, which tries to correct the abandonment of Local Attention heads observed in the initial layers. It consists of substituting a Local Attention head for a ConvAttention head in the first six layers of the encoder.

Finally, the $multiformer\_v2$ is built more strictly from the analysis. It incorporates 3 different MHMA configurations. In the first 3 layers, it uses 1 head of Local Attention and 3 heads of ConvAttention. The next 5 layers (from the 4th to the 8th) use 3 Local Attention heads and 1 ConvAttention head, to finish the remaining 4 layers with 2 heads of each type.

In general, it is clear that, whereas the baseline uses few heads in most layers, Multiformer architectures[3] force the model to have a more uniformly distributed contribution between heads.

5 Results

First, it can be observed from Table 1, that the efficient architecture based only on Local Attention ($local\_attention$) already obtains the same results as the baseline, suggesting the presence of unnecessary computations in self-attention. Unlike previous works (Alastruey et al., 2021), this architecture maintains the convolutional layers, so the amount of global content within the attention mechanism is higher using the same window size. On the other hand, while the architecture based exclusively on ConvAttention ($conv\_attention$), manages to achieve baseline results in English→French (en-fr) and English→Spanish (en-es), its score in English→German (en-de) drops 0.2 BLEU, suggesting the need for a higher resolution extraction of representations for that language pair.

Secondly, analyzing the heads contribution of the baseline architecture, we can observe that the heads contribution tends to accumulate in few heads. This means we obtain similar conclusions than Voita et al. (2019), but for the ST setting. Furthermore, our work goes one step further, showing that those architectures where the heads contribution is uniformly distributed, obtain a higher performance. This finding confirms that, in ST, some heads on a regular Transformer tend to learn irrelevant information. This shows that MHSA might not be as capable as expected of extracting different kinds of patterns, unless it is biased on purpose towards doing so.

In particular, all Multiformer variants improve the results obtained by the baseline and the $local\_attention$ and $conv\_attention$ architectures. However, these improvements are not equal in all languages pairs, and go from 0.15 to 0.57 BLEU for $multiformer\_lc$, from 0.13 to 0.69 BLEU for $multiformer\_v1$ and from 0.29 to 0.45 BLEU for $multiformer\_v2$, becoming the latter the architecture with the most robust gains.

6 Conclusions

In this paper, we present the Multiformer, the first Transformer-based model that allows to combine different attention mechanisms in the MHSA module. This helps the model extracting different types of token interactions from each head, hence preventing the appearance of irrelevant heads. By applying this diversity of attention patterns with efficient mechanisms, the model is able to maintain both local and global context across encoder layers while being more efficient. Experiments on 3

[3]More details in Table 2 in the Appendices.

language pairs show that all Multiformer architectures outperform the results achieved by the S2T Transformer in the ST task, with an improvement up to 0.69 BLEU for the English-Spanish direction in the $multiformer\_v1$.

7 Acknowledgements

This work was partially funded by the ADAVOICE project, PID2019-107579RB-I00 / AEI / 10.13039/501100011033, and the UPC INIREC scholarship nº3522. We would like to thank Javier Ferrando for his advice on the heads contribution analysis.

References

Belen Alastruey, Gerard I. Gállego, and Marta R. Costa-jussà. 2021. Efficient transformer for direct speech translation.

Antonios Anastasopoulos, David Chiang, and Long Duong. 2016. An unsupervised probability model for speech-to-translation alignment of low-resource languages. In *Proceedings of the 2016 Conference on Empirical Methods in Natural Language Processing*, pages 1255–1263, Austin, Texas. Association for Computational Linguistics.

Iz Beltagy, Matthew E. Peters, and Arman Cohan. 2020. Longformer: The long-document transformer.

Luisa Bentivogli, Mauro Cettolo, Marco Gaido, Alina Karakanta, Alberto Martinelli, Matteo Negri, and Marco Turchi. 2021. Cascade versus direct speech translation: Do the differences still make a difference? In *Proceedings of the 59th Annual Meeting of the Association for Computational Linguistics and the 11th International Joint Conference on Natural Language Processing (Volume 1: Long Papers)*, pages 2873–2887, Online. Association for Computational Linguistics.

Yuchen Bian, Jiaji Huang, Xingyu Cai, Jiahong Yuan, and Kenneth Church. 2021. On attention redundancy: A comprehensive study. In *Proceedings of the 2021 Conference of the North American Chapter of the Association for Computational Linguistics: Human Language Technologies*, pages 930–945, Online. Association for Computational Linguistics.

Alexandre Bérard, Laurent Besacier, Ali Can Kocabiyikoglu, and Olivier Pietquin. 2018. End-to-end automatic speech translation of audiobooks. In *2018 IEEE International Conference on Acoustics, Speech and Signal Processing (ICASSP)*, pages 6224–6228.

Roldano Cattoni, Mattia Antonino Di Gangi, Luisa Bentivogli, Matteo Negri, and Marco Turchi. 2021. Must-c: A multilingual corpus for end-to-end speech translation. *Computer Speech & Language*, 66:101155.

Krzysztof Marcin Choromanski, Valerii Likhosherstov, David Dohan, Xingyou Song, Andreea Gane, Tamas Sarlos, Peter Hawkins, Jared Quincy Davis, Afroz Mohiuddin, Lukasz Kaiser, David Benjamin Belanger, Lucy J Colwell, and Adrian Weller. 2021. Rethinking attention with performers. In *International Conference on Learning Representations*.

Fahim Dalvi, Hassan Sajjad, Nadir Durrani, and Yonatan Belinkov. 2020. Analyzing redundancy in pretrained transformer models. In *Proceedings of the 2020 Conference on Empirical Methods in Natural Language Processing (EMNLP)*, pages 4908–4926, Online. Association for Computational Linguistics.

Mattia A Di Gangi, Matteo Negri, and Marco Turchi. 2019a. Adapting transformer to end-to-end spoken language translation. In *INTERSPEECH 2019*. International Speech Communication Association.

Mattia Antonino Di Gangi, Matteo Negri, Roldano Cattoni, Roberto Dessi, and Marco Turchi. 2019b. Enhancing transformer for end-to-end speech-to-text translation. In *Proceedings of Machine Translation Summit XVII: Research Track*, pages 21–31, Dublin, Ireland. European Association for Machine Translation.

Linhao Dong, Shuang Xu, and Bo Xu. 2018. Speech-transformer: A no-recurrence sequence-to-sequence model for speech recognition. In *2018 IEEE International Conference on Acoustics, Speech and Signal Processing (ICASSP)*, pages 5884–5888.

Long Duong, Antonios Anastasopoulos, David Chiang, Steven Bird, and Trevor Cohn. 2016. An attentional model for speech translation without transcription. In *Proceedings of the 2016 Conference of the North American Chapter of the Association for Computational Linguistics: Human Language Technologies*, pages 949–959, San Diego, California. Association for Computational Linguistics.

Marco Gaido, Mauro Cettolo, Matteo Negri, and Marco Turchi. 2021. CTC-based compression for direct speech translation. In *Proceedings of the 16th Conference of the European Chapter of the Association for Computational Linguistics: Main Volume*, pages 690–696, Online. Association for Computational Linguistics.

Magdalena Igras, Bartosz Ziółko, and Mariusz Ziółko. 2013. Length of phonemes in a context of their positions in polish sentences. In *2013 International Conference on Signal Processing and Multimedia Applications (SIGMAP)*, pages 59–64.

Diederik P. Kingma and Jimmy Ba. 2015. Adam: A method for stochastic optimization. In *3rd International Conference on Learning Representations*.

Goro Kobayashi, Tatsuki Kuribayashi, Sho Yokoi, and Kentaro Inui. 2020. Attention is not only a weight: Analyzing transformers with vector norms. In *Proceedings of the 2020 Conference on Empirical*

Methods in Natural Language Processing (EMNLP), pages 7057–7075, Online. Association for Computational Linguistics.

Simon Kornblith, Mohammad Norouzi, Honglak Lee, and Geoffrey Hinton. 2019. Similarity of neural network representations revisited. In *Proceedings of the 36th International Conference on Machine Learning*, volume 97 of *Proceedings of Machine Learning Research*, pages 3519–3529. PMLR.

Guodong Ma, Pengfei Hu, Jian Kang, Shen Huang, and Hao Huang. 2021. Leveraging Phone Mask Training for Phonetic-Reduction-Robust E2E Uyghur Speech Recognition. In *Proc. Interspeech 2021*.

Paul Michel, Omer Levy, and Graham Neubig. 2019. Are sixteen heads really better than one? *Advances in neural information processing systems*, 32.

H. Ney. 1999. Speech translation: coupling of recognition and translation. In *1999 IEEE International Conference on Acoustics, Speech, and Signal Processing. Proceedings. ICASSP99*.

Sara Papi, Marco Gaido, Matteo Negri, and Marco Turchi. 2021. Speechformer: Reducing information loss in direct speech translation. In *Proceedings of the 2021 Conference on Empirical Methods in Natural Language Processing*, pages 1698–1706, Online and Punta Cana, Dominican Republic. Association for Computational Linguistics.

Kishore Papineni, Salim Roukos, Todd Ward, and Wei-Jing Zhu. 2002. Bleu: a method for automatic evaluation of machine translation. In *Proceedings of the 40th Annual Meeting of the Association for Computational Linguistics*, pages 311–318, Philadelphia, Pennsylvania, USA. Association for Computational Linguistics.

Niki Parmar, Ashish Vaswani, Jakob Uszkoreit, Lukasz Kaiser, Noam Shazeer, Alexander Ku, and Dustin Tran. 2018. Image transformer. In *Proceedings of the 35th International Conference on Machine Learning*, Proceedings of Machine Learning Research. PMLR.

Elizabeth Salesky, Matthias Sperber, and Alan W Black. 2019. Exploring phoneme-level speech representations for end-to-end speech translation. In *Proceedings of the 57th Annual Meeting of the Association for Computational Linguistics*, pages 1835–1841, Florence, Italy. Association for Computational Linguistics.

Matthias Sperber and Matthias Paulik. 2020. Speech translation and the end-to-end promise: Taking stock of where we are. In *Proceedings of the 58th Annual Meeting of the Association for Computational Linguistics*, pages 7409–7421, Online. Association for Computational Linguistics.

Christian Szegedy, Vincent Vanhoucke, Sergey Ioffe, Jon Shlens, and Zbigniew Wojna. 2016. Rethinking the inception architecture for computer vision. In *2016 IEEE Conference on Computer Vision and Pattern Recognition (CVPR)*, pages 2818–2826.

Yi Tay, Mostafa Dehghani, Samira Abnar, Yikang Shen, Dara Bahri, Philip Pham, Jinfeng Rao, Liu Yang, Sebastian Ruder, and Donald Metzler. 2021. Long range arena : A benchmark for efficient transformers. In *International Conference on Learning Representations*.

Ashish Vaswani, Noam Shazeer, Niki Parmar, Jakob Uszkoreit, Llion Jones, Aidan N Gomez, Łukasz Kaiser, and Illia Polosukhin. 2017. Attention is all you need. *Advances in neural information processing systems*, 30.

Elena Voita, David Talbot, Fedor Moiseev, Rico Sennrich, and Ivan Titov. 2019. Analyzing multi-head self-attention: Specialized heads do the heavy lifting, the rest can be pruned. In *Proceedings of the 57th Annual Meeting of the Association for Computational Linguistics*, pages 5797–5808, Florence, Italy. Association for Computational Linguistics.

Changhan Wang, Yun Tang, Xutai Ma, Anne Wu, Dmytro Okhonko, and Juan Pino. 2020a. Fairseq S2T: Fast speech-to-text modeling with fairseq. In *Proceedings of the 1st Conference of the Asia-Pacific Chapter of the Association for Computational Linguistics and the 10th International Joint Conference on Natural Language Processing: System Demonstrations*, pages 33–39, Suzhou, China. Association for Computational Linguistics.

Sinong Wang, Belinda Z. Li, Madian Khabsa, Han Fang, and Hao Ma. 2020b. Linformer: Self-attention with linear complexity.

Ron J Weiss, Jan Chorowski, Navdeep Jaitly, Yonghui Wu, and Zhifeng Chen. 2017. Sequence-to-sequence models can directly translate foreign speech. *Proc. Interspeech 2017*, pages 2625–2629.

Biao Zhang, Ivan Titov, Barry Haddow, and Rico Sennrich. 2020. Adaptive feature selection for end-to-end speech translation. In *Findings of the Association for Computational Linguistics: EMNLP 2020*, pages 2533–2544, Online. Association for Computational Linguistics.

Tianfu Zhang, Heyan Huang, Chong Feng, and Longbing Cao. 2021. Enlivening redundant heads in multi-head self-attention for machine translation. In *Proceedings of the 2021 Conference on Empirical Methods in Natural Language Processing*, pages 3238–3248, Online and Punta Cana, Dominican Republic. Association for Computational Linguistics.

Name	MHMA Configurations		
conv_attention	$12 \times \left(4\times\ Conv\,(5,2) \right)$	-	-
local_attention	$12 \times \left(4\times\ Local\,(64) \right)$	-	-
multiformer_lc	$12 \times \begin{pmatrix} 2\times\ Local\,(64) \\ 2\times\ Conv\,(5,2) \end{pmatrix}$	-	-
multiformer_v1	$6 \times \begin{pmatrix} 1\times\ Local\,(64) \\ 3\times\ Conv\,(5,2) \end{pmatrix}$	$6 \times \begin{pmatrix} 2\times\ Local\,(64) \\ 2\times\ Conv\,(5,2) \end{pmatrix}$	-
multiformer_v2	$3 \times \begin{pmatrix} 1\times\ Local\,(64) \\ 3\times\ Conv\,(5,2) \end{pmatrix}$	$5 \times \begin{pmatrix} 3\times\ Local\,(64) \\ 1\times\ Conv\,(5,2) \end{pmatrix}$	$4 \times \begin{pmatrix} 2\times\ Local\,(64) \\ 2\times\ Conv\,(5,2) \end{pmatrix}$

Table 2: Multiformer architectures. The notation for each configuration is as follows: $N_{layers} \times \left(N_{heads} \times Attention\,(hyperparameters) \right)$.

A Detailed Experimental Settings

The training has been performed using the label smoothed cross entropy loss (Szegedy et al., 2016) and the Adam optimizer (Kingma and Ba, 2015). The learning rate has been set to $2 \cdot 10^{-3}$ with an inverse square-root scheduler and 10,000 warm-up updates. We have set a maximum number of 32,000 tokens for the construction of the mini-batches and an update frequency of 5. The training has been hosted on 2 NVIDIA GeForce RTX 2080 Ti GPUs until the completion of 50,000 updates. For a better performance in ST, models have been pretrained in ASR (Bérard et al., 2018).[4] For this pretraining, all the parameters have been set as in ST, with the exception of the learning rate, which has been set to $1 \cdot 10^{-3}$.

For the S2T evaluation of the architectures, we averaged the 7 checkpoints around the best one and then computed the BLEU score (Papineni et al., 2002).

To visualize the layer-level relevance of each head (Figure 3), we computed the median of the contributions (§3) of each head for all the tokens in 500 random samples. Since we want to observe which head is the most relevant during training, the en-de training partition was used.

[4]For the use of the ASR pretrained encoder in ST training, the best checkpoint has been used, being this the one that obtains the lowest loss.

Defending Compositionality in Emergent Languages

Michal Auersperger and **Pavel Pecina**
Charles University
Faculty of Mathematics and Physics
{auersperger,pecina}@ufal.mff.cuni.cz

Abstract

Compositionality has traditionally been understood as a major factor in productivity of language and, more broadly, human cognition. Yet, recently, some research started to question its status, showing that artificial neural networks are good at generalization even without noticeable compositional behavior. We argue that some of these conclusions are too strong and/or incomplete. In the context of a two-agent communication game, we show that compositionality indeed seems essential for successful generalization when the evaluation is done on a proper dataset.

1 Introduction

Compositionality is a property of language that describes its specific hierarchical structure. Multiple atomic units (e.g., words) can be combined to produce more complex units (e.g., sentences), while the meaning of the larger units can be inferred from the simpler parts and the way they are combined.

Of course, there are inherently noncompositional structures in language, idioms being a prime example. If someone is *making waves*, it usually means that the person is causing trouble and no water is implied. Still, many reputable researchers (Nowak et al., 2000; Pinker, 2000; Fodor and Lepore, 2002; Lake et al., 2017) have seen compositionality as a key ingredient that enables language to be used productively, i.e., in an infinite number of novel situations. Often, this productivity is juxtaposed with the learning of Artificial Neural Networks (ANNs), whose performance is known to suffer when tested in new scenarios.

Recently, a strand in the literature has been making waves (*sic*) by calling into question the proposed benefits of compositionality. Various papers have shown that ANNs can generalize well to unseen contexts (be productive) even if they work with internal representations that are noncompositional (Kottur et al., 2017; Andreas, 2019; Baroni, 2019; Chaabouni et al., 2020; Kharitonov and Baroni, 2020).

The goal of this paper is to counterbalance these claims.[1] More precisely, we would like to relativize some of the stronger conclusions that are provided and show (by running modified experiments) that the reported experimental results can be harmonized with the view that compositionality is necessary for successful knowledge transfer.

We will do this by first providing an overview of the related research in Section 2. Then in Section 3, we give our arguments against some of the presented assumptions and/or conclusions. These arguments are further supported by experiments that are described in Section 4. We conclude the paper with a short discussion in Section 5.

2 Emergent languages generalize without compositionality

Much of the critical research comes from experimentation with languages that emerge during a communication game. Here, two agents (ANNs) are trained to communicate in order to perform a certain task. The first agent (sender/speaker) encodes the input into a message, a sequence of discrete symbols. The second agent (receiver/listener) does not have direct access to the original input, but only sees it as represented by the message. The receiver's goal is to transform the message into a desired output.

The output can take many forms depending on the task: reconstructing the input fully (Chaabouni et al., 2020; Andreas, 2020) or partially (Kottur et al., 2017) or reconstructing the input after going through some deterministic transformation (Kharitonov and Baroni, 2020).

Inputs can be conceptualized as representations of objects by means of independent nominal at-

[1] We consider the cited research valuable and important. In some cases we argue with some statements that were not even the main topic of the paper in question.

Proceedings of the 2022 Conference of the North American Chapter of the Association for Computational Linguistics: Human Language Technologies: Student Research Workshop, pages 285 - 291

tributes, e.g., *blue circle, red square, orange triangle* for two-dimensional input vectors (color and shape). A uniform random sample of all such objects is then held out for testing, the rest of the data (or its part) is used for training.

Andreas (2019) and Chaabouni et al. (2020) develop custom metrics to measure the compositionality of messages passed between the sender and the receiver. The metrics compare each message to the corresponding input and try to assess to what extent each part of the input (attribute value) can be isolated in the message regardless of the context (i.e., other attribute values). They report runs in which models communicate through messages with low compositionality scores, but still achieve good generalization on unseen data.

Kharitonov and Baroni (2020) replace training the first agent (sender) by hand-coding the messages. This gives them the advantage of having direct control over the emergent language. They find that good generalization can sometimes be achieved using a non-compositional language (sometimes leading to even better results than using a compositional language).

3 Allowing compositionality to have an effect

Our main argument is that the process of selecting the test data plays a crucial role in evaluating the effects of compositionality. Sampling examples with uniform probability is a mainstay in machine learning, and algorithms have been shown many times that they can perform very well under these conditions. However, once we move away from the static world of i.i.d. data samples into the dynamic world of ever-changing distributions, the limitations of such models become obvious.

We argue that this is where compositionality is supposed to be helpful. Analyzing the world (or data points to keep the discussion down to earth) through a hierarchy of parts and their relations enables inferring a 'rule-based algebraic system', which is 'an extremely powerful generalization mechanism' (Baroni, 2019). Systematic compositionality exploited by human learners enables them to be sample efficient, i.e., quickly learn a new task seeing just one or a limited number of training examples (Lake et al., 2017). Therefore, we conclude that showing compositionality not being correlated with generalization on in-domain held-out data is not very informative. Instead, it is preferable to control the exposition of certain patterns in the training and testing data as illustrated by, e.g., the SCAN benchmark (Lake and Baroni, 2018).

We also point out that Andreas (2019) and Chaabouni et al. (2020) implement both agents (sender and receiver) as relatively standard encoder/decoder architectures with recurrent (LSTM, GRU) layers. These architectures are not necessarily known for their ability to produce or utilize compositional sequences.

The assumption seems to be that when running an experiment many times (with different random initialization of the models), some runs will be successful in the sense that the agents will develop a more or less compositional language by chance. Moreover, the degree of compositionality would have to be large enough to influence the generalization of the models (should such an effect be real). We do not think this assumption is justified.

Kharitonov and Baroni (2020) avoid a part of the above problem by creating compositional messages manually. Their main conclusion is that one can devise different tasks, and in some of them a compositional representation of the input data might even prove disadvantageous. Indeed, it is possible to create, for example, an arbitrary bijective function from the input space to the output space and train a model to learn such a mapping. Not surprisingly, such a model will fail at the test time. However, if we first encode the input with the same arbitrary transformation (thus creating a non-compositional representation of the input data), the model is then asked to learn the identity function, which it might achieve quite well. Therefore, we agree with the conclusion that 'in isolation from the target task, there is nothing special about a language being . . . compositional.'

Yet, as mentioned above, compositionality is often discussed in conjunction with natural language or human cognitive abilities more generally. In the lived experience of biological species (to be less human-centric), it is reasonable to expect that the 'underlying factors of variation' or 'explanatory factors' (Bengio et al., 2013) behind the input data a) repeat in many different situations and b) are directly relevant for different tasks. For example, it is reasonable to expect that many languages have a word for *water* rather than a word for *water and the wind is blowing*, simply because the first is more useful. Therefore, we believe that the em-

Model	train	in-domain test	out-of-domain test
sender (ours)	1.00 ± 0.01	1.00 ± 0.00	$\mathbf{0.99 \pm 0.06}$
sender (Chaabouni et al., 2020)	1.00 ± 0.04	1.00 ± 0.03	0.83 ± 0.19
receiver (ours)	1.00 ± 0.00	1.00 ± 0.00	$\mathbf{1.00 \pm 0.02}$
receiver (Chaabouni et al., 2020)	1.00 ± 0.02	1.00 ± 0.00	0.44 ± 0.32

Table 1: Learning alone experiment: Comparing the accuracy (mean $\pm$ std over 20 runs) of two types of architecture in different data splits. Each agent (sender/receiver) is trained independently of the other by using fixed messages.

phasis on compositionality in research can be more than 'a misguided effect of our human-centric bias' (Kharitonov and Baroni, 2020).

4 Experiments

We follow the communication game experiments of Chaabouni et al. (2020). We create a set of instances, each of which is represented by i_{att} attributes. Each attribute has n_{val} possible values. The messages passed between the agents are limited by the maximum length (c_{len}) and the size of the vocabulary (c_{voc}). The receiver's goal is to reconstruct the input.

As messages are sequences of discrete symbols, which prevents gradients from passing through, the sender must be trained with the REINFORCE algorithm Williams (1992). The receiver is trained using backpropagation. We use the EGG toolkit (Kharitonov et al., 2019) to implement the experiments.[2]

We focus mainly on the setting of (i_{att} = 2, n_{val} = 100, c_{len} = 3, c_{voc} = 100). In this case, the dataset contains isntances such as $(12, 34), (0, 99), (99, 0)$ etc. We create three splits. The *out-of-domain (OOD) test set* contains all pairs where 0 appears, apart from three examples: $(0, 0)$, $(0, 1)$, and $(1, 0)$. The *training set* contains these three zero examples together with 90% of the remaining (nonzero) examples (random sample). The rest of the data constitute *in-domain (IND) test set.* In other words, we designate a special symbol (0), which appears only in a limited number of contexts in training. We then separately evaluate how the models perform on unseen examples with ordinary symbols (IND test set) and on unseen examples with the special symbol (OOD test set).

Given the absence of any incentive for the models to develop compositional messages during training, we opt for architectural biases in our experiments. We use the models that have been proven to be successful in OOD generalization in the SCAN benchmark (Li and Bowling, 2019; Russin et al., 2020; Auersperger and Pecina, 2021). Each agent is implemented as a separate seq2seq encoder-decoder architecture with recurrent layers and a modified attention mechanism. Details are provided in Appendix A

4.1 Learning alone

We first want to know whether the architectures used for implementing the agents are capable of achieving systematic compositionality on their own, that is, outside of the context of the 2-agent communication game. To do this, we handcode the messages that are to be created (sender) or received (receiver) and train each agent using regular backpropagation on the corresponding task.

We first create an arbitrary bijective mapping from the input vocabulary to the message vocabulary. Furthermore, to introduce variability in the length of the messages, we duplicate the occurrences of all tokens with odd indices in the message vocabulary. For example, having a mapping $tr: 0 \to 3, 1 \to 8, 2 \to 2, \ldots$, we produce (among others) the following input–message pairs: $(0, 0)$ – $(3, 3)$, $(1, 0)$ – $(8, 8, 3)$, $(2, 1)$ – $(2, 2, 8, 8)$.

We train 2 types of agent for both sender and receiver comparing our architecture with the default used by Chaabouni et al. (2020). There are 500 training epochs and 20 runs with different random initializations for each agent. The results are presented in Table 1. They show that at least for this simple task, adding architectural bias helps with compositional generalization to out-of-domain data. The results also suggest that the default architectures are unlikely to provide systematic generalization in the communication game since they are unable to achieve it even if their communication partner does never make mistakes (i.e. the messages are guaranteed to be produced/received correctly).

We experimented with limiting the capacity of the default architecture to see if such kind of regularization could help with generalization perfor-

[2]The code is available at `https://github.com/michal-au/emlang-compos.git`

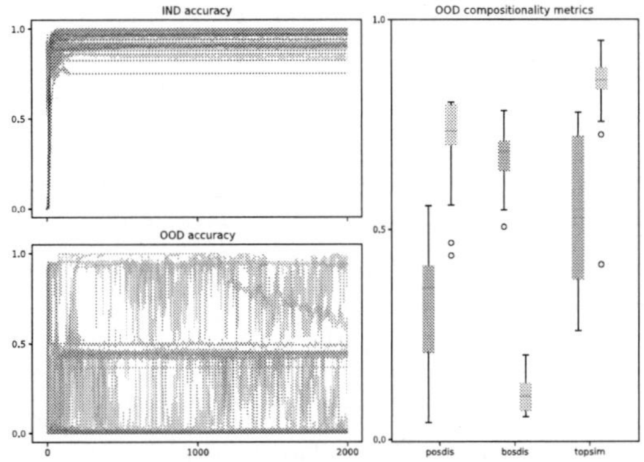

Figure 1: Communication game experiment: Training and OOD accuracy during training. Compositionality measures at the end of training. Orange represents runs of our architecture, blue represents runs of the architecture used by Chaabouni et al. (2020). There were 20 runs for each architecture.

mance. Besides the original size (500), four additional sizes of hidden layers were tested (100, 200, 300, 400). For the default receiver, a smaller capacity (100) improved the OOD accuracy from 0.44 ($\pm$0.32 std) to 0.81 ($\pm$0.21 std).

We point out that it is the out-of-domain test set that reveals the difference between the architectures.

4.2 Communication game

Having seen that in some tasks our architectures are capable of approaching systematic compositionality, we turn our attention to the full communication game. We train both the default and our modified architectures on the full task for the maximum number of 2,000 epochs. Similarly to Chaabouni et al. (2020), we use early stopping when training accuracy reaches 99.999%, however, we evaluate all the runs, even those that never reach perfect training accuracy. Each experiment was repeated 20 times with different random initializations. The training progress is visualized in Figure 1 and the results are given in Table 2.

The experiments demonstrate that our changes to the default architecture lead to some out-of-domain generalization, but we were unable to guarantee such behavior for each run (accuracy 0.42 ± 0.27 std). In contrast, the original architecture does never succeed (accuracy 0.00 ± 0.01 std).

We evaluated the three compositionality metrics used by Chaabouni et al. (2020) and found significant differences between the two architectures. In two of the metrics, namely *positional disentanglement* and *topographic similarity*, we achieve higher scores than the original architecture, while in *bag-of-symbol disentanglement* the situation is reversed. We show the relationship between compositionality and generalization in Figure 2.

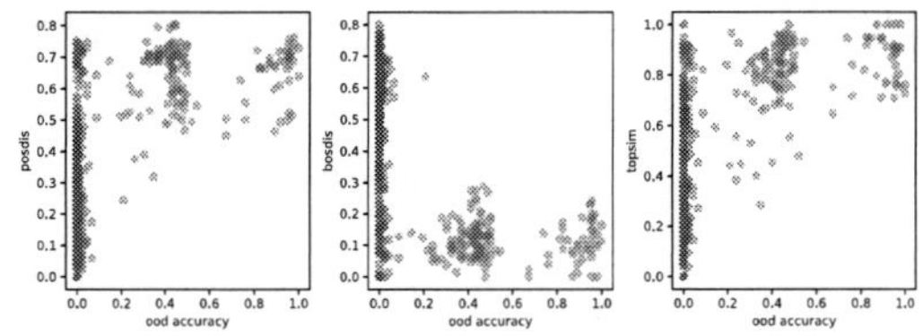

Figure 2: Compositionality measures and generalization in out-of-domain dataset. Successful generalization was possible only with large posdis and/or topsim scores.

Both Andreas (2019) and Chaabouni et al. (2020) claim that compositionality is not a necessary condition for good generalization, but that it might be a sufficient condition (Chaabouni et al., 2020). Choosing the out-of-domain data for evaluation and training models whose architecture is biased towards utilizing composationality of a language, we arrive at the opposite conclusion: compositionality is a necessary but not sufficient condition for good generalization. In other words, we often observe runs where both agents communicate through relatively compositional messages, but fail to generalize. However, we never observe a run where generalization is successful in spite of a low compositionality (posdis or topsim) score.

However, given the size of the input space (100×100) and the proportion of training data (about 90%), we did not expect to find such a noticeable difference in performance in the in-domain test set. This suggests that such test data is not completely agnostic to the notion of compositionality (which is somewhat contrary to our previous argumentation). Yet, we still maintain that the out-of-domain dataset is much more informative with respect to evaluating the benefits of compositionality.

Similarly to the previous experiment, we tested additional sizes of hidden layers of the original architecture (100, 200, 300, 400) but were not able to match the IND accuracy of our architecture.

Looking at the OOD generalization performance of our models, it is notable that most models operate in one of three regimes: the accuracies tend to cluster above 0, below 0.5, or below 1. Manual inspection of the agents' communication showed that most of the time agents successfully reconstruct the

Model	train	IND test	OOD test	posdis	bosdis	topsim
Chaabouni et al. (2020)	0.99 ± 0.07	0.91 ± 0.09	0.00 ± 0.01	0.32 ± 0.15	0.67 ± 0.07	0.53 ± 0.18
ours	0.99 ± 0.03	0.98 ± 0.05	$\mathbf{0.42 \pm 0.27}$	0.71 ± 0.11	0.11 ± 0.04	0.83 ± 0.11

Table 2: Communication game experiment: Accuracy (mean ± std) measured in different data splits, Three compositionality measures of the messages (mean ± std) evaluated in out-of-domain test data.

non-zero symbols, which means that most of the errors are caused by wrongly reconstructing the zero symbol. These errors are also systematic, meaning that, given the position in the string, the zero symbol is replaced by the same symbol regardless of its neighbor. Thus, agents successfully reconstructing zero at both positions achieve accuracies close to 1, agents successfully reconstructing zero only in a single position achieve scores close to 0.5 and in the rest of the runs, agents fail regardless of the position.

5 Discussion

There are many questions that remain for further analysis. The distinction between the in-domain and out-of-domain data is not clear-cut. One might object that seeing just one or two examples of a given symbol in the training data is too little for ANNs to learn its embedding and reliably map it close to other 'similar' symbols in the semantic space (Lake and Baroni, 2018; Loula et al., 2018). This is actually the issue as it seems that human learners unlike ANNs are able to succeed in such a scenario and work with limited data or, in other words, 'not-yet-converged embeddings'. See Lake et al. (2017) for a more thorough discussion.

The goal of this paper was to show that some conclusions in the literature on compositionality are too strong or incomplete. However, there are other arguments that remain untackled. Baroni (2019) gives examples of neural networks that generalize (partially) well to out-of-domain data. For instance, Dessi and Baroni (2019) show that a simple convolutional network is enough to improve accuracy from 1.2% to 60% in a difficult task from the SCAN benchmark. Gulordava et al. (2018) demonstrate that a language model is capable of preferring grammatical nonsense sentences (certainly not seen in training) to ungrammatical ones. In general, the practical success of ANNs in many applications can serve as a proof of their strong generalization abilities (Lake and Baroni, 2018; Baroni, 2019).

In response, we would like to point out that such success often coincides with new developments in neural architectures (convolutional NNs in vision, attention in NLP). These developments might actually point in the direction of compositionality. A trained convolutional NN actually detects primitive shapes (at least by the filters in the lower layers) and combines these into composit representations. Similarly, a trained attention-based encoder-decoder language model represents each input as a sequence of contextualized embeddings of the original units. Some of these embeddings might primarily represent the corresponding input units, and others might represent their collections.

We also acknowledge that for practical applications, especially in the short term, focusing on compositionality is not guaranteed to help (Kharitonov and Baroni, 2020). The most practical way so far has been to enable training on as much data as possible. However, it is likely that such an approach will eventually result in diminishing returns.

There are many potential aspects that favor compositional behavior: inductive architectural biases (e.g., attention); limited channel capacity relative to the input space (Nowak et al., 2000); ease of transmission within the population (Chaabouni et al., 2020); generalization pressure (contrary to Chaabouni et al. 2020), if such a pressure is allowed to have some effect (e.g., by meta-learning); .... It is also possible that systematic compositionality might emerge[3] only as a result of multiple such factors.

Acknowledgements

The work was supported by the grant 19-26934X (NEUREM3) by the Czech Science Foundation.

References

Jacob Andreas. 2019. Measuring compositionality in representation learning. In *International Conference on Learning Representations.*

Jacob Andreas. 2020. Good-enough compositional data augmentation. In *Proceedings of the 58th Annual*

[3]As is often the case, *emerge* here means *somehow come about* and is used to hide the fact that the authors cannot explain things any further.

Meeting of the Association for Computational Linguistics, pages 7556–7566, Online. Association for Computational Linguistics.

Michal Auersperger and Pavel Pecina. 2021. Solving SCAN tasks with data augmentation and input embeddings. In *Proceedings of the International Conference on Recent Advances in Natural Language Processing (RANLP 2021)*, pages 86–91, Held Online. INCOMA Ltd.

Marco Baroni. 2019. Linguistic generalization and compositionality in modern artificial neural networks. *Philosophical Transactions of the Royal Society B: Biological Sciences*, 375(1791):20190307.

Yoshua Bengio, Aaron Courville, and Pascal Vincent. 2013. Representation learning: A review and new perspectives. *IEEE Transactions on Pattern Analysis and Machine Intelligence*, 35(8):1798–1828.

Rahma Chaabouni, Eugene Kharitonov, Diane Bouchacourt, Emmanuel Dupoux, and Marco Baroni. 2020. Compositionality and generalization in emergent languages. In *Proceedings of the 58th Annual Meeting of the Association for Computational Linguistics*, pages 4427–4442, Online. Association for Computational Linguistics.

Junyoung Chung, Caglar Gulcehre, Kyunghyun Cho, and Yoshua Bengio. 2014. Empirical evaluation of gated recurrent neural networks on sequence modeling. In *NIPS 2014 Workshop on Deep Learning, December 2014*.

Roberto Dessi and Marco Baroni. 2019. CNNs found to jump around more skillfully than RNNs: Compositional generalization in seq2seq convolutional networks. In *Proceedings of the 57th Annual Meeting of the Association for Computational Linguistics*, pages 3919–3923, Florence, Italy. Association for Computational Linguistics.

Jerry A. Fodor and Ernest Lepore. 2002. *Compositionality Papers*. Oxford University Press UK.

Kristina Gulordava, Piotr Bojanowski, Edouard Grave, Tal Linzen, and Marco Baroni. 2018. Colorless green recurrent networks dream hierarchically. In *Proceedings of the 2018 Conference of the North American Chapter of the Association for Computational Linguistics: Human Language Technologies, Volume 1 (Long Papers)*, pages 1195–1205, New Orleans, Louisiana. Association for Computational Linguistics.

Eugene Kharitonov and Marco Baroni. 2020. Emergent language generalization and acquisition speed are not tied to compositionality. In *Proceedings of the Third BlackboxNLP Workshop on Analyzing and Interpreting Neural Networks for NLP*, pages 11–15, Online. Association for Computational Linguistics.

Eugene Kharitonov, Rahma Chaabouni, Diane Bouchacourt, and Marco Baroni. 2019. EGG: a toolkit for research on emergence of lanGuage in games. In *Proceedings of the 2019 Conference on Empirical Methods in Natural Language Processing and the 9th International Joint Conference on Natural Language Processing (EMNLP-IJCNLP): System Demonstrations*, pages 55–60, Hong Kong, China. Association for Computational Linguistics.

Satwik Kottur, José Moura, Stefan Lee, and Dhruv Batra. 2017. Natural language does not emerge 'naturally' in multi-agent dialog. In *Proceedings of the 2017 Conference on Empirical Methods in Natural Language Processing*, pages 2962–2967, Copenhagen, Denmark. Association for Computational Linguistics.

Brenden Lake and Marco Baroni. 2018. Generalization without systematicity: On the compositional skills of sequence-to-sequence recurrent networks. In *Proceedings of the 35th International Conference on Machine Learning*, volume 80 of *Proceedings of Machine Learning Research*, pages 2873–2882, Stockholmsmässan, Stockholm Sweden. PMLR.

Brenden M. Lake, Tomer D. Ullman, Joshua B. Tenenbaum, and Samuel J. Gershman. 2017. Building machines that learn and think like people. *Behavioral and Brain Sciences*, 40:e253.

Fushan Li and Michael Bowling. 2019. Ease-of-teaching and language structure from emergent communication. In *Advances in Neural Information Processing Systems*, volume 32. Curran Associates, Inc.

João Loula, Marco Baroni, and Brenden Lake. 2018. Rearranging the familiar: Testing compositional generalization in recurrent networks. In *Proceedings of the 2018 EMNLP Workshop BlackboxNLP: Analyzing and Interpreting Neural Networks for NLP*, pages 108–114, Brussels, Belgium. Association for Computational Linguistics.

Thang Luong, Hieu Pham, and Christopher D. Manning. 2015. Effective approaches to attention-based neural machine translation. In *Proceedings of the 2015 Conference on Empirical Methods in Natural Language Processing*, pages 1412–1421, Lisbon, Portugal. Association for Computational Linguistics.

Martin A. Nowak, Joshua B. Plotkin, and Vincent A. A. Jansen. 2000. The evolution of syntactic communication. *Nature*, 404(6777):495–498.

Steven Pinker. 2000. Survival of the clearest. *Nature*, 404(6777):441–442.

Jacob Russin, Jason Jo, Randall O'Reilly, and Yoshua Bengio. 2020. Compositional generalization by factorizing alignment and translation. In *Proceedings of the 58th Annual Meeting of the Association for Computational Linguistics: Student Research Workshop*, pages 313–327, Online. Association for Computational Linguistics.

Ronald J. Williams. 1992. Simple statistical gradient-following algorithms for connectionist reinforcement learning. *Mach. Learn.*, 8(3–4):229–256.

A Appendix

A.1 Architecture

Both the sender and the receiver are implemented by the following encoder-decoder architecture:

The **encoder** produces two embeddings (size 500) for each input symbol, one syntactic and one semantic. A uni-directional GRU (Chung et al., 2014) layer (size 500) transforms the syntactic embeddings to contextualized embeddings.

The autoregressive **decoder** embeds the last produced symbol (or the start-of-sequence symbol) (size 500) and transforms it with another GRU layer (size 500). This contextualized embedding is then used as a query in the dot-product attention (Luong et al., 2015) and matched against the contextualized embeddings produced by the encoder. The attention weights are then used to produce the weighted sum of the semantic embeddings of the input symbols. This vector (size 500) is added to the query and transformed by a linear layer to the output symbol logits.

Exploring the Effect of Dialect Mismatched Language Models in Telugu Automatic Speech Recognition

Aditya Yadavalli **Ganesh S Mirishkar** **Anil Kumar Vuppala**

Speech Processing Laboratory
International Institute of Information Technology, Hyderabad
Gachibowli, Hyderabad, Telangana, 500032
{aditya.yadavalli, mirishkar.ganesh}@research.iiit.ac.in
{anil.vuppala}@iiit.ac.in

Abstract

Previous research has found that Acoustic Models (AM) of an Automatic Speech Recognition (ASR) system are susceptible to dialect variations within a language, thereby adversely affecting the ASR. To counter this, researchers have proposed to build a dialect-specific AM while keeping the Language Model (LM) constant for all the dialects. This study explores the effect of dialect mismatched LM by considering three different Telugu regional dialects: Telangana, Coastal Andhra, and Rayalaseema. We show that dialect variations that surface in the form of a different lexicon, grammar, and occasionally semantics can significantly degrade the performance of the LM under mismatched conditions. Therefore, this degradation has an adverse effect on the ASR even when dialect-specific AM is used. We show a degradation of up to 13.13 perplexity points when LM is used under mismatched conditions. Furthermore, we show a degradation of over 9% and over 15% in Character Error Rate (CER) and Word Error Rate (WER), respectively, in the ASR systems when using mismatched LMs over matched LMs.

1 Introduction

Automatic Speech Recognition (ASR) systems are rapidly becoming part of our everyday lives through voice assistants such as Siri, Alexa, and Google Assistant. Since these voice assistants can now perform various day-to-day tasks exceedingly well, they have now become an integral part of many devices such as phones, televisions, music players, and smartwatches.

Accurate and reliable ASR systems for Indian languages would have a significant impact due to two reasons: Firstly, India is home to many languages and dialects. Many of these languages and dialects do not have a written form. Secondly, a considerable amount of the population in India cannot read or write, as evidenced by the low literacy rates.[1] This leaves such people with only one mode of communication – the spoken form.

Despite the advances made by spoken technology research in recent years, dialect or accent variation proves to be a huge challenge.[2] Huang et al. (2001) show that accent variation contributes most to speech variability after gender. Biadsy et al. (2012); Elfeky et al. (2018) show the amount of degradation in ASR performance when it is not trained on dialect-specific data. Therefore, currently, state-of-the-art systems, including those of Google and Microsoft, use dialect-specific ASR systems.

However, multi-dialect ASR is an attractive solution in scenarios where sufficient dialect-specific data or information is not available. Therefore, Liu and Fung (2006); Rao and Sak (2017); Jain et al. (2018); Yang et al. (2018); Fukuda et al. (2018); Jain et al. (2019); Viglino et al. (2019); Li et al. (2018); Deng et al. (2021) attempt to improve multi-dialect ASR systems.

Liu and Fung (2006) use *auxiliary accent trees* to model Chinese accent variation. These are decision trees that model accent-specific triphone units and have a similar function as the decision trees that are used for state-tying of standard triphones. Rao and Sak (2017) show that grapheme-based Recurrent Neural Network-Connectionist Temporal Classification (RNN-CTC) ASR models outperform their phoneme-based counterparts when trained and used in multi-dialect English conditions. Furthermore, they study modelling phoneme recognition as an auxiliary task to im-

[1] https://censusindia.gov.in/2011-prov-results/data_files/mp/07Literacy.pdf

[2] In this paper, we use the words, 'dialect' and 'accent' interchangeably. However, we make one important distinction between dialect and accent: accent differences are largely constrained to the spoken form while dialect differences are not.

Proceedings of the 2022 Conference of the North American Chapter of the Association for Computational Linguistics: Human Language Technologies: Student Research Workshop, pages 292 - 301

Dialect	Sentence
Coastal Andhra	ప్రతి పౌరుడు ఓటు తప్పక వేయాలండి
Rayalaseema	మాకు మా పల్లెటూరు అంటే చానా ఇష్టము
Telangana	గా ఫుట్బాల్ గురించి అయితే నాకు మస్త్ గా తెలుసు రా బై

Table 1: Sentences of Different Dialects Taken from the Dataset

prove grapheme recognition and show improved performance when tested on multiple English dialects. Yang et al. (2018); Jain et al. (2018) explore the benefits of learning an accent classifier and multi-accent acoustic model under a multi-task learning framework. Viglino et al. (2019) explore incorporating various accent embeddings into a multi-accent End-to-End ASR model. All of these multi-accent studies report significant relative Word Error Rate improvements in their ASR models on various English accents. Li et al. (2018) incorporate dialect-specific information at the acoustic feature and textual level into multi-dialect End-to-End ASR and report that such a model outperforms dialect-specific End-to-End ASR systems. Zhang et al. (2021) propose a Transformer-based (Vaswani et al., 2017) encoder to simultaneously detect the dialect and transcribe an audio sample. More recently, with increased interest in self-supervised learning, Deng et al. (2021) explored self-supervised learning techniques to predict the accent from speech and use the predicted information to train an accent-specific self-supervised ASR. They report that such a model significantly outperforms an accent-independent ASR system.

Many researchers have previously studied the effects of dialect mismatched acoustic models in ASR systems. However, to the best of our knowledge, we are the first to explore the effects of a dialect mismatched Language Model (LM) in ASR systems.

Our language of interest in this paper is Telugu. Telugu is a South Central Dravidian language primarily spoken in two states of India: Telangana, and Andhra Pradesh. As previously mentioned, low literacy states in these states has motivated researchers to build Telugu ASR systems (Srivastava et al., 2018; Diwan and Jyothi, 2020; Bhanuprasad and Svenson, 2008; Vegesna et al., 2017; Diwan et al., 2021). However, they largely concentrate on building ASR systems for "standardised" Telugu. While Mirishkar et al. (2021b) collect dialect-specific Telugu data, they do not conduct any ASR experiments on individual Telugu dialects. We conduct our experiments on three regional Telugu dialects, i.e., Telangana, Rayalaseema, and Coastal Andhra. A considerable portion of dialect variation in Telugu can be seen in the lexicon, grammar, and occasionally semantics. Additionally, since Indian languages are considered to be low-resource in nature, adding external text to the LM is a solution that has gained interest (Pham et al., 2020; Karpov et al., 2021; Mirishkar et al., 2021a; Klejch et al., 2021). While such a method has shown significant benefits in their ASR systems, we argue that if proper care is not taken in matching the dialect of the external text with that of the ASR, it could lead to degradation in performance. These are the primary motivations for us to conduct this study. To this effect, the following are the major contributions of the paper:

- We show significant degradation of the perplexity scores of the LMs when tested on a different Telugu dialect.
- We use these LMs in a dialect mismatched ASR and report degradation of over 15% WER in such a setting compared to matched setting.

The rest of the paper is organised as follows. In Section 2, a brief description of the three dialects used in this study is given. In Section 3, we describe the dataset used in the study. In Section 4 and Section 5, we describe our experimental setup and discuss results under matched and mismatched settings. We conclude the paper with Section 6 and discuss possible future directions.

2 Telugu Dialects

All Telugu dialects can be broadly classified into three regional dialects: Telangana, Coastal Andhra, and Rayalaseema. The formation of these dialects is primarily due to the influence of neighboring states, and the regional culture (Mannepalli et al., 2016). The Nizams ruled the Telangana region, whose official languages were Persian and Urdu. Thus, one can see the influence of Urdu with many nativised Urdu words present in Telangana (Ithagani, 2014). Here are some such examples: కాకా, జాగా, దవాఖానా .[3] There is also some influence of the neighboring states' languages like Kannada on Telangana. The Coastal Andhra dialect is largely influenced by Sanskrit as well as Tamil due to historical and geographical reasons (Shivaprasad and Sadanandam, 2020). Finally, the Rayalaseema dialect is influenced by neighboring states' languages, i.e., Tamil and Kannada (Shivaprasad and Sadanandam, 2020). Interested readers are referred to Table 1 to see a few sample sentences of each dialect from the corpus. We also discuss these sentences in detail in Appendix B.

3 Dataset

We conduct our experiments on a corpus of three Telugu dialects collected by Mirishkar et al. (2021b). It is a crowd-sourced read speech corpus collected from the native speakers of the regional dialects of Telugu. In Table 2, we present dataset statistics we use in this study.[4]

Dialect	Train	Test	Vocabulary
Coastal Andhra	70.90K	1.99K	91737
Telangana	84.88K	2K	115505
Rayalaseema	65.32K	1.99K	90093

Table 2: Number of utterances in training and test set in each dialect (K for thousand)

All audio used in this study is mono channel, sampled at 16KHz with 16-bit encoding. The prompt given to the speakers is hand-curated. Therefore, we were able to ensure that the datasets across dialects have no domain mismatch. This allows us to study dialect mismatch better, which is our primary interest in this study.

3.1 Analysis

Since the dataset used in this paper is crowd-sourced read speech, we found a number of speakers not speaking in their native regional accent but in the "standardised" Telugu accent. However, the prompt given to the speakers is hand-curated which reflects the variations exhibited by the three dialects of interest. Additionally, we focus on dialect mismatched LMs in this paper. These reasons motivated us to limit ourselves to a textual analysis.

To analyse the three dialects, we choose to fine-tune *IndicBERT* (Kakwani et al., 2020) on a dialect classification task. *IndicBERT* is an ALBERT (Lan et al., 2020) based pre-trained multilingual model. It achieves state-of-the-art results on many Indic benchmarks and is trained on *IndicCorp* (Kakwani et al., 2020), one the largest publicly available Indian corpora.

To fine-tune *IndicBERT*, we use the same transcripts provided to the ASR models for training. We tokenise the input sequence using *IndicBERT*'s pre-trained tokeniser. We add a classification head to the pre-trained model. We use an initial learning rate of 1×10^{-5} with an Adam optimiser (Kingma and Ba, 2015). We train this model for 10 epochs. To get t-SNE representations, we take the sentence representations of the fine-tuned model and use *sklearn*'s implementation with default parameters.[5]

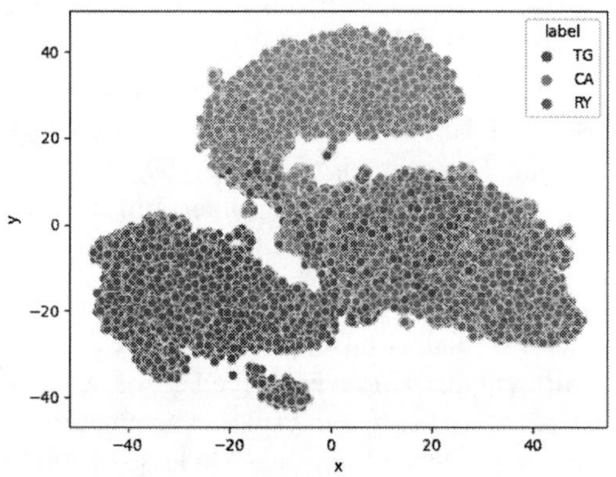

Figure 1: t-SNE plot of IndicBERT sentence representations of the three Telugu dialects. In this plot, TG is Telangana, CA is Coastal Andhra, and RY is Rayalaseema.

Figure 1 shows the t-SNE (van der Maaten and Hinton, 2008) plot of the sentence representations of *IndicBERT*. It can be observed that each of the dialects form its own cluster with some overlap with the other dialects. Out of the three, Ray-

[3] transliteration of the words using the WX notation (Gupta et al., 2010) are as follows: kAka, jAgA, xavAKAnA

[4] A more detailed analysis of the data used in this paper has been provided by Mirishkar et al. (2021b). We refer interested readers to their paper.

[5] https://scikit-learn.org/stable/modules/generated/sklearn.manifold.TSNE.html

alaseema cluster overlaps most with both Coastal Andhra and Telangana dialects, which shows that Rayalaseema dialect has a lot of similarities with both Coastal Andhra and Telangana dialect.

4 Experimental Setup

All of the ASR experiments are conducted using ESPnet (Watanabe et al., 2018). The input acoustic features are 80-dimensional log mel features extracted on the fly. We choose to use the Conformer model (Gulati et al., 2020) as it was able to achieve state-of-the-art performance on many standard datasets. The encoder of the ASR uses 12 Conformer (Gulati et al., 2020) blocks with 8 attention heads while the decoder uses 6 Transformer (Vaswani et al., 2017) blocks with 4 attention heads. We train both the encoder and decoder with a dropout rate of 0.1. All the models are trained based on the Hybrid CTC/Attention architecture (Kim et al., 2017; Watanabe et al., 2017). The training is done within the Multi-Objective Learning (MOL) framework. The CTC loss term helps the Attention model converge faster. The training objective (L_{MOL}) is as follows:

$$L_{MOL} = \lambda \log p_{ctc}(c|x) + (1-\lambda) \log p^{*}_{att}(c|x)$$

Here, λ is the multitask coefficient which should satisfy the following condition: $0 \leq \lambda \leq 1$. We found λ set to 0.3 while training and 0.4 while decoding gave us the best results for our datasets. c is the output unit. This could be characters, subword units, or words. Using words as output units could lead to two major issues: Out of Vocabulary (OOV%) cannot be handled well. The number of output units could be very high, especially in an agglutinative language like Telugu, which could lead to data sparsity. Chiu et al. (2018) show that using subwords over characters leads to better performance of End-to-End ASR systems. Thus we opted to use subwords as the output units. We used SentencePiece (Kudo and Richardson, 2018) to tokenise the words into subwords.[6] We found a vocabulary of around 500 tokens to give us the best performance on all the three datasets. We refer readers interested in how vocabulary size affects the performance of ASR of different Telugu dialects to Appendix A. Finally, x, in the above equation, is the input acoustic features.

We take mucs21_subtask1[7] recipe in ESPnet since it is tuned to perform well on a similar sized Indian dataset and make the following modifications: Change the initial learning rate to 5×10^{-4}, and use early stopping with a criterion to stop training the model if its performance does not improve for 5 consecutive epochs on the validation set.

We train an independent 16 block Transformer LM with an embedding size of 128 and a hidden encoder size of 512 for a maximum of 25 epochs. Finally, the decoder uses an LM weight of 0.6 to predict a sequence of subwords.[8] This method of integrating LM into the End-to-End ASR is known as Shallow Fusion (Kannan et al., 2018) and it is shown to give better results than other forms of integrating LM into the End-to-End ASR (Toshniwal et al., 2018). To decode, we use beam search of size 10 to predict the sequence.

5 Results & Discussion

In this section, the results of the experiments conducted are reported, and briefly analysed.

Biadsy et al. (2012) experiment the effectiveness of cross-dialect ASR in Arabic by experimenting with cross-dialect Acoustic Model (AM) and training the LM on target dialect data. In this paper, we take the exact opposite approach, i.e., train the AM (in this case, End-to-End ASR before the independent LM is fused) on the target dialect data and experiment by using a cross-dialect LM. We do this to test the effectiveness of the LM and thereby the ASR in cross-dialect conditions.[9] No external text was used to train LMs as it is difficult to obtain dialect information of external text.[10]

We report the performance of the LM both in terms of extrinsic metric, i.e., CER and WER of the ASR which uses the LM in question as well as an intrinsic metric, i.e., perplexity. Table 3 shows the performance of ASR systems in terms of CER and WER in both dialect matched and mismatched settings.[11]

[6] We used no external text to train the tokeniser.

[7] https://github.com/espnet/espnet/tree/master/egs2/mucs21_subtask1

[8] The rest of the weight is given to the CTC/Attention Hybrid Model.

[9] This is only possible because all dialects we experiment with share a common orthography

[10] For the rest of the paper, when we refer to a setting as mismatched consider only the LM to be mismatched.

[11] Even though WER is the most widely used metric, we report CER as we find WER to be not as reliable for agglutinative languages like Telugu as it is for analytic languages like English. However, in this paper, both the metrics are largely in agreement with each other.

Dialect/LM	None	Coastal Andhra	Telangana	Rayalaseema	All Dialects
Coastal Andhra	11.6/36.4	11.6/34.3	14.0/38.7	14.8/39.4	**11.2/34.3**
Telangana	7.6/27.9	16.7/40.1	7.6/25.4	17.0/40.9	**7.5/24.7**
Rayalaseema	8.6/26.5	8.2/25.4	7.9/25.1	**7.7**/24.2	9.0/**23.0**

Table 3: CER/WER(%) with Dialect Matched & Mismatched Language Models

As expected, ASR performs best when the LM is trained on all dialects outperforming ASR systems under matched conditions by approximately a WER of 1%. Since the dialect-specific text in our setup is not heavily skewed towards one dialect, the ASR performs well on all dialects. However, text collected from most external sources are heavily skewed towards the "standardised" Telugu dialect. Therefore, in the remaining part of the section, we focus on ASR systems where its LM is trained on a single dialect.

From Table 3, it can be observed that the average WER of the ASR in matched conditions is 27.96% and average CER is 8.96%. On the other hand, the average WER of the ASR in mismatched conditions is 34.93% and the average CER is 13.1%. This absolute difference of 6.97% in WER and 4.14% in CER of the ASR shows that having a dialect-specific LM can lead to the superior performance of an ASR. Moreover, our experiments with having no LM in ASR show that such a system can outperform ASR in mismatched conditions by upto 13% absolute WER. This shows that when the LM of the ASR is trained on text from a different dialect, it can *actively* hinder the performance of the ASR.

From Table 3, we can also observe that there is dissimilar amount degradation across all the three dialect ASR under mismatched settings. Telangana-specific ASR under mismatched conditions leads to over 15% WER drop compared to matched conditions. This is primarily due to the data imbalance in the dataset we used. Telangana dialect has most amount of data which leads to a superior performance when the LM is trained on it. However, when it is trained on other dialects, it is not only of different dialect but also trained on significantly lesser amount of data, which leads to an inferior model. On the other hand, Rayalaseema-specific ASR is robust to dialect mismatch with only slightly above 1% drop in performance compared to matched conditions. This is because Rayalaseema has a significant overlap with both Telangana and Coastal Andhra as shown in Figure 1. Since it has similarities with both Coastal Andhra and Telangana dialect, it performs relatively well even under dialect mismatched conditions.

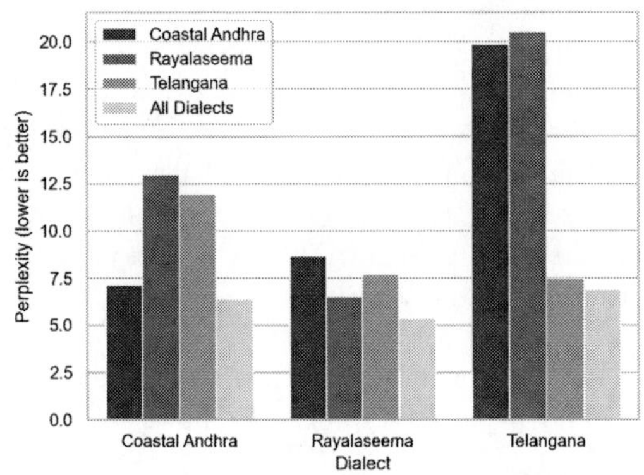

Figure 2: Perplexity in Cross-Dialect Conditions

Figure 2 shows the perplexity scores of LMs in dialect matched and mismatched settings. One can draw similar inferences from the perplexity scores as from the WERs of the ASR systems under different conditions presented in Table 3.

As expected, the perplexity of the LM trained on all the dialects is the least. LM's perplexity under matched settings much better in all the three dialects compared to mismatched conditions. As discussed before, Telangana LM is highly sensitive to dialect mismatch, with perplexity increasing by over 13 points. LM trained on Coastal Andhra and Telangana and tested on Rayalaseema leads to the highest increase in perplexity, i.e., 5.82 and 13.13 points, respectively. On the other hand, Rayalaseema LM is most robust to any dialect mismatch.

6 Conclusion & Future Work

This paper studies how LMs perform under dialect mismatched conditions. Our experiments reveal that LMs perform poorly, with the perplexity score increasing sharply in dialect mismatched conditions. We use the mismatched LMs in ASR systems to study how they are affected. Similar to what we have observed with perplexity scores of the LM, we notice a significant degradation in the performance of the ASR with over 15% difference in WER in dialect mismatched conditions when compared to its matched counterpart. Furthermore, through our study, we show that mismatched LMs can *actively* hinder the performance of ASR by comparing it to ASR systems with no LM. These findings show the importance of careful curation of external text when training a dialect-specific ASR system.

These experiments have also led to an interesting finding: Rayalaseema dialect is more robust under dialect mismatched conditions as it shares a lot of similarities with both Coastal Andhra and Telangana.

In the future, we plan to improve the LM and thereby the ASR in dialect mismatched conditions using various adaptation techniques available in the literature. We hope that our future work would lead to LMs that are more robust to dialect mismatched conditions, thereby leading to improved ASR systems.

Acknowledgements

We would like to thank the anonymous reviewers for their valuable feedback. We would like to acknowledge Technology Development for Indian Languages (TDIL), Ministry of Electronics and Information Technology (MeitY), Government of Republic of India for supporting us for the pilot project on "Crowd Sourced Large Speech Data Sets To Enable Indian Language Speech - Speech Solutions".

References

Kamadev Bhanuprasad and Mats Svenson. 2008. Errgrams a way to improving asr for highly inflected dravidian languages. In *IJCNLP*.

Fadi Biadsy, Pedro J. Moreno, and Martin Jansche. 2012. Google's cross-dialect arabic voice search. In *2012 IEEE International Conference on Acoustics, Speech and Signal Processing (ICASSP)*, pages 4441–4444.

Chung-Cheng Chiu, Tara N. Sainath, Yonghui Wu, Rohit Prabhavalkar, Patrick Nguyen, Z. Chen, Anjuli Kannan, Ron J. Weiss, Kanishka Rao, Katya Gonina, Navdeep Jaitly, Bo Li, Jan Chorowski, and Michiel Bacchiani. 2018. State-of-the-art speech recognition with sequence-to-sequence models. *2018 IEEE International Conference on Acoustics, Speech and Signal Processing (ICASSP)*, pages 4774–4778.

Keqi Deng, Songjun Cao, and Long Ma. 2021. Improving accent identification and accented speech recognition under a framework of self-supervised learning.

Anuj Diwan and Preethi Jyothi. 2020. Reduce and reconstruct: Improving low-resource end-to-end asr via reconstruction using reduced vocabularies.

Anuj Diwan, Rakesh Vaideeswaran, Sanket Shah, Ankita Singh, Srinivasa Raghavan, Shreya Khare, Vinit Unni, Saurabh Vyas, Akash Rajpuria, Chiranjeevi Yarra, Ashish Mittal, Prasanta Kumar Ghosh, Preethi Jyothi, Kalika Bali, Vivek Seshadri, Sunayana Sitaram, Samarth Bharadwaj, Jai Nanavati, Raoul Nanavati, Karthik Sankaranarayanan, Tejaswi Seeram, and Basil Abraham. 2021. Multilingual and code-switching asr challenges for low resource indian languages. *arXiv preprint arXiv:2104.00235*.

Mohamed G. Elfeky, Pedro Moreno, and Victor Soto. 2018. Multi-dialectical languages effect on speech recognition: Too much choice can hurt. *Procedia Computer Science*, 128:1–8. 1st International Conference on Natural Language and Speech Processing.

Takashi Fukuda, Raul Fernandez, Andrew Rosenberg, Samuel Thomas, Bhuvana Ramabhadran, Alexander Sorin, and Gakuto Kurata. 2018. Data augmentation improves recognition of foreign accented speech. In *INTERSPEECH*.

Anmol Gulati, James Qin, Chung-Cheng Chiu, Niki Parmar, Yu Zhang, Jiahui Yu, Wei Han, Shibo Wang, Zhengdong Zhang, Yonghui Wu, and Ruoming Pang. 2020. Conformer: Convolution-augmented transformer for speech recognition.

Rohit Gupta, Pulkit Goyal, and Sapan Diwakar. 2010. Transliteration among indian languages using wx notation. In *KONVENS*.

Chao Huang, Tao Chen, S. Li, Eric Chang, and Jian-Lai Zhou. 2001. Analysis of speaker variability. In *INTERSPEECH*.

Venkanna Ithagani. 2014. Linguistic convergence and divergence in telugu-urdu contact situation: A study with special reference to telangana dialect.

Abhinav Jain, Vishwanath Pratap Singh, and Shakti Prasad Rath. 2019. A multi-accent acoustic model using mixture of experts for speech recognition. In *INTERSPEECH*.

Abhinav Jain, Minali Upreti, and Preethi Jyothi. 2018. Improved accented speech recognition using accent embeddings and multi-task learning. In *INTERSPEECH*.

Divyanshu Kakwani, Anoop Kunchukuttan, Satish Golla, Gokul N.C., Avik Bhattacharyya, Mitesh M. Khapra, and Pratyush Kumar. 2020. IndicNLPSuite: Monolingual corpora, evaluation benchmarks and pre-trained multilingual language models for Indian languages. In *Findings of the Association for Computational Linguistics: EMNLP 2020*, pages 4948–4961, Online. Association for Computational Linguistics.

Anjuli Kannan, Yonnghui Wu, Patrick Nguyen, Tara N. Sainath, Zhifeng Chen, and Rohit Prabhavalkar. 2018. An analysis of incorporating an external language model into a sequence-to-sequence model. *ICASSP*.

Nikolay Karpov, Alexander Denisenko, and Fedor Minkin. 2021. Golos: Russian dataset for speech research. *Interspeech 2021*.

Suyoun Kim, Takaaki Hori, and Shinji Watanabe. 2017. Joint ctc-attention based end-to-end speech recognition using multi-task learning. *2017 IEEE International Conference on Acoustics, Speech and Signal Processing (ICASSP)*, pages 4835–4839.

Diederik P. Kingma and Jimmy Ba. 2015. Adam: A method for stochastic optimization. *CoRR*, abs/1412.6980.

Ondřej Klejch, Electra Wallington, and Peter Bell. 2021. The cstr system for multilingual and code-switching asr challenges for low resource indian languages. In *Proceedings of Interspeech 2021*, pages 2881–2885. International Speech Communication Association. Interspeech 2021 : The 22nd Annual Conference of the International Speech Communication Association ; Conference date: 30-08-2021 Through 03-09-2021.

Taku Kudo and John Richardson. 2018. Sentencepiece: A simple and language independent subword tokenizer and detokenizer for neural text processing. In *EMNLP*.

Zhenzhong Lan, Mingda Chen, Sebastian Goodman, Kevin Gimpel, Piyush Sharma, and Radu Soricut. 2020. Albert: A lite bert for self-supervised learning of language representations. *ArXiv*, abs/1909.11942.

Bo Li, Tara N. Sainath, Khe Chai Sim, Michiel Bacchiani, Eugene Weinstein, Patrick Nguyen, Z. Chen, Yan-Qing Wu, and Kanishka Rao. 2018. Multi-dialect speech recognition with a single sequence-to-sequence model. *2018 IEEE International Conference on Acoustics, Speech and Signal Processing (ICASSP)*, pages 4749–4753.

Yi Y. Liu and Pascale Fung. 2006. Multi-accent chinese speech recognition. In *INTERSPEECH*.

Kasiprasad Mannepalli, Panyam Narahari Sastry, and Maloji Suman. 2016. Mfcc-gmm based accent recognition system for telugu speech signals. *International Journal of Speech Technology*, 19(1):87–93.

Ganesh Mirishkar, Aditya Yadavalli, and Anil Kumar Vuppala. 2021a. An investigation of hybrid architectures for low resource multilingual speech recognition system in indian context. In *Proceedings of the 18th International Conference on Natural Language Processing (ICON)*, pages 205–210.

Ganesh S Mirishkar, Vishnu Vidyadhara Raju V, Meher Dinesh Naroju, Sudhamay Maity, Prakash Yalla, and Anil Kumar Vuppala. 2021b. Cstd-telugu corpus: Crowd-sourced approach for large-scale speech data collection. In *2021 Asia-Pacific Signal and Information Processing Association Annual Summit and Conference (APSIPA ASC)*, pages 511–517.

Van Tung Pham, Haihua Xu, Yerbolat Khassanov, Zhiping Zeng, Chng Eng Siong, Chongjia Ni, Bin Ma, and Haizhou Li. 2020. Independent language modeling architecture for end-to-end asr. *ICASSP 2020 - 2020 IEEE International Conference on Acoustics, Speech and Signal Processing (ICASSP)*, pages 7059–7063.

Kanishka Rao and Haim Sak. 2017. Multi-accent speech recognition with hierarchical grapheme based models. In *2017 IEEE International Conference on Acoustics, Speech and Signal Processing (ICASSP)*, pages 4815–4819.

S Shivaprasad and M Sadanandam. 2020. Identification of regional dialects of telugu language using text independent speech processing models. *International Journal of Speech Technology*, 23(2):251–258.

Brij Mohan Lal Srivastava, Sunayana Sitaram, Rupesh Kumar Mehta, Krishna Doss Mohan, Pallavi Matani, Sandeepkumar Satpal, Kalika Bali, Radhakrishnan Srikanth, and Niranjan Nayak. 2018. Interspeech 2018 low resource automatic speech recognition challenge for indian languages. In *SLTU*, pages 11–14.

Shubham Toshniwal, Anjuli Kannan, Chung-Cheng Chiu, Yonghui Wu, Tara N Sainath, and Karen Livescu. 2018. A comparison of techniques for language model integration in encoder-decoder speech recognition. In *2018 IEEE Spoken Language Technology Workshop (SLT)*, pages 369–375.

Laurens van der Maaten and Geoffrey E. Hinton. 2008. Visualizing data using t-sne. *Journal of Machine Learning Research*, 9:2579–2605.

Ashish Vaswani, Noam Shazeer, Niki Parmar, Jakob Uszkoreit, Llion Jones, Aidan N. Gomez, Lukasz Kaiser, and Illia Polosukhin. 2017. Attention is all you need.

Vishnu Vidyadhara Raju Vegesna, Krishna Gurugubelli, Hari Krishna Vydana, Bhargav Pulugandla, Manish Shrivastava, and Anil Kumar Vuppala. 2017. Dnn-hmm acoustic modeling for large vocabulary telugu speech recognition. In *MIKE*.

Thibault Viglino, Petr Motlícek, and Milos Cernak. 2019. End-to-end accented speech recognition. In *INTERSPEECH*.

Shinji Watanabe, Takaaki Hori, Shigeki Karita, Tomoki Hayashi, Jiro Nishitoba, Yuya Unno, Nelson Enrique Yalta Soplin, Jahn Heymann, Matthew Wiesner, Nanxin Chen, Adithya Renduchintala, and Tsubasa Ochiai. 2018. ESPnet: End-to-end speech processing toolkit. In *Proceedings of Interspeech*, pages 2207–2211.

Shinji Watanabe, Takaaki Hori, Suyoun Kim, John R. Hershey, and Tomoki Hayashi. 2017. Hybrid ctc/attention architecture for end-to-end speech recognition. *IEEE Journal of Selected Topics in Signal Processing*, 11(8):1240–1253.

Xuesong Yang, Kartik Audhkhasi, Andrew Rosenberg, Samuel Thomas, Bhuvana Ramabhadran, and Mark A. Hasegawa-Johnson. 2018. Joint modeling of accents and acoustics for multi-accent speech recognition. *2018 IEEE International Conference on Acoustics, Speech and Signal Processing (ICASSP)*, pages 1–5.

Jicheng Zhang, Yizhou Peng, Van Tung Pham, Haihua Xu, Hao Huang, and Chng Eng Siong. 2021. E2e-based multi-task learning approach to joint speech and accent recognition. In *Interspeech*.

Vocab/Dialect	Coastal Andhra	Telangana	Rayalaseema
500	**11.6/34.3**	**7.6/25.4**	**7.7/24.2**
700	11.8/35.0	7.9/25.5	8.2/25.1
1200	13.3/36.5	7.9/25.6	8.7/25.6
2500	15.3/38.1	8.7/25.9	10.0/27.1

Table 4: CER/WER(%) for Different Vocabulary Sizes

A Experiments with Different Vocabulary Sizes

In this paper, we conducted experiments with the following vocabulary sizes: 500, 700, 1200, 2500. Table 4 shows the performance of the ASR under these settings. We found that using 500 tokens results in best performance in all 3 dialect-specific ASR systems. We also conducted preliminary experiments by reducing the vocabulary size beyond 500 tokens but we could not find any noticeable improvement.

B Example Sentences

Table 5 presents the example sentences along with their transliterations using the WX notation (Gupta et al., 2010) and their translations. In Coastal Andhra, we notice the usage of the word "aMdi" frequently. In the example sentence, this word is fused with another word "veyAli" to become "veyAlaMdi". In the example Rayalaseema sentence, we notice the usage of the word "chaana". This is specific to the Rayalaseema dialect. The corresponding equivalent words in Coastal Andhra and Telangana would be "cAnA" and "masw", respectively. In Telangana, we notice the influence of Urdu/Hindi. In the example sentence, the words "masw" and "bE" have its origins in Urdu/Hindi.

Dialect	Sentence with Transliteration and Translation
Coastal Andhra	ప్రతి పౌరుడు ఓటు తప్పక వేయాలండి prawi pOrudu otu wappaka veyAlaMdi every citizen should vote without fail
Rayalaseema	మాకు మా పల్లెటూరు అంటే చానా ఇష్టము mAku mA palleVtUru aMte cAnA iRtamu we like our village very much
Telangana	గా ఫుట్బాల్ గురించి అయితే నాకు మస్త్ గా తెలుసు రా బై gA PutbAl guriMci ayiwe nAku masw gA weVlusu rA bE I know a lot about football

Table 5: Example Sentences of Different Dialects

Author Index

Association for Computational Linguistics
209 N. Eighth Street
Stroudsburg, Pennsylvania 18360

ISBN 978-1-7138-5621-4

CURRAN ASSOCIATES INC.
proceedings.com